ALSO BY SHAUN CONSIDINE

Barbra Streisand: The Woman,
the Myth, the Music

Bette & Joan: The Divine Feud

MAD AS HELL

MAD
AS
HELL

The Life and Work of
Paddy Chayefsky

SHAUN
CONSIDINE

Random House
New York

Library of Congress Cataloging-in-Publication Data
Considine, Shaun.
Mad as hell: the life and work of Paddy Chayefsky / by Shaun Considine.
p.   cm.
Includes bibliographical references and index.
ISBN 0-679-40892-4
1. Chayefsky, Paddy, 1923–1981.   2. Dramatists, American—20th century—Biography.
3. Screenwriters—United States—Biography.
I. Title.
PS3505.H632Z57   1994
812′.54—dc20   93-46154

Manufactured in the United States of America
on acid-free paper
24689753
First Edition

Book design by Oksana Kushnir

For the first and foremost Paddy in my life—
my father, Patrick James Considine,
of Clooney, County Clare, Ireland

CONTENTS

Why Paddy Chayefsky? That was the question most commonly asked when this book was a work in progress. The answer was standard. Chayefsky was one of a rare circle of writers. He achieved considerable success in three media: television, where he was one of the prime creative forces behind the Golden Age of Drama; theatre, where he had notable success with his plays *Middle of the Night* and *The Tenth Man;* and film, where he became the only single screenwriter in movie history to win three Academy Awards, for *Marty, The Hospital,* and *Network.*

In the early 1950s, Chayefsky, described as "a poet of the streets," made an immediate impact on millions of TV viewers with his naturalistic dialogue and his unique ability to expose the very soul of the people he was writing about. His appeal was universal. He wrote of common but good-hearted people: a homely butcher, a spinster schoolteacher, a confused accountant— ordinary, everyday human beings who did not reflect the cosmetic, elitist ideals packaged by Hollywood and Madison Avenue. Moving on to films and becoming more infatuated with language, Chayefsky further defied cinematic standards by writing literate scripts loaded with dazzling, provocative dialogue delivered by unlikely heroes intent on leveling the icons and sacred institutions of our time. Passionate with indignation at the dehumanization and deperson-alization of society, Chayefsky on screen dissected the U.S. military (*The Americanization of Emily*), the medical establishment (*The Hospital*), the TV industry (*Network*), and the scientific community (*Altered States*), while on the stage he lampooned communism and the Internal Revenue Service and, in a personal fit of pique and ego, debated and defied the greatest force of all—God—in *Gideon.*

"I'm as mad as hell and I'm not going to take this anymore!" was Howard Beale's war cry for the people in Chayefsky's *Network*. Some twenty years earlier, Chayefsky had added another popular expression to the national vernacular: "Well, whaddya feel like doin' tonight?" I first heard that line at the Metropole Cinema on O'Connell Street in Dublin, Ireland, where I was raised. As a young student, my enthusiasm for *Marty* was such that I sat through two showings, thereby missing an exam for an all-important government job. Inevitably that meant: emigration. Three years later, in June 1958, at a small theatre on the West Side of Manhattan, I saw my second Chayefsky film, *The Goddess*. This quintessential study of a neurotic, tortured Hollywood movie star was said to be modeled on the reigning sex symbol of the day, Marilyn Monroe. The script was compelling, as was Kim Stanley's tour-de-force performance in the leading role. Yet despite that and the rave reviews, the film failed at the box office. Not long after, with the psychological unraveling and the untimely demise of Monroe, which Chayefsky had augured to a fine, twisted hair in his script, *The Goddess* became a cult classic, often shown at revival houses and in college film courses.

The movie would also lead to a memorable encounter between this writer and Chayefsky in 1977. *Network* had just been released and I was on hand to interview its creator for an entertainment publication. The meeting took place in a midtown restaurant, and all was copacetic for the first fifty minutes. Then I mentioned *The Goddess* and Marilyn Monroe. The air above us suddenly grew thin. The tableware began to rattle and the framed celebrity photographs hanging on the wall began to shake. A torrent of hot verbal lava spewed forth from the mouth of Chayefsky, who was hissing and crackling with articulate fury in my direction. The eruption was so sudden and searing that a precise register of what he said was not made. In essence, he called me an asshole. Marilyn Monroe was *not* the model for the character he wrote in *The Goddess*. Furthermore, the film was *not* one of his favorites. It was a flawed work, best forgotten, now and forever, amen.

Chayefsky died in 1981. He was only fifty-eight. By the end of the eighties, with the proliferation of national cable and the VCR market, his films began to be seen with regularity again. Included with the staples—*Marty, Network, The Hospital*—was *The Goddess*. After a fresh viewing of the latter, I learned by chance that the producer of the film, Milton Perlman, lived in my neighborhood. We met, and some facts emerged about the production. For starters, Marilyn Monroe was indeed the model for the story. She was also Chayefsky's first choice to play the part. He forwarded the script to her, and her response came via her husband at the time, playwright Arthur Miller. They threatened to sue if Paddy dared to make this film. He blithely proceeded, keeping an active and upper hand in all phases of the production. Along with personally selecting the entire cast, Chayefsky coproduced, codirected, coedited, then marketed and publicized the film in the U.S. and Europe.

Paddy Chayefsky was never a mere writer, I soon learned. He was a plenary artist, who insisted on total involvement in the production of his work. In the area of motion pictures, none of his contemporaries—Arthur Miller, William Inge, or Tennessee Williams—had the power and autonomous control that Chayefsky had. Consequently, in an industry known for its propensity to kowtow to the star, the director, the executive producer, Chayefsky's tight involvement and dogged professionalism irritated and exasperated many. As the stories on the making of his films and the staging of his TV and Broadway plays accumulated, I felt there was a book here. Along with the creation of the work, the focus would be on the production of Paddy Chayefsky's greatest hits, and a few of his more notable misses.

Working on spec for the first of the three years this exploration would take, I decided to use a chronological approach. Thankfully, most of his colleagues from the formative period, the Golden Age of Television, were available. Writers J. P. Miller, Tad Mosel, David Shaw, Horton Foote, Sumner Locke Elliott, and Gore Vidal enthusiastically gave of their time, agreeing collectively that the star writer of that mythical era was Chayefsky. He was also the first to cross over to movies—with *Marty,* which brought him minimal cash but maximum creative control. He wrote the script, chose the director, approved the cast, and insisted on being retained as an associate producer *and* the associate director of this, his maiden film. "Rampant ego" was Hollywood's explanation for his excessive privilege, but in my research, as I slowly gathered the details of that production, I found that Chayefsky's vigilance was not unwarranted. In interviews with the principal creative talents on the picture, it was mentioned that *Marty* had come close to being a stillborn classic. When queried, the executive producer and the studio executives denied this, until, in a fortuitous turn, I came across the United Artists files, which confirmed that owing to a lack of interest and financing *Marty* was almost aborted in midproduction. With its ultimate worldwide success and the bestowal of Hollywood's top honor, the Academy Award for Best Picture, the exigencies of its production were naturally concealed and/or conveniently forgotten by many. But not by Paddy Chayefsky. The lesson learned was that no one could be trusted and that he alone was responsible for the preservation of his carefully crafted dialogue and quixotic vision. With that dictate in mind, he proceeded to pit his will against some of the most formidable figures in the theatrical and motion picture fields.

When I went through Chayefsky's archives (stored in Madison, Wisconsin), it was staggering to see the amount of time and detail he had put into his work. His preliminary research was prodigious. He had done character studies for even the secondary roles, along with numerous drafts and endless revisions for each scenario. Outlines for subsequently abandoned projects were included. These were sometimes dashed off two or three at a time, and frequently came on the heels of a recently completed project. He would finish one script or play, then immediately go on to the next story, expand or discard that, and start another. "That's my trade, man! That's my trade! I'd crumble into the coffin without my trade," says the old man in *Printer's Measure*. For Chayefsky, his work was his addiction. Having no hobbies and few outside interests, he was a man who was never satisfied, who was constantly in fast-forward, always geared for the next play, the next movie, the "Big One"— the ultimate, significant, meaningful *opus*. For a biographer, this obsession naturally raised some questions. What was Chayefsky trying to prove? And whom was he trying to please? Himself? His critics and peers? His dominant mother? His tenebrous wife?

In Wisconsin, another question surfaced. Beyond the volume of scripts, outlines for plays, numerous reviews, newspaper clips, etc., there was very little personal documentation, and no papers pertaining to his work after 1970, when he wrote his strongest trilogy of films, *The Hospital, Network,* and *Altered States.* This material, I learned, was in the possession of his widow, Susan Chayefsky, who lived in Manhattan. I was not the first to approach her. Two previous biographers and a documentary producer had contacted Mrs. Chayefsky, who was strict in her refusal to release the material or cooperate with any book, film, or testament to her late husband.

Temporarily circumventing this obstacle, I continued my research, locating most of the needed documentation elsewhere and tracking down and interviewing many of the people who worked on Chayefsky's last trio of films. Arthur Hiller, Sidney Lumet, and Arthur Penn, the directors who had worked closely with him during the 1970s, generously shared their recollections. Producer Howard Gottfried, Chayefsky's partner for that decade, also agreed to meet and talk openly about the productions of *The Hospital* and *Network* and about Chayefsky's final film, *Altered States.* The playwright Herb Gardner, who, along with the late Bob Fosse, was Chayefsky's closest friend, also provided important insights into him and their relationship. By now, one hypothesis had emerged as fact. Most writers tend to put a large part of themselves into their work. Early on, many people had assumed, but Chayefsky had never acknowledged, that *Marty* was based on him. When the details of the last third of his output were assembled, the biographical correlation was obvious. It was clear that the raging suicidal Dr. Bock, in *The Hospital,* and Howard Beale, the manic suicidal anchorman in *Network,* were also Chayefsky clones. The leading question became: What happened here? What caused this drastic shift from the positive, good-natured Marty to the pessimistic, self-destructive, mad-as-hell Bock and Beale?

It was his family that drove him crazy, some of his associates believed. His seldom-seen wife, fiercely jealous of his work, made his life miserable (and after his death was supposedly determined that he remain "a forgotten writer"). His sole offspring, a son, once rebellious, was now said to be seriously "troubled." Others intimated that it was Chayefsky's family who were the tormented ones. They were "the victims of his psyche," one playwright remarked.

In August 1991, two and a half years after this book was started, one last attempt was made to talk with the Chayefsky family. This time the word came back that Susan Chayefsky was a recluse and an invalid. The surviving son was living somewhere in Manhattan; no address or telephone number was given. If he wished to talk, he would call on his own. Early that September, Dan Chayefsky did phone. The timing was right, he said. Emerging from protracted therapy, he said it also helped that his father had been dead for ten years, making the subject less painful. "I can be more objective and not feel as if I'm drowning in it," he said.

A preliminary meeting was held. The portrait of Paddy Chayefsky presented by his son resembled significantly the one presented by his friends and associates. He *was* a man of complexity and frequent rage. With considerable candor and insight, the younger Chayefsky attempted to clarify where that anger came from, while helping to fill in the stretches of the book where vacancy or speculation existed. There was also enormous curiosity on his part. As a writer himself, respectful of and fascinated by his father's legacy, Dan Chayefsky was eager to learn what I had uncovered about the work. In the exchange, what was surprising was how little he knew, not about the writing itself or about the projects produced or abandoned, but about his father's alliance with so many of the leading people in the entertainment business. "We were close. We lived in the same house for twenty years. And yet I know so little about that side of his life. Why is that?" Dan Chayefsky asked.

I didn't have an answer. What I did know was that the book I had written would have to be amended to include the information that was now being made available. In numerous and lengthy follow-up talks with Dan Chayefsky and other members of the family circle, hitherto unknown aspects of the writer's private life began to emerge. Facts about his physical and psychological health, his habits and fears, were revealed, showing a side of Chayefsky that his friends and colleagues obviously knew little about. It was known that Chayefsky had been in psychoanalysis and psychotherapy, but the duration, on and off for twenty-five years, had not been disclosed. Also, in the early 1970s the outwardly confident, jocular Chayefsky was diagnosed and treated for depression, from which he had suffered for most of his life. Few of his friends and colleagues were aware of this—nor were they, or his family, aware of other aspects of Chayefsky's life. He had a sensitive political past no one knew much about. There was also a curious romantic contretemps that remained hidden.

Chayefsky was said to be prudish, almost Victorian, in his attitude toward sex. His associates and his son shared that belief. Yet I learned from three separate sources that Chayefsky had once had an extramarital romance, serious enough for him to consider breaking up his marriage. True, this was an isolated case, but since it was with one of the leading movie stars of that day, surely his friends, his partner, his brothers would have known or been told about it.

There was no clear-cut explanation for the other numerous contradictions in Chayefsky's behavior, until one evening, after dinner with close friends of the family, I was shown some snapshots of Chayefsky. They were taken at his last birthday party, at the River Café in 1981, six months before he died. The host was Bob Fosse, and for the occasion he had ordered two cakes. One was inscribed to Paddy Chayefsky; the other to Sidney Aaron, the pseudonym Chayefsky used on the credits of his last film, *Altered States*. I didn't make any connection at that point, but two nights later, at three o'clock in the morning, I awoke with the image of Chayefsky cutting Sidney Aaron's birthday cake. Then it occurred to me: Was it possible that there were *two* Chayefskys? Paddy, the publicly invented persona, and Sidney, the private man? Sidney was his given name, the one he grew up with and answered to for the first twenty years of his life. It was also the name, in its Hebrew form, that he used for his last production company, Simcha Productions.

Was that the answer? Did Chayefsky have a divided self? Was Sidney the core character, the serious creative one who could write about anger but never express his own, and Paddy the loud, extroverted one who could demolish mountains when crossed? Was Paddy the cocky, overconfident one, the one who took talent and fame for granted, while Sidney stayed passive, polite but insecure about his looks and about his work, which never gave him a true sense of accomplishment?

Everyone has more than one self, but the others usually stay in place, removed, in their subconscious. In pursuits and professions that demand discipline, self-absorption, confidence, and high visibility, that other self is often cultivated and encouraged. For display and defense, to cope and survive, actors, artists, athletes, frequently have to rely on their more assertive alter egos when situations infringe or threaten their senses and livelihoods. Writers, a more solitary lot, also develop a more active second self, one that is usually displayed in but confined to the pages and the characters they create.

Attempting to find out if any duality of selves existed in Chayefsky's work, I went back to his scripts and plays. Nothing significant arose until 1977. During the publicity for *Network*, Chayefsky stated that the characters of mad prophet Howard Beale *and* the conventional good guy, Max Schumacher, were patterned on himself. Another, more pertinent connection emerged on his next film, *Altered States*. Chayefsky admitted up front that the genesis for this script was the metamorphic split-self classic, *Dr. Jekyll and Mr. Hyde*. That story, suffice it to say, was a study in the extreme, as was *Altered States*. There was no literal transmogrification with Chayefsky, but there were two personalities, two extremes, with separate hues and sensibilities which existed on and off the printed page. They shared, however, the same intellect and the same abiding passion for the work, during the creation of which Sidney, the archperfectionist, was painstakingly diligent, which led Paddy, snared by the image of omnipotence, to become obsessed with control, which eventually almost destroyed them both.

For further validation I returned to Chayefsky's son. Having lived with and observed his father closely for more than twenty years, and being highly sensitive and perceptive on his own, Dan Chayefsky had to have some thoughts on this. His response was prompt. "He *did* have two personalities," the son confirmed. "One was really sensitive and quiet, often depressed and brooding and emotional. The other was almost hyper, turned on, a nightclub act, a pinball machine, like Robin Williams or Liza Minnelli."

Paddy was obviously the showman that protected Sidney. "Paddy was a persona, whereas Sidney was the vulnerable being he was born with," said Dan Chayefsky. "In the work there is some incredible sensitivity—real genius, and at times you wouldn't be able to tell that from talking with my father. In public he'd be one person, gregarious with everyone. Then alone he'd be morose, very withdrawn, unable to share his thoughts with anyone."

With that discovery, two tasks had to be undertaken. The book I had written was on the life and work of Paddy Chayefsky. Sidney Chayefsky's side had to be inserted in the proper places. Although this was not going to be a definitive psychological study, *nor* an extended treatise on the life of a split personality, it behooved me to determine when and how the initial Chayefsky identity crisis occurred, and if it was ever resolved. Medical experts claim that a split in the self occurs during the early years of a person's childhood. Chayefsky's oldest brother, Bill, was still alive. Apologizing, he said he doubted he could contribute much because he was seven and a half when Paddy was born. But again, in follow-up talks with Bill Chayefsky, new facts about the early years began to emerge. These were discussed with others, including Dan Chayefsky, until at the end of one last marathon session, the first and last chunks of the enigma revealed themselves. Something that Paddy Chayefsky had once confided to his son was revealed. That led to an image, followed by another, then substantiation, and suddenly there it was: the paramount pieces of the mosaic appeared and settled into place. To complement and supplement the vast, colorful vista of Chayefsky's professional life, I now had the vital intimate beginning, a turbulent sensational middle, and an explosive critical culmination—all the necessary ingredients of any good Chayefsky story.

To a visionary like Paddy Chayefsky, an artist so clearheaded and prescient about the ills and condition of human society, it must have seemed ironic that in his own life he could not discern where the roots of his personal turmoil and powerlessness began. In his writing he spoke often of an unknown sense of horror and helplessness. "I tell you! . . . I feel I am in somebody's hand, and they squeezing my bones!" the ditchdigger, Mario Fortunato, cries out in Fifth from Garibaldi. "I felt a shaft of terror that chills me even now," says the title character in Gideon. "I saw myself and all men for what we truly are, suspensions of matter, flailing about for footholds in the void, all the while slipping back screaming into endless suffocation."

His final script, Altered States, was to be the empirical demonstration of this, the source of man's rage and terror. Six months after the film was released, Chayefsky became gravely ill. Lying in his hospital bed in a coma, hooked up to an IV, he was seized by terror again. "He kept yanking the tubes out of his arms," his son said. "It was frightening. His eyes were closed, and the medical staff were trying to hold him down. They taped a wooden board on his arm to keep the tubes fastened, but he kept fighting and ripping them out. I don't know if he was doing it compulsively, if he was aware of it and just didn't give a damn. But obviously, being restricted like that was terrible for him. That fear was far worse than dying, because he never knew what caused it."

PART 1

THE FORMATIVE YEARS

Parental Influences

His parents, Harry and Gussie, were Russian Jews, born in 1888 and 1889, a time when people of their creed were relentlessly oppressed and persecuted. Because Harry Chayefsky's father had served for twenty-five years in the czar's army, his family was allowed to live in relative comfort in Moscow.

Of medium height and slim build, Harry at age eighteen had a winning smile and an adventurous nature that was easily influenced by the revolutionary forces around him. In 1907, as the key leaders of the rising Socialist movement were being arrested and imprisoned, the young man, identified as a member of the cause, had to use his father's influence to secure an exit visa and a ticket, and he hastily left Moscow for the safety and promise of America.

Farther to the south in the Ukraine, in a small village called Velikye Bubny on the Black Sea, about forty miles from Odessa, Gussie Stuchevsky lived with her family. Her father owned a dry-goods store in the village of seventeen hundred, which had only three Jewish families, so "naturally they hated each other," she would recall. Strong-willed and Orthodox, Gussie in childhood found the core of her existence in the Torah, which for centuries had strengthened and protected Jews during their wanderings and afflictions. Possessed of a keen mind and voracious intelligence, as a teenager Gussie had an abiding interest in books, not boys. Among her favorite authors were Gorky, Dickens, and Tolstoy. Of *Anna Karenina* she said, "How a man could describe so carefully how a woman feels I will never understand."

Denied entrance to any school or college of higher learning, in 1909, after a further outbreak of state-backed pogroms and penalties, Gussie and her brother, Abe, joined the mass exodus of Jews that went to America. In New York they settled with an older sister, Becky, who lived in the ghetto on the

Lower East Side. Working by day as a seamstress in the Garment District, at night Gussie attended school at the Educational Alliance, a five-story settlement building at Jefferson Street and East Broadway. Here she learned English, expanding her vocabulary each day by reading newspapers and magazines. Her verbal proficiency and pride were such that years later, when her playwright son brought her backstage to meet one of the stars of his show, Edward G. Robinson, Gussie declined a reversion. "When Paddy introduced my mother, Robinson began to speak to her in Yiddish," said Bill Chayefsky, "but she spoke to him in English. It was the funniest thing I ever saw. He kept insisting on using Yiddish, and she would talk only in English, which she used in its correct grammatical form."

Fully intending to attend a city college, to study medicine or law, the young woman found her plans altered one hot summer afternoon when, five thousand miles from home, a transient hero, Harry Chayefsky, "fished a half-drowned Gussie out of the waves of Coney Island." According to their future son, this was their introduction, and he recounted their ensuing courtship in his TV play *The Big Deal.* "He used to take me to the Hippodrome in New York City," the mother says. "At that time, the Hippodrome was the big date of dates. They used to have big spectacles there, like circuses. It used to cost a dollar. In those days, a dollar was a dollar. I never knew where he got the money."

In *The Big Deal,* the father, who the writer admitted was based on his own, is spoken of as kind, generous, with "an open hand to everybody," but he didn't have a job. "He was always in this business or that business. He was always what we used to call a sport," says the mother. In reality, Harry Chayefsky had worked regularly as a house painter before finding a job delivering milk by horse and cart for the Perth Amboy Milk and Cream Company in New Jersey. His ambitions, however, were tepid until he met Gussie. Hers were strong and clear. America was "the golden land," that was what she had been told. She didn't intend to work in the garment sweatshops or to live in the crowded tenements on the Lower East Side forever. Her escape would be through education and hard work. And maybe someday she would be famous, "another Emily Brontë or Madame Curie," she said. Harry Chayefsky pushed her to accept more intimate esteem as his future wife and the mother of his children. Gussie politely declined. Marriage to her signified a big house, with bright, active, educated children, and that could be provided only by a man who had drive and a hunger for upward mobility.

Soon, Harry Chayefsky requested a change in duties at the Perth Amboy Company. He stopped delivering milk and was given a desk job. Good at math, he found he liked accounting and making deals. On weekends he went with Gussie to visit the farmers in northern New Jersey. He signed them to contracts for future milk deliveries, thereby eliminating the middleman, the traditional milk broker. Harry also saved his salary and borrowed from friends, and soon he became a part owner of the Perth Amboy Company. Eventually he bought the largest share, took control, and renamed it Dellwood Dairies. With his position as president of the new company came Gussie's hand. They married and settled in Perth Amboy in a small rented apartment whose kitchen was furnished with an extra set of dishes and utensils, required for the kosher meals Gussie would serve for the rest of her life. In 1916, their first child, William, was born. Four days after his birth the family moved to a larger place in Mount Vernon, New York, where a year later another son, Winn, arrived. Six years after that, on January 29, 1923, on Bailey Avenue in the Bronx, where they had relocated temporarily, the family was blessed with its third and last child—another boy, Sidney, who in later years would be known to the world as Paddy Chayefsky.

At birth, it was obvious that Sidney had inherited his mother's immutable curiosity and intellect. All of her boys had minds of their own, she said, but Sidney was different. As he lay in his crib his eyes would follow her every move, and he listened so avidly when she spoke that she was sure he understood her every word. For the first ten months, when they lived on Bailey Avenue, the emotional bond between mother and son was obviously tight. Gussie was very happy then. Her dreams were fulfilled. She had her own family, all boys, and Harry, now quite prosperous, was in the midst of building a new house, the mansion of her dreams, in Mount Vernon, New York.

In October 1923, when the house was close to completion, it was up to Gussie to supervise the interior decoration and to purchase the many new pieces of furniture. This meant that she was frequently absent from their home on Bailey Avenue. The older boys were in school but she felt that the baby, Sidney, was in good hands, tended to by her mother, who had come to America after the death of Mr. Stuchevsky in Russia. Assigned to look after the baby during the day, it was the grandmother who unwittingly ruptured and impaired the natural order of things. Not used to the vagaries of fall weather in her new country, before taking the baby out in his carriage each morning Mrs. Stuchevsky would dress him in warm clothing, then wrap him in layers of blankets. On the street or in nearby Van Cortlandt Park, as the day got hotter, the baby in his carriage would struggle to rid himself of the oppressive swaddling. His grandmother would reinforce the covers, which made the baby cry, then scream. Grandmother Stuchevsky, described as a gruff, peasantlike woman, would then wipe her forefinger on her black shroudlike tunic, stick it in the baby's mouth, poke around roughly, and say aloud in Russian, "Ah! Another new tooth is coming." She would then wrap the baby so tightly in the carriage that he resembled a creature in a cocoon, with only his little head sticking out. Unable to breathe and afraid to cry out lest his small mouth be violated again, he would feel his anger and frustration implode. This sense of despair, of helplessness, of feeling unloved and abandoned, would remain, leaving his primary self and his autonomy ungrounded for most of his life, it has been suggested.

His happiest early memories would always be of the large new house on Fifth Street in Mount Vernon. It was here that Sidney Chayefsky showed the first signs of being gifted. When he was two he displayed an innate ability to memorize words. At two and a half he could "speak intelligently," and by three he was discoursing. His mother exalted these qualities and was naturally pleased with her wunderkind. She became his first mentor and teacher. She introduced him to books, not the usual children's fairy tales but realistic stories and novels. "Everything should be true to life, that was her attitude," said Bill Chayefsky. "A play or a story should be realistic. She didn't believe in fantasy." Together, she and Sidney devoured the classics, pausing to look up the more obscure words in the dictionary. Her favorite book was James Fenimore Cooper's *The Last of the Mohicans,* parts of which young Sidney learned to read, using the proper locutions and appropriate dramatics. This delighted the mother even more. And the boy, having won her love and attention, basked in the pleasure he provided.

It was in the house at Mount Vernon that the performing side of Sidney emerged. The place was always filled with people: visiting relatives, friends, neighbors who dropped in for an hour and stayed all day. "I remember constant talking, laughing, singing, dancing, card playing, eating, and drinking," he said. "Sometimes the parties went on until two and three o'clock in the morning." There were two distinct groups involved. Gussie had her "Russian intelligentsia" circle, and Harry had his vagabond gypsy friends. For his mother's group, the boy sometimes read a passage from a book or gave a recitation. For Harry's troupe, he would sing the verse of a popular song. The theatrical talent was inherited from *him,* his father said. Before he got married Harry had been a member of an amateur theatre company in Perth Amboy, and was considered to be quite an able actor. "Some actor," Gussie observed. "Ten words at a time he couldn't remember."

Harry did play "a damn good mandolin," and the banjo and the balalaika. And he instilled in his boys a love of the theatre. On weekends he would gather the three of them in his car and drive down to New York City, to lower Second Avenue, where the Yiddish theatre was located. It was here that Sidney had his first "spiritual experience." In the theatre one day, as a humorous sketch was about to unfold onstage, the youngest boy laughed at the precise moment a punch line was being delivered. His father picked up on his mirth, then his brothers, and soon the entire theatre was united in a geyser of laughter and enjoyment, like one big family. "I felt so warm, so connected to everyone," he later said. "I discovered then that humor was a very wonderful thing."

Gravity, however, was never far from the boy's impressions. Balancing the parental scale, Mrs. Chayefsky made sure that her influence was felt by her sons. Striving for more culture, she insisted that each one take piano lessons. Of the three, Sidney had the best ear. At age four he could play classical pieces, with or without sheet music. At five he was "giving cute little concerts in velvet suits at PTA meetings." He played with such skill and enthusiasm that "for a time there was talk of a career as a concert pianist." Undoubtedly this was largely Gussie's hope, that Sidney, the jewel in her crown, would provide the renown and success unattainable to her. In one of his TV plays, *Catch My Boy on Sunday,* Chayefsky wrote of a mother whose intense goal in life is for her youngest son to be a child star on television. The woman is not a typical stage mother, attracted to the money or the neighborhood cachet. Her son is the source of her emotional sustenance. She needs the boy's success to prove to her dead father that she is worthwhile. "I just wish he was alive today to see how wonderful I turned out with my children," the mother says.

Having his environment changed from one of great receptivity to one of great expectation must have had a profound effect on Chayefsky as a boy. While extending his own ego, his sense of grandiosity, it instilled in him the drive to excel, to do better than everyone else in his class. At the same time, having been made a part of someone else's psyche meant that the crystallization of his own independence and identity was further impeded. Years later, when this stage of his development was discussed in analysis and it was suggested that primary damage might have been done at this time, he reacted with fury. "Don't you say a fucking word against my parents," he warned the analyst. "They were *perfect!*"

Gussie apparently agreed. As far as she was concerned she only wanted the best "for all my boys." In 1928, proceeding with her splendid vision of Sidney's becoming another Horszowski or Josef Lhévinne (prodigies who played Carnegie Hall), Mrs. Chayefsky bought a baby grand piano and stepped up his tutoring. Using the inducement of special treats—homemade cheese blintzes or store-bought cream-filled éclairs—the mother managed to persuade the boy to increase his practicing time to three hours a day. The extra regimen took its toll. At that age, Sidney wanted to be outdoors. Henceforth, when obliged to play the piano, there were occasions when he did rebel. He would run through andante pieces, deliberately hitting the wrong notes. One day, prior to an important recital, he broke into an unexpected burlesque of one of his father's popular songs. In later years, pointing to the piano that he kept in his Midtown Manhattan office, Paddy Chayefsky said that one of his greatest joys in life was "playing good music badly." At that same time, he had another piano in his apartment on Central Park West. There his son would often see him sitting at the baby grand with his eyes closed, playing almost flawlessly a classical composition by Chopin or Tchaikovsky.

In *Catch My Boy on Sunday,* because the mother's misplaced ambition is hurting the child and their marriage, it is the father who steps in and puts a stop to the boy's acting career. In the Chayefsky family, another, more prevalent force curtailed Sidney's budding career as a prodigy performer. In October 1929, when he was six and a half, the stock market crashed. With it, the good life for the Chayefskys and millions of other American families came to a sudden halt.

In the bleak period that ensued, as factories and companies shut down and farmers in the Midwest burned grain in winter because it was cheaper than coal, the dairy distributors in the East dumped milk into the rivers and canals because people didn't have money to pay for it. With the collapse of the U.S. economic system, many small-business owners filed for bankruptcy, but not Harry Chayefsky. To him, that would have been a dishonor. "He was a very moral man," his son Bill remembered. "He insisted on paying off all his debts."

Hoping to recoup his fortune, Harry Chayefsky sold the mansion in Mount Vernon and went into the construction business. He built houses in the Kingsbridge section of the Bronx, including one on Tibbett Avenue, which became the new home for the entire Chayefsky clan, including two grandmothers (the paternal one had arrived from Moscow sometime before). Sidney's reaction to the move and the changes in the standard of living was one of confusion and deprivation. His stature as boy wonder, along with the privileges provided, had suddenly vanished. What frustrated him even more was that, being the youngest, he was told nothing. "It was as if I no longer existed," he said. During the day the adults moved around him in slow motion, acting as if he weren't there. At night the former atmosphere of spontaneity, of joy and laughter, was replaced with one of solemnity and hushed voices. In the parlor, his grandmothers would whisper and moan softly in Yiddish about the calamity and poverty that had followed them to America. In the kitchen, his father would sit for hours holding his mother's hand, trying to reassure her about their future. "My mother used to get so miserable and my father always tried to understand," Marty Pilletti tells Clara in *Marty*. "He'd talk and talk to her. I adored my father, because he was always so kind."

Unfortunately, things got worse for the Chayefskys. When the banks failed and mortgage loans were stopped, Harry was forced to sell the houses he had built at a big loss, including the one they lived in on Tibbett Avenue. They moved back to an apartment on Bailey Avenue. "Then we had some rough times," said Paddy. "But there was always food on the table," said Bill

Chayefsky, "maybe not the best food, but we never went without meals, and my father always managed to find the money for our education."

Undaunted, through the early 1930s Harry Chayefsky continued to pursue other get-rich schemes. When these failed to materialize, Gussie turned against him. The hardening of her character would later be used by her son in his TV plays. In the scripts of *The Sixth Year* and *The Bachelor Party,* the wives speak of their men as having never grown up, while they themselves have had to become callous and tough. "Somebody has to have an idea of what's to be done," the embittered mother in *The Sixth Year* tells her daughter. For his part, as the gifted boy, the chosen "entertainer," Sidney Chayefsky obviously felt it was his responsibility to lift everyone's spirits. This moral but cumbersome task was an obligation that would stay with him for the rest of his life. "There is always that guilt that kids have; they believe when something bad happens in the family it's their fault," says Dan Chayefsky. "Early on he acquired that tendency to put the burden on himself, to help everyone, to take the responsibility. His perception was enormous, and at times that leads to terrible depression. He could feel people's pain and he wanted to help, but what could a kid of that age do? Also, part of him, the childlike ego part, must have been very angry over the changes. But he never expressed it, and that inner struggle left him very torn at times."

As the tension between his parents increased, Sidney sided with his mother—apparently for the wrong reason. The pervading unpleasantness was over money, his father's foolish investments, the boy believed. But there was a larger issue at stake. Harry Chayefsky, perhaps in retaliation for being looked upon as a failure by his wife, had an affair. This was doubly wounding to Gussie because the woman he chose to sleep with was the wife of a man she revered— her local rabbi. The infidelity was brief, but the shame lingered with Gussie for many seasons. She mentioned nothing of this, then or later, to Sidney, who eventually found out about it from his first cousin. The enforced secrecy, and the fact that Gussie, despite her mammoth pride and religious convictions, elected to keep the family together, would become ingrained principles scrupulously enforced by her son when he became an adult.

Growing up in the Depression did have some positive aspects, especially in terms of honing the skills of a future writer. With funds for extraneous spending severely limited, most families had to rely on the airwaves for the current news, sports, and entertainment. "All we had was this old wooden radio," Chayefsky once recalled. "On Saturday or Sunday nights we would listen to the variety shows or the weekly dramas. They were wonderful to cultivate your ear and your imagination. You'd hear these voices and sound effects coming out of the box, and you'd have to imagine what the people looked like and what was going on. The basic plot and dialogue were given, but it was up to you to supply the visuals."

Around the kitchen table, when the radio was off, there were "unlimited and unending discussions of every topic: economics, politics, the theatre," recalled Winn Chayefsky. Each boy was encouraged to contribute to the conversation, and Sidney, being the youngest and the smallest, may have felt he had to talk the loudest and the fastest to be heard.

Thanks to the pervasive curriculum at home and his superior intellect, Sidney excelled at classroom oratory when he attended Public School 7. "I was offensively precocious," he said. "One of those kids in the front row with his hand up all the time." Being too smart too often naturally did not endear him to the slower, tougher boys in class. The taunts usually began at recess or after school, and always included someone mocking his first name: "Si'ney." "He had a lot of trouble with his name," said Dan Chayefsky. "And he was always aware that kids could be very cruel to each other." To react with anger or violence was to lose dignity and power, that's what Gussie told him. It was his father, the mild-mannered Harry, who ultimately stimulated Sidney's rebellion and defense. After finding employment as a milk broker, Mr. Chayefsky moved his family back to Tibbett Avenue, to a two-family house next door to their Aunt Rose. The new location was three blocks west of Broadway, between 233rd and 234th streets. Like most of the neighborhood, their block comprised Italians, Irish (who worked as domestics and servants in nearby Riverdale), and "a few Jews." The Chayefskys lived on the second floor of the house; the O'Connors, the owners, lived beneath. On the other side of them were the Catalanos. During the first weeks of this third and last move, Sidney tended to stay indoors with the family. After school, he would go to the front room to talk to his grandmothers or do his homework. Meanwhile, in the kitchen, Gussie, with her omnipresent book, stood by the stove and prepared dinner. When the smell of the overcooked food reached Sidney's nose, he'd go to the open window, yell out to his brothers on the front stoop, and say, "Hey, guys, the meat's burned, dinner's ready."

In June, when school let out, Sidney continued to hang around at home, until one day his father took him by the hand, brought him downstairs, opened the front door, and said, "Go! There are children your age out there. Get in trouble." That's when Sidney discovered he had another talent, one that would provide a new identity. Some of the kids gathered at the end of the block he recognized as hostile idlers from school. Unwilling to fight or play the "feeb" as he approached them warily, a cover strategy popped up, seemingly out of nowhere. At closer range, before the neighborhood gang could scowl or say anything, Sidney attacked, with his tongue. Like a sudden, biting summer squall, he let loose with a rapid, nonstop, brilliant, absolutely incisive commentary on everything that stood or moved on Tibbett Avenue. The linguistic storm, charged by a rich, pungent vocabulary, mesmerized and captivated the hostile forces. It also amazed and thrilled Chayefsky himself, and made him aware of an ally he could now rely on. "In the thirties in the Bronx you weren't supposed to walk around as a sensitive, creative, talented person," says Dan Chayefsky. "If you did you got yourself killed. So in order to survive he created this persona and he put on a show."

His audience was mostly Irish and Italian kids, and Sidney was soon welcomed into their homes, which would later provide the settings for some of his television and movie scripts. There was a distinct similarity between the two groups—"very close family ties among emotionally volatile people," he said. Each nationality had traits that appealed to him. The Italians were generous, passionate, and noisy, openly demonstrative in their feelings toward one another. The Irish weren't as "mushy." They served lousy food, but around the table their dialogue was reckless and sparkling. With ease they orchestrated topics, mixing fun with profundity and bravely ridiculing such important things as religion, politics, and death. And in a fight, where an Italian "could bite your ear off just as soon as look at you," the Irish, using their combative wit and pithy prose, could deliver a verbal uppercut that would bring foes down faster than any fist or blow.

Although his mother was not responsive to Sidney's new street image, or to his habit of shooting craps and playing cards instead of practicing the piano, his father and the other Chayefsky males approved of the changes. It was a perfect match, putting his brother in with the Irish, Bill Chayefsky believed. "They liked to talk, and his vocabulary was unbelievable. I never met anybody whose command of words was as large as his, even as a kid."

At the age of twelve, Chayefsky entered De Witt Clinton High School, an all-boys public academy in the Bronx. Abe Pasternak, a classmate of Chayefsky's, remembered him as "tremendously bright, with the gift of tongues, and always the centerpiece of a crowd of guys." "My pals" was how Chayefsky referred to his group, all of whom signed their names to a page in his school notebook. The names—Bernie Rossen, Howard Newman, Jay Rosenblatt, Irving Gaft—were all Jewish. In school he had one set of friends, mostly intellectual, while at home, on Tibbett Avenue, there was a different claque, with Damon Runyon–type monikers such as "Crooked-dollar Joe" and "Scrambled-eggs Willie," with whom he learned to smoke and had his first taste of alcohol. As he cultivated a love of sports, he maintained the same social diversity. During baseball season, Sidney went with his Jewish school pals to the nearby Polo Grounds, to cheer on the Giants. Concurrently, he was also part of the basketball team at St. John's, the local Catholic church on 238th Street. His Catholic chums, he said, had something the Jewish people didn't—

the ritual of confession. "Imagine," he said, "you can sin and carouse to your heart's delight, then get rid of all that guilt by spilling your guts to a priest."

His ventures into alien religious territory did not upset his mother; she made sure that Sidney embraced the faith of his forefathers. Being Jewish had remained important to Gussie. In Mount Vernon and the Bronx she continued to keep a kosher kitchen where pork was verboten and all dairy products were segregated. In other Orthodox matters, her beliefs were so strong that when her oldest son, William, at age twenty-five fell in love with a Gentile girl, she proceeded to break up the relationship.

The practice of Judaism was an art form that required talent and discipline, and with his mother's urging, Sidney diligently applied himself. His proficiency was such that at age six, during Hanukkah, when he lit the candles at four o'clock each day, he could recite the blessings in both Hebrew and English. At ten he knew the Mishnah by heart, and at twelve he was the star student at Hebrew school, next to the storefront synagogue on West 234th Street, where he was bar mitzvahed at thirteen. That was the year it was noted in the synagogue records that young Chayefsky became "a legend," when on a few hours' notice he substituted for a leading actor in an important religious play.

In his teens, Chayefsky began to turn his attention to another communal art form: the movies. In the mid- to late 1930s, as President Roosevelt's New Deal program was slowly restoring prosperity to America, it was estimated that 60 percent of the country attended the movies each week. Intermittently, the Chayefsky family formed part of that statistic. Their visits were sporadic because the parents could not always agree on the movie of choice. Mrs. Chayefsky preferred dramas, or movies "that told you something." *Anthony Adverse* and *Death Takes a Holiday,* both with Fredric March, were her idea of solid entertainment. Mr. Chayefsky preferred a good comedy with Cary Grant, or a musical with Fred Astaire and Ginger Rogers, whose stellar charms greatly impressed the youngest member of the Chayefsky family.

Sidney and his friends often went to the RKO Marble Hill on 231st Street. As they got older and braver they would frequently take the bus or hitch a ride east, over to Fordham Road, where the big movie palaces were located. Loews Paradise was the major showcase. Inside the massive theatre, past the columns of Greek statuary, the entire ceiling of the auditorium was painted blue, with floating clouds and inverted twinkling lights that dimmed on cue as the giant stage curtain parted and the main feature began. As they entered their teens, Chayefsky and his group were partial to adventure and tough-guy pictures. But they found they could actually enjoy a comedy or a corny musical, if it featured Carole Lombard or Jean Harlow or any of a bevy of blond chorus-type girls who didn't appear too bright but had terrific legs and bosoms. Afterward, the real fun was going across the street to Crumb's Ice Cream Parlor, where if the timing was right they would approach girls, using the best or worst lines from the movie.

With his pals, Sidney seldom had trouble talking to girls. He was funny but never fresh. On his own, on a one-to-one basis, it was a different matter. Sidney was shy with the ladies. Then there was the matter of his size. In his family his brother Winn, at five foot ten, was the tallest. Bill was five foot eight and a half. And Sidney, favoring his mother, was only five foot six. "He never spoke about his being the shortest," said Bill. "Which led me to believe that it didn't bother him." But it did. As a teenager, hoping to rectify the situation, Sidney increased his food intake and did special stretching exercises. But instead of becoming taller, he grew wider, until he began to resemble "a compact office safe." Still, he did have a handsome face, deep-set eyes, and a shy but devilish smile which attendant to his irrepressible humor made him attractive to people, especially those of the female gender.

In April 1938, three months after he turned fifteen, the annual spring dance was held at De Witt Clinton. The boys had a choice: they could bring a girl, if they had one, or they could choose a dance partner from among the girls who had been invited from the neighboring schools. Since this was his social debut, Sidney prepared for a week in advance. His mother bought him a new shirt, new shoes, new socks, and a new tie. She ironed his best suit, and he borrowed his father's fourteen-karat-gold rolled tie clip and cuff links. On the big evening the family bathroom was his, reserved from six-thirty to seven. Anyone who "had to go" during that time was sent by Gussie downstairs to the O'Connors' or next door to Aunt Rose's. Having no facial hair yet to shave, Sidney stood in front of the medicine cabinet and washed and dried and combed and uncombed his hair, while practicing his opening lines of contact with his future partners. "May I have this dance?" with a polite bow? No, that was too formal. "Shall we?" accompanied by a jerk of the head toward the dance floor? That was cool, but too flip. And what if he stumbled or stood on a girl's toes? Or if his sweaty palms left a huge stain across the back of her dress? Girls in white dresses required special attention. Talk, yes; dance, no. Because first impressions were everything.

Arriving fashionably late, twelve minutes past the slated hour, Sidney was relieved to see some of his pals in a cluster by a side door of the school gymnasium. Standing together, they watched as the seniors hogged all of the best-looking girls for the opening numbers. Then, by design, one of the teacher-chaperones announced that the next dance would be by girls' invitation only. Moving slightly apart, Sidney and his pals stood awkwardly at the edge of the dance floor. As the music began, the contingent of females slowly fanned out in twos and threes, shyly stalking their prey around the gymnasium. Sidney and his pals were ignored; then he spotted a trio of girls heading from the right. His heart began to thump. He knew *he* was on their dance card. He was right. They stopped first before him.

"How about this one?" one of the girls pertly asked. There was a dramatic pause for inspection, then a reply.

"No," the brassiest one of the trio answered. "He's too short and fat."

And they moved on, leaving a devastated teenager in their wake.

Years later, Chayefsky would put a variation on that brutal rejection in his TV play *Marty*. At the time, the actual experience destroyed him, said Dan Chayefsky. "It was so crushing. He became nauseated and embarrassed. He wanted the floor to open up and swallow him." While permanently halting the final formation of his converging teenage identity, the experience at the school dance wiped out whatever self-confidence Sidney had accumulated. His world collapsed, sending him into an excruciating cycle of depression. "He told me he had severe moods before, but this one almost destroyed him. It was a consuming, overwhelming experience for him," said Dan Chayefsky.

At night Sidney began to have recurring dark dreams. In these he either was being suffocated to death or was left abandoned as a small child on a street corner in some strange town. Throughout the day, he constantly thought of suicide. Standing on the platform of the subway at 231st Street, he would find himself transfixed by the deadly third rail. It would be so easy and quick to jump down and electrocute himself. "The only thing that stopped him was that he didn't want to hurt his parents," said Dan Chayefsky.

"The time of death is determined by God, and none dare anticipate His decree"; that's what the Talmud says. So in the temple, Sidney prayed to God to ease his pain or to take his life. When He refused, the boy retreated further. He became more morose and aloof. He stopped talking. At home during mealtime, when his mother said he was "in one of his moods," Sidney gave up eating. When, for no discernible reason, he lost his temper and snapped at one of his grandmothers, the guilt from that became almost unbearable. And then one evening, walking alone, the solution came to him. The emotional numbness was suddenly lifted when he realized that there was a place where he could put his evolving feelings and energies, a place where no one could touch him. It was in a special craft that he had slowly cultivated over time—his writing.

In lower-middle-class Jewish families, writing was always considered a highly respected career. That's what Sidney had always been told. His mother had once written a book in Russian. His father boasted that one of the players in his poker group was a writer, whose byline appeared regularly in "the only paper of importance," *The New York Times*. Having been born literate, it was a natural progression for Sidney to combine his massive vocabulary with his active imagination. He showed his first story to Mrs. Daly, his English teacher at De Witt Clinton. She encouraged him further by urging that he contribute his work to *The Magpie,* the De Witt Clinton magazine. "He was extremely modest, very modest," said Mrs. Marcella Whalen, literary adviser of the magazine. "He'd poke a piece of work at me and ask, 'Will you have time to read this?' His contributions had been revised so meticulously they needed no editing or proofreading. There were never even typing or spelling errors."

One of his first published pieces in the school magazine was an open letter he wrote to his cousin Hesh. It was about a girl named Jane, who was pretty and fun and one of those rare types "who can carry a conversation." But Jane was in love with his friend Buddy, who has "a wow of a build and got there first," and that left Sidney as "the stooge . . . the beaten warrior." Closing the letter, he told his cousin that he was going to forget Jane and consider a career on the stage, and "I wouldn't tell this to nobody but you, but I'm inclined to think I'm a swell fellow. I mean I'm not bad looking. I sing well. I guess she doesn't know what she's missing."

After he was rejected at the school dance, Sidney's short stories in *The Magpie* had more of an edge and centered solely on males. One of them, "No Dice," was about an art student addicted to gambling who attempts to break the bank at Monte Carlo. "Vice is nice, but virtue won't hurtue," the randy young gambler concludes after calling his father to bail him out of debt. Another short story, "Two Punch Wilson," tells of a tough boxer who longs to be in "the pugilistic hall of fame," that is, on the front page of the *Police Gazette.* He gets his wish when, in a rash career slip, he's arrested for burglarizing a house.

When asked about it years later, Chayefsky said his earliest writing inspiration came from dime-store novels, the slick magazines, and the classics. "Neo-Wodehouse, you know, with a touch of Dickens," he said. To protect his creative aspirations, he donned an armor against criticism. When his stories appeared in the school magazine they were casually dismissed by the other student writers, including a later professional critic, Seymour Krim. "We had teethed on highbrow literature and were full of pretentious dreams and literary theories," said Krim. Dismissing Chayefsky's talent as "pedestrian . . . downright crass," Krim said that the "criticisms rolled right off his back. He wasn't the least bit swayed by us."

In his last year at De Witt Clinton, Sidney canvassed for and got the job as editor of *The Magpie.* The position and his more authoritative demeanor did not go unnoticed. "He wore a vest all the time, a sweater vest. That was his identification," said his friend Abe Pasternak. "He was like a school monitor, in the hall a lot, going from his classroom to the head office, and he didn't walk, he kind of strutted. If you stopped him, he seldom wasted time on hello.

He'd begin to talk, and it didn't matter what the topic was, the words would shoot out of him like bullets." Chayefsky was articulate but also uncompromising, Pasternak recalls. "After he gave his opinion on something he was ready to walk away. There was no further discussion. He always had to have the last word."

"The last word? The last *ten* words," said Herb Gardner, a friend in later years. "The last word to Chayefsky was an epilogue."

"But people always listened to him," said Pasternak, "because he had kind of an aura about him. Part of it came, I guess, because he was not very tall—five foot five or six at most—so it was kind of like he had a Napoleonic complex."

In June 1939, at the age of sixteen and a half, Chayefsky graduated from De Witt Clinton with an A average. In the school yearbook, when asked to give his ultimate ambition, instead of listing "doctor," "lawyer," or "humanitarian," he wrote, "Muckraking." When he was voted the class wit, the magazine's literary adviser, Mrs. Whalen, was taken aback. "I was surprised, because he gave me the impression of being shy and quiet," she told the *New York Post* in an interview in 1960.

After working through the summer in his Uncle Abe's printing shop in Manhattan, in the fall of 1939 Chayefsky enrolled in "the Harvard of the Jewish middle class," City College of New York. Though majoring in accounting and the social sciences, he said he wanted to be a writer—but he had no idea what application he had to fill out. He did join an English literature class taught by Professor William Bradley. "I remember him chiefly because he was frequently raising his hand in an attempt to argue with me," said Bradley. "Perhaps that indicated that he was at least one member of the class who was listening to my lecture."

In his second year, Chayefsky enrolled in a short-story class presided over by a legendary CCNY professor, Theodore Goodman. A tough mentor who puffed cigarettes furiously throughout class and harangued some students for being too middle-class and others for being too bohemian, Goodman thought nothing of throwing the inattentive or insubordinate out of his classroom.

Playwright William Gibson had attended Goodman's class two years earlier. He recalls the professor as "extraordinary . . . very witty . . . a great entertainer. He had a passionate dedication to literature, which was infectious and gave aspiring students the feeling that their interest in writing was somehow confirmed by some bishop." Chayefsky's impression was somewhat different. "As a teacher he could be savage and cruel," he said. "Not in the Russian sense, but cruel as a cold winter—a natural force, not a malicious force." Goodman contributed little to the style or content of his later work, Chayefsky believed, but he did impress upon him the dictum that every writer should learn "to stand alone, because no one would give him guidance or show approval."

"He insisted that we write about what we knew," said Gibson. "People tended to write stories that were derived from magazines—like *The Saturday Evening Post*. He was very tough on them. One guy wrote a story about condoms, about finding these white balloons on a beach. Goodman would not discuss this story in the classroom. He was very uptight about that. Yet at the same time he was a passionate exponent of James Joyce, one of the first to bring Joyce into the classroom when *Ulysses* was banned."

"Our textbook was *Dubliners,* by Joyce, so I got to be a big fan of his in those days," said Chayefsky. "The Dead" was "one of the finest stories written," he added, "but *Ulysses* was too obscure, too topical. I mean, you really had to know Dublin in 1904 to know what the hell he was talking about."

Because none of his English teachers ever gave him any personal encouragement, Chayefsky said he squandered his writing talent in college. His literary output was limited to writing "satirical ditties and songs for classmates." These were inspired by the comedians he heard on radio and saw in vaudeville. "Milton Berle used to do parodies of popular songs," said Abe Pasternak. "One of them was called 'Roll On, You Mississippi.' That was the original title. But instead of singing those lyrics, Berle used the names of the subway stops along the Brooklyn-Bronx IRT subway line." Chayefsky penned similar material. His cover versions were set in the Bronx. One popular favorite was "When the Moon Comes over the Causeway." In college he wrote a song satirizing a student vigilante group. "They were our local witch-hunting, Red-hunting committee," he said years later, prudently neglecting to divulge that he was a part of the leftist faction that was being antagonized.

At nineteen, Sidney considered a career in professional sports. Earlier he had volunteered for the college basketball team, but at five foot six inches, he did not get past the preliminaries. In football, bulk, not altitude, is the most critical physical factor, and being 183 pounds, with huge arms and shoulders and a solid chest, he tried out and was selected to play pocket guard for the Kingsbridge Trojans. "In those days you played defense and offense. There was no platooning," he said. "I was the running guard who pulled out and led the interference." Acting as a block during one overly violent play, Chayefsky wound up mangled and bloody on the ground. He pulled himself together and managed to get back in the huddle, whereupon the leader spat at him to "get in there and *fight*." With that command, the dazed, squat player said to himself, "What the hell am I doing here?" And that ended his career on the gridiron.

The following May, Sidney received a bachelor's degree in social sciences from City College. There was no ceremony. The year was 1943; America was at war, and two weeks before graduation he was drafted. When his induction notice arrived, his father assured him that this would be "an adventure," that like his older brothers he would now get to travel and see many interesting places and people. His mother cried, cursed Hitler and Hirohito, then packed a cold lunch for her son to take on the subway down to Whitehall Street, where he would be examined and sworn in. Sitting half naked on a bench for two hours, Sidney and the other scared recruits were then relayed "like so many cattle" through the rudimentary physicals. "If you could walk and talk and see out of both eyes, they took you," he said.

During World War II, the initial culture shock of being in the Army, even for those of just average intelligence and awareness, was considerable. For Chayefsky the adjustment to boot camp was enormous. This was the first time he had been away from home, from his mother who cooked and cleaned and picked up after him, and away from Tibbett Avenue, whose insularity brought him a sense of safety and notoriety. As a raw recruit he had his first encounter with depersonalization. Stripped and shorn of his civilian identity, he was reduced to a name tag and a number, then shipped as a potential robot-soldier to a basic-training center at Camp Carson, Colorado. During his first week, after marching for miles in the rain, then wriggling on his back under barbed wire at night, Sidney poured out his bitterness in a letter to Professor Bradley, his old teacher at CCNY, who had assured him that he would "like the Army." What was there to like about being yelled at and bullied by an illiterate redneck sergeant who needed an interpreter to translate his orders? And what was the purpose of spit-shined boots, gleaming brass buckles, and a haircut clipped so close to the bone that his skull was shining? "Presumably this was meant to dazzle the enemy and reflect the bullets during battle?" he asked. Professor Bradley wrote back and congratulated Sidney for using his time constructively, by keeping a journal. Sidney took the hint and began to transfer his anger and frustration onto paper. Again, the process helped to lift his spirits. His other self, the cocky alter ego, slowly emerged, making him bolder and more assertive. Opposed to and inept with guns, on the rifle range the day he was tested he deliberately positioned himself next to a sharpshooter who was cross-eyed. Lying prone, they fired four shots at the same time. "I missed every shot and he got four bull's-eyes, on *my* target," Chayefsky crowed.

The Army made him grow up, he later stated. It also gave him a new name. Listed on the official Army roster as Sidney NMI (No Middle Initial), one Sunday morning Chayefsky was awakened at five o'clock to serve kitchen duty. He had to be excused, he told the duty officer, so he could attend Mass. "Yesterday morning you said you were Jewish," the officer replied. "Yes, but my mother is Irish," said Sidney. "O.K., Paddy," said the officer, and the name stuck.

It was a perfect fit, Chayefsky learned. "Paddy" had character, caprice; it appealed to his sense of swagger. Wearing it for a while, he also found it gave him more confidence. As Paddy, he felt he had a certain poetic license to publicly buck the system, to stand up for his rights against bullies and bigotry. "There was a lot of anti-Semitism in the Army," said Dan Chayefsky. "So he had to fight a certain battle for himself. Even then he was concerned because he felt that people picked on Jews and he didn't like anyone [being] picked on—Jews, blacks, anybody."

From Camp Carson, Chayefsky informed his family and friends of his new identity. "When he wrote and told me he was now 'Paddy,' I went along with it. I thought it suited him fine," said Bill Chayefsky. His mother wasn't as amenable. "She never called him Paddy, always Sidney," his brother said.

Sidney was Gussie's creation, and Paddy was his, that's how Chayefsky saw the scheme of things. In defiance, or perhaps to assert his new identity, in the Army he proceeded to break a few of the religious ordinances set up by his mother. He ate his first bacon. "He had never eaten pork before," said Dan Chayefsky. He also changed his age, making himself older, and his vocabulary became more colorful. "Be the cursed and not the curser," the Scriptures say, and most of the time, Sidney dutifully followed that injunction. For Paddy, however, obscenity soon became a second language, and he would also dispense with humility. In the Torah, the forty-eighth qualification frowned on self-glorification. Sidney had always followed that tenet, putting the greatest value on learning and scholarship. Paddy went along with the injunctions concerning knowledge and hard work, but as far as he was concerned any accomplishment of note deserved to be acknowledged and broadcast as far as the human ear could hear.

And so it came to pass, in the summer of 1943, that Sidney Chayefsky was retired and "Paddy" Chayefsky came to the fore. He and Sidney would continue to serve each other well. Sidney had the talent, the genius. He was the silent creator, the one who thrived on isolation, until he was stuck, and then it was Paddy who would come to his aid, taking the unformed material and ramming it past friends and colleagues, to be discussed and fixed. Then he would retreat, leaving Sidney in peace to get the job finished, when he would reemerge as Paddy the producer, the protector, the agent, who wheeled and dealed and pushed to get the most money and the best creative terms for poor Sidney. However, with the swagger and the support there would also be frequent doubt and discord. Because, as Archie Leach, Thomas Lanier Williams, and Norma Jean Baker would likewise find, a simple name change to Cary Grant, Tennessee Williams, or Marilyn Monroe might help to prop the core and sell the façade, but it could never erase the fears of the original dark companion.

Paddy Goes to War

When PFC Paddy Chayefsky scored in the top five in the written part of the basic-training tests, he was asked to join the Army's Advanced Service Training Program. "He had the nerve to ask them *where* he would be trained," said Bill Chayefsky. "When they said Fordham College, he told them, 'I'm your man.' That meant that while Winn was stationed down South and I was off on a ship in the Pacific, Paddy returned to the Bronx and got to go home on weekends."

A fellow student-soldier in the ASTP was Larry Mayer, who said that a part of the course was to study German, for intelligence work in Europe. "Paddy already knew the language from high school," said Bill Chayefsky. "But he told me the course at Fordham was so intensive that in a few weeks he wasn't only talking German, he was thinking in German."

Although he was taken with the adventurous prospects of the program, of working as an underground agent or a spy in France or Germany, the newly named Paddy Chayefsky did not adapt his dress or decorum accordingly. "He verged on the sloppy, but not slovenly," said Mayer. "He had a short, stumpy kind of figure, and when he had his military cap on he would tilt it in such a way that he looked impish and cocky." Part of this was calculated, Mayer believed. Chayefsky was aware of his appearance, but no one ever discussed it with him because his personality was too strong. "He had a comic, jocular, ironic presence," said Mayer. "He was somebody you didn't laugh at—but he made you laugh at things around him. He was very cocky, but whether it was a shell, a put-on, or an act, or if it was actually the real Paddy, one didn't know."

When the regular day students at Fordham invited the Army members to try out for their college revue, Chayefsky attended the auditions with Mayer as moral support. "He went to the piano and sang a song with very unusual lyrics, which he wrote himself. It was satirical, with a wry commentary on urban life." After the song, the students thanked him politely and he was dismissed. "The Fordham regulars weren't at all interested in what Paddy was doing, and he felt, and rightly so, that he had been given short shrift," said Mayer.

Confined to campus during the week, when Chayefsky couldn't rustle up a card game in the evenings he spent his time in the college library. Here he would be exposed to a writer whose work and psyche would cast a strong shadow in later years: Edgar Allan Poe, who had once lived in a cottage adjacent to the Fordham University complex. The first volume Chayefsky was steered to was *Marginalia,* a collection of aphorisms, comments, and notations that the poet-critic-essayist had made in the margins of books he read. One Poe meditation proved to be of immediate interest to Chayefsky. On the ambivalence of genius, Poe spoke of the "fate of an individual gifted, or rather accursed, with an intellect *very* far superior to that of his race."

On a further visit to the library, Chayefsky was directed to a biography of Poe, which told of his extreme self-absorption, his fear of suffocation and premature burial, and his frequent thoughts of suicide. A highly romantic idealist, with the fine manners of an amiable southern gentleman (when sober), Poe was also secure and very fond of his own work. Upon presenting a copy of "The Raven" to a friend, he enthusiastically called it "the greatest poem that ever was written." Sensitive and responsive to criticism (good and bad), when he lived in the Bronx Poe began a series of sketches entitled *The Literati of New York City,* which were short essays profiling the writers and editors of the day, some of whom had either praised, printed, or rejected Poe's many literary submissions. Writing of a former publisher and fellow critic, Charles F. Briggs, Poe recklessly disparaged his looks, character, and writing ability. Of Briggs's talent to judge other people's work Poe said, "Mr. Briggs has never composed in his life three consecutive sentences of grammatical English." In retaliation Briggs printed a savage portrait of Poe, cutting his physical height from five foot eight inches to five foot two; zeroing in on Poe's extremely pointed chin, he said it "gives his head on the whole a balloonish appearance, which may account for his supposed light-headedness."

Chayefsky's delight and further immersion in Poe's literary attacks were soon curtailed. That fall, many of the soldier-students at Fordham were transferred. Larry Mayer was assigned to an intelligence training unit at Camp Ritchie. He wasn't sure what happened to Chayefsky. "Maybe his German wasn't good enough, or he deliberately fouled up, but he did not make it to Camp Ritchie," said Mayer. Bill Chayefsky said that his brother never finished the course. "The war was escalating in Europe and they needed more infantry-men," he said. "So the Army, which had trained Paddy so thoroughly to speak and to think in German, took him out of intelligence and sent him to a heavy-weapons platoon, which he thought was stupid, but he had to go along with it."

Assigned to the 413th Infantry Regiment at Camp Croft, Chayefsky did not conscientiously adapt to his new role as a gung-ho soldier. When he and a new Army mate, Milton R. Bass, were promoted to private first class, they refused to sew on the stripe that accompanied the promotion and the paltry pay hike. "Consequently, we were treated as plain old dogfeet, rather than with the dignity to which our rank entitled us," said Bass.

As a second machine-gunner, Chayefsky was sent overseas with the 104th Infantry Division, which, after the invasion of Normandy, was the fourth wave to land. In Belgium, while a massive assault was being prepared farther north against the Germans at the Battle of the Bulge, the 104th Infantry Division headed west, toward the enemy border. Upon capturing a disbanded German unit, Chayefsky, the only infantryman to speak the language fluently, was put in charge of interrogating the prisoners. If they didn't talk, he was told not to allow them to go to the bathroom. Their pain and discomfort unnerved him, so he ignored the command. As punishment he was assigned as a foot soldier on the advance scouting patrol. "These guys had the privilege of moving ahead of the troops, ferreting out snipers and hostile gunfire. Then they went back and reported that somebody was shooting at them. Terrible way to make a living," said Bass.

On one reconnaissance detail, Chayefsky was seriously injured when, report-edly, he stepped on a land mine. Rushed to a nearby MASH unit, his first concern was for his parents. "The usual procedure when anyone was wounded was for a telegram to be sent to the family," said Bill Chayefsky. "Paddy knew that would scare the hell out my mother, so he had the lieutenant of the medical unit write a letter saying that he was injured but was O.K. Of course she didn't believe a word of that until she heard from him directly."

Transferred to a hospital in England, while recuperating Chayefsky com-posed a letter proudly telling his parents that he was the first man in his company to receive a Purple Heart. Garson Kanin, a captain in the U.S. Army's Special Service Division, recalled meeting him at this time. While making a tour of the hospital ward, Kanin paused in front of Chayefsky's bed. "I looked down at his chart and it said 'Paddy Chayefsky,' which made you stop right there," said Kanin. After remarking on the incongruity of the names, the captain asked the soldier how he had become injured. "What happened was that I took a dump," Paddy replied.

"Tell me more," said Kanin.

"We were out on a patrol and I had to take a dump," he continued. "The sergeant said, 'Go ahead, but don't take too long.' So I stepped out of line and went into the woods, dropped my pants, and I sat down on a mine. Jesus, it goddamn nearly blew my ass off.''

"He turned the entire painful experience into a big joke," said Bill Chayefsky. "It became Paddy's favorite war story."

Impressed with his wit and delivery, Kanin had Chayefsky assigned to the Special Service Division. With the director Carol Reed and the actor Peter Ustinov as England's creative delegates and the actor Claude Dauphin representing France, the Allied group were working on *The True Glory,* the definitive documentary on the Allied invasion of Europe. It was Chayefsky's job to interview some of the American soldiers who took part in the landing. He also added his own account of military duty, which wound up on the final sound track.

With his foot in the door, Chayefsky was also not shy about exploring the other branches of show business housed within the Special Service Division on the base. Sitting in on rehearsals of the shows scheduled to play at Army camps in England and France, Chayefsky remained singularly unimpressed. The skits and jokes, written by people who had "never seen combat," were flat. He would write his own show, he decided. With a fellow patient, pianist-arranger Jimmie Livingston, he wrote five songs and the book for a "musical smasher." He then wangled a meeting with Staff Sergeant Curt Conway, the theatre unit's producer-director. "Until I met Chayefsky, I thought I was the sloppiest soldier in the Army," said Conway. "Bedraggled is the best description [of Chayefsky]—his shirttail was always riding out, and one trouser leg always out of the boot. He was generally unimpressive until you found he had a charming sense of humor." Upon hearing Chayefsky's songs, Conway, who had been with the Group Theatre in New York, asked to read the book of the show. "It was very dirty, full of latrine humor," he said. "But it was clearly one of the most talented things I'd read in a long time."

Conway arranged for Chayefsky and Livingston to join his section, then went to work on the show with the pair. Paddy was eager and prolific, but frequently off the mark, he recalled. "He would bring me a scene that was a gem—but had nothing to do with the story line. I'd say, 'This has to go,' and he'd say, 'O.K., what do you want?' "

The main setting of the play was a military hospital ward, where a combat casualty, "Paddy Ostrinowski," having written the book and lyrics for a show, goes in search of a partner to write the music. One candidate is hired, then fired. "Because yesterday he wrote a song. The first eight bars were from Gershwin, the second eight bars, a direct steal, note for note, from Jerome Kern," says Ostrinowski. "A plagiarist?" his friend Looie asks him. "No," says Paddy O. "With him, it was research."

With luck, Ostrinowski finds another collaborator, a pianist who "when he strikes a chord, women bear children." Together they write ten songs, including one titled "Fugue de Manic Depressive," which features a chorus of soldiers pleading to be released from war duty because of various emotional disorders. In a solo number, Paddy Ostrinowski sings and talks of his yen for "a big girl for little me." Amazon women, and "aggressive lasses who'll throw all the passes," were his type. And so what if he was short? He could "straddl'er without Adler. I can navigate'er, without an elevator." What he lacked in size he could make up in science, because talent was talent, and Paddy O., a playwright, was also a genius. There wasn't a woman alive who wouldn't want to feed and nurture him, he said, just to be a chapter in his autobiography.

With two acts and eight scenes completed, a cast of fifteen, including eight females to play nurses, patients, and the love interest, was hired. Conway also suggested that Chayefsky join the show. He balked. He was "the writer," not an actor. When told that with his book chores finished he might be reassigned to active duty at the front, Chayefsky reconsidered. The decision literally saved his life. "Most of his former infantry division were killed in the assault on Berlin," said Bill Chayefsky.

NO T.O. FOR LOVE
BOOK AND LYRICS BY PFC PADDY CHAYEFSKY
MUSIC COMPOSED AND ARRANGED BY PFC JIMMIE LIVINGSTON

Such were the title and credits on the program announcing the Army show that premiered in January 1945 in a military depot two hundred miles north of London. "We toured Army camps and played in every conceivable and inconceivably difficult situation," said Chayefsky. "I must have ended up with ten years of theatre experience from that one show."

"Paddy treated the whole thing like we were doing a Broadway musical out of town," said Conway. "After every performance he'd bring me changes he wanted to make in a song or in someone's lines. We had nothing to lose, so if they were any good, I put them in before we hit the next camp. And the funny thing is the show kept getting better and better. So good, in fact, we were asked to take it up to London."

On May 28, 1945, *No T.O.* [*Table of Organization*] *for Love* opened at the Scala Theatre in the West End, and enabled Chayefsky to become a part of a legitimate theatrical milieu. His new friends included composer Marc Blitzstein and an established British actor, Laurence Olivier, who took him on a tour of London's bombed-out streets one night after a performance. In the audience another evening was Broadway director Joshua Logan, who was so impressed with the "diamond-bright lyrics" of the show that he went backstage to meet the writer. When summoned, Paddy was cool. "I told him how much I liked his work," said Logan, "expecting him to warm up a bit and become a very friendly person. But not at all. He knew they were great. He'd written them."

In June 1945, when the war with Germany ended, a new Special Service unit was assembled in Paris. The producers were Joshua Logan and Alan Campbell, a writer known mainly for being married to Dorothy Parker. Among the talents recruited to entertain the troops on active duty were the actors Mickey Rooney and Dan Barton and a future director, Arthur Penn. From England, Chayefsky and the entire company of *No T.O. for Love* were dispatched to join the new unit, which was stationed in a camp set up on the grounds of a château eight miles outside Paris. Dan Barton later recalled that he was rehearsing for Clifford Odets's *Golden Boy* when he was asked one day if he had met "this crazy guy, Paddy Chayefsky." He replied, " 'Nobody is named Paddy Chayefsky.' And then I met him and he bowled me over with his wit and talent."

Regular curfews and military restrictions were frequently ignored at the camp, especially on weekends, when most of the staff chose to be in Paris. Chayefsky's first sighting of the recently liberated City of Light came from the back of a jeep which he and three others had stolen from the Army's motor court. "None of us had much money, but that didn't matter," said Barton. "The war was over and we were like gypsies in show business. There was a lot of socializing and parties going on."

Arthur Penn shared a hotel room in Paris with Chayefsky and watched him wash his socks in the bidet. Another time they drove to the south of France to appear in a French movie. "Claude Renoir, who was the nephew of Jean Renoir, was the cameraman," said Penn. "He was doing this movie in Marseilles and he needed some GIs. So Paddy and I volunteered. We went down there for a few days, appeared in the movie, but we never found out what happened to it."

Throughout his time in France, Chayefsky continued to write. "He showed me some lyrics he was doing for a musical on Clare Boothe Luce," said Penn. "The scenes were good, but at that time he didn't have that great gift for the supernaturalistic dialogue that he would write for *Marty* and the other Philco TV shows. He seemed to be more taken with the musical-theatre format. Why that caught his fancy, I don't know."

Dan Barton said that comedy seemed to interest Chayefsky the most; he would spend hours explaining the different types of comedy to the actor. For example, he told Barton, "Jewish humor is completely funny because it's completely honest and completely logical. And that's why it can be universally understood by everyone."

Larry Mayer, Chayefsky's Army pal from Fordham, also commented on the farcical side of Chayefsky. "The contrast between the impish, puckish fellow I knew and the sensitive writer that came later surprised me. That sense of personal insight into the nuances of human behavior, and into the bittersweet parts of urban life, was not evident during the war years to me, or for that matter to anyone else."

Throughout the summer of 1945, as productions of *Golden Boy,* Thornton Wilder's *Our Town,* and *No T.O. for Love* were staged in France and Germany, the stress of future battle was still a factor for many in the performing unit. "The war in Japan was still going on, so we were all sweating it out, particularly those in infantry, because we could be recalled any minute," said Penn. "The conventional wisdom was that there was going to be a massive landing in Japan, much like D Day in Europe. So everyone was kept on alert. Then all of a sudden they dropped the atom bomb on Hiroshima, and the war was over. I remember we were all relieved, but also shocked by the swiftness of it all."

> When I got outta the Army, Clara, I was lost.
> I didn't know what I wanted to do.
> I was twenny-five years. What was I gonna do?
> Go back to my old job? Fifty cents an hour?
>
> Marty Pilletti, *Marty*

In Europe, after V-J Day, members of Josh Logan's Special Service unit were offered a substantial pay raise if they would stay and entertain the young army of occupation that was coming into Berlin and other parts of Germany. Arthur Penn was among those who agreed to stay as stage manager. With ambitions of his own, Paddy Chayefsky opted to go home to New York, where he was sure that a civilian career in show business awaited him.

His return to the Bronx was not the one he envisioned. His parents, relatives, and the neighbors on Tibbett Avenue were overjoyed to see him, but they failed to comprehend that he was a far different person from the young man who had left them. It wasn't merely that he had been to war. He had a new name, and the respect and friendship of people they had never heard of. "The sad thing to realize was that I had moved beyond them," he said.

That fall, wearing his brown Eisenhower jacket and alternately carrying *An Actor Prepares,* by Stanislavsky, or *The Craft of Comedy,* by Athene Seyler and Stephen Haggard, Chayefsky was a frequent visitor at Louis Shurr's office in the Paramount Building at 1601 Broadway. Shurr and his brother, Lester, whom Paddy knew from Paris, were theatrical agents, representing Bob Hope, Dan Dailey, and others. Chayefsky hoped they would be able to have his Army show restaged in a theatre in New York. But Broadway producers gave the same reply. The war was over. Audiences didn't want to hear or see what went on in an Army hospital, even if it was funny. Chayefsky said he would gladly make revisions. He was willing to change the background, write new lyrics and a new book for an entirely different revue. Again, there were no takers, and soon Chayefsky found himself sitting at Walgreens or the Astor drugstore in Times Square, "discussing with all the other Army talents how lousy the established stars were and the pitiful condition of the theatre."

Soon the money he had saved in the Army began to run out, and Chayefsky was forced to face another unpleasant condition of postwar times—unemployment. Work was not that easy to find. As millions of other returning GIs had learned, the job market in their absence had been filled with women, younger men, or machines. Chayefsky had a degree in accounting, but no experience. Scouring the want ads and visiting offices, he found that no openings existed. He applied for lesser jobs, as a store clerk, a salesman. As the rejections piled up, his spirits went into a tailspin. The abundance of confidence that Paddy had acquired during the war began to erode, and Sidney's bouts with depression returned. In *Marty,* the main character spoke of the confusion and despair he felt when he came back from the war, and how he thought of taking his life by jumping onto the subway tracks. The nights were the worst for Chayefsky. The bad dreams in which he was being crushed or suffocated to death returned.

The protagonist of *Marty* would survive civilian life by becoming a butcher. In real life, Paddy had to settle for getting his old summer job back. He went to work as a messenger-apprentice in his Uncle Abe's print shop on West Twenty-eighth Street in Manhattan. It wasn't show business, he said, "but the place had lots of character." Dank and dark, the floors stained black from years of spilled ink, the print shop held a certain mystique for him. As a kid he had learned there was a special skill involved in the composition of type. His uncle was an artist from the old days when books were made by hand. He would print them and bind them and etch the leather covers. The old man taught Chayefsky to distinguish the different kinds of typeface, and about quality paper. It had to look good and feel good. "If it offended your fingers, it had no rag content."

His new responsibilities in the shop included inking the presses and cleaning them. In between those chores he also made deliveries, which he welcomed, as the fresh air helped to clear the vapors of kerosene from his head. One afternoon, two months into the job, he was delivering a batch of office stationery to a building in Times Square when he spotted a familiar face. It was the director-playwright Garson Kanin, whose hit play *Born Yesterday* had just opened on Broadway. "My wife [actress Ruth Gordon] and I were walking along, somewhere near the theatre district, when I saw Paddy, carrying some packages," said Kanin. "We stopped and talked about what he was doing. I asked him if he was writing. He said, 'Who has the time? I have a job.' After a while we exchanged phone numbers, and on the way home I told my wife about him. She was fascinated. She thought he was so colorful and interesting. That night she said to me, 'You know, Garson, that guy we met today is so talented, why don't we subsidize him so he can write something?' "

The Kanins gave Chayefsky five hundred dollars, which would enable him to quit his job and write a play. "I didn't have a clue on how to do that," he said, "so I went out and bought a book of plays by Lillian Hellman. Then I sat down at the typewriter and copied *The Children's Hour,* word for word. I studied every line of it and kept asking myself, 'Why did she write this particular line?' "

After studying the preciseness of Hellman and the dramatic techniques of Ibsen, Chayefsky scrutinized the orthodox structure of *The Front Page,* written by Ben Hecht and Charles MacArthur. "It was a well-made play," he said. "I got something out of that, too."

"But then," Kanin said, "he became a nuisance. Paddy was full of ideas, and he used to come up to the office every three or four days with a new play. I told him that a play was supposed to take a little longer, and to stick to just one idea."

Put Them All Together was the title of the play he finally chose to write. "Needless to say, it was about a Jewish family in the Bronx," said Chayefsky. "Part Hellman, part Hecht. I was influenced by Clifford Odets as well." The play's central character was Willie, a twenty-four-year-old former soldier who lives with his parents in a three-room apartment in the west Bronx. The father is passive but smart. Every day he reads *The New York Times,* "the paper that never makes a mistake." The dominant figure in the play is the mother, Mrs. Sack. Feisty, intelligent, and strong, she's "got a lot of drive," says Willie. "If she was Lady Macbeth, Pop would still be King of Scotland." Mrs. Sack loves her sons, especially her youngest, Willie. She calls him "the genius," because he was so bright in kindergarten. Mr. Sack calls him "the talent," because Willie wrote a musical show while in the Army. "It was a smash success," the father tells a local gossip. "Who in the neighborhood doesn't know?" the woman replies. Other characters are introduced in the first scene, including the older son, George, who comes home for a visit from England with a British bride. "The English are worse than the Irish," the gossipy neighbor opines. "You turn your back on them, they'll break your legs."

As the house fills up, Willie says he needs more space, a room of his own, because "plays aren't written in revolving doors." His mother stoically suffers his complaints. Someday she's going to write a book herself, she says. "The name of the book will be 'I Was the Mother of a Playwright.' And the first sentence of the book will be 'Better you should be dead than be the mother of a playwright.' " Willie says he loves his family but there's something hard, something cold, within him that worries him. He is a person who takes, and doesn't give, his mother says, advising him to "always write comedies because in your whole life you'll never understand how completely a person can suffer."

In Act II, Willie announces his plans to go to California, where all his wartime show-biz friends are now located. He's sure he'll get a job there, writing for the movies. The mother is concerned and, like Gussie Chayefsky, overpossessive. She wants Willie and his brother to stay at home, where she can love and care for them. Willie tells his mother he would appreciate it if she didn't love him so much. He also advises his brother that "at some point in your life, George, you gotta give your mother the brush. It's as callous as that." When his mother collapses, Willie is stricken with remorse. "Now and then I get so selfish I could cut my throat," he says. "My mother has a heart attack, and all I can think of is a screen credit. Boy, I can see I'm gonna be a real bastard when I get to be a big shot." Changing his mind, Willie says he will stay home, whereupon his mother confesses she faked the heart attack and urges the young man to leave. "Go pack your bags. Get ready. I'll go to the movies someday. I'll see your name. I'll be happy."

The Lure of the Dream Factories

Early in the summer of 1947, when his play was half completed, Chayefsky decided to emulate his fictional character, Willie, and go to Hollywood. "I went only because my family kept saying, 'If it's writing and show business you want, Hollywood is the place for you. Go!' So I went," he said.

On the way to California, he lucked into the hottest poker game on the train and ended up winning thirty bucks. Upon his arrival at Union Station in Los Angeles, feeling flush, he took a cab directly to Universal Studios, where his Manhattan sponsors, Garson Kanin and Ruth Gordon, were working on *A Double Life,* starring Ronald Colman and directed by George Cukor. After welcoming Chayefsky to the lot, Kanin and Gordon also managed to find him a job—not on the movie, but in the studio's accounting office, where he worked in the budget and audit department.

The daily digit routine was boring, but Paddy soon took care of that. Under the pretext of "computation confirmation," he found numerous excuses to leave the office and visit the various movie sets, where he would introduce himself to people who would later be beneficial to his writing career. Included were manager-agent Harold Hecht, Hecht's impending star client, Burt Lancaster (making his feature debut in *The Killers*), and Michael Gordon, who was directing Fredric March and Ann Blyth in *Another Part of the Forest.* Gordon recalled inviting Chayefsky to a party at his house. "I was living in the Valley and he came and performed," said Gordon. "The songs he sang were satirical, self-composed. He was debunking all that crappy lyricism in popularity at the time." During his performance, Chayefsky left his cigarette burning on the piano. "It was at the top of the treble clef," said Gordon, "and it burned right through the keys. It wasn't a Steinway, but it was a good piano. You had to forgive him because he was such a darling guy, so full of ideas, bubbling with a marvelous sardonic slant.''

Very little writing was done on that first trip to Hollywood, Chayefsky later confessed. Not that the time was wasted. Under the GI Bill, he was a part of the T-shirt brigade that studied acting at the Actor's Lab theatre on North Las Palmas Avenue. Curt Conway, his Army patron from London, was on the staff. "There was a very fervid group of teachers and talent at the Lab," said Conway. "Michael Chekhov, Jules Dassin, and Joe Papp were there at the time. Paddy was always very quiet and observant in class. He never got up onstage to do a scene, but offstage he kept everyone entertained."

At Universal, the frequent absences from the office eventually cost Chayefsky his job. To keep him going, Garson Kanin managed to get him two days' work as a bit actor in *A Double Life*. Also in the supporting cast was actress Betsy Blair, who remembered Chayefsky as gregarious, outspoken, and opinionated. Talking politics, she said, he was "uninhibited, ambitious, intense, but wise like an old man." They had enormous arguments; still she invited him home to dinner. She and her husband, MGM star Gene Kelly, lived on Rodeo Drive in Beverly Hills. Within an hour of his arrival, Chayefsky was arguing with Kelly over the merits of American movies versus European films. "Name me one good picture Hollywood made in the last ten years!" Chayefsky insisted. Kelly mused while Chayefsky pushed on. "Name me one film to compare with *Open City* or *Shoeshine*!" Kelly began his list: *Dodsworth* . . . *Citizen Kane* . . . *Double Indemnity* . . . *The Ox-Bow Incident* . . . Chayefsky was amazed when Kelly named twenty.

"Paddy was not going to be intimidated," said Blair. "He was being abrasive in a movie star's house, but it was okay because you could see he was valuable. You could see he was smart. And he did have gentleness and that sweet smile." When told later that Chayefsky was musically inclined and played the piano, Blair was surprised. He made no attempt to entertain at their house. "He must have been stricken with shyness, which seems surprising to me in retrospect," she said. "But then again, the piano in those days was monopolized by Lennie Hayton, Saul Chaplin, or Lenny Bernstein."

When the big day arrived for his appearance as a bit player in *A Double Life*, Chayefsky got some precoaching from Curt Conway. In the movie they played a tabloid team, a reporter and a photographer, assigned to cover a murder scene. The victim was Shelley Winters, in her first big role. She knew Chayefsky needed the money from this job, so she deliberately fouled up the scene. Lying on a bed, strangled to death by Ronald Colman, Winters was supposed to remain motionless as Chayefsky photographed her corpse. "It was late, toward the end of the day," said the actress. "I began to twitch and run out of breath during the complicated dolly shot. That way Paddy could come back the next day and get another hundred bucks."

Winters was under the impression that he wanted the money to buy a car so that he could return to New York to get married. The real purpose of the trip, however, was to see his father, who was in poor health. Shortly before the war, Harry Chayefsky had suffered a stroke. "He could talk, but it seriously affected him physically," said Bill Chayefsky. "He could never walk too well after that."

With his pay from *A Double Life*, Paddy bought a secondhand, beat-up Pierce-Arrow and drove straight across the country to New York. Upon his arrival, his mother assured him that his father was fine, improving each day. Shortly thereafter came a knock on the door. In the midst of a card game at a neighbor's house, Harry Chayefsky had collapsed and died from another heart attack.

They had had their differences in the past, but "he was a good man, and I loved him," said Paddy, who with his brothers said Kaddish at the funeral. Bill Chayefsky later expressed his regret that their father had not lived long enough to see his youngest son become a famous writer. "I know Paddy would have liked that, and my father would have loved it."

The death of his father made Chayefsky realize that time was of the essence. Instead of returning to California, he elected to stay in New York and finish his play. Sidney, the serious side of him, was pleased with that decision, but soon Paddy the dilettante was goofing off again. Part of this was reflected in the revisions. In a new draft, Mrs. Sack, the writer's mother, complains how her gypsy son is now spending his time, hanging around downtown with his actor friends, staying out for three days at a stretch with bums and drinkers. "Ma, I'm twenty-four years old," says Willie. "I spent a year and a half in Paris, six months in Hollywood. Don't be shocked."

In February 1948, with a new title, *M Is for Mother*, the play was completed and shown to a director, Ezra Stone. "Garson Kanin sent him to me as a promising playwright," said Stone. "We met at the Belasco Theatre, where I was directing Gertrude Berg in *Me and Molly*. I recall Paddy was not too comfortable about having to go around to stage-door alleys and peddle his wares, and I couldn't blame him."

The two went to a nearby restaurant for coffee. Stone's recollection of Chayefsky was of an angry young man whose brow almost covered his eyes. "His chin was deep into his chest, and the teeth were kind of set. I think he was impatient to be established and having a hard time putting bread on the table."

Stone read the play, but was not captivated. Meantime, another copy had been sent to the director Michael Gordon at Universal Pictures in Hollywood, who recommended that the studio hire Chayefsky as an apprentice writer. "I was given a six-month contract," said Chayefsky. "It was a job, nothing as impressive as a contract," Gordon corrected.

Being a playwright from New York provided a few privileges. "I was allowed, for example, to drive onto the lot," said Paddy. Actors, directors, even the stenographers were also given that access, but the screenwriters were told to park across the street, in one of the public paying lots. The reason for that was Hollywood's lingering distrust of writers' working methods. "When the studios hire a director, they can see him direct, or an actor act, or a typist type, but they can't see a writer think, and that frightens them," said Chayefsky.

At night after work, the grousing about the hierarchical studio system continued at a show-business hangout on Sunset Strip, which Chayefsky would later use in *The Goddess*. "It was called the Glorifried Ham 'n' Eggery," he said. "They had lamps on the ceiling in the shape of frying pans." Next door was a bar called the Black Swatch, where unemployed actors and writers huddled together, swapping stories of Hollywood's nepotism and favoritism. Good writers were a useless commodity in California, Chayefsky would argue. "If you've got talent, you can't work out here! What do they want talent for? They hire a bunch of nephews who jump around on a typewriter with their bare feet, and that's a script!" The actors had it twice as hard, because they couldn't release their creativity or show their worth unless someone hired them. The constant waiting and stress made them restless and self-indulgent, he said. "They go into black moods of depression or yak it up for hours in bars and saloons, breaking up reluctantly at four in the morning to return either to empty apartments or impatient wives."

Although his perception and writing talent were prodigious, the outlines Chayefsky turned in to Universal in 1948 were not marketable, Michael Gordon said. So prematurely, after six weeks his employment at Universal was terminated and Paddy went back to New York.

Subletting a friend's apartment in Greenwich Village, he stuck to a regular schedule. For three hours in the morning, from eight to eleven, he worked on short stories or ideas for future scripts. Over breakfast at a coffee shop on Bleecker Street and Seventh Avenue he would read Maurice Zolotow's theatre column in the *Times*. That usually left him "with a sick ambition," so he would take the subway uptown to Times Square to look for work. Dropping in at Lester Shurr's office was equally disheartening, but it sometimes gave him the chance to shoot the breeze with other unemployed talents like Dan Barton, Alex Nicol, and John Forsythe. "We had a group that always hung out together," said Barton. "We called ourselves 'The Boys' Club.' All of us were actors, except for Paddy. He was doing this, doing that, into everything."

Leaving Shurr's office, Paddy would head uptown to Hanson's luncheon-ette, a popular show-biz hangout at 1650 Broadway. Here, for a twenty-five-cent minimum, one could sit in a booth, trade stories, hustle agents, and find out what comics in town were looking for material. Chayefsky had his stan-dards. Unlike other aspiring writers, he would never hang around the stage door at the Paramount or the Roxy, pitching jokes to the headliners as they came out. Hustling Milton Berle at his front table at Lindy's on Fifty-second Street could be the exception. If Berle liked a joke, he'd pay five or ten dollars on the spot. When a sale was made, Chayefsky would go back downtown to celebrate over a Chinese dinner in the Village. Or he'd take the No. 1 train up to the Bronx, for a free meal and a fresh nudge from his mother. Gussie by this time had stopped complaining about his nomadic life. She encouraged his career. "Listen, you want to be a writer, you've got to write," she said. "You submit, and they'll reject. But you've got to keep writing."

"My family were wonderful to me when I was struggling," said Chayefsky. "Although each one had their problems, they'd help to keep me afloat, take it as a matter of course." His brother Bill recalled that Paddy seldom borrowed because "he always managed to make money, selling jokes or doing stand-up comedy at clubs and private parties."

In 1948, Chayefsky heard of a Broadway role that he thought was tailor-made for him, that of a tough little sailor in the forthcoming comedy *Mister Roberts*. The part was small but meaty, and the director, Josh Logan, was an old friend. But the morning Paddy showed up at the Alvin Theatre to read, there were eight hundred guys waiting outside to audition. "Since it was shortly after the war, there were many young men who had read the novel and had felt as I did that it was their own story," said Logan. Chayefsky did get to audition the following week, but the part went to Harvey Lembeck.

"It was a very frustrating time for all of us, but especially for Paddy," said Dan Barton. "He was very confused as to what he wanted to do. He wanted to be an actor, he wanted to be a writer, he wanted to be a comic and a lot of different things."

Abe Burrows, writer of such satirical material as "Syphilis on Parade," a skit on a public health feature, had his own radio show in 1948, *Breakfast with Burrows*. Chayefsky contributed three sketches to the show and tried to get himself booked as a guest performer. Leonard Sillman, producer of another radio revue, *New Faces,* did hire him. "He came on one night and sang a song about the Champs-Élysées of the Bronx—Mosholu Parkway," Sillman re-called. "He sang it in a hoarse, deadpan style that was funny and fresh." At the end of the broadcast, Sillman suggested that Chayefsky expand his topical material. He told him to "get it out of the Bronx."

That fall, Chayefsky took Sillman's advice. He wrote an outline for a story set in New Jersey. The theme was a concern that would dominate his later work—the dehumanization of man in modern society. His leading character, John Hodges, having turned sixty-five, has been forced to retire from his job as a handset operator in a printing firm. Age had nothing to do with intelligence or ability, Chayefsky argued. So why should the elderly, who had proven skills, experience, and wisdom, be automatically pushed out of the work force when they reached a certain age?

In the opening scene of *A Few Kind Words from Newark,* Hodges decides to write a letter of protest to the boss of his company. But this being the postwar era of ravenous big business, with large corporations gobbling up smaller companies, Hodges doesn't know whom to send his letter to. Chayefsky describes the small printing company as "a subsidiary of the Cincinnati Publishing Service, whose stock is held by the Stimson Iron Foundry, Inc., which in turn has been recently swallowed up in a merger by the Bullock-Finch Nut and Bolt Co., Inc., whose parent organization is American Hardware, Inc., Ltd., whose directorate is interlocked with Allied Steel, Inc., which is one of the subsidiaries of the incredibly complex corporate structure, General Motors."

Hodges deduces that if no one in his company knows who the man at the top is, they also wouldn't know what he looks like, so he decides to impersonate the big boss. He grows a beard, dyes his hair, and, as the president of General Motors, pays a visit to the Newark printing firm, where he magnanimously abolishes the retirement policy, thereby reinstating his old job.

Incorporating some delectable subplots and supporting characters, Chayefsky finished the story and sent it to the William Morris Agency, whereupon further episodes of benign confusion ensued. The story was written as a movie treatment, but mostly in prose; hence it wound up on the desk of the fiction agent Helen Strauss, who thought it was a novella and sent it on to Maggie Cousins, an editor at *Good Housekeeping* magazine. The piece was accepted, and when published, an offer came in from Twentieth Century–Fox for the movie rights. Chayefsky did not take issue with any of this because the money involved was $25,000, a considerable sum in those days, especially for one who was subsisting on the scant sales from jokes and skits. Another plus was that he was asked to write the script for the movie, which meant an additional $250 per week.

As he headed west on his third Hollywood trip in two years, Chayefsky's anticipation was notably keen. This time out he was going to work at one of the giant studios: Twentieth Century–Fox. It had made two John Ford classics, *The Grapes of Wrath* and *How Green Was My Valley,* and had also produced that year's Oscar winner, *Gentleman's Agreement,* directed by Elia Kazan, the first movie to deal openly with anti-Semitism.

Arriving at Union Station, Chayefsky was met by a studio representative with a car, then whisked to the popular Roosevelt Hotel, where he would stay for the duration of his employment. Added respect was tendered when the writer checked in at the studio the following day. Along with his own parking space, he was assigned a private office and a secretary. Upon meeting the top story executive, he was told that he would have two months to work on the script, and that a top star, William Powell, had been tentatively assigned to play the lead. When Chayefsky was ushered into the Fox commissary for lunch, he noted the first sign that he might not actually be in the Garden of Eden. Director Elia Kazan had summed up the commissary scene two years before when he arrived at Fox to direct *A Tree Grows in Brooklyn*. In the massive studio restaurant, Kazan noted that the center tables were reserved for the stars, surrounded by their agents, makeup men, and assorted friends. The directors sat in a special section, against the best wall, looking out at the executives, producers, and cameramen, who were seated at other prominent tables across the room. At a remote table near the kitchen and rest rooms were an isolated group. They were not a part of the joviality, nor were they table-hopping like the others. Their dress was tamer. They had no fashionable tans. "They laughed in a hysterical way, giddy or bitter. They were the writers," said Kazan.

Having been to Hollywood before, Paddy Chayefsky was not unmindful of the trials and travails to which screenwriters were subjected. Their fabled stories were piled as high as the cash paid for the ignominy they suffered. A cross "between a doormat and a groundhog" was how Ben Hecht, writer of more than three hundred movies, described the scribes' station in Hollywood, and to keep them underfoot "all you had to do was gag them with a thousand-dollar bill." Ever mindful that in the blueprint stage of movies a plot and the spoken word were vital (but secondary to the action and images), the studios encouraged writers to submerge their own personalities, and any sense of an individual voice or style. Their homogeneous efforts, when approved, were then passed down an assembly line of experts, who imparted their individual specialty. These included a construction man, a dialogue expert, and "a polish person," who would add some laughs and sharpen the "garbage" (the words) if needed. "If one writer on a picture is good, ten are ten times better," F. Scott Fitzgerald said during his tenure at MGM. Those who fought to preserve the value of their contributions, or believed they had a personal gift or unique talent, were strongly disciplined or dismissed. Writers either made peace with the realities of the system or took the money and ran, frequently castigating the town, the people, and/or the climate as they departed. "Hooeyland" was Theodore Dreiser's parting epithet. "A sewer" was Bertolt Brecht's malediction, characterizing his employment there as "a chrysanthemum in a coal mine." In 1946, Evelyn Waugh was at MGM adapting his novel *Brideshead Revisited* when the industry censors demanded changes. He withdrew his book and returned to England. Of the fabled, glamorous movie capital he said, "Morticians are the only people worth knowing."

In 1948, the same studio order was in effect, but Paddy Chayefsky was convinced that he would not be subjected to any of the writers' indignities of yore. He had a strong insider on his side, he believed. The producer assigned to his story was Lamar Trotti, a man with such Fox movies as *The Ox-Bow Incident* and *The Razor's Edge*, both of which received Oscar nominations for Best Picture, to his credit. A third cited film was *Wilson*, which Trotti had written and which remained the all-time favorite of mega–studio boss and producer Darryl Zanuck.

When they met, Trotti and Chayefsky became good friends. Trotti loved Chayefsky's story. It had warmth and depth and human integrity, he said. Opened up and carefully transferred to the big screen, it was a potential winner. The producer then made some suggestions, which Chayefsky accepted. Three weeks later, when a first draft was completed, Trotti had only one critical comment. He said that Chayefsky wrote too fast, that a movie script needed more time, otherwise the other executives on the lot wouldn't consider it "an important project." Tackling his second draft, Chayefsky heeded Trotti's counsel. He wrote more slowly. This enabled him to ponder and insert vital details he had overlooked before. Trotti loved those pages, too, and he and Chayefsky discussed other ideas for movies that they could make together for Fox. Their tight accord led to a little guilt on Chayefsky's part. When he went to lunch at the studio commissary, Chayefsky felt bad for the regular staff writers. While they moaned and complained about "the crap" they were churning out for pictures starring Betty Grable, June Haver, and Tyrone Power, he had to remain mum about his literary good fortune. Then one Friday, by chance, he overheard another writer talking about a script he was working on for William Powell. For a moment Paddy got paranoid. Powell had been mentioned as the star of *his* script. He asked about the locale. It was set in a small town outside Los Angeles. Paddy was relieved. His locale was New Jersey. Then the guy added that Powell was playing a character who tries to save his job by impersonating the owner of the company. Paddy excused himself from the table. He was about to become very ill, and very angry.

When he checked in with the head script supervisor, his worst fears were confirmed. Behind his back, his script had been purloined and put on the writers' assembly line. He called Lamar Trotti. The producer had left for Palm Springs for the weekend. That night, Chayefsky went to the Black Swatch for words of support, but all he got were more horror stories about how writers were treated in Hollywood. For example, did he know that at Warner Bros., screenwriters were not permitted on the set of their pictures unless they had written permission from mogul-chief Jack Warner? Nor were they allowed to see rushes or invited to the previews or premieres. "If a writer wanted to see his own picture, he went to a theatre, paid the ticket price, and saw the picture with the general public," said Casey Robinson, scripter of *Dark Victory* and *Now, Voyager.*

The following Monday morning, as soon as he got to the studio, Chayefsky went after Lamar Trotti. The producer, who would be credited as writer of the final picture (titled *As Young as You Feel*, released in 1951), was polite and sympathetic. This was normal studio procedure, he explained. The "procedure" had to be changed, Chayefsky insisted, then demanded to see the big boss, Darryl Zanuck, who remained unavailable. "I stormed and ranted," said Paddy. "And the more I raved, the more they 'respected' me."

He also called William Morris, his agency in L.A. They said they'd get back to him. He waited two days, then made his decision. There would be no compromise. This meant quitting his job and leaving his generous salary at the studio.

Boarding the train for New York, Paddy turned around and bestowed his parting blessing on Tinseltown. As far as Darryl Zanuck, Jack Warner, and all the other studio moguls were concerned, they'd have to bend down and kiss his ass "in Macy's and in Gimbel's window" before he would ever consider writing for Hollywood again.

More Serious Intentions

Back in New York, the first item on Chayefsky's agenda was to review his standing with the William Morris Agency. "I don't believe that Helen [Strauss] was really doing anything more for him," said her assistant, Esther Pollock. "She handled Robert Penn Warren, Betty Smith, and Bob Considine, many of the top writers, so she didn't give that much time to Paddy." Pollock recalled that she was the one who dealt mostly with Chayefsky. "We used to go to Toots Shor's for free lunches on the agency, and I really was fascinated with him. He was an egalitarian. He believed so much in human rights. And he could be very sharp with his humor. Later, after he left the agency and became a big success with his plays, Helen regretted not giving him more of her attention."

The option money from Fox, which was paid in full, did enable Chayefsky to relax for a while. He didn't have to hustle jokes or perform in nightclubs. The financial security also enabled him to give some serious consideration to settling down with a female partner.

Since that callous rejection of Sidney Chayefsky at the school dance when he was fifteen, his friendships with women had remained platonic. "His sexuality became muted. That's the best way to describe it," one source stated. "And he learned to compensate for it, by putting his drive in his writing and his career." During his college years Chayefsky, in his public persona as one of the boys, liked to give the impression that he was something of a roué with the girls. "We would wander around as a pack on Fordham Road," said Paddy. "When we spotted a looker I'd be the first to yell, 'Hey, hi yuh, honey!' " Curt Conway recalled that in London during the war, Chayefsky seemed awkward and somewhat adolescent when females were around. "He was uncertain and didn't seem to know very much about them," said Conway. Chayefsky had one encounter in London that he would later use in one of his movie scripts. During a late night of carousing, his soldier friends tried to fix him up with a woman they met standing in the doorway of a closed pub. "I'm afraid you fellows have the wrong idea about me," the girl says in Chayefsky's re-creation of the incident in a preliminary draft of *The Bachelor Party*. "You guys are working under a misconception." The men walk off, leaving their game but nervous buddy with her. She looks at him, then mutters, "All right, come on." Upstairs, in her small dark flat, she turns her back on him. Slipping out of her dress, she attempts to hold on to her dignity by saying, "Listen, I don't want you to think I don't have a job. I got a job. I work." Hearing sobs, she turns around and sees her gentleman caller sitting on a chair, crying. "Ashamed, bewildered, and deeply frightened, he sits miserably, bent on the wooden chair, horrified at his own lack of control," Chayefsky wrote. The woman is startled, a little frightened. Her visitor stands, turns away from her, hides his face with one hand, and with the other reaches into his pants pocket and takes out some loose bills. He places them on the bed, then stumbles out of her room.

Part of Chayefsky's fear and sexual diffidence could have been due to the injuries he suffered from his encounter with the land mine. "When I was a kid, I saw him naked," his son, Dan, said. "His buttocks were badly scarred. They looked as if pieces had been cut out of them, and the explosion hit very close to his private parts." It was easier to cover up his fear with an act, which was Paddy's forte. With women, he knew he was "no Gable," he said in his Army revue. There were definite advantages in that attitude. He didn't have to waste time and energy playing cool games. Also, by treating females not as sex objects but as fellow travelers, he could engage in a more vivid and objective study, which might prove invaluable to his writing. As "a pal" to women, Paddy felt he did not have to watch his language, either, or play the passive, polite gentleman that Sidney was raised to be.

After the war, in New York, Dan Barton double-dated with Chayefsky. On occasion, the actor escorted a gorgeous showgirl from the Copacabana on a tour of the city, with Chayefsky in tow. "We were riding along in the upper tier of a double-decker bus on Fifth Avenue," said Barton, "when Paddy suddenly turned to the girl and said, 'If somebody was writing a story about you, do you know what they would call you?' And she said, 'No. What?' And very charmingly, he said, 'Big Tits.' " Another time, Barton brought Paddy along when he visited a wealthy female friend for cocktails. "All she did was talk about herself, and talk about money, which didn't settle very well with Paddy. At the end of the evening, when we were leaving, she put out her cheek so I could kiss her goodbye, European-style. And then she put out her hand to Paddy, and said, 'It was so nice meeting you.' He took her hand and said, 'Goodbye. It was wonderful meeting you. And fuck you.' "

Unbeknownst to Barton and the rest of the Boys' Club, during this time Chayefsky had a semi-steady girlfriend. Her name was Susan Sackler. "She came from a very liberal Jewish family, up on Allerton Avenue in the Bronx Park East," said Esther Pollock. "That was Odets country, a Socialist co-op. They had study groups and workshops, before the banks moved in and eventually took it over."

Susan Sackler had lustrous dark auburn hair and porcelain skin, and was a petite five feet tall. She lived in an apartment in Greenwich Village, where she studied modern dance. "She always wore the usual dancer's outfit: a white blouse, black skirt, and black flats," said Mike Ryan, an actor friend of Chayefsky's. Her outfits might have looked standard, but they were custom-tailored, made by a dressmaker friend. Smart and well-read, Susan was also very adept at holding her own in conversation with Paddy. They had heated discussions and disagreements, which led to frequent collisions and partings. During his third trip to California, he wrote long letters to Susan. When he returned, he brought her home to meet his mother. Gussie gave her approval, and in February 1949 they were married in a Bronx synagogue, with only the immediate family present. "None of us knew about it," said Ryan. "The way I found out about it was when I called Paddy and asked if he was going to join our regular Friday-night poker game. He said, 'I can't. I got married last week.' And that was it. He dropped out of sight, and for a long time the only time I would see him was if I bumped into him making the rounds."

Married life obviously inspired him. In the course of two months, Chayefsky wrote three short stories and a novella, *Go Fight City Hall,* about civic corruption in Cambridge, New York. Although he had a new agent, Flora Roberts, none of this material was sold, but Roberts did get him a job writing jokes and skits for Robert Q. Lewis, a radio comic. But on April Fools' Day, after two weeks on the job, he was fired by Lewis. "It was under very friendly terms," he said. "I just couldn't write gags."

He was no longer interested in comedy. Serious drama now took precedence. Shortly before, he had been exposed to a daring new play on Broadway, *Death of a Salesman,* written by Arthur Miller. Chayefsky had seen the play the week after it opened. The father-son connection, and the theme of a proud but broken man desperately trying to make a comeback, were achingly familiar. At the play's final curtain, as the audience rose to their feet to applaud, Chayefsky was already out of his seat, on his way to the men's room. Locking himself into a stall, he stood with his head slumped against the wall, weeping copiously for the father he had failed to mourn two years before. The next day he wrote a letter of appreciation to Miller, who would become the abiding focus of Chayefsky's new passion—and of his discontent in the years ahead.

Abandoning *Put Them All Together,* Chayefsky started a second, deeper work. Entitled *The Man Who Made the Mountains Shake,* the new play was set in an Italian-American section of Boston in 1922. Mario Fortunato, age fifty-two, is an immigrant and frustrated ditchdigger in the Boston navy yard. He has seven sons, one of whom he hopes will restore his former pride and strength. Mario dreams of having a famous boxer in his family. Vinnie, the oldest boy, with seventeen victories in the ring, tells his father he is quitting. "I don't like the noise! I don't like the smella the rosin! . . . Whaddya want from me, Pa! I don't wanna fight!" he says. The youngest boy, a frail adolescent, is then put into training. Through fear of the ring and his father, he loses his first fight and tries to kill himself.

This play had size, it had passion, said Chayefsky. It was destined to be "a major contribution" to the theatre. But first it had to be nurtured and refined. In June 1949, he found the perfect place for the incubation process. It was a brand-new theatrical group called the New Dramatists, which provided readings and in-house discussions of plays by new writers. The group had been started by two other aspiring playwrights, Robert Anderson and Michaela O'Hara. Expressing the need for some kind of a workshop or rallying point for young playwrights, Anderson and O'Hara appealed to the established playwrights Howard Lindsay and Russel Crouse, who enlisted Richard Rodgers, Oscar Hammerstein II, and Moss Hart as the benefactors and muses for the beginners' conclave. A meeting place was also donated, a room on the top floor of the Hudson Theatre on West Forty-fourth Street, which Lindsay and Crouse owned. Among the first students were Anderson, O'Hara, William Inge (whose first play, *Come Back, Little Sheba,* was about to open on Broadway), William Gibson, and Paddy Chayefsky. "It was an extraordinary group, some of whom were almost ready to burst," said Anderson. "Every two weeks we traipsed up to that small room on top of the Hudson Theatre. The best part of it was that you would sit and listen to people like Maxwell Anderson, Elmer Rice, Elia Kazan, and Josh Logan talk to you about the theatre."

The discussions were invaluable, Chayefsky later recalled. "I learned the first rules of playwriting there. Howard Lindsay, for example, told us that the audience must know at the beginning of each act who they're for and who they're against. Josh Logan gave us something he learned from Hal Roach, the old silent-movie producer, and that was 'When does the villain kick the dog?' You've got to let the audience know who to root for." On another level of craft, Moss Hart told the group always to make sure they knew why they were writing something, and not to put it down on paper "until you've got the whole thing cold." There were also free theatre tickets for members. "Seeing all the plays, you came to know what was boring on stage and what wasn't, what would work and what was plain dull," said Chayefsky.

When the first draft of his new play was completed, a reading was given at the New Dramatists. "It had some wonderful speeches in it," said Anderson. "The theme and background seemed to be influenced by Clifford Odets and Arthur Miller. But you could not say that to Paddy. He could be very difficult, you know."

"Paddy was a very interesting, somewhat pugnacious, talkative, uninhibited character," William Gibson recalled. "He was full of ego. There was a certain ebullience of ego that just came out of him all the time."

"I talked more than I wrote," Chayefsky agreed, "because I wanted to be provoked to write something better, something imaginative and important."

"At the meetings Howard Lindsay would rebuke Paddy," Gibson continued. "He would say to him, 'All you're interested in is options. You have to be interested in getting a play produced, you can't live on options.' But the fact is, all of us were young writers—we wanted an option because that was the first step that would acknowledge our legitimacy. It was how you kept alive—both emotionally and financially."

During this time, Chayefsky found another staunch supporter in Robert Anderson's wife, Phyllis. As head of the play-reading department at the Theatre Guild, Phyllis Anderson had brought *Come Back, Little Sheba* to the attention of the Guild producers. "Bill Inge dedicated the play to Phyllis," said Anderson. "She was wonderful with writers, and therefore Paddy was always eager for me to feed her his plays."

After she read *The Man Who Made the Mountains Shake,* Phyllis suggested to the Theatre Guild that they produce it. "They weren't that enthused about it," Robert Anderson recalled, "and it wasn't something that she could do on her own." Instead, Phyllis gave the play to a close friend, Molly Thacher, who had been with her at the Yale Drama School. Thacher was likewise a staunch supporter, a "mother hen" to such formative talents as Robert Anderson and actor Montgomery Clift. Her interest was of special significance because she was married to Elia Kazan, the director of two of Broadway's most outstanding dramas, *A Streetcar Named Desire* and *Death of a Salesman.* For Chayefsky, whose admiration for Kazan bordered on hero worship, it was hoped that Kazan's patronage and steerage would be the force that would at last launch the playwright's name in the theatre.

In an interview for *Horizon* magazine in 1960, Chayefsky said that he wrote *The Man Who Made the Mountains Shake* "for Elia Kazan." But in 1992, Kazan said that it was his wife who was mainly connected with Chayefsky. "Molly had a great enthusiasm for Paddy and his play," he said. "He was at our house a lot. He and she put in a lot of time on the work, the details of which seldom came to my attention because I was busy elsewhere."

Chayefsky also claimed that he and Kazan worked on the play for more than a year, and that he had "gotten quite broke, following Gadge [Kazan] around." Kazan confirmed that in the summer of 1951, when he and his wife went to California for the filming of *Viva Zapata!*, Chayefsky followed them. "He came and stayed with us in Malibu," said Kazan. "He and Molly worked on the play while I directed *Zapata*." That fall, when the movie was completed, an announcement appeared in the *New York Herald Tribune*. It said that among the batch of scripts that Kazan was considering to stage on Broadway that season was "the more likely possibility—*The Man Who Made the Mountains Shake* by Paddy Chayefsky." Kazan, who did direct *Camino Real* by Tennessee Williams that season, followed by *Tea and Sympathy*, written by Robert Anderson, the following year, said he had no recollection of any commitment to do the Chayefsky play. "I don't know where that news item came from; maybe Paddy planted it. It could have come from me. But I never had plans to do it. Molly kept urging me to get involved with him, but I just had other things going and I never got around to it."

That winter, almost broke, Chayefsky was forced to put the play aside and look for work that would provide income. A job adapting scripts for CBS Radio came through Robert Anderson, who also vouched for Chayefsky's ability. "I had been with the Theatre Guild of the Air since 1948," he said. "Then when *Tea and Sympathy* was being prepared for Broadway, I went to the Guild and told them I was busy elsewhere but that I had a terrific new writer for them. I suggested Paddy. They said they would use him, but only if I agreed to redo the scripts if he didn't work out."

Known for its fine adaptations of plays and classic novels, the Theatre Guild of the Air would enable Chayefsky to examine the fine art of distilling a story to fit the concentrated span of broadcasting, while also giving him the chance to study the inherent techniques. "Radio required an exact technical skill," said Anderson. "You had an hour, less commercials, to tell *David Copperfield* or *A Farewell to Arms*. That's an enormous job of condensation, and of supplying dialogue where originally there wasn't any. You learned about structure, about dramatic essentials, and you pared the whole story down to those essentials."

Chayefsky's first assignment was to adapt George M. Cohan's *The Meanest Man in the World*. The script was accepted and aired in February 1952, with James Stewart and Josephine Hull in the leading roles. Two other adaptations, *Tommy* and *Over 21*, were followed by *The Spectacle Lady*, a documentary-drama for Du Pont's "Cavalcade of America." Describing his brief time in radio, Chayefsky said, "It's the most demeaning form of writing, but marvelous for your professional sense of humility. They don't need you—they just hire you, for seven hundred fifty dollars a script, and if you worked on it more than a week, you were a fool."

In March 1952, Chayefsky's legitimate play, *The Man Who Made the Mountains Shake,* was finally optioned by producer Richard Davidson and Robert Anderson. It was "tentatively set for Broadway that fall," a press announcement stated. To solidify the venture, Chayefsky felt it was up to him to get a star for the leading role of the Italian father. He had an actor in mind—a favorite from his youth, Fredric March. He didn't know March, nor could he go through the normal channels, because having fired the three people who had represented him over the past four years, Chayefsky didn't have an agent. One day he read in Ed Sullivan's column that March was scheduled to present an award that night at a dinner at Sardi's. Chayefsky waited outside the restaurant for two hours, and when March walked out, Chayefsky handed him the play.

March read the play and liked it. He suggested to his agent, Bobby Sanford, that Sanford contact the playwright. Sanford, however, deemed the play unworthy of his star client. "When Paddy heard this, he became a wild man," said Mike Ryan. "He went up to Sanford's office and threatened to throw him out the window. He terrified the guy." A former dancer and actor, Sanford had a very theatrical demeanor. "He called everyone 'dear' or 'darling,' " said Ryan. "And here was Paddy, like a wounded, bellowing bull before him." To calm him down, Sanford said, "Darling, I hear you're a fabulous writer. Tell me about yourself." Chayefsky took the cue and calmly gave the agent his credits. Sanford listened, then told him to go straight home, pick out the best of his plays and short stories, and bring them right back to him.

Chayefsky did as he was told, and oddly enough, Sanford read them. In their next meeting, as his agent Sanford told Chayefsky he had set up an appointment for him at CBS. Paddy growled that he wasn't interested. He had already adapted four scripts for CBS Radio, and the experience had left him feeling miserable. "But, *darling!*" said Sanford. "I'm not talking about CBS *Radio.* I am talking about *television.*"

Television in the early 1950s was still in its infancy, both technically and in the size of its audience. Its growth had been stunted four years before, when the U.S. government had imposed a freeze on the number of stations allowed to transmit TV signals, setting a limit of 108. In 1952, at almost the same time that Chayefsky was scheduled for a meeting at CBS, the legislative restrictions were lifted. Overnight the number of stations jumped to 308, and the number of homes equipped for television would soon soar from 190,000 to 32,000,000. To cater to this new mass of viewers, additional programming was needed in a hurry. In New York, where most of the TV fare was produced, the call went out for writers, especially playwrights who would know how to fill the slots for the dramatic shows that were about to be scheduled. But New York's theatrical community chose to ignore this sudden cry for its services. "There was a real look-down-the-nose attitude toward television," said Robert Anderson. "In those days you were considered selling your soul, a disgrace, if you did either television or movies. But it kept you alive."

To cover the necessities—rent, food, cigarettes—Chayefsky agreed to meet with a programming manager at CBS. The day before, he dashed off a ten-page outline for a TV comedy entitled *The Senator and the Lady*. It was about a politician and his wife stranded in Washington during the postwar housing shortage. The roles were written specifically for Spencer Tracy and Katharine Hepburn, Chayefsky told the CBS executive when they met. But Tracy and Hepburn wouldn't *spit* on TV, the executive explained. They were much too big for the smaller screen, as were most Hollywood stars.

Rather than waste an opportunity, at the meeting Chayefsky managed to toss out a few more story ideas. Impressed with his imagination and energy, the CBS story executive asked if he would be interested in writing for "Danger," a weekly dramatic series. The premise of the show involved the leading characters in some sort of perilous situation. When that was established, the climax and resolution had to be wrapped up in twenty-four minutes. The directors of the series were "two refugees from the theatre," actors Yul Brynner and twenty-seven-year-old Sidney Lumet.

On April 22, 1952, *Hello Mr. Lutz*, a story about a union leader who is assassinated in a phone booth, was shown on CBS. It starred Maria Riva, Marlene Dietrich's daughter, and future director Martin Ritt. The writer, Paddy Chayefsky, received $700, but no satisfaction. "It was a horror," he said. "I wrote it out of snobbery." His next script for "Danger" was crafted better, but that show didn't come out as he envisioned it either—because he wasn't invited to attend rehearsals. "Our schedules were so hectic," said Sidney Lumet, "[that] sometimes we literally shot from the scripts as they came in from rewrites. But Paddy's scripts were so good they never needed rewriting. That's why he was never called in."

"I made a vow that I would never again do a show in which I wasn't in attendance at all the rehearsals," said Chayefsky. To ease his pique, his agent set up another meeting, this time at NBC with Fred Coe, a producer who would be pivotal in changing the course of Chayefsky's life and career.

Fred Coe was born in Mississippi and raised in Nashville. He had acted in and directed plays at community theatres before heading north to study drama at Yale University. After the war he joined NBC as a production assistant. Within eight months he was promoted, without additional pay, to writing, directing, and producing TV programs. "Anyone who had half a brain, who volunteered and was willing to work long hours, could pick up ten years of experience in a month," he said. In 1948, the Philco Corporation, manufacturers of washing machines, refrigerators, and TV sets, became the sponsor of a new Sunday-night anthology series at NBC, the "Philco Television Playhouse." Coe was the producer and director for the first two seasons. The shows were re-creations of old plays such as *Dinner at Eight* or works by Shakespeare. "Those were the only properties available, because Hollywood owned the rights to the more current plays," said Coe. "To them we were the enemy, the competition, so they consistently refused to give us the rights to broadcast." Condensations of famous novels were also aired. In 1952, with an alternate sponsor, the Goodyear Tire Company, and with television about to expand, Coe began to look around for new writers. Not only would they be used to adapt other people's work, but "they might come up with some original ideas for plays of their own," he said. Among those added to the regular Philco staff of David Shaw and Robert Alan Aurthur were Sumner Locke Elliott and Horton Foote. In July 1952, Paddy Chayefsky was brought in to talk to Coe. "We met up at NBC, in the furious little office he had on the fourth floor," said Chayefsky. "He told me what he was looking for and that he would guarantee his writers freedom and total participation. Not only would we be involved in all rewrites and the rehearsals, but if we chose we could have a say in the casting."

Serendipitously, Coe also had a story in mind for Chayefsky's maiden assignment. "I usually kept some material I liked tucked away on an office shelf, something I'd read which I thought might make a good show," he said. "I gave Paddy a little story from the *Reader's Digest*. It was called 'It Happened on the Brooklyn Subway.' " The story was about a photographer who, on his way to work one day, reunites a man and his wife, each of whom believes the other has perished years before in a Nazi concentration camp. "The writer of the article drew the conclusion that God had been riding the Brooklyn subway that day," Chayefsky surmised.

Using the rules he had learned at the New Dramatists, and his own fertile imagination, Chayefsky proceeded to refashion the story until it was "only vaguely related to the original." The plot of the original was anemic. There was no opening crisis or closing resolution for the leading characters. In his revision, Chayefsky changed the leading character from a photographer to a middle-aged cantor. He wakes up one morning. It is the eve of Rosh Hashanah, the Jewish New Year, but he decides he cannot sing in the temple. Why? Because he has lost his faith in God. Why? Because of "the sadness in the world." The crimes, the famines, the wars. "Is God a mortician, that he desires all this tragedy?" the cantor asks a colleague.

With a crisis established, Paddy proceeded with his narrative. The cantor is urged by a colleague to talk with a rabbi, a wise elder who lives in New York

City. On the way to the city by subway the old man is given the wrong instructions by a platform guard. He gets on a train that goes in the opposite direction. Standing in the last car he sees a woman who has opened the last door and is about to throw herself on to the tracks. He stops the woman. They talk. She is Dutch, a widow who has lost her husband and children at Auschwitz. The cantor escorts the distressed woman home, then returns to the subway. Riding back to his original express stop, he meets the same guard on the platform, who shoves him on the wrong train again. Angry and upset, on the second train he shares his frustration with a fellow passenger, a young man, who is also Dutch. Recognizing the accent, the cantor asks about the man's background. He hears a similar sad story. The young man is from Utrecht, and he lost his wife and children at Auschwitz. "Of course, this is foolish, but could you tell me, was your wife's name Marya?" the cantor asks. Suddenly alert, the young man says "Yes." At the next station, the cantor leads the man to a telephone. He calls the young woman he met earlier. He asks for her husband's name. It is the same as the young man's. Over the telephone, the couple weep as they are reunited.

After the climax, Chayefsky came in with the resolution. The cantor, after reconciling the couple, returns to his original subway stop. He goes in search of the platform guard, to tell him that even though he put him on the wrong train, twice, something wonderful happened. At the station he finds out there is no such guard on duty, that day or any other. Standing on the outdoor platform, the cantor looks up at the sky and whispers: "And ye shall know Him in the strangest costumes and in the strangest places." The cantor, with his faith in God restored, sings at the synagogue that evening. Raising his voice in the age-old hymn for the occasion, as the notes grow louder, he turns to face the congregation. "His eyes are glistening," wrote Paddy Chayefsky. "The choral voices crescendo to a roar. Fade out. The End."

On Sunday night, September 14, 1952, three days before Rosh Hashanah, the play, retitled *Holiday Song,* was shown on the "Goodyear Playhouse" (which shared the Sunday-night slot with the Philco show). "It was a big success for Joseph Buloff, the actor who played the cantor," said Chayefsky. "He got something like four thousand letters. I got maybe two or three. But my mother watched the show that night, and when I called her she said, 'Very nice, Sidney, very nice.' For her, that was high praise indeed."

Both Fred Coe and the sponsors of the show were also pleased, and Chayefsky was asked to contribute another play. He agreed to do so, but he said he was no longer interested in doing adaptations. He wanted to do original stories only. "Adaptations were fast and easy," said the writer Mel Goldberg. "We all needed the money, but not Paddy. He felt he had things of his own to say. He had the image of himself as a fine writer and he wasn't going to compromise his talents for a fast buck."

MAD AS HELL ■ 49

By refusing to submit himself to deadline pressures, Chayefsky took the opportunity to study this new medium. As a member of the Fred Coe "family" he was allowed to spend as much time as he wanted watching the other shows in production in the Philco-Goodyear series. "In the beginning, Paddy was in the control room constantly," said production supervisor Milton Meyers, "and he had a thousand questions."

"The beauty of those days was [that] everything was an experiment," said Chayefsky. "The cameras, the equipment [were] rudimentary, and the studios themselves were tiny." The intimacy of the small screen would also enhance the stories he was about to write. "Television drama could not expand in breadth," he said, "so it must expand in depth." In that "marvelous medium of the ordinary" you could go in very close with a very small moment, he told critic Cecil Smith. "You can take an emotion too delicate for the stage or the movies and shade this slight thing and let it grow." Because the grandiose and complex were not possible, Chayefsky decided to focus on small sections of people's everyday lives, probing each one with a succinct but subtle precision. "The man who is unhappy in his job, the wife who thinks of a lover, . . . your father, mother, sister, brothers, cousins, friends—all these are better subjects for drama than Iago," he wrote in an anthology of his television plays published in 1955.

Five months after *Holiday Song* was telecast, the second Chayefsky play was aired on NBC. *The Reluctant Citizen* was a cameo from his family's history. Set in 1946, it was based on the plight of an elderly cousin, a refugee who spent much of his time at the Educational Alliance, the Jewish settlement house on the Lower East Side of Manhattan. The old man has been savagely treated by the Nazis during the war. Because of his terror of anyone in civic authority, he is reluctant to apply for citizenship in his new country. At the settlement house he meets a young social worker who recognizes the fear and emptiness the immigrants face. "I've got all these old people, and I want them to realize what rich lives they have!" the social worker says. "I want them to learn they don't have to depend on their children. That they don't have to be afraid of being old. That they can be useful and productive citizens."

The TV play, with Joseph Buloff as the elderly immigrant and James Daly (father of Tyne and Timothy) as the compassionate social worker, was directed by Delbert Mann. A tall, amiable, gentleman from Tennessee, and a close friend of Fred Coe's, Mann, with an unobtrusive interpretative style and infinite patience, would guide Chayefsky through most of the television shows and movies he wrote in the 1950s. As a director, Mann's finest gift was his ability to see the whole show in its proper shape, "and to never lose the forest for the single trees," said the writer in tribute.

By January 1952, Chayefsky's third script was completed for Philco-Goodyear. It was called *Printer's Measure*. The setting was familiar: the printer's shop where Chayefsky had worked for his uncle. The teleplay opened by showing the friendship between a compositor and a young boy who works in the shop. The boy shares the elderly man's love for and pride in the old style of printing. Together they choose the type and set it by hand. "I get a real kick out of it," says the boy. "When I go out on deliveries, I always wear my apron, because I want everybody in the street to know I'm a printer." The crisis comes when an "interloper," a product of the Machine Age—a modern linotype printer—is installed. This creates a wedge between the two friends. It is also a threat to the old man's craft and livelihood. At the end of Act II, when the boy announces his plans to go to school to learn about this new form of printing, the old man slaps him across the face. That evening he takes a sledgehammer to the new machine. In Act III, the forgiving boy tells the elderly printer: "The world changes, Mister Healy. The old things go, and each of us must make peace with the new." "You're a good kid," the printer says, reconciling with the boy and with the changes he must make in his work and his attitude.

With the script perfected to the precision of commas and semicolons, and with actors Pat O'Malley and Martin Newman expertly cast in the lead roles, in rehearsals the only unusual occurrence was that Chayefsky, wandering around, discovered the idea for his next project. This would be the one that established his name. It would also become the most highly acclaimed TV drama of the decade. Some historians would go so far as to call it the most outstanding live drama in the history of television. It was a simple story set in the Bronx. The name of the play was *Marty*.

Marty: A Television Classic

Because of the limited space available at the NBC television studios, rehearsals for the Philco-Goodyear shows were held at various sites in midtown Manhattan. One location was the Palladium Ballroom on Seventh Avenue. Another was the ballroom of the Abbey Hotel on Fifty-third Street. On Friday nights the Abbey Ballroom was also used as a gathering place for single men and women. It was called the Friendship Club.

In February 1953, when the Philco-Goodyear group was at the hotel rehearsing *The Reluctant Citizen*, Paddy Chayefsky strolled around the ballroom and his attention was caught by the hand-lettered signs on the wall. One of them read: "Girls, please dance with the man who asks you. Remember, men have feelings, too." During a break, the writer went to director Delbert Mann and said, "You know, there's a story here. What if we focused on a girl who comes to one of these dances?" Mann, eager to get on with rehearsals, said, "Sounds good to me, go talk to Fred."

Almost two months passed before Chayefsky spoke to Fred Coe about the idea. By then the focus and locale of the story had been altered. Instead of concentrating on a girl who goes to a lonely-hearts dance club in Manhattan, he changed it to a man who goes to a dance hall in the Bronx. The motivation—to meet a girl who would help ease the emptiness in his life—remained the same. Fred Coe, when told of the idea, said, "Write it, Pappy [a name Coe bestowed on favored colleagues]."

The lead character, Marty, was originally conceived as a short, overweight Jewish accountant who lives at home in the Bronx with his widowed mother. This was revised in the first draft. "Paddy had already done three shows for us with a Jewish background," said Delbert Mann. "So he made the background Italian. The whole family relationship of mother and son, all of that was so typically Italian at that time, as was the Irish and Jewish element in the Bronx. These were families that Paddy knew so well and it was that knowledge, and the fondness he invested in them, that made the story so deeply moving."

A butcher by trade, Marty is amiable and respectful to all, but at heart he is a lonely little man. Having looked in vain for a girl every Saturday night of his adult life, he now prefers to spend his free time with his mother or his unmarried pals. When his mother pushes him, he reluctantly agrees to go to the Waverly Ballroom for one more night of "heartache." At the ballroom he is approached by a stranger who offers him five dollars to take his blind date off his hands. "Are you kidding?" says Marty. "You just can't walk off onna girl like that." When the guy hustles another stag into accepting the deal, Marty follows them. He sees the woman who is being bartered sitting at a table. She is Clara, Marty's female counterpart, blatantly plain but a good soul. She also has pride and politely refuses to be palmed off on another escort. As the two men walk off, Clara is obviously shaken by the rejection and doesn't know what to do. She gets up from the table, then proceeds nervously toward a fire exit. Marty follows. Out on the fire exit she stands with her back to him. Her head is lowered, her shoulders are trembling. Very softly, Marty says, "Excuse me, miss. Would you care to dance?" The girl turns to him. Her face is streaked with tears. Her lips are trembling. "Then, in one of those peculiar moments of simultaneous impulse," Chayefsky wrote, "she lurches to Marty with a sob, and he takes her to him." Later, on the dance floor, exchanging confidences about their past experiences with rejection, Marty and Clara find they are enjoying each other's company. A solid friendship and romance begins.

"I set out in *Marty* to write a love story," said Chayefsky, "the most ordinary love story in the world." Determined to shatter the shallow and destructive illusions—propagated by cheap fiction and bad movies—that love was simply a matter of physical attraction, he deliberately created a hero who wasn't handsome and a heroine who was not pretty. "I wanted to write a love story the way it would literally have happened to the kind of people I know," he said.

"The basic story, the characters and the relationship, were already in Paddy's mind," said Mann. "This was just a way of unlocking the emotions he was already thinking about."

With the principal characters established, Chayefsky worked on the subsidiary figures. Marty's widowed mother, Mrs. Pilletti, loves her son and wants him to get married, but at the same time she is scared of being left alone, of winding up as "a lonely old woman," like her widowed sister. On the morning after Marty has met and brought Clara to his house, Mrs. Pilletti, like Chayefsky's own mother, tries to break up the relationship because Clara is not one of their own kind, i.e., Italian. "What kinda family she comes from?" Mrs. Pilletti asks. "There was something about her I don't like. It seems funny, the first time you meet her she comes to your empty house alone. These college girls, they all one step from the street."

Marty's best friend, Angie, and his pals in the neighborhood bar also try to dampen his interest in Clara. To them she's "a dog." These are guys he knew firsthand, Chayefsky said. "Certainly I and everybody I know have at least once in our lives brushed off a girl we rather liked because our pals said she was unattractive."

On Monday, May 11, Chayefsky was working on the story when he got a call from Coe. The producer was in trouble. A script scheduled for the following week had not worked out. Coe asked Chayefsky, "How are you coming with that lonely-hearts idea?" Chayefsky said, "Well, I've finished the first act, I'm in the middle of the second, and I've got the third kind of blocked out in my mind." Coe said they were stuck, and could he have it by that Thursday? "Paddy hemmed and hawed," said Mann, "and finally said, 'O.K., I can give you two acts tomorrow, and the third act by the end of the week.' "

As Chayefsky worked "straight through, three nights and three days," to finish the script, Coe and Mann went into preproduction with the two acts already completed. "Pages were copied and distributed through NBC very quickly," said Mann. "The only adjustment in our normal schedule was that we had to delay rehearsals one day until Paddy had finished the last act."

During the casting process, Martin Ritt was set to play Marty. But when his name appeared on the political blacklist of that time, he was replaced by Rod Steiger, a relative newcomer, who was paid $500 for the role. Agent George Baxt said he suggested Nancy Marchand for the part of Clara. "I was young then, and had this bony face," said Marchand. "I was never a cutesy little girl, so I tended to be cast in character parts, which was really a blessing." In the supporting roles, Esther Minciotti was hired to play Marty's mother; Joseph Mantell was cast as his possessive pal, Angie; and Lee Philips was set as Marty's cousin Thomas. Auditioning for the role of the cousin's wife was a young actress named Anne Italiano. Her looks and name (later changed to Anne Bancroft) were considered "too ethnic," so a blond actress, Betsy Palmer, was given the small but integral part of the family outsider, Virginia.

Coe, Mann, and the entire cast were already gathered for rehearsals when Chayefsky arrived with the finished pages of Act III. "The fact is, we all read the completed play for the first time that morning," said Coe. "Rod was there, and Nancy, and all of the other actors," said Mann. "We sat around the table and as we went through the script everybody would sort of look at one another in silence and say, 'Is this as good as we really think it is?' " "The writing was beautiful," said Marchand. "It dealt with language and the rhythm of language. And Paddy was very specific about what he was saying, so you never had trouble reading his lines. They fell right out of your mouth."

The construction was compact, very close to perfection, the director believed. "To my recollection only one change was made, by NBC," said Mann. "Paddy originally called the play *Love Story*. But the network and the ad agency said that with such plain characters as these they could never sell that title to the public."

As the reading of *Marty* progressed that morning, Marchand said she felt a curious sense of *déjà vu*. They were gathered at the Abbey Hotel, in the ballroom where the original Friendship Club had held its dances. "They were the inspiration for Paddy's story," said Marchand, "and as I looked around, I saw all these barren little chairs lined up against the walls. Posted over them were those gentle but sad little signs that reminded people 'to dance with the people who ask you.' You could almost see all the Martys and the Claras sitting in those lonely chairs under those signs."

Chayefsky commented later that he did not consider *Marty* to be either sad or dramatic. It was "character satire," he said. "We were satirizing lower-middle-class social values. In rehearsals we all laughed like hell." Nancy Marchand said she had no recall of anyone laughing: "It was too touching, too beautiful."

Marty was obviously a character based largely on the emotions and feelings of Sidney Chayefsky, and though Paddy Chayefsky was loath to admit publicly to that side of himself, some of his colleagues were aware of the connection. "*Marty* was based on Paddy's personal experiences," said Mann. "In the story he was stripping off layers of himself and laying some things bare. He never said that to me, but I made that assumption and I held to it all these years."

"Yes, we all thought that *Marty* was based a lot on Paddy," Rod Steiger said. "But we didn't go up and ask him, because it was about such a lonely man, and such a man hungry for love, it would have been a rather embarrassing situation for him and all of us."

During rehearsals, the intimate correlations ignored, Chayefsky was open to discussions for changes. "I worked a few times in Paddy's plays," said Marchand, "and the wonderful thing is that he was always there when you needed him. During the run-through he would make notes, and if he sensed you were having trouble, during the break, in a very low-key manner, he would ask if he could help. I would tell him whatever problem I was having. He would listen and say, 'Yes. I see.' Then he would go over to a corner of the room where he had his little typewriter and he would tap away. He would come back and say, 'How's this?' The new lines were always perfect. He knew exactly how to fix things. He understood not only his characters but how the actors were playing them."

Ma, when are you gonna give up? Sooner or later,
there comes a point in a man's life when he
gotta face some facts, and one fact I gotta face
is that whatever it is that women like, I ain't got it.

Marty Pilletti, *Marty*

With the actors, director Mann said that his only problem was to curtail the
emotions of Rod Steiger. A Method performer from the Actors Studio, Steiger
worked from the inside, and with feelings that were very close to the surface.
In the scene in Act I where the mother urges her aging son to put on his blue
suit and go to the Waverly Ballroom and meet a nice girl, Steiger as Marty
argues that there was nothing at the Waverly Ballroom for him but another
night of rejection. His mother has to face the facts, because "Blue suit, gray
suit, I'm still a fat little man, Mama. A fat little ugly man."

"In rehearsals, Rod was so deeply moved by this, the tears would gush from
his eyes," said Mann. "This was a tricky thing. If the emotion spilled over-
board too big, too soon, it would hurt the play."

Less was always more to Mann, Betsy Palmer stated. "In theatre there's a
fine line called the 'aesthetic distance.' It means you can go to the edge of an
emotion, then pull back. If the tears are a little too real or the nose runs, then
the audience might pull back into themselves. You touched them a little too
closely and that isn't what good theatre is about."

On Saturday afternoon, May 23, the first run-through was done at NBC's
Studio 8, at Rockefeller Center. "This was to give the actors a feel for the sets,
and for us to figure out the best camera shots," said Mann. In scene 2 of Act
I, Marty and Angie were to sit in a booth of the local bar and discuss what to
do on that Saturday night. The dialogue—"Well, what do you feel like doing
tonight?"—and the direction were, as one critic later remarked, "revolutionary
in their simplicity." The two actors, each reading a section of a newspaper,
were not supposed to show much animation, or move too much, Mann
instructed. "The camera wasn't to move either. Nor was there any cutting
from one actor to the other. What we were trying to convey was the utter
naturalness and quiet of two friends aimlessly discussing a way to fill up their
Saturday night."

The following afternoon, Sunday, May 24, hours before the broadcast, the
cast and technical staff went through a complete run of the play, with camera
setups, music, and sound effects, all timed and adjusted to fit the prescribed
one-hour-show format. A full dress rehearsal followed from seven to eight that
evening. "Nancy Marchand had this long beautiful hair," said Betsy Palmer.
"So what they did was put it in a net and they tied it back on her head." Rod

Steiger didn't look too Italian, "so the makeup people put little rubber rings into his nostrils, just to spread them a little," said production supervisor Milton Meyers.

As the clock moved closer to nine o'clock, showtime, the usual fear and nervousness set in. "These shows were done live, so there was always a lot of stomach jitters and cold sweat," said Meyers. "The most frightening thing was the countdown," said Rod Steiger. " 'Ten, nine, eight, seven, six . . . ,' and I was ready to bolt for the door and run home." Chayefsky was there but stayed in the control room. "The writers felt they were giving birth, so they were always kept off the floor," said Meyers.

Just before the on-air buzzer sounded, the director gave one last note to Steiger. "I said, 'Remember, Rod, hold back the tears at the end of Act I.' "

When the show began, Mann was with Coe and Chayefsky in the control room. "All went well and then that scene came up. Paddy and Fred and I looked at each other as if to say, 'Well, here we go.' And Rod did it. He held the tears back. He let the audience cry for him. It was heartbreaking, the best-controlled performance that he has ever given in his life."

At the top of Act II, the introduction to the dance-hall scene in the Chayefsky script reads: "Fade in: Exterior, three-story building. Pan up to second floor . . . bright neon lights reading 'Waverly Ballroom.' " "That big sign was nothing more than a large sheet of black cardboard," Meyers said. "We punched out the letters in the front. Then when the scene came on, we had a stagehand behind the cardboard, with a lamp in his hand. He kept flicking the lamp, on and off, as the camera panned up the flat of a building."

Nancy Marchand has said that she has no actual recall of what went on in her scenes as the shy wallflower. "Isn't it strange? I remember the rehearsals, and what happened after, but I have no lasting impression of what happened during the telecast. All I remember is understanding and liking Clara very much. Her feelings were universal. A lot of girls, even if they're attractive, think they're not."

The memory of Chayefsky's own rejection at his school dance fifteen years before was transposed into the character of Clara. Dancing with Marty, she tells him of the last time she was at the Waverly Ballroom, when she sat on the sidelines for an hour and a half without moving a muscle. "Now and then, some fellow would sort of walk up to me and then change his mind," she says. "I just sat there, my hands in my lap. Until ten o'clock, when a bunch of kids came in swaggering. They weren't more than seventeen, eighteen years old. Well, they swaggered down along the wall, leering at all the girls. I thought they were kind of cute, and as they passed me, I smiled at them. One of the kids looked at me and said: 'Forget it, ugly, you ain't gotta chance.' I burst out crying. I'm a big crier, you know."

"So am I," Marty answers. "I cry alla time. Any little thing. I can recognize pain a mile away."

The exchange of confidences, the tentativeness and awkwardness as the ordinary couple stumble through the first steps of their courtship, kept viewers at home glued to their TV sets that night. "Audiences felt uncomfortable by the story, but they would not turn the TV set off," wrote John Crosby in the *New York Herald Tribune.*

"I was only thirteen or fourteen at the time," playwright John Guare has recalled. "But I remember sitting in my living room in Jackson Heights with my parents, watching that show. We were held absolutely spellbound."

"I don't think any of us had ever seen such a beautiful story on television before," said actress Eva Marie Saint.

"What Paddy gave us that night was a story about 'the losers,' " said CBS producer Sonny Fox. "Audiences were so used to seeing shows about 'the winners,' the beautiful [heroes and] heroines. Marty and Clara were essentially 'the nerds,' two people easily dismissed. But they were real people, with real emotions, dealing with real situations that are still with us today."

At the end of Act III, after his family and his best pal, Angie, have continually tried to discourage his interest in Clara, Marty makes his stand. Slamming his fist on the counter of the bar, he heads for the phone booth in the back, with Angie at his heels. Sitting down in the phone booth, Marty turns to Angie and says in a low intense voice: "You don't like her. My mother don't like her. She's a dog, and I'm a fat ugly little man. All I know is I had a good time last night. I'm gonna have a good time tonight. If we have enough good times together, I'm going down on my knees and beg that girl to marry me."

At that juncture, Marty is to shut the door on Angie and begin to dial Clara's number. "I put the dime in and I could not remember what came next," recalled Rod Steiger. "As I was dialing the number, I was soaked with perspiration inside my suit from head to foot, thinking this is a terrible time to blow everything, in the last scene. Then it suddenly occurred to me that the audience had not read the script. So I thought: 'I have every right to say what I was thinking.' So when the number connected I said, 'Hello.' And I ad-libbed something over the phone about being nervous and 'maybe you'd like to do something tonight, go to the movies or something?' "

"When that last scene faded out, and the final credits rolled, everyone in the studio was very quiet," said Meyers. "The show was over, but no one said anything."

"Instinctively, we knew we had done something," said Steiger. "All the souls were singing at the same time, thanks to the material."

On Monday morning, May 25, the praise and enthusiasm went public in New York City. People on the subway, on the streets, in their offices, were saying, "Hey, did you see that show about that guy in the Bronx last night?"

"I was walking on Fifth Avenue, and it was crowded," said Nancy Marchand. "This lady stopped me and said, 'Didn't you do that show last night?' I said yes. She said, 'Oh, you did your part so sweet.' I thought that was wonderful."

"Everywhere I went cab drivers and truck drivers were yelling 'Hi, Marty' to me," said Steiger. "I ran into Elia Kazan and he said, 'What did you do last night? The whole town is talking about *Marty*.' Then he told me to go over and see Budd Schulberg, to read for the part of Marlon Brando's brother in *On the Waterfront*."

In *The New York Times,* critic Jack Gould wrote a glowing essay about the show. "At that time TV plays didn't get much attention, just a paragraph or a line," said Eva Marie Saint. "An entire column, and a good one at that, was earthshaking."

"The reaction was the same from outside of New York," said Mann. "That week the mail started to come in. There were thousands and thousands of letters, more mail than for any show we ever did. People would say, 'That's my story. That's my life. How did you tell it so true, so faithfully?' "

"Millions of people were affected," said Saint.

"I guessed I touched a nerve," said Paddy Chayefsky, for once at a loss for words.

The Golden Age of Television

It may seem foolish to say, but television,
the scorned stepchild of drama, may well be the
basic theatre of our century.

Paddy Chayefsky, 1953

With the broadcast of *Marty*, an era in cultural entertainment began that was later to be known as the "Golden Age of Television." It was a time when a wide array of original scripts were telecast live, sometimes twenty-five in one week, by the three major networks. Among the sponsor-named showcases were "Kraft Television Theatre," "U.S. Steel Hour," "Revlon Theatre," and the "Philco"/"Goodyear" playhouses, which both critics and viewers considered the best series of all.

The success of the Philco-Goodyear programs was largely due to the predominance of good writers on the staff. They included David Shaw, Robert Alan Aurthur, Sumner Locke Elliott, Reginald Rose, Horton Foote, and Paddy Chayefsky. "All of our writers were writing about the audience they knew," said the show's producer, Fred Coe. "They were saying to the people, 'This is your life, this is what's going on, and this is one shred of understanding about that life.' That's why that drama was important and significant—and that's why Philco-Goodyear produced such a crop of first-rate writers."

The abundance of the best literary talent at Philco-Goodyear was attributed to the respect and attention they received. "Writers love to be loved, and Fred did that. He discovered them and nurtured them, carefully and creatively," said Robert Alan Aurthur. "Fred had the best story sense in the business," said Chayefsky. "You could pitch him the barest outline for a play. He'd say, 'Sounds like a good idea, go ahead and write it.' That was the deal."

In the summer of 1953, Tad Mosel was a young ticket seller at Northwest Airlines. "Writing plays like crazy" in his spare time, he decided to submit one to Coe at NBC. Not long after, a secretary called and made an appointment for him to meet with the producer. "That first day Fred said to me, 'How many plays would you like to write for us?' " Mosel recalled. "Can you imagine saying that to a kid?"

J. P. Miller was working in a TV appliance store, "writing plays on the side and starving to death." He didn't consider writing for television, simply because he didn't own one. "Then one day a guy in the shop, a TV repairman, gave me a cathode tube, you know, a picture tube. I put it in a cardboard box, painted the box maroon, and that was my first set." Tuning in to the Philco-Goodyear series on Sunday nights, he saw a play by Paddy Chayefsky, then another by Horton Foote, and a third by Tad Mosel. "I said, 'Jesus Christ, these guys really mean it. This is not just bullshit. This is the real thing. These people are trying to do something good.' "

Miller wrote a fifty-minute script and sent it to an assistant to the story editor at Philco-Goodyear. She called and asked, "Who's your agent?" He didn't have one, he replied. A meeting was arranged with Coe. "Just going into his presence scared me, because I had no credits," said Miller. "But Fred said, 'We like your play, do you know any other stories?' I said yes, and told him one. He said, 'Go home and write it, Pappy, you've got a job.' "

"It was a wonderful time," said Chayefsky, "the closest thing to bohemia that I ever lived in. All the writers hung out together in a creative klatsch. We were really intimate friends. We spent all day up on the fourth floor of NBC. We were accused of all sorts of things—they called us the Diamond Typewriter Brigade."

"Yes, that's true," writer David Shaw said. "There was a wonderful camaraderie. We played cards, swapped jokes and stories, goofed off downstairs in the Rockefeller Center drugstore. There were also parties and dinners, and late at night, if you were having trouble with a script deadline, there was always someone to call."

"We all liked each other's work," said Sumner Locke Elliott. "We learned from each other. We weren't competing. If Tad Mosel did a good script, we all felt good for him. If Horton Foote had a show on the next week, everyone watched it. And when Paddy started writing his plays, he taught me a great deal about simplicity."

The writing part came easy because of Fred Coe, Chayefsky said. "He never stomped on you. He only helped you. We never had to turn in an outline for him to give to the network, for them to muddy up. He had that kind of power."

When a script was approved, it was presented as the writer wrote it. "Fred worked on the same premise as the Dramatists Guild, that the writer was God, that you can't change anything without his consent," said casting director Ethel Winant. " 'Philco' and the rest of the good dramatic shows grew out of that belief. It never occurred to anyone not to consult the writer all through production. The writer was the engine. 'If it's not on the page, it's not on the stage,' that was the rule. And even though Fred knew exactly what he wanted to do, he worked with the writer to attain that end."

J. P. Miller believed that Coe's method, of never "stomping" on the writer, worked especially well for Chayefsky. "Paddy could skid out on a turn, just like any of us could. But with insight and a little persuasion, Fred could bring him back on the right path. He had this knack of gently milking the best stuff out of you. He never used a battering ram. By inference, by evocation, not by direct confrontation, Fred was able to send any writer home to make the changes and feel that he had been *inspired*."

Another reason the Philco-Goodyear anthology series was so effective during this period was because "a producer, not a committee, was in control," said TV historian Eric Barnouw in *Tube of Plenty*. That meant there was a minimum of interference during production. "We were never troubled by anyone—not the networks, not the agencies," said Chayefsky. "It was like having the ship steered for you," Sumner Locke Elliott agreed. "Fred kept everyone off the bridge."

Coe occasionally allowed the sponsor or a representative from the ad agency to watch from the control room during rehearsals. "But if one of them set foot on his set, there would be an explosion," said Elliott. "And if something went wrong, he took the rap. If the show was bad, Fred would say, 'Well, next time we've got to come up with something better, that's all. Got any ideas, Pappy?' "

Chayefsky was paid $1,200 for his script of *Marty*, which he said was hardly commensurate with the three months he worked on it. Money, however, was not the priority. "All your life you aim for a time when you're doing what you do for no other reason than that you like it, and I love writing," he said.

"Everything back then was on a much smaller scale," actress Nancy Marchand has recalled. "There weren't people sitting on your doorstep saying, 'Look, baby, you've got to have this script in by X date, because we're going to be a seventeen-million-dollar show and we're going for a big killing here.' It was all much more human than that."

The Philco-Goodyear unit helped to stabilize its connection with the writers by including them in all stages of the production process. That included soliciting their input on the casting of the plays they had created. "The idea was that the writer often had someone in mind when he wrote his script. So we continued that collaboration when the casting began," said Ethel Winant. "As soon as I got a script I'd call Paddy or Tad or Reggie, and I'd say, 'Do you want to come over, or could we have lunch and talk about what you think?' "

Sometimes the writers did not approve of the actors chosen to perform in their plays. "I can remember standing outside the NBC building one day, arguing with Paddy and Reggie about a piece of casting," said Winant. "In the end it frequently worked out. Because often you knew something about the actor that they didn't know, or you *hoped* you did. We were looking at new actors in plays and showcases that the writer didn't know of, so frequently we had more of an insight into what they could do."

The bold new talent from the Actors Studio were popular choices, including Kim Stanley, Geraldine Page, Eva Marie Saint, James Dean, Paul Newman, Joanne Woodward, John Cassavetes, Anthony Franciosa, Eileen Heckart, and Maureen Stapleton.

"Some of the directors at Philco-Goodyear *insisted* on people from the Actors Studio," said agent-writer George Baxt. "Vincent Donehue cast most of his show from their roster."

"Basically we used people that no one else wanted to hire," said Winant. "In the beginning, the established theatre actors wouldn't do television; and of course the motion picture stars totally ignored us. So we looked around, in summer stock, in the New York workshops, the Equity Library Theatre, and we would find all these new people; these incredibly talented kids like James Dean and Steve McQueen."

"In those days, no one knew who James Dean *was*. He was a nobody, but a *talented* nobody," said Baxt. In one Philco-Goodyear show, *Run Like a Thief*, written by Sam Hall, Dean was given the leading role of a young waiter training to be a maître d' in a restaurant. "His co-star was Kurt Kasznar, who was also from the Studio, but older, and a real bastard, loathed by everybody," said Baxt. "During rehearsals he was giving Jimmy Dean a very hard time. On the night of the telecast, Paddy Chayefsky showed up and words were exchanged. I'm not sure what was said, but I know the situation was tense. But with actors from the Studio, you could expect that. They always brought extra luggage to a performance."

Trained toward "naturalistic" emoting, the Method actors were always eager to act in Chayefsky's TV plays. "Paddy's dialogue was so alive and realistic," said Sumner Locke Elliott. "Everything was there in his writing, so the actors didn't have to do their customary probing and searching, looking for 'the meaning' of the text."

Chayefsky said that he "liked all actors, even bad ones," but with acolytes of the Method he often objected to the lengthy pauses they inserted gratuitously into his dialogue. "In rehearsals Paddy would say to me, 'I don't want these long Actors Studio pauses,'" said director Arthur Penn. "But then on camera, when he saw what the actors were doing in those moments, he responded to it, because he was very enamored of good work."

For actors as well as writers, the new medium had pluses and minuses. The continuity of the live shows pleased the stage-trained performers. However, the rudimentary aspects of television, the nascent technology and limited physical space, often provided tensions and dramatic touches not called for in the scripts. "Studio 8, where the Philco-Goodyear series was shot, was a former radio studio and it was tiny, minuscule compared to the soundstages they have today," said Milton Meyers.

"That's why they called our shows 'closet-dramas.' They were literally filmed in a closet," said Chayefsky.

"We had only two cameras, which could never be raised too high because the ceilings were so low," said Meyers.

"There were no exterior shots," said Mann. "All of the sets were crammed into this small studio, and the actors would literally walk or run from one set to the other."

"And forget about putting a fire or a flood in your script," said Chayefsky. "The fire department wouldn't allow it. All you would get would be some wisps of smoke or a small puddle of water."

Special effects were limited or improvised. When an earthquake or tremor was called for, the turret holding the lens was jiggled. "One night we were in the middle of a shot when the lens popped out and dropped on the floor," recalled Arthur Penn.

"Lights would go out, sets would collapse, props would vanish," said Tad Mosel. "But you kept going because this was live, there were no retakes."

"There was one early show," said Meyers, "where Grace Kelly was supposed to be in bed, alone in a room, when suddenly, in the background, viewers saw this prop man in a corner, sweeping the dust up off the floor."

Paul Newman recalled the time when a corpse was lying on a road. "As the actors in the foreground were delivering their lines, with the camera still on him, the corpse got up, brushed himself off, then walked offstage."

Another night, Eva Marie Saint was to deliver a long speech while sitting at a picnic table and wearing a bathing suit. On camera, during the speech, out of the corner of her eye, she could see the assistant director waving frantically. "I was giving the speech all I had," said Saint. "Until finally I looked down and saw that my bathing suit had slid down below my bosoms. There I was on live television, with my bare bosoms showing. So I just sort of slid under the table and fixed it and continued talking."

There was no cutting to commercials when mishaps or mistakes happened, because the commercials were also done live, in the same studio. When one act of the play was coming to a close, the stagehands would quickly draw a drape on a traverse rod across a section of the set, then wheel in the product—a Philco television set, a refrigerator, or a Goodyear tire. As the scene faded out, Camera 2 went to the product and the commercial began.

At times the studio floor was so crammed with sets and product that actors who were not needed for the scene at hand were asked to wait outside in the hallway. "My favorite Philco story had to do with Fred Coe and the nun," said Summer Locke Elliott. "One Sunday night there was a show with Kim Stanley. Towards the climax, at the end, this nun was supposed to enter. The show was running long, so Fred decided to eliminate the next-to-last scene, and get right to the climax. As the floor manager ran outside to alert the nun, Fred had his eye on the clock and he began to panic. Unfortunately the mike to the floor was left open, and as the seconds were ticking away, while millions of viewers were listening, Fred's voice boomed out over the air: 'Get the nun on—get the fuckin' nun on.' "

"Anything and everything could happen, and it did," said Chayefsky. "But that was the beauty, the excitement of being live."

The live medium was a phenomenon, said Gore Vidal, whose original script *Visit to a Small Planet* was shown on the Goodyear program on May 8, 1955. "We were the auteurs," said Vidal. "Millions of people switched on to see our plays, not the actors and *never* the directors. We created an art form that flourished for a decade, and vanished forever."

Horton Foote, reminiscing in 1991, wasn't as sentimental about the period. "I think it's been romanticized," he said. "But it did give the writers freedom to do whatever they could according to their talents."

"In the dictionary the 'golden age' is not described as 'a zenith,' " said Tad Mosel. "A golden age is a flower. It's a time when things bloom and blossom, and that's what television was in those days. It *was* a golden age, and not a 'so-called golden age,' as critics later called it. It was golden because people like Fred Coe and Paddy Chayefsky were there. *They* were golden people. There was also gold dust in the air, an excitement and generosity of spirit that I've never experienced since. Everyone cheered the others' successes, and when needed, they mourned the failures."

"And there *were* failures. We wrote some real stinkers," said Robert Alan Aurthur. "But even if a play bombed, a writer would be back in a few weeks or months with another play, another chance," said Mosel.

"And that was the true joy of that age," said Chayefsky. "We didn't have the terrible burden of producing something significant every time we did something. You could get an idea and say, 'Is it substantial enough? Is it sturdy enough to merit an hour show?' Then you'd go home and write that for television. It didn't have to be important, because it went on every week consistently. Some weeks were good, some lousy. It was a terribly *young* thing. That kind of enormous energy. It was for youthful people, which we were then."

The press exposure and celebrity accorded the writers, especially those at Philco-Goodyear, was unusually high, but again, the credit for this must go to producer Fred Coe. "Fred insisted that the writer's name be first on the opening credits, and that it be the last name listed at the end, *after* the producer and director," said Delbert Mann. "Promote the writers, they're all we have" was Coe's instruction to Johnny Friedkin, the publicist from the show's ad agency.

"Johnny reinforced what Fred believed in, a love and respect for the writers," said Horton Foote. "He was responsible in many ways for bringing all of us to the public's attention."

It was agreed that of the group, Paddy Chayefsky was the most adept at promoting himself. He loved to talk, and to eat, and it was the job of the press to listen, then pick up the meal check. The "most impure motives" were useful for a beginning writer, he later told author-interviewer John Brady. "Just to get your name in the columns is not an improper motivation for a writer, when you're a kid, when you're young. The need for fame and notoriety I think is part of the package that brings you into show business."

"Paddy did have a knack for publicity," said Johnny Friedkin. "Reporters and columnists loved him because he always had an angle for them, and good quotes for their stories." But if the talent had been lacking, the press wouldn't have bothered with him. Friedkin recalled that Chayefsky had a hard time getting any press until *Marty* was shown. "Then the interest in Paddy and the show soared spontaneously," said *Variety*. "*Marty* broke new ground for all of us," said Tad Mosel. "After the fact, other writers would say, 'Well, I could have written stuff like that.' But the fact of the matter is that Paddy did it first and he did it best."

The pinnacle in approbation came when *Life* magazine, largest in circulation and mainstream acceptance, devoted four pages of one issue to the Philco-Goodyear writers. The magazine called it a "New Era for Playwrights," noting that "if William Shakespeare were alive today he might well be writing for television." Extolling the show's shining roster of writers, the magazine then singled out Paddy Chayefsky as "the undisputed best" of the lot.

Gore Vidal, speaking in 1991, went along with the consensus. "To write a live drama in fifty-odd minutes for two or three cameras was as intricate a task as writing haikus or practicing precision bombing," said Vidal. "There were not any of us who could do it with ease. Of the lot, it was Paddy's natural form; it was my, agreeably, acquired one."

"If there was envy among us, it was the kind that kept us on our toes," said Mosel. "We didn't want to write like Paddy Chayefsky, but we wanted to be as good as he was."

In July 1953, two months after *Marty* was shown, Chayefsky's next play, *The Big Deal*, was telecast. The model for the story of an elderly man who tries to recapture the success of his youth was Chayefsky's father, Harry. Having once made and lost a fortune in the construction business, Joe Manx in *The Big Deal* dreams of making one last big score. To take a prospective backer to lunch, he borrows some money from his working daughter, who pleads with her disapproving mother not to deflate Joe's dreams or push him into taking a lesser job as a building inspector. "It isn't in him. He likes big things. It would kill him to be a little man," she says. The "painfully real and uncommonly perceptive script made the play the highlight of the summer season," said *Variety*.

In October 1953, TV viewers eagerly tuned in to the next Chayefsky play, *The Bachelor Party*. The canvas for this story was much wider. Instead of confining the plot to one central figure, Chayefsky intended to show what happens when a group of men try to recapture the fun and freedom of their youth during a night on the town. The characters include Charlie, a young accountant, whose wife has just become pregnant with their first child. Also featured is Kenneth, another young husband who rides the subway to work each day thinking of other women; Walter, a family man and bookkeeper who talks only of the war and the fun he had with his soldier pals in Paris; and Arnold, the thirty-two-year-old nervous groom whose family has arranged his match with a woman he doesn't know. "What am I going to do with her, Charlie?" the terrified Arnold asks his friend. "She's one of these quiet ones. I'm not much of a talker myself. Somebody's got to do the talking."

Discussing the interwoven construction of the play, Chayefsky said that "no matter how delightfully any character is written, he is a bore if he serves no definite plot purpose. For example, George Bernard Shaw will drag in any number of peripheral characters just to indulge a dissertation." Of his compelling naturalistic dialogue Chayefsky said, in a statement that would later come back to haunt him, that he tried to write his TV plays as if they "had been wiretapped. I tried to envision the scenes as if a camera had been focused on the unsuspecting characters and had caught them in an untouched moment of life."

The reviews for *The Bachelor Party* were positive. "Chayefsky makes a habit of writing for TV as if he had invented the medium," said critic John Crosby in the *Herald Tribune*. "He has an uncanny ability for making his characters come to life as full-bodied people who talk and act in a manner that permits audience identification," *Variety* agreed.

Five months later, in March 1954, Chayefsky had completed the script of a TV play that some of his supporters would remember as his best after *Marty*. This was *The Mother*, the story of Mrs. Fanning, a recently widowed woman who at the age of sixty-two decides to go out and enter the work market. "I don't want to be some old lady living with her children," she tells her married daughter. "If I can't take care of myself, I just as soon be in the grave with your father." She finds a job in a garment factory, but is fired after the first day when she sews five dozen sleeves to the wrong side of a batch of dresses. Scared and tired, she calls her children that night and announces that she will sell her house and move into "a room somewhere with some other old woman." In the meantime she asks her daughter, Annie, if she can move in with her temporarily. Mrs. Fanning spends one night with Annie, during which she discusses how to dispense with her furniture and silver. "Is this what it all comes to," she asks, "an old woman parceling out the old furniture in her house?" Her daughter assures Mrs. Fanning that she will fit in and be happy in their household. But early the following morning, Mrs. Fanning packs her valise and tells Annie that she can't stay with her, that she's going out to look for another job. "I'm a woman of respect," she says. "I can take care of myself. I always have. Work is the meaning of my life. It's all I know how to do. I can't change my ways at this late time."

"The play took place in a dress factory and none of us knew what one looked like," said Philco-Goodyear supervisor Milton Meyers. "So Paddy took Delbert Mann, Otis Riggs, the set designer, and me down to this place down on Seventh Avenue. It was lunch hour, and there were rows and rows of sewing machines—with bins and racks between them. At the end of the room there was an elderly woman, brown-bagging her lunch at one of the machines. We walked down there and Paddy said, 'Ma, I'd like you to meet some of my friends.' It turns out that the mother in the play was his mother, except he gave her an Irish name."

Bill Chayefsky confirmed that the character in *The Mother* was indeed Mrs. Chayefsky. In 1950, with all of her sons married and gone, the independent and indomitable Gussie had no one to take care of. So she went back to work as a seamstress. "It had been thirty-four years since she worked, but she picked herself up and went down to the garment district," said Bill Chayefsky. "They needed help and she was hired. She didn't remember much about sewing, the business had changed, so she got fired after the first day. So the next day, she went to another place, got another job, learned a little bit more, then got fired again. A third job followed. She was dismissed again. But by this time she had learned a lot more. So by the fourth time she was adept at what she was doing and she kept that position." That job was important to her. " 'If you can't produce, you shouldn't be alive.' That was my mother's philosophy," said Bill Chayefsky. "Young or old, a person had to be productive, every day of their life."

The veteran actress Cathleen Nesbitt was cast as the mother in the TV play, and Maureen Stapleton played Annie, the daughter. On the Monday morning after the broadcast, Tad Mosel remembered, he, Paddy, and the rest of the Philco-Goodyear writers were gathered in Fred Coe's office. "We were being photographed for a magazine article when Fred's secretary came in and interrupted the session. She was breathless, almost shaking. She said to Paddy, 'Mr. Chayefsky, Marlene Dietrich is on the telephone.' We were all as awed as he was when he came back and told us that Dietrich had seen the show the night before and she identified with the mother." That was the wide appeal of Chayefsky's work, Mosel believed. "Most of us were satisfied, thrilled, to elicit responses from the farmer in Iowa or the woman in Minnesota, but Paddy could make Marlene Dietrich see herself in a sixty-six-year-old garment worker."

That same month, an item appeared in the New York *Journal-American*. It stated that Chayefsky had been asked to write a movie script for United Artists. That news in itself was not unusual, considering how popular the writer had become. The wonder of the situation was that the script was to be an adaptation of a play that had already appeared on television, which was still the enemy and rival of the powerful motion picture industry.

Marty: The Motion Picture

In the four years that had passed since Paddy Chayefsky departed Hollywood in a huff, swearing not to return until they kissed his rear in two department-store windows, the movie industry had gone through an unexpected cycle of changes. A major blow came when attendance at theatres began to drop drastically. This was attributed to the free competition—television.

After instituting a ban preventing their product and their contracted per-formers from appearing on the new medium, the studios proceeded to try and lure audiences back into their theatres with new technical improvements, including making movies in 3-D, CinemaScope, and stereophonic sound. "They tried everything except the real novelty: three-dimensional material, new and better stories," said Elia Kazan.

Another dire blast hit Hollywood in the early 1950s, when the United States Supreme Court ruled that the major studios had to divest themselves of their large movie theatre chains. As the booking monopoly ceased, the independent movie outfits such as United Artists began to prosper. Run by two sharp lawyers in New York, Arthur B. Krim and Robert Benjamin, who took over the company with borrowed funds in 1951, UA specialized in releasing low-cost movies and films imported from Europe. Krim and Benjamin then gam-bled on two independent filmmakers, John Huston and Stanley Kramer. When *The African Queen* and *High Noon* became artistic and financial hits, the two lawyers were able to go to the major banks and secure letters of credit to finance future films. Then they spread the word to other maverick producers and stars that UA could provide the money and the "psychological climate" to nurture their creative and capitalistic souls. Among the maverick talents that joined the company at this time were Otto Preminger, Frank Sinatra, John

Wayne, and a very ambitious, ingenious producer-star team named Hecht-Lancaster.

Born in the Bronx, Harold Hecht was a dancer turned agent whose main client, actor Burt Lancaster, became his producing partner in the late 1940s. By 1952 they had scored with two tremendous box-office hits, *The Flame and the Arrow* and *The Crimson Pirate*, which enabled them to set up a lucrative deal with Arthur Krim and Robert Benjamin at United Artists. Their first release for UA was *Apache*, which grossed triple its cost the first year. By 1954, three other movies starring Lancaster were scheduled for UA, at which time Hecht decided to add a separate, smaller production to their slate. The property he had in mind was *Marty*, which he had seen on television the previous year.

Harold Hecht and Paddy Chayefsky knew each other. They went back to 1947, when Paddy was making the rounds at Universal Studios, chatting up producers and directors to further his career. In 1948, Hecht was filming a quickie, *Kiss the Blood Off My Hands*, with Lancaster, when Chayefsky asked him to read some of his work. "In fact for a long time Hecht was Paddy's only and very captive audience. Paddy would make him sit still while he read him plays nobody wanted," said one reporter.

In 1953, when Hecht went after *Marty*, Chayefsky said he wasn't interested. He didn't want his small story turned into a big Hollywood movie, he said. In fact, he was stalling, because Philco-Goodyear producer Fred Coe was trying to raise money on his own to make the film. When that didn't materialize, Hecht returned with a second offer, which Chayefsky also resisted. Still mindful of the ignominy he had previously suffered in Hollywood, he coolly asked for a few guarantees upfront. He wanted the same creative deal he got at Philco. He would write the new script, in New York, and do all the rewrites and revisions. "You spill your guts into the typewriter, which is why you can't stand to see what you write destroyed or degraded into a hunk of claptrap by picture butchers," he said. Full consultation on casting was also requested, and the director had to be the man who had directed it on TV, Delbert Mann.

Amazingly, Harold Hecht agreed to everything, making Chayefsky the "associate producer." Too fast, Paddy thought that evening, so the next day he added one more stipulation. Having been up and down Hollywood Boulevard a few times, he knew he needed more creative protection. He told Hecht he had to be on board as the "codirector." That way, if Hecht or Lancaster decided to fire Mann during filming, Chayefsky would be able to step in and take over the direction, and thus preserve the intrinsic values of his script. "Paddy did indeed ask for and receive codirector status on the movie version of *Marty*," said Mann. "He paid his fee to the Directors Guild, and later asked for it back when he was sure I was locked in to the job."

On February 5, 1954, a memo was circulated at United Artists detailing the company's financial allotments for future Hecht-Lancaster films. These included *Trapeze,* set to pair Lancaster with Montgomery Clift, at a budget "not to exceed one million dollars, excluding stars' salaries." The last film mentioned on UA's memo was *Marty,* to be produced at a cost of "not over $150,000, including 10% for overhead; and no producer fee." From that amount, a payment up front of $13,000, and 5 percent of any future profits, was allocated for the script, by Paddy Chayefsky. "Originally his fee was fifteen thousand, but they were only going to give Del eight thousand, so Paddy cut himself back to thirteen and they gave the extra two thousand to Del," said publicist Johnny Friedkin.

Work on the script went fast. Chayefsky did not change or expand his original TV play. "There's no way of opening up that story any wider than it is," he said. "Essentially, it was a portrait, and a portrait can only be done in detail and depth."

Clara's background, which was barely touched upon in the TV version, was developed further. Her meeting and blossoming romance with Marty was explored at greater length. The only trouble Chayefsky had was keeping in mind "that a motion picture must move all the time. In television you more or less set up your camera and let the play go by. For the movies you have to be a whole lot more inventive."

In June 1954, with a first draft completed, the writer went to Los Angeles for two weeks of story conferences. "Those I hate," he said. "That's when I'm no good at all." Back in New York, working on a second draft, Chayefsky was visited by Jim Hill, Hecht-Lancaster's story editor, a handsome, polished bachelor who would wed Rita Hayworth a year later. Prior to meeting with Chayefsky, Hill attended an afternoon baseball game with singer Helen O'Connell. Arriving at his hotel suite he learned that two or three other beautiful women had dropped by, along with Chayefsky, who had watched the ball game while waiting. "Jesus," said Paddy, referring to the sportscast when Hill arrived. "The cameras spent more time looking at you and O'Connell than they did on the game." The two men were talking about the script for *Marty* when Paddy stopped to mention "the broads who dropped by." Hill nodded, then continued talking about the script, until Paddy broke in again. "Can I ask you something?" he said. Hill nodded yes. "What in the hell does a guy like you know about a fat ugly butcher from the Bronx?" Hill laughed and said, "Absolutely nothing," and from then on, he added, "we became the best of friends." Hill never worked with Chayefsky on the script. "Nobody did. We made suggestions. Paddy would come to me to try things out, but that was it."

When the script was completed, Chayefsky said, "I honestly feel that *Marty* in film form is a better play than it was on TV. There, it ran forty-eight minutes. The film will run a little over ninety minutes."

The Casting

While the second draft of the script was being done, Harold Hecht was in Mexico making *Vera Cruz*. In a letter to Arthur Krim in New York he discussed the casting of the leading role of Marty. "I believe that Marlon Brando can play it," he said. "We would then of course have an entirely different picture from its previous conception, although I don't think that it would necessarily cost much more money."

On May 14, when the second draft was completed and accepted, Bob Blumofe, the vice president in charge of West Coast operations for UA, sent another memo to Krim. Of the script he said, "It has some wonderful qualities. It rings with truth and honesty. It is about real people with real problems. I see tremendous opportunity for audience identification." Regarding the leading role, Blumofe felt it was "a waste of time to talk back and forth the way Burt and Harold are apparently doing about whether Marlon Brando is right for the part. I say he's not only right but the picture cries for him or someone like him in talent and box office stature. Artificial means can easily be used to make him physically unattractive."

In closing his letter, while urging that someone should go to work on getting Brando "immediately," Blumofe said he would like to offer an alternate recommendation. "I don't know whether anyone else has thought of this as yet, but I am going to suggest it and run. It's *JACKIE GLEASON!*" Don't think of Gleason "as an out-and-out low comic," Blumofe suggested. "Rather think of him in his character of Ralph the bus driver on his TV show."

Chayefsky and Delbert Mann had their own thoughts on the casting. They wanted Hecht-Lancaster to hire the original actors from the TV version. Rod Steiger had completed *On the Waterfront* and was making the film version of *Oklahoma!* when he was summoned to meet with Lancaster and Hecht. They offered him the lead in *Marty*, along with an ironclad seven-year employment contract. Steiger said no to the latter. He didn't feel they should be allowed to own him and choose his future film parts. "I have the right to make my own mistakes. If I want to go to bed with somebody, I want to be the one to choose," he said; and that was the end of Steiger for *Marty*.

According to Jim Hill, it was Burt Lancaster who came up with the actor to play the leading role. In Mexico to film *Vera Cruz*, Lancaster had his eye on a supporting actor in the cast, Ernest Borgnine, whose screen time thus far had mainly been limited to playing sadistic bullies. "Burt and I were riding back from the set one day," said Hill. "We were bullshitting about this and that and Burt said, 'You know who could play Marty—Ernie Borgnine.' That was how it happened, just like that. It was Burt's idea."

Borgnine recalled it differently. "It was Bob Aldrich, the director of *Vera Cruz*, who first suggested me. Delbert Mann was in Mexico, visiting the set, picking up pointers because he had never done a Hollywood picture before. He had the script of *Marty* with him and Aldrich asked to read it. A couple of weeks later at a party, Del asked him, 'Who do you think could play the part?' Aldrich said, 'I can't think of anybody but Ernie Borgnine.' And everyone said, 'Ernie Borgnine? But Christ—he's a killer. He plays nothing but these tough guys.' And Aldrich said, 'Don't kid yourself. He could do it.' Evidently that got around to where Burt said something to Harold Hecht, because not long after the ball started rolling in my direction."

As per his contract, Paddy Chayefsky had to give his counsel on Borgnine. That July, in California, Chayefsky and Mann were flown upstate by private plane to a place called Lone Pine, where Borgnine was making *Bad Day at Black Rock* with Spencer Tracy. "I knew they were coming," said Borgnine, "so that day when I was leaving the set early, Tracy stopped me. 'Where the hell are you going?' he said. 'Anybody that leaves the set early is *me*.' I told him I had to go read for a part. And he said '*Read?* Goddammit, you're not supposed to be reading for parts anymore.' And he asked what the part was. I told him that it was for the lead in *Marty*. And he said, 'Don't worry. You're going to get it. When you come back here tomorrow, you tell me that. Because you're going to be a star, and a big one.' And I thought, 'Well sir, out of your mouth to God's ears.' "

Paddy Chayefsky's ears were not as receptive. Sitting in Borgnine's motel room when the actor arrived, he did not appear to be too cordial. "He and Del had a rough crossing from Los Angeles to Lone Pine," Borgnine recalled. "Their stomachs were still a little upset and then I walked in. I was dusty, with a three-days' growth of beard, and a cowboy hat on. I could tell right away that Paddy thought this was a lost trip for him." Borgnine went to the bathroom to wash up, and when he came out he knew that Mann and Chayefsky had been talking. "I decided to be up front with them," he said. "I told them how much I liked the script but that if I wasn't right for the part that was O.K., that I'd help them find someone else." Chayefsky grunted and said, "Let's get started."

In the motel room, with Mann stretched out across the bed, Chayefsky began by reading the part of the customer in the butcher store with Borgnine as Marty. "The very first thing out of the box," said the actor, "was Paddy yelling, 'Jesus Christ! Hold it! Hold it!' " A little nervous, Borgnine asked what was wrong. Chayefsky told him that he was playing the Bronx character with a western twang. "Oh my God," Borgnine said. Throwing his Stetson on the bureau and pulling his shirt out of his pants, he started the scene again.

The reading went on, with Chayefsky suggesting the actor use different tones and inflections. "It began to get better and better," said Borgnine. "We were moving along at a fairly fast clip. We finally got to the part at the end of the first act, where my mother in the movie asks that I put on my blue suit and go down to the Waverly Ballroom, to look for tomatoes. And I said, 'Ma, don't you understand? I'm an ugly man. I'm a fat, ugly little man.' And I turned away, because I had started to cry. Tears were coming out of my ears. When I turned back to Paddy, who was playing the mother, I saw he was crying too. And out of the corner of my eye, I could see Del was also close to tears. That gave me the most wonderful feeling in my life; to think I had accomplished something that could affect people this way."

Neither Chayefsky nor Mann made a firm commitment to Borgnine at that time, but the actor felt confident. The next morning when he went back to the *Bad Day at Black Rock* set, Spencer Tracy came up to him. "He looked and said, 'Well?' And I said, 'I think I got it.' And Tracy said, 'Goddammit, I told you so.' "

> You don't like her. My mother don't like her. She's a dog,
> and I'm just a fat, ugly little man. All I know is
> I had a good time last night. I'm gonna have a good time tonight.
> If we have enough good times together, I'm gonna go down
> on my knees and beg that girl to marry me.
>
> Marty Pilletti, *Marty*

For the role of Clara, the spinster schoolteacher, Chayefsky and Mann again asked for the actress who had played her on TV, Nancy Marchand. But she was passed over because the producers wanted a new face. "I was not necessarily disappointed," said Marchand. "I have always had a lot of faith in my future. If that didn't come along there was a reason because something else nice was going to happen, and later on I did work in two of Paddy's other movies."

In Hollywood, auditions for Clara were held at the Hecht-Lancaster offices on the Goldwyn lot. Among the actresses considered were Cloris Leachman and Betsy Blair. Upon reading the script, Blair said, "Only twice in my life have I ever read something and known it was great. One script was *Death of a Salesman*, which Gene [Blair's husband, Gene Kelly] was asked to do; the other was *Marty*."

Born in New Jersey, Blair had begun her career as a dancer, then acted on Broadway before marrying Gene Kelly and moving to California. After the birth of their daughter she played a few minor parts in films, then more or less withdrew to become the Metro star's wife. When her name was mentioned for *Marty*, Delbert Mann said she was "too young and too pretty" for Clara. Chayefsky knew better. Seven years before, on the set of *A Double Life*, he had watched Blair perform a bit part. She had played a rather sedate-looking model who is asked to impersonate a femme fatale. "You want sexy? I can be sexy," she says earnestly. "You want chic? I can be chic." Her lines were minimal, said Chayefsky, but Blair delivered. She was what he and the pros called "a real actress," and he insisted that Hecht and Lancaster meet with her. "So I went and read for them," Blair recalled. "I was dying to be in it. I went back and read again. They didn't have any money for screen tests, so I read a third and fourth time. The last time, the secretary said to me, 'I think you must have the part because the great stone face—Burt Lancaster—had a tear in his eye.' "

Within weeks, after the rest of the cast was chosen, a problem arose with Blair. United Artists informed the producers that she would not be allowed to work in the movie because her name was on a list of Hollywood people connected to various left-wing political causes. These were the blacklist years, when the anti-Communist hysteria and paranoia was dictating the terms of employment—or unemployment—of thousands of American citizens.

Blair recalled, "Harold Hecht said to me that he was sorry he had to ask me to see a lawyer, and write a crawling letter, but that he must because the Un-American Activities Committee was very hot on everything connected to him. I knew at the time that that was nonsense. I had my own 'bad reputation.' "

When apprised of this, Chayefsky stood firm. He insisted that Blair not be replaced. He also tried to help her write a letter to her congressman in California. "I was supposed to say that I was sorry but that people had misled me," she said, "but I couldn't do it very well." Blair's husband stepped in at that point. "Gene felt that I deserved the part since I had read for it so many times, and it was a great script. He then went to Dore Schary [head of MGM], and said that Dore knew me well, knew that I was not about to overthrow the country." For emphasis, Kelly told Schary that production on his latest musical would come to a halt unless the studio head intervened. "So Dore Schary called the American Legion in Washington and they cleared me for the film."

On the morning of September 6, 1954, rehearsals for the movie of *Marty* began at the Palladium Ballroom in New York. "This is where the real fun is," said Chayefsky. "Making the thing come to life. Giving it tone and quality. Cutting it, trimming it, changing it, making it tight."

"We rehearsed it like a play," said Blair, "which enabled us to shoot it rather quickly when we began to shoot."

Three days of exterior shots were scheduled for the Bronx, with the interiors to follow on a soundstage in Hollywood. The Bronx location scenes had been carefully chosen in advance by Harold Hecht and Chayefsky. "We drove around in Harold's Cadillac for two whole days," said Paddy, "pointing and picking out spots we both grew up in. At one point we were having so much fun we considered adding some new stuff to the script, but we both knew we couldn't afford those kind of indulgences."

On September 20, the opening shot, of the busy shopping strip on 186th Street and Arthur Avenue, was filmed. That night the unit moved over to Boston Road and Tremont Avenue, where the news store–luncheonette scenes between Borgnine and Blair were filmed. "Paddy was there every minute," said Borgnine. "But he never bothered anyone too much. In the beginning he said to me, 'Do you have a tendency to blow up during the lines?' I said what I usually do is learn my lines to a point where I know them by heart, and unless I'm hit by a Mack truck I just keep going and do my part the best I can.' Paddy said, 'That's all I want to know. Just keep going and keep it moving. Any mistakes, we'll dub them in later.' "

Arriving on location the second evening, Borgnine asked Chayefsky and Mann about the first day's rushes. They were good, he was told. "Period. That's all they said. Never another word about rushes or anything else."

That night, across from the RKO Chester movie theatre at West Farms Road, Chayefsky sat calmly on a fire hydrant making further changes in his script as the deafening IRT train ran overhead on the elevated tracks. He was "developing certain points, rounding out the minor characters, so you get to know them better," he told one reporter.

Later, sitting in Hecht's Cadillac, with its new push-button doors and windows, Chayefsky told another visitor that "this is as alluring as it's going to get all night." Making movies was *not* the glamorous thing it was cracked up to be. "The monotony of the technical things could drive you crazy," he said. "Lights blazed, failed, then blazed again," the reporter wrote in his notes. "Grips yelled when children, no respecters of rope, suddenly appeared under-foot. Young men in dungarees, girls on their arms wearing shorts or pedal pushers, watched, elaborately casual, as if they too could act if anyone asked them."

On the third and final night in the Bronx, the services of Chayefsky the former actor were put to use. Marty and Clara have left the luncheonette and are strolling along the avenue when from across the street some of Marty's friends, sitting in a parked car, yell for him to ditch her and join them in a party with some hot nurses. An extra actor was needed to sit in the car and Chayefsky was recruited. "He didn't want to do it, but to save time and money he agreed," said Mann. "You can barely see him in the back of the car. He had one line of dialogue, and you can recognize the Bronx accent right away."

"His one line was 'Yeah, Marty, he's a good guy,' " said Borgnine. "And no one ever knows that's Paddy until I point it out."

"I had to rejoin the actors' union for that," the writer grumbled. "One hundred forty dollars for membership and I made something like sixty-seven net for the role."

At three-thirty that morning, the last shot of the Bronx schedule, set up at East 204th Street and the Grand Concourse, gave the cast and crew some trouble. "It was the one where I'm waiting for a bus, after dropping Betsy off at her apartment house," said Borgnine. "I'm supposed to be a happy guy. I had a terrific time with her. How do I show it?" Chayefsky and Hecht and Mann deliberated, making various suggestions, until eventually Borgnine spoke up and said, "Hey, you guys. Why don't you let me as the actor try one."

As the cameras rolled, Borgnine did the scene his way. "I stood there, at the bus stop, with my hands in my pockets, and this grin of realization comes on my face. It says, 'My God! Finally, I've got a girl.' I look up and see the bus sign. This is a big night, what am I taking a bus for? I reach up, and pow!—I hit the bus sign. Then I run out on the street and yell for a taxi."

That was the take used. The location shots were completed on September 18. The next day, a Saturday, the company flew to California for the filming of the interior scenes at the Goldwyn studios. Arriving at the studio early on Monday morning, Chayefsky was given some dire news: shooting on *Marty* had been suspended indefinitely.

"They were junking the movie, that's what I was told," said Ernest Borgnine. "In fact, they never intended to finish it in the first place. The whole thing had been planned as a tax write-off."

A Primer in Movie Economics

The previous year, when producer Harold Hecht had first broached the idea of making the movie of *Marty,* everyone told him he was crazy. *Marty* had been seen on TV not long before, for free. Why would audiences want to pay to see it a second time in movie theatres? But Hecht persisted. He assured United Artists that he could make the film without stars, for very little money. They could book it in art theatres, and even if it flopped there, they would make their money back from sales to the foreign markets, where the TV version had never been seen.

In February 1954, when UA had given their O.K., the budget was $150,000. By May, with Marlon Brando being considered to play the title role, Bob Blumofe at UA was emphasizing to Arthur Krim that "we simply must make it at $550,000 or even $600,000 with the strongest name possible." That August, when Ernest Borgnine and Betsy Blair were signed, the total budget had been pared back to $286,000. But by this time, according to a flurry of memos exchanged within United Artists, Hecht-Lancaster was bogged down in a labyrinth of accounting and financial difficulties surrounding a number of their productions. The situation was brought to a head by *Vera Cruz,* the Western they were in the process of completing.

With Burt Lancaster and Gary Cooper headlining, *Vera Cruz* had originally been budgeted at $1.25 million. This was to include Cooper's salary of $200,000. In mid-May, when the picture was on location in Mexico, the budget had risen to $1.37 million, and Hecht-Lancaster was obviously having a cash-flow problem. Separate accounts were supposed to be set up for each movie, including *Apache* (already in release), *Vera Cruz* (in production), and *The Kentuckian* and *Marty* (set to roll that September). But apparently the producers were funneling cash from one account to the other to stay afloat, much to the disapproval of United Artists, which was supplying the financing for each film. On May 12, in a memo to Arthur Krim, Bob Blumofe stated that the *Vera Cruz* company was asking for more money to cover the cost-of-living expenses "for Burt and Harold" in Mexico. The memo also mentioned that an original $100,000 that had been advanced to Hecht-Lancaster as producers earlier that year had gone to Gary Cooper to pay the first part of his salary. A second $100,000 was "desperately needed."

On May 21, United Artists' chief accountant, Al Bollengier, advised Arthur Krim that at this time "no separate overhead accounts were being maintained by Hecht-Lancaster, but all overhead items, as paid, were being charged to *Vera Cruz.*" This, the memo stated, made it difficult to keep track of miscellaneous expenses, such as the $2,500 needed each month for glossy publicity photographs of Burt Lancaster (who received "in the neighborhood of 12,000 requests per month"), and the $500 per week that would be required on June 5 for Paddy Chayefsky to polish his script.

To untangle the Hecht-Lancaster financial situation, in late June United Artists sent Al Bollengier to California, where he was to work "for the next three to six months" with Hecht-Lancaster's accountant, Ernie Scanlon, on "methods and procedures." Bollengier would also hold the purse strings, acting as the disbursing agent between the bank, Bankers Trust, and Hecht-Lancaster.

In July, when *Vera Cruz* had wrapped production and was in postproduction, United Artists learned that the picture had gone $250,000 over budget. In a flurry of calls and exchanges, it was decided that the first profits from *Apache,* due any moment, would be held as a pledge for the penalty charge for overruns on *Vera Cruz.* That penalty payment in turn would be used as a promissory note for *The Kentuckian,* set to roll in September. The latter, budgeted at $1.2 million, was of paramount importance to Burt Lancaster. He was not merely producing (with his new full partner, Jim Hill) and starring, he was making his debut as the director of the movie, "in CinemaScope and glorious Technicolor." As for the "pissant *Marty,*" due to be made that same month, in plain old black-and-white on a shoestring, the only mention found in UA's correspondence at that time was to the $14,000 that had been advanced as "overhead" payment to Chayefsky for his script. When and where the rest of the money for *Marty* was to come from had obviously not yet been established.

In September, while Lancaster and Jim Hill were on location shooting *The Kentuckian,* Harold Hecht was in New York with Paddy Chayefsky, shooting the three days of exteriors for *Marty.* The money for that, calculated at $27,000, came from profits he received from Warner Bros. for previously released films. The rest of the financing for *Marty*, Hecht assumed, had been or was in the process of being put into the film's account in California by United Artists. But when Hecht and the *Marty* company returned to Los Angeles on the weekend of September 15 to begin shooting interiors, they found out that no sets had been built and that no crew or technicians had been hired, the reason being that the cupboard for *Marty* was bare. Not a penny of cash was on hand in its production account.

"There was a problem with money, that's all I knew," said Chayefsky. "But I never could figure out who was screwing who here."

According to other memos and sources, United Artists and Hecht-Lancaster were playing hardball on another issue. When the producers signed their original contract with UA in June of 1953, their agent, Lew Wasserman, managed to get them some nifty terms upfront. Instead of the standard 30 percent distribution fee that UA charged its independent producers, Wasserman had the fee lowered to 25 percent. The company's usual share of profits was 50 percent, but Hecht-Lancaster got a 75–25 deal, with the larger slice going to them. Arthur Krim and Bob Benjamin were said to be "always sore about those terms," because it set a "bad example for the industry." But they couldn't say no because Lancaster's movies were making large sums of money at the box office. Then when *Marty* came along, without Lancaster in the cast, the movie company decided to use that film to rearrange the terms.

Marty would be subject to the regular distribution terms and a fifty-fifty split of the profits, UA told Harold Hecht in August of 1953, which the producer would not agree to. With or without Burt Lancaster in the film, this was a Hecht-Lancaster production and he wanted the same deal as in their existing contract. UA's response was to dig in their heels, which meant they would not proceed to arrange the financing of the film. According to Max Youngstein, UA vice president in charge of operations, his colleagues couldn't have cared less if the film was made or not. "I loved Paddy Chayefsky and his writing," said Youngstein in 1991. "But some of the people associated with me weren't as hot on the project. To them it was a crapshoot. To do a picture about a fat, ugly Italian butcher was a gamble, a very difficult subject."

Up front, Hecht also encountered resistance from his partner Burt Lancaster. "From the beginning *Marty* was all Harold Hecht," said Jim Hill. "He saw the thing on television and fell in love with it. Neither Burt nor I was that impressed." But Hecht persisted, for another prevailing reason. He wanted to make a movie *without* Burt. At five foot four, Hecht was eager to step out from behind Lancaster's six-foot-one star shadow, to prove to Hollywood that he could make a movie on his own, one that could enhance his reputation as a producer of "distinguished quality."

When Hecht insisted on proceeding with his plans for *Marty*, Lancaster recruited Jim Hill as his producing partner on *The Kentuckian.* Hence, when *Marty* began filming, then ran out of money, Lancaster and Hill were far from the scene, on location in Kentucky for their film. "Burt and Jim Hill were like two Rover Boys, always off somewhere kicking up dust solely in the interest of themselves. They didn't give a shit for Harold or his movie," said one UA source.

"They sort of tolerated the idea of doing *Marty,*" said the company's publicist, Walter Seltzer. "They weren't terribly enthused about the project. It was Harold's baby. There was some idea they would humor Harold and let him do it, because the worst that could happen is that there would be a tax loss."

"What they planned to do," said Ernest Borgnine, "was make half of it, then shelve it." Betsy Blair, who was told nothing of the problem with the financing, recalled that when the rushes of the New York scenes were shown to the executives, there was more enthusiasm. Borgnine said it was the accountants who resolved the situation. "Their tax man told them that there was a new tax law that said you have to finish the picture, show it once, and then you can shelve it. So they said, 'O.K., finish it.' "

Early in October 1954, while the principals of the film were waiting it out in Los Angeles, the United Artists records show that the company did proceed to raise the cash to finish *Marty.* That month a confirmation of the bank loan was sent from Bankers Trust to United Artists. The officer in charge of approval was H. L. Golden. In his memo of October 5, 1954, he said, "While in Europe last month, I received the following cable from Arthur Krim, president of United Artists: 'Would you want finance *Marty* to be made by Hecht-Lancaster black and white without stars at approximately three hundred forty thousand dollars with last ninety thousand guaranteed. All Hecht-Lancaster assets as well as UA and UA guaranteeing as much of balance as necessary. Was about to submit to Chemical but occurred me you have Hecht-Lancaster priority and might want to do this one. Please cable. Regards.' "

"I replied as follows," said Golden. " 'Agree that as part Hecht-Lancaster program we should finance *Marty*. However in view financing entire budget and no stars we should have hundred percent UA guarantee plus 10 percent distribution fee deferment and pledge Hecht-Lancaster interests we now hold under *Gabriel Horn* [*The Kentuckian*] deal in support their last 25 percent guarantee.' "

On October 28, 1954, a follow-up memo from Golden said that the loan agreement was "now in the process of being drawn." The budget had been reduced to $319,674.63. "Of this amount we will loan $319M," said Golden. "United Artists will provide the $674.63 and the completion guarantee, which will carry anything beyond that."

On November 3, an "Office Rushgram" informed Arthur Krim of UA that for the purpose of "tax benefits," Hecht-Lancaster had formed a new producing unit within their company called Steven Productions. So that they "should have substantial capital when it begins," the producers asked that $75,000 be sent to them immediately, to be deducted from the eventual disbursement of funds from Bankers Trust. Obviously this was sent because by November 15, the sets for *Marty* were being built and the company had resumed production.

"While they were putting up the sets on the Goldwyn lot, we shot the Waverly Ballroom scenes in a dance hall in downtown L.A.," said Delbert Mann. "The entire movie, including the scenes shot in New York, took twenty days. Much of this was due to the men and women on the crew. They worked like dedicated sophomores."

The speed was helped by the script, which during the hiatus had been trimmed and tightened by Chayefsky. "It was perfect, it just flowed," said Ernest Borgnine. "Betsy and I felt we couldn't do anything wrong, because the words felt so right."

In the living-room scene, when Marty is rebuffed while trying to kiss Clara on their first date, producer Hecht made a suggestion to Borgnine. He wanted him to cry with his eyes open. "I looked at him as if to say 'What is this man thinking? How can you cry with your eyes open?' " said the actor. "That's when Paddy got mad and threw him off the set. 'Get the hell out of here,' he said. And he kept him away as much as possible."

Hecht would be there, however, standing tall, when *Marty* ran into trouble again. Two days after the movie was wrapped, while watching a rough cut, Chayefsky and Delbert Mann felt that another scene was required. "We needed to elongate the time in between Sunday afternoon, when Marty's friends make fun of Clara, and the evening, when he decides to call her," said Mann. "So Paddy wrote a scene where he's pacing back and forth on the front porch, trying to make up his mind on what to do."

Some retakes were also required for the Saturday-night scene between Marty and Clara in his living room. "I don't remember the specifics, what went wrong there," said Mann.

"Now that you bring it up, I do recall the retakes," said Borgnine. "What happened was that those scenes were photographed too dark." The fault for that lay with Chayefsky. "Paddy got into a big fight with Joe LaShelle, the cinematographer," said Borgnine. "Joe was first-rate. He did *Laura* and a lot of good Hollywood pictures. But Paddy kept telling him, 'I want this done like a goddamn movie in Europe. I want it *dark*.' [Laughter] And Joe LaShelle was saying, 'But, Paddy, you won't be able to see anyone.' But Paddy kept arguing, 'I want it dark.' He wanted *Marty* to look like what he called an 'art film.' "

The retakes and the new scene would cost more money, which United

Artists refused to put up. "Harold needed an extra twenty thousand dollars to finish the picture," said Walter Seltzer. "But Arthur Krim and Ben Benjamin at UA dug in their heels and said, 'Absolutely not—not another nickel.' " Hecht had to come up with the completion cash himself, which he did by taking out another mortgage on his Los Angeles house.

When the retakes and new scene were done, Chayefsky and Mann worked on the final edit, then returned to New York to resume their work in television. Early in December, the finished film was shown to Burt Lancaster. Also in attendance were Borgnine and his wife. "There were only six or seven of us in the screening room," said Borgnine. "Burt and Harold Hecht were seated in the back, and when the picture was over there was great silence. The lights came on slowly and the first people to get up were Burt and Harold. Burt said to Harold, 'Why didn't you shoot more?' And Harold said, 'They wouldn't let me,' meaning Paddy and Del. With that, Burt picked up Harold by the lapels, held him up against the wall, and said, 'What do you mean they wouldn't let you?' And he had to explain that Paddy wouldn't let him add or change a thing. It was a very funny scene."

Any talk of shelving the movie and taking a tax loss was now obviously forgotten. During the second week in December 1955 a print of the film was sent to New York to be shown to the UA brass. Bernie Kamber, who was employed by Hecht-Lancaster as their East Coast publicist, recalled the reaction within the company. "One of the top executives said it would make a good second feature, meaning as the bottom half of a double bill."

That was the original plan. UA had two big movies they planned to release that spring. One was *Not as a Stranger*, with Robert Mitchum and Frank Sinatra playing surgeons. The other was *Gentlemen Marry Brunettes*, a musical extravaganza starring Jane Russell and Jeanne Crain. Both films would turn out to be stiffs.

"Who told you that? Burt?" Arthur Krim said angrily when asked some thirty-five years later of the original plan to release *Marty* as a second feature. "I don't know what they're all talking about. I only remember we felt we had a nice picture on our hands, but we were thinking in terms of art-house distribution."

Max Youngstein, Krim's partner, said, "without naming names," that there were those in the company hierarchy who were ready to throw *Marty* away. "It was considered too offbeat. It didn't go along with what the rule book of the industry was. I felt that we could do just as well by breaking the rules if you believed the picture was good. And I thought *Marty* was a very romantic love story. It had the smell of truth to it because the people didn't look like Greta Garbo and Robert Taylor, and because it had Paddy's gritty honesty."

In mid-December, Harold Hecht and Chayefsky met with Youngstein and

Bill Henneman, the head of UA sales and distribution. Without stars, this would be a hard film to sell, they all agreed, but putting their heads together they came up with a plan. They would open the movie in only one market—Manhattan. With good reviews they hoped *Marty* would then be easier to break around the country. Chayefsky, a tyro where the marketing of movies was concerned, had only one suggestion. He wanted to keep the movie out of a big theatre, and away from the easy glitz and prurience of Times Square. *Marty* was "an art film," he insisted, and he wanted a small dignified "cinema" for its debut. Henneman agreed, stating he had already found the perfect New York showcase. He had screened the movie for Alan Perry, the general manager of the Sutton Theatre, a 540-seat house on the East Side. Perry loved the movie and agreed to book it, but there was one slight problem. There would be a delay involved. The hit British comedy *Genevieve* was being held over at the Sutton, with two other films set to follow. That meant *Marty* couldn't open until April 1955, more than four months away.

Chayefsky didn't like that. It was too long to wait. But Hecht told him the extra time would allow them to lay the groundwork for the publicity. The producer also knew that United Artists, by virtue of the agreement they had with Bankers Trust, were limited in the amount of money they could spend on prints and merchandising. Only two hundred copies of the film could be made, and the publicity budget, including advertising, could not exceed $50,000. Therefore, *Marty* would need all the free coverage it could get from the media.

Throughout January and February, publicist Bernie Kamber would recall, he literally had to camp out on the doorsteps of Manhattan's columnists and reviewers, to get them to attend a screening of *Marty*. "They'd say, 'Who's in it and what's it about?' People were being very blasé and difficult."

One evening, by chance, Kamber got the boost he needed to generate a buzz for *Marty*. "I used to go to the Victoria Barber Shop every Friday night at six o'clock," he said. "In those days you got a haircut every week. In the barbershop for a shave one night was Walter Winchell. He'd come in every night from the St. Moritz, where he lived. We weren't buddies. No way. You couldn't be pals with Winchell. If he wanted to be friendly with you, fine. You didn't say hello unless he said hello first. But this evening he came over to me and said, 'What's doing?' I told him about the picture *Marty,* and how I couldn't get anyone to see the goddamn thing at a screening. The following week he wrote it up in his column. He said that *Marty* was going to be one of the great sleepers of all time. And all of a sudden that same day my phone never stopped ringing. That was the power of Winchell. He never saw the movie but he started it off for us."

In the meantime, in Hollywood, UA publicist Walter Seltzer was working on an ad campaign. "We didn't have the money for a professional illustrator," said Seltzer, "so I gave this guy, Harold Tritel, who was a window decorator, fifty bucks to do a sketch."

The pencil sketch of a short, heavyset man, shown from the rear, sitting dejectedly in a telephone booth, reaching up to dial the phone, would be used throughout the life of the movie. The model for the sketch was not Ernest Borgnine but the writer and original inspiration for the character—Paddy Chayefsky. On Sunday, April 3, a week before the movie was set to open in Manhattan, the sketch appeared in an ad in *The New York Times*. To make up for the lack of name performers in the movie, a gaggle of star names circled Marty in the phone booth, giving their collective endorsement. "Marty is a honey!" said Jane Russell. "What a man is Marty!" said Charlton Heston. "We like him! We like him!" said Dean Martin and Jerry Lewis.

On April 12, 1955, the Manhattan reviewers had their say. "A trailblazer and triumph for the spirit of the small people," said the *New York Post*. The movie's hero was what the author intended him to be: "a Hamlet of butchers," said *Time*. The script was loaded with accurate and vivid dialogue, "so blunt and insensitive in places that it makes the listener's heart bleed, while striking a chord of humor with its candor, and colorfulness," said *The New York Times*. Chayefsky's ear for everyday speech was almost without equal among current playwrights, *Cue* magazine chimed in. "His delicately turned sentences spring and sparkle into a thousand subleties of tone and shading, and are so accurate that hearing them is like listening to your own heartbeat."

"If there was one bad review, I didn't see it," said Chayefsky.

During its first week's run, *Marty* played to packed houses and took in $20,500. A "terrific" sum, said *Variety,* comparing it to the $30,000 *Blackboard Jungle* and *East of Eden* had earned in the larger houses in Times Square. During week number two, the take for *Marty* was $20,700, with standing room only. However, later that month, when released in other cities, the film "fell right on its ass," said Bernie Kamber.

Outside of New York, the movie's ethnic urban appeal was limited. And due to the lack of funds, there was no way of publicizing the picture or the stars. "Most people across the country didn't know who the hell Ernest Borgnine or Betsy Blair were," said Kamber. "Today they put you on talk shows or hook you up to satellites," said Borgnine. "But back then they didn't have that kind of access. And UA wasn't going to spend the money to send us out on tour, especially with a movie they predicted was going to go into the toilet."

Early in May, Betsy Blair flew to New York on the way to London with her husband and daughter. Two interviews were arranged, with a New York columnist and a wire-service reporter. Her openness and honesty were disarming, but Blair didn't have "the oomph" that sold pictures, UA declared. "I'm a plain ordinary-looking human being. I would have never been considered for the role if I were a Marilyn Monroe. I don't feel that's what womanhood is, or that movies should be some fairyland," she told the United Press. Dispelling the fantasy angle further, the actress told the second interviewer, "Nobody looks like those beautiful people in the movies. Even those people in the movies aren't like that off the screen. Except perhaps Elizabeth Taylor. She always looks beautiful. But she's rare."

With the prospects of a national breakthrough for *Marty* fading, one last distant hope remained. Arnold Picker, the head of UA's global distribution, had submitted the film in March to the festival committee in Cannes. Against formidable competition, *Mister Roberts* from Warners and *The Long Gray Line* from Columbia, *Marty* was picked to be shown as the American entry in competition at the festival that May. In a memo informing Arthur Krim of this, Picker said that "off the record, because I cannot use this officially, the selection committee considered *Marty* one of the finest motion pictures it has ever been their privilege to see."

When this good news was relayed to the press, the first naysayer heard from was Hollywood columnist Hedda Hopper. Cannes never gave its top prizes to American films or its performers, Hopper commented. United Artists apparently shared her pessimism. They decided not to spend the money to send either Ernest Borgnine, Paddy Chayefsky, or Delbert Mann to the festival. Betsy Blair would be there with Gene Kelly, who was part of an MGM caravan of stars sent to Europe to boost the studio's summer releases. From UA, Arnold Picker would be attending with Stanley Kramer and Olivia de Havilland, publicizing their medical soap-drama, *Not as a Stranger.*

At the Cannes opening festivities, Betsy Blair was aggressively bypassed by the press and photographers covering the arrival of MGM stars Grace Kelly, Doris Day, and a "heavily guarded Esther Williams." The first film shown was *Bad Day at Black Rock;* during the screening, when villain Ernest Borgnine harassed good guy Spencer Tracy, the audience hissed and booed. The following night, when *Marty* was shown, the audience en masse swung over to Borgnine's side. "I have never seen such a reaction to a film," Blair recalled. "They applauded after certain scenes and cheered at the end."

The following morning, as three budding starlets, Terry Moore, Sophia Loren, and a French newcomer, Brigitte Bardot, posed and pouted on the beach, the photographers abandoned the nubile beauties to pursue Betsy Blair as she walked alone on the avenue. "Overnight, from being an insignificant *festivalière,* she became the most photographed woman in Cannes," said the London *Daily Express.* Musing with humor on the situation, Blair recalled that as the excitement for *Marty* escalated, various executives from United Artists began to arrive in France. In *Variety* that week, under the section marked "To

Europe," Arthur Krim's name was listed. Harold Hecht also flew in from California and was seen on the veranda of the Carlton Hotel having an animated one-sided conversation with Miss Bardot, who spoke no English.

On the evening of May 11, the last festival film shown was *Carmen Jones*. Earlier that day the prestigious Office Catholique International Cinema award had gone to *Marty*, so it was assumed that the big prize on the final night, the Palme d'Or, would go to *Bad Day at Black Rock, East of Eden,* or *The Country Girl.* When the announcement was read, the Golden Palm went to *Marty*, "for its general merit, and in particular for the script by Paddy Chayefsky, the direction by Delbert Mann—and the acting by Ernest Borgnine and Betsy Blair." As "The Star-Spangled Banner" played, Betsy Blair stood on the stage next to Harold Hecht, holding the coveted statue. "My one regret," she said, "was that Paddy wasn't there, because the reception was so wonderful."

At midnight, the announcement came clacking over the teletype machines in newsrooms in the United States. This was "the first time an American film had won the top prize at Cannes," the bulletin reported. The following day, the news was heralded by newspapers across America, and clips from the movie were shown on the morning TV news shows. "That was the stamp of approval we needed," said Walter Seltzer. "Nothing could stop *Marty* after that."

At United Artists it was heartily agreed that the ad budget should be increased from $50,000 to $150,000. "New bookings came in, but we were choosy," said Max Youngstein. In New York, the film continued to run for an unprecedented thirty-nine weeks at one theatre only, the Sutton. "That was the first time that people from the suburbs ever went to a movie on the East Side," said Bernie Kamber. "They'd come in on the subway from Queens or from the Bronx, get off at Fifty-ninth Street, walk two blocks south, then stand on line for *Marty*."

When other long lines began to materialize in Los Angeles, the movie studios' most devoted clarion, Louella Parsons, was forced to acknowledge the consequences of the event. "Five years ago, I never dreamed Hollywood would make a movie out of a TV drama," said Parsons. "But it has finally happened. Only because *Marty* is as good as it is has the wall between Hollywood and TV crumbled at last. I'm mighty glad to see this come to pass."

CHAPTER 9

Upward Mobility

In the David and Goliath victory of television versus Hollywood, there was no gloating by the catalytic hero, Paddy Chayefsky, nor did he consider going over to the other side. When *Marty* had completed filming in Hollywood the previous November, he had told Cecil Smith of the *Los Angeles Times* that he "had little use for Hollywood" and was planning to return to New York, to write for television, for "the rest of my life." In a subsequent self-penned article in *Variety*, when the movie was beginning to emerge as the sleeper of the year, Chayefsky felt once more compelled to stand by the medium that spawned him. He said he resented the inference that because *Marty* was a hit he had "graduated from the minor leagues and made good in the big time." There was nothing minor about television, he declared. "The simple truth is the best writing done in our country is being done on television."

On September 9, 1954, *Middle of the Night*, the story of a fifty-year-old garment-industry executive (E. G. Marshall) who falls in love with his much younger secretary (Eva Marie Saint), was shown on the "Philco Television Playhouse." A "rich and meaningful drama," said the New York *Journal-American*, commending Chayefsky for his sensitivity and "sure sense of drama that's so often lacking in TV drama."

On December 12, 1954, *Catch My Boy on Sunday* was telecast. The drama of a frustrated mother who pushes her ten-year-old son into a career as an actor starred Sylvia Sidney and was directed by Arthur Penn. It "was not Chayefsky's greatest work," said *Variety*, "but even a lesser script from his atelier deserves attention." Five months later, another original script, *The Catered Affair*, had been completed. It would be Chayefsky's last for television.

Paddy's colleague the writer David Shaw said that he was partly responsible for Chayefsky's writing *The Catered Affair.* When Shaw saw *Marty* on TV, he was one of the few who had seen "the laughs" in the story. He suggested to Chayefsky that he write a comedy. "Sometime later I bumped into him and he said, 'Listen, I'm doing that comedy you suggested. It's about two young people who want a small wedding but the bride's mother keeps making the wedding reception larger and larger.'"

The play is set in a railroad-style apartment in the Bronx where an Irish American family lives. The ruler of the roost, Aggie Hurley, a full-time housewife, is approaching sixty and has no sense of how closed off her life has become.. There has never been any real contact or affection between her and her husband or her children. She doesn't care where her daughter works, or what boys she dates, "as long as they [are] from the neighborhood." When the daughter announces she is getting married, the mother insists on having a big "proper" wedding. The wedding will ease her guilt for neglecting the girl, and also show the neighbors that Aggie Hurley is as good as her future in-laws. But the daughter doesn't want a big wedding, and Aggie's husband, a cabdriver, or "hackie," wants to save the money so he can buy his own cab. The mother obstinately persists with her plans, and only when the entire household has been disrupted, and the wedding almost called off, does she stop to examine her motives, and realize how barren her life really is. "This is a comic premise," Chayefsky said, "with plenty of jokes, and the total effect should be that of a very yakky show, with emotional depth."

When Fred Coe received the script of *The Catered Affair* he decided this production should be "an event." The movie of *Marty* had just been released, hence TV audiences would be primed for another Chayefsky quality program. With the blessing of NBC, the budget was increased, making it possible for the writer to receive the top fee of two thousand dollars. It also enabled the producers to hire one of his favorite actresses, Thelma Ritter.

In the pantheon of character actors, a category of talent to which Chayefsky was especially partial, Thelma Ritter was a true star. In 1948, when he was under contract to Universal, to give him an idea of what they wanted in stories the studio screened *Miracle on 34th Street* for him. "Now do you see what we're looking for?" they asked. "Yes," said Paddy. "You want me to write something for Thelma Ritter."

That movie, set in a Manhattan department store, had been Ritter's Hollywood debut. Embodying the tough crust but compassionate heart of South Brooklyn, where she was born, Ritter walked off with the best reviews and was signed to a long-term contract at Twentieth Century–Fox, where writer-director Joseph L. Mankiewicz created two parts for her: Sadie, the wisecracking maid in *A Letter to Three Wives,* and Birdie Coonan, the acerbic dresser and confidante of Margo Channing in *All About Eve.* Nominated in succession for four Academy Awards, Ritter was scheduled to start another picture when the Chayefsky television script arrived at her door. She read it, sent her regrets to Fox, and agreed to play Aggie Hurley for a tenth of her movie salary.

According to Fred Coe, Paddy was "in hog heaven" when he and Ritter met for rehearsals of his TV play. But no overt compliments or flatteries were exchanged, just the normal professional cool and efficiency, with intermittent glances of worship exchanged by both parties.

The week of the broadcast, the pairing of Ritter and Chayefsky warranted two pages of coverage in *Life* magazine. The reception for the play itself, broadcast on Sunday night, May 22, 1955, was mixed. "Bitter," "disappointing," and "unpleasant" were some of the critical comments. It was "an unfocused piece," Chayefsky admitted fourteen years later when, after Ritter's death, he wrote an appreciation for *The New York Times*. Of the play he said, "The first act was farce, the second was character-comedy, and the third was abruptly drama. There aren't a dozen actresses who could make one piece out of all that; Miss Ritter, of course, did."

Over the summer of 1955, the demand for Chayefsky the TV writer continued. In July, columnist Marie Torre reported, "Milton Berle is telling everyone that Paddy Chayefsky will come up with an original play for his fall series. Chayefsky denies it." Berle wasn't the only "luminary" that Paddy had turned down, Torre stated. Others spurned were Danny Kaye, Sid Caesar, and Bob Hope. Chayefsky, despite his earlier avowals of allegiance to television, was inwardly at odds with that loyalty for some time. The Philco-Goodyear stories of everyday people no longer challenged him. "Elemental passions are the easiest things in the world to write," he said. "I can write elemental passions with one hand." And although part of him exulted in the attention and the camaraderie at Philco, Sidney, his creative side, felt compelled to move on. He wanted what his mother insisted was the goal of every true artist— substance and respect. Some of that had come earlier that year when Simon and Schuster published a book of his TV plays. Chayefsky made room for the book on a shelf in his office "right next to the plays by Shakespeare and Ibsen." In a preface to one of his TV plays, he outlined his next step, to become a serious playwright. Bidding an official goodbye to television, he said that although the medium had been kind to him, he came "out of the legitimate theatre," and he wanted to go back again.

Producer Fred Coe tried to assist in that move for Chayefsky and the rest of the Philco-Goodyear writers. During the summer of 1955, Coe announced he was forming a cooperative group to be called Playwrights '56. It would be analogous to the Playwrights Company formed in the 1930s by Maxwell Anderson and Elmer Rice. Coe's group would include Horton Foote, Tad

Mosel, David Shaw, Robert Alan Aurthur, and Chayefsky. "The idea was that we would produce our own plays on television and on Broadway." said Mosel. "The hits would sustain the failures and we would all share equally in a percentage of the company."

Meetings were held and discussions continued, until Chayefsky backed out. He was "more concerned with his own identity than reality demands," Robert Alan Aurthur said. "He seemed to think that by signing a contract to the effect that we were legally equal, it would make his talents no more nor less than anyone's in the group."

"I knew he wasn't in favor of the idea," said Mosel. "In the first place, Paddy did not want to be part of a group. But also there would be an economic imbalance. Because some of us would write hit plays and some would not. The ones who wrote the hits would suffer and the ones who wrote the bad plays would benefit. But that was the point of the group. Even when the Playwrights Company was formed, Elmer Rice did not have one successful play, but by God, the Playwrights Company put them all on."

Robert Anderson, the new head of the Playwrights Company, said he also tried to get Chayefsky to join his group. Anderson had optioned Paddy's original play *The Man Who Made the Mountains Shake*, retitled *Fifth from Garibaldi*. "Fredric March and Florence Eldridge were very interested in doing the play," said Anderson. "We had several meetings with them. Freddie was very fond of Paddy. He would sit there and read some of his speeches. There were wonderful speeches, but the play needed more work, and we needed a director, because Kazan was tied up with something else."

Jed Harris was a stage director of repute on Broadway. In the 1920s, '30s, and '40s, he had directed some of Broadway's most popular plays, including *Our Town, The Front Page, The Royal Family,* and *The Heiress.* A man of divergent myths, described as endlessly creative and energetic, Harris was possessed of "one of the most interesting self-devouring egos I have ever met," said Noël Coward. "He suggested to my mind that strangely ruthless insect, the praying mantis." Having earned and lost considerable fortunes over the years, and built himself a widely publicized reputation as a lout with the ladies, by the late 1940s, as his genius began to decay, Harris began to unleash his bad spirits in public. At the premiere of Arthur Miller's *Death of a Salesman* in 1949, Harris called it "a stupid play" because "there is no drama in an ass like Willy Loman."

After directing Miller's *The Crucible* in 1953, Harris was a viable name again, and Anderson and Chayefsky believed he had the talent and temperament to stage *Fifth from Garibaldi.* "We went to see Jed," said Anderson. "He was a very truculent, mercurial man. He was in, he was out, he led us on a merry chase."

Paddy added his own twists to the course, Anderson recalled. "He would say no a thousand times first, then on the way out the door he would say, 'Well, maybe we can think about that.' "

Jed Harris finally signed the contract to direct *Fifth from Garibaldi*. "Then in a matter of a week—he tore it up," said Anderson. "Paddy was furious— very angry. And that was the end of the play as far as I know."

In 1955, in his haste to be on Broadway, Chayefsky elected to dispense with creating a new plot or characters for a play. As he had done with the movie of *Marty*, he proceeded to remodel material that originated on television. The script he chose to expand was *Middle of the Night*.

In the original TV version, Chayefsky said, he had barely probed beneath the surface to explore the psychological and social ramifications of why an older man falls in love with a much younger woman, and of what happens. When apprised that in the theatre the theme of age versus youth was as old as the proscenium itself, Paddy remained steadfast. "All the beauty some poets find in dreams can be found in the involved relationship of a middle-aged man who is concerned about impotence and a highly neurotic girl of twenty-four who devours everyone she knows in her desperate search for love," he said.

Expanding the girl's background, he decided that she had never known her father. He had deserted the family when she was six. As a youth the girl escaped to the movies, sometimes attending four and five a week. As a teenager, confusing sex with affection, she gave herself to boys in the park. Married at nineteen to a handsome musician, she learns that their only communication is physical. In the night, when she asks him to hold or talk to her, he reaches over and begins to feel her leg. When he gets a job to play in Las Vegas, she decides she would rather stay in New York and be lonely on her own. Contemplating divorce, she spills out her troubles to her boss. A widower thirty years older, he finds he is attracted to the girl's dependent, childish nature, and he falls in love with her. She is attracted to him, too, and that pleases him enormously. "I didn't know it, but it's important," he says. "She needs me, you understand? It's been a long time since somebody needed me."

The conflict in the play arises when the couple's families object to the relationship. His sister, who is also his housekeeper, worries about the loss of her position. She tells her brother that he is making a fool of himself, that the girl is obviously a tramp and after his money. The girl's mother, a lower-middle-class bigot who complains about the increase of Puerto Ricans in their neighborhood, objects to the man because of his age and because he is Jewish. The girl's best friend says that in a few years an older man won't be able to satisfy her sexually. Therefore she should stay with her younger, better-looking husband. "You had a good marriage with George," the friend advises. "You paid the rent and you went to bed. What more are you looking for?"

By June 1955, Chayefsky had the first two acts of the play completed and went looking for a director. Garson Kanin had a hit play on Broadway that year, having directed *The Diary of Anne Frank*. He worked with Chayefsky on *Middle of the Night* and assumed he was going to direct. Then he heard otherwise. "Paddy, for all his talent and charm, could be a little shit," said Kanin. "He had discussed *Middle of the Night* with me. Then he turned around and gave it to Josh Logan."

Chayefsky insisted that that had happened by chance, not design. Josh Logan was in Hollywood, finishing up preproduction on *Picnic*, when he attended a screening of *Marty*. "I was so excited by Paddy's writing I decided I would find him come hell or high water," said Logan. "As it turned out, he was staying in the same hotel, the Beverly Hills Hotel. I sent him a note asking if he had any new ideas, any new plays. And before I knew it he was on the phone and we were meeting downstairs."

Paddy gave Logan the two acts of the play. The next day Logan called and said, "Look, I'll take a chance. I'll do it and guarantee to get it backed without the third act." Putting up $50,000 of his own money, Logan got the play. He became the director, and coproducer with ANTA (the American National Theatre and Academy). In August, with $10,000 added to the financing by Chayefsky and his wife, Susan, and another $40,000 from other sources, the contracts for the *Middle of the Night* production company were signed. Off the top from the financial pool, $5,000 immediately went to Logan, and Chayefsky as playwright received $10,000, his original investment. When the play opened he would still share in the investors' profits, and as playwright he would also receive the standard 15 percent of the weekly gross, plus 60 percent of all income from foreign and film rights, which Chayefsky had retained in his new corporation, Carnegie Productions. Becoming a playwright for Sidney's sake obviously suited Paddy, who now reveled in the role of "the entrepreneur."

In October 1955, it was announced that *Middle of the Night*, "from the pen of the Bronx TV and movie writer," would be presented on Broadway in February 1956. The playwright and the director had their first clash on the matter of casting. Chayefsky had rewritten the original story for Fredric March, whom he wanted to play the elderly widower, but producer-director Logan found it difficult to get the actor to sign a contract. Salary and "the extras" were said to be one obstacle, until it was rumored that March was holding out for a far weightier dramatic prospect, *Long Day's Journey into Night*, by the late Eugene O'Neill. Discussions for this were under way between O'Neill's widow, Carlotta, and director José Quintero. When Josh Logan became aware that March was stalling because of the O'Neill play, he sent a copy of *Middle of the Night* to Edward G. Robinson in California.

Robinson had been a star in movies during the 1930s and '40s, but by the early to mid-'50s, he was playing featured roles. Dabbling a bit in television, he knew the only way he could kick his career into high gear again was to return to Broadway. Absent from the stage for thirty-five years, he harbored doubts about his prospects—until the play by Chayefsky arrived. "I read two acts of it and was deeply impressed," Robinson said. "When I read the third act I knew that this time I had to take the plunge."

For the role of the younger girl, actress Eva Marie Saint was sought. When she appeared in the original TV version her performance was warmly praised, with one critic noting that Saint was "now beginning to emerge as a gifted actress instead of a merely beautiful girl." Chayefsky hoped that Saint would repeat the role in his legitimate-stage version, but the actress had won a supporting Oscar that year for her film debut in *On the Waterfront,* and her agent told Chayefsky and Logan that they were now swamped with offers. These included the lead in a movie with Bob Hope and the possibility of a contract with Warner Bros., where Saint might play in *Summer and Smoke* and *The Rainmaker.* In early November, Louella Parsons reported: "Eva Marie wants to return to Broadway to appear in Paddy Chayefsky's play, but I believe one of the Warner pictures will be next for the girl everyone in town is saying will be the next Grace Kelly."

Ethel Winant, who had cast the Philco TV shows, recalled getting a late-night call from Chayefsky. She recommended a newcomer to him: Gena Rowlands. "I used Gena a lot in those days," said Winant. "I told Paddy that she was both talented and beautiful and was right for the part."

Rowlands did frequently meet with the playwright and the director. "Gena was forced to read for the role nine or ten times, as the producers hoped Eva Marie Saint would return to New York," one New York columnist stated.

By late November, unwilling to wait any longer for Saint, Chayefsky and Logan decided to go with Rowlands. Her salary would be $250 a week, compared to the $2,500 per week that Edward G. Robinson was to receive. Rounding out the cast were Anne Jackson, Martin Balsam, and Lee Philips. Chayefsky's old Army friend and patron, Curt Conway, now blacklisted from movies and TV, was brought in as understudy for Robinson, and Audrey Peters was hired as a substitute for Rowlands. Peters had auditioned and been approved before Chayefsky was told that she was married to his publicist pal from Philco-Goodyear, Johnny Friedkin. "You did right by not telling me upfront that you're married to Johnny," Paddy told her. "If I had known I probably wouldn't have given you the job."

On December 19, 1955, when rehearsals for *Middle of the Night* began, Josh Logan, who had directed *Mister Roberts, Annie Get Your Gun,* and *South Pacific,* said that his biggest problem was having Paddy Chayefsky in the same room. "He sat or stood beside me and whispered instructions into my ear the entire time."

In January, during the out-of-town tryouts in Wilmington, Delaware, Chayefsky expressed confusion about the audience's reaction. He wrote *Middle of the Night* as a very serious play, yet the people in Delaware were reacting as if they were witnessing a comedy. "Pursued by television techniques," he said he never stopped to think that with a live audience in the theatre, some of his more pungent lines would inspire mirth. "I remember telling Josh Logan 'That's not a laugh line, that's meant to be a chuckle.' And Josh said, 'But Paddy, eleven hundred chuckles in a theatre make a loud noise.' "

"They love it too much," Chayefsky told Logan at one point in Wilmington, and proceeded to eliminate the laugh lines. "I tried to persuade him that he had written some of the funniest lines ever heard on a stage," said Logan. But Chayefsky insisted, "This is an august play. It has nobility, it's a serious play. It shouldn't be getting all those laughs."

"Paddy and Josh fought like cats and dogs on the road," said Audrey Peters. "Most of their disputes were over the rewrites that Paddy insisted on doing. He tried to rewrite the entire play."

By the time the company had reached Philadelphia, Chayefsky had changed the ending five times. In the tradition of Ibsen and Chekhov, whose ranks he was eager to join, the play, he felt, should end on a note of "resigned despair." "I urged him to leave us with some hope," said Logan, "and before long he had a sparkling, warm, and uplifting finish."

During the run in Philadelphia, an impediment in casting became visible. Rowlands's reviews ranged from tepid to cold. She "begins on a note of rather inexplicable hysteria, but after that she deals competently with a part that isn't easy to believe at best," said one critic. "Gena was scared," said Ethel Winant. "I went to Philadelphia to see her. It was an overwhelming role to play, the second lead. She didn't have the confidence she gained later in life. It was an uncertain performance. She was very good, she had a lovely quality, but it didn't have the strength or confidence of a theatre actress. She didn't have the theatrical energy required for that kind of role." Chayefsky sat with Rowlands in her hotel room and tried to explain the character. "Gena didn't improve, and Paddy was sure she was going to sink the play," said George Baxt.

On February 8, 1956, *Middle of the Night* opened at the ANTA Theatre in New York. With five thousand dollars left in the budget for "overcall," the producers decided to host a gala black-tie premiere and postperformance party. Every visiting star and resident celebrity, together with supportive friends and family, including Chayefsky's two brothers, his sister-in-laws, and his mother, Gussie, was invited to attend. "I was there," said Tad Mosel. "All of us from TV showed up to give Paddy moral support."

The opening-night crowd applauded everything, including "the hero's sister bringing on a dish of apples," said one observer. The professional critics were not as easily seduced. At the party afterward, Logan said he was faced with "the strangest set of notices I had ever seen." Walter Kerr of the *New York Herald Tribune* praised Logan's direction and welcomed Chayefsky's Broadway bow as "a profitable debut." George Jean Nathan of the *Journal-American* described the play as "another one of those first shown on television, which has stopped over in the theatre on its way to the movies," then dismissed the entire proceedings as "a juvenile study of mindless characters." Richard Watts of the *New York Post* liked the play and the staging but roundly panned the performance of Gena Rowlands, who "approaches her opening scene as if she were playing a young Medea"; while William Hawkins of the New York *World-Telegram* said the play had "situation, rather than a story," and Gena Rowlands was "a remarkably versatile and efficient young actress, able to imitate any known emotion."

"The word at the party, after the reviews came in, was that Paddy had a big flaming flop on his hands," said George Baxt. "Everyone forgot they had a little thing in their corner called Edward G. Robinson."

At nine o'clock the next morning, the lines were three deep around the block at the ANTA Theatre. Stars sell tickets and the New York theatregoers wanted to see Robinson. "The second wave of reviews, from the weekly and monthly magazines, and from columnists and the like, were wonderful," said Logan. "They were rapturous in their applause for Robinson. Gena was also praised and became much stronger as the run proceeded." The reinforced support, which guaranteed a long run, delighted everyone. "Everyone but Paddy," said Logan.

Paddy fumed. Paddy stewed. Then Paddy fought back for the sake of his serious playwright self. The critics did not give his Broadway bow the respect it deserved, he said. Dashing off a series of letters on his typewriter, he chastised certain reviewers for taking such wild, subversive shots at his work. Obviously *they* were wrong, he said, because *Middle of the Night* was playing to packed houses, and such people of prominence as Walter Winchell and Joan Crawford were calling the play "the best of the year."

Saving his last volley for *The New York Times,* which called the play "average drama, less successful in the theatre where size is more important," Chayefsky wrote a short article that he urged the paper to print. In it he said that if Arthur Miller had achieved his prominence in television, even *Death of a Salesman* might have been called "a little play."

"I could not escape the feeling that I was being looked down upon as a nouveau riche," Chayefsky wrote in the *Times,* "who had elbowed his way into an aristocratic home. And while the gentry were by noblesse oblige dutifully courteous, they could not help raise an eyebrow at my choice of necktie."

The First Oscar

On the afternoon of February 13, 1956, less than a week after *Middle of the Night* opened on Broadway, the production manager, Wally Fried, drafted a telegram to Josh Logan, then in Nevada scouting locations for the movie *Bus Stop*. That morning the Oscar nominations had been released in Hollywood, and two movies Logan had worked on, *Picnic* and *Mister Roberts*, were cited in the Best Picture category. Also on the list for Best Picture was the low-budget sleeper of the year, *Marty*. Any chance of victory for the latter was slight, the sages said. Louella Parsons predicted that *Marty* would garner a few accolades, but "not an Academy Award, because the production is too slight and lacks big-salaried actors."

Newsweek agreed with Louella. This was a time when millions of dollars were being spent on color pictures and "ever-widening screen processes," they said. So it was doubtful that Hollywood "would cut its own throat by conferring its highest honors on a conventional black-and-white movie."

Producer Harold Hecht, who had fought against all odds to get *Marty* made, was determined to keep the momentum of its release going. The previous year he had pressured United Artists to put more money into the picture's promotion. At Hecht's insistence a large chunk of the increased advertising budget was spent sustaining interest in the movie in the New York market. This concentration paid off, not only in a lengthy unprecedented run at the Sutton Theatre, but in East Coast citations and awards at the end of the year. The first tribute came from the Newspaper Guild of America, which awarded their plaque "for excellence" to Chayefsky. Follow-up honors came from the New York Film Critics, who honored *Marty* with awards for best movie and best script.

But that was New York, where *Marty* was a sentimental hometown favorite. In Los Angeles, when the preliminary nomination lists were being compiled, it was not considered to be "a blue-chip entry." The strong candidates were those from the major studios, including *East of Eden, Rebel Without a Cause, The Seven Year Itch, The Rose Tattoo, Bad Day at Black Rock,* and *Love Is a Many-Splendored Thing.*

To ensure that *Marty* received an adequate share of attention during the preliminary nominating phase, Hecht-Lancaster publicist Walter Seltzer was assigned the task of touting the movie's merits, regardless of cost or practicality. "When the movie first opened in L.A.," said Seltzer, "Hecht got this wild idea. He suggested we call everyone in the Los Angeles phone book, and tell them that *Marty* was in town. I told him, 'Harold, that will take months, years.' "

During the voting season, Seltzer arranged special screenings for the town's most influential opinion makers and talkers. "I didn't ask them to come see *Marty,* I brought the picture to their homes," said the publicist. Seltzer supplied the food for the evening, along with a print and a projectionist. "I called beforehand, and asked them what they wanted to eat during the picture. For Georgie Jessel, we sent over corned-beef sandwiches. In all, we did forty to fifty of those special screenings."

Marty was a tough sell in Hollywood, but the consistency and the personal approach moved the campaign along. In New York, Paddy Chayefsky made his contribution. When *Marty* was released in Los Angeles, Paddy wrote a letter to columnist Sidney Skolsky, thanking him for his kind words about the movie, adding, "It is something of a shock to see my name in your column." In an article for *The New York Times,* which appeared during the voting primaries, a somewhat tractable Chayefsky did a dramatic about-face in his views on Hollywood. He said that the town's film industry was much maligned. Those frequent outbursts and claims of nepotism and depravity had been exaggerated. Los Angeles was "not the wild, rootless town" he had known ten years before, "where everybody changes his number every week." The studio producers and executives he met were not the idiots "they are frequently supposed to be," he continued, and furthermore, he had a wonderful time making *Marty.* "Script and production conferences were on as high a level as any conferences I have ever sat in on in the theatre," he stated, and for what it was worth, he wanted to clear the record by saying that a writer did not have to compromise his talents in Hollywood, that "good films can be made there as well as anywhere else."

"He sounds a little like Goldilocks to me," said Ben Hecht, writer of *Scarface* and *The Front Page.* "He's had one success and one success usually gives a fellow feverish ideas about who he is and what he can do. But after you've had four or five successes and about fifty failures, you change your mind."

That February, when the Oscar nominations were released, *Marty* received a whopping seven in the major categories. Along with Best Picture, it was cited for Best Director (Delbert Mann), Best Actor (Ernest Borgnine), Best Supporting Actress (Betsy Blair), Best Supporting Actor (Joseph Mantell), Best Cinematography (Joseph LaShelle), and Best Screenplay (Paddy Chayefsky). The writer evinced surprise. "I'm shocked," he said. "They put Betsy in the category of Best Supporting and she's in most of the movie."

For the last lap of the race, the bid for the awards themselves, Harold Hecht, now joined by his formerly reluctant partner Burt Lancaster, decided to pull out all the stops. According to *Time,* the campaign, which included trade-paper ads, 16mm prints for home viewers, rhinestone cleavers, and aprons (the butcher angle), cost $350,000, which was more than the entire cost of the movie itself. "That figure was absurd," said Seltzer. "We didn't spend any-where near that amount. I know, because United Artists was paying for the promotion, and along with making us account for every dollar spent, they deducted the costs from Hecht-Lancaster participation in the final profits."

On the big night of March 21, a dual telecast of the Oscar ceremonies was broadcast from Hollywood and New York, with the preponderance of stars and glitter out west. Early arrivals at the RKO Pantages Theatre in Los Angeles were Harold Hecht, Burt Lancaster ("We're going to take 'em all!" said Burt), Tony Curtis and Janet Leigh, and "another hot twosome—Natalie Wood and Tab Hunter." Among the actor nominees present were Betsy Blair, Ernest Borgnine, Susan Hayward, Peggy Lee, Frank Sinatra, James Cagney, and Jack Lemmon.

At the Century Theatre in New York, the "smattering of celebrities" included cohosts Claudette Colbert and Joseph L. Mankiewicz and newylweds Debbie Reynolds and Eddie Fisher, scheduled to present and perform. On hand in the press room backstage was Jayne Mansfield, whom NBC publicists promised to trot out if there was a slack in New York winners. Mansfield's "connection with the Academy Awards no one could figure out," said colum-nist Dorothy Kilgallen.

Although they had been urged to join the Hecht-Lancaster contingent in Hollywood, Chayefsky and Delbert Mann opted to remain in New York. "Paddy stayed put because he was scared," said United Artists vice president Max Youngstein. "*Marty* was a long shot. We felt that Ernie Borgnine might win, but the rest of the awards would go to *East of Eden* or *Mister Roberts.*"

Chayefsky had vacillated in his position on the Oscars. Prior to the ceremo-nies, he nonchalantly told one New York reporter that he didn't care if he won or lost, "but I prepared a short speech so I wouldn't look like a fool."

Newsweek got the other take. "You hear a lot of people say that if they don't win they'll manage to live, but I want that Oscar," said Paddy. "I'll die if I don't get it."

Sitting in the Century Theatre, Chayefsky was calm for the first hour, as the awards went to the Hollywood artists and technicians responsible for *Picnic*, *The Rose Tattoo*, and *To Catch a Thief*. In the final hour, "two or three events before the writing award, I began to get jittery," he said. Anna Magnani appeared on film from Rome to read the Best Screenplay nominees: "Mildred Kaufman for *Bad Day at Black Rock*, Richard Brooks for *The Blackboard Jungle*, Paul Osborn for *East of Eden*, Daniel Fuchs and Isobel Lennart for *Love Me or Leave Me*, and Paddy Chayefsky for *Marty*." Opening the envelope in New York, Claudette Colbert paused, smiled, and said, "Paddy Chayefsky . . . for *Marty*." As a roar of approval went up from the New York crowd, Paddy later recalled, "I froze. I managed to get up there but I couldn't remember my speech. I'm told I did manage to say, 'Thank you.' I never believed that winning a prize would do that to me."

In New York the second major award for *Marty* quickly followed. The Best Director award went to Delbert Mann. In Hollywood, at that point, the main drama was unfolding offstage, in the audience. Producer Harold Hecht, on his big night, was drunk. "Harold was celebrating early," said Youngstein. "He was drinking in the lobby before and during the show, and was feeling no pain. With Paddy and Delbert winning in New York, we felt we might get Best Picture in Hollywood. But Harold was barely able to stand up. So while we were in the lobby, pouring black coffee into him, someone went to Burt Lancaster and asked him to accept if *Marty* won for Best Picture.

Onstage, as Grace Kelly read off the Best Actor nominees and announced the winner, "Ernest Borgnine . . . for *Marty!*" the UA contingent in the lobby were still sobering up Harold Hecht. Escorting him down the aisle, they placed him in a seat as Audrey Hepburn appeared to announce the final award, for Best Picture. The winner was *Marty*, and Hecht made it to the stage, alone. Composed and coherent, sounding "as if he were running for office," the producer said he was "very fortunate to live in a country where any man, no matter how humble his origins, can become president. And to be part of an industry where any picture, no matter how low its budget, can win an Oscar."

"We were in shock by then," said Delbert Mann. "I don't remember what Paddy said, if anything."

While Hecht and Lancaster spent another fortune on their post-Awards party, where Kim Novak "had a workout trying to keep her backless and almost frontless dress up," the New York contingent celebrated at a supper party in a nearby hotel. Refusing to pose for a photograph with Mansfield and Monique Van Vooren—"That's not my kind of publicity"—Chayefsky coolly told reporters that he wasn't surprised that his movie had taken the top prize: "I would have been disappointed if we hadn't won," he said. "I believe *Marty* was the year's best."

That indifference was an act, his sister-in-law Terry Chayefsky said. She and his brother Winn baby-sat for the Chayefskys that night. "I know he was thrilled and excited, as we all were," she said.

His first call that night was to his mother, who had one slight reservation. She wished he had used his real name, Sidney. That way old friends and relatives would have made the connection. "She was very proud of him," said Bill Chayefsky. "But my mother's attitude was always: 'I have three sons. I'm proud of all of them.'"

More Hollywood Gold

In the spring of 1956, after establishing his name on Broadway as a hit playwright and winning the first of his Academy Awards, Chayefsky took a well-deserved vacation in Florida with his wife, Susan, and their infant son, Danny. With the boy's birth the year before, the Chayefskys had decided they needed more spacious accommodations. The place they chose was an apartment at Eighty-first Street and Central Park West that had eight rooms, including a library, which Chayefsky stocked with books by James Joyce, William Faulkner, Edgar Allan Poe, Charles Dickens, James Thurber, and his own volume of television plays. At first they rented the place, but with his success assured on Broadway, Chayefsky purchased the apartment. At the same time he leased an office in Carnegie Hall on Fifty-seventh Street. The office was a necessity, he explained. Show business entailed a lot of "schmoozing," and a lot of yelling. "It wasn't fair to the kid to be exposed to all that," he said, "so I got my own place in Midtown." Describing his daily work habits, he said he walked downtown each morning at eight-thirty, stopped off for a container of coffee and a bagel, opened his office, sharpened a lot of pencils, and hoped that the phone would soon ring. "When it doesn't, I say, 'Stop fooling yourself. Get to work.'"

Immediately after the movie *Marty* had been released, the Hollywood studios, impressed with the praise and the burgeoning profits, went on a stampede buying up other original plays that had appeared on television. Among the seventy-five properties they acquired were *Patterns* and *Requiem for a Heavyweight,* by Rod Serling; *Twelve Angry Men,* by Reginald Rose; *The Rainmaker,* by N. Richard Nash; *The Rabbit Trap,* by J. P. Miller; and *Billy the Kid,* by Gore Vidal.

Two additional TV plays by Chayefsky were also bought, *The Bachelor*

Party, and *The Catered Affair,* which MGM bought for $50,000, a reasonable price, because the writer did not come with the purchase. Chayefsky would be available for consultations, but the adaptation for the film version of *The Catered Affair* would be done by Gore Vidal. "MGM was eager to compete with TV, rather late in the day," said Vidal, "so they thought that if they bought up the TV talent they could get the audiences we had. I signed a studio writer's contract with them, just for the amusement—to see what a big studio was like, in what I suspected at the time would be their last days."

To some, the story of a lower-middle-class Irish American family from the Bronx whose lives are disrupted by a family wedding did not seem to be material suited to the polished, urbane Vidal. "I forget whose idea it was to get me to adapt Paddy. Not mine certainly," said Vidal. "But the logic, though skewered, was understandable. One of the new TV lords would adapt another one." Per his agreement with Sam Zimbalist, who would produce the movie, Chayefsky did agree to write a preliminary treatment of the story, which, he said, "in short, was about the emptiness that faces millions of American women in their middle years." The basic flaw in the television version was the muddled movement of the main line, he believed. Desperate for her daughter's love, the mother, by insisting on a fancy wedding, finds that the distance between them is insurmountable. "In the end, the mother has got to learn her life lies with her husband," said Chayefsky; rather than "painfully settling down to living with each other's bad habits, they must come to an understanding of each other."

This was "a comedy," Chayefsky again insisted, "because in the end of the story, the mother does achieve an understanding of herself and the beginning of love for her husband. The incident of the wedding is just the gimmick out of which she achieves this understanding."

"If you want all the prizes, you gotta write shrill" was Paddy's sole advice to Vidal. "He was cynically convinced that reviewers only reacted to a lot of noise on the screen or in the theatre. He had a point," said Vidal. Chayefsky had no approval over the final script, the adapter believed. "I was the writer, not he. Also, under the studio system, I was not autonomous, but a pencil in the hand of the producer, Sam Zimbalist, a conventional but good man."

Directed by Richard Brooks, and starring Bette Davis, Ernest Borgnine, and Debbie Reynolds, *The Catered Affair* was exploited by the studio for the full advantage of the recent *Marty* Oscars. In the ads and lobby posters, much to the chagrin of Miss Davis, then in her galactic decline, MGM concentrated on Borgnine's more timely appeal. A full-sized photograph of the actor was shown, sans Davis, in the displays. And inserted in the upper-left corner of the layouts was a smaller sketch of Paddy Chayefsky seated at his typewriter. In bold letters, the headline read ERNEST BORGNINE AND PADDY CHAYEFSKY— THE ACADEMY AWARDS TEAM DOES IT AGAIN!

In its review of the film, the *New York Herald Tribune* said that "Chayefsky has a sure ear for the folk idiom of New York, and Gore Vidal preserves [it] in his screenplay." *Life* magazine predicted that the movie was a surefire winner because it "has the same elements of love and frustration, the same sharp look of truth as *Marty*."

The film was not a success, however. Bette Davis blamed the studio. "MGM didn't spend a *dime* promoting it," said the actress in 1973 when she told this writer that *The Catered Affair* was "the most unappreciated but self-satisfying performance of my career."

The movie did very well in Europe, "particularly England," said Gore Vidal. "It was [Chayefsky's] most admired movie pre-*Network*. I used to tease Paddy about that."

The Bachelor Party

Tandem to the release of *The Catered Affair*, United Artists had hoped to have their next Chayefsky picture in theatres later that summer. The rights to *The Bachelor Party* had been bought by Hecht-Lancaster the previous year. Chayefsky agreed to write the screenplay, but for reasons not explained until later, he was lax in completing it. Three months after the Oscars, in June 1955, writer David Shaw received a Saturday-morning telephone call from Chayefsky. "I was at home and he opened with 'Listen, you have kids, little kids, don't you?' which is typical Paddy dialogue. I said, 'Yes, why?' He said, 'Well, that means you're going to be home tonight.' I said, 'Yes, why?' And he said, 'Listen, I'm working on the movie version of *The Bachelor Party*, and I'm stuck. I've got to talk to somebody about it.' I asked him when it was due. He said, 'Monday.' We laughed, and I said, 'O.K., come on over.' I hung up, and the phone rings again. It's Paddy. 'Listen, do you have the book of my television plays?' he asked. I said, 'Yes.' 'Well, read *Bachelor Party* before I get there,' he said and hung up."

That evening Chayefsky arrived at Shaw's apartment on East Seventy-fourth Street. "It was a terribly hot night. We didn't have an air conditioner. So he and I sat in my kitchen until two o'clock in the morning, with the refrigerator door open to cool off. We screamed with laughter. Paddy was always marvelous in a working situation. He went home, and maybe three weeks later he called and said, 'Listen, they want rewrites.' We met again. When you work with Paddy, all the ideas are his. But now he was challenging me. 'Why do we have this in here, and why do we have that?' I listened, and sure enough he came up with the answers, too."

On television, *The Bachelor Party* had not materialized as Chayefsky had envisioned it. He wanted to show the emptiness of an evening on the town, and emptiness is one of the most difficult of all qualities to dramatize. Also, the story was supposed to be a multiple characterization, exposing the problems and anxieties of four men whose youth had been sacrificed for adult ambitions. But because of the limitations of time and physical space on television, the full, woven fabric of the story could not be shown. Chayefsky believed that much more could be accomplished in the movie version. The lead character would still be Charlie, with the other characters expanded but existing to shape the main story line. The device of cutting from one story to the other as the main plot moves to it climactic point could be achieved by the extra time and the facility of film.

With a rough first draft of *The Bachelor Party* completed by late June, Chayefsky went to California for script conferences with Hecht-Hill-Lancaster. On his previous trips, solo, he had usually stayed in a hotel. This time out, accompanied by his wife and young son, he needed a house, and per his contract one was supplied by the producers. It was a comfortable house located on North Palm Drive in Beverly Hills that had been occupied previously by Marilyn Monroe during her marriage to Joe DiMaggio. All was serene for two days, until Chayefsky checked in for work at Hecht-Hill-Lancaster. Originally the producers had worked out of an office on Santa Monica Boulevard. Early in 1956 they leased two buildings in Beverly Hills. The "authors' building" was an old house whose living area had been converted into small but comfortable offices for the writers. Through the parking lot on the main thoroughfare at 202 North Canyon Drive was the partners' main office building. The interiors were sumptuous: wall-to-wall carpets, solid mahogany desks, purple velvet divans, and original paintings by Matisse and Utrillo hanging on the walls. Even the bathrooms were fancy, with black marble floors and gold fixtures; over the sinks, where paper towels had once sufficed, plush purple towels with H-H-L embroidered in real gold thread were stacked. "They went crazy and built a private men's room for themselves," said Walter Seltzer, "with three wash basins, three booths, and three urinals so Burt and Harold and Jim Hill could stand and pee together."

More amused than impressed by the ultra-fancy decor and fixtures, Chayefsky's spirits turned dour when story editor, and new full partner, Jim Hill began to discuss the expensive slate of movies planned by the company. Films starring Laurence Olivier, Katharine Hepburn, Alec Guinness, Audrey Hepburn, Charles Laughton, and Elizabeth Taylor were planned, from scripts or plays by George Bernard Shaw, Tennessee Williams, John Van Druten, Clifford Odets, and James Thurber.

Chayefsky was convinced that much of Hecht-Hill-Lancaster's new fortune, and all of its current prestige, came from *his* creation, *Marty*. He received part of the acclaim, but very little of the profusion of cash that flowed into the company had made its way into *his* bank account. From the current gross of $5 million for *Marty,* his participation thus far had come to $25,000. Then again, that was considerably more than Ernest Borgnine received, Paddy soon learned. According to legal papers the actor was about to file, it appeared that prior to its distribution of profits, H-H-L had done some skimming off the top before the profits from *Marty* were distributed to each participant. They had paid themselves a bonus of $50,000 each, with another $100,000 lopped off for their agent, Lew Wasserman.

When Chayefsky heard of this he called his agent in New York. Bobby Sanford told him there was nothing they could do about his contract for *The Bachelor Party.* They had got a good deal, $40,000 plus points, when they signed the contract. But that was *before* the Oscars, Chayefsky argued. His price had easily doubled since then. And surely *he* deserved a bonus? Sanford called Hecht-Hill-Lancaster with that suggestion. They came back and said they'd be happy to give Chayefsky a bonus, if he would sign a multiple-picture deal with them, which would include the movie rights to *Middle of the Night.* Chayefsky's reply via Sanford was that the producers could "go fuck themselves."

Deliberating for a while, Chayefsky eventually found a way to make H-H-L part with more cash. In his contract he found a clause that said, "While working on the script for *The Bachelor Party,* the proprietor (the writer) must have accommodations commensurate with his New York residence." To Paddy, eight rooms on Central Park West in New York were equal to a mansion in Beverly Hills. So he asked for a new house, in a better neighborhood. Furthermore, it had to be fully staffed, and he needed two cars, one for him and one for his wife to drive to the market.

"Paddy was an extraordinarily good human manipulator," said J. P. Miller, who was in California at that time working for H-H-L on his script for *Rabbit Trap.* "He knew his way around a scrap as very few writers do. Most writers, if they get into a fight or a bad situation on a movie, call their agents. But Paddy knew Hollywood and he didn't back down. He would go head to head with anybody—and at the same time he had this incredible writer's sensitivity. That's a rare combination which many of us don't have. He was that rare breed of talent and fighter."

Hecht-Hill-Lancaster, upon checking Chayefsky's contract, found that he was right about the accommodations clause, and they were obliged to move him out of Marilyn Monroe's honeymoon cottage and into a far more lavish mansion. "Most of us poor writers were living in Hollywood or Beverly Hills," said J. P. Miller. "And here was Paddy, lording it up in Bel Air."

"It was an estate with thirty-two rooms on Copa D'Ora," said Johnny Friedkin, who visited from New York with his wife, Audrey Peters. "There were two wings to the house," said Peters. "The main living room looked like a hotel lobby, with enormous chairs and couches. There was an Olympic-sized pool way down at the end of an expansive lawn. With the cars, the servants, and everything, it was very grand."

Premieres and parties were a natural part of the Hollywood landscape, and that summer Chayefsky sampled the high life. "Paddy got a big kick out of movie stars. He was a little kid," said Peters. "We went to a few premieres, and one night we went to Eddie Albert's house. Eddie had done *The Bachelor Party* on TV, and he wanted to be in the movie. So he invited the four of us to this dinner party at his house. There were a lot of people there and it was very strange because after dinner Eddie Albert and his wife, Margo, performed. You had to sit there and watch them. You couldn't wander around, and at one point Eddie bawled out the butler because he served a drink in the middle of a number. When they finished one song, the other guests would shout out, 'Sing what you sang last night.' We looked at one another and realized that Eddie was auditioning for Paddy. The whole thing was *for* Paddy. We couldn't wait to get out of there, but Paddy loved every minute of it. He was like Marty in Hollywood, taking everything in."

To serve their writers and speed up the completion of scripts, Hecht-Hill-Lancaster had installed two full-time secretaries in the authors' building. In the beginning, when Chayefsky went to work he would spend an hour kibitzing with the secretaries, then go to his office and shut the door. All calls were to be held, he said, unless they were personal. Emerging at noon, he would go to lunch with J. P. Miller or other friends. When he returned, if he returned, he would shut the door, come out at five, and go home. When the secretaries delivered the writers' work to the main building that evening, there weren't any pages from Chayefsky. The problem, apart from his lingering pique at the producers and the distractions of his new social commitments, was that he didn't have anyone in Hollywood to "talk story" to.

"Burt Lancaster and Harold were guys you could respect when it came to scripts," said J. P. Miller. "Burt was nobody's fool. He was a damn good story analyst. He knew what made a story go, as did Harold, but at this time their operation was bigger than they could handle, so they were busy elsewhere. That meant Paddy and I wound up having to deal with Jim Hill. We resented him because he had a clichéd mind. His way of criticizing something was to say something like 'Why don't you do it more like the scene in *Ninotchka* or *Sunset Boulevard*?' Everything he suggested was lifted from some other picture."

With *The Bachelor Party* scheduled to begin shooting at the end of August, and United Artists breathing down their necks for a new Chayefsky picture, the executive producers tried to pressure Paddy. When that happened he stopped going to the office. His contract said he could work at home. When the producers phoned he was unavailable. "Burt Lancaster used to call all the time," said Audrey Peters, "but Paddy would not talk to him."

David Shaw was at his home in East Hampton, New York, when he received a frantic call from Harold Hecht. "He said to me, 'Listen, we got a problem on *Bachelor Party*. We're not getting along with Paddy. He won't talk to me. He won't talk to Burt or the UA guys. He'll only talk to you.' "

Hecht asked Shaw to come out to California. "I said, 'I can't do that. I'm working on my own thing.' Hecht said, 'But you gotta come out.' He offered me a lot of money for a short time. So I went."

Chayefsky was delighted to see his old pal. "Can you believe this?" he said to Shaw. "These cruds want rewrites." "I stayed about a week," said Shaw. "Paddy wouldn't go to the office. We worked in his home. But again, all I did was sit there. The ideas were his. He'd talk a little, then go upstairs and write a scene. He'd come back down, and I'd be at the pool, and he'd read what he had written. I'd say, 'Gee, Paddy, that's terrific.' We'd talk some more. He'd go back upstairs, write some more, then read it to me over cocktails. And that's how my week in California went."

When Shaw left, Chayefsky agreed to return and work in Hecht-Hill-Lancaster's authors' building. His sounding board there was J. P. Miller, who was trying to work on his script for *Rabbit Trap*. "I'd be in the middle of something and the door would fly open," said Miller. "Paddy would burst in like a typhoon. He wouldn't knock or anything, just barge in and say, 'Japes, I got to bullshit a little about this scene. I don't know how to make it work. Goddammit, it goes great then suddenly stops in the middle. There's something wrong here. Let me tell you about it.' And he wouldn't wait for me to say anything. He would talk for ten minutes, recap the scene, say what he thought about the characters, what they meant to each other, what was making the scene go. Then he'd yell, 'That's it. I got it. O.K., thanks, Japes.' And he'd leave with the problem solved and through all this I never got to say a fucking word."

By August the script for *The Bachelor Party* was completed, the film was budgeted at $750,000 (double the cost of *Marty*), and casting began in Los Angeles. Although Eddie Albert and the rest of the actors from the TV version were passed over, Hecht and Lancaster agreed with Chayefsky's suggestion that only theatre people should be used for the key roles. Don Murray, who had just completed *Bus Stop* with Marilyn Monroe, was chosen for Charlie. His party companions would be Jack Warden, E. G. Marshall, Larry Blyden, and Philip Abbott as the frightened groom-to-be. Patricia Smith was cast as Charlie's wife, and Nancy Marchand was brought from New York to play his unhappily married cousin. Another female part, newly added to the story, was "the Existentialist." Chayefsky described her as young, attractive, a "nothing-shocks-me-I've-seen-everything girl," who meets the wandering men at a party in Greenwich Village and proceeds to challenge Charlie's mind and his marital fidelity. In all, her scene would come to less than four minutes, but for many viewers it would remain the most memorable one in the movie.

To read for the role, Chayefsky later recalled, "a stream of Hollywood starlets" trooped in and out of the Hecht-Hill-Lancaster offices before he and director Delbert Mann zeroed in on one candidate, Carolyn Jones. She was twenty-five, had played bit parts in thirteen Hollywood movies, and with "a career going nowhere" had been urged by her husband, a struggling actor-writer-producer named Aaron Spelling, to audition for the small part in the new Chayefsky picture. "I read for Paddy and the director twice," said Jones. "Intuitively I could sense that they liked me but something was bothering them. It turned out to be my hair. I was a blonde, a natural blonde, and they wanted a brunette. 'No problem,' I told them, 'I'll dye my hair.' I became a brunette and my entire career changed."

Jones, who eventually received an Oscar nomination for her performance, said she originally could not comprehend the character. "She had lines like 'My martini has no olives, the scotch no rocks.' She was one of those Greenwich Village intellectual dummies. I was from Texas, and there I was in Hollywood with all these New York theatre people involved. Finally, I said to Paddy, 'You've got to get somebody else because I don't know how to play this part. I don't know a girl who would say lines like these.' "

Chayefsky asked Jones to stick with the project. Days later, when she was in the wardrobe department being sewn into her dress for the 1950s vaccuum-sealed look, he showed up with new pages. "I was facedown on the floor, being fitted, when he shoved the script by my face on the carpet. 'Now read this,' he said." After being lifted up by two assistants, Jones read the new lines where her character, desperate for even the illusion of affection, says to the indecisive young husband as he kisses her, "Just say you love me—you don't have to mean it."

"Now, *that* character I understood," said Jones. "Paddy defined her so well. She was no longer for New York audiences but for audiences—especially men—everywhere. Even guys in places like the Midwest have approached me with the request, 'Say that line again.' "

"That was what made Paddy's writing so memorable," Nancy Marchand recalled. "His characters were wonderful on their own, but now and then he would come in with a line of such intimacy and truth that audiences would catch their breath. They recognized that truth. And no doubt those lines came from Paddy's experiences. He was a very deep soul."

In September, *The Bachelor Party* began filming in New York. Shooting in the subway, in a restaurant on the East Side, in a strip club on the West Side, and on the streets of Greenwich Village, Chayefsky said he had such a good time he was lax with his own script. "It needed tightening, more time, but everyone was telling me how great it was that I didn't bother listening to myself."

Originally United Artists had planned to release the movie in late December, to qualify for the Academy Awards. When the company saw the edited film they changed their minds. "It didn't affect us the way that *Marty* did," said Max Youngstein. "Paddy had lost it as far as I was concerned, he did not get us involved with these people's emotions. It was what I called a gray picture, oatmeal. And there were no stars. You could say the same for *Marty*, but the tug between those two people—Borgnine and Betsy—was so real, and has seldom been re-created."

When *The Bachelor Party* was released in April 1957, the critics were equally lukewarm in their appraisal. *Variety* commended the keen, insightful script and the sharp performances, but said it wasn't another *Marty*. "However, with hard sell, *Party* can be a box-office winner."

That hard sell never came, Chayefsky complained. Beyond sending Carolyn Jones on tour "with a Don Loper wardrobe," United Artists did not aggressively market the picture. Instead, they spent most of their time and money pushing another Hecht-Hill-Lancaster film, *Sweet Smell of Success*. Chayefsky believed that this bitter but dazzling drama, starring Burt Lancaster and Tony Curtis in a script written by Ernest Lehman and Clifford Odets, had helped to bury his smaller picture. "*Sweet Smell of Success* was a better film, with bigger stars and stronger performances," said Youngstein. "It later became a cult picture, but we didn't make any money from that either."

Chayefsky said he got screwed on *The Bachelor Party*. Going in, he was supposed to received 5 percent of the profits. Then Hecht-Hill-Lancaster docked him three points for being late with the script. Ultimately, the movie never did return a profit, and a few years later, H-H-L, overextended and nearly broke, closed its offices and disbanded. "All of us stayed in touch," said Jim Hill. "Different projects were discussed with Paddy's name attached from time to time." Hill spoke to Chayefsky about adapting Charles Dickens's *Dombey and Son,* although the period and locale might not be Chayefsky's forte, he admitted. "The thing that made Paddy great was that he had to know the people," said Hill, "just as Clifford Odets did. When they went to work on characters, they gradually made them their own."

In tribute to Harold Hecht, who established his name worldwide, Chayefsky said, "Working with Harold on *Marty* and *Bachelor Party* gave me a fresh respect for what producers have to do to get a movie made." He also learned a valuable lesson about Hollywood business ethics from Hecht. "Harold told me: 'They can screw you, and you can screw them, but if you want to keep on working, both of you need a short memory.' "

CHAPTER 11

Contention on Broadway

Although *The Catered Affair* and *The Bachelor Party* generated little or no revenue, *Middle of the Night* continued to play to packed houses on Broadway through 1956 and 1957. As playwright and investor, Chayefsky's average weekly royalty check came to $2,700, then a considerable sum. The play also provided ancillary disputes and conflicts that apparently were now indispensable for sustaining his art and his zest for life.

His first opponents were the critics who dared call *Middle of the Night* "a little play." As soon as they had been properly chastised, Paddy took on his star, Edward G. Robinson. Along the Great White Way their frequent and colorful contests were referred to as "The Bronx Bomber versus Little Caesar."

When Robinson had initially been suggested for his play, Chayefsky said he was a lousy choice. "He's a gangster," he said. Josh Logan settled that matter by having Paddy meet with Robinson in a suite at the Stanhope Hotel, the walls of which had been temporarily decorated with art from Robinson's vast collection of Impressionist works (which would be sold the following year to the Greek shipping tycoon Stavros Niarchos for $3 million). That high touch of culture obviously swayed Chayefsky, but during rehearsals it was learned that Robinson had lied to the producers about his height. Onstage, his leading lady, Gena Rowlands, wearing high heels, towered above him. The sets, doorways, and other actors had to be scaled down to accommodate the star (Rowlands was told to wear flats). "Paddy was the same height as Eddie," said Wally Fried, the play's production manager, "so he didn't make too much fuss about that. Actually I think he enjoyed that Eddie insisted everybody come down to his size."

But Chayefsky's ardor for Robinson cooled considerably after the reviews came in. He didn't begrudge the actor the raves he received, but was miffed that the high volume of praise tended to diminish the worth of the play itself. Robinson did not help matters by overlooking Chayefsky's participation and importance. This was Chayefsky's first play on Broadway, and he felt that Robinson went out of his way to ignore or downplay the writer's contribution. "It was a very sensitive time for Paddy," said Wally Fried. "Robinson was older and respected, and being that the theatre is about surrogate family, perhaps Paddy was looking for some kind of personal praise or endorsement. But being a star and an actor, Robinson felt he didn't have to bother with those mundane formalities."

Transferring his ire from the critics to Robinson, Chayefsky soon found comfort in the grievances he discovered. First, as an investor he objected to the money and perks the actor had been granted in his contract. Along with his salary of $2,500 per week against 10 percent of the gross, Robinson was receiving out-of-pocket expenses (not to exceed $150 per week), first-class hotel accommodations at the Stanhope, a Cadillac (no earlier than a 1954 model), and a chauffeur who doubled as a masseur and dog walker. Robinson's contract also mandated that he receive a box-office statement of the attendance at each performance, and a recap and certified check at the end of each week. If he spotted irregularities he would question Wally Fried, who if the problem warranted it would refer the matter to Paddy Chayefsky, who in Josh Logan's absence was acting as coproducer. Chayefsky for his part was determined to ensure they were getting their money's worth. He would show up most evenings at the theatre to assess Robinson's performance. "Paddy would stand at the back of the theatre and make notes of the things that Eddie was doing which distracted from his play," said Fried. "Eddie would sometimes use his cigar as a prop, which Paddy felt was provoking the audiences to laugh at the wrong moments. Naturally that annoyed the hell out of him, because he felt his play was Eugene O'Neill material."

In April 1956, three months after the play opened, Robinson informed Chayefsky and the producer-director, Logan, that he was leaving when his six-month contract was up. Paddy, seemingly pleased, instructed his agent, Bobby Sanford, to inquire about the availability of other actors, specifically James Cagney, Melvyn Douglas, Claude Rains, and Orson Welles. Those were his first choices. Logan, who along with his wife, Nedda, owned 25 percent of the play, felt that it was in their best interest for Robinson to continue in the role. In a letter to Chayefsky, Logan remarked on the excellent business the play was doing and on the recent good notices from the British critic Kenneth Tynan. "It is really quite rewarding to know that a man of his brilliance appreciates your writing so very, very much," said Logan. In a minor key, the director went over a second list of Chayefsky's suggestions for a replacement: Paul Douglas ("just doesn't seem right"), Luther Adler ("too theatrical"), Lee J. Cobb (no comment). Easing the way back to Robinson, Logan said that he hoped Paddy would allow him "to continue on it" so that the play would "run as long as humanly possible."

Chayefsky wouldn't budge, nor would Robinson, who in his heyday at Warner Bros. had matched his intractable will against the likes of Jack Warner and co-star Bette Davis. According to Fried, the problem by now had to do largely with the movie rights to the play. In April 1956, Chayefsky was quoted as saying that he had three major studios bidding for it and that he wanted Spencer Tracy or Paul Muni to play Robinson's role. That insensitive remark, said Fried, forced Robinson to employ "a face-saving device to offset the public rejection the announcement carried." He gave his notice, declaring that he wanted to take on one of several movie offers that had come in for him.

At Logan's request, Fried arranged a conciliatory meeting between Robinson and Chayefsky. "I'm afraid it did not turn out well," said Fried. "Paddy lost his temper and told Robinson that the movie was his business and that he did not feel obligated to talk to any actors about it. He was quite blunt about it. All this despite the fact that I had told him it would be courteous and wise to talk to his star about his plans to make an inexpensive picture, with an inexpensive actor playing his part." Noticing that Chayefsky was "a bit contrite" the following day, Fried said that Paddy's dislike of Robinson would be something he would get over "when he discovers years from now that Eddie is not his father."

Developing a bad cold "augmented by prostate trouble," Robinson informed Fried the next day that he did not want his condition aggravated ("so that the play would become distasteful to him and unconsciously—because Eddie is a pro—cause him to leave before his contract is up on June thirtieth," said Fried to Logan). Showing he meant business, Robinson at the same time instructed his agent, Abe Lastfogel, to line up some definite movie work for him that summer.

Meanwhile, in California, Josh Logan, stuck between a rock and two hard places (he was directing Marilyn Monroe in *Bus Stop* at the same time), decided to dispatch his wife and partner, Nedda, to New York, to heal the rifts. A woman of "quicksilver sensibilities," Nedda Logan in her day was known to have soothed the temperaments of such theatrical divas as Jeanne Eagels, Mary Martin, and, more recently, Marilyn Monroe, who had named Nedda as "next-of-kin" when she left the set and checked into a hospital, suffering from "nerves and fatigue," during the filming of *Bus Stop*.

On May 14, Mrs. Logan flew to New York to talk to the disgruntled Robinson and the querulous Chayefsky. Four days later, mission accomplished, she returned to California. At her urging, Chayefsky had agreed to curb his temper and ego and to make up with Robinson for the good of the play and the sale of the movie rights. A new run-of-the-play contract was then offered to Robinson. If he consented to sign on for at least one more year, he would receive the same salary and perks, but his cut of the weekly gross would be raised from 10 to 15 percent.

On June 1, Robinson signed the new contract. In a follow-up letter, Josh Logan praised Wally Fried for "steering the ship" and suggested that an ad be taken out announcing Robinson's re-signing and congratulating Chayefsky for their continued success. "I realize that Paddy has been a thorn in the side of the play," said Logan. "But it's not much bigger than our star with all his personal illnesses." Another reason for the ad would be to "save face" with Chayefsky, the director concluded. "I would love to approach him someday to write a little better ending, before we go on the road, just for his own sake so that the notices might be better."

But according to cast members, throughout the year and a half that *Middle of the Night* ran in New York, Chayefsky never stopped writing new endings. "He hated the 'soft finish' that Logan insisted upon in Philadelphia," said one witness, "so after the opening he kept showing up at the theatre with corrections." In the late spring of 1957, Martin Landau replaced Lee Philips in the role of George. He later recalled that Chayefsky was constantly at the theatre during rehearsals with his revisions for the last scene. "That scene had nothing to do with me," said Landau. "It was between Eddie and Gena Rowlands's characters. Paddy wanted a deeper, more complex ending. We were supposed to close in New York, then pick up later to tour across the country, so Paddy was insistent that a new ending be inserted. He would come in every day with a new scene. This went on for weeks. Even after we closed on Broadway and reconvened for the tour, he would come into the theatre with his new pages. While the rest of us were sitting in the audience, Paddy would be on stage with Robinson. He would hand him the pages. Eddie would read them, and say: 'Yass, very good. Yass! Yass!' And then he'd tap his cigar and say, 'Yass, waal, Paddy, we'll stick to the old one.' And Paddy would say frantically, 'But you don't understand. The old one ties it up too neatly.' And Eddie would say, 'We've done four hundred and seventy-five performances so far, and the audiences seem to like the play—so we'll stay with the old ending.' "

The enmity between Robinson and Chayefsky diminished slightly before the tour began. When told by his understudy and road director, Curt Conway, that Chayefsky had performed onstage in England during the war, Robinson slapped his knee and said, "I suspected he was a frustrated actor after all!" On the road in Washington, D.C., Robinson invited Chayefsky and Martin Landau to be his guests at the Press Club. "On a napkin, I drew a caricature of

Paddy and one of Eddie," said Landau. "And Eddie drew one of me, until we were all doing pictures of one another into the early hours of the morning." The next day Chayefsky saw the matinee and evening performances. "He still wanted to make changes," said Landau, "but Eddie wouldn't hear of it."

By the time the company reached California, it was divulged that the movie rights to the play had been sold to Columbia Pictures. Robinson asked Chayefsky about his re-creating his part on film. Nodding pensively, Chayefsky replied, "We'll see, Eddie. We'll see."

Paddy and Marilyn Monroe

Because the movie version of *Middle of the Night* could not be made until the play ended its tour, Chayefsky, with time on his hands, decided to write another script for Columbia Pictures. One idea he had was "a story about show business." This had been on his mind since 1950, when the movie *All About Eve* had just been released. Despite its critical and widespread appeal, Chayefsky found the film bogus, "a musical comedy of the theatre."

"Maybe Anne Baxter can get a job as a star's understudy without any previous experience, but I'd like to meet the producer of that show," he said. "And the idea that this strumpet can step on a stage and give a performance of 'fire and music' just like that could only happen in Hollywood."

He had yet to read or see or hear anything that exposed one inch of an actor's or a writer's or a director's genuine self, Chayefsky commented further. "Anne Baxter in *All About Eve* could have been a ladies' room attendant, for all the motivations given to her. Why does a girl like that take her ambition into the theatre instead of going into politics?"

He had some authentic stories of the theatre to tell, which were "real and more actual, and a great deal truer," Chayefsky said again, in 1954. One was called *The Five-Day Clause*. It was about a struggling New York actor, making his daily humiliating rounds, begging to see agents and "chasing television directors around the CBS building." Another story he worked on was loosely based on that of a friend of his: After seducing various female casting agents, a struggling actor gets his big break in Hollywood by sleeping with the male star of the picture. *There's No Bizzness Like Show Bizzness* was the title of that script. In 1955, a revised version was optioned by Fred Coe for a ninety-minute TV dramatic original, to appear on NBC. Upon reading the outline, NBC asked for changes, which Chayefsky would not consider. Six months later he pitched the concept to Columbia Pictures as part of a two-picture deal. "The two movies were *Middle of the Night* and the show-business story, which would be done first," said Milton Perlman, Chayefsky's new producing partner.

Reexamining his Hollywood script, Chayefsky found it needed changes. Another movie about a disillusioned actor, *The Big Knife*, had appeared not long before. Rather than abandon the idea, Chayefsky decided to switch the gender. He changed the actor to an actress, a beautiful, seductive girl who after sleeping her way to the top begins to unravel psychologically, destroying herself and those around her. Chayefsky also had a real-life model for his doomed heroine, one of the leading sex symbols of the day, Marilyn Monroe.

Although little was known or ever publicized about any connection between Monroe and Chayefsky, their paths had crossed several times. Back in 1951, when Monroe signed a seven-year contract with Fox, her starlet status was solidified by *As Young as You Feel*, which was based on Chayefsky's story. He wasn't on the set during filming, but Elia Kazan was, and a torrid affair ensued. "A simple, eager young woman" was Kazan's remembrance of Marilyn, "a decent-hearted girl whom Hollywood brought down, legs parted." When asked years later if Paddy Chayefsky, his houseguest in Malibu at that time, had used Monroe as the prototype for his doomed star in *The Goddess*, Kazan said, "Marilyn was just a kid when we first met. She wasn't desperate, or the kind of tragic figure that Paddy wrote in *The Goddess*. Although I guess there were parallels."

By 1954, after twelve movies, hundreds of photo sittings, and many sexual favors, which she considered part of the training program, Monroe had become the leading female star at Twentieth Century–Fox. With other voracious needs to fill, including her desire for respect, she walked out on her Fox contract, flew to New York, and joined the Actors Studio. Carroll Baker, who was then competing with Monroe for the lead in *Baby Doll*, described her rival's entrance at the Studio. "If her hips weren't gyrating, she was winching her shoulders, or swinging her pink fuzzy tits, or making that sucking fish-pucker mouth," said Baker. "Everything about her stated, 'I'm yours. Take me. Use me.' " In the doorway, past the many students who were "tripping over one another" in an effort to get close to the blond star, Baker said she spied Elia Kazan and Paddy Chayefsky with their eyes fixed on Monroe. "Oh, boy, would I like to fuck that," said Chayefsky.

In her own good time, Marilyn would get around to Paddy. Writers, after all, were her specialty. In Hollywood thus far she had conquered such stalwart skeptical types as Clifford Odets and Ben Hecht. Odets found her "spontaneous, tender and original . . . a coquette playing somewhat for your affection and esteem." Ben Hecht, with *Twentieth Century, Nothing Sacred,* and *Notorious* among his credits, found himself more than willing to answer to Marilyn's beck and call. He spent four months working on a project for her, not as a scenarist but as a ghostwriter, transcribing her memoirs. When the manuscript was completed, Marilyn "wept and wept for joy at what I had written," Hecht told his agent. But at the insistence of her new husband, Joe DiMaggio, she refused to allow the book to be published.

After ditching DiMaggio and her studio, Marilyn established her own production company in New York, where she proceeded to dazzle and seduce the best writers in town. "I don't want to be rich. I just want to be wonderful," the breathy, luminous star told everyone, and they listened, intently. In fact, the assemblage of literary talent, male and female, straight and gay, that Monroe bowled over in Manhattan was extraordinary. Tennessee Williams, a Pulitzer Prize winner, at their first meeting told her she could have the lead in *Baby Doll* or play Maggie in his premiere production of *Cat on a Hot Tin Roof.* Truman Capote offered her Holly Golightly from his novella-in-progress, *Breakfast at Tiffany's.* Sir Terence Rattigan, writer of *Separate Tables,* was flying from London to Hollywood to discuss the sale of another play, *The Sleeping Prince.* At Idlewild Airport, where he stopped between planes, he was paged by Marilyn. She kidnapped him, brought him by limo to the Barberry Room in Manhattan, and before the entrée arrived she had the rights to *The Sleeping Prince* sewed up for her company. "She labors like a field hand to please everybody," said Truman Capote of Monroe's bewitching technique. "She wants to make of each of us an affectionate protector, and consequently we, her audience, her acquaintances, are flattered, pitying, aroused."

In May 1955, accompanied by Eli Wallach and Anne Jackson, Monroe attended the NBC telecast of *The Catered Affair,* featuring a friend and fellow performer from Fox, Thelma Ritter. A few months later she and Chayefsky were formally introduced at a party at Lee Strasberg's home. "Strasberg was guiding Marilyn's career at the time," said Martin Landau, "and he wanted her to meet the best writers in town." Chayefsky, normally forward and loquacious, found himself at a loss for words when caught in Monroe's golden gaze. "Gee," said the Oscar-winning writer, "I thought you'd be much fuller." Marilyn, whose innate gifts included a delectable sense of humor, casually assumed her photo pose. Elbows pressed to her torso for cleavage, her right foot wrapped around her left, she coyly asked Chayefsky, "Where do you think I ought to be fuller?"

After capturing his sexual id, Marilyn proceeded to ravish Chayefsky's ego. She spoke with admiration and knowledge about his work, the TV plays, and the movie of *Marty,* which she had seen not long before, in Boston. Giving the supreme compliment to a writer, Marilyn then whispered some of his lines, accurately. Eventually the conversation got around to business, hers. With rapt interest, Marilyn asked Chayefsky about his current output, and whether there was anything he was writing that might be suitable for her, something serious, something wonderful. Chayefsky, his natural confidence restored, said that he did indeed have something in the works. He had a play, *Middle of the Night,* that was due to open early in the new year, and the female lead was one that she might be interested in for the movie version.

> This girl is so sweet, I can't tell you.
> A neglected girl. She's so hungry for love, like
> an orphan. She has to know twenty-four hours a day
> that you love her. She's a baby.
>
> The Widower, *Middle of the Night*

Marilyn had no trouble persuading Paddy to let her have an advance copy of his play. She read it in one night and called him the next day. She told him she was in love with the part of the secretary, the beautiful young woman with the soul of a child. On February 8, 1956, when *Middle of the Night* opened on Broadway, the star showed up accompanied by her business partner, photographer Milton Greene. After the play, she and Chayefsky and Greene were seen "in a huddle over the movie rights." The following day, Marilyn appeared at a packed press conference in the Plaza Hotel. This was to announce her first independent film, *The Prince and the Showgirl*, based on Terence Rattigan's *The Sleeping Prince*. After posing for pictures with Rattigan and co-star Laurence Olivier and gently chastising a cynical reporter for suggesting that she might have broken the thin strap of her low-cut black velvet dress deliberately, Marilyn took the time to send a telegram and to call Paddy Chayefsky. Congratulating him on the reviews for his play, she made him promise that he would not give the screen rights to anyone else. A similar vow was extracted from director-producer Josh Logan.

According to Monroe's lawyer, Irving Stein, *Middle of the Night* was listed in their files that season as a possible joint venture between Marilyn Monroe Productions and Chayefsky's company, Carnegie Productions. Whether or not Paddy Chayefsky ever realized his fantasy of being intimate with Marilyn has never been established. He did, however, throw himself into revising his play for her. Putting all other projects on hold, including his long-overdue script of *The Bachelor Party* for Hecht-Hill-Lancaster, that spring Chayefsky restructured the female role in *Middle of the Night* for Monroe. The business aspects of the movie sale were handled by Herb Jaffe at Bobby Sanford's agency. "Three studios are bidding," a *Variety* item declared: "Warners, Columbia and Twentieth Century–Fox."

In May, when Chayefsky's first draft was completed, he began to encounter difficulty in reaching Monroe and Milton Greene. She was finishing *Bus Stop* in Hollywood, and Greene was traveling back and forth to England, arranging *The Prince and the Showgirl*. In June, Chayefsky was told that Marilyn had a new "literary adviser," another writer she had been seeing, sub rosa, for more than a year. This was the man that Chayefsky had once planned to surpass professionally—Arthur Miller.

> No, you're not a slut. You're a baby.
> Every time life gets a little tough for you, you
> want somebody to take you in their arms, anybody,
> some guy in the street and rock you to sleep.
>
> The Widower, *Middle of the Night*

While Monroe was openly seducing New York's literary set, very few people knew that on the sly she was bedding down with the titan of the theatre himself, Arthur Miller. Oddly enough, that alliance also went back to 1951, when Marilyn had been working on *As Young as You Feel* and Miller had been in Hollywood trying to sell a script to Harry Cohn of Columbia Pictures. Introduced by Elia Kazan, Miller said of that first meeting with Marilyn, "I desperately wanted her and decided I must leave tonight, if possible, or I would lose myself here."

Miller left for New York, where over a period of time he received notes and letters from Marilyn. Already married, he told her to forget him, because he "wasn't the man who could make her life happen as she imagined it would." But Marilyn persisted. "I'll follow you. I swear I will. I wish we were married. I'd make you a good wife. I swear I would. You'll never be sorry. Never!" Those were the words the desperate love-starved girl spoke to the writer in Chayefsky's subsequent script, *The Goddess*.

When Monroe relocated to New York, Miller was part of the attraction. He tried to resist her, he said, by staying close to home in Brooklyn with his wife and two children. But Marilyn's siren call wafted across the river from Manhattan and soon he and she were meeting for clandestine, passionate liaisons on Long Island and elsewhere. In New York their covert affair was witnessed by actor Martin Landau. After a session at the Actors Studio one afternoon, he and Ben Gazzara and Elia Kazan escorted Marilyn to a restaurant in Times Square. "It was Child's restaurant on Forty-fourth Street, and we had a table by the window," said Landau. "Across the street was the office of Kermit Bloomgarden, who was preparing *A View from the Bridge*." Over drinks, the actor noticed that Marilyn wasn't really with them. Following her gaze, he saw the object of her attention. High up, framed in a window of the building across the street, was Arthur Miller. "He stood there for the longest time, with his foot on the windowsill, looking down at her," said Landau. "I was the only one who noticed, and nothing was said. Only later did I put it all together."

By February 1956, when Marilyn showed up with Milton Greene for the opening of Chayefsky's play *Middle of the Night*, news of her involvement with Miller had begun to surface. The consensus among the theatrical intelligentsia was that Miller would never leave his wife and family for, as one producer put it, this "blond fantasy shiksa." To respectable men, especially respectable Jewish men, "Marilyn was a girl you fucked but didn't marry."

In June, after converting to Judaism and standing loyally by Miller during his troubles with the House Un-American Activities Committee in Washington, Monroe did marry Miller, much to the consternation of the New York vanguard. Josh Logan and Elia Kazan openly expressed their dissatisfaction with the union, as did Norman Mailer, who harbored his own exalted fantasies of the star. Mailer did not think that Marilyn should be married to anyone, because "she belonged to all men."

Chayefsky's reaction to the marriage was overshadowed by the indignation he displayed concerning the movie version of his play. He had spent considerable time and energy revising *Middle of the Night* for Monroe. While she and Miller were honeymooning in England, word was relayed to Chayefsky that Marilyn had read his script and was not interested in doing the movie anymore. To soften the blow, he was asked if he wanted to write the script for a biofilm, *Harlow*, that Monroe was considering for Fox. "That was a bone they threw to him," said Herb Jaffe. "Paddy was angry, and rightly so. He had spent months reworking *Middle of the Night* specifically for her, and to a degree the movie sale depended on her."

That wasn't the only deal that was affected, Milton Greene soon found out. "We had made commitments to other writers and directors. I tried to tell Marilyn we couldn't do business like that. She was vague, in a fog, when it suited her."

It was up to Greene to inform everyone that their services were no longer required. His own connection to the star would also soon be severed by Arthur Miller. "I got aced out of my own company," he said. "And there was nothing I could do about it."

Neither could all those hoodwinked writers—except for one, Paddy Chayefsky, who would spend the next two years of his life writing and producing *The Goddess*. This original script would intimately depict the rise and fall of a major Hollywood movie star whose unquenchable ambition and shattered life were eerily similar to Marilyn Monroe's.

CHAPTER 12

Writing the Script

You know what I used to do when I first
came out here? I used to go into bars and let men think
they could pick me up. Just to talk to somebody.
I never drank in those days, I just used to sit with those
guys till they got drunk and then I'd go home. I was so lonely
I used to have the shakes like I had palsy. But I never
went home with any of those men. I just couldn't stand the
thought of somebody touching me. I came close
to going crazy in those days.

Rita Shawn, *The Goddess*

What would later surprise many about Chayefsky's script of *The Goddess* was not that he had used Marilyn Monroe as his prototype, but that he captured her inner longing and despair so accurately. After her death, Clifford Odets would write that Monroe always traveled with a "dark companion," an omnipresent twin that took precedence during her bleak earlier life of rejection and deprivation. People who saw "only the gorgeous foliage of her life could not even imagine on what subsoil her roots were feeding," said Odets. Chayefsky, who had his own dark, Stygian side, certainly understood Monroe's fragmented psyche, and he transposed it with considerable intuitiveness and empathy into the character of Rita Shawn. When questioned about his original muse, however, he was emphatic in declaring that his inspiration came from "any number of actresses in popularity at that time."

But the first draft of *The Goddess* was clearly based on Monroe. Among the parallels between Marilyn Monroe (née Norma Jean Baker) and Rita Shawn (née Emily Ann Faulkner) were that they were born in the same year, 1926, and that both were illegitimate and never knew their fathers. In early childhood their mothers tried to abandon them. Norma Jean's mother went crazy; Emily Ann's tried to palm her off on relatives. As young girls they fantasized about movie stars. Norma Jean's idol was Jean Harlow. Emily Ann's was Ginger

Rogers. Both girls married young, Norma Jean at sixteen, Emily Ann at seventeen. Divorced, then revamped into starlets, they looked and dressed the same. "A little too blond, with glistening lips, wearing high heels too high, the hips undulate more than necessary and her breasts are almost bursting against the material of the dress which was carefully selected as a size too small" was Chayefsky's description of Rita Shawn as she is first seen walking along Hollywood Boulevard. Dramatically, both starlets were limited. "She can't act," Chayefsky said of Rita, "but she's a good comedienne, and very sensual. She has what a studio executive called 'the quality of availability,' which makes every man in the audience think they could make her if they only knew her."

Struggling to become established in Hollywood, Rita Shawn, like Marilyn Monroe, employs sexual guile and submission to get parts. "How nice do I have to be?" she asks one casting executive. "If you're not Bette Davis, you gotta be very nice," she is told. After her nude calendar photos were exposed, Monroe redeemed herself and got further national publicity when she married America's ex–baseball hero, Joe DiMaggio. Chayefsky's heroine, after posing for "provocative pictures," also marries a retired baseball star. As well as past careers, the husbands share some of the same characteristics. Both loathe the prurient aspects of their wives' profession. When Monroe posed with her skirts flying above her waist for a street scene in *The Seven Year Itch*, DiMaggio stood on the sidelines looking grim and tight-lipped. "His eyes are slitted with cold fury, and he is flourishing a magazine," says Chayefsky in his script as Rita Shawn's husband throws the publication featuring her sexy pictures across the room. On the domestic scene, the two men appeared sluggish. "Joe DiMaggio bored Marilyn," columnist Sidney Skolsky said in his memoirs. "His lifestyle added up to beer, TV, and the old lady. Marilyn ran second to 'Gunsmoke' or 'The Late Show' and a can of beer, night after night after night." "Why don't you shave?" Rita Shawn says coldly to her once athletic husband. "You haven't been out of this room in two days. You sit there watching television all night long. It's a wonder your eyes don't fall out of your head." After eleven months of marriage, Rita divorces her ex–sports hero. Marilyn Monroe walked out on DiMaggio after nine.

Arthur Miller, Monroe's next groom, is not overlooked, either, in Chayefsky's story. Reversing the chronological order of marriages, Chayefsky used a facsimile of Miller for his goddess's first husband, whom he describes as "a tall, thin writer with a gaunt face and a morbid interest in Eugene O'Neill." The latter obsession, however, was more clearly linked to Chayefsky than to Miller during this time. *Long Day's Journey into Night* had opened on Broadway the previous November, and the import of O'Neill was clearly evident in the first drafts of Chayefsky's *The Goddess*. Along with giving his writer character the same fictional surname (Tyrone), Chayefsky invested him with a comparable background. O'Neill's autobiographical figure had a miserly father, a mother who was an addict, and a brother who winds up in a sanitarium. Chayefsky's John Tyrone speaks of similar familial afflictions, except that his mother's habit is alcohol, not morphine. In dubious homage, perhaps, Chayefsky refers to O'Neill in his script as "that great Irish peddler of death."

With the help of O'Neill, Chayefsky also hoped that *The Goddess* would dispel his reputation as a writer of inarticulate characters and colloquial dialogue. "*Marty! Marty!* That's all I hear about," Chayefsky had complained to his sister-in-law, Terry. "He was always afraid that the public would only know him for that one movie," she explained. The critics were also at fault, his son said, for perpetuating the image of him as a stenographic writer. "They used to say his dialogue sounded as if it were tape-recorded, and that annoyed him," said Dan Chayefsky. "I'd like to find a tape recorder as clever as I am in dialogue," the writer declared, insisting that he spent hours trying to make those realistic lines sound right. "The whole labor of writing is to make it look like it just came off the top of your head."

To make his intent clear, Chayefsky decided to divide his script for *The Goddess* into three acts, like a theatre play. That would avoid making it too ponderous, "although theatre audiences like a little tedium," he said. "It makes them feel they're in the presence of something weighty." When cautioned that the rich, bombastic language in his soliloquies was too close to O'Neill's, Chayefsky was hurt, said Milton Perlman. When another acquaintance mentioned the heavy influence of O'Neill on his script, Chayefsky became angry. "So what!" he retorted. "O'Neill in his day was influenced by Strindberg." Perlman said he urged Chayefsky to use his own language and technique, which he eventually did. "And, as it transpired, his own dialogue was striking," said the producer. "His human insights and character studies in *The Goddess* turned out to be extraordinary."

In Act I, Chayefsky shows the goddess as a young girl growing up unloved and rejected in a small southern town. Act II focuses on her struggling, promiscuous days as a starlet in Hollywood. In Act III, with stardom and fame achieved, the goddess is a psychological cripple, addicted to pills and alcohol, unable to love or relate to anything beyond her own career and pain. Because Marilyn Monroe's mental instability and drug use were not widely known at this time, Chayefsky, getting no credit for his prescience, was accused of using director Josh Logan as the source for his material. During the making of *Bus Stop*, Logan had been a witness to the grueling self-torture and the "sad reliance" on pills that were part of the daily ritual of getting Monroe to perform. Logan, however, denied that he contributed knowingly to Chayefsky's script. "It was suggested to me that because I was working with her and with Paddy at the same time, that I betrayed some confidences. But that wasn't true," he said in 1974. "Perhaps Paddy and I did talk of Marilyn. After all, she was being considered to play the girl in *Middle of the Night*. But regarding the pills and such, I never mentioned any of that. Also they were not as much a problem for me as they were further on, for Billy Wilder and John Huston. Nor did I ever see Marilyn's mean side, or envision that she would have such a tragic end. Paddy was very perceptive about that, very clairvoyant. That was one of his gifts."

By December 1956, Marilyn Monroe and Arthur Miller had completed *The Prince and the Showgirl* in England and had returned to the United States. Early in January, Chayefsky forwarded the first copy of his script of *The Goddess* to Marilyn in Amagansett, Long Island, where she was temporarily living.

"I guess it was a bold move on his behalf," said Perlman, "but it was a very good script, and Paddy and I both felt she might want to do the movie."

According to Chayefsky and others, Monroe did read the script and she very much wanted to play the leading role. "Maybe Marilyn didn't quite see *The Goddess* as biographical," Martin Landau theorized. "Clearly it was analogous, but maybe she felt that it was just a damn good part."

"Marilyn certainly could look the part of the goddess, but I don't think she could have handled Paddy's dialogue," said J. P. Miller.

Actress Geraldine Page, who had once seen Monroe perform in Eugene O'Neill's *Anna Christie*, said, "She could handle the heavy stuff wonderfully."

"But that was at the Actors Studio, in that little church, with all your friends around you," said J. P. Miller. "On a regular stage where you have to project night after night, or on a soundstage when you are given a script like the one Paddy wrote, I really doubt if Marilyn could have done it. She was not a verbal actress. Marilyn was a counterpuncher. Her face was a movie actor's face. All you had to do was push the camera up on her and you'd get a reacting emotion. But if she had to do a lot of talking on her own, I don't think she could have carried it."

The acting challenge was never put to the test, because shortly after Monroe read Chayefsky's script of *The Goddess*, she gave it to her husband and literary adviser, Arthur Miller. He hated it and "felt honor-bound to change her mind," said Perlman. "Arthur controlled her thinking process. He was leading her down the path of great American culture. He wanted her to be more than just the sex symbol he married. He sent back word to Paddy and me that very definitely we were not to make this movie. In his wrath I was sure he was going to challenge Paddy to a duel, and me second. He also spoke to friends of mine, asking how I could be involved in something that was so injurious to this innocent little lady."

Marilyn Monroe and Arthur Miller were not the only ones opposed to the making of *The Goddess*. At one point, Chayefsky and Perlman were without a studio. When they submitted the idea to Jack Cohn, the head of Columbia Pictures on the East Coast, he was all for it. Then his brother, Harry, president of the studio in California, tried to persuade Chayefsky and Perlman to drop the project. "He did not want us to make the picture," said Perlman. "He thought it was a diatribe against the motion picture business, that we were biting the hand that feeds us. Paddy explained that what we were trying to do was make a movie depicting the horror of the success drive in society."

At one point in their discussions Cohn said to Chayefsky, "This Rita dame in the story, it's *my* Rita, isn't it?" referring to his studio's all-time great sex goddess, Rita Hayworth. "Cohn also thought we were putting down the studio concept, and him personally," Perlman said with humor, "when actually it could have been any studio. But it *was* his studio and Paddy did model the mogul in his script on him."

Cohn never gave Chayefsky or Perlman a firm answer. "He didn't say yes or no," said Perlman. "However, in Hollywood, he was surrounded with opinion makers. One of which was this lady who worked with him, Lillian Burns. He sent her to New York to speak to us."

Dubbed "Tinkerbell" by an earlier boss, Cecil B. De Mille, because she was "fierce and faithful and small," Burns had been in show business a long time. As a talent counselor at MGM, she had molded and tutored such budding goddesses as Lana Turner, Ava Gardner, and Elizabeth Taylor. "Speak low and develop a thinking heart" was Burns's opening advice to starlet Kim Novak when Burns went to Columbia Pictures in 1955 with her husband, the director George Sidney. Her side duties included evaluating scripts for Harry Cohn. "She read for him," said Perlman, "because I don't think Harry knew how to read." When Burns came to the script of *The Goddess,* which could have been about Lana or Ava or any of her precious former wards, she swooped into Cohn's office and declared the script "disgraceful."

Dispatched to New York to meet with Chayefsky and Perlman, Burns "went on and on about what she and Mr. Cohn disliked about the script," said Perlman. "Until finally Paddy said, 'Just what did you find so objectionable about it? After all, it's a legitimate theme, highly critical of the success drive.' And she came back with 'Well, we think . . .' which made Paddy rise to his feet. 'Who the hell are you to *think?*' he said. And he began this long harangue, finishing up with, 'And you can go back to California and tell Harry Cohn that he can go fuck himself.' "

After that the independent producers decided to offer the script to Arthur Krim and Max Youngstein at United Artists. They had done *Marty* and *Bachelor Party* and had financed a recent bold attack on Hollywood, *The Big Knife,* which made Chayefsky think they would have the guts to make his picture.

By 1991 Arthur Krim's recall of any particulars was vague. "*The Goddess?* Was that the movie about Marilyn Monroe?" he asked. "I have a feeling we would have not wanted to get into that. Because you know, I was working very closely with the Kennedys and I knew Marilyn Monroe very well. In fact her last public appearance was at our house. She came with Jack and Bobby after the president's birthday party in Madison Square Garden. We were very fond of Marilyn. She was a lovely person."

Max Youngstein said that he also considered Monroe "a dear friend," and that there were things in Chayefsky's script that he didn't appreciate. "I didn't like the approach. So I turned it down," said Youngstein.

Milton Perlman disputed this. "UA wanted to do it. Absolutely. We had discussions with Arthur Krim and with Max Youngstein. Max said, 'Hey, look—am I going to give you a bid which you'll take back to Columbia and it'll bounce back and forth?' "

"Paddy played those games very well," Youngstein concurred. "You could expect that from him."

"And that's what happened." said Perlman. "Harry Cohn called and said, 'We hear you're talking to UA.' Paddy said, 'Things are free at this point, aren't they?' Harry said, 'Hell no! You have a contract with us for two pictures. We're not going to let you break that. And how could you think we'd desert you?' [Laughter] Then after we signed with him, he tried to change the script—desperately. He was a strange fellow, very crude. He had no understanding of what we were trying to do."

With Marilyn Monroe a definite no, Chayefsky and Perlman had to find an actress to play the goddess. The budget of $500,000 could not accommodate a Hollywood glamour queen, which was all right, "because most of 'em can't act anyway," said Paddy.

In New York, the performers considered were Lee Remick, Carroll Baker, and Piper Laurie. Remick was ruled out as too young and wholesome. Baker reportedly read the Chayefsky script and wanted the part, but her studio, Warner Bros., was releasing Monroe's *The Prince and the Showgirl* and gave Chayefsky the excuse that they needed Baker to play the Diana Barrymore role in *Too Much, Too Soon.* Piper Laurie, having fled a jejune starlet's career in Hollywood a short time before, was in New York and agreed to read for the producers. "She was excellent," said Perlman. "We came very close to signing her. But Paddy kept stalling."

"Paddy wrote himself into a corner," said the film's publicist, Johnny Friedkin. "He wrote a part for the most beautiful girl in the world, who also had to be the best actress. Obviously he had written it with Marilyn Monroe in mind, but when she wouldn't do it, he had to make up his mind in the final casting. What did he go for, the looks or the ability?"

In February 1957, while Piper Laurie waited to hear, another strong candidate emerged, Kim Stanley. A leading star of the Actors Studio at that time, Stanley's awesome talent elicited exalted, lasting praise from those who saw her work. "She was the most brilliant and unforgettable stage performer of our generation," said J. P. Miller. "A truly heroic actress," said director Joseph Anthony. "She inhabits a dilemma and fills it with bountiful humanity. I don't know for whom she plays—her father maybe . . . maybe God . . . but she isn't just performing for the people in the house."

Of Irish, Cherokee, German, and English stock, Stanley was raised in New Mexico and Texas, shuttled between parents who were legally separated. In school she acted in plays and wrote "turgid poetry," but most of the time, she said, "I simply counted. I counted everything: leaves on trees, pickets on fences, cracks in pavements, in a kind of contained rage. I did it in anger and out loud to hear my voice, to be sure that I was real." At twenty, armed with a bachelor of arts degree in psychology, Stanley turned her attention toward acting. In New York she studied with Curt Conway, whom she married, then joined Lee Strasberg's studio on West Forty-fourth Street. In 1954, after appearing on Broadway in *The House of Bernarda Alba*, she asked to read for the role of Millie, the thirteen-year-old tomboy in William Inge's *Picnic*. She was told that at twenty-nine she was too mature for that part. Swiping one of her infant daughter's diapers to bind her breasts, she showed up for the audition and got the role. Two years later she was given the lead in another Inge play, *Bus Stop*. Broadway was hers after that opening, and among the stars and notables that flocked to see the play was Marilyn Monroe. Actually, Marilyn went a few times, but never backstage to compliment the cast. "She must have been embarrassed," said Stanley when she learned that the superstar intended to play her part in the movie version.

Because Monroe got to do *Bus Stop* on the silver screen, there were those who said it was only professional justice that Stanley would play Marilyn in Paddy Chayefsky's sensational script *The Goddess*. Her decision had nothing to do with vengeance, the actress replied. Other scripts had been offered, but she chose *The Goddess* because it was the first one that interested her. "I'd be a fool to turn this one down," she said. "It's not any slice-of-life. The character delineation reaches out—in places it's like O'Neill."

One major deterrent stood in the way of Kim Stanley's playing the role, namely Milton Perlman, Chayefsky's partner. Because of Stanley's Junoesque looks, he felt that the concept of the movie would be changed drastically. "Kim was an exceptional actress, but she was not a sex goddess," said Perlman. "The part called for a young animal. It had to be someone like Marilyn Monroe, who aroused the animal instinct in everyone. The electricity in the script came from this. The story was about this neglected young girl who becomes sexually active when she's sixteen or seventeen. The fever begins then and you build from that. That's what *The Goddess* was all about."

Perlman also raised the matter of Stanley's age to Chayefsky. She was thirty-two and looked it. So how could they get away with her playing a sixteen-year-old? "This is the *movies!*" Chayefsky answered. Stanley was going to lose weight, and a good cinematographer would do the rest.

Her age and looks taken into account, Chayefsky had also been cautioned that Stanley was not easy to work with. Professionally and privately she was as tortured as Marilyn Monroe. Said to be inhabited with "a terrifying tension . . . something like a high C held too long," Stanley did not take to fame kindly. Her bouts with melancholia and alcohol were well known. "Kim was very neurotic, very self-destructive," said George Baxt. "We both went to the same husband-and-wife psychiatrist. She was always trying to commit suicide, by putting her head in the gas oven, then later telling everyone in town about it. She tried it one night, shoved her head in the oven, and the next day when I arrived for my session she was sitting in the outer office, waiting for her shrink. I was silent, until finally she looked at me and said, 'Well, say something!' I said, 'Kim, why don't you put a phone in your oven?' She stomped out. And that was that."

The "work" was everything to Stanley, and hers was a life-or-death approach to acting. Akin to Marilyn Monroe, whose unique luminosity on the screen was often achieved through arduous retakes and through physical and psychological turmoil for herself and others on the set, Kim Stanley was also prone to serving up hell with her art. During the out-of-town tryouts of *Bus Stop,* her director and friend, Harold Clurman, said he aged twenty years trying to restrain the actress's insecurities offstage. On opening night, she checked in before the performance covered in perspiration and with a temperature of 104 degrees. Literally pushed on the stage by Clurman, "She was superb as usual and well enough after the performance to go out with friends." Other unusual symptoms appeared throughout the run of *Bus Stop, Show* magazine reported. "She would turn purple, her temperature would go up, her eyes would disappear. She was magnificent once she got there, but oh, the struggle to get her onstage." Watching her throw up in the wings one night, her co-star, the talented, no-nonsense Elaine Stritch, briskly admonished, "Honey, save that shit for the Actors Studio. O.K.?"

Paddy Chayefsky held firm with his choice of Kim Stanley to play the lead in *The Goddess.* Only a major star of the theatre would have the dramatic ability to bring his momentous script to life on the screen, he felt. He also told Milton Perlman that they had a formidable ally in their corner, one who would assist them in restraining and guiding the actress when needed. This was his old friend Curt Conway, who was also Stanley's ex-tutor and current husband.

During the out-of-town tryouts for *Bus Stop*, Conway was frequently recruited when the actress became too distraught. "Harold Clurman would call Curt, who would fly up to Boston or wherever the show was playing," said Martin Landau. "When that happened I would have to take over his acting class. Apparently, Curt was the only one who knew how to control and calm her down."

To ensure his help on *The Goddess*, Chayefsky gave Conway a supporting role in the picture. With that in place, he told his lawyer to prepare a contract. Kim Stanley was going to play the lead in *The Goddess*. Informed of this, Milton Perlman said he felt the project was doomed. "It was the beginning of the end for the movie," he said, "and for our partnership."

Paddy the Producer

Chayefsky said that early on, when he had Marilyn Monroe in mind to star in *The Goddess,* he spoke to Elia Kazan about directing. In 1992, Kazan claimed he had never considered directing either the movie or Monroe. "No, never. I wouldn't have directed Marilyn," said Kazan. "I liked *The Goddess,* very much. Paddy and I spoke about other things, in general, but not *The Goddess.*"

"Kazan wouldn't do it," said Milton Perlman. "He would never be subservient to Paddy. We spoke to a few other people, then Bobby Sanford suggested John Cromwell." A courteous, patient man of flair and humor, Cromwell was an accomplished director of "women's pictures." His credits of the 1930s and '40s included *Of Human Bondage,* with Bette Davis, and *Since You Went Away,* with Claudette Colbert and Jennifer Jones. In 1949, after completing the all-female prison drama *Caged,* Cromwell was "gray-listed" for his political leanings. With no further work available in Hollywood, he moved to New York to resume his career as an actor and director. In 1953, when *Fifth from Garibaldi* was optioned by the Playwrights Company, he and Chayefsky met to discuss his staging the play. "Then Paddy changed his mind," said Cromwell. "He said he no longer liked the play and he didn't want it produced." Four years later, apprised of Cromwell's expertise with strong actresses, Chayefsky asked him to direct *The Goddess.* "It delighted me to do it; it's a devastating portrait of the film colony, and well deserved," said Cromwell.

Two members of Elia Kazan's production team who had worked on *A Face in the Crowd* and *On the Waterfront* were also hired: George Justin, production manager, and Charles Maguire, assistant director. The two had several preproduction conferences with Chayefsky and Cromwell, the purpose of which was to lay out as tight a shooting schedule as possible, to keep the production costs to an absolute minimum. "The tenor of the conferences went something like this," said Chayefsky the producer: " 'Do we absolutely need that big Hollywood party scene? Because it will cost a fortune to construct such an elaborate set, to rent such expensive costumes, to hire two hundred extras, and to spend one whole day of shooting on this one scene.' And the answer was 'No, we don't absolutely need it.' And the scene was cut from the script." Chayefsky the writer didn't mind these cuts, because he knew that the budget was only $500,000, and anything spent over that came out of his pocket.

By early June, the script had been pared from an original draft of 140 pages to 115. The estimated shooting schedule was thirty days, which included a week of location filming outside Baltimore, Maryland, and another week of shooting in Hollywood. With the exception of some scenes to be filmed at a mansion in Beverly Hills, all of the interiors would be done on a soundstage in New York. "That endeared us to Harry Cohn," said Milton Perlman. "He wanted to have nothing to do with us or the movie."

In mid-June some minor changes were made to the script. Rita Shawn's character remained intact, although those portions of the script written with Marilyn Monroe in mind had to be altered to accommodate Kim Stanley's physical and facial differences. "She's not particularly pretty" was added to the section where the agent describes Rita Shawn's "quality of availability." Eliminated for obvious reasons was the line "She can't act"; and in the closing scene with the studio head in Act II, the mogul's lecherous appraisal of Rita was changed from "You're very sensual" to "You're a strange type, but the audience response to you has been very exciting."

On the advice of his lawyers, Chayefsky changed the profession of the two leading male characters to avoid any legal hassles with Joe DiMaggio and Arthur Miller. The ex-ballplayer became an ex-fighter named Dutch Schultz, and the brooding writer, John Tyrone, became John Tower, a brooding New York book editor.

A Columbia stock player, the athletic Lloyd Bridges, was picked to play the ex-boxer, and Steve Hill, who had recently appeared with Kim Stanley in *Clash by Night* on TV, was cast as John Tower. When the script was in an early draft, Chayefsky had considered using Ginger Rogers in the role of the mother, who was seen only in the early scenes at that stage. Later, when he elongated the time span and showed the mother as an older woman and a religious fanatic, it ruled out casting Rogers, much to her regret. "I met Paddy once, and he seemed to like my work in the movies," Rogers recalled. "There were rumors that he would offer me a role in *The Goddess.* I only wished he had, because he seemed to me to be the type of fellow whose company I would enjoy."

"If it had been Ginger as the mother and Marilyn as the daughter, we would have made twenty million dollars," said Perlman.

New York stage actress Betty Lou Holland originally read for the mother role in Chayefsky's office on Fifty-seventh Street. "At that time *The Goddess* script did not have the mother as an older woman—just the early scenes to establish the rejection of the child," said Holland. "I thought the script was brilliant, and naturally I identified with the lead character. But I knew at the time they wanted Marilyn Monroe. When Arthur Miller refused to let her do the movie, Paddy went after Kim Stanley, and he expanded the part of the mother. He called me in again and I was flattered that he trusted me to play it, because I was in my early thirties, the same age as Kim. Actually, in *Picnic,* I was her understudy."

Rounding out the cast, five-year-old Patty Duke was brought in to play the goddess as a young girl, and Joan Copeland was hired to play her aunt. The latter choice was viewed by some to be either a cynical or safe move on Chayefsky's behalf. Joan Copeland's brother was Arthur Miller, which made her Marilyn Monroe's sister-in-law.

For the later sequences, Werner Klemperer was cast as the Hollywood producer more concerned with his studio's next picture than with the mental well-being of his star. For the goddess's hawklike secretary-companion, said to be an amalgam of two members of the Monroe support-team, Natasha Lytess and Paula Strasberg, actress Elizabeth Wilson was chosen. When subsequently asked whether her character, akin to Lytess (once referred to as "my husband" by Monroe), was sexually involved with her star employer, Wilson told writer Arthur Bell, "It was implicit in the script that I was in love with the goddess character. But probably nothing happened between us."

On Monday, July 22, 1957, *The Goddess* commenced shooting in a process studio on West Fifty-fourth Street in Manhattan. Sitting in a 1949 Cadillac convertible, Kim Stanley played Emily Ann, at age sixteen, talking to a teenage boy. The publicist Johnny Friedkin recalled the difficulty of these opening shots. "This was the first movie Kim had ever done, and here she was playing a sixteen-year-old. Why Paddy decided to begin with that scene, I don't know. Kim was nervous enough without having to try to look like a teenager."

A different concern was expressed by the coproducer, Perlman. In the two months since Kim Stanley had been signed, she was supposed to be in physical training. "Kim had promised on her mother's grave that she would lose weight," he said. "This was a wonderful opportunity for her. I offered to send her to one of those health camps so she could get in shape. She didn't go. She felt her performance would be so brilliant it would overcome every physical problem."

For two hours, while the makeup and hair experts worked on Stanley,

Arthur Ornitz, the cinematographer, who would later be commended for his gritty work on *Midnight Cowboy,* struggled with gauzes and filters to make her look younger. By ten A.M. the team was ready and the first scene was shot. A reporter from the *Herald Tribune,* invited to watch the opening-day shoot, noted that as the Cadillac was being bounced up and down to simulate motion, the writer-producer, Paddy Chayefsky, "began circling the set, looking rather like a honeybear nosing out sweets." With sweat dripping off his brow, Chayefsky made bets with the grips on how many takes the scene would require. "The first take went brilliantly, with Miss Stanley going through six minutes of film without a fluff or a hesitation," the reporter wrote. "Look at that girl," Chayefsky the producer said proudly. "There's just one like her in a generation. Laurette Taylor . . . now this one. She's going to make me look very good."

Two days later, at 7:30 A.M. the *Goddess* company assembled at the Gold Medal Studios on East 157th Street in the Bronx, where the bulk of the interior scenes would be shot. Hung across the vast soundstage a sixty-foot union banner urged: LET'S KEEP 'EM IN THE EAST. Formerly the old Biograph Studio, where D. W. Griffith shot some of his early classics, the place had been bought and renovated by "two junkmen" who had not splurged on essential comforts such as air-conditioning. The spartan conditions at the studio did not bother her, Kim Stanley said later, but the lack of preparation for the work did. "I was promised three weeks' rehearsal, which turned out to be me standing in front of a camera." Steve Hill and Betty Lou Holland had a different recollection. "There were rehearsals, maybe not three weeks, but there were rehearsals," said Holland. "For the technicians and sound people," Stanley insisted. "All the performers were told was where the chairs were, where they were going to stand, which is the least important thing about acting, in my opinion."

Upon seeing the first day's rushes, Stanley asked to redo her scenes. "I knew what I was doing wrong when I saw those scenes," she said, "but by then Paddy said it was too late. There was no *time* for improvements. The *economics* of the thing prohibited that."

As the producer, Chayefsky actively limited expenses. "The production of an art film is a shoestring business, damned by haggling and skimpiness," he explained. "The lower the budget the more chance of profit, so the whole idea is to keep costs down." To get to the studio in the Bronx each day, the actors and crew were told to use public transportation. "Most everybody went by subway," George Justin said. "I doubt whether we even picked Kim up by car." Chayefsky declared that he was also forced to make sacrifices as the writer: once the picture began to shoot, he would not allow himself any major changes. Minor alterations stemming from improvisations by Kim Stanley and the other actors were allowed, within reason. "I'm as vain as can be about my relations with actors," Chayefsky stated. "If they're improvising actors, I make no fuss about their cavalier attitude towards the script, but I ask the right to choose the part of their improvisation that stays in. In some parts of *The Goddess,* Kim Stanley rose to heights of improvisation, and you know, much as I could have killed her, she had moments of magnificence."

On Monday morning, July 29, as the sets in the Bronx were being struck so they could be rebuilt for subsequent scenes, the *Goddess* company boarded a train to Maryland for a week of location shooting. In Baltimore, part of the company checked into the Hotel Emerson, while Chayefsky, Perlman, Cromwell, and the principals traveled fifteen miles farther, to Ellicott City, where the Depression and early-1940s scenes would be filmed. "That town was an incredible sight," said Steve Hill. "I don't know how they found it, but it was perfect. The homes, the streets, were right out of that early period."

A documentation of the location filming was kept by Betty Lou Holland. "Every morning we were awakened in Baltimore at six A.M.," she said. "Then after breakfast we were all piled into a bus and we drove to Ellicott City. There were no trailers or special dressing rooms for the actors to change or be made up in. The wardrobe department had taken over a little rods and reels and ammunition store, where we all had to dress and undress. We were in there with the local people, who were extras, both men and women, each scurrying to find a private corner or a spot behind the clothes rack. Eventually we had to become uninhibited about the whole thing."

On days when the sun went in or it rained, schedules were hastily rearranged. Holland was having lunch one day in the company motel when a frantic production assistant rushed in to tell her there had been a change in plans. "Because of rain they had switched the afternoon's shots inside, to a dime-store scene with my little girl, Patty Duke. Well, the dime-store scene was four years after the scene I had done that morning, so I was rushed back to M'lady's store, in a car, with Paddy Chayefsky giving me new lines to learn with a local lady who had never acted before. After my hair was reset and I was costumed we ran down the street to the dime store, did the scene in four takes, then I was hustled back to wardrobe for the opening bus scene, where I'm 23. But my legs were swollen, I was also tired, so instead of looking young and pretty, I'm sure I looked 102."

The pressures of time and lack of continuity eventually ignited an open war between Kim Stanley and Chayefsky. "Obviously the fault was mine," the actress said with lingering, unconcealed bitterness twenty years later to film historian John Kobal. "I was limited by my own lack of knowledge and technique in the medium. Maybe Marlon Brando and Shirley Booth can do it, but I could not get used to playing a 16-year-old girl one day, a woman of 35 the next, and then in the following take become 21. I lost the continuity."

"Kim had her problems, as everybody knows," said Charles Maguire. "But she was there all the time, and like most good stage actors she always had her lines and movements prepared. And being a stage actress, she found the process of filmmaking very difficult." Betty Lou Holland said she wasn't aware of Stanley's being unhappy. "She was working so hard all the time. At one point she said to me, 'Boy, they really earn it!' Meaning that making movies wasn't easy."

According to Steve Hill, director John Cromwell wasn't too helpful. "He never spoke a lot, or communicated, or explained too much. It was almost like he was concentrating on the camera part of it, making sure we hit our marks. Kim and I talked a lot about that. It wasn't a smooth experience for either one of us. There wasn't much input in terms of interpretation, or delivery, or anything in terms of acting."

Stanley said later that Cromwell was "the last of the great gentlemen. But Paddy would not let him do his work." According to Marie Kenny, the continuity supervisor, it was a codirecting job, between Chayefsky and Cromwell. "And Paddy was not as overt about it. I think he and John had a lot of discussions offstage, before we started shooting, and then John would take over."

"Cromwell was just an old, good, solid motion-picture director," said Johnny Friedkin. "The question one could ask was Why did Paddy hire him?"

The opinion of outsiders was that Chayefsky hired Cromwell because he knew film. "Cromwell could take care of the camera part of it, and Paddy could direct the actors, that's what I was told," said Martin Landau. "At the same time, Steve Hill was giving tips to Kim Stanley. So she had directions coming from Cromwell, from Paddy, and from Steve. To say the least that confused her, especially since this was her first movie."

On Thursday, August 1, the picnic scene, where the desperate Emily Ann (Stanley) pleads with the young soldier-writer (Steve Hill) to marry her, was filmed in a field outside Ellicott City. Lying on the ground beside them and the director was Paddy Chayefsky, giving the couple his points on the scene. "Don't beg so much," he told Stanley, "just let him know he'll be getting a good deal." "I'd make you a good wife. I swear I would. You'll never be sorry. Never," says Emily Ann.

It was "nitpicking," said Marie Kenny when critics later carped that Stanley was too old in those scenes. "It never bothered me because Kim *acted* so young. In one scene I was so enthralled with her acting that when she stopped and asked me something, about where her hands were supposed to be when she picked up the shot, I had no idea of what she was talking about. In all my years on movie sets that's the only time that happened."

When the time approached for Stanley to play the goddess in mental decline, thick clouds of dissent began to hover over the location set. A conscientious and dedicated artist, Stanley was never one to "wing" a performance. She steadfastly embraced the tenet of the Actors Studio, that an actor had to live a part, not merely act it. Disinclined to rely on instinct when preparing a role, as Chayefsky did with his writing, Stanley's research was prodigious. For background and character insight, she would visit libraries and museums, study paintings, photographs, people—their movements, gestures, and patterns of speech—not for the purpose of imitation but for essence and assimilation. In 1953, when Harold Clurman reviewed her performance as the thirteen-year-old girl in *Picnic,* he said that her speech reflected some of Marlon Brando's vocal mannerisms. Stanley angrily told Clurman that these were *not* mannerisms. She was attempting to act as if "the character was wearing braces on her teeth." Once, when *Bus Stop* was playing on the road, shortly before Stanley was to enter for a scene where she was to register chill she was seen wandering outside in an alley without her coat in 15 degree weather.

During the rehearsals for the funeral scene, where Rita Shawn shows up drunk and tries to throw herself into her mother's grave, screaming "I want to die, I want to die," Stanley said she felt like she was "shooting pool in the dark." She had no intellectual understanding of the hopelessness and utter despair her character was feeling. The creator and writer, Chayefsky, was not forthcoming with help. "He never spoke in any depth about the characters we were playing," said Steve Hill. "He always spoke about what the 'concept' was. But an actor cannot play a concept."

Chayefsky was being deliberately evasive, reluctant to talk about the goddess character because of Marilyn Monroe, whose real-life misfortunes were making headlines at that time. During the second week in August, when *The Goddess* company was rehearsing the funeral scenes in Maryland, Monroe was rushed to a hospital on Long Island, New York, suffering from depression and an overdose of Nembutal. On the set of *The Goddess* the unit's still photographer took a picture of Chayefsky and John Cromwell reading a newspaper with a front page headlining the star's latest affliction. The look on Chayefsky's face in the photograph (which he would later have framed and hung on a wall in his New York office) was one of concern. His solicitude toward Marilyn was undoubtedly equaled by his concern for the state of his production. What if she died *before* his film was completed?

Monroe rallied and Chayefsky remained silent about any link between her and his movie, which made Kim Stanley more curious. When she first read the script, she said, she did not think of Marilyn Monroe. "Somebody more like Jayne Mansfield occurred to me . . . any number of people like that, who've had tragic private lives." Posing for publicity portraits that would be used as background ambience in the movie, Stanley said she did borrow some of Marilyn's patented mannerisms, the "wet lips and a come-on look. But it's a routine business, and Marilyn does it better than most."

In Maryland, growing increasingly frustrated about the character she was playing, Stanley spoke to her co-star Joan Copeland, Monroe's sister-in-law. Referring to the script, Copeland told Stanley that "Arthur wanted Marilyn to sue." Determined to settle the question of whether or not her role was based on Monroe, Stanley sent a note to Chayefsky. "I got his message back saying it wasn't Marilyn," she said. "And he was so adamant about it. I wondered if it *was!*"

At that point the filming schedule began to slow down considerably. The last scenes scheduled for Maryland were also the final ones in the movie. After collapsing at her mother's funeral, the disoriented and distraught Rita Shawn is put to bed in her mother's house. There, she is visited by her ex-husband, who pleads with her to see their young daughter, who is waiting outside on the street. Rita refuses this request and sinks deeper into despondency. Kim Stanley, a devoted mother, could not understand this cruel rejection of a child. Also, the Marilyn Monroe she knew and heard about at the Actors Studio was not like this. "Anyone who had any largeness of spirit loved Marilyn," Stanley insisted, begging Chayefsky to allow her to "insert some moments of lightness" into her performance. "I kept thinking that girl was so hopeless—she should at least *try* to be happy."

But Chayefsky refused to change the bleak nature of his character, or the script. It was frozen, perfect, he said. "That bugged the hell out of me," said Stanley. "He wanted to prove he was 'an epic writer,' and I'm quoting now. These are words I've heard from his mouth. It was one thing for Paddy to write a script he considers meaningful, but it was something else for him to stand there on the set *telling* us that every day. And whether the character was taken from Rita Hayworth, or a combination of Marilyn and Rita and all the other people who were unfortunate in Hollywood, you can't tell me those girls didn't have a good time! *Don't* tell me that! I know both of them had a terrific sense of humor."

Consistent with the minuscule budget, only one week of filming had been scheduled for Maryland. "We were supposed to leave that Sunday," said Betty Lou Holland. "But for whatever reasons that developed we stayed over for a second week." The blame lay with Kim Stanley, Chayefsky believed. Once the actress thought that he was inhibiting and/or impairing her work, he became "the enemy." The distrust led to delays and further animosity, with Chayefsky aggravating the situation by bluntly telling her during one private meeting that her real problem was with "the bottle!"

The situation between Chayefsky and Stanley became "frightening," said Milton Perlman, adding that Chayefsky was not without error in the matter. "Paddy had that great complex about proving himself all the time. His impatience and frustration created an atmosphere that wasn't easy to work with."

"He was a talented but tough little guy," said George Justin, "with a big ego. His experience as a playwright made him a god, and he carried that into the movie world."

As an actress, Kim Stanley was also deified, and rightly so, said Perlman. "No one can dispute that her talent was extraordinary. But she was a very emotional creature, irresponsible. She had this grudge against the world, about life, about living. She screamed at me one day, 'You never wanted me for this part!' Which was true, but I also told her I respected her as an artist and hoped she would do a bang-up job."

The shoot was four days behind schedule when Chayefsky took an evening flight to La Guardia Airport, in New York. His mission was to bring back Curt Conway, Stanley's husband.

But when Conway learned of the problems, he told Chayefsky he wanted nothing more to do with his wife or her career. "Their marriage was on and off all the time," said Martin Landau. Shortly before *The Goddess* began filming there had been a party to celebrate the couple's reconciliation. "It was on the East Side and seventy-five or eighty people showed up," Landau recalled. "It was supposed to be a festive occasion, but in front of everyone they began to argue. It was the worst fight they ever had and it literally ended their relationship." When told of the details of the marriage's demise, Chayefsky sympathized with Conway and no longer pressed for his help. He would deal with the problems on *The Goddess* on his own.

On August 8, Chayefsky returned to Baltimore. The onus of seeing the production through was now solely on his shoulders, as Perlman had departed, saying he wanted nothing further to do with the "unpleasantness" between Chayefsky and Stanley. On the way back to the location, determined to catch up, get back on schedule, and finish the film, Chayefsky proceeded to cut pages from the script "which were not dramatically vital." As for his star, when Chayefsky arrived back in Ellicott City he composed a legal brief in which he informed Stanley that if there were any more delays he would shut the picture down and the responsibility for putting the other actors and the crew out of work would be hers. As the producer, he could not afford "to spend any more time arguing with the lead actress for a more profound insight to her acting, or with the cameraman to give us a more exquisite shadowed mood in the lighting," he commented later. "The point was that no 'art film' was half as good as it should be. An art film must be low-budget, and low-budget means you sacrifice some art."

On August 12, shooting resumed at the Gold Medal Studios in the Bronx. A four-page scene in which Rita Shawn, up-and-coming Hollywood star, was seen "buoyant and hysterically gay" surrounded by her friends in a bar was reduced to one page. Leaving out "the comedic stuff" broke Stanley's heart, she said, "because nobody doesn't try to laugh once in a while. I mean, even Hamlet had some lines of humor."

Stanley claimed that as a hard-nosed producer Chayefsky also tried to further sabotage her confidence. "He would come in in the morning and say, 'I saw the rushes last night, and they were terrible.' And I said, 'When are we going to reshoot them?' He said, 'We're not.' And this was the beginning of the day. It's terribly stupid because it's awful hard, even with willpower, to get that out of your head."

The tension and boredom were "piling up like banana peels in a monkey cage," said writer Helen Dudar, detailing the shooting of one scene for the *New York Post*. The leading lady was becoming fretful; the ever-present author was turning into a nag. For perhaps the twentieth time, Stanley as Rita Shawn prepared to light a cigarette, the key prop for the scene being filmed. "With a persistence by now beyond count," wrote Dudar, "Paddy Chayefsky, author of *The Goddess*, and director by reason of anxiety rather than appointment, repeated, 'Now remember there should be a lot of smoke. I want more smoke.'" Stanley then announced that unless Chayefsky left the set she would not continue to perform. Chayefsky left. The work resumed. Stanley settled down to light the cigarette once more. "Suddenly from high above the scenery, where Chayefsky was perched, came a voice, 'Now remember, more smoke. More smoke!'"

As the tasty word of the tempest spread through the corridors and watering holes of Manhattan, the requests to visit the *Goddess* set poured in from other members of the press. One such request came from Lillian Ross, who had written a remarkable series for *The New Yorker* on the disasters and ego wars that surrounded the making of John Huston's *The Red Badge of Courage*. "That also became a best-selling book," said publicist Johnny Friedkin. "And now she wanted to take another insider's stab on the making of *The Goddess*. I told her, 'Miss Ross, I know your work, and I enjoy reading it, but regarding Paddy Chayefsky and Kim Stanley, if you think I'm going to allow these two people to be set up and destroyed by you—because basically they both have self-destructive tendencies—you're out of your goddamn mind.' I also told her if she came up to the studio she wasn't going to get in. The woman could be a killer. She was the type of writer who would say very sweetly to Paddy, 'Oh, Mr. Chayefsky, tell me how does the camera work?' She would quote Paddy, and Kim, and they'd come out looking like assholes."

On Sunday, September 1, one week behind schedule, the *Goddess* company went to California for the final week of shooting. "The crew consisted of our cameraman, his assistant, a grip, an electrician, the soundman and myself," said Charles Maguire, the assistant director. "Nobody had ever done that before. Hollywood always went on location, but no one ever went on location to Hollywood."

After shooting in the Polo Lounge and the lobby of the Beverly Hills Hotel, the company moved to Grauman's Chinese Theatre. On days three and four the unit took over a mansion in Beverly Hills, where Rita Shawn, psychotic superstar, resided. "The place we rented belonged to Noah Dietrich, an associate of Howard Hughes," said Maguire. "It had a pool and there was a sliding roof over the living area, which facilitated the filming."

"My one memory of that shoot," said Marie Kenny, the continuity supervisor, "is that on the morning we were driving to the house, Paddy was telling us a story about Harry Cohn. The rumor at the studio was that Cohn had Kim Novak's dressing room bugged. We were riding along in one of Columbia's cars, and in the middle of Paddy's story, we heard a loud clunk, followed by a terrible scraping sound. Something had fallen out of the bottom of the car. It was almost as if Cohn was listening and pushed a button. We stopped dead on the road, and Paddy said something to the effect that Cohn probably had our car wired too."

At the mansion, preparing for her scenes as the elderly mother, who is there to care for her movie-star daughter after her nervous breakdown, Betty Lou Holland made notes of her character's situation. "This is the first time the mother has seen her daughter in eight years," Holland wrote. "She is not there because the thing is to be there. It's her Christian duty." The daughter must be saved, so the mother "gives her the only thing she knows anything about—her religion."

On Thursday afternoon, the street outside the mansion in Beverly Hills was closed off for shooting the scene in which Rita, having lost her faith in God, screams at her mother for deserting her once more. "Nothing I do pleases you," Kim Stanley yelled viciously from the front door as Betty Lou Holland exited to a waiting cab. "All you know is to run off on me. I hate you so much. You never cared whether I lived or died. I never want to see you again, not even in your grave. I hope your heart just explodes. I hope you die."

Watching the scene from an adjacent lawn was the Hollywood columnist Sidney Skolsky, who was astonished at Stanley's precise performance. "What's the movies coming to when an actress does it perfect on her first try?" Skolsky asked Chayefsky. "She's the greatest," Chayefsky said. "Difficult. Wants things her way, but compromises when she realizes her way isn't always best."

Stanley agreed to do an interview with Skolsky, in which she said she wasn't buying the hype she was hearing about the movie. The words "great" and "brilliant" were being used too loosely, she said. "They keep telling me that when I see the picture with music, I'll love it. But I felt like an amateur. It was only as we approached this last week that I began to feel as if I belonged." Of the town itself, Stanley said Hollywood was "a fantasy place, with pink houses and weird architecture. It's charming all right, but it's only for children."

On Friday night, after a final scene on a Columbia soundstage was filmed, the wrap party was held at Trader Vic's. When informed that the movie had come in at a mere $25,000 over budget, and had taken only thirty-five days to shoot, Chayefsky came back with "Thirty-five days? It seemed more like thirty-five years to me."

"A Real Octopus, That Man"

Actually, as far as production went,
I was a meddler. I meddled from one end
of the business to the other.

Paddy Chayefsky, 1958

When filming of *The Goddess* was completed, Chayefsky proceeded to spend another ten months editing, marketing, and publicizing the film. In New York, Carl Lerner, who had edited *Red River* and *Twelve Angry Men*, worked for seven weeks on the footage of *The Goddess* with John Cromwell. Their first cut of two hours and forty minutes was pruned by half an hour and shown to Chayefsky and the executives of Columbia Pictures. Columbia suggested further trimming, reasoning that theatres in the major cities would not book any film over two hours long. Chayefsky went along with this. "The producer of an art film that does not make a profit will not be given the chance to produce any more films, art or otherwise, and a lot of good his esthetics will do him then," he said. But Cromwell, after viewing the film again with Carl Lerner, said that any further cuts would harm the film considerably. He and Chayefsky discussed the matter heatedly. "We started arguing so much that I just walked out," said Cromwell. " 'All right,' I told him. 'If you want to cut the picture, do it yourself.' It was a foolish thing to do because Paddy did not know the first thing about the technique of motion pictures."

Milton Perlman's account differed from Cromwell's. "Paddy didn't cut the movie on his own. He continued working with Carl Lerner. Carl was a very good editor, very patient, the only man I had known who could handle Paddy. He was married to a German psychiatrist."

Lerner knew that he couldn't go after someone like Chayefsky frontally, but had to go around him. "And that's what he did, very discreetly," said Perlman. Their cut came in at two hours and five minutes. Then Columbia, with an eye to the eventual release on the wider theatrical circuit, said the film could not be put on a double bill unless it was shortened further. They suggested that

Chayefsky cut the entire funeral sequence, "because pictures with funeral scenes don't sell." While insisting on keeping that segment, Chayefsky agreed to trim within the "long-winded soliloquies," and some of the peripheral characters. Another twenty minutes were excised from Act II and from the Hollywood scenes to "achieve popular pace, and to avoid a sagging epic," Chayefsky told critic Archer Winsten; but at one hour and forty-five minutes, *The Goddess* was still "a major work."

The musical scoring by Virgil Thomson helped fill in some of the gaps, Betty Lou Holland believed. "It underscored the haunting despair of the goddess, and the loneliness of the mother, wandering around her daughter's big Hollywood mansion," she said.

When the film was ready to be seen, Johnny Friedkin set up a screening for Kim Stanley and *Life* magazine, which was doing a feature on her. After seeing the picture, Stanley left the screening room in tears. This was *not* the movie she had agreed to do. "More than an hour was cut, mostly the transitions and gayer moments," she exclaimed, putting all the blame on Chayefsky. Editing was an art form of its own. "It's a craft and a discipline that has *nothing* to do with playwrighting," she said.

After promising her agent and Columbia that she would not bad-mouth the movie, Stanley told another reporter that the film looked "as if it were in its second week of rehearsals," and that she was so bad she wanted "to crawl out of the screening room in embarrassment." The reporter, obviously taken with the film and her strong performance, asked her whether she would change her opinion if the reviews were positive. "Of course not," said Stanley. "You have to have a standard of your own. What matters is how you feel."

Milton Perlman didn't believe it was her performance or the eliminated scenes that upset Stanley; it was the shock of seeing how she looked on the big screen. "The camera is a wicked thing. And Kim never accepted the responsibility that she was supposed to be at her peak at all times. Both she and Paddy had assumed that her art, her performance would overcome everything. Well, that does work on stage, or on the smaller screen in television, but on a movie screen, which is ten feet high and forty feet wide, the flaws can be quite obvious and fatal."

"Kim had to know in her heart of hearts that she didn't look the part," said Friedkin. "However, her acting was absolutely breathtaking. I still get chills when I think of certain scenes she did in that movie."

In January 1958, when Walter Winchell told his readers that "Kim Stanley hates *The Goddess,* and refuses to publicize it, although it's an odds-on favorite to bring her an Oscar nomination," Chayefsky knew that he would have to promote the movie on his own. In a lengthy article he wrote for *The Saturday Review* entitled "Art Films—Dedicated Insanity," and in an interview with

Variety, he predicted that *The Goddess* "will be a great picture, a classic," then proceeded to rap the movie industry for its outdated selling methods. "Nobody knows how to sell these days—the exhibitors, the studio don't know what they're dealing with," he said. "You can't advertise a picture as 'for perverts only' and sell the public. That doesn't work today."

"Paddy is an expert in everything," a theatre figure told the reporter Helen Dudar. "You'll find he has an expertise in directing, selling, photography, promotion, sales—everything it takes other people fifteen or twenty years to learn. A real octopus, that man. He has to have a hand in everything."

In February 1958, "more disaster" struck. Just as plans were under way to distribute the film, Harry Cohn, the president of Columbia, died of a heart attack. His brother, Jack, had died the year before, so now Chayefsky was left without anybody to yell at in the company. "They were tough characters, but they got things done," said Johnny Friedkin. The remaining members of the executive staff, according to Chayefsky, were "banging their heads on the boardroom table, wailing, 'What'll we do? What'll we do?' They don't know sales or movies from a hole in the ground."

The Columbia sales staff did know enough about "big" pictures, such as *The Bridge on the River Kwai,* which was raking in a fortune for the company. But with his smaller film, they told Chayefsky they couldn't find a theatre in New York that would show it. This was because all the small houses were booked with Brigitte Bardot films and English comedies. They also said the title of his movie was too obtuse, like something out of Greek mythology. Among the new titles they suggested were: *Shoot for the Stars, The Beautiful Nothing, One Sin, Her Sin, My Sin,* and *Lovers Are Losers.*

His title must remain, Chayefsky insisted. He then took on the added responsibility of booking the movie himself. It was his idea to open *The Goddess* "like a play, out of town." Ben Sack, who owned four movie theatres in Boston, was a personal friend of his. A colorful, unorthodox salesman, Sack had made a lot of money when he booked *Marty* in two of his theatres. When contacted about *The Goddess,* Sack told Chayefsky he would be honored to be the one chosen to open it. "Boston has never had a world premiere," Sack told his local press, "but they'll know they have one when I get through."

April 16 was the date set for Boston, with openings in Baltimore and Philadelphia scheduled for the following week. In the ads and posters, Columbia's merchandising department took a salient approach toward the film. THE PUBLIC DISROBING OF A GENERATION, their ad copy read, featuring a distraught but sensuous Kim Stanley in a nightgown, clutching a bedpost in desperation. At the bottom left, adding public identification and literary significance, appeared a sketch of Paddy Chayefsky sitting at a table pounding away at his typewriter. And with it, presumably to convey humility or add a further scholarly touch, the inscription "written expressly for the movies by paddy chayefsky" appeared in lower case.

A GALA WORLD PREMIERE! the Boston papers announced a week before the official opening, promising ∗TELEVISION ∗MUSIC ∗LIGHTS∗ CELEBRITIES∗ and a marching band. On April 13, three days before the opening, Chayefsky arrived for a blitz of promotion arranged by Sack. Breakfasts, luncheons, and dinners were scheduled with the TV, radio, and print media, along with a question-and-answer symposium scheduled at Harvard University. "No theatrical writer has been so warmly greeted, or so widely quoted, since Sean O'Casey stormed into town some years ago to defend *Waiting at the Gates* when it was banned in Boston," columnist Elliott Norton declared.

At Harvard, the night before the premiere, Chayefsky confided to the university's drama teachers and students that he had received a nasty letter from Arthur Miller, "who had erroneously assumed that *The Goddess* was based on the life of his wife, Marilyn Monroe." Miller was the best of the current playwrights, Paddy added, "if he can shake off his sense of writing for posterity."

The following day, *The Boston Globe* printed an account of Chayefsky's evening at Harvard, along with his comments on the New York critics' abuse of power. "Writers suffer more from the nine incompetents—who are usually drunk—than they would from the most violent personal onslaught" was the quote used. "Complete fiction. I've never seen a drunken critic in my life," Paddy roared in his reply to the *Globe* editor, denying he ever said such a thing. In New York, days later, *Variety* covered the entire commotion, calling it "Chayefsky's Boston Brannigan," while in another section of the trade paper, the movie reviewer gave his assessment of *The Goddess:* "Semipoetic semirealistic melodrama . . . may have exploitation values, if hurried to market." Chastising Chayefsky for attempting to break "the jinx" of doing movies about Hollywood ("they have a reputation of being slow at the box office"), the *Variety* critic said the writer was also "guilty of the bogus qualities" with which he charged the Celluloid City. "It would have been a better story," the critic opined, "if Chayefsky had stuck to the Bronx instead of trying a transplant to Hollywood and Vine."

In Los Angeles the same day, the *Hollywood Reporter*'s reviewer called the film "labored, stylized, and pretentious." Chayefsky's script was at fault, that reviewer felt, jingoistically observing, "Nowhere in it do we find the touches of gallantry nor of the hard work for self-improvement which mark the life of most stars."

The trade papers aside, when the reviews from the regular critics in Boston,

Philadelphia, and Baltimore came in, they cast a much warmer light on Chayefsky's first independent production. "A tour-de-force," said the *Boston Herald*. "Magnificent . . . written by a current somewhat god of writers named Chayefsky," said the *Boston American*. "There is beauty, integrity, compassion and terrible reality in the writing," said Mildred Martin of the *Philadelphia Inquirer*.

"Most of the out-of-town reviews were raves," said Chayefsky. "But they didn't mean a damn thing, because at that point Columbia Pictures had already sold us out."

"Columbia threw the picture away," said Perlman, "before the Boston reviews were in. Instead of arranging a good booking in New York they sold the movie to a small theatre for fifteen hundred upfront for the entire length of the run. That for us was the final outrage."

"We were stuck," said Chayefsky. "The Cohns were gone. The new regime was either scared or stupid. They didn't know what to do with the movie, how to handle it. I kept telling 'em, 'Wait. Have patience. We need time for this film to break.' But they chickened out and dumped the film in this out-of-the-way theatre on the West Side of Manhattan."

"Columbia wasn't going to even release *The Goddess* in New York," said Johnny Friedkin, "but then Harold Hayes of *Esquire* published Paddy's script in its entirety in the magazine. I also got some of the New York critics to come in to see the film. They were floored by it, and that's the only reason we got an opening."

On June 24, 1958, the day after it opened at the West Fifty-fifth Street Playhouse, the New York reviews appeared. "A shattering but truly potent film," said Bosley Crowther of *The New York Times*. "Kim Stanley is brilliant. Equally fine and expressive is Betty Lou Holland. John Cromwell has beautifully directed an excellent cast that makes the film fairly quiver with emotion."

"Here is a substantial advance in the work of Chayefsky and a substantial contribution to the season's major movie dramas," said Alton Cook of the *New York Herald Tribune*. "His dialogue has acquired a new depth and clarity in expressing ideas and characters."

The following week the news magazines added their praise. "Actress Stanley triumphs!" said *Time*. And *Newsweek*, devoting a full page to its coverage, complimented the director and the cast, then said of the writer, "Chayefsky is of course the prime mover in the whole work. His satire is sometimes crude, but it has bigness and generous anger, and his too physical sense of reality is a limitation that helps to concentrate his force and sharpen his impact. At his best he has an earthy weight and vigor that suggest a more amenable Von Stroheim, a pocket Zola."

With the positive New York notices, Columbia Pictures looked like fools,

Milton Perlman said. "Within days, people were lined up around the block on Fifty-fifth Street. Paddy and I demanded that a new agreement be made with the theatre. We had a massive blow-out with sales executive Leo Jaffe."

"In the wake of excellent business and generally good reviews, Columbia is now making strenuous efforts to renegotiate its 55th St. Playhouse deal," *Variety* reported in its July 9 issue.

"Nothing happened in New York," said Perlman. "It was outrageous. Paddy and I went to the head of Columbia's sales department, who said, 'What can we do? The movie doesn't have it.' Which was bullshit. So many of the critics and audiences were going back a second and third time to see it. Everywhere I went that summer, people were talking about *The Goddess*."

"I thought it was wonderful," said Chayefsky's TV colleague, David Shaw. "Bob Aurthur saw it around the time I did. 'How did you like it?" I asked him. He said, 'I liked it so much, I had a headache for three days,' which meant that it was so good it stayed with him."

"What surprised me," said Steve Hill, "was that the first time I saw the film, I felt some of it, especially the Hollywood scenes, didn't come off. But then these great reviews came in, and it went on to become sort of a cult film, making such an impression on so many people. But I think that was more the gift of the script than the actors."

In August 1957, hoping to duplicate the success and prestige accorded *Marty* at Cannes, Chayefsky arranged for *The Goddess* to be shown at a film festival in Brussels. "It attains the purest classicism . . . a masterpiece from Paddy Chayefsky, the most intelligent writer Hollywood has been known to attract," said *La Libre Belgique* after its screening. On closing night, competing against *Raintree County, The Old Man and the Sea,* and *Touch of Evil, The Goddess* was awarded the Jury's Special Prize "for exceptional qualities."

After festivals in Berlin and Venice, Chayefsky went on to Great Britain to show the film out of competition at the Edinburgh Festival. The following week it opened at the Curzon Theatre on the West End in London. Dilys Powell, the estimable reviewer for *The Sunday Times,* said *The Goddess* was not a complete success, but a bold adventure. "It brings to the cinema, for once, analysis of character on the intellectual level of a serious contemporary novel," she said. In British *Vogue,* critic Penelope Gilliatt found the film to be "savage, overheated, given distinction by Kim Stanley's frenetic performance." There was some fraud involved in Chayefsky's story, Gilliatt felt. "The divinity is a Hollywood idol who has ludicrously been identified as Marilyn Monroe. But the woman in the film is a born drug-taker, an introvert who hasn't set foot outside her own frontal lobes for years; whereas Miss Monroe is visibly milk-fed, and stammers with excitement when she meets people."

Back in the United States, as the film continued to play to capacity audiences in only one New York theatre, Bosley Crowther, in a follow-up article in the *Times,* remarked: "How this remarkably fine picture, which has already copped an award in Brussels and may yet win a few over here, happened to land in this small theatre instead of a larger house on Broadway, is one of the lasting sagas of real goofing that its distributors would rather not recall."

In Hollywood, the once powerful and now fading boosters of the film industry Hedda Hopper and Louella Parsons shared judgment on *The Goddess.* "Is this the compassionate writer who gave us *Marty?*" Hopper asked in her column. Parsons said she hadn't seen the film, and furthermore, "I don't know of anyone who has." But the film *was* seen and appreciated in Los Angeles, especially by those with their own private screening rooms. In one of his legendary memos, David Selznick, producer of *Gone With the Wind,* urged the French author Romain Gary to see *The Goddess.* "It has many things wrong with it, particularly from a standpoint of wide popularity," said Selznick. "But it has many things in it that are brilliant too, and Chayefsky has again proved that he is one of the most original and gifted modern dramatists."

Hecht-Hill-Lancaster executive Jim Hill, who was married to Rita Hayworth by this time, recalled that the movie was booked into a small theatre in Brentwood. "Let's go see if it has anything to do with you," he said to his wife. She enjoyed the movie, but as far as reflecting her life, the sublime Hayworth said "it didn't even come close."

And what of Marilyn Monroe? What was her reaction to the movie? She was in Hollywood making *Some Like It Hot* when *The Goddess* was released, and reporters who visited the set were warned not to mention it. The writer Adela Rogers St. Johns, who had been asked by Fox to write the script of *Harlow,* inadvertently brought up the Chayefsky film. Marilyn remained silent for a spell, St. Johns reported, then in an impromptu flash of enthusiasm she whispered, "Wasn't Kim Stanley marvelous?"

That appreciation was not shared by Monroe's fellow actors. At Oscar time the following February it was deemed certain that Kim Stanley would be cited. "For her performance and her reviews, Kim should have had at least a nomination," said Johnny Friedkin, "but a publicity buildup was part of the game and Kim wasn't interested in that." Stardom meant nothing to her, her ex-husband Curt Conway agreed. "Kim can't be judged by conventional standards; her integrity from her own point of view is extraordinary. Neither you nor I would have the courage to carry out her ideals."

Paddy Chayefsky did receive an Academy Award nomination for his script. He didn't win, but he remained steadfast in his defense of the movie and in his insistence that he did not base his tragic star on Marilyn Monroe. "Jesus Christ! You too?" he yelled at this writer nearly two decades later. "The movie was *not* based on Monroe. The girl in the story came from the South. Why couldn't she be Ava Gardner?"

· "*The Goddess* isn't a Hollywood story either," Chayefsky said at the time of its release. "I wanted to say something about a condition that exists today. And this is the best way. I think *The Goddess* is one of the best things, if not *the* best thing, I ever wrote!"

CHAPTER 15

Psychiatric Assistance

I'm an arrogant, opinionated, arbitrary human being.
I'm a megalomaniac—a prima donna. But I'm never
a prima donna in the office and in discussion.

Paddy Chayefsky

In 1955, in an essay for his book of TV plays, Chayefsky commented on how many people were currently turning "into themselves, looking for personal happiness." Masses of "disturbed human beings" were flocking to psychiatrists and counseling clinics. Others were reading advice columns and books, looking for "ways of achieving personal adjustments to life," he said, neglecting to divulge that he too was in psychoanalysis and had been for some time.

Around the start of his tenure at the Philco-Goodyear show, Chayefsky considered consulting a psychiatrist, which at the time was viewed as the thing to do. This was the fifties, and many Jewish writers, artists, and the secular bourgeoisie were making a cult of psychoanalysis. Chayefsky's rationale for seeing a shrink was that it was helping him with his work, to gain more understanding of his ordinary but repressed characters. That assertion was accepted with amusement by some of his television associates, who felt that the practice of lying on a couch, talking nonstop with little or no interruption from a paid presence he could not see, was the perfect pastime for the compulsive Chayefsky. "Here was a man who couldn't or wouldn't shut up," said J. P. Miller. "In fact, Paddy was the only guy in our whole group who could outtalk me."

It was the pitch of Chayefsky's orations that impressed Robert Anderson. "He reminded me of Sam Spiegel [producer of *The African Queen*]," said Anderson. "Once I was at Spiegel's apartment in the Beverly Wilshire and Sam was standing over me screaming and yelling. I said, 'Sam, please, I can't take people yelling at me.' He said, 'I'm not yelling, I'm talking loud.' And Paddy was like that. He was screaming, but he believed he was only talking loud."

When Miller and Chayefsky were in California writing for Hecht-Hill-

Lancaster, they would sometimes go out for lunch in Miller's car. "I was the driver, with Paddy in the front seat as a backseat driver," he recalled. "He'd be talking nonstop, then give instructions. If you were coming up to a red light, he'd say, 'It's a red light! It's a red light!' I'd say, very calmly, 'Yes, I see that, Paddy.' And then we'd drive on and if I was too close to another car, he would scream at me, 'Look out, we're going to crash, we're going to crash!' " One day, Miller stopped the car in the middle of Sunset Strip. He turned to Chayefsky and said, "Listen, you son of a bitch, if you don't shut your fucking mouth, I'm throwing you out of this car and you can walk home." Chayefsky shut up for five minutes, until Miller found he missed the incessant talk. "With Paddy, that was his way of having fun. He was only happy when he was driving everyone crazy."

Others believed that some hidden trauma had prompted Chayefsky to see a psychiatrist. "Something happened that spooked Paddy," said Mike Ryan. "There was a fear there, a tenseness, a suspicion he didn't have before." The actor Alan Manson knew Chayefsky from Curt Conway's acting class in the early 1950s. "Paddy could be great fun, with a wonderful sense of theatre," said Manson. "But he was not what you'd call a natural man. There was a driven quality there. He was always sort of looking over his shoulder, as if the Furies were after him."

Success had unnerved him, said Johnny Friedkin. "It happened so fast. For him it was like winning the triple crown. He made it big on TV, in the movies, and on Broadway within a period of two years. That was a lot for anyone to handle."

"When I first clicked, I had an anti-success complex," Chayefsky remarked. "I said that I wouldn't change a bit, and I went to great trouble to prove I was the same old Joe. I learned better. I wasn't the same person I had been. We all change in time, one way or the other."

Fame when it first arrived certainly satisfied Paddy, the public persona. With each new credit and accolade, his stature and hubris increased, but in time small cracks began to appear in the fictive shield. As the outer man grew, Sidney, the inner one, felt diminished, unhappy, and at times painfully self-conscious about the charade that was being played. This was apparent from the episodes of grandiosity that were staged on occasion. During preproduction of *The Bachelor Party,* actor Philip Abbott recalled dining with the Chayefskys in the Bel Air mansion that Paddy had forced the producers to supply. During the meal, Mrs. Chayefsky, described by Abbott as "a gracious woman and a marvelous hostess," was at the head of the table and wanted to ring the floor buzzer. She was small and "had to stretch her foot way out and kind of search around the floor for it," said the actor. Noticing this, her husband exploded. "What the hell are we doing out here living in a big house with a swimming pool and buzzers for servants anyway?" Chayefsky asked.

Sometime later, in New York, Audrey Peters bumped into Chayefsky on Central Park West. "I said, 'Paddy, how are you?' And he said, 'Oh God, I've got such problems.' I became very concerned, thinking something had happened to Danny or Susie. I said, 'What's the matter, Paddy?' And he said dejectedly, 'Well, I don't know whether to go to Africa this summer or not.' And I thought, 'Oh come off it, Paddy. I remember when you would call my husband to ask if he could get you a good table at Sardi's, and what wine to order with dinner.' "

When the fame came and stayed, part of Chayefsky grew suspicious of the attention being paid. Mel and Offi Goldberg were family friends from the early 1950s and were the godparents to Chayefsky's son, Danny. "We used to have terrific fun when Paddy and Susie lived on Riverside Drive," said Mel. "We'd drive over to Palisades Park to hit baseballs. Paddy was always down-to-earth and very funny. No one could tell a story like he did. Then sometime after *Marty* and the Oscars, in the middle of one humorous discussion, he became very morose. 'People only like me because they think I'm funny,' he said. That was the first time I saw that conflict that was going on inside of him. The psychiatry began sometime after that."

His success led to introductions to various members of the Upper West Side intelligentsia. At one social gathering Chayefsky met Ernst and Marianne Kris, psychoanalysts who had been a part of Sigmund Freud's inner circle in Vienna (Marianne's father had been the Freuds' pediatrician). When they were first introduced, Ernst Kris, who was also Jewish, expressed amusement and curiosity about Chayefsky's obviously adopted first name. Paddy gave forth with his usual war yarn, and when the laughter subsided, Kris solemnly inquired after Chayefsky's "original self—Sidney." Whatever happened to him? Silence was followed by discomfort. It was a stupid question, Chayefsky later told Mike Ryan. Actors, writers, people in the arts, changed their names all the time. "So do crooks and criminals," said Ryan, which made Chayefsky even more defensive. There was nothing duplicitous about his name change, he blasted at his friend. He chose it because it had more bite and commercial appeal. But the new name hadn't altered his life or his thinking in any way.

When Chayefsky moved to Central Park West, he learned that Ernst Kris lived farther south, at number 135. Kris, who was also an art historian, had collaborated on a book entitled *Legend, Myth and Magic—The Image of the Artist,* which was one of the topics covered when the doctor and the playwright got together for what was described as "informal discussions." Among the writers discussed were Jonathan Swift and Edgar Allan Poe. Both possessed above-average intelligence and creativity, which coexisted with emotional immaturity and frequent fits of anger. Rage always gave a split person a sense of unity, of aliveness, Kris noted in a subtle preamble to Poe's short stories, in which the most striking characters grappled with dissociation and with a condition referred to as a "bi-part soul." This fragmentation, according to Freud, was due to damaged narcissism in infancy or childhood, which caused the injured self to arm itself with a tougher, more grandiose identification, usually enhanced and strengthened by an approving parent or guardian. Chayefsky apparently listened with only one ear to this hypothesis. He was more eager to push on with what he considered his priority. Because of his long-term nightmares, in which he was either being crushed or asphyxiated, he wanted to learn more about Freud's popular *Interpretation of Dreams,* which he had read in the original German during the war. Kris and Chayefsky discussed Freud's essays, but it is doubtful that they ever confronted Chayefsky's primal fears and seminal duality—which were now becoming more pronounced—because in February 1957, Ernst Kris died suddenly.

That summer of 1957, when *The Goddess* was in production, Chayefsky began to openly express concern about his anger. One particular outburst frightened him. He and his wife had been on a plane returning from California. It was night and their infant son would not stop crying. The boy was changed, and fed, then carried back and forth through the narrow aisle of the first-class section. But the baby would not stop screaming, until, losing all control, Paddy seized the child and threw him into an empty seat. "He was terrified and concerned about what he did," Dan Chayefsky said later. "He also tried to use it, in *The Goddess.*" In the scene where teenager Emily Ann Faulkner is trying to calm her newborn baby, Chayefsky instructed Kim Stanley to yell at the baby, then throw her down into her crib. But Stanley refused. It wasn't the truth, she said; she couldn't feel it.

As the writer and producer of that film, Chayefsky's anger toward Stanley, "who would never do what I told her," began to magnify and to become unsettling, even to him. "Sometimes I find myself dealing unpleasantly with people, talking to them as if they were animals," he said. "And I get physically sick. I just get sick, but it's the only way you can get things done with some people. Yet I cannot bear to humiliate them, and get twice as ogreish about it as I need be." When he was crossed, Chayefsky's entire body would tighten like steel. He'd scowl, clench his fists, glare, then the verbal avalanche would begin. "He could level armies with that tongue of his," said Mike Ryan, "if he didn't explode first, because his whole body would shake in a fit of apoplexy. For the most part, he looked like a monster child having a tantrum."

Appropriately enough, the analyst he chose to see at this time was Katharine Frankenthal, a noted child psychologist who was short, spoke with a heavy German accent, and smoked a cigar. Close to seventy, Frankenthal was a devout disciple of Freud and believed that chronic rage came from unconscious feelings of helplessness and impotence, which usually had their origins in early childhood, when true autonomy was blocked by trauma. Chayefsky willingly went along with that theory, but he offered nothing to substantiate his own case. He had no memories of any early trauma, or of any unusual anger being expressed or directed toward him. Somewhat defensive, perhaps out of loyalty to his parents, his assertion then and later was that his childhood had been normal and happy. His family was solid and nurturing, he insisted.

In an essay written for his book of TV plays, Chayefsky did divulge that in *Marty* he "ventured lightly" into such areas as the Oedipal relationship between the bachelor son and his overpossessive mother. In analysis, however, Paddy spoke only of how proud he was of his mother, how Gussie had overcome repression in Russia to educate and improve herself in America. Harry Chayefsky, his father, took up most of Chayefsky's time in the analyst's office. Chayefsky spoke about his father's humor, his music, his enjoyment of life and people, emphasizing his father's good points repeatedly, and divulging very little about his relationship with his mother. Therefore, it surprised him considerably when Dr. Frankenthal, after six months of sessions, gave her diagnostic impressions.

The notion was familiar. Chayefsky's obsessive traits of workaholism and perfectionism and his increasingly uncontrollable anger were indicative of a personality emotionally arrested at an early stage of development, Frankenthal told him. To overcome the fear and helplessness he experienced as a child, Sidney Chayefsky felt compelled to compensate. He began to rely overly on his intelligence and his communicative and performing skills. These brought attention and approval, which warded off his feelings of abandonment. A new self had emerged out of these defenses, one that served to entertain and take care of Sidney and everyone around him. In the creation of this second, superresponsible self, Sidney felt forfeited, "dehumanized." His parents compounded this misrepresentation. By encouraging the boy to believe that life's meaning lay in their and other people's approval, Sidney's true development was impeded. The realization that he was being praised and loved not as Sidney but as this other, new self sowed the first seeds of frustration. When grown, the other, dominant self, now identified as "Paddy," was less inclined to repress the feelings of frustration and rage. His tyranny, however, was directed toward outsiders rather than toward the real cause of his pain, his parents, specifically his mother, who had used him to bolster her lack of self-esteem.

After absorbing this, Chayefsky said his first reaction was to jump on top of the elderly, squat Dr. Frankenthal and throttle her lifeless. His better self prevented this. Calmly, Chayefsky told the doctor that his mother was a loving, self-made, self-reliant, intelligent, decent woman, who had more self-esteem than Sister Kenny and Eleanor Roosevelt combined, and no half-cocked quack was going to tell him otherwise. Reeling from the force of the patient's retort, the good doctor said she never meant to imply that Mrs. Chayefsky was ignoble. His mother was undoubtedly a victim of her own early oppression as a Jew in Russia and later as a woman with ambition in America. As adults, however, some parents tend to impart their own frustrated ideals, dreams, and unconscious distortions to their pliant offspring, under the guise of what's "best for the child." The inherent damage inflicted by this process always leads to subsequent anger and to redress on the part of the emotionally abused child, which was why Chayefsky deep down wanted revenge on the one who unconsciously oppressed that critical primary stage of his life, his mother.

With barely contained fury, Chayefsky walked out on that session with Dr. Frankenthal. A few weeks later he returned after she "apologized," he told his son. Their sessions continued indefinitely but were eventually ruptured anew when Frankenthal trespassed on another area that Chayefsky was particularly sensitive about—his sexuality. As a staunch Freudian, Frankenthal was convinced that sexual feelings thwarted (or nurtured) in childhood prove to be the entire foundation for the negative (or positive) feelings and affects in a person's adult life. Chayefsky vehemently disparaged that principle. "My father was a man who believed very much in his spirituality," said Dan Chayefsky. "If you look at his work from that time, it is full of spirituality. Therefore he refused to accept Freud's theory. He needed someone like Jung, who believed that spirituality was equally important. Of course, his own sexuality at the time was underplayed, which is putting it lightly."

He was almost Victorian in his attitude toward sex, others noted. In *Altered States,* Chayefsky said that among Jews, especially "very religious Jews, the young men were encouraged to marry early to dispose of the lusts of the flesh, so as to get on with the more significant business of studying holy law." That might explain his earlier uneasiness when sexual matters were discussed among his friends. "The Mickey Spillane bit in *Marty,* where the guys are talking about women and their bodies, and Marty gets embarrassed, that was Paddy," said Mike Ryan. "Oh, he'd put on a show with the guys at times, but in an intimate one-to-one discussion about sex and women, he was very uneasy." In 1958, while promoting *The Goddess* in Boston, he told one reporter that he could not understand " 'the big-bosom philosophy' " of America. "Our attitudes towards sex and life have become truly alarming."

In a scene that eventually was cut from *The Bachelor Party,* the Existentialist asks, "What is our age today, really? We eat the finest foods, but we have no sense of taste. We are married to people we do not like, raise children we do not know, work in jobs we have no interest in. And men and women, what are they? They have been elevated from animals to machines, and sex, what is that? Two derricks generated by an ignition." Twenty years later, the same metaphor appeared in *Altered States.* Sex was then described as "some kind of electrical affinity for each other, a communal ionization."

"If you spoke to my father," said Dan Chayefsky, "you'd swear he was asexual. Which of course isn't exactly the case, because I'm here." But that was the purpose of sex, Chayefsky senior believed. It was either for procreation or "an animal thing," he told Mike Ryan. "That's how he looked on it, which I thought was kind of sad," said Ryan. "But obviously that's what he was either taught as a kid, or he learned it growing up. Remember, this was not an attractive little guy. Probably he never had a girl or a woman who took the time to give him affection or show him what real physical love is." Which is why, it could be further deduced, there are so few love scenes in his plays and movies.

In *Marty,* his first autobiographical work, the lead character, in an unusually coarse impulse, suddenly grabs Clara for "one lousy little kiss." In *The Hospital,* Dr. Bock, the George C. Scott character, ravages the girl on the couch in his office, climaxing in seconds. "I arouse quickly, consummate prematurely, and can't wait to get my clothes back on and get out of that bedroom," says Diana Christensen, Faye Dunaway's character in *Network,* whom Chayefsky admitted was partly based on himself.

Dan Chayefsky speculated that suppressing his physical feelings, Paddy Chayefsky relocated that energy in his work. "He preferred to say, 'Fuck this, I'm not going to deal with it. I'll write instead.' " ("I'm goddamn good at my work and so I confine myself to that. All I want out of life is a thirty share and a twenty rating," says television executive Diana Christensen in *Network.*) "That attitude obviously was not going to sit well with a strict Freudian psychiatrist such as Dr. Frankenthal," said Dan Chayefsky. "So after a year or so, he left her."

From a psychological and social perspective, Chayefsky's marriage provided considerable curiosity and speculation over the years. The collective view of Susan Chayefsky was that she was attractive, soft-spoken, and very shy. "She barely made an impression," said Robert Anderson, "except as being very sweet, very self-effacing. It was pretty hard with that overpowering personality of Paddy's for her to say or do anything as long as he was around."

Her husband's compulsions were not the governing factor, however. Susan Chayefsky had her own carefully concealed neuroses, which went back to her childhood. Described as "a beautiful child, sensitive, and very bright," the girl's initial identity had been undermined and suppressed by her parents when she was very small. Her mother, said to be very attractive and vain, was "a woman in constant flight from her children, herself, and especially her husband." Mr. Sackler was Prussian, with a mustache and a rough guttural voice that was used frequently to mock and belittle his family. Susan, who was the smartest and most vulnerable, became the prime target of his abuse and ridicule. Shamed but eager for approval when she entered school, she became the hardest worker in the class. When she was told that she scored the highest in New York City in a citywide math competition, and was to be awarded a gold medal, she was certain that someone had made a mistake. When assured that she was indeed the winner, she ran home to tell her parents. When no one reacted with any enthusiasm, the young girl went to her room, sat on the floor, and told the family cat her good news. This rejection and the emotional impact of the scene would be reenacted in *The Goddess*, played by the child actress Patty Duke.

When Susan was a teenager, her mother either died or walked out on the family (the exact details were kept from all outsiders); for compensation the young woman relied on others to boost her self-esteem. She became meticulous about her clothes and appearance. Delicate, petite, and possessed with natural grace, at nineteen she was studying dance in Manhattan when she was asked to join an established performance company. She was semi-established when she met Paddy Chayefsky at a party in a Greenwich Village apartment. His oration and ebullience dominated the room and gained Susan's attention, especially since he did not seem to notice her until the party was almost over and he curtly asked if he could walk her home. As in the scene where Marty and Clara meet in *Marty*, Paddy carried most of the conversation that first night, while Susan responded with a quiet but genuine interest in his ambitions and his work. "She dominated the entire evening," he said later, "by saying absolutely nothing about herself." As their courtship proceeded, the writer found himself drawn to the seemingly passive but fierce nature of this attractive, intelligent girl who had experienced such a tragic, loveless early life in the Bronx. That was the crux of their relationship, their shared pain, a friend of that time surmised. "They became each other's support team. It was Sidney and Susan against the world, which they felt was a very cruel place. There was so much emphasis initially on that shared pain that later on, when they tried to dislodge themselves from it, there was enormous frustration."

As his wife, Susan Chayefsky could show she had a strong side. Her formidable mother-in-law was possessive and expected her sons to continue living with her even after they wed. Winn Chayefsky and his bride, Terry, who were married shortly after Paddy and Susan, adhered to Gussie's wishes and moved in with her. Susan Chayefsky, however, would have none of that. "She put her foot down," a family friend said. "Susie told Paddy that she wanted to get as far away from Tibbett Avenue as possible and he agreed with her." The newlyweds settled in Greenwich Village and were apparently very happy. "That was another world for them," said Dan Chayefsky. "They were like bohemians back then. They were different. They went to the coffeehouses and jazz clubs, and had a lot of fun." Susan was everything to Paddy—wife, mother, business partner, and professional booster. "She told me how she used to listen to him on the radio when he was a comic," said Dan. "He wasn't very good at it and he swore that if he didn't make it as a writer in six months he would quit and become a shoe salesman." Those six months stretched to three years, and when success came, Susan Chayefsky's role changed almost overnight. When Chayefsky became the hottest writer on television, he had an agent, an accountant, and a publicist, with producers and reporters calling each day soliciting his time and attention. That meant Susan was essentially out of a job. Her steady and expert counseling was no longer required. Her frustration must have intensified since in the interim she had forsaken her own career at her husband's insistence.

"If a woman has got a spark, it's her right and privilege to make a thing of herself," Chayefsky said in his TV play *Printer's Measure*. Those were the sentiments of Sidney, the writer. Paddy, the public self, was much more of a chauvinist, however. As the man of the house he had the career. "Typical of his generation, my father was restricted by all sorts of credos that were very self-defining," Dan Chayefsky said. "When he married my mother she had a possible career as a dancer. She had talent and she was asked to go with a show on the road. And he wouldn't allow it. He had this old 1940s macho attitude. 'No wife of mine is going to go on the road.' That was his attitude. Part of it was realistic. Dancers do get lonely on the road and take up with others. He was not comfortable with that idea, so she went along with him."

Initially, Susan Chayefsky felt that her husband would have a modest career as a writer and that their life together would be quiet and simple. When the fame came, "the Paddy persona took over like a vortex, a tornado, and she didn't have anything to hold on to," said Dan Chayefsky. "My father could always get up in the morning and go to his work. My mother now had nothing."

Chayefsky, for his part, did encourage his wife to pursue outside interests, according to other family members and friends. Susan Chayefsky enrolled at Columbia University and received top grades, but dropped out. She then became a very accomplished and sensitive photographer of children. But impeded by the lack of support in her own childhood, she lost faith in her abilities. Her compassion became a more abiding vocation.

In the early 1950s, Phyllis Anderson, wife of the playwright Robert Anderson, was stricken with cancer. "She had a horrible five-year battle," said her husband. "Many of the writers she had worked with and encouraged stayed away, but Paddy and Susan came frequently. They would visit her at home or in the hospital. Paddy would tell her what he was up to, all the stories of his latest battles, and Phyllis loved it. Susie was also very good, very sweet to her. She would call and help in any way she could." When other good friends,

Johnny Friedkin and Audrey Peters, had a baby who almost died from sudden infant death syndrome, it was Susan Chayefsky who stepped in to help. "She came to my house and sat with me for twelve hours, saying over and over again that it wasn't my fault," said Peters. "Later on, I never saw Susie much, but I never forgot that kindness."

As Paddy Chayefsky's career and popular public persona grew, his wife's social appearances became less frequent. "During the Philco-Goodyear years, Fred Coe and NBC would have various dinners and parties. Susie went to a few, then we stopped seeing her," said Arthur Penn. In California, during the making of *The Bachelor Party* in 1956, Audrey Peters noted, to get Mrs. Chayefsky to attend a party or a show was a major production. "We would have to drag her kicking and screaming, and then once she got there she had a marvelous time. She was always the last to leave."

Upon becoming a hit playwright on Broadway, Chayefsky believed a new social image was in order. His ideal of married show-business couples was embodied by Garson Kanin and Ruth Gordon and Howard Lindsay and Dorothy Stickney. At his urging, Susan tried to adapt to his social fantasies. She purchased an appropriately fashionable wardrobe and decorated their lavish Central Park West apartment in flawless taste, but the period during which she played the perfect hostess and celebrity wife was short-lived. "They had a few parties in the beginning, and Susie showed up at the openings and premieres occasionally, but she couldn't seem to carry it off quite as well as Paddy," said Audrey Peters. Chayefsky tried to help his wife develop a public persona, but the attempts boomeranged. Instead of acquiring élan, Susan began to become more insecure and fastidious about her appearance and actions, which gave some people the impression that she was behaving in a superior, haughty manner. In 1957, when plans for *The Goddess* were under way, Chayefsky invited those involved with his first independent production to meet at his house. When Susan Chayefsky entered the room mid-discussion, the men rose, and one of them, a legal assistant, tried to bring her into the group by explaining the specifics of their talk. Without warning, Susan became agitated and very angry. "I know what you're doing," she screamed at the man. "You're talking down to me because I'm a woman."

It was a "very embarrassing situation," Chayefsky said later. It served to widen the rift between his professional and private lives.

That year Susan Chayefsky also entered analysis. "She and Paddy went to this husband-and-wife team on the Upper West Side," said Audrey Peters. "And from what I recall of the time, she did make an effort to keep up with him."

In June 1958, when Paddy went to Europe to publicize *The Goddess*,

Susan went with him and was at his side at all of the public events. At the end of the tour they rented a villa on the Riviera "with a reputable French cook," then went to Paris, Munich, Vienna, and Switzerland. "When we're in Rome we're at the Excelsior," Paddy told Archer Winsten of the *New York Post.*

CHAPTER 16

The Tempest Continues

In May 1957, the last TV show credited to Chayefsky appeared on CBS. *The Great American Hoax,* starring Ed Wynn, was announced as a special event, but the network was remiss in not divulging that Chayefsky did not write the script. The show was an adaptation of the 1951 film *As Young as You Feel,* which in itself was an adaptation of the 1949 Chayefsky original story, "A Few Kind Words from Newark." "Second-hand Chayefsky still stands head and shoulders above most of his contemporaries," said the New York *Morning Telegraph,* and the paper's TV critic entreated the writer to "come on home where you belong. Your talents are sorely missed."

But Chayefsky wasn't going home again, columnist Atra Baer reported, the reason being his asking price of $25,000 for a ninety-minute drama. "We didn't know the TV industry had moved to Las Vegas," said Baer.

The issue of money was "a sheer canard," Chayefsky blasted back. He had never asked for $25,000 from any TV network, and even if he had, that was not an exorbitant sum. "As everyone knows, there are women in TV who earn $100,000 a year, simply for opening refrigerator doors and babbling about deep-freeze compartments," he said.

It wasn't his desire for compensation that was keeping him away from TV. "Rather, it's because I demand a respect for writers that on the whole doesn't exist in television today." That respect had to include involvement in casting, the choice of a director, "and, most important of all, the right to be the only one to cut and revise my scripts." If the right producer asked him, Chayefsky said, he would do a TV script for nothing. There were few takers, however, because in the two years since he left the Philco-Goodyear series, network programming had changed drastically. With the switch to film and to production in Hollywood, live original drama had ceased almost entirely. The airwaves were filled with moronic fairy-tale Westerns and quiz shows, which brought in high ratings. "What television is doing is out of stupidity, not fright," said Chayefsky.

According to the broadcasting historian Eric Barnouw, the decline of good anthology drama in the late 1950s, especially by Chayefsky and the other first-class TV dramatists, was due to the growing influence of Madison Avenue sponsors. "Most advertisers were selling magic," wrote Barnouw. "Their commercials posed the same problems that Chayefsky's dramas dealt with: people who feared failure in love and in business." In their cheery commercials, the sponsors posed a quick solution, "a new pill, deodorant, toothpaste, shampoo or girdle," while it was obvious that Chayefsky's heroes and heroines needed a deeper, more lasting remedy for their unhappiness. Furthermore, Paddy's people were usually ordinary and unglamorous, which might not only disturb viewers but would also counteract everything the advertising stood for.

On another level, the sponsors were also exerting more control over the scripts and the content of the shows. Barnouw points out that in one play set in New York, the Ford Motor Company ordered that the Chrysler Building be painted out of the city skyline. Cigarette manufacturers insisted that only the heroes, and not the villains, be shown smoking on TV. In 1959, the American Gas Company ordered that the word "gas" be deleted from the TV drama *Judgment at Nuremberg*, "making it sound as though six million Jews perished in —— chambers," said the critic Jeff Greenfield.

If anyone could lift the quality of TV drama and ease the new limitations imposed on it, that person was Fred Coe. The producer resigned from NBC in December 1957 and went to CBS the following year, to present original dramas on "Playhouse 90." One of the first of the Philco writers he recruited for the program was J. P. Miller. "I was walking along Fifth Avenue one day and I bumped into Fred," said Miller. "He told me he was going to produce three 'Playhouse 90's and he wanted me to write one of them. I told him I didn't want to be a writer anymore. I was tired of writing, period. I had recently come back from California, having had a bad experience on my movie with Hecht-Hill-Lancaster, and on another film. So I was quitting writing. I intended to buy a boat and go out to Riverhead and become a fisherman."

Hoping to change his mind, Coe told Miller he was only interested in doing shows on really strong subjects—such as divorce, insanity, and current social problems. At home that night, Miller later recalled, he couldn't sleep. "I was lying awake and I was thinking about alcoholism. I had an uncle who lived with us during the Depression. He was an alcoholic, and smoking in bed one night he fell asleep and our house burned down. I got to remembering that and somehow or other this little story took shape. It was now one o'clock in the morning and I called Fred, who was out in East Hampton. I called him right then, and told him the idea, a love story about two people who meet and like to drink and then the booze becomes more important than they are to each other. Fred said, 'I like it, Pappy. Write it.' "

When *Days of Wine and Roses,* with Piper Laurie and Cliff Robertson, was presented on "Playhouse 90," Paddy Chayefsky was watching. He said he got "homesick" that night. The following day he called Fred Coe and met with him and the director Gordon Duff. A short time later CBS announced that Chayefsky was returning to TV, not for a single show, but for a series, which would focus on a prevailing interest of his—modern-day psychiatry. "I've been thinking of making nine one-and-a-half-hour films with the American Psychiatric Association," he told the press. One of these would deal with an actual case of a woman "relieving anxiety over menopause by throwing a pass at one of her son's friends; another would be on the tortures of a man discovering that he is homosexual."

Chayefsky submitted full outlines and partial scripts for three shows to CBS. They were eager to proceed until the matter of final approval over the scripts was raised. "Once they got control," Chayefsky said, "it would be so dehydrated it wouldn't be worth doing. They would try to make the subject matter more palatable, and it can't be done that way; it can only be done as art."

From CBS he went to ABC, who also "begged for the series" but would not give the writer final approval of his scripts. The loss would be to the viewers, he said, who would be deprived of seeing real issues dramatized. "The networks felt they couldn't challenge the complacency of their viewers," he said. "You could give them some conflict, one or two philosophical moments, and a crisis, but the whole thing had to be tied up with a pink bow. That way, at the end of the show viewers could turn to their partners and say: 'Oh that was nice, dear. Shall we have some SpaghettiOs for dinner tomorrow night?' That kind of insidious brainwashing and crass manipulation was the real sickness on TV."

Susskind Versus Chayefsky

I believe in therapy but not in analysis.
An analyst I met socially told me I would never
need it. He said, "You're a man
who makes your neuroses work for you."

David Susskind

It was a toss-up as to who disliked whom the most. Chayefsky at one point conceded, saying he had no feelings whatsoever for David Susskind because as far as he could determine the man was "a cipher, a nonentity, and you can't have feelings good or bad for someone that doesn't exist."

Known as "Mr. Humility," Susskind began his career in the late 1940s. As an agent at MCA, representing Dinah Shore, Dean Martin, and Jerry Lewis, he said he quickly learned the valuable rules of "conniving, plotting, and below-the-belt punching." Representing performers was, however, heart-breaking and ulcer-making. "I hated being an agent," he said. "You worked your heart out for an actor and when they hit the big time they turn on you, because you remind them of the time when they were nothing." In New York, Susskind formed Talent Associates with another ex-agent, Al Levy, and they managed the directors, writers, and producers who worked on the Philco TV show. In time, with most of the talent in their corner, Susskind and Levy decided to "package" the show and sell it to the advertising agencies who represented the sponsors. Susskind and Levy got 10 percent of the budget, plus another 10 percent from each writer and director they represented. One holdout from the Philco stable was Paddy Chayefsky.

Susskind was "a self-hating, closet Jew," Chayefsky believed. In 1953 Susskind had tried to interfere with Paddy's first Philco script, *Holiday Song*. Susskind said the story was "too Jewish." He wanted the main character changed to a priest or a minister. "No, let's leave it as one of those cantor guys," said Fred Coe.

When Chayefsky scored with this show, then later with *Marty*, Susskind tried to get him to sign with his management firm. Paddy remained with Bobby Sanford, and for as long as he could he stayed clear of Susskind. The agent-turned-packager then became a producer, taking over the Philco show one summer when Fred Coe was on vacation. Two years later, Susskind was responsible for bringing the Philco-Goodyear hour to an end. Writer Robert Alan Aurthur and director Gordon Duff were at the advertising agency one day, ready to pitch future episodes. They were discussing a new script, *The Five Dollar Bill* by Tad Mosel, when Susskind began to moan about "another neurotic boy and neurotic mother swimming on a neurotic lake." Duff continued with the story, until Susskind suddenly jumped to his feet and yelled, "Quit it! I'm sick of hearing this crap. Forget *The Five Dollar Bill*. Mosel is finished in television! Chayefsky is finished in television!" Thrusting his finger at Aurthur, he concluded, "And you're finished in television. The people don't want that kind of stuff anymore."

After the Philco-Goodyear series ended, Susskind continued packaging, then went into producing full time. He made some flops before putting some very distinguished shows on television, including *The Bridge of San Luis Rey* and Somerset Maugham's *The Moon and Sixpence*, with Laurence Olivier in his American TV debut. ("Who's Laurence Olivier?" the Madison Avenue agencies reportedly asked. "My answer was 'He's Vivien Leigh's husband,' " said Susskind.)

As his self-propelled legend and bombastic ego grew, Susskind began to take credit for amazing accomplishments outside his realm. His press releases stated that he had "discovered" Paddy Chayefsky and produced the original version of *Marty* on TV. In January 1956, when *Middle of the Night* was trying out in Philadelphia, Chayefsky called Susskind in New York. *The New York Times* had just interviewed Paddy and they had mentioned Susskind's assertion. "Tell them you *didn't* discover me," Chayefsky shouted over the phone.

"He was raving," said Susskind. "He said nobody discovered him but himself and that I was to call the paper immediately and tell them that." Susskind agreed to do as Paddy ordered. He dialed the number of the paper. When the operator came on, he said, "I did not discover Paddy Chayefsky." Then he hung up.

The downside of success, said Susskind, was that it made you peculiarly vulnerable to jealousy from enemies. "I'm very vivid, I suppose. A very strong-minded and positive individual. This thing with Paddy Chayefsky now. I find Paddy's moaning about loneliness a bore. I think his writing is without real moment and we collide."

In 1958, intent on getting out "of this sick rat race of using big stars" in TV shows and desirous of establishing his own name as "marquee value to the public," Susskind created a new show for a local New York station. It was described as a two-hour "enlightening, unrehearsed, free-association" talk show, to be produced and hosted by him. The program would not feature any stars or celebrities hawking their latest product. His guests would be distinguished and important figures on the cultural, social, and political scene. "The name of the show was 'David Susskind's Open End,' " said Tad Mosel, "which always struck us as kind of funny, although David never saw the humor of it." Mosel, along with J. P. Miller, David Shaw, Robert Alan Aurthur, Sumner Locke Elliott, James Lee, and Paddy Chayefsky were the invited guests for the premiere program that fall.

The show was broadcast from a small studio in New Jersey. "It was live," said Mosel, "and prior to going on, David took us all out to a posh dinner in Manhattan, where a lot of cocktails were served. Then he transported us to New Jersey by limo. He had plied us with so many drinks beforehand, God knows what we said on the air."

THE DISGRUNTLED CADILLACS was how a *Time* magazine headline described that distinguished panel, illustrating the coverage with a photograph of only one guest, Paddy Chayefsky. Kay Gardella of the *Daily News* also singled out Chayefsky for solitary inspection. "Of the seven men, the one who bit hardest the hand that once fed him was Paddy Chayefsky of *Marty* fame," said Gardella.

"A malevolent juggernaut that's gonna chew me up" was Chayefsky's description of the medium that wouldn't allow him to do a series about the anguish of menopause or the torments of homosexuality. "But you could try a TV Western with a homosexual horse," cracked David Shaw. When James Lee mentioned having written a script a few years back about a blacklisted actor, Robert Alan Aurthur said that he had been told by "powerful forces" in TV that blacklisting had never existed. Those were the days of "total optimism," an era of false advertising brought on by President Eisenhower's promise to wage "total peace," said Lee, which brought a fresh wave of moans and grumblings from Chayefsky.

"On the panel I was sitting next to Paddy," Tad Mosel recalled. "He always loved to talk, and on this night he never stopped. When the others were speaking, Paddy's voice would go lower, but he'd keep on talking, then when there was a silence he would simply raise his volume." The country was racing as fast as it could into anonymity, which was why the TV medium was plunging into massism, said Chayefsky. "We're all trying to be conformists these days, and a TV writer carries a very low mark of prestige."

Riding back to New York in the limo, Chayefsky had second thoughts about the running oratory and negative comments he had delivered on live TV. "He didn't want to do the show in the first place," said Aurthur, "and now he was afraid he'd made a fool of himself." In Manhattan, Chayefsky told the limo driver to keep driving around, because he did not want to go home. "Finally the driver turned and asked us where we wanted to get off," said Aurthur. "Paddy groaned and said, 'Take me to Central Park and drop me off in the middle of a lot of muggers.' "

"That was the wonderful blunderbuss aspect to Paddy's personality," Arthur Penn said later, commenting on Chayefsky's acute fluctuation in behavior. "He would storm in where angels feared to tread. He had an opinion about everything. But there was a combination there—almost as large as I've ever seen it—of absolutely total narcissism, and then a sudden independent collapse of ego."

Garson Kanin gave a further impression. "I think it's fair to say—and nothing against him—Paddy was a little crazy. I don't think there is any important writer who's completely sane. If he was, he wouldn't be a writer— or a painter, or a poet, or a sculptor. I don't mean clinically insane—but his reactions aren't normal, and his perceptions certainly aren't normal. And Paddy, more than most, was a little bit cuckoo. Someone once said, 'You don't love your friends in spite of their faults, you love them *because* of their faults.' Paddy's faults were part of his whole makeup, part of his psyche, part of him."

CHAPTER 17

Middle of the Night: The Movie

By March 1958, *Middle of the Night* had finished its road tour and Chayefsky proceeded to work on the screenplay. In its third incarnation, he said that he was at last satisfied with the work. The play was "abysmally written—dreadful," he said. "I couldn't believe it had been a Broadway hit and was forced to come to the conclusion that it was really Edward G. Robinson, and not the play, that kept it going for two years."

Even with that tardy acknowledgment of Robinson's contribution, Chayefsky was not about to give him the role in the movie. As originally planned, he gave the part of the older man who falls for his secretary to Fredric March, which called for particular changes. The play's overtly Jewish characteristics and references would have to be cut. "That was really the origin of the story," said the director, Delbert Mann. "In the TV version, with E. G. Marshall, he was no more Jewish than Fredric March. The people around him clearly were—as were the attitudes, the vernacular, the business that he was in. All of that suggested he was Jewish, but it was never made a point of. So we went back to the original approach."

The play had also been "much too clinical," Chayefsky said. "And not believable." The culmination of the affair between the older man and younger girl happened too easily and too quickly. In the movie it would be more protracted, awkward, and desperate on the part of the man. This would make the film *his* story. "It's his thinking, his progression, his decision that counts, and the girl is there only so long as she serves that purpose," said Chayefsky.

Enlarging the Fredric March character meant that the part of the young, emotionally insecure secretary, once slated for Marilyn Monroe, was now in essence a featured role, not a starring one. Chayefsky was therefore surprised when two leading movie stars were interested in playing the smaller part. The first of these was a ravishing, violet-eyed brunette, the top female box-office star of the day, Elizabeth Taylor.

Three years before, Taylor had seen the play on Broadway. Her escort that night was the flamboyant promoter-producer Mike Todd. He introduced Taylor to Chayefsky, who, attracted by her luscious looks, her quick wit, and her facility with four-letter words, became an instant ally. Todd encouraged their friendship and as a trio they planned to make movies together. One project discussed was *Don Quixote;* another was the life and work of poet Edna St. Vincent Millay. But then in March 1958, thirteen months after his wedding to Taylor, Todd died in a plane crash. The following June, Taylor was in New York on a mission of mercy to help her friend Montgomery Clift. He had suffered serious facial and body injuries in a car crash not long before, which had led to a desperate reliance on painkillers and alcohol. "If you don't have the brains to eat, fall down," another friend, actress Nancy Walker, advised the actor. Elizabeth Taylor had an antidote. Work was the answer. But there was *no* work, Clift lamented. When his face was damaged, the offers for movie roles had stopped coming in. Taylor, who would survive countless calamities, including near-death illnesses and scalding public censure, told Clift to get a grip on himself. Self-pity sucked. And forget sitting around waiting for producers to call. As a team they would make their own movies. They would commission a script, hire a director, then offer the package to the studios.

Never one to dally when the lives of others were in jeopardy, Taylor went to work immediately. She told Clift that when it came to scripts, she knew one of the best writers in Manhattan—Paddy Chayefsky. She called Chayefsky and apprised him of the situation, and they made an appointment to meet for drinks at the Russian Tea Room. Chayefsky arrived with Delbert Mann. "We sat in a booth at the back of the restaurant, on the left side as you go in," said Mann. "Liz was by Monty's side. The text of the meeting was her telling Monty that he was all right and that he could still act. It was kind of chilling and eerie. She wanted Paddy to write something for them to do together. It wasn't about a specific project. And I don't believe anything ever came of it."

There was a follow-up call, however, two weeks later, from Taylor's agent, Kurt Frings. Taylor had been scheduled to make another independent film, *Busman's Holiday,* about a beauty-contest winner on her way to Florida when her bus gets hijacked. The financing for that fell through, and Frings asked Chayefsky if he had anything in the production pipeline that Taylor could do. Paddy had the script of *Middle of the Night.* Fredric March was signed, but not the girl. According to casting director Everett Chambers, Columbia Pictures had been "pushing Paddy to think more in terms of having a star in the role." Chayefsky mentioned this to Frings, who asked to see the script. It was sent that night by courier. Two days later, the agent said that if the money and billing could be worked out, Elizabeth Taylor would do *Middle of the Night*.

In late August, Taylor made a three-day stopover in New York en route to France for some rest and recuperation before starting *Middle of the Night*, due to roll that October. The plan was for her and Chayefsky to meet the next day, to talk about the script, the schedule, her clothes, etc. That evening, alone in her hotel room, Taylor received a call from Eddie Fisher, a close friend of her recently deceased husband. He was also in town alone and suggested they meet for dinner. Taylor agreed. Dancing followed dinner, and at the end of the night, as the best friend of a dead man would do, Fisher escorted the beautiful widow back to her hotel room. They had a late-night drink, and after that came what has been called "the longest goodbye in history." Fisher and Taylor reportedly did not come up for air for several days. She missed her meeting with Paddy Chayefsky and her flight to France. The roar of the ensuing scandal was heard around the world. Fisher left his wife, Debbie Reynolds, for Taylor, who overnight went from being America's favorite widow to Mary Magdalene. In the midst of the scandal and headlines, Paddy Chayefsky remained sanguine and loyal as ever to Taylor. Discussing the bad timing and the loss to his movie he said, "Imagine what would have happened if she had met *me* for dinner first?"

Reverting to his original concept of casting a featured actress in his movie, Chayefsky was considering a newcomer, Hope Lange. But then the name of a second major star took precedence in the proceedings. Columbia Pictures, still insisting on a marquee attraction, suggested an actress from its own roster, Kim Novak.

Five years before, when *Middle of the Night* opened on Broadway, while many of the first-nighters stood in the aisles gawking at Marilyn Monroe during the intermission, a lesser-known celebrity, Kim Novak, sat farther down in the orchestra section. Over the past sixteen months the formerly brunette and overweight model from Illinois had been revamped and renovated by Columbia Pictures. Her body was toned down, her hair was stripped of its color and tinted a bluish blond, and her voice was altered, reduced to a whisper—until "this former tough Polish broad from Chicago became this ethereal 'where-am-I-what-are-you-saying-to-me?' girl," said Jack Cole, the studio's choreographer. Small parts led to featured roles in *The Eddy Duchin Story* and *Pal Joey*, until her first taste of dramatic potential in the recently completed *Picnic* made Novak want more, namely significance and esteem. This, she felt, could only come with roles such as the one Paddy Chayefsky had created in *Middle of the Night*. "It had a dimension that my other parts lacked," she said. "The girl wanted an older man, a father image. But my boss, Harry Cohn, couldn't believe I'd want to touch such a topic."

Paddy Chayefsky agreed with Cohn. He told him and his brother, Jack (who had bought the play), that there was no way he would allow a lavender-haired amateur to appear in his movie. Two years passed. Novak became a star with *Picnic*, then appeared in *Vertigo*, directed by Alfred Hitchcock, who when asked how he got Kim to act, replied, "I used the psychological approach. You see, she's a bit confused. On the one hand people are telling her she's America's top woman star, on the other, that she's nothing but a dumb ox. I convinced her the truth lay somewhere between the two."

In September 1958, when Elizabeth Taylor took herself out of Chayefsky's movie, Kim Novak stepped up her campaign. The timing was now more favorable. Harry and Jack Cohn were dead, and her contract with the studio was up for renewal. Through her agent, Norman Brokaw, Novak let the new regime at Columbia know that, owing to her current heavy draw at the box office, a more favorable contract was in order. It had to include more money, and the right to choose her future movie roles. Top of the list was *Middle of the Night*. Columbia, which was putting up the entire financing for the film, duly notified Chayefsky, who was also being prodded by his casting adviser, Everett Chambers. "I thought Kim could do it," said Chambers, "and Paddy finally acquiesced."

Through Norman Brokaw, Chayefsky relayed the word to Novak that there would be no star frills on his picture. It would be made in New York on a limited budget of one million dollars. He was going for realism. There would be no glamour. The film would be photographed in black-and-white on the streets of New York, and all the interiors would be done at the Gold Medal Studios in the Bronx. To get there, Novak would have to travel like the rest of the actors, by subway.

To counteract their female star's lack of dramatic training, Chayefsky and Delbert Mann brought in a strong supporting cast of New York actors. Martin Balsam and Lee Philips were retained from the stage production, and Joan Copeland was hired in lieu of Anne Jackson, who had asked Chayefsky for too much money. Others added to the cast were the veteran Warner Bros. character actress Glenda Farrell, as Novak's biased mother, and Lee Grant as the best friend. Grant had made her film debut ten years earlier as the neurotic shoplifter in *Detective Story*, for which she won the best actress award at Cannes and an Academy Award nomination, but she had not worked in films since. "I was blacklisted," she said. "Except for one minor picture, I wasn't allowed to act in movies. Then Del and Paddy came along. They were such decent people. What they tried to do was crack the blacklist."

On December 15, 1958, rehearsals began at the Palladium Ballroom on West Fifty-third Street. The first to arrive was Paddy Chayefsky, with a fresh growth of facial hair. The beard made him look "more like a writer," he said.

The last to arrive, thirty minutes late, was Kim Novak. It wasn't a deliberately delayed star entrance. She was visibly nervous—"shaking," said Delbert Mann. "This was a new experience for Kim. Here she was faced with a very high-powered, theatrically experienced company. She was very frightened."

The idea of rehearsing a role before shooting surprised her, Novak said. "I never saw the script of my first two movies. On the set they would say, 'Don't bother with that, just get out there and do as you're told.' Alfred Hitchcock wouldn't even discuss the part with me." Nervous and soft-spoken during the initial readings at the Palladium, Novak soon learned that although she identified with the confused emotions of the girl she was playing, none of it was registering in her voice or face. The carefully constructed blank persona and the roles she had played in Hollywood did not permit any display of feelings.

"Kim had not done a part like this before," said Chambers. "She didn't know how to break the role down, or what a subtext was either. To play this character she had to get inside herself, to show some of the emotions the girl was feeling. 'Look left. Look right. Look at the camera.' That's all she was taught in Hollywood, and it worked there, but not in New York." Her co-star Lee Philips, aware of how unsteady and unsure Novak was, said that during a break he tried to help. "I went to her and said, 'Listen, if you want to get together after time, I'll rehearse with you.' And Freddie March, who had his eye on her, cautioned, 'Don't listen to that son of a bitch, you know what he wants.' "

By the end of the second week, with no visible improvement from Novak, Chambers said that Chayefsky and Mann considered firing her. "They were thinking about going after Hope Lange again." But Chambers had some experience as a dialogue coach. The Christmas weekend was coming up and he volunteered to try and work with her. "They agreed," he said. "And that's what we did for the next three days."

Chambers said he worked straight through the holidays, teaching Novak how to act. "Most stars learn to play what they do best, themselves." he said. "Burt Lancaster always played Burt Lancaster, and Jimmy Stewart played Jimmy Stewart. Once in a while they'd break out and do something different, but most of the time they like to keep it safe, to stay within the image. Novak was like that too. She had a fixed façade which she gave to the camera, to everyone. I was determined to get past that."

In the first big scene there is a lengthy sequence where the girl pours out her feelings of confusion and despair to the older man; it takes up four pages of dialogue. "Kim couldn't remember all the lines," said Chambers. "She didn't have that kind of concentration to get through it. So we went over it line by line, again and again, and Kim kept holding back. I wanted to break through the bullshit, get past the defenses, so the character would be closer to her, closer to her own feelings."

Chambers kept at her into the early morning hours, when a flash of the former tough Polish broad came through. "At one particular point, it was close to three in the morning, Kim began to yell at me, 'I can't do it. I can't do it,'" Chambers recalled. "There was a Christmas tree behind her and she swung her hand around and smashed one of the ornaments. Later she denied this ever happened, but it did. I yelled at her to repeat the gesture, but as part of the scene, and to talk *louder*. Together we smashed every ornament on the tree. By dawn we were finished. The place was a shambles, but the character she was supposed to play was finally emerging."

At the rehearsal Monday morning Novak performed the scene for Delbert Mann, Paddy Chayefsky, and Fredric March. "She was extraordinary," said Mann. "It was a literal transformation."

"They realized she could cut it," said Chambers, who for his Pygmalion-in-reverse duty was given a bonus by Paddy Chayefsky and was retained to coach Novak for the duration of the production.

> If you weren't such a decent man, you'd
> probably make out a lot better with me. I mean
> if you were just on the make I'd probably be saying
> to myself, "Well, I'm pretty lonely and he's a
> gentleman." The way I've been feeling lately, who cares
> anyway? I think what really scares me to death
> about you is that you might really fall in love with me.
>
> The Girl, *Middle of the Night*

On January 5, 1959, production began at the Gold Medal Studios in the Bronx. Neither Kim Novak nor Fredric March was asked to take the subway; cars were provided for Novak and March, who was also given his own wardrobe assistant. A hair stylist was retained for the actress, but to acquaint her with the character's plebeian background, Chayefsky decreed that the star should do her own makeup. Her wardrobe was to be similarly modest. Meeting with a New York costumer, Frank Thompson, Novak agreed to an off-the-rack woolen coat and plain tailored skirts and blouses. But for one special sequence the star managed to sneak in an expensive black cocktail dress, designed by her regular Hollywood couturier, Jean Louis. "As long as it doesn't come out of my budget, and she stays within character, she can wear whatever the hell she likes," said Chayefsky.

The tough New York crew represented a hurdle to Novak. "Most of them had worked with Elia Kazan, and they didn't have much respect for Kim," said Johnny Friedkin. "The crew were basically a jolly lot," said George Justin, the assistant producer. "Kim was not an extrovert but she began to enjoy the informality of the whole thing. When we had to change or switch things around, she would pitch in. And during the breaks she began to play cards with the men."

"The biggest problem I had as assistant director was to get her off the stage when she wasn't working," said Charles Maguire. "The whole crew liked her so much that after a setup was done, they stood around talking to her. That interfered with their work, so I had to say to her, 'Hey, Kim, you're finished. Get out of here. Go home.' "

Delbert Mann said Novak gained confidence as she went along. Fredric March helped her and the others, but Chayefsky stayed clear, preferring to kibitz with Lee Grant and Glenda Farrell. "I adored him," Farrell told an oral historian at Columbia University. "He is every actor's dream of a writer. His perception of people is so great that most anybody can take a Chayefsky character and play it and be good in it. It's very hard to hurt one of his characters. They're drawn so beautifully and so carefully, and the dialogue is so sparse and true."

During the second week of filming, Chayefsky learned that having a big Hollywood star in his cast could ease his production problems. That Tuesday night, the company was scheduled to shoot at Eighty-fourth Street and Columbus Avenue, on Manhattan's Upper West Side. "The cops wouldn't give us clearance to shoot there because they said it was a rough neighborhood," said Johnny Friedkin. Upon learning that Kim Novak was involved, the police agreed to provide a clearance and protection, but only if the star agreed to show up at their Policeman's Ball. "Kim was a good sport and she agreed to do it," said Friedkin. "She got all dressed up and I went with her to the ball, in a police car, with the siren going, the whole works."

On the set, Novak was not as cooperative with visiting reporters. "Paddy always liked to have the press around," said Johnny Friedkin, "but not Kim. She was nervous and most of the stuff they were looking for was pap." One day, as a favor, the press agent sneaked a journalist onto the set. "Then he proceeded to stand in front of her, in her key light," said Friedkin. "Kim asked him to move and he did a whole column on what a bitch she was."

Upon reading this report, Chayefsky sprang to the defense of his star. He called his friend, Leonard Lyons, a columnist at the *New York Post,* and told him Novak had been given a bum rap. She was a doll to work with, and he would personally value and appreciate it if Lyons would set the record straight. He did, and the relationship between Chayefsky and Novak began to warm considerably. When she raised questions about the script, instead of referring her by rote to her director, the writer conferred with her personally. Paddy was also more generous in his praise for her work. "She was the first one there in the morning, the last to leave at night, and she showed a tremendously keen intelligence for both the script and character delineation," he said.

Novak said she, too, owed a lot to Chayefsky: "Whenever I came across a line that I didn't quite feel, I'd say to Paddy, 'What did you mean by that?' In Hollywood you *never* see the writers. They're hidden away somewhere for fear they might think up complications. Nobody's supposed to rock the boat out there but the director."

By the third week of filming, Chayefsky was not averse to driving up to the Bronx each morning with Novak. In the evening he often accompanied her downtown to view the rushes of the previous day's shoot. Soon it became evident, at least to some, that his interest was more than professional, that Paddy was heels over head in love with his star, Kim Novak.

"Kim used him for security," said Audrey Peters, who had a small role in the picture. "There was nothing calculating about it. Paddy was enamored, just in awe of this movie star."

"Kim was very vulnerable and she needed reassurance, constant reassurance," said Lee Grant. "She was also darling. A lot of times when actors get nervous they close up, and they put distance between you. She didn't. Kim was open and needy and she expressed it."

"When she talked, she grabbed ahold of you," said Peters. "The physical contact was always there. Even with women. I saw her once in the office with Delbert Mann. She was rubbing up against him. The poor man was walking backwards and he walked right into the wall."

"I know that Paddy was intrigued by her. As we all were," said Delbert Mann. "Kim was a very attractive girl, very feminine. It is entirely possible she and Paddy had a romance, but it wasn't something I had any personal knowledge of, nothing we ever discussed."

A producer who later worked with Chayefsky said he knew of the romance. "He mentioned it, a little surprised—awestruck, really—that someone like Kim Novak would be interested in him," said the producer. "Kim had Paddy thinking he was seven feet tall, a blond, blue-eyed WASP," said Audrey Peters.

"Kim was a very seductive person," Everett Chambers said. "On the set of *Middle of the Night* she needed the recognition of everybody. So she would use her sexuality to seduce them. I don't mean physically—but to rapture them, so that maybe she could call the shots on the production."

But surely Chayefsky was impervious to those movie-star games? He had been on the Hollywood scene for some time now.

"Yes, but not with Kim Novak," Chambers said, laughing. "This was a sensational-looking woman. She had a pair of tits you would not believe, and she never wore a bra."

"Kim was every man's sexual fantasy come true," said Johnny Friedkin. "At that time she was so beautiful, at her prime. I'll never forget the New Year's Eve party at George Justin's house. Kim showed up in the black dress she wore in *Bell, Book and Candle*, the one with no back. There wasn't a wife in that room who wouldn't have fucking killed her, because their husbands didn't look at them all night."

As for Chayefsky's spouse, Susan, she knew of his interest in Novak, because he had told her. Fifteen years later a variation of her reaction would be put in *Network*. When William Holden's character tells his wife that he is having an affair, the wife, played by Beatrice Straight, rages at him, then cautions him to be careful. She does not want him to be destroyed by this other woman. Susan Chayefsky had the same strong sense of what was happening on *Middle of the Night*, and although she remained at a distance from the set, she knew exactly how far the romance would go.

Considering the strife and turmoil that had accompanied Chayefsky's first independent film, *The Goddess*, the production of *Middle of the Night* was an exercise in ease and restraint. Adapting to the vagaries of winter weather, by the fourth week of January the company was only two days behind schedule. "MARCH WITH MANN! FIGHT WITH FREDDY! JUMP WITH JOE [LaShelle]!" George Justin exhorted the crew in one work bulletin. In another, Justin (promoted to full producer by Chayefsky) told the technicians that "if we keep this good pace up, Paddy will soon stop running to the analyst."

On January 29, Chayefsky's thirty-sixth birthday, a giant card with individual pieces of hair stuck to a facial sketch was presented to him. "Since you've put your beard in each of these departments, here's a gift from us," the inscription read. The card was signed by each member of the crew and cast, except for Kim Novak, who gave Chayefsky her own card, and an expensive pipe, to further his writer's image. That same weekend, Chayefsky and Novak made a tour of his New York. With Novak sporting a dark wig they went to the Village, visited book shops and jazz clubs, and he encouraged her to audit classes at the Actors Studio. Akin to Arthur Miller's fixation on Marilyn Monroe, Chayefsky was convinced that with his guidance and collaboration as a dramatist, Novak could have a respectable career. Discussing her work in *Middle of the Night* with Jesse Zunser from *Cue*, Chayefsky said, "She does a wonderful job. She's not a great actress, but she's got talent and with roles that fit her she can be terrific. You'll see."

To another reporter, when asked if there was any special message in the movie, a visibly milder than usual and enrapt Chayefsky replied, "I just say, live and be happy. Stop looking for hidden, inner, obtuse meanings—you'll just get lost. Live, love, find the beautiful and enjoy it. Love is life. Keep loving and keep falling in love. Find beauty and you've found that which is worthwhile in life."

Veering from the two previous productions of the May-December love story, Chayefsky made a change for the movie version. In a moment of weakness, the Kim Novak character, although betrothed to Fredric March, has sex with her ex-husband. The following morning, sitting on a bench in Central Park, she confesses her transgression. Reacting with fear and anger, the older man spurns her. Later, realizing that his dreams of a new life are also being dashed, he forgives and returns to her. "It is better to be unhappily in love, to be sickly in love, to be neurotic, diseased, gruesome, sordid, as long as it involves the passions of life. It is better to be all that than to be careful," he says.

On Friday night, February 13, when the film was completed, Kim Novak hosted a "black velvet" (champagne mixed with Irish stout) party for the crew in her apartment. The following night, the official wrap celebration was held at Toots Shor's. In a rare burst of largesse, in addition to paying for the party Chayefsky individually thanked the cast and crew members for their contribution to what he prophesied would be "an important cinema classic."

In the weeks that followed, instead of returning to Hollywood, Novak stayed in New York while Chayefsky worked with Delbert Mann on the editing. Speed was of the essence because they wanted to unveil the film on the spring festival circuit. Early in March a cut was ready to be shown to Novak and the executives at Columbia Pictures. When her opinion was solicited after the screening, Novak blushed and said she was the wrong person to ask for an objective appraisal. Chayefsky wasn't as impartial. The movie was "going to be an enormous hit, and Freddie and Kim will both win Oscars," he proclaimed.

That weekend a public sneak preview was held in New Jersey. Attending were the Chayefskys and Johnny Friedkin and Audrey Peters. "Coming back in the limousine Paddy kept praising Kim's performance, how at one point she made this gesture of lifting her hand. And we all looked at one another. He completely lost his sense of reality," said Peters.

Chayefsky went so far as to ask his wife for a divorce. "Susie said, 'Don't be ridiculous,' " said Friedkin. "She knew that he was just in awe of this movie star, and thought he was being silly."

On March 15, the picture opened a film festival in Argentina. Chayefsky and Delbert Mann were present, but Novak, a promised guest, was said to be "worn out and exhausted" and did not attend. The reaction to the movie was positive. In New York, further good news came when Columbia announced that the film had been chosen as the official American entry at Cannes. During the week of May 15, Chayefsky and Novak, accompanied by her parents, flew to France. On the plane was the *New York Post* columnist Earl Wilson. "Give me some secret I can expose of Kim," Wilson said. Paddy rubbed his Vandyke beard and said, "Well, we drove around New York together—and you know what she did while she was in my car, don't you?" "No, what did she do?"

Wilson asked, poised for a scoop. "She had her hair done," said Paddy, tugging his beard again.

In Cannes, Chayefsky checked into the Carlton Hotel while Kim and her parents moved into the Château l'Horizon, a villa owned by Aly Khan. "In the face of close scrutiny by the press, Khan stayed in Paris but dispatched an army of servants to entertain the Novaks," one reporter explained. The following afternoon, another of the multidinous press dispatchers noted that "the new Kim" arrived at a press conference wearing a spectacular straw hat and "carrying a heavy volume of Herodotus, the Greek philosopher, where it could plainly be seen by photographers." At the official evening screening of *Middle of the Night*, Novak gave the voracious media what they were looking for. Dressed in a low-cut white tulle gown and mobbed by the crowd, it took her "more than ten minutes to walk the fifty yards to her seat." The follow-up reaction to the film and to Kim, the dramatic actress, was less feverish. At a party at the Eden Roc Hotel afterward, Novak was somewhat subdued, until another visiting U.S. star, Cary Grant, came to her table and asked her to dance. The two were photographed on the floor in close embrace. "We danced and danced and danced," said Kim. "I loved his sense of humor." At five A.M. she left the party with Grant. Seemingly forgotten was her friend the writer-producer Paddy Chayefsky.

The following day, Novak threw a party on Aly Khan's yacht for Cary Grant. When later asked about the matinee idol, she said, "It was not a big romance. But how could I *not* be attracted?" No mention was made then, or after, of any romantic attachment to Chayefsky.

Offering an overview of the Novak-Chayefsky contretemps, Audrey Peters said she did not believe that there was anything "malicious or mean" in Novak's behavior. "Those things happen on movie sets. When the picture is over, so is the romance. Whether or not Paddy was hurt by it, who knows? Certainly he had to know it wouldn't last."

Apparently Chayefsky was grateful for his encounter with the star. While it probably helped to fulfill fantasies that he may have harbored, he never boasted of the affair. Sidney Chayefsky was too much of a gentleman for that. Novak touched him deeply, of that there is no doubt. Echoing the Fredric March character in *Middle of the Night*, who believed in any kind of love, "even if it's sick or selfish—as long as it gives a person a reason to live," Chayefsky told an interviewer, Nora Sayre, the following year, that "it is better to suffer a genuine emotion and live than to be numb."

From Cannes, Chayefsky traveled to London alone to prepare for the opening there. Those reviews, and the ones in New York, were mixed. Bosley Crowther in *The New York Times* recognized the gravity of the plot. "This is loneliness, boy, and it is grim," said Crowther. *Time* magazine praised the performances of Fredric March and, "amazingly," Novak. The work had greater cogency than the Broadway play, the magazine said, and had a "deeper maturity than *Marty*. In fact, it is the first sustained passage of mature feeling and thinking that has appeared so far in the course of Chayefsky's lucrative celebration of the commonplace."

The film had a short run in theatres. Chayefsky's marriage continued, however, with a renegotiation of rules, it was said. Whatever the precise terms, there were no further known infatuations or affairs for Paddy in the future. For a time, Susan Chayefsky appeared to be more social, dining in public with Chayefsky and his friend Elizabeth Taylor and Taylor's new husband, Eddie Fisher. The occasion coincided with the Chayefskys' tenth wedding anniversary, and when asked by columnist Earl Wilson whether they would give their secret for a happy marriage to Fisher and Taylor, Susan replied, "So who says we're happily married?" Having changed her hair to blond, she was later at Paddy's side when he was invited to a formal dinner at the White House. Elegant, faultless, and observant, Mrs. Chayefsky took special pride in telling friends that whereas the first lady, Jacqueline Kennedy, had a crease in one of her long white gloves, hers were "perfect." At the opening of Chayefsky's next play Susan Chayefsky appeared again, wearing an ivory-colored satin coat and gown that she had designed. But this would be one of her last photographed appearances. Soon after that she began to retreat again, leaving Chayefsky to make the social rounds on his own or with his show-business pals and their wives.

"In those days there used to be a group of us—David Shaw, Delbert Mann, and Bob Mulligan," said Johnny Friedkin, "and we all thought the first marriage that would break up was Paddy and Susie's. But the first to go was Audrey and me. Then one day Paddy and I were talking and he said, 'You know, Johnny, Susie and I don't have the greatest marriage, but we're both neurotic as hell and this is probably as well as we're ever going to do.' "

CHAPTER 18

Using the Anger

The writer has only one obligation—
to stay alive and try to please himself.

Irwin Shaw

Although he would continue in analysis, then therapy, on and off for the rest of his life, in 1959, after *Middle of the Night* was released, Chayefsky claimed he was no longer looking for ultimate answers or psychological realignments that would lead to a happier, more serene, so-called "normal" existence. "The aim of psychoanalysis, as I understand it, is not to make you solve problems or even to change or 'adjust,' but to make you enjoy what you are," he told interviewers Nora Sayre and Robert B. Silvers of *Horizon* magazine. Life was not logical or orderly, but full of spontaneity and chaos. Furthermore, "Some of the most neurotic, miserable, poorly married men I've met in my life are among the most fascinating and interesting people I know," he said, "as are confirmed bachelors, homosexuals, lechers of the worst sort who suffer the tortures of the damned. I enjoy these people more than others. As for the women, the kookier they are, the more attractive they seem."

Autoanalysis also allowed Chayefsky to impart his newfound theories and philosophies. One tenet he prevailed upon himself, and his wife, to accept was that "Despair is an existential state and necessary to man's uncertainty of life." Selfishness and self-interest, he insisted, were "the basic motivations of men. And, as long as we know that, we can get along very well in this world."

People assume that everybody else's unhappiness is a demand on themselves, he went on. "We are hardly in this world for the purpose of making other people happy; we are lucky if we can get in a few moments of the stuff ourselves. And to hell with togetherness. Togetherness hasn't quite worked out. Let's face it. It was a feminine institution, and men couldn't get into it comfortably. In the little world I live in, there has been a distinct reassertion of the male as master of the house, and so on."

Madness in artists was "a higher form of sanity," Edgar Allan Poe had claimed. Chayefsky, without championing that cause, did sanction the use of anger in legitimate protest over one's rights. Instead of suppressing it and letting it harden into resentment, or using it as he had previously, as a battering ram to abuse and control people, he would endeavor to utilize his anger appropriately in the future, with dignity and conviction. As for the world, it *was* a fucked-up place, he said. War, crime, injustice, did exist. The only permanence was change, nothing remained the same, and the most important and enduring thing for an artist was his work. The zest and vitality for that could be generated by love and enthusiasm, or by its polar extremes, hate and indignation. The major figures throughout time knew that. "When I am angry I can write, pray, and preach well," said Martin Luther, "for then my whole temperament is quickened, my understanding sharpened, and all mundane vexations and temptations gone." Poe, Van Gogh, Ibsen, Tchaikovsky, and others endeavored to make their anger and rage work for them. Some succeeded, some perished. The solution was to not permit the minor frustrations of life to impede the energy or swamp the fury needed for the larger canvas. To survive one had to be smart, resilient, a survivor. To thine own self be true; don't wallow, don't be a victim, and above all, said Paddy Chayefsky, "Don't let the bastards win."

That summer, the writer carried his converted pique abroad. In the spring of 1959 a new cultural exchange program had been initiated between the United States and the Soviet Union. Among the American works sent to the USSR was *Marty*. "The ice was beginning to break with the Russians," said UA chief Arthur Krim. "We had a motion picture exchange and they decided to pick *Marty*, because they thought it would show the seamier side of American life, a butcher's life and all that." The opening night in Moscow was "a revelation," said Krim. "The Russians were absolutely enthralled that a butcher could have so much, his own house, a room for his mother and aunt, a phone that worked." The movie would play in the Soviet Union for two years; "Even though they paid us nothing, we felt good about it," said Krim, "because it was the first picture in the American-Russian exchange."

Because of the film's success, in July 1959 its creator was invited to be a member of the first writers delegation to visit the Soviet Union. At the Russian embassy in New York, when asked the purpose of his visit, Chayefsky wrote "Kicks." Also in the U.S. delegation were historian Arthur Schlesinger, Jr., literary critic and writer Alfred Kazin, and *Atlantic* editor Edward Weeks.

In Moscow, the first question from the group of participating Russian writers concerned unemployment in the United States. Chayefsky estimated the number at two million. No, the Russians corrected, the number was four million. "Oh really?" Chayefsky shrugged. "I'll accept that. I'm sure you can out-statistic me. But believe me, at least half of those four million unemployed

Americans went around job-seeking in their own cars." Boasting of their deep universal cultural attachment, the Russians announced that unlike the Americans, *they* recently celebrated Ernest Hemingway's sixtieth birthday. "Oh, you shouldn't have," Kazin replied. "Hemingway doesn't like to be reminded of his age."

In the Soviet Union, Chayefsky had "a stunning gift for deflating pomposity and clearing through the claptrap with quick, effective answers," Arthur Schlesinger recalled. His response to the Russians "was real and so swift—and sometimes so outraged," Edward Weeks added. "He would get almost uncontrollably angry in discussions of writing and censorship." When Schlesinger diplomatically asked the Russian writers about the need for external guidance in their work, Chayefsky, impatient at the delayed response, delivered the question more bluntly. "What about censorship from the Communist party?" he asked. There were no rejected stories, one Russian writer answered. "I've never had a story turned down either, but that's because I didn't write anything I thought would be turned down," Chayefsky retorted. "What I want to know is—would you print *Lady Chatterley's Lover?*" The answer was "nyet." Chayefsky's point, said Weeks, was "that the worst kind of censorship is the kind that takes place in your own mind before you sit down to a typewriter."

Most of the time in Russia, "we were lectured at by people telling us how communism had solved all the problems of humanity," said Schlesinger. "The Soviet Union," said Chayefsky, "is like a husband and wife who keep telling everyone all the time how happy they are." When they weren't being lectured at, they were being deceived, not on high-policy matters but on minor things. "We were lied to casually, contemptuously, and persistently, on petty issues," said Schlesinger.

After visiting a weary and cynical Ilya Ehrenburg, and Leo Tolstoy's house, the group was taken on a tour of the Mosfilm studios and shown some recent work. "There were no polemics, no politics, just technique," Chayefsky noted. "Bad movies, but great camera work." At the theatre he sat through a performance of Arthur Miller's *A View from the Bridge,* which "lasted four hours or less, depending on how long the actors took to smoke their cigarettes onstage."

When Chayefsky said he wanted to go to Velikye Bubny, the Ukrainian village where his mother was born, he was asked, "But why? They have a poor collective farm there. We could show you a better collective nearby." They did everything possible to divert his attention from the request, said Weeks, "until Paddy said, 'All right, you've lied to me consistently. I'm pulling out of the conference and going home.' "

With this, Chayefsky was allowed to fly to Kiev, where a car and driver were assigned to take him to his mother's village the following morning. The car arrived at his hotel four hours late, then drove at fifteen miles an hour on the seventy-five-mile journey to Velikye Bubny. When Chayefsky finally reached the village, old friends of his mother's family, who had never seen an American before, tried to welcome him. But after ten minutes, Chayefsky's driver told him that if they were to catch the last available plane back to Moscow that night, they had to return to Kiev at once. On the return trip the car went eighty miles per hour. At the airport there was no late plane scheduled. "After this, I really don't believe you have a Sputnik," said Chayefsky.

"When Paddy finally rejoined us twenty-four hours later," said Schlesinger, "he had already shaped this saga of Communist manipulation and mendacity into a marvelous story, at once hilarious, wrathful, and touching. I had admired the writer, and now I loved the man."

> Once I put the living world ahead of my
> writing, and it was a serious mistake, that is,
> for my writing. I got a lot of writing done that way,
> but it was a bit fraudulent. The living world
> demands some fraud, you see.
>
> Paddy Chayefsky, 1959

That summer, after the lukewarm response to the film version of *Middle of the Night,* and after he had abandoned his plans to write further scripts for Kim Novak, Chayefsky said he was returning to his true calling, the legitimate stage. The play he chose to write, *The Tenth Man,* would be the most successful of his theatrical career.

For some time, Chayefsky wanted to do a play with a Jewish background. In 1957 he had tried to buy the rights to his first Philco-Goodyear story, *Holiday Song,* but they were too expensive. His mother referred him to a book of Yiddish plays, where he came across the work of Szymon Ansky. Born in Vitebsk, Russia, Ansky had described himself as living a divided life "on the border between two worlds." During his early rebellious years, at war with the imperial restrictions imposed on Jews and eager to move beyond the confines of shtetl life, Ansky (né Solomon Rappoport) renounced his faith and proceeded to speak and write in Russian instead of Yiddish. Relocating to St. Petersburg he posed as a non-Jew until 1891, when the czarist police exposed his duplicity and threw him into prison. Upon his release, Ansky left for Paris, where, in 1902, he became a cofounder of the Socialist-Revolutionaries party. The latter would enable him to renew his passion, spiritually and artistically, in the Jewish nationalist cause. Before publicly reconverting to Judaism he began to speak and write in Yiddish again. In 1909 he created his short story "Behind a Mask." "The Sins of Youth" came in 1910, and in 1912 Ansky began his most famous work, *The Dybbuk,* a four-act play that would later become one of the most frequently performed works in Jewish repertory theatres around the world.

Featured for centuries in Yiddish folklore, a dybbuk is the angry, tortured soul of a dead person that inhabits the body of a living person, rendering him or her incensed or insane. Chayefsky, growing up in the 1930s, frequently heard the word applied to him, "in jest of course," he said. The Ansky play, which dealt with the exorcism of a young bride possessed by the soul of a dead lover, was set in the 1860s. Chayefsky said that his loosely adapted version would be updated, set in an American synagogue in current time. It would not be a place of ostentation or wealth, but "a shabby converted storefront" similar to the one he and his family had attended on 234th Street in the Bronx.

Plunging into "four months of the most enjoyable research," Chayefsky found it was impossible to study Jewish mysticism without studying the medieval Catholic church. "And that led me into pagan rituals and the way they have been adapted into Christianity." He also investigated the practices of psychiatry versus the supernatural for the casting out of demons and evil spirits.

In the outline for his story, his central character is a young girl possessed by the soul of a dead woman—"the whore of Kiev, a companion of sailors." After the girl is psychoanalyzed and treated without improvement, her parents plan to have her committed to an insane asylum. To prevent this her grandfather brings her to the local synagogue, where he requests that she be exorcised in a traditional ceremony. To perform this, a minyan, a group of ten men, is needed. Recruited off the street, the tenth man is a young lawyer, Arthur Landau. In the throes of a nervous collapse, he is an arrogant, unhappy, disillusioned human being. The character's surname came from the actor Martin Landau, but most of his background, his attitudes, and his contemporary malaise were expropriated directly from Paddy Chayefsky.

Because his parents were poor, Arthur Landau spent his first twenty years condemning the rich "for my childhood nightmares." Life was merely dreary if one was sane, but unbearable "if you're sensitive," he says. Reproaching society and his mother for his lower status, as soon as he was professionally established, he moved away from home. He lived by himself for a while, then, to escape the constant loneliness, got married. "Needless to say, we told each other how deeply in love we were," says Landau. "We wanted very much to be happy. Americans, you know, are fanatic about being happy." Making ardent love became a drain on his energy, so the young lawyer turned into a workaholic and was quite successful, which enabled him to avoid his wife entirely. "For this deceit," he says, "I was respected by everyone, including my wife, who was quite as bored with me as I was with her." The couple decided to have a child, "because we couldn't possibly believe we were that miserable together." After that, Landau began to drink and behave badly. When he failed at suicide he began to visit a psychoanalyst, but even that proved to be futile. "Life is utterly meaningless," he tells the possessed girl he meets in the synagogue. "I have everything a man can get out of life—prestige, power, money, children . . . and all I can think of is I want to get out of this as fast as I can."

Close to tears after his confession to the girl, the lawyer switches his bearing to one of composure. He does have "a theatrical way" when he wants to, he says brightly. The possessed girl, in turn, thinks he is wonderful. After comparing notes on their psychiatric histories, she corrects a mistake he made regarding the Scriptures. King Solomon did not write Ecclesiastes; it was written by an anonymous Jewish scholar in Alexandria. "I wouldn't put much stock in it," she tells him. "Weariness was all the rage among the Hellenized Jews." Staggered by her intelligence and beauty, the lawyer discovers that he is falling in love with this "amazing kid."

Commenting on the romantic outcome of the story, Chayefsky said: "I was finally able to give myself a delightful problem of craft—to marry off, to the audience's satisfaction, a lunatic and a suicidal maniac within five hours of their meeting each other. I suspect that's very much the way Shakespeare must have felt when he wrote *Richard III*."

The conflict in the play comes when the lawyer and others in the minyan object to the exorcism that is about to be performed. Skepticism and modern-day psychiatry are pitted against old-fashioned faith. At the climax, when the cabalistic ritual is conducted, an oblique surprise is presented to the audience.

Perhaps because of his own analysis, in *The Tenth Man* Chayefsky felt secure enough to allow the disparate sides of his nature to be exposed. Seven years before *Holiday Song* he had said he wanted to do a comedy in the fashion of Shalom Aleichem, "but it came out a rather ponderous spiritual message." With *The Tenth Man,* he intended it to be "a throwback to the old stylized folk comedies of Europe," and he accomplished that goal. In his second draft, while adhering to the critical vein of the story, Chayefsky proceeded to embellish the play with his inimitable candor and abundant jaunty humor. To build toward the exorcism ceremony, he inhabited the synagogue with a group of eccentric but lovable old cronies, no doubt held over in memory from his youth. Among the members of the minyan are a cranky leftist atheist, a whimsical philosopher, and a pious but cynical civic-minded citizen. In tandem they open the play complaining about the weather and their relatives ("My daughter-in-law, may she grow rich, buy a hotel with a thousand rooms, and be found dead in every one of them"). They reflect on their burial plots ("Old fools," says one, "discussing their graves as if they were country estates"), then argue about dybbuks, and the correct way to conduct an exorcism. For spiritual contrast, a pious old cabalist prays constantly in the background, while downstage, a younger, materialistic rabbi, "a go-getter," talks on the phone, drumming up business in an attempt to increase his dwindling congregation. His recruiting methods include starting a little league baseball team and a drama group and holding weekly raffles and bingo games to bring in more money. He is so busy, he says cheerfully, that this morning he "almost forgot to come to the synagogue."

When the play was near completion, Chayefsky had lunch at Sardi's with Josh Logan, who had directed the writer's last work on Broadway. "We sat down and he began talking about this new play he had written," said Logan. "And I could tell by the tone of his voice and his excitement that he was madly in love with it." As Chayefsky talked on and on about the modern young rabbi and the funny old men in the synagogue, Logan began to get "more and more nervous that he had never brought up any word of a director." Finally Chayefsky said, "The director's got to be really smart, really sharp, really chic. I really think this can be one of the best things I've ever done." After a short pause, Logan asked tentatively, "Paddy, is it by any chance something that might be right for me?" "Oh, good God, no!" said Chayefsky, "this one needs class."

It was Garson Kanin who introduced Chayefsky to a director with class. "Paddy and I had become friends again," said Kanin. "I read the play and he asked me to direct it. I said it would fail if I did it, because being Jewish I knew these characters and I wasn't excited by them. They didn't have any color or glamour for me. So I suggested that Tony [Tyrone] Guthrie do it."

Described as a loud, clear English voice in the commercial theatre, Tyrone Guthrie began his career as a director in England and Canada. In 1946 his legend was established in New York with an outstanding sequence of plays: *The Matchmaker, Tamburlaine, Six Characters in Search of an Author,* and an opulent, rousing production of *Carmen* at the Metropolitan Opera.

With the suggestion and endorsement of Kanin, Chayefsky immediately sent a copy of his play to Guthrie, who resided in Ireland. "After that," said Kanin, "Paddy's partner and producer, Arthur Cantor, called me up and said, 'What the hell is the matter with you, getting Paddy all confused? Are you putting him on? Why did you tell him that a British Shakespearean director should do his play?' "

A versatile artist who would "direct anything that gives me a challenge," Guthrie was very taken with the style and irreverence in Chayefsky's play, and cabled a positive reply. He liked the work and suggested they meet in New York for a sounding of minds and an inspection of egos. Known as "a dictator in the theatre" who seldom yielded to opinionated artists, when asked about his adroit staging of Shakespeare's plays, Guthrie attributed his facility to the fact that "Willie was seldom in the theatre during rehearsals."

When they met, Guthrie and Chayefsky found they had a few qualities in common. Counter to his florid professional reputation, the director was a man of unadorned personal style and few encumbrances. He seldom traveled with luggage, preferring to stow his belongings in a string bag or large army knapsack. His appearance was likewise adventitious. With his clipped mustache and short hair, his everyday attire consisted of sandals, no socks, old trousers, a clean but unironed short, and a gaudy scarf tied around his neck. Chayefsky's sartorial mode was equally vagrant.

As a bona fide Celt, Guthrie was also drawn to Chayefsky's adopted name, and his abiding humor. Then there was the matter of their respective heights. Chayefsky was five foot five and Guthrie was said to be six foot six or seven, depending on the view of the awestruck observer standing below him. "Ninety-two feet tall and like a windmill" was actress Coral Browne's summation. Being too tall was "as bad as being too short," said Guthrie, and as a youth he "suffered agonies"; that was the bond that brought the two men closer. "It all fell into place very quick," Chayefsky told the *Herald Tribune*. "We met in New York, signed the contracts, then Tony brought in a set designer to work on the sets and lighting over the summer."

The designer chosen was one whose credits satisfied Chayefsky's standards of stature. David Hays was affiliated with the successful revival of Eugene O'Neill's *The Iceman Cometh,* and the American premiere of *Long Day's Journey into Night*. His preliminary sketches and plans for *The Tenth Man* were discussed via calls and correspondence with Guthrie, who was back in Ireland that summer. The director, although in absentia, was a very strong presence, a confident pipeline between all the contributors, Hays said. And that September, prior to Guthrie's arrival, the set designer scouted various storefront synagogues in New York. "These were on the Lower East Side," he said. "They were narrow little stores—about the same size as a shoe store. Just big enough for your minyan of ten and maybe ten others."

With Guthrie and Chayefsky in tow, the designer then visited a Hasidic center in the Williamsburg section of Brooklyn. There was no deep philosophical discussion. They were there just to see the place. "I remember how funny Tony looked," said Hays. "Before going into the synagogue, Paddy and I had placed yarmulkes on our heads. So Tony, who was very tall, plopped a white handkerchief on top of his head and swept in after us. He looked so utterly ridiculous, and the sextons inside regarded him with enormous suspicion, but

Tony was totally unfazed. He knew that there was nothing he could possibly do about it."

When the casting got under way, Chayefsky told agents that he wanted "a compelling but neurotic Romeo and Juliet" for the young couple in his play. Risa Schwartz, the daughter of the famed Yiddish actor Maurice Schwartz, was cast as the possessed girl. For Arthur Landau, the cynical, disillusioned lawyer, John Cassavetes and Mike Nichols were Chayefsky's first choices. Guthrie suggested a Canadian actor, Donald Harron, who had worked with him at Stratford. "I was out touring the U.S., playing Jimmy Porter in *Look Back in Anger*," said Harron. "My agent kept sending my reviews to Chayefsky and he eventually agreed to see me."

On a Sunday, his only day off, Harron flew from San Francisco via Dallas to New York for the meeting with Chayefsky. "I met with him and Tony Guthrie in Paddy's office for about fifteen minutes," said Harron. "There was no audition, no reading, just a chat about miscellaneous things. Then they said goodbye, and I was out on the street not long after, saying, 'Why the hell did I come all this way for?' Later I found out that thanks to Tony, I already had the role. It was just that Paddy wanted to take a look at me."

For the subsidiary characters, the old men in the synagogue, Guthrie said he relied almost entirely on Chayefsky's recommendations. Jewish actors who had played vaudeville and the Yiddish theatre were brought in. Jack Pearl, a well-known radio comedian, was hired to play Zitorsky, the wry philosopher; David Vardi was cast as the harried sexton or shammes; and the nightclub comic Lou Jacobi was asked to audition for the role of the atheist who is in the synagogue because it's winter and he has nothing better to do with his time. "They sent for me and asked me to show them what I thought would be the general attitude of an amicable atheist," said Jacobi. "I am neither an atheist nor always amicable. But I tried to put the two together and they must have liked it because I got the role."

Gene Saks had been in *Middle of the Night,* and was recommended by Chayefsky to play the brash young rabbi who tries to boost attendance in the synagogue by holding bingo games. "Paddy asked me to come in and meet Guthrie, who said, 'Do you play comedy?' I said, 'Yes.' He said, 'Jolly good!' And that was that," said Saks. "I didn't have to read."

On the first day of rehearsals, Guthrie addressed the cast and said he hoped they would "put up with someone who is a total goy." The purpose of rehearsals was to find out where they were going and to have a good time on the journey. On the second day of readings a problem arose. Jack Pearl was obviously unhappy with his part. In his youth, Pearl had been a star in the *Ziegfeld Follies* before creating the character of Baron Munchausen ("Vass you dere, Sharlie?") on radio. Celebrity, wealth, and retirement followed, until, at seventy-five, Pearl wanted one more turn in the spotlight. During rehearsals for *The Tenth Man,* however, he found his role too small. "He hated the part," said Gene Saks. "He would have an occasional line here and there. They were very funny lines, but this was an ensemble piece and Jack wasn't happy. In rehearsals he'd be talking to the actors onstage and seldom paid attention. When his turn came, everything would stop, and Guthrie would say, 'Jackie boy, your turn.' And Pearl would say, 'What? What?' And someone would say, 'It's your line. Your line.' And the line would be something like 'Me too.' And he'd do the line, 'Me too.' Then under his breath he'd say, 'Some part.' "

Donald Harron was aware of Pearl's dissatisfaction when he bumped into actor Jack Gilford in the village. Harron told him the producers might be looking for another actor to play Zitorsky. "He obviously contacted Paddy," said Harron, "because a few days later, Jack Pearl left the play and Gilford took over."

"Gilford was wonderful in the part," said Saks, "as were the others. These were first-class middle-aged Jewish actors—very serious about their work. Guthrie never had to tell any of the actors *how* to act. They really knew their business. They were very comic and adept. But they had to be under the hand of someone they respected, because during the performance there was also a lot of shoving around and upstaging, a lot of fights. David Vardi was this terrific little Israeli actor, and Lou Jacobi, who was kind of monstrous to work with, was very paranoid about him. Jacobi was sure that at times Vardi was upstaging him—which he was."

During the religious rituals and the exorcism ceremony, the ensemble of character actors were often at odds as to the correct interpretation. "When you get ten Jews together there's always ten different ideas as to how things should be done according to custom," said Saks. "For instance how do you wear the prayer shawl? Do you wear it over your head, half over your head, whatever. So they would argue amongst each other and then speak to the director. 'Doctor Guthrie,' they would say, 'which way do you want it?' And Guthrie would chuckle. 'Don't ask me, gentlemen,' he would say. '*You* are the Jews!' "

Guthrie and Chayefsky agreed there would be no touching or "sweet kissy-poo" in the love scenes between the possessed girl and the lawyer. Both men were disinclined toward physical displays of affection onstage, although unspoken gestures of lust and desire were not ruled out. Once, in a production of *Hamlet,* Guthrie suggested that Laurence Olivier put his hand up Ophelia's dress during the soliloquy.

At the other extreme, to avoid having the play stereotyped as "a religious work," Chayefsky stressed that the work was "catholic—with a small *c.*" With the exception of the word "dybbuk," and a few others referring to the Scripture and holy rituals, not one Yiddish or Hebrew word was uttered. There were to be no obvious accents either. The actors were to speak in cultured tones and even the prayers were to be spoken in English, though sung to the ancient melodies. At Guthrie's suggestion Risa Schwartz was coached by a voice teacher to give her voice strength and timbre in the scenes where the girl, possessed, had to scream.

Known as a fearless and stern director, who was hell on actors who were late or slacking, Guthrie admitted, "Yes, I'm nippy at times, like a sergeant major. When you've got a large group together—someone has to spin the ball." Yet the work process on *The Tenth Man* was relatively free of clashes and reproach. The main surprise expressed along Theatre Row was how well the distinguished director and the brash playwright were getting along. Hays recalled that Chayefsky "was always present, and always in Guthrie's ears, but we never heard any of it."

Donald Harron also remembered the Guthrie-Chayefsky relationship as marvelous and easy. "There was this kind of idolatry going on. Paddy loved the idea of working with this strange creature who came from classical theatre. And Tony obviously adored Paddy. He considered the play to be like Shakespeare and naturally Paddy was very taken with that."

Alan Manson, who played one of the ten men in the minyan, said that Guthrie relied considerably on Chayefsky for his insights into Jewish life. "Here was a man who had never been in a synagogue in his life. He and Paddy came from completely different worlds, and together they were creating this wonderful magic on stage, because at the core there was a trust and great fondness between them." The director's staging was "as creative as the script," Chayefsky acknowledged. Guthrie's blending of the religious mysticism with the dramatic aspects, while seamlessly moving the sections from comedy to ritual to farce, was "miraculous," the enamored playwright exclaimed.

A devotee of choreography, Guthrie devised the placement and movements for each actor. "When he was staging the opening scene, where the old men come in and have their conversations, he had them move around each other, in almost kind of a dance pattern," said Saks.

"The part which I laugh out loud about today was a piece of business that happened in the first act," said David Shaw, who visited Chayefsky during rehearsals. "One old Jew comes in. It's winter and he's freezing and he starts peeling off clothes—one thing after another. He is this skinny old man, and finally the last thing he has on is a football jersey, with a big number on the back. I fell apart when I saw that, it was hysterically funny. Later, when Paddy was preparing the play for publication, I asked him, 'Paddy, that idea of the football jersey, was that yours or Guthrie's?' He said, 'Oh no, that was Tony's idea.' I said, 'Are you putting it in the book of the play?' and he replied, 'You bet your ass I am.'"

Guthrie's keen eye for color and bold sense of setting added immeasurably to his reputation. He relished innovation and the unconventional. For one revival of *Hamlet* he had alpine peaks dominating the stage. *The Tenth Man* production had "the bold shadings of an etching or lithograph," said *The New York Times*. "We all thought the David Hays set was wonderful," said Saks. "It was something I had not seen before, or since. The upstage part was lower than the downstage, it was like a sunken living room. Some of the actors who had very few or no lines prayed there. It gave the play a background, great depth which added but was not intrusive to the main drama being played on the raised forestage."

"The lighting was unique too," said Harron. "The whole effect was like a Rembrandt painting."

The coup de théâtre came at the climax of the exorcism scene. The stage went black. The sound of a body hitting the floor was heard. Moments passed, and when the lights came up the audiences saw that it was not the young girl who had been freed of demons. It was the young lawyer.

On September 25, the *Tenth Man* company was in Philadelphia to try out the play. Describing Guthrie as "an assassin in terms of story," Chayefsky said that he had to "stand ceaseless guard against the director's ambushes." After the first preview performance they found they were thirty-five minutes over, so the official cutting began.

"The original script was like a plum cake, and wonderfully so, but very rich," said Harron. "Paddy was in love with words. And even though I loved my part and what I had to say, I did have to go to Guthrie and ask him if he could get him to cut the two or three adjectives that were in front of every noun. 'It's a little purple,' I told Tony, and very discreetly he managed to have it done."

Describing the changes as minor, Chayefsky said he sharpened a line here and there, and "cut out the 'wisdom'—the philosophizing and sermonizing—so that the dramatic action will speak for itself."

On October 1, two days before the official opening in Philadelphia, Guthrie announced to the cast at rehearsals, "Gentlemen! I know I'm hopelessly goy, but aren't we opening this play on Yom Kippur?"

"Of course he was right," said Alan Manson. "So they postponed it, and Dr. Guthrie got his one good suit pressed and went to shul with Paddy."

"I can still see them walking down the street that evening," said Saks. "They both had blue suits on, with their hair slicked back, like two little yeshiva boys."

That same evening, over holiday dinner, Guthrie convinced Chayefsky to change the ending of the play. Originally it closed with the old men trading traditional Yiddish daughter-in-law curses. Guthrie wanted something less comic, and suggested ending on "a note of Talmudic disputation." On the spot, Paddy gave him the new ending. The young lawyer, having found his passion for life restored by his concern for the girl, asks God for the capability to love, then leaves the stage. The old men discuss what has just transpired, and one of them says, "He still doesn't believe in God, he simply wants to love. And when you stop to think about it, gentlemen, is there any difference?"

To perform the new closing, Chayefsky chose Arnold Marle, a distinguished European actor who was playing the old cabalist. "He was perfectly cast," said Manson, "because Marle was a mystic himself. He was also a very obstinate and stubborn man. He insisted on reading the two lines directly into the one key light above him. And Guthrie said, 'Arnold, dear. Would you just sort of throw the line away, and walk upstage as you say it?' But Marle refused to do this. So Guthrie took the line away from him and gave it to George Voscovec. Guthrie didn't want to do this, but Marle would not take his direction. Making it so melodramatic would have spoiled the ending."

The opening-night performance in Philadelphia brought an elitist response from the professional critics. They praised the play but wondered if the general public would enjoy it. But the response from audiences was favorable, and ticket sales were brisk for the entire run. During the second week one negative blast came from an unexpected source. A local conservative rabbi, reacting to Chayefsky's picture of an enterprising, modern-day rabbi and other religious matters, took to his pulpit and said the play was "a distortion of Judaism, desecrating, insulting, and ugly."

"A lot of the objection to the play was that Paddy didn't show Jews in a good light," said Gene Saks. "By that they meant, Why don't you show them in a synagogue in a better-class neighborhood, like on Fifth Avenue. 'Show us like we really are!' " David Hays said that he was sitting in a Horn & Hardart cafeteria in Philadelphia with an electrician from the company when they overheard two men talking about the play. "Gee, the synagogue was so shabby," one said. "Aw, come on!" his friend replied. "I remember our first synagogue was in a gas filling station."

On November 5, 1959, the day of the New York opening, Frank Farrell of the *World-Telegram and Sun* said, "No matter how the play registers with critics, it will have no comparison with previous ventures, because this time out, Paddy Chayefsky avoided all riots and cooperated completely with producers, stars, directors, et al."

During that night's premiere performance the playwright sat in a rear-aisle seat at the Booth Theatre. Before the first act was over he was up, pacing at the back of the theatre, counting the laughs and judging the audience's reaction.

"The only previous New York review we got came from *Variety*," said

Donald Harron, "and it wasn't good. So there was trepidation all around. Also, opening-night audiences in New York are tough, so most of us were petrified. After the show we all trooped over to Sardi's. It was like a wake. No, not a wake, a funeral. And then the reviews started to come in and they were absolutely glowing."

"Praise the Lord for an imaginative play that restores the theatre's self-respect," said Brooks Atkinson of *The New York Times*. Walter Kerr of the *Herald Tribune* declared *The Tenth Man* "an original, a first, an inventive play by a writer of real talent." *Newsweek* followed with "Cheers for Chayefsky . . . a common man with a touch of the priest and the poet."

Kenneth Tynan, the critic for *The New Yorker*, while finding the dialogue "as meaty as I have heard since the heyday of Clifford Odets," did express some reservations. As a gentile, Tynan said he got most of the Jewish expressions, but found that "the performance of the stage Jews displayed the same kind one finds, and abhors, in stage Irishmen," and that for most of the evening he felt "that I was watching an image of the Jewish people that was as limited in its way as the image of Uncle Tom."

Prepared for an attack similar to the one from the rabbi in Philadelphia, Chayefsky lined up support from New York Jewish religious and political leaders prior to the opening. Free house seats were made available to the rabbis of various districts and to the executive members of the leading Jewish organizations.

Rabbi Louis Malamud was the cantor of the Actors Temple on Forty-seventh Street and Eighth Avenue. He knew about show business because his congregation included Georgie Jessel, Sophie Tucker, and Eddie Fisher. After attending the play as a guest of Chayefsky, Rabbi Malamud gave his assessment of the play to *Variety*. He was enthusiastic about the acting, he said, "but the plot is a mishmash. It would be better on Second Avenue. *The Music Man* is a better show."

Other rabbis expressed their opinion in letters printed by *The New York Times*. One purist objected to the "contrived happy ending." In the Ansky play *The Dybbuk*, the girl, when abjured of her demon, collapses and dies. Chayefsky's heroine lives. So why wasn't he faithful to the original? "Because it's *my* play," said Paddy. "And with due respect to Mr. Ansky, there is no copyright on dybbuks."

The playwright was also admonished for implying that a mystical exorcism of a dybbuk, or demon, could succeed where medicine and psychiatry had failed. That was misleading, said Rabbi Dr. Louis I. Newman, rabbi of the Rodeph Sholom Temple on West Eighty-third Street. Although he believed in a supernatural world "above and beyond our own world," said Newman, in this world we "must learn from science and ethics, not mysticism."

But the cantor of Rodeph Sholom, Gunter Hirschberg, observed that the essential point of the play was *not* Jewish cabalistic practices as opposed to modern psychiatry, but a charge against materialism. "Just who is possessed in the play—the boy, the girl, the rabbi, or the atheist?" he asked, then surmised, "We are a possessed generation, aren't we? And in all of us lives a dybbuk."

Wisely, this time out Chayefsky did not enter the fray. *The Tenth Man,* which would run 624 performances in New York and be produced in eight foreign countries, was never intended to be "the intellectual's meat," he said. It did not lend itself to deep scrutiny and "was meant to be amusing, nothing more." He also recognized that it was the best thing he had ever written, so he could afford to say "to hell with it, that's what my play means. It is an orgasmic play. It's finished. It does its job."

A DECADE OF ADVERSITY

Cudgeling Among the Literati

In March of 1960, the plays nominated for Tony awards brought to a close a decade of American theatre not to be equaled again. Among the original musicals nominated were *Gypsy, The Sound of Music,* and *Fiorello!* The dramatic plays were *Sweet Bird of Youth, The Miracle Worker, The Best Man, Toys in the Attic, A Raisin in the Sun,* and *The Tenth Man.* Tyrone Guthrie was nominated for best director, and Paddy Chayefsky for best dramatist, but when the final votes were tabulated, the awards went to Arthur Penn and William Gibson, respectively, for *The Miracle Worker.*

That May, a month after the awards, Chayefsky was invited to speak at a playwrights forum at CCNY, his alma mater in Harlem. On the panel was William Gibson, who knew Chayefsky from their days at the New Dramatists group ten years before. After the forum the two writers shared a cab downtown. "Both of us at this time were making a lot of money," said Gibson. "But Paddy didn't seem happy about it. 'You make a lot of money and you never get rich,' he said. Also on that occasion at CCNY I had been talking about new plays and playwrights. I had always appreciated anyone who had helped me when I was starting out, so I was interested in giving a hand up to younger people. Paddy was wary about this. 'Bill,' he said, 'I don't seem to have your passion for other people's work.' "

Geniuses, it is said, harbor a jealous nature, and writers of note seldom indulge in homage to their own. Chayefsky had learned this when his name first went into orbit. In fact, there were those who dared openly to dismiss his work. Dorothy Parker had been a literary light since her days in the Algonquin set of the thirties. By the late fifties she was living on alcohol and unemployment checks, holed up in a less than genteel hotel in New York. Her reduced

circumstances notwithstanding, Parker still managed to lift her cane of approbation and take a whack at the artistic community from time to time. One day,
during an interview with *The Paris Review,* after casting a somewhat jaundiced
eye on the current theatrical terrain, the legendary Parker said dramatic vision
was mandatory for all good writers. "It's the difference between Paddy
Chayefsky, who just puts down lines, and Clifford Odets, who in his early plays
not only sees but has a point of view."

Another distinguished curmudgeon of this time, S. J. Perelman, said he was
aghast at the "unconscionable amount of publicity" Chayefsky was receiving.
"It's now at the point where you wouldn't mind if you never heard his name
again," said Perelman, while the junior macho novelist Norman Mailer, after
praising Clifford Odets "for giving us *Waiting for Lefty* in the nineteen-
thirties," peevishly asked, "What have the nineteen-fifties brought us but
Marty?"

In the newer group of writers, Gore Vidal possessed a mordant wit, versatil-
ity, and an unsparing self-confidence. He liked a number of playwrights "as
people," Vidal remarked. "For some reason they bring out my protective and
pedagogic instincts. I like to reassure them, to help them, to give them reading
lists." When inclined, he would also lend his time to writing reviews and
ratings of their work for various publications. In 1959, when Arthur Miller
released a collection of his plays in a book, Vidal covered the occasion for *The
Partisan Review.* He admired Miller as "a writer-cripple," Vidal said in his
opening critique. Evaluating Miller's preface, Vidal noted that the playwright
"with paralyzing pomp" split his infinitives and crushed the syntax before
ascending to the throne as "our prophet, our king, our guide in the dark. The
only thing wrong is he does not write awfully well."

Vidal and Paddy Chayefsky also sparred occasionally during the fifties and
early sixties. After Vidal adapted *The Catered Affair,* which Paddy praised, but
not to Gore's face, the two had a temporary tiff over a collection of TV plays, to
be published by Ballantine Books, which Vidal compiled and for which he had
written an introduction. "I thought I would try to raise, as it were, the very low
estimate that 'intellectuals' then had of TV drama," Vidal recalled. "Paddy
thought that my preface, on writing for TV versus the theatre, was demeaning to
'The Art,' and said that if it stayed in the book he would remove his play." With
"uncomplaining nobility," Vidal removed his preface, and relations with Chayefsky cooled until later, when, "as Broadway dramatists, we were amiable."

In March 1960, Vidal's play *The Best Man* opened on Broadway. The
plot—two rival presidential candidates threaten each other with calumny and
blackmail—was sharp and timely, given that this was an election year. The only
conflict of sorts was that Vidal's *The Best Man* was housed directly across the
street from Chayefsky's *The Tenth Man,* and audiences were sometimes

confused as to which play they were attending. A woman in a cartoon in *The New Yorker,* watching the old Jewish men scurry back and forth onstage in Chayefsky's play, turns to her matinee companion and asks, "Which one is supposed to be Richard Nixon?" The confusion was repeated when a theatre magazine printed a glowing essay on the Vidal play, but inadvertently illustrated the piece with a photograph of the theatre marquee of Chayefsky's play.

Thirty years later, Vidal said that he always admired the way Chayefsky controlled his first three films: "Had they made money," he said, "he would have had a splendid career." He also "liked" Chayefsky's work, he said. "Though I did not value it as highly, perhaps, as he did. But then my close friends in those days were Tennessee Williams and Bill Inge."

From Odets to the Bible

In 1959, after the Broadway production of *The Tenth Man* was launched, Chayefsky told *The New York Times* that he was working on a unique story idea, to be done as a play or a movie, with Elia Kazan directing. "This isn't double talk," he stated. "Kazan and I wanted to work together for several years. I've got the idea in mind, and some of it is down on paper."

The concept was a satire of famous writers. "It's a spoof on American literature, from World War I up to the present," he said. "There will be a variety of scenes, each of which will be carefully done in a famous writer's literary style. It should be really wild as a story." His inspiration was Virginia Woolf's novel *Orlando,* in which she satirized various British historical and literary figures. "If Mrs. Woolf can satirize English literature, why can't I satirize American playwrights and novelists, and call it *Mrs. Orlando?*"

It would be three plays in one, he decided, each written in a different style, combining drama, farce, and musical comedy. Mrs. Orlando would be in each play, as a literary groupie, "a gal who just can't help falling in love with American writers." In the first act, she falls in love with the ghost of Eugene O'Neill. In the second and third acts, both "farcical in form," the targets of her ardor would be Clifford Odets and Arthur Miller.

Chayefsky's combat with Arthur Miller and his professional struggles with the specter of Eugene O'Neill were already documented. The name of Clifford Odets was poked at sporadically. In the thirties, Odets was the voice for millions of Americans struggling with the horrifying dilemma of the Depression. His unique dialogue and dramatic vividness influenced a generation of writers to come, including Arthur Miller, who, according to Odets, "never approached or acknowledged the slightest influence from me to him." (Of Eugene O'Neill, Miller told *The Paris Review* that he "never meant much" to him, that O'Neill was "a finished figure" when he started to write in the forties.) Paddy Chayefsky was more forthcoming about Odets. In an interview, he said that it would be difficult to find "a writer of my generation, especially a New York writer, who doesn't owe his very breath—his entire attitude towards the theatre—to Odets. Arthur Miller is an obvious example." That done, Chayefsky went on to say that as far as he was concerned Odets had "yet to write his best play." This was in 1960, when Odets's theatrical résumé included *Waiting for Lefty, Awake and Sing!, Paradise Lost, Golden Boy, The Big Knife,* and *The Country Girl.*

Some friendly fire had erupted between Odets and Chayefsky before that. In 1956, the two had met in California, in the offices of Hecht-Hill-Lancaster. Chayefsky was working on *The Bachelor Party,* and Odets was busy with *Sweet Smell of Success.* Jim Hill recalled, "Clifford was a god! The most talented writer of his day." Chayefsky was equally talented, but different, Hill continued. "Paddy was young, full of piss and vinegar, and Clifford had had his day. But as a craftsman, he was first class. And he liked Paddy's work. I'm almost sure of that. I remember I used to tease them about each other all the time."

William Gibson also had known Odets, at the Actors Studio, where the elder writer taught drama for a few semesters; later, the two became social friends. Odets was "astonishing . . . generous . . . the best talker I ever heard in my life, no matter what the topic was," said Gibson. As a writer he was better than O'Neill, "a genius . . . the only American playwright I truly love." The petty rivalry between Odets and Chayefsky was one-sided, Gibson believed, but Odets was aware of it. After he had written *Golden Boy,* the story of a young violinist who reluctantly becomes a boxer, Chayefsky wrote *The Man Who Made the Mountains Shake,* the story of an idealistic young man who grudgingly becomes a boxer. *The Big Knife,* Odets's lacerating attack on the Hollywood movie industry, came in 1949, followed a few years later by *The Goddess,* which Chayefsky called his "exposé of a stinking town." Five years after that, Odets wrote *The Flowering Peach,* a bibical comedy of human righteousness. Soon to come from Chayefsky would be *his* biblical play, *Gideon.* "Look at that," Odets said to William Gibson at that point, "when I write a play about the North Pole, that young man writes one about the South Pole."

There was no rancor in Odets's comment, Gibson added, because, "as playwrights, amongst ourselves, we tend to be a funny, cantankerous lot."

> Do not presume to matter, Gideon,
> for in the house of God you matter not. To love me,
> Gideon, you must abandon all your vanities. They are
> presumptuous and will come between us.
>
> The Angel, *Gideon*

By June 1960 Chayefsky had abandoned *Mrs. Orlando.* It was "too much of an in-joke," he told one reporter. In reality, the idea of sparring onstage with the big three of American drama no longer interested him at that juncture. He had found a far greater subject to tackle: God.

The idea had come to him that spring, he said, when he was in Israel, researching a script based on the fall of the second temple. Traveling south to Beersheba one weekend, with nothing to read in his hotel, he found himself immersed in the Bible. "And there it was," he said, "the story of Gideon."

In Chapter 6 of the Book of Judges, in the year 1100 B.C., the Lord was offended by the Israelites' worship of false idols, so for seven years He had allowed a seditious tribe, the Midianites, to rule Israel. Heeding their cry for release, the Lord decided the Israelites should conquer and oust the Midianites. To effect that mammoth task, he chose an ordinary farmer, Gideon, to act as leader of the Israelites. When confronted by the Almighty in person, Gideon would not accept that God was God. He wanted proof, some extemporaneous miracles performed on the spot. "Other men in the Bible needed just one miracle to accept God—the burning bush sufficed for Moses—but God kept performing miracle after miracle for Gideon, and Gideon didn't buy them," said Chayefsky.

The humor of the situation, and the idea that this wasn't God testing Gideon but Gideon testing God, was a good premise for a play, Chayefsky believed. He also had some lingering religious doubts of his own to air. In his youth, owing to his mother's strong influence, Sidney Chayefsky had been both pious and diligent. He had gone to the temple daily, attended yeshiva, and studied the Bible regularly. "God's hand is in everything," his mother said frequently, but Sidney wondered about that during the Depression, when poverty and suffering were everywhere. At fifteen, when he was burdened with his own depression and suicidal feelings, he asked God for help, but the Lord was busy elsewhere. "Paddy" stepped in then and saved the day. He did it again during the harsh basic training period in the Army. His attendance at the formal religious observances decreased considerably at that time. He still believed in God, but further doubts were raised when he was stationed in London, working on the war documentary *True Glory.* The British combat photographers were the first to bring in footage of the Nazi concentration camps. Viewing the atrocities and human destruction, Chayefsky asked in horror where the hand of God was when this was allowed to happen.

Stationed in Paris, Chayefsky read the writings of Friedrich Nietzsche, who rejected Christianity because it emphasized life in the next world instead of this one, because it taught men how to die, not how to live. Paddy was particularly taken with the German philosopher's concept of the *Übermensch* (superman), and the idea that God had nothing to do with destiny, that each human was in charge of his or her own life, and death. Quoting Nietzsche on the subject of mortal control, in an early draft of *The Goddess,* Chayefsky said that it was the comforting thoughts of suicide that helped get his writer character "through a lot of bad nights." God's involvement in human existence was not entirely dismissed or discounted, however. In 1960 Chayefsky would turn to the Lord again, when a personal matter shrouded his life. It had to do with his beloved mother.

Through the years, despite his marriage and busy career, Chayefsky had remained very close to Gussie Chayefsky. She was always there for him. In the fifties, as his star was ascending, his greatest pleasure was to have his mother share in everything. He invited her to each premiere and play opening. During the production of his movies in New York, he would frequently have Gussie brought to the set, where he would place her in the director's chair so that the actors could be brought forward to pay respect. For her part, Gussie knew that it was her duty never to let her youngest son get a swelled head. With each new triumph she reminded him that there was a Divine Force out there, greater and more lasting than any prize or glory from show business. Her famous son always listened and remained respectful of her religious beliefs.

In the last part of the decade, Mrs. Chayefsky, almost seventy, left Tibbett Avenue and moved to Scarsdale, to live with her son Bill and his family. She continued to work, however, in a garment factory in White Plains. "She went to and from work by private car, which Paddy paid for," said Terry Chayefsky. "The car cost him more than she made each day, but he knew that this job was very important to her." In 1960, during a medical examination, it was discovered that Gussie had terminal cancer. Her illness became protracted and agonizing. When she was hospitalized, Paddy visited each day, sitting by her bedside, holding her hand and watching as she slipped in and out of consciousness. His mother's suffering was "terrible, terrible," he said, laying the blame on God. "Why did He allow this?" he asked. "She was a good woman, a good, good woman, a dear woman. Did she need to enter death without being able to make a sound?"

"Paddy took my mother's illness very hard," said Bill. "We all did. 'Why should the good suffer? This was not a just God.' That was his reaction."

In August 1960 Mrs. Chayefsky died. After sitting shiva with family and friends, Paddy went to work on his play. In his adaptation he made Gideon into "the first Existentialist." Dubious about the existence of God, and emphasizing will over reason, all infinites were dispensed with. "Existentialists only know the world they see," said Chayefsky, "which gives them reason for despair." At the outset, Gideon is a simple but stubborn man, something like Marty, "a good hearted guy who's not a dummy but is thought of as one." Later, as the play proceeds, so that he can hold his own in the stormy debates with God, Chayefsky made Gideon more articulate and intelligent. He also changed the story. In the Bible, after capturing the elders of Succoth, who were sinners and miscreants, Gideon has them put to death at the Lord's request. In his version Chayefsky made Gideon more compassionate. The elders are also Hebrews—"our people"—so why should he kill them? Gideon asks. Man has three main passions, Chayefsky explained in his notes. The first is his passion to love, not to be alone. The second is the passion to create, to write, or paint, or build cities. The third is the passion of hatred, "and this one I don't understand at all," he said. "Why must we kill?"

Having made Gideon more assertive against God's will and commands, Paddy then imbued him with some homegrown vanity. Following his first victory against the Midianites, looking for compliments, Gideon asks God whether he thought he handled his battle duties well, whether he spoke and looked and behaved like a general. With humor and patience, God agrees that Gideon cut "a splendid figure" and calls him vain, "a pompous ass." "Yes, so I am," Chayefsky's Gideon cheerily replies. "Like all modest men, I am impossibly vain. I amuse even myself, strutting about, shouting—well, not really shouting; I'm cleverer than that at the charade. What a peacock I am! Oh it is amusing, isn't it?" Pushing for more stature, after the final battle is won Gideon asks the Lord to make him a king. God answers that He Himself is the King of Israel, and to suggest they need another would mean He is inadequate. Gideon, in a burst of temper, says that he is not asking for much. He did not intend to usurp the Almighty's throne. He only wants a "nominal crown and a few trappings, . . . perhaps a modest palace?" God cautions against this presumptuous vanity. He wants total devotion and submission, which makes Gideon angrier. All he wants is "a bit of pomp" because he likes to preen. Furthermore, isn't that what God promised—"to exalt me above my fellows"?

With his apprenticeship over, and eager to write "at greater depth," Chayefsky said that this new work would release him from the common burden of being known as an urban dramatist. "Realism has sort of had it," he told *The New York Times*. "Albee, Richardson, the new playwrights, not one of them's realistic. I was bored with it more than most people."

Many critics had failed to notice that in his last play, *The Tenth Man*, his dialogue had been more stylized than realistic; in *Gideon*, Chayefsky intended to go even further, by straying as far north from the vernacular as possible. He was going to write the entire play in *verse*. "Verse and the Bible?" asked W. J. Wetherby, correspondent for the *Manchester Guardian*. "From the man who gave us the simple colloquialism of 'Hey, Marty, whaddya want to do tonight?' This could be comparable to Elvis Presley switching to grand opera." Chayefsky explained to Wetherby that he had to change his style because the current social-comment play was much too transitory and didn't have lasting power "unless the writer is a brilliant wit like Shaw, and even he looks tacky fifty years later."

Chayefsky believed his progression to verse and poetry was a natural evolution. His interest had been sparked by Elizabeth Taylor. "Liz wanted to make a movie about Edna St. Vincent Millay, so I started to read her poetry," he told the *London Standard*. "In researching her life I read the other poets she was interested in." His own favorite was Edgar Allan Poe, who was "a great poet," said Chayefsky. "It's a matter of sensibility, you know."

Being a poet was also a respected profession. His mother told him that. In fact, when she lay dying, Chayefsky wrote some couplets about her agony. As she tried to breathe, he leaned in to decipher her wretched whispers. "Are you all right, Ma?" he asked. She shook her head with monumental slowness, no. "So this is death then," he wrote. "Not a soft sleep, but a succumbing, a drowning, an asphyxiation. For the first time, I am afraid."

"I saw myself and all men for what we truly are, suspensions of matter, flailing about for footholds in the void, all the while slipping back screaming into endless suffocations," said Gideon in his cry to the Lord.

In Westport, Connecticut, where he rented a house for the summer, Chayefsky added more "trumpets of grandeur" to his speeches, with the insertion of euphonious but obscure words. "I collect words like some people collect stamps," he explained, but for the benefit of their readers, when the play of *Gideon* appeared in *Esquire* the editors felt compelled to include a pony upfront. The decoding list included *apogeny* (loss of reproductive function), *immane* (that which is vast), *pschent* (a double crown, headdress of Egyptian pharaohs), and *rodomontade* (vain boasting, empty bluster).

"Every word was checked and gone over to be sure it wouldn't ring false," said Chayefsky. "I hate period pieces that use modern jokes. I want the play to be looked on as authentic."

The dueling debates between God and Gideon came from issues germane to the writer: his willfulness and doubts regarding God's supreme authority. "Gideon cannot believe in God because it means giving up the illusion of his own significance," said Chayefsky. "Cannot? Or will not? Or prefers not? The specific illusion that Gideon would like to keep is that he has created his own eminence, that the people love him because he is a good man and a good leader, that he knows right from wrong, and that he is more than just God's power."

Wrestling further with his own issues through Gideon, Chayefsky asked why God should be the star, the only *primo don*? Why should He get all the credit? "The sun does not revolve around the earth, you imbecile; the earth revolves around the sun," the Lord tells Gideon. But that is "patent nonsense,"

Gideon argues, then begs to be released from the covenant of love between them. "Are you suggesting some sort of a divorce between your God and you?" the Lord asks. Gideon says yes. He is a plain man, subject to imperfect feelings. "I shall betray you many times," he says, "and you shall rise in wrath against me and punish me with mighty penalties." Startled, the Lord asks, "You do not love me?" Kneeling before Him, Gideon confesses, "I tried to love you, but it is too much for me. You are too vast a concept for me . . . I cannot love you, God, for it makes me a meaningless thing."

"Man cannot accept his insignificance," said Chayefsky. "He is driven by a terror of being utterly insignificant. Some passion drives him to get above himself."

After a third and final draft of the play was completed, in New York that fall Chayefsky showed it to Fred Coe, who agreed to produce it on Broadway, with Arthur Cantor as coproducer. The only director Chayefsky would consider was Tyrone Guthrie. "He improved *The Tenth Man* by at least twenty-five percent," he said. "So I went out and wrote another one fast because of him."

In December the play was sent to Guthrie in Ireland. In February 1961 it was announced that Guthrie had read the work and enthusiastically elected to have double duties on the project. He would direct *and* act in *Gideon*. "At six foot seven, Mr. Guthrie decided he would like to play the role of God," said the *Herald Tribune*. He had performed once on the stage in his youth, and acting had remained a covert aspiration, the director explained. But within a month he changed his mind. By April, Guthrie was still in as director, but out as God. Chayefsky's favorite actor, Fredric March, was now considering the part, "if terms for his appearance can be worked out." By June, the terms were agreed to, and March was signed.

Suggested actors for the role of the shepherd Gideon were Peter Sellers, Anthony Franciosa, and Robert Morse, but Guthrie preferred to "give a leg up" to a newcomer, as he had with Donald Harron in *The Tenth Man*. Visiting the director one day was a Scottish actor, Douglas Campbell, who had worked with Guthrie before. After reading the play, Campbell suggested that he could effectively play the title role. "I daresay you could," said Guthrie.

"Tony [Guthrie] said the decision belonged 'to the powers that be,'" Campbell recalled. "Fred Coe and Arthur Cantor would have been very glad to have somebody else, but when I read for Paddy he thought I was the bee's knees. It was his sole desire that I play Gideon. I think he was wise enough to realize that he needed a well-trained classical actor for the part. There was a lot of range required and your usual run-of-the-mill Method actor in New

York wasn't going to be able to do what was required. They could do very well with it, but not what Paddy wanted."

Campbell was hired, and the actor Alan Manson was cast as the tribal leader, Hezekiah, with a newcomer, George Segal, as Purah, Gideon's servant.

The play would open the following November, at the Plymouth Theatre. "It will be a huge production with plenty of scenery, soldiers, and even a belly dancer," said the press announcement, "and though Mr. Chayefsky is straying from his customary locale, he is reportedly taking his celebrated Jewish humor with him." When he was asked to comment about the change in his dramaturgical mode, the quasi-poetic language, Chayefsky commented that as a playwright he felt it was his moral duty to grow, to expand in style and theme. "Few people want stature today," he said. "They seem to be trying to get rid of the stature they have, to be trying to lose size."

"While any aspiring dramatist might be happy with Chayefsky's fluency and polished craft, it is his thirst to be recognized as a true prophet that few serious critics will slake," reporter Helen Dudar surmised.

As he had on *The Tenth Man*, Guthrie brought to *Gideon* an innovative conception for staging. In discussions with Chayefsky and the set designer, David Hays, Guthrie explained that they should do whatever they could to alter the frame of the proscenium at the Plymouth Theatre. "He tore up the orchestra pit and extended the stage area into it," said Chayefsky. "He dug trapdoors into the floors so as to have actors leaping up from below. If he could, I think he would have smashed down the wings, bulldozed a hole into the back of the theatre, anything in fact that would have broken the reasonableness of that platform. He was in short prepared to treat the play as something as close to nonrepresentational art as theatrical comprehensibility allowed."

Guthrie told David Hays: "Listen, I want a very steep set. I want the actors to really work, to scramble hard to get up to the top of the hill." *Gideon's* rostrum was really nothing more than a barren crag raked at a precipitous 45 degree angle, said Chayefsky. "The actors looked as if they were about to pitch into the pit."

For the most part, Chayefsky kept clear of the actors during the critical stage of the readings. "He was very good that way," said Campbell. "He would never insist that he had any kind of point of view that wasn't yours. He let you sort of mull it out for yourself." There was only one reported flap between the writer and director. During one scene, when Chayefsky asked what Guthrie was striving for, the director imperiously but disarmingly admonished him, "Don't question what I am doing. I am a genius."

"He *was* a genius," said Alan Manson. "Guthrie's direction of *Gideon* was above and beyond anything I had ever seen. There was a moment in the play, at the end of Act One, when God performs the last miracle for Gideon.

Witnessing this, Gideon kneels down and worships God, reciting a verse that Chayefsky had written in iambic pentameter. Guthrie had an expression he used in rehearsal: 'It wants to be this,' he would say. And in this scene he said to Campbell: 'Dougie, this wants to be sung.' And he turned to this Israeli, a Yemenite actor, who was also in the scene playing a soldier. Guthrie said, 'Meir, could you give me a Yemenite tune?' And spontaneously, Meir started to hum a tune. As he hummed, Douglas picked up on it and he put Paddy's words to it. And at the end of it, as he finished with the words 'Oh I love you Lord,' he reached up to touch the hand of God, much like the Michelangelo image in the Sistine Chapel. It was done extemporaneously, but it ended the act on such an exalted note. Paddy was there and he was thrilled, out of his mind with joy. He had that infinite trust in Guthrie, who to put it mildly also exalted Paddy's work. He elevated it to the highest degree."

During the out-of-town run, in Philadelphia, there were minor changes. Some of Paddy's big words and a few of the deeper but irrelevant musings were cut. Coe and Cantor also added their "contributions," according to Douglas Campbell. "They felt it should be more like *The Tenth Man*. But Tony of course was very strong. He had a wonderful precision in putting 'the experts' in their place."

On November 9, 1961, *Gideon* opened before a black-tie audience at the Plymouth Theatre in New York. Disaster almost struck during the first act. Fredric March as God was about to make his first speech. "He was supposed to have a single light from directly overhead," said David Hays. "That afternoon, unfortunately, we had a photo call. That meant we had to change the lighting circuits. In those days we didn't have elaborate light systems or computers. We had plugs and replugs. So during the photo session they were changed and we forgot to replug for God's spotlight." As March began his speech he was left in darkness. Hays, sitting out front, instantly realized what had happened and raced backstage with his assistant. Neck and neck with them was Paddy Chayefsky.

As the plug was reconnected and the light was slowly brought up on March speaking as God, Chayefsky began to shout backstage at the electrician. "That man is fired!" he bellowed. "Which is not a great thing to yell at a man who is working to correct the mistakes," said Hays. "But Paddy had really lost his head. Fred Coe arrived, then Tyrone Guthrie, who said, 'Happily, I'm here too late to do any real damage.' Which was the kind of humor the situation needed."

With the sweat running down the middle of his back, Hays went outside the theatre for a breath of fresh air. "I walked out onto Forty-fifth Street and there's Paddy. He came up and grabbed me by the lapel of my tuxedo and said, 'You ruined my show. Ten years of my life is destroyed.' I said, 'Come on,

Paddy. I didn't ruin *all* of it.' He said, 'Well, just three years of it, then.' And then he began moaning: 'Why is it you write plays and then other people come in and ruin them?' I said, 'Come on, Paddy, write novels then.' Which wasn't a nice thing to say but it calmed him down, because he brought me across the street, where we had a drink and a chat until the show was over."

John McLain, the drama critic for the New York *Journal-American,* led off with the positive notices. Describing the opening-night audience as "wildly enthusiastic," with March and Campbell giving "two towering perform-ances," McLain said the play "had exceptional warmth, weight and dimension. It is an unqualified hit." John Chapman of the *Daily News* said it was a lovely play, written with simple distinction "and staged most beautifully by Guthrie"; while a competing tabloid, the *Daily Mirror,* found the Chayefsky work to be "distinguished . . . stirring . . . humorous."

There were also those with reservations. "*Gideon* has distinction and a haunting fascination," said the *New York Post,* "but I can't help feeling that in the second half, Mr. Chayefsky courageously plunges in beyond his depth." Walter Kerr of the *Herald Tribune* said it was "a fine feast . . . for vegetarians," but he longed for the entrée, "for the thrust of knife and fork against satisfying substance, for psychological meat and potatoes." In accomplishing the difficult task of making the dialogue simple, candid, and humorous, Kerr believed, the playwright had dallied at a simpler level. In his concentration on the clashing debates and their encores, Chayefsky had forgotten that it was a play he was writing. "The repetitions made the evening stand still," said Kerr.

Thirty years later Chayefsky's colleagues offered their perspectives. "*Gideon* was terrible!" said Garson Kanin in 1991. "Thornton Wilder, who was my mentor, once said to me, 'The most difficult thing that faces a writer is that he has to find his subject.' Certainly all too frequently I failed to find my subject. And with *Gideon,* that was not Paddy's subject. He wrote a play outside of himself, and that's not an impulse that makes for good writing. Just because you think something is classy at the moment doesn't mean you should write about it. And that was Paddy's mistake on several occasions."

Gore Vidal believed that Chayefsky had a problem when it came to the why of what he was doing. "He had a good ear for the dialogue of the proles and he was observant when it came to the behavioral subtleties," said Vidal. "But when he had to imagine anything or, indeed, *think,* he did not even rise, as he once proclaimed to our general delight, to lyricism. To his credit, he tried to break out in that *son of J* thing [*Gideon*], but he did not have much imagination, and Western civilization had passed him by (not a bad thing, from one view)."

In the first three months of its run, *Gideon* was a sellout. Then, after the regular New York theatregoing audience was depleted, the box office began

Sidney Chayefsky, newly renamed Paddy, poses for an Army photographer in London, 1945. *(Wisconsin Center for Film and Theater Research)*

The Golden Age of Television: producer Fred Coe (front center, with glasses)
with his Philco-Goodyear staff. Clockwise from front left: associate producer
Gordon Duff and writers Harry Mulheim, Tad Mosel, Sumner Locke Elliott,
Robert Alan Aurthur, Paddy Chayefsky, David Shaw, Thomas Phipps,
and N. Richard Nash. (Absent are J. P. Miller and Horton Foote.)
(courtesy of Delbert Mann)

Betsy Blair played Clara to Ernest Borgnine's inimitable Marty, for which he
won the Oscar for Best Actor. *(Springer/Bettmann Film Archive)*

Screenwriter Paddy Chayefsky jubilantly accepts his Academy Award for *Marty* from actress Claudette Colbert. It would be the first of Chayefsky's three Oscars. *(UPI/Bettmann)*

The Catered Affair, starring Debbie Reynolds, Ernest Borgnine, and Bette Davis, was scripted by Gore Vidal, adapting Chayefsky's teleplay. *(The Bettmann Archive)*

The Goddess. Kim Stanley as Rita Shawn, the doomed Hollywood star, whom Chayefsky closely patterned on Marilyn Monroe. Lloyd Bridges, in the doorway, played the Joe DiMaggio counterpart. *(Photofest)*

November 1961. Tyrone Guthrie, Fredric March, Douglas Campbell, and Chayefsky at Sardi's on the opening night of *Gideon*, the playwright's lyrical, combative discourse on the omnipotence of God. *(UPI/Bettmann)*

Startled, perhaps, by the rich, bombastic Chayefsky speeches they had to deliver in *The Americanization of Emily,* Julie Andrews and James Garner huddle together for a publicity still. *(Museum of Modern Art Film Stills Archive)*

In Los Angeles, the principles connected with Chayefsky's last stage play, *The Latent Heterosexual,* gather for an amiable photo call. Seated (from the left) are Chayefsky, Zero Mostel, producer James E. Doolittle, and Jules Munshin. Standing are director Burgess Meredith and Norman Kean, general manager of the APA-Phoenix repertory company. *(courtesy of James E. Doolittle)*

Hollywood, 1968. Chayefsky and his thirteen year-old son, Dan, visit with Gwen Verdon, Shirley MacLaine, and Bob Fosse during the making of the movie version of *Sweet Charity*. *(courtesy of Gwen Verdon and the Library of Congress Music Division)*

April 1971. A benign George C. Scott looks on as writer-producer Paddy Chayefsky explains how a scene should be played in *The Hospital*. Scott's amusement was short-lived. *(courtesy of Barbara Robinson)*

"I'm as mad as hell," says Howard Beale, Chayefsky's frenzied mouthpiece in *Network*, urging his TV viewers to rise up and rebel against the fear and manipulation that are paralyzing their lives. Peter Finch won a posthumous Oscar for his performance. *(Museum of Modern Art Film Stills Archive)*

Faye Dunaway as *Network*'s ruthless Diana Christensen, the UBS network's head of programming. *(Museum of Modern Art Film Stills Archive)*

It was like "an abortion . . . a major separation from something you've invested in and cherished," said Chayefsky of his tumultuous displacement from the production of *Altered States*. With the writer off the premises, director Ken Russell (at left) explains his concept of the script to actors Blair Brown and William Hurt. *(Museum of Modern Art Film Stills Archive)*

January 1981. In New York City, at a luncheon party six months before his death, Chayefsky shows off a birthday cake inscribed "Sidney Aaron." *(courtesy of Terry Chayefsky)*

to decline. Fredric March and the play were nominated for Tony awards, but lost to Paul Scofield and *A Man for All Seasons*. To jack up attendance, Chayefsky personally appealed to Ed Sullivan to put Fredric March on his TV variety show. But he was told that even on a Sunday night, ten minutes of God speaking blank verse would be taxing for Sullivan's middle-class audience. Another promotional opportunity arose when Fred Coe brought in a group called Dynamic Theater Networks, who wanted to broadcast two perform-ances of the play to a paying audience in an auditorium in Rochester, New York. If the closed-circuit showing was profitable, they would transmit the play to other cities across the United States. The live telecast was done but it wasn't a success and the national plans were canceled. That April another setback befell the production. Fredric March's agent told them that his client had been asked to make a movie with Sophia Loren in Germany, and therefore he would not be renewing his contract when it expired on May 5. When informed of this, Paddy Chayefsky exploded. "Can you believe this?" he fumed. "I give him the best role of his life, to play God, an actor's dream. And he wants to quit to do a movie with a spaghetti actress?"

Douglas Campbell felt that March wasn't too happy in the play. On paper the role of God looked larger, but on stage it was Gideon who had the stronger part. Chayefsky tried to persuade March to stay. Over a pleasant lunch, the actor confessed that he had already signed for the movie with Loren, and he asked if he could leave a week earlier. Chayefsky said no. March then raised the matter with Equity. "An offer to star with Miss Loren is not an act of God, under Equity's rules," the union decided, and March was forced to pay the *Gideon* producers $10,000 to leave a week earlier.

The playwright and producers frantically sought a replacement. Chayefsky suggested Spencer Tracy or Lee J. Cobb, but neither actor was available. Eventually it was decided to move up Douglas Campbell to play God. To stress the importance of this, the press were reminded that a comparable switch had been made the previous season when Laurence Olivier had taken over his co-star Anthony Quinn's role in *Becket*. But the transposition did not work for *Gideon*. The box office was healthy for the first week, then began to slide. Four weeks after the change was made, the play closed. "God was not dead," said Chayefsky, "He was respectfully being ignored."

When the prospects of a road tour failed to materialize, Chayefsky would still not concede. He believed it was his best work and with speed he attempted to remount the play elsewhere. He flew to London to talk to his friend Laurence Olivier, who expressed a keen interest in directing and starring in *Gideon* at the new Chichester Festival. Chayefsky's hopes were further buoyed when Olivier suggested that if the play was a hit at Chichester they would bring it to London. A film option was also discussed, to star Olivier as God and Peter

O'Toole or Albert Finney as Gideon, with filming to commence in Israel and England the following summer. These stellar plans never went further. If he felt disappointment, "he never discussed it," his son commented later.

William Gibson recalled writing a letter to Chayefsky. "Actually I wrote two," he said. "One was after *Gideon* opened. The second was from Israel after the play had been published. I was there researching the life of Golda Meir for a project I was doing. Golda had a son named Gideon, so I brought along a copy of Paddy's play and I read it on the plane. Once again, I was tremendously moved by the scene where God pleads with Gideon not to forsake him. Anybody who has had a father-son theme in his life would be moved by that."

Gibson said he heard nothing from Chayefsky in reply to his letters.

Political Gleanings

In the aftermath of *Gideon,* Chayefsky remained ambivalent about the existence of a Greater Power. "I think there is a God, but it is all so incomprehensible and I don't see why I should concern myself," he said. "I worry about me, my life, and the people around me. There's enough down here to keep me busy."

At noon, on Sunday, August 5, 1962, two months after the play had closed, he was in his apartment in New York when the news came over the radio. Earlier that morning, Marilyn Monroe had been found dead in Hollywood, a victim of an overdose of barbiturates. Some people made the connection between her demise and that of the tortured star in Chayefsky's *The Goddess,* including *Show* magazine, which asked the writer to cover Monroe's funeral in Hollywood. Chayefsky declined, because "I am not a journalist"; *Show* assigned the piece to Clifford Odets. In Roxbury, Connecticut, when Arthur Miller was asked if Chayefsky's movie *The Goddess,* "in which a girl with many problems marries at sixteen, becomes a movie star, and then descends into drugs and drinking," was mirrored on the life of his late ex-wife, Miller replied that the Chayefsky script was third-rate and had "a shallow, sociological approach."

"I thought it rather a takeoff on Marilyn, but I could have been easily mistaken about that," Miller said later. "A takeoff rather than the tragic piece it wanted to be." At that time he also denied that there was ever any "serious friction" with Chayefsky over his script of *The Goddess.* "I certainly never held it against him. It was just a less than good performance, something we all fall into," he said. However, the enmity between the two writers, at least from Chayefsky's corner, would remain constant through the early sixties, erupting again over a scheduling of theatrical projects. Miller was working on a play that would re-create stark installments of his life with Monroe. Chayefsky's new work, which he hoped would be the one that would finally propel him past all existing rivals, was described as a historical epic, "the greatest real drama of our time": the Russian Revolution. "I generally favor revolutions," said Paddy. "They show spirit. We should have them regularly."

It was his interest in "antiquity and the moralities" and his Russian roots that prompted the creation of *The Passion of Josef D.*, Chayefsky claimed. But as with most of his radical work there was a personal cause, a disaffection, a hidden betrayal involved.

Like so many millions of oppressed Jews in Russia, Chayefsky's parents had been ardent supporters of the Bolshevik revolution and hoped the uprising would put an end to the pogroms and the repression their people had suffered under the czars. In his youth, Harry Chayefsky had also been attracted to socialism, which he forsook when he married and found financial success in the dairy business. After he lost his fortune during the Depression, his interest in Marxism was rekindled. For many reduced and indigent families in the Bronx, the Socialist party was an enormous support system. In every crisis and emergency the party members were there first—before the church, before the authorities—with food and comfort and words that the afflicted could understand and respond to. It was not their fault that they were poor and hungry; it was the current political system that had failed them. The Socialist doctrine brought nobility to the suffering of not only Jews, but the many Irish, Poles, and Italians who joined the union and labor movements that sprang up in the 1930s. Their lives had worth, promise, entitlement, they were told. The union gave them a home, a purpose, a true sense of brotherhood. The party provided discipline and a plan. It made them feel inventive, alive, filled with responsibility for one another and for a better world.

The adventure and danger of the times captured the attention of the youngest member of the Chayefsky clan. As his father and friends sat around the kitchen table, smoking cigarettes and drinking tea in glasses, Paddy was enraptured by the stories of the war in Spain and of Trotsky, the exile and outlaw who was establishing his own Marxist wing in Mexico. At De Witt Clinton High, many of Chayefsky's pals' parents were bona fide members of the Communist party. These boys, the best and the brightest in class, also belonged to the Young Communists League, which combined with their academic distinction gave them a strong sense of morality. Lying, cheating, and stealing were forbidden in the Y.C.L. They could play cards for the sport, never for money. And sex? You could flirt, maybe neck on a third or fourth date, but petting or intercourse were sternly discouraged. Although they approved of these virtuous ordinances, Chayefsky's parents, who voted twice for Franklin D. Roosevelt, refused to allow their son to join any Communist club or league. Karl Marx's doctrine was fair and fine, Gussie Chayefsky remarked, but where was God in this new civilization the Communists were building? For Harry and Gussie there was also the matter of the Moscow trials. The new Russia was supposedly free of anti-Semitism, yet by the late 1930s many of the original Jewish leaders of the Bolshevik revolution had been tried and executed in the course of Stalin's show trials and purges.

Resistance to the truth was strong, particularly among adolescents and passionate liberals who, in the interests of defense and world peace, felt it was better to side with the stronger Soviet side. At seventeen, Paddy Chayefsky was attending City College, known as a hotbed of radicalism. The most dedicated and fearless students on campus were Communists. Caught up in the vibrancy, the history of the times, students viewed the party as an immediate electrifying link to Russia, to the war in Europe, and to the entire world, which only *they* were capable of saving. During his sophomore year at CCNY, Chayefsky attended his share of Marxist meetings and social events, which included party picnics in Van Cortlandt Park and dances held in the community halls of the Communist-sponsored cooperative housing projects on Allerton Avenue in the East Bronx. Chayefsky was also adept at handing out mimeographed sheets of the lyrics he wrote satirizing the red-baiting bullies on campus. His assertiveness, talent, and qualities of leadership duly drew the attention of the CP recruiters downtown. Good organizers were at a premium, and for a time Chayefsky was almost seduced. Ultimately, though, he held back, not only because of the caution expressed by his parents, but also because he was gradually becoming discontent and suspicious of the party's working system. Looking beyond his own smart circle of friends, he noticed how the operation treated its lower-echelon members. The timid, the lost, confused adults and adolescents beset with sexual and social fears had joined the Communist party to feel less lonely and fearful. After being assured that they would be given support, structure, a family, these timorous, desolate souls were pushed out on the street each night to be jeered at, spit on, and possibly beaten as they tried to hand out petitions and sell their fixed quota of copies of *The Daily Worker.*

When he questioned the danger and the humiliation, Chayefsky was told that this was "party procedure." These brave volunteers were the foot soldiers, the first to be sacrificed for the greater good of the revolution. Everyone and everything was subordinate to the dictates and future of the party. Individual suffering, humiliation, even pleasure, any sense of self was trivialized. The personal was suppressed and despised. It had to be abandoned for the sake of the collective. When apprised of this, Chayefsky's participation at meetings became less than composed and he acquired the mark of a troublemaker. In 1940, the writer Budd Schulberg had been expelled from the party when he refused to let their literary police influence the writing of his novel *What Makes Sammy Run?* Earlier, Elia Kazan quit when V. J. Jerome, the CP's cultural czar, tried to persuade him to exert more control over the Group Theatre. The theory offered for Chayefsky's early defection was that the party attempted to control his creativity. That conjecture was unsound because he was not doing any serious writing at that time. By all accounts, he never was an actual party member, so he couldn't have been expelled for his heretical questions and behavior. But he could be barred from meetings and ostracized, betrayed at a later date by his former comrades and supposed friends. Chayefsky's ultrasensitivity to rejection and disloyalty may account for the considerable anger and hate he would ever after display toward the Communist party. "Watch out for the Commies," he told his friend Eddie White in 1975. "They were a treacherous lot and not very nice to begin with." Their methods of punishment were ruthless, Budd Schulberg recalled. "If they got down on you they were just as destructive as the SS in Germany."

In the notes for his Russian play, Chayefsky said that he was attracted to the subject of communism because of its founding leader, Lenin. Here was a man who set out to change the world in his image, and succeeded, becoming a god to his people. "The viewpoint is that man cannot live without some form of a god (or religion), someone the people can fix their futile dreams and lives on," Chayefsky explained. The evolution for him, as a writer, was inevitable, he emphasized. In his last play, there was Gideon, who couldn't believe in God because he couldn't bear the burden of being insignificant. In this new play, based on Vladimir Ilyich Lenin, the father of the Soviet Union, Chayefsky intended to show "what happens when man thinks *he* is God."

After voraciously consuming every bibliography, biography, and book written on Lenin and the Russian Revolution, Chayefsky began to assemble his dramatic dossier. In the process, a curious parallel between the Bolshevik leader and the Bronx playwright began to emerge. In Lenin's youth, he and his family were close but not necessarily happy. His mother came from good stock, a family that was part of a previous intelligentsia, which gave her a sense of superiority and "the rather poignant aspiration to breeding." His father was a self-made man, a provincial intellectual who had plodded his way up the civil service ladder. "He was dutiful, sober, earnest, sad and defeated—just the sort of father a boy can't respect," said Chayefsky.

Lenin, like Chayefsky, was bright and precocious in school. "A clamorer in class, a hand-raiser, he learned his lessons too quickly. Where did he get the stubborn literalism that was to mark him all his life?" Chayefsky asked in his notes. "Equipped with genius, yet he distrusted fancy, never ventured into possibility, always ground deeper and deeper into existing fact. Equipped with extraordinary intelligence and sensitivity, . . . he lacked originality."

That was his point of departure, Chayefsky said. Lenin was never really a revolutionary, he was an artist. "For him it was all a grand mural, splashed and washed with color. If Lenin had been less literal, he would have been a poet; being literal he became a moralist." With this realization, Chayefsky decided to switch protagonists. Originally this was to be a story about a man who decided to change an ugly world in his own image, to convert injustice to justice, war into peace, and self-interest into brotherhood. But from his vantage as supreme ruler, Lenin saw that the world had rigidly remained the same, "unjust, warlike and selfish." Paradise on earth was a complete fraud, an illusion. The moral of this, Chayefsky believed, was that when anyone in power "thinks he knows the truth—thinks he can attain the ideal state for mankind—it leads to war. It's better to recognize that man can never be perfect. At best he is an aspiring beast and must be controlled."

In Chayefsky's telling, Josef Stalin, Lenin's number one acolyte, is such a beast. In the beginning Stalin's god is Lenin; his religion is socialism. With time, as his political power grows, Stalin becomes a zealot and a barbarian, obsessed with converting the world by force. Lenin, sensing the danger of Stalin's ambition, attempts to stop him. To strip him of his illusions, he tells him that he, Lenin, is *not* a god, and that there is no ultimate truth in communism. "Communism," said Chayefsky, "is a bullshit philosophy." Stalin, terror-stricken, disputes this. He cannot live without these beliefs; his godless life is meaningless without them. Lenin knows this, but before he can strip Stalin of power and remove him from office, he suffers a stroke and dies. Stalin then steps forward and appoints himself successor, ruler of the Soviet Union. "To set the system up," he decides twenty million people must die.

"Let's face it, it is Stalin's show," said Chayefsky, abandoning eight months of work on Lenin to concentrate on the more villainous protagonist of the story. *The Passion of Josef D.* became the title of the play and once more Chayefsky threw himself into research, reading additional books and translations of Russian articles on Joseph Stalin. In all, he filled five journals with 200,000 words of facts and details of Russian and Soviet lore. Then in January 1963, Chayefsky received some negative capitalistic news from his accountant. He was running out of available cash.

The situation was thus, Irving Gaft, his accountant told him. *Gideon,* his last play, had closed losing a third of its production costs. Royalties from the foreign and stock productions of his two earlier plays were still coming in, but these were slight, as were the participation checks from his movies and the books of his plays. Chayefsky had investments, but if liquidated in the current soft market, he would have to take a loss. The bottom line was that if he wanted to continue maintaining the very comfortable lifestyle he and his family were accustomed to on Central Park West, he would have to put his political play aside and seek a more immediate and lucrative assignment.

His agent, Bobby Sanford, suggested that he write something for the movies. Seldom humble where Hollywood was concerned, Chayefsky envisioned this as a fast, simple chore. He would pitch one or two original story ideas to a producer, write the script in a few weeks, then resume his more important work for the theatre. But in February 1963, when his agent called the studios in California, he learned that owing to the lackluster take on Chayefsky's last three movies, no one was eager to commission another original script. An adaptation of a current hit play or novel was a different matter. But Chayefsky didn't do adaptations, he said. His name and career had been founded on original material. He didn't welcome or need anyone to lay the groundwork for his seminal talent. However, as the records would show, doing a rewrite or a polish of someone else's work was a different matter.

Two years before, in the spring of 1960, when Chayefsky had turned up in Israel on the set of *Exodus,* an immediate report was issued that he was not there to doctor the script by Dalton Trumbo. He was there "on invitation" from the producer-director, Otto Preminger, and would "be on the set for a while." Not long after that, in New York, Chayefsky had done some work on the script of *Butterfield 8* as a favor for his pal Elizabeth Taylor. She wanted him to add some spine and strength to the smaller role her current consort, Eddie Fisher, was playing in the film. At that same time, perhaps in a bid to boost Fisher's declining career, Taylor asked Chayefsky to adapt his own play, *The Tenth Man,* for them. Nothing came of that, but a short time later, another possible Taylor-Chayefsky collaboration was discussed, this time for the multimillion-dollar movie version of *Cleopatra.*

Chayefsky's time on *Cleopatra* was apparently brief. According to the producer, Walter Wanger, he sent a "very interesting letter about his views on the script, but they would require six months for the rewrite. We don't have the time." Comedian Jackie Gleason then ambled onto the scene in 1961. The "Great One" wanted Chayefsky to write *Gigot* for him. This was the story of a dumb but sweet-natured Parisian mute that Gleason created. He felt that only Chayefsky had the sensitivity and talent to write his masterpiece. The two spent many hours discussing the story, until Chayefsky suggested they switch the locale from Paris to Brooklyn. After Gleason rabidly dismissed him from the project, Paddy said the only reason he got involved in the first place was because Orson Welles was supposed to direct. "There weren't many people in Hollywood that could get Paddy excited," said Bobby Sanford. "But occasionally, his interest could be poked with a name like Orson Welles, or John Ford. Paddy loved big talents and class projects."

The Americanization of Emily

In Hollywood during the spring of 1963, Marty Ransohoff was not yet a name synonymous with class. A former TV producer of "Mr. Ed" and "The Beverly Hillbillies," Ransohoff had an independent production deal at MGM. With two films already set up, *Boys' Night Out,* with Kim Novak, and *The Wheeler Dealers,* with James Garner, the producer was looking for a "quality" project. "I'd rather have a good film that makes five million than a lousy film that makes eleven million," he said. His quest for quality led to the purchase of a novel written by William Bradford Huie. Described as "an honest *Farewell to Arms* love story," the book was *The Americanization of Emily,* a wartime love story set in London. Five writers, including Huie, had worked on the script before Ransohoff spoke to Chayefsky. "Marty was looking for more of a romance story," said director Arthur Hiller, "and he thought Paddy was right for the job."

On a quick trip to California, Chayefsky met with Ransohoff and stuck to his position that he didn't do adaptations. Ransohoff deftly reminded him that even Shakespeare did adaptations, that most of his plays had come from other people's stories. Ransohoff then delivered the clincher. He mentioned that he already had a director and a top star interested in doing his war movie: William Wyler and William Holden. These two were definitely "class acts" in Chayefsky's opinion, and he agreed to at least look at the material.

On the flight back to New York, Chayefsky read the Huie book. The background, London during World War II, was familiar. The plot, that of a raffish American Navy lieutenant, a "dog robber" (one who procures luxuries and women for his military superiors) who falls in love with his British driver, Emily, was amusing, but predictable. The "hook" for Chayefsky came on page eighty-eight, where the admiral of the Navy talks of his distrust and frustration with General Dwight D. Eisenhower, the commander of the U.S. Army.

Eisenhower, according to the admiral, was a man who spoke in platitudes, "thinks in platitudes," and almost lost the battle in North Africa. Now that the main event of World War II, the landing at Normandy, is about to unfold, the admiral fears that Eisenhower plans to steal that campaign, too. The Navy, "the runt of the litter," would do all the preliminary work on the assault, then Ike and his Army would move in and take all the credit. "They've got motion picture producers and big film crews here to publicize it," says the admiral. "The Army, the Air Force, the Coast Guard, *Life* magazine—photographers are crowding one another." The Navy isn't doing enough, the admiral concludes, so to influence "public opinion," he instructs the lieutenant to spare no expense in producing a film "which will show schoolchildren how the Navy made Normandy possible."

Chayefsky, having worked on *The True Glory,* the definitive documentary of the war, was captivated by this aspect of the Huie story. The setup for the script had to be the Navy versus the Army, in celluloid combat for World War II. That rivalry was the fulcrum of the piece, around which the love story and all the other characters would revolve.

Making some preliminary notes on the plane, Chayefsky thought of ways to strengthen the plot. In Huie's book, the dog-robber hero, Lieutenant James Madison, dutifully carries out the admiral's order. He assembles a film crew, photographs the Allied invasion, then returns home to live happily ever after with his English bride, Emily Barham. Naturally this leisurely premise was too tame for Chayefsky. What if, in addition to the order to document the Navy as arriving first at Normandy, the admiral also insisted that the first dead man photographed be one of his division? That way the Navy could erect its own statue—a Tomb for the Unknown Sailor. And what if that first victim of the assault were to be the commander of the unit himself, Lieutenant James Madison, who, sensing the personal danger, refuses upfront to have anything to do with this mad mission?

Landing at La Guardia Airport, Chayefsky called Ransohoff. He told him he would write the script but only if he could change the entire story. Ransohoff said, "Send me some pages." Within a week, Chayefsky had completed forty pages of a scathing satire of the U.S. military. "There was nothing 'small' about Paddy," said his friend Mike Ryan. "He was prepared to take on the Army, the Navy, the entire U.S. military." Playwright Robert E. Lee agreed. "Paddy loved to battle windmills. He was one of the most quixotic men I've ever known. And we need Quixotes. We need them to charge these windmills, otherwise we have a society and a civilization which is all wind."

At MGM, Ransohoff read the material, then gave it to Bob O'Brien, the head of production. "He loved it, too," said Ransohoff, "and we moved quickly after that because we needed the script in three months." Chayefsky's fee was $100,000, plus "full creative approvals." That meant he would do the script, the rewrites, and be allowed to stay on the film set throughout production, making whatever changes were needed.

His first step was to verify the facts contained in Huie's book. "I'm Jewish and I thought I should be sympathetic at least with World War Two," said Chayefsky. "But I did some research. If you read the generals' memoirs after the war you find each pointing out the others' blunders." In checking out the account of the D-day landing, everything was accurate. "I couldn't catch one mistake in the reportage," he said. "Huie was a wonderful reporter."

Retaining the casual sardonic aspects of Huie's book, Chayefsky proceeded to add more of an edge to the characters. Originally, Lieutenant Madison was a novelist from an upper-class background. Chayefsky changed his civilian occupation to that of a night manager of a diplomatic hotel in Washington, which prepared him for the procuring duties required in the Navy. He also gave him a new first name. James was too formal, as was his middle name, Monroe, so he became "Charlie." Exploring his motivations for refusing to take part in the invasion at Normandy, Chayefsky considered making Charlie a pacifist. But audiences wouldn't buy a pimp and a pacifist in the same basket. Examining the situation further, Paddy asked himself why *he* personally balked at returning to the front in 1945. Because he was afraid of getting his wounded ass shot off again, he admitted. That was it, he decided. Charlie was afraid. "Not merely afraid," said Chayefsky. "The guy was a dedicated coward."

"Staying alive is instinct," Chayefsky wrote in his rapid notes. "Men aren't heroic by nature. And what's wrong with that? Courage, yes, but do they have to be noble too?" If everyone obeyed his first real impulse and ran like a rabbit at the first shot, how could anybody get out a second one? Tacked on to that practical view of survival, the writer then gave the character some of his personal philosophies on war. To maim and kill and destroy in the pursuit of peace was the most immoral and absurd act that man was capable of. Chayefsky's thoughts on this and other martial matters would be the grist for some dandy theatrical speeches.

The heroine of the story, Emily Barham, would also be transformed to Chayefsky's specifications. In the book, she is described as "an English virgin," meaning that she has had no Americans, and could count the number of Englishmen on one hand. Chayefsky gave Emily a more active, albeit slightly morbid, sexual past. When her husband, father, and brother are killed in the war, she almost goes insane. Working days as a volunteer nurse in the hospital, at night she finds herself in ten-shilling hotels, "administering last rites" to brave but doomed soldiers about to return to duty at the front. "I take these things badly. I fall in love too easily, and I shatter too easily," she says, requesting a transfer from the hospital to work as a driver for the American military. Here she recaptures her spunk. In Chayefsky's hands, Emily refuses to be "Americanized"—to accept food or luxuries in exchange for physical and social favors. When Charlie Madison, whose charm and largesse is obviously appreciated by the other female drivers, takes the foreign liberty of patting Emily on the fanny, she turns and slaps him, hard, across the face.

Emily also resents Charlie's cavalier attitude toward the war. "It's all one big Shriners' convention for you Americans, isn't it?" she tells him.

"You America haters bore me to tears," he replies. "Europe was a brothel long before we came to town."

With his lead characters, as well as the conflict of their opposing stance on the war and other matters, established, Chayefsky then asked, "How do we get them into bed by page six?" To pierce Emily's British reserve, he has

Charlie call her a prig. "Am I really?" she asks a fellow driver. She agrees to serve as a fourth at bridge at one of Charlie's officer parties, but she refuses his offer of a cocktail dress to wear at the do. Watching him operate at the party, Emily finds she is drawn to his unabashed roguish charm. When he returns to his room after ministering to the admiral, he finds Emily sitting on his bed. "I've had it with heroes, Charlie," she says, and their affair begins.

The crisis in Chayefsky's script comes when Charlie is assigned by the admiral to go to Normandy. His attempt to avoid active duty ultimately turns Emily against him. At first her only interest is in his staying alive, but being noble of heart, she rejects his furtive schemes. "Since you are cowardly, selfish, and ruthless, I can't help but despise you, detest and loathe you," she tells him. Through a change of plans, Charlie is forced to take part in the invasion. Landing on the beach at Normandy under German fire, he begins to run the other way and is shot by his Navy associate, Bus Cummings. Charlie stumbles into a mine; it explodes and he is presumably killed.

For the wrap-up, Chayefsky has the Navy proceed with plans to glorify their first casualty. They announce that they will erect a statue in his honor. Charlie, who is not dead, only wounded, reads about their intentions on a boat back to England. Emily is overjoyed to see that he is alive, but she objects when Charlie contemplates exposing the entire Navy scheme to the press. That is a noble gesture on his part, but who, or what purpose, would it serve? "Good Lord!" says Emily, "all the while I've been terrified of becoming American-ized, and you, you silly ass, have turned into a bloody sentimental English-man!" That was *it*, Chayefsky realized. It wasn't the nylons or candy bars, but the desentimentalization of her feelings about the nobility of war that was the true Americanization of Emily.

"Having someone as gifted and as skillful as Paddy helped us enormously," said Ransohoff's production assistant, John Calley. "He was a real artist. He did the script as he saw it, with no compromises to speak of—no studio pressures that I recall. Of course, it helped us because he was a serious heavyweight. As a consequence of that, the studio tended to treat him with more respect than they did with the sort of collaborative scripts they were so used to at the time. You'd have five or six writers on a project. Everyone would sort of put their paw print on it. But not with *Emily*. That was Paddy's exclusive property."

By late June the first completed draft was enthusiastically approved by MGM, and by William Wyler and William Holden, who agreed to sign on for the picture. The first choice for the female lead, described in the book as twenty-two, blue-eyed, and blond, was Julie Christie. Ransohoff and Calley spoke to the actress in London. Having recently completed her first feature role, in *Billy Liar*, Christie said that she had had it with films for a while. "She decided she didn't want to do Emily," said Calley. "She wasn't keen about it. At the time Julie was working with a British repertory group and I think she was more interested in theatre."

Another possibility, and one heartily endorsed by Paddy Chayefsky, was the British actress Diane Cilento. Twenty-nine-year-old Cilento's credits included *Rattle of a Simple Man* and the current film *Tom Jones*. "She was a strong contender for Emily," said Arthur Hiller. "But by that time Ransohoff was also talking with Julie Andrews."

Andrews was in Hollywood making her first movie, *Mary Poppins*. Calling herself "the British square of all time," she begged her agents to "please let me do something whacky or mad or sexy or whatever." When she read Chayefsky's script of *Emily* she said, "Oh, I wanted it, I wanted it so badly." To prove she could act in movies, she had her agent show Ransohoff and William Wyler some footage from *Mary Poppins*. "We saw twenty minutes," said Ransohoff, "and Willie said, 'She's going to be a big, big star.' And we signed her."

The film was budgeted at $3.15 million, and production was due to begin in London on September 15—but a problem with William Wyler surfaced in early August. "Everything was all set and laid out and then Wyler decided he wanted to wait a few weeks before he went to London," said Calley. "He was dawdling. He just didn't seem to want to leave his house in Malibu."

The dilemma was over Paddy Chayefsky's script. "When we made the deal with Willie, he thought the script was brilliant," said Ransohoff. "Then he began to ask for changes, serious changes. I told him, 'Willie, two months ago you said it was brilliant; we haven't changed it.' "

Wyler was the director of *Dead End, Jezebel,* and *Ben-Hur*. He was also responsible for two wartime classics, *Mrs. Miniver* and *The Best Years of Our Lives*. "Basically, Willie was a traditionalist," said Ransohoff. "He had directed these two very sentimental war movies, and here was a script written by Paddy that was very iconoclastic. So Willie began to have second thoughts. He was concerned with some of the more outrageous stuff that Paddy had written."

On August 12, Chayefsky met with Wyler at his beach house in Malibu. "Willie wanted the script softened," said Ransohoff, "and neither Paddy nor I wanted to do that. We felt if we were going to do the movie we had to go with the script Paddy had written."

At that stage, things with Wyler became "very difficult," said Ransohoff. Wyler insisted on bringing in his own writer. "Out of deference to him and his reputation, his credentials, I had to let him do that," said Ransohoff. "I said to him at the time, 'Look, I think you're wrong. I don't think you can rewrite Paddy.' But I did let him try, because how can you deprive a director of Wyler's stature from trying to improve a script?"

When Wyler's revised script came in, Ransohoff said: "No, absolutely not." He didn't like the new material. Things became difficult again. Wyler gave an ultimatum: It was either him or Chayefsky. Ransohoff chose Chayefsky.

Concurrently, a conflict had also arisen with the star of the picture, William Holden. It wasn't the script that concerned Holden. He had already played a far shoddier patriot in *Stalag 17*. Holden and his agent, Charles Feldman, wanted to change the leading lady. They asked that Julie Andrews be removed and replaced by Capucine. "She was the girlfriend of one, or both, of them at the time," said Calley. When Ransohoff refused to do this, Feldman, a considerable power, proceeded to give the producer and MGM a very hard time. Using the defection of Wyler as an excuse, Feldman invoked his client's right of approval of a new director, and sent a list of fourteen names to the studio. They included Howard Hawks, who told MGM he would direct but only if he could produce; and Joseph Mankiewicz, who said no because of his own battle fatigue from the recently completed *Cleopatra*. Others on Feldman's list were David Lean, George Seaton, John Sturges, and Billy Wilder. "Patently useless choices," said Ransohoff, because all were busy elsewhere. Two meetings were then arranged with another director, Blake Edwards. His "onerous terms" included a rewrite of the Chayefsky script, "to accommodate an ending which he would approve." He also wanted to recast the leading lady, whom he considered "wrong" for the role. Julie Andrews was too wholesome and sweet to play Emily. "She has lilacs for pubic hairs," Edwards said, an opinion he undoubtedly rescinded a few years later when he married her.

In a memo to Feldman, Ransohoff said he was aware that the agent was playing hardball regarding directors so "as to avoid your contract with us." He also gave him and William Holden a deadline to come up with a suitable choice. At the same time, Ransohoff had an alternative in mind. He was considering giving the assignment to a Canadian newcomer, Arthur Hiller. Hiller was working at MGM on *The Wheeler Dealers* when he got his hands on a copy of the Chayefsky script. "I fell in love with it," said Hiller. "This was the one time I really went after a project. I called Ransohoff all the time. I tracked him down at the Bel Air Hotel in the midst of his divorce. I kept after him until he agreed to let me direct the picture."

Ten minutes after the deadline with Feldman and Holden had passed, Ransohoff called them and announced that Hiller was the new director. Feldman threatened to sue, but they agreed to forgo the legalities for the proper compensation. To settle Holden's contracted fee of $600,000, against 10 percent of the gross, Feldman told MGM his client would graciously withdraw for an immediate payment of $150,000.

On September 3, an interoffice memo at MGM stated that the second lead of the picture, James Garner, had been moved up to number one. "It was always in the back of our mind, that if William Holden backed out, we'd use Jim," said Calley.

James Coburn was then brought in to play Bus Cummings, the Navy lieutenant who shoots the cowardly Charlie Madison at Normandy. "Take a lot of movies of this man, sailor," says Cummings, standing over the lifeless body on the beach. "He was a coward. But he ran in the face of the enemy. He's the first dead man on Omaha Beach. And he was from the Navy." That character, a "real gung ho son of a bitch," was mostly Chayefsky's invention. A variation appeared in Huie's book. "He was married, an Irish Catholic with the name of Kennedy," said Paddy. "Naturally, with a Kennedy in the White House we had to give him a new name. I also made him into a rampant womanizer, which gave us some trouble with the censors later on."

A first-class company of supporting players rounded out the cast, including Joyce Grenfell as Emily's dotty mother, suffering from "menopause and the bombs," and Melvyn Douglas as the admiral of the Navy intent on competing with the Army on D day. In his metamorphosis into a Navy publicity hound, the admiral was made "temporarily insane, because you can't have sane admirals sending men to their deaths for a naval publicity stunt," said Chayefsky. Prohibited from thrashing the admiral's nemesis, General Eisenhower, Chayefsky did manage to include a subtle but deft swipe at the Army leader and future Republican president. On D day, moments before the assault on Normandy commences, Eisenhower's words of morale are broadcast over the ship's loudspeakers. "You're about to embark upon the Great Crusade . . . the eyes of the world are upon you," says the general, while in a tight close-up a combat sailor is seen throwing up in his helmet.

In their preliminary discussions, Ransohoff agreed with Chayefsky that *Emily* should not be made in color. "It was a black comedy, and a period piece, so my father said it would be better in black and white," said Dan Chayefsky. On October 14, 1963, shooting commenced in England. After six days the producers decided to pack up and go home. "We were having too many problems," said Calley. "There was a complicated series of exterior shots we were very close to getting, but the crew would never stay after six o'clock. It was always difficult to get any cooperation out of them, so we told the studio we wanted to bring the company back to California."

Chayefsky was on hand in London, and also at the MGM studio in Culver City. "I treated him like a partner," said Ransohoff. Hanging around with the supporting cast, Chayefsky took special delight in spinning out stories about his Army days in London for Garner and James Coburn. "The most dangerous man in the world," was his description of the character that Coburn was playing. "And the way that Paddy wanted me to play him was with a certain sense of fun," said the actor. "We talked about the guy all the time, and when we were shooting he'd come up to me afterwards and say, 'That's it! You're doin' it perfect!' And that made me enjoy playing the role even more."

James Garner, however, had trouble performing Chayefsky's lines. Apparently his earlier career, modeling bathing suits, had not provided him with any solid theatrical experience. His subsequent emoting technique came on the TV Western series *Maverick,* in which his character "seldom rode a horse, was slow on the draw, and was untrustworthy and self-centered," said the writer Tedd Thomey. The dialogue on that series was also sparse, so when confronted with Chayefsky's profuse speeches in *The Americanization of Emily,* Garner was in a quandary as to how to get through them.

The problem manifested itself in one particular scene, where Garner was supposed to express Chayefsky's philosophy of war to Emily and her mother. In take after take, as Andrews and Joyce Grenfell sat by patiently in character, Garner's delivery wavered from flat to frenzied. "It was a Friday afternoon and I said, 'Let's leave it to Monday,' " said Arthur Hiller. "I talked to Jim over the weekend and found out the problem. He had so much respect and admiration for Paddy's script that he was playing each line like it was the best line in the movie—because Paddy's dialogue lends itself to that. I said, 'No, Jim, you just play the character and the dialogue will take care of itself.' "

Working with Chayefsky was "a collaboration in the truest sense of the word," said Ransohoff. "If Arthur, or Julie, or any of the actors felt uncomfortable or wanted changes, everyone felt comfortable in discussing them with Paddy."

From material in the studio's files, it is obvious that there was considerably less latitude with the industry's official censors. At the outset, Chayefsky was told by the MGM standards and practices department that there were certain words and scenes in the book that could not be put in his adaptation. "Sloane's Sluts," the name of the drivers' unit that Julie Andrews worked for, had to be eliminated. Also, the connotation of "whoring," used in reference to the executive party scenes, had to go.

When Chayefsky's initial drafts were submitted to the Motion Picture Alliance Association, their protests came fast and frequent. Regarding the Garner and Andrews characters, the MPAA objected "that the boy and girl are attracted to each other physically the moment they meet and start a sex affair at that moment." This was deemed immoral. At that point, MGM informed the censor group that Chayefsky was in the midst of doing "a number of very forceful speeches by both the boy and the girl which adequately supply the missing voice of morality." Also, regarding some "offensive" language, the MPAA was assured that Chayefsky would eliminate "those 'hells' and 'damns' which were not dramatically essential."

On October 22, 1963, in a letter to MGM, the censors asked for further changes. Referring to Emily's confession of sleeping with wounded service-men, her line "I couldn't say no to them, could I?" had to be cut, along with her copulation dialogue with Charlie Madison—"Oh, Lord. I hope I don't get pregnant." "Oh, Lord, I hope you do," he replied.

The final dissension and impasse came over a scene Chayefsky had written for Charlie. On the eve of D day, in a bogus show of bravery, he drops by Bus's bedroom to tell him he's changed his mind, that he'll go to Normandy Beach after all. "Underneath it all, you're a pretty gutsy guy, Charlie, aren't you?" says Bus. "I don't know what came over me before. I showed the white feather, I suppose," Charlie replies sheepishly. The dialogue was acceptable to the censors; it was the mise-en-scène that rankled them. In the background, as Charlie delivers his heroic words, Chayefsky had three "nameless broads" cavorting in the nude. This was "objectionable and totally unacceptable" to the MPAA board.

MGM duly assured the censors that the scene would be keyed to develop the humor and the fact that the girls are "presumably" naked; and that Charlie would ignore them completely while delivering his speech. The emphasis "will not be on actually seeing them nude."

Chayefsky agreed to amend the scene slightly. He changed it from three nameless broads to two. One was in bed, filing her nails, presumably naked under a sheet. The other stood separately, wearing panties, but topless. When Charlie enters the bedroom, Number Two girl grabs a towel to cover herself. In deference to Charlie's officer's uniform, Bus snaps at her to "stand at attention!" The girl (played by Judy Carne) drops the towel and stands rigid and topless, her back to the camera. "At ease, sailor," Charlie tells her, then, averting his eyes from her naked chest, delivers his ersatz patriotic speech to Bus.

The censors on the board were emphatic in their response to Chayefsky's sly revisions. They objected that the scene showed "an officer of the armed forces who apparently devotes all of his time to hitting the hay, and also the nudity element." Their resolution was to have the naked women "stay under the covers and not be hopping around. The audience is to catch no glimpse of them." Furthermore, they said, it would add "some comedy effect, if the girls wore provocative nighties."

The censorship code back then was "preposterous," Ransohoff recalled three decades later. "We all felt they were taking themselves much too seriously. They refused to see that the way Paddy had set it up it was a very funny situation. There is a big difference when nudity is used for comedy and when it is used for lust." Among the actors, it was said that the conservative "family man" James Garner approved of "the watchdog actions of the MPAA," while James Coburn commented that "a little titty never hurt anyone."

On Friday, November 22, 1963, the cast were rehearsing the risqué party scene when John Calley came on the set and announced that President John F. Kennedy had been shot in Dallas. "We stopped immediately and people clustered around a radio," said Coburn.

"Julie was there, and Jim Garner. Everyone was stunned," said Calley. "It was just a nightmare. We were all put in a daze. People gradually wandered off by themselves, and we shut the production down for a few days."

Chayefsky's Russian Revolution

Bland is for blancmange and Paddy
was a man of pungency. He was a genius. Not being
one myself, I can say that with objectivity. He
was a true genius, but his problem was one of
splattering, of wanting to get into everything. Sometimes
that's good. Sometimes it's disastrous.

Playwright Robert E. Lee

The day of the president's assassination, Chayefsky was in New York, immersed in his own historical chaos, preparing to mount his epic play on Joseph Stalin.

Throughout the preproduction and filming of *Emily,* he continued to work on *The Passion of Josef D.* This led to an overrun and exchange of material from one project to the other. In the play, Lenin finds that despite his efforts to bring justice and brotherhood to the world, everything remains unjustly the same. "Nothing is real. Nothing is true. The human condition is relentlessly uncertain," he says. A variation of that statement also wound up in the mouth of Julie Andrews in *Emily.*

In fleshing out the character of Joseph Stalin, Chayefsky applied another religious diversion. When Stalin was seventeen, under the influence of his mother he entered an ecclesiastical seminary. But instead of becoming a priest, he became a revolutionary. "Not that there's much difference, except being a Bolshevik demanded a nobler nature, and didn't pay half so well," said Chayefsky. Stalin's faith in God, Chayefsky determined, began to deteriorate when he was forced to watch his wife die a long and pitiful death from the plague. "Tell me, God, is the end really terrible? Are the last hours, for even the good people, really terrible?" said Stalin, quoting almost verbatim the verse that Chayefsky wrote at his mother's deathbed.

With the Russian leaders firmly established, Chayefsky brought in a third character, Nadya, Stalin's second wife and the victim of his burgeoning ambition. The daughter of a fellow revolutionary, Nadya was young and beautiful and helped to ease the emptiness and despair Stalin felt after the tragic death of his first wife. Early in this second marriage Stalin is happy. Nadya is his anchor. She supports and encourages his dreams of political greatness, but once the new Soviet regime is established, Stalin no longer has to rely on her. "Nadya does not give him the sense of significance that Lenin does," said Chayefsky. "His love for Nadya simply makes being a brute endurable, even enjoyable. But Lenin makes Stalin feel more than a brute." Eventually Stalin stops sleeping with Nadya, staying in his office or in a separate part of their house. Though Nadya remains deeply in love with her husband, she resents his work and appears in public with him only on important occasions. When she reproaches Stalin for his lack of interest in her and their children, he begins to abuse her. His temper and cruelty start to unravel her mind. She consults a neurologist, but she cannot leave Stalin. He alone is her meager existence, "the only act of faith" she is capable of. As a last resort, she decides to betray him. Meeting with his superior, she apprises Lenin of his disciple's true barbaric, political nature. Nadya wants Lenin to strip Stalin of his power and position. That way he will return and love her again. Before Lenin can do this he suffers a stroke and dies. Stalin succeeds him as the supreme ruler of the Soviet empire, leaving Nadya more isolated than ever. She has no recourse but to commit suicide, at age thirty-one. The fault is not his, a stubborn, unrepentant Stalin declares. She got the idea from reading a book, and furthermore "she died an enemy."

In a somewhat defensive analysis of the character, Chayefsky subsequently said that his portrait of Nadya came "from the few facts that were known about her." Then he admitted he "contrived the relationship" between her and Stalin. However, the similarity to Chayefsky's own marriage and his voracious self-interest was never divulged.

A Home for *Josef D.*

Because of his disillusionment with Broadway and the "economic futility" of putting on a serious play there, Chayefsky said that he wanted his Russian play to be shown in a repertory theatre. "He is even thinking about raising funds for construction of a playhouse, preferably near one of the city's big universities," a press report stated.

In July 1962, Chayefsky had spoken to Robert Whitehead, a coproducer of the newly formed Lincoln Center Repertory Company. The original plan was to establish a permanent company to perform new works by American authors. Among those asked to contribute were Lillian Hellman, Arthur Miller, William

Inge, Edward Albee, and Paddy Chayefsky, who had a preliminary meeting with Whitehead. When the play was in its second draft it went to Whitehead, and an announcement appeared in *The New York Times* that *The Passion of Josef D.* had been chosen to launch the Lincoln Center Repertory Company that fall. The director of the play would be the man who first brought fame and stature to Arthur Miller, Elia Kazan. "We've talked of working before," said Chayefsky, "but our schedules always clashed. This year the time is ripe."

Another attraction for Chayefsky was the Lincoln Center theatre itself, then in construction. A mobile stage that could be mechanically transformed to present plays of any kind, from realistic proscenium to intimate area, was planned. "You can do chronicles, pageants, anything with a wide-open theatre like that," Chayefsky said. "I'm writing the play for that kind of theatre."

In attempting to capture the scope, the actual historical events of his play, the writer found that the revolution was giving him "more trouble than it did to the czar." To compress and interpret those seven years of unrest on a stage meant that he would have to use the techniques of musical theatre. "When you have only thirty-five people to represent five hundred thousand, you have to." Chayefsky said he intended to have songs, and some choreography, but this should not suggest to anyone that they were about to see *Oklahoma!* or *South Pacific.* There would be no full orchestra or dancers leaping out of the wings; the songs would be performed a capella, in lusty, seamy, cabaret style, analogous to the boulevard theatre of the German expressionists.

He hastily amended any presumption that because his new work had a sociopolitical motif, performed in a music-hall carnival background, it was therefore inspired or influenced by Bertolt Brecht (the revival of whose *Threepenny Opera* was then in its fourth year at the Theatre de Lys in Greenwich Village). Not so, said Chayefsky. To him, Bertolt Brecht was less of a playwright and more of "a scene-wright." "His poetry is a bit too stark, at best third rate. To use the metaphor of another art, he is more of a caricaturist than a painter, a charcoal illustrator rather than an artist. At his very best, he is Daumier rather than Goya or Rembrandt."

If there was a muse for his Russian play, it was the master, Tyrone Guthrie, Chayefsky said. "Guthrie regarded all plays as a musical score, with its modifications, its crescendos and climaxes." In rehearsals for *Gideon* he was like a conductor. During one difficult verbal sequence with the supporting cast, Guthrie paused to solve it. "After a moment," said Chayefsky, "he was seized with the idea of doing the whole scene musically. He turned his back on the players and directed the scene by sound. He gave one line to a tenor, another to a basso. He had two actors do a phrase in duet. Then a sudden full chorus of all the actors, with one voice rising out of the shout in solo. By lunch, he had organized the scene into something of an a capella cantata."

Witnessing this brought exhilaration to Chayefsky, and led him to investigate whether any other directors had used the technique. "I did research into the use of music in drama, needless to say for the purpose of plagiarizing any useful technique I could find, but I found nothing quite as original as Guthrie's way of doing it."

The three-act play was complete: eleven scenes, each written in a different style to "achieve a complexity of colors for scenes representing farce, burlesque, high drama, high comedy, expressionism, and the absurd school." Chayefsky handed a copy of his play to the administrative board of the fledgling Lincoln Center Repertory Company, along with his concept for the production and for the estimated cast of seventy-five actors to play three hundred roles. The reaction from the board was enthusiastic, but the follow-up was lax. Ultimately Chayefsky was given good and bad news. They loved the play. The significance and scope demanded that it be presented on the stage of their new theatre. However, that theatre would not be ready for at least another twelve months. In the meantime, eager to launch their repertory group, they were going to present another play in a smaller theatre downtown on West Fourth Street. The new play was called *After the Fall.* The writer was Arthur Miller; the director was Elia Kazan. When apprised of this, Chayefsky "turned red, then purple," then kicked a large-sized hole in the wall of his agent's office.

The company had obviously been contemplating producing the Miller play, described as "an autobiographical drama," for some time. In a more rational mood, with no intimation of being irked or feeling second best, Chayefsky sent a letter to the repertory board at Lincoln Center, saying that he was taking his play back. "I liked that play. I tried to do it with Lincoln Center," said Kazan. "I wanted Paddy to be one of our main authors, along with Miller, but I failed."

Not long after this, Chayefsky's artistic ego was buoyed when he learned that another, more prestigious repertory company was interested in doing *Josef D.* Sir Laurence Olivier, after reading the work, telephoned the writer and told him he wanted to launch the play at his new National Theatre in London. Paddy's euphoria was short-lived, however. Olivier's "literary manager," Kenneth Tynan, subsequently rejected the play—"for ideological reasons," he said. It might have been "a little too revisionist," Chayefsky commented. "There were a lot of hidden political biases in the theatre, at that time, disguised under some other form," Elia Kazan observed. "It didn't amount to shit, because a few years later it was all over."

With no other repertory companies equipped with the space or the budget to mount his epic work, the playwright had no other alternative but to allow it to be done in a commercial venue—on Broadway. Arthur Cantor agreed to coproduce *The Passion of Josef D.* and Chayefsky said he was hopeful that Tyrone Guthrie would come in again to stage it. "He wanted Tony to direct, and for me to do something in it," Douglas Campbell recalled, "but we were totally taken with something else, probably the new company in Minneapolis." The directors Peter Brook and Jerome Robbins were also approached, but both were "unavailable." What he needed was "a strong fellow with a big imagination to handle a widely covering script," Chayefsky said, talking to others before finding the perfect candidate—himself. The opening was set for the week of November 11, with a cast that he would personally select.

Rod Steiger, George C. Scott, Martin Landau, Peter Falk, Rip Torn, Jack Lemmon, Charles Bronson, and Christopher Plummer were among the actors initially thought of to play Joseph Stalin. For the co-starring role of Lenin, James Mason, Donald Pleasence, Joseph Wiseman, Werner Klemperer, Herbert Berghof, and Luther Adler were contemplated, and Adler was eventually chosen. To play Nadya, Stalin's beautiful, tormented wife, the various names submitted by agents were Ina Balin, Claire Bloom, Susan Kohner, Janet Margolin, Suzanne Pleshette, and an odd newcomer, Barbra Streisand.

On June 26, in Arthur Cantor's office on West Forty-fourth Street, Chayefsky saw twenty-seven actresses, including Olympia Dukakis ("at 1:40 P.M.") and Brenda Vaccaro ("1:45 P.M."). In July and August, he considered Susannah York, Melinda Dillon, Susan Oliver, Estelle Parsons, Carroll Baker, Lois Nettleton, Zoe Caldwell, and Elizabeth Hubbard. On September 17, Chayefsky called in Brenda Vaccaro for a second reading, followed by Elizabeth Hubbard, who got the role.

That left only Stalin to be cast. By early September, two actors, Peter Falk and Charles Bronson, had emerged as final contenders. Falk was offered the role, but turned it down to do a movie. On Tuesday, September 10, Chayefsky had lunch with Charles Bronson. The following day Bronson auditioned and it was announced that he would play the role. A week later, with the report that the play's opening had been postponed to January, a casting change was noted. Charles Bronson was now out. The role of Joseph Stalin would be played by Peter Falk. "He's always been the one we wanted," said Chayefsky.

Chayefsky confessed that the only problem he had at this time was in getting the writer of the play to modify it to the director's point of view. The immediate problem was one of linear style. "The piece cannot be presented simply as a series of cabaret acts," he said. "Also, the overall tone of the piece is religious, cathedral." To execute that concept, Will Steven Armstrong was asked to create the sets and lighting. Domingo A. Rodriguez was hired to design the costumes, which would involve one hundred changes, from peasant babushkas for the women to the authentic tunics worn by Stalin. Retained to supervise the makeup and hair, including twenty-four mustaches, ten goatees, four full beards, and twenty-two wigs, was Richard Corson. And after composer David Amram gave Chayefsky an audition tape, with thirty voices, all his own, sung in Russian style, he was commissioned to write the score.

By November it was obvious that additional funds would be needed to finance the play, and Arthur Fogelson, a Texas industrialist-rancher, was brought in as a coproducer. In December, a third money man, Mark Lawrence, was added to the production masthead, and the opening was now set for February. In December, the rest of the actors were hired. Alvin Epstein, who had studied dance with Martha Graham in New York and mime with Marcel Marceau in Paris, was cast in the role of Trotsky. "All of my background was important for the kind of performance that Paddy wanted," said Epstein. "Not only for Trotsky but for the other parts he wanted me to do in the play."

On January 2, rehearsals began on the roof of the New Amsterdam Theatre on West Forty-second Street. "The writer has been barred from the theatre. I'm mutilating his script at will," said the playwright-director. With the press in attendance, the opening scene featuring Peter Falk as Stalin was performed. Lying on a bench when a kindly old jailer enters with a bundle of clothing and food, Stalin is told to get up. There has been a revolution, the czar has been arrested, and he is free to leave. As Stalin gets dressed, he and the jailer exchange talk about the revolution, Lenin, and the bright future for Mother Russia. Bidding him farewell, Stalin then stabs the kindly old jailer in the back and steals his boots. The moral of the scene, Stalin declares, stepping to the front of the stage, is "When a barefoot fellow tells you he is revolting against tyranny, watch out; he's only after your boots. There you have the class struggle in a nutshell."

Chayefsky's plan as a director was to rehearse for three weeks, then give preview performances on Broadway. "I get so isolated out of town," he explained. "I find myself going back to New York three or four times a week. Here you go home after a day's work. You don't find yourself sitting in a bar or club generating panic. Out of town you get suspended in midair and lose contact with reality and lose faith in yourself."

The play was "architecturally sound," Chayefsky believed, so there was no need for any extensive rewrites. That conserved time and energy for his supervisory chores. As a writer he was normally "a benign influence" with actors. As a director he felt he tended to scare them. To forestall that problem, he prepared at home, "by becoming an actor, reading all the parts and asking myself questions performers might raise." As for the physical aspects of the play, Chayefsky's unannounced intention was to distract audiences from the nonlinear plot by giving them dazzling, inventive staging, such as Tyrone Guthrie had done with *Gideon*. Alvin Epstein said that he and the rest of the cast knew what Chayefsky was up to. "As regards movement, complexities of staging, that kind of virtuosity, we were very aware he was attempting to present a Tyrone Guthrie production," said Epstein. "The writing of the play demanded that. It was a very daring piece of work. It alternated between vaudeville and drama, which was groundbreaking for Broadway at that time. All of that loosening of linear structure on stage did not come until later."

Within the dramatic vignettes, Chayefsky had written a special song for Epstein to perform. "This was in the Trotsky sequence," the actor recalled. "Paddy had staged it rather spectacularly. I came down a long flight of stairs, wearing a huge white wig, and singing like a high soprano, in falsetto, very loud. This was the artifice he was tracing within the development of the Russian Revolution, and it was a very effective piece of theatre. If Tyrone Guthrie had been the director it would have been far more successful, because essentially Paddy was having enormous difficulty bringing it all off."

Directing the actors, pacing the crowd scenes, conducting the choral group, synchronizing the sound effects, and supervising the mechanical, motorized sets, Chayefsky was taxed with details that burdened his time and spirit. When cues or props were off or missing, he tended to react in a nonprofessional manner, with considerable fury. "I have no ability to deal with other creative people, except to respect them," he said. "A director needs meticulousness, patience, ingenuity. I have none of those things, so therefore I could never get anyone to do what I wanted."

According to the company press releases, the audiences at the preview performances in January were "wildly enthusiastic." Describing the play's dialogue as "terse, pungent, vernacular with a semipoetic level," the media announcement stated that Peter Falk was "magnetic . . . hypnotizing . . . he possesses star quality." Unreported were the nightly boos that greeted Chayefsky's theatrical interpretation of Leon Trotsky. The co-leader of the revolution didn't have substance, Chayefsky said earlier in his research. "He was all goose quills and parchment. He ended his days writing manifestos for *Liberty* magazine." Hence in his dramatic translation, Chayefsky made Trotsky into a caricature. Dressed in a white Afro wig, strutting on stage, orchestrating and taking credit for the revolution, his gross depiction offended staunch supporters. Each night die-hard Trotskyites trooped into the Ethel Barrymore Theatre to express their dissatisfaction. "Imagine paying money to sit in the front rows and jeer?" said Chayefsky, refusing to change the character. Trotsky was *not* presented as a clown, he insisted, but as "an actor, uncommonly vain and gracelessly arrogant . . . posturing before the mirror of history . . . a man who would have gladly given his life to the revolution if only he could be sure the audience was large enough."

During the show's previews, choreographer-director Jerome Robbins was said to be "giving tips for improvement" to Chayefsky. Following another performance, an old-time Metro star, Greer Garson (married to the coproducer Fogelson), went backstage to encourage the cast. "She was there to spread cheer and goodwill," said Epstein. Chayefsky's attempts to persuade Garson's husband to infuse more money in the play so as to extend the previews and delay the opening did not work, however. On February 11, 1964, *The Passion of Josef D.* officially opened. The first-night audience was rapt and respectful through Act I, which dealt with the exposition and the revolution. In Act II, the vaudeville aspects began to tax the viewers. In the civil war segment, two businessmen sat at an outdoor café with bullets flying on either side of them, while they discussed the military situation in song. Nothing had changed, they said. What had been lost in privilege would be made up in profit. Then one of the men stood up on the table, took out a knife, and slashed his throat. As the blood gushed out "by the bucketful," he reached up for a rope, arranged a noose around his neck, and, dangling in the air, put a pistol in his mouth, then blew his brains out. That scene "symbolized the self-destruction of the Russian bourgeoisie," said Chayefsky. But many in the gasping, nauseated opening-night audience missed the point.

By the start of Act III, those who remained in their seats were counting or commenting on the varied styles of the work. "As the curtain rose," said critic Norman Nadel, "a gentleman in the row behind me whispered, 'Now it's Wagnerian.' And sure enough, there sat Luther Adler as the aging Lenin on a hexagonal tiled platform like a launching pad for Valkyries. All that was lacking was the orchestra to begin an hour of delayed resolutions."

"Embarrassingly highfalutin'," the *Daily News* decreed. "Crude . . . sardonic . . . oversimplified," said the *Times.* George Oppenheimer of *Newsday* said that the story of Stalin was lost in the exasperating diversions of the Brechtian vaudeville, while Whitney Bolton of the New York *Morning Telegraph* said that the pedantic method of sonorously announcing historical events by day and date was patronizing. "Surely those who elected to produce this play did not jump up in ecstasy and astonishment when they received the script from Mr. Chayefsky and cry: 'Look, look, Paddy has discovered the Russian Revolution!' " said Bolton.

"*Josef D.* didn't work because the circumstances, the events of the Russian Revolution, were so outrageous, so incredible, that for a dramatist they created a very strong magnetic field," said Chayefsky's colleague Robert E. Lee. "That tends to distort the dramatization. It doesn't quite ring true. You may say, 'But that's the way it was.' Still, it's difficult to translate. I know. I did a play based on John Reed's *Ten Days That Shook the World.* It never worked on the proscenium. The canvas wasn't big enough."

The general consensus was that Chayefsky the director had shortchanged Chayefsky the writer. "What impulse is it that makes a playwright feel that he and he alone can and should direct his own play?" asked *Newsday*'s Oppenheimer. "Had Mr. Chayefsky, purely in the capacity of playwright, been witness to his play at rehearsals, run-throughs, and previews, changes might have been made before the opening."

Those changes weren't possible, said Lee. "Becoming a director diminishes the writer. He may have more control and more power, but he loses the writer's perspective, the chance of looking at something with a broad, objective eye."

Although the performances of the leading actors were praised, the negative assessment of the play itself was immediately felt at the box office. The day after it opened the cumulative take was $735. It was decided the play would close that Saturday. Arriving at the theatre on Saturday for the matinee, Chayefsky was told they had 92 percent capacity. Meeting with his three producers in the lobby, Paddy urged them to extend the run for one more week. They agreed, and with the remaining $20,000 in overcall, they decided to run an ad in the four metropolitan papers that Monday. Immediately assuming the job of press agent, the playwright-director grabbed some blank ledger sheets from the box office and composed the ad himself. Calling it "the Miracle of Forty-seventh Street," he wrote a stirring revolutionary plea from the producers to the public to support this play. Quoting the wildly mixed reviews, from "red-blooded satire" to "Brecht shampoo," he said that "the United Press adored it, the Associated Press abhorred it." With "bravos and berations matching each other in passionate conflict," what was one to make of such a reception? Especially since at that very moment, the matinee audience was cheering the performances of Peter Falk, Luther Adler, and "a virtuoso cast of 35 performers." In summation, it was up to the public to save this "most important theatrical adventure, this extraordinary experience, written and directed by one of the most brilliant and audacious of American playwrights."

On Monday, when the ad appeared, an interview with Chayefsky was published in *Newsday*. It stated that he was making extensive cuts and revisions, and that his play had been misinterpreted. "I didn't get the point across. This was not meant to be heavy drama. It was meant to be nightclub material. But when you've got Lenin and Trotsky in the act, it's not easy to see the vaudeville aspects," he said.

Throughout the week he made changes, which were inserted into the play each night. In a column plug in the *Post*, it was said that "first nighters wouldn't recognize *Josef D*. Paddy Chayefsky has tightened the play and added laughs." But on Saturday, February 15, after seven performances, *The Passion of Josef D*. closed permanently. When asked for his reaction, Chayefsky said,

"Nobody likes to get slugged. But I'm in good spirits. I allow one day for rancor and that's it." But his rancor lasted much longer this time. On Sunday, February 23, a week after the play had closed, the final death knell was sounded in the theatrical section of *The New York Times*. A "fucking vicious post-mortem" was Chayefsky's assessment of this notice, adding, "they're not satisfied in killing the play, they want to bury the playwright with it."

In his original review of *Josef D.*, Howard Taubman, the drama critic for the *Times,* described it as "garish distortions." He panned Chayefsky for his "intoxication with the thunder of the English language," his adoption of "the techniques of Brecht," and his "disservice to history" by depicting Trotsky as a clown and Lenin as a man disenchanted with socialism and the party he established. In his second essay, printed after the play had closed, Taubman further charged Chayefsky with distorting and changing the facts, and with being less than just to the figures of the Russian Revolution. His portrait of Stalin as brutish and ruthless was credible, but to show Lenin ending his days feeling that he and Russia had been betrayed by the Bolshevik revolution made Chayefsky guilty of "sentimentality, if not arrogance." To presume to transform Lenin into the image of a self-questioning Western man, and have him "wind up as the voice of anticommunism, was going entirely too far," the critic felt. Creative privilege to rearrange and re-create history was the right of all playwrights, Taubman said, but a responsibility to truth had to be retained because liberty was not license to stand history on its head. And "to put into Lenin's mouth words that twist his philosophy is to be the victim of wishful thinking." Furthermore, it was "childish" and a "dangerous illusion" for Chayefsky to use Lenin like this when the evidence showed the Soviet leader had not "abandoned hope in the Soviet future or in his commitment to it."

Chayefsky of course did not take any of this with head bowed. Before his anger had subsided, he was at his typewriter banging out a reply to Howard Taubman. In all, his rejoinder to the *Times* went through five protracted drafts and consumed most of his energy for a period of three days and nights.

"You have done me a great disservice," Chayefsky said in his first draft to Taubman. He asked for an apology on specific points, namely on the matter of his erroneous depiction of Trotsky and on his usage of Brechtianism. "Your review was irresponsible. If nobody else holds you to account, you must take that responsibility yourself," he told the critic. "At any rate, I don't fault you for lack of integrity or suggest you are a vulgar propagandist because we disagree."

By draft three the contrivance of the relationship of Stalin and his wife was acknowledged, but it was "arrantly untrue," said Chayefsky, that he made Lenin the voice of anti-communism. "Communism, in itself, is not even mentioned in my play. There is not a single political comment made, for or against communism." And by reviewing his play as a political tract and considering it "a grotesque and perilous fantasy," Chayefsky suggested, Taubman was "running off into the last refuge of a scoundrel."

His final transcript, fifteen pages, was not addressed to Taubman, but to the editor-in-chief of the *Times*. The first few weeks after a play opened were fairly touchy ones for a playwright, he said, especially if the notices weren't good. "When wounded, even the most sensible of us turns into something of a paranoid." One may adopt airs of unconcern, along with a patronizing tolerance of critics, "but underneath we rumble and rankle and make a half a dozen false starts on angry, cutting articles about the decline of the American theatre and other such statuesque themes." But a writer should contain himself against such measures, said Chayefsky, because "if there is anything more tiresome than a fatuous, prolix, criminally ignorant critic, it is surely a playwright smarting from bad notices."

The whole point of his play, he said, "was that humanitarianism and the idea that man is an essentially decent creature are illusions, and therefore the Russian revolution as a moral triumph must be considered humbug." Offering his "interpretation" of the characters and events, he wanted to enclose *his* source material, which was the last essay that Lenin wrote, in which he attacked Stalin. But as far as he was concerned, Chayefsky said, he didn't think it was "the business of critics of the arts to decide what is historically true and what isn't." As for the danger of the "perilous fantasy" of his play, Chayefsky believed it was far more perilous to resist threatening realities by clinging to moral aspirations that had already proved to be illusory. Such persistence and dangerous reliance was what his play was about, he concluded; "it was entirely possible that man will destroy himself to preserve his damned dignity."

It has never been established whether Chayefsky ever sent any of these rejoinders to the *Times*. If he did, the paper did not print them. The premise of his play, that communism was bogus and that the Soviet empire would eventually fall, did prove valid, however. "Paddy predicted a lot of things," Bill Chayefsky said. "He saw a lot of things that no one else did. He would discuss things with me, and I'd say, 'Paddy, I'm not so sure about that.' And sure enough, five or ten years later it actually transpired." That unusual foresight was of little comfort to the writer at the time, however. The failure of his Russian play affected Chayefsky greatly. "That was the first time I remember seeing him really depressed," his brother said.

CHAPTER 22

Further Negation

Following the failure of *The Passion of Josef D.* and the loss of its entire production cost of $160,000, Chayefsky hoped to recoup his career, professionally and financially, when the film of *The Americanization of Emily* was released. The movie had its world premiere on October 27, 1964, at the Loews State Theatre in New York City. "It is astonishing and very stimulating to listen to what is being said in *The Americanization of Emily*," said Bosley Crowther of *The New York Times*. "Sarcasm laces through it like fumes of acid through a chemistry lab, and boisterously ribald situations bespeak tensions that are solemn and sad. It is a fiercely funny picture. And what it says is tart and profound."

Most of the notices "from the critics of importance" were glowing, and that pleased and reassured the writer. "He told me what a relief it was to get some good reviews after one of your plays was killed by the critics," said Dan Chayefsky.

The film did not, however, succeed at the box office. This was partly attributed to its anti-heroic theme.

"Is World War Two itself fair game for laughter?" Judith Crist asked in the *New York Herald Tribune* the Sunday after the movie was released. In *Show* magazine, author-essayist Arthur Schlesinger, Jr., posed the same question. While praising the film for "an abundance of delights" and for succeeding in catching "certain less admirable aspects" of the military bureaucracy in action, Schlesinger believed the anti-war theme was more suitable to the First World War. "To write this way about the Second World War invites the conclusion that it is not only unpalatable to most audiences (outside Germany) but, most important, is wrong."

"Some reviewers became very emotional," said Arthur Hiller. "They saw the film as anti-war. It wasn't. It was the anti-glorification of war, that's what Paddy was saying."

"We make heroes of our dead and shrines of battlefields; as long as valor remains a virtue, we shall have soldiers," Chayefsky wrote.

"Paddy also said loud and clear in the picture that there are times when you *have* to go to war to defend your country," said Hiller. "Paddy served. And so did I. We didn't walk away when we were called. In *Emily,* what he was saying was, 'Let's not glorify all this. Don't name streets after heroes. Don't build statues. Don't make it so heroic and noble that our children will want to go to war to become heroes.' "

The timing of its release hurt the movie, James Coburn believed. "President Kennedy was dead. Lyndon Baines Johnson was in the White House. The war in Vietnam was escalating. And here we were talking about shutting things down, saying let's not get involved in any more wars. I don't know, it's strange, but there is a great deal of pressure that the politicians put on film companies before they release pictures—pressures that a lot of people don't like to advertise. Probably some of that happened with this."

Another factor that impeded the initial success of *The Americanization of Emily* was the now popular pristine image of its leading actress, Julie Andrews. *Mary Poppins* had been released the month before, and many critics were shocked at the idea of their favorite nanny shacking up with soldiers and sailors, sympathy be damned. A further deterrent came when Andrews did not aggressively publicize the film, as James Garner and Chayefsky had done. Reportedly she did not like her performance and considered herself "a little lost in the part." There was also the matter of her burgeoning Hollywood career. *Mary Poppins* was a gigantic hit, soon to be followed by another million-dollar musical, *The Sound of Music.* Hence, to protect her image and career, her retinue of advisers may have felt that it was best that Andrews not get involved with any bureaucratic controversy over *Emily.* Years later, when the film (described by columnist Liz Smith as "too good for its time, and now a classic for the cognoscenti") attained cult status Andrews was still trying to throw off the shackles of the wholesome and dulcet image solidified by *Mary Poppins.* When asked what would have happened if *Emily* had come first, Andrews was quoted as saying, "I might have had a different career."

Looking back, the other principals said they had no regrets concerning the film. Director Arthur Hiller, who would later work with Chayefsky on *The Hospital,* said in 1990, "Of all the films I've done, *Emily* is still my favorite. I think Jim Garner would say that too, and Jim Coburn."

"The important thing to remember is that all of those things we talked about in the film came about," said Coburn. "Certainly it took the heroism out of war. That was Paddy's astuteness. He was like Shaw in that respect, able to bring down all the sacred cows, but with humor, and paradoxical turns. That's why audiences later embraced the film and ultimately recognized how good Paddy's script was."

The Adaptation Years

In 1964, after the tandem failure of *Josef D.* on Broadway and *Emily* on the screen, Paddy Chayefsky's usual self-confidence was seriously impaired. He attempted to write a series of outlines for future plays but soon abandoned them. The most "dreaded time" of a writer's life was at hand, he said. At forty, he felt his career was over. He was in his "fallow period," a stage when, stripped of any original thoughts or ideas, he was forced to work as a hired hand, writing adaptations of other people's material.

His contemporaries also fared badly during this time. The political and social climate was not conducive to creative work for established writers. The old ideology and conventions were being flouted, onstage and off. It was a good time, said Tennessee Williams, "to head for the hills, or take a nice, long nap." Horton Foote won his first Oscar that year, for his adaptation of *To Kill a Mockingbird*. That ensured employment in Hollywood, which he refused. "Back then I never felt a part of the movie process," said Foote. "And I was never that inclined to take on the studios, as Paddy did. He was very forceful, a fighter. Also, I was more interested in writing for the theatre, which at that time there wasn't very much of either. Broadway was in a transition which didn't seem to include us." Foote's solution was to transplant himself and his family to New Hampshire, where he continued to write plays for small, noncommercial theatres.

But Chayefsky, as much as he would rail about the acquisitiveness and superfluous luxuries of a materialistic world, was not about to pull up stakes and leave Manhattan for some bucolic but spartan existence. He enjoyed the splendor and convenience of his eight-room apartment on Central Park West. He couldn't write or exist outside New York City. He needed the noise, the attention, the masochism of the daily contest as it was played out in the urban arena. "Paddy was hooked on New York, and on the games that go on in show business," said Mike Ryan. "This was a guy who felt he wasn't alive unless there was some confrontation going on in his life. He also had to constantly prove to the world, and to himself, that he was still a player at the big table. In that respect he was very much like Clifford Odets."

Clifford Odets. Now there was a talent that had once inspired awe and reverence in playwrights. But in 1964, just the mention of his name caused Paddy Chayefsky to shiver and break out in a cold, clammy sweat. "I think

Paddy's fear at that time was that he was going to be swallowed up and destroyed by the Hollywood system, like Odets was," said Mike Ryan. There was always that "ethical allegory," that implacable struggle American writers were faced with, Odets had said early in his career. " 'Do I work for art or money?' That is the question most creative people have to consistently ask themselves." For twenty-five years, Odets balanced that quandary by going back and forth from New York to the "tinted hills" of Los Angeles, writing movies to finance plays that frequently failed. He was further dispirited by the political witch-hunt of the fifties. By the early 1960s, to support his family Odets was working in the medium where Chayefsky had begun—television. In 1963 he was writing a Western series for Richard Boone when he fell ill and died of peritonitis at the age of fifty-seven. The conflict between art and money was there to the end, William Gibson said in his eulogy. "Clifford never surrendered. He struggled and struggled. He was miserable out there. All of his dreams were of escaping from it, of writing plays and coming back to the theatre. If you surrender you don't have dreams and aren't so unhappy. He never made peace with his defeat."

That would not happen to him, Paddy Chayefsky vowed. He would never be vanquished by Hollywood; nor would he ever live in that town. His plan was to take their money and run.

Having worked harmoniously with Marty Ransohoff on *The Americanization of Emily*, Chayefsky agreed to adapt *The Cincinnati Kid* for him. This was based on a novel by Richard Jessup and it promised to be a "class" production, starring Spencer Tracy and Steve McQueen as two poker players competing in a marathon game. "This was to be *The Hustler* with a deck of cards," said Ransohoff. "I kind of knew that Paddy would go for it because he had quite a reputation as a cardplayer himself." Chayefsky belonged to two floating poker games, one in New York, the other in Los Angeles. Among the players in Los Angeles were Tony Curtis and Walter Matthau; those in New York included Reginald Rose, J. P. Miller, Neil Simon, Johnny Friedkin, and Chayefsky's future producing partner Howard Gottfried. "The early games were usually held at Reggie's house," said Miller, "and Paddy was our dependable loser."

"It was his attitude," said Gottfried. "Paddy would walk in and say, 'O.K., let's see how much I'm going to drop tonight.' And he'd lose."

In a group consisting largely of writers, the dialogue was notably mundane. "It consisted of 'I raise—two bucks' or 'I pass,' or whatever. Those were the lines," said Miller. "Except for Paddy. He'd keep talking in a continuous stream, about every subject under the sun, very opinionated. Doc Simon was quiet, never funny, just listening, taking in whatever was worth remembering for further use."

As the stakes went higher, Chayefsky became nervous. He was losing close to a thousand dollars a night. By this time the Manhattan band was meeting in a room rented for the night at the Warwick Hotel. One evening the game was almost raided by the police. "They were playing for a lot of money," said Dan Chayefsky, "and the house detective got wind of it and broke it up. If he had called the police it would have made the newspapers, which scared the hell out of everyone." The group lay low for a while, and when it reconvened it was in somebody's home. The stakes went lower and Chayefsky resumed his dialogue. "He would talk and talk," said Miller, "until it was his turn and one of us would say, 'Paddy, you in or what?' And he'd say, 'What's the bet? What's the bet?' He'd make the bet, then he'd continue talking."

For his first draft of *The Cincinnati Kid,* dated March 1964, Chayefsky put in considerable time and energy setting up the background and atmosphere leading into the big modern-day game. Adhering to the book, wherein old-time card sharp Lancey Hodges arrives in Cincinnati to challenge the local younger champion, Chayefsky went to Ohio and spent four days driving around, soaking up the local color. Back in New York, after writing eighteen pages of an outline, he found it didn't work. The story didn't "hang," he said. The problem was the locale and the period, said Ransohoff. When he agreed to do the script he had believed there was a "mystical essence for poker players, an almost Arthurian ethic among cardplayers. After his research, he found out that was horseshit."

With Ransohoff's approval, Chayefsky backdated the story to the 1930s and changed the locale from Cincinnati to New Orleans. He worked until the end of June 1964, when a fourth draft came out to his liking. He forwarded it to Ransohoff in California and the next day the writer took off on a twenty-one-day vacation to Europe and Egypt with his wife. In a scrupulously detailed schedule, with maps and diagrams, Chayefsky charted each step of their daily itinerary. The record in part read: "July 2, arriving in Frankfurt, Germany, at 8 A.M., flying time approximately 9 hours. Departing at 1 P.M. that same day for Cairo, flight time 5 hours and 5 minutes. Departing Cairo the following afternoon at 1 P.M. (total time in Cairo: 18 hrs. 5 min., with sleep, and 2½ hrs for sightseeing)."

On his return to New York, Chayefsky unpacked his bags, brought his clothes to the cleaner's, visited his office and the bank, then took off the following day for California. The purpose of this trip was to meet Sam Peckinpah, the man who would direct his script of *The Cincinnati Kid.* Brilliant, obsessive, self-destructive, manipulative, pathological, and clinically paranoid, Peckinpah was not in the best of spirits the day Chayefsky came to call. He had just come up from Mexico where Charlton Heston, on horseback and brandishing a sabre, had tried to run him down because of too many retakes on *Major Dundee.* Six hundred thousand dollars over budget, Peckinpah had also been pestered in Mexico by executives from Columbia Pictures. When two men in suits came to visit the set, the irascible director reportedly had them stripped and bound and left in a desert motel forty miles from the location.

In Hollywood, Peckinpah opened the meeting with Chayefsky with a sneer. He had read the script and was surprised. He never would have guessed that Paddy was "a fairy." That was the only explanation for the aggregate cerebral and dainty approach he brought to the material. A man keenly interested in action scenes as violent and bloody as possible (to which *Straw Dogs* and *The Wild Bunch* would later attest) and in members of the opposite sex ("Women have very complicated plumbing, that I am fascinated with," he told the New York *Daily News* critic Kathleen Carroll), Peckinpah said Chayefsky's script had neither. It was loaded with fancy, obtuse dialogue, and the women were used as decorative but inanimate props. Picking up the script, Peckinpah said, "*This* is so much puke!" Then he threw the bound copy at Chayefsky's head, grabbed a nearby bottle of tequila, and retired to the can.

Chayefsky claimed that during the entire meeting he remained his "calm and professional self," even after Peckinpah had returned from the john and told him where his script and the empty bottle of tequila should be placed. The orifices were the usual, but left untouched, because Peckinpah with his last wind let out a very loud belch—which must have exhausted him, said Chayefsky, "because seconds later he was sprawled out, facedown, fast asleep on the floor."

The final decision came when Chayefsky went to Marty Ransohoff and told him he had a choice to make. It was either him or Peckinpah. "This time he chose the director," said Chayefsky.

"Well, that's not quite my memory," Ransohoff said in 1990. "I don't think Paddy was too crazy about Peckinpah, and vice versa. But Paddy was dealing directly with me, as were Spencer Tracy and Steve McQueen. What I wanted the movie to be was a gunfight with a deck of cards. It was supposed to be a licorice stick, an entertainment. And I told Paddy, 'For God's sake, whatever you do, don't make this a mint julep. Don't make it the end of the era of the Mississippi Gambler. Forget that. It's got to be a gunfight between Lancey and The Kid.' But somehow, Paddy never got a handle on the story. When it came to character and dialogue, he was first-rate, but to do a straightforward commercial story, Paddy couldn't come through. He couldn't get a handle on the ending of the script."

John Calley felt that this was not a major disappointment for Chayefsky, "For Paddy, it was 'pay day.' " He received his full fee and Ransohoff gave him another assignment. Spy movies such as *The Ipcress File, Funeral in Berlin,* and the burgeoning James Bond cottage industry were in vogue. So Chayefsky was given the task of adapting an Alistair MacLean espionage thriller, *Ice Station Zebra*, with a class actor, Gregory Peck, tentatively attached.

"Paddy did a hell of a good job on that adaptation," said Ransohoff. "He gave us a good set of bones to go in on, but again, the problem was the ending. As you know, Paddy was very verbal. He gave us an ending that would have gone more with an Agatha Christie story, like *Ten Little Indians*. The director, John Sturges, and I felt we needed big action stuff up on the North Pole. So we brought in another writer."

He and Ransohoff remained friends, but when MGM tried to put Chayefsky's name in the final movie credits, he made them take it off. "He was right," said Ernest Borgnine, who played the Russian villain in the film. "The picture had a very bad ending. All these guys shooting at one another at the North Pole. It was a mishmash. And the funny thing is it wound up as one of Howard Hughes's favorite movies. Go figure."

Inactivity and Diversion

For a brief time, Chayefsky worked on another adaptation, *Three Lives for Mississippi*, from a novel by William Bradford Huie. This he abandoned, along with the few original story ideas that came up from time to time. His creativity stopped completely at one point, his son recalled. "He would wake up every morning, go to the office downtown, and with sheer willpower he would sit at his typewriter. But nothing came out of him." The enduring emptiness and sense of impotency magnified his anger and the despair he felt for the people and strife around him. "My father loved mankind but I think he felt that God was not very supportive," said Dan Chayefsky. When his son was nine, another boy the same age was pursued by a gang of tough kids in Central Park. To escape he ran across a transverse that overlooked a busy traffic causeway. The boy fell and was killed by the oncoming cars. "My father raged and fumed over that," said Dan Chayefsky. "He went around our apartment for hours, fantasizing how he would strangle the boy's killers. Somehow he put the burden on himself to feel the pain and to help everyone else. He felt that he had to be responsible because God wouldn't do it anymore."

The loss of his own inner support confused Chayefsky further. Previously, when Sidney, the sensitive, creative side of him, felt blocked or lost, Paddy, the more energetic, positive one, came to the rescue. Paddy brought aid, bolstered his confidence, and always managed to find an assignment or to make a deal that would revive their cause and their spirits. But by 1965, after a long string of critical failures and script rejections, Paddy too had lost his confidence. "He had been famous for six or seven years, then it all went away," said Dan Chayefsky. "That part of him that made the success happen could not understand what went wrong, or how he could pull himself out of the slump and his misery."

To get him out of the house, Susan Chayefsky suggested that he take a teaching job. He did this for one semester, teaching a writing course at City College. It was much tougher than writing, but he found he enjoyed it and got tremendous satisfaction from some of the students. On his own he also read extensively, mostly nineteenth-century novelists and biographies of writers who had led troubled lives. Edgar Allan Poe, described as the quintessential struggling American writer, and the master of rhythmic expression, received Chayefsky's renewed intense attention. But perhaps to keep the image of his self-created talent intact, or to avoid comparisons to his own dark quirks and personality, he made only the barest of mention of this interest. Yet the absorption was there. In 1965, when Chayefsky's son, Dan, was in grade school, the boy asked for help with a school paper on Poe's short story "The Black Cat." Chayefsky senior assisted with a discourse on Poe's entire work. "His knowledge was vast," said Chayefsky junior. "This was not just a peripheral thing." Chayefsky subsequently brought home and played a long-playing record of an actor reciting "The Raven" for Dan, who remembered becoming quite frightened, which didn't seem to deter his father's absorption.

A New Best Pal

For relief perhaps, or to lift the continuing downward spiral of his career, Chayefsky periodically considered writing in a genre for which he wasn't known: musical comedy. In 1959, Harold Arlen, composer of the scores for *The Wizard of Oz* and *A Star Is Born,* collaborated with Chayefsky on a song for the movie of *Middle of the Night.* It was never used because the financial negotiations could not be worked out. After that, Chayefsky and Arlen discussed doing a musical version of *Marty,* but this never got beyond the title of the opening song, "So, Marty, When Are You Gonna Get Married?" In 1963, composer Jule Styne reportedly asked Chayefsky to write the book for *Something More,* a musical that opened and closed on Broadway in a single week (sans Chayefsky's contribution). By 1965, the word on Music Row was that Chayefsky was working on a show with one of the hottest talents on Broadway, director Bob Fosse, whose distinctive choreography—an amalgam of jazz, ballet, burlesque, and kinetic street moves—was to become as synonymous with his name as the colloquial urban writing style was with Chayefsky's. But their collaboration was only geared toward scholarship and toward a friendship that would become the most intimate and enduring of both men's lives.

His prodigious talent and credits (*Damn Yankees, New Girl in Town, Redhead*) aside, Fosse did not find it easy to connect with Chayefsky when they first met over dinner at writer David Shaw's house in Amagansett in 1959. The dancer-director said, in jest, he had "to audition for twelve years" to be Chayefsky's friend. "Yes, that's true, but Bob was not that easy to get to know either," said Gwen Verdon, the star and main influence on Fosse's best productions, who was present at that introductory dinner. Shortly thereafter she was given an award by *Dance* magazine. They needed a celebrity presenter, and Fosse, figuring Chayefsky had a gift for language, asked that he make the presentation. "Well, Paddy came and got up on the podium," said Verdon. "He made this speech, which was really one sentence, but it went on and on, beautifully punctuated and spoken. It was almost two paragraphs long, with no period, no full stops, and it continued for what seemed like two to three minutes. When he did stop, he looked up from the paper he was reading from, and said, 'How's that for a hunk of prose?' And Bobby burst out laughing. He thought that was hilarious. From that time on there was a sort of a tentative feeling out of one another."

Bob Fosse revered writers. He had been named after one, Robert Louis Stevenson, the author of *Treasure Island* and *The Strange Case of Dr. Jekyll and Mr. Hyde*. Fosse also had a strong alter ego, Bob Riff, a name taken from his first dance act in high school. His youth had been strange and schizophrenic, "a pull between Sunday school and my wicked underground life." While the public at large knew the performer as sunny and cheerful, eager and always polite, an eternal Peter Pan, the other side of Fosse could be cynical, stubborn, and morose. He was obsessed with perfectionism and details and had a constant need to keep proving himself. "Bob was a very brilliant artist, but conflicted," said Howard Gottfried. "Both he and Paddy had their very dark sides, their demons. I think those demons are what brought them together more than anything—that and genius. It was an interesting combination of genius and conflict. Both felt very torn and misplaced at times. In their own minds they could not find out where they really belonged or establish themselves with any kind of sense of regular contentment."

As their friendship evolved, Chayefsky, who was only four years older, became "the Professor." He took over Fosse's literary education. He suggested the books and plays Fosse should read, and brought him together with other writers. He also introduced the Norwegian-Irish Methodist to "Jew food" at the Carnegie Deli on Seventh Avenue. Herbie Schlein, the congenial maître d', was a friend to both, but felt closer to Fosse. "I considered Paddy to be one of the most brilliant men I ever met in my life," said Schlein, "but I didn't understand him. I was afraid of him, because he had such an extensive vocabulary, and mine was limited." Chayefsky could be very private and reserved, Schlein remembered. "Fosse was private too, but he was always friendly, a very special man once you knew him. The combination of the two of them together worked so well. They were like two brilliant kids that played together, joked together, and were serious together. In show business everyone says they're 'best friends' with everybody; but with Paddy and Bob, right from the beginning everyone knew there was something very real between them."

The lunches at the Carnegie Deli led to frequent dinners, where they were sometimes joined by Gwen Verdon, who by this time was married to Fosse, and by Susan Chayefsky. "Susie came along occasionally," said Verdon. "We also saw her at the Shaws' in Amagansett, but after a while she stopped coming." In the mid-1960s, Fosse decided to get an office closer to Chayefsky, on the eleventh floor at 850 Seventh Avenue. Chayefsky's office was an efficiency apartment that had been converted into two rooms. The larger one had a desk, a chair, a sofa, and a baby grand piano in the corner. The kitchenette had a sink, a hot plate, and filing cabinets filled with correspondence, press clips, and story ideas. Fosse took a corner office down the hall, and together after work the two men would walk home to their apartments on Central Park West. "And then Paddy discovered that Bob was nuts about baseball," said Verdon. "When the final games of the World Series were on, Paddy would come to our house. In the television room we had two sets. That way they could watch the end of the baseball series and the beginning of football. The room would be filled with pretzels, potato chips, and beer, all that stuff." Joining the two men on occasion would be Verdon and Fosse's young daughter, Nicole. "Paddy was so patient with children who were exploring and learning," said Verdon, "with his son Danny, and with Nicole." One day, when the men were watching a baseball game, Nicole stood in the doorway until Chayefsky gestured for her to join them. "Unfortunately he gestured towards a bowl of pretzels which were to the left of him," said Verdon. "So Nicole went over and sat on the pretzels. She knew exactly what she was doing and Paddy also knew she was going to do it. Then he wouldn't acknowledge that she had done it. And Nicole just sat there, as if everything was normal. The two of them would put one another on all the time. And that was very much the relationship with Bob and Paddy."

In the exchange of entertainment and influence, although Verdon knew that Fosse admired writers and aspired to be one himself, she wasn't aware that Chayefsky had any musical talents or experience. She had seen the piano in his office but had never heard him play. He did sing for her, once. "We were at our house in East Hampton and he was on the patio lying down in the sun. Nicole came out and when she saw him she started to put flowers all around him until he looked like someone who was laid out. All he needed was a coffin. And gradually everyone in the house came out to look, and Paddy began to chant, like a rabbi, as if he was at his own funeral. It was hilarious."

Chayefsky and Fosse shared a strong interest in foreign films. Together they would sometimes visit the Thalia and the Symphony revival houses on the Upper West Side of Manhattan. A film on their repeat list was Federico Fellini's *Nights of Cabiria*, starring Giulietta Masina. There was a musical here, Fosse believed. Updated and relocated to New York, the story of the meek, victimized prostitute would be perfect for Gwen Verdon. With Chayefsky in tow, Fosse frequented the dime-a-dance halls and the tango joints in Times Square where he intended to place his musical. He also asked Chayefsky to write the book. That would kill the friendship, Chayefsky told him, urging Fosse to write the play himself.

"The Professor" was there each day to push and encourage and grade Fosse's writing. "Paddy always read everything and anything that Bob had written," said Verdon. "He would tell him about form and structure, and Bob listened to everything he said, because he trusted him so much." It was a mutual reliance, Herb Gardner felt. "And there was a good reason for that. Instinctively they were the same in many ways. There was absolutely nonexistent bullshit between these two guys. I mean it scared them about each other because they would always hear the truth from each other."

Eventually Fosse turned over the writing of the musical, retitled *Sweet Charity*, to Chayefsky's poker partner Neil Simon, and he concentrated solely on the direction and the choreography. On the night of January 29, 1966, the musical comedy opened at the Palace Theatre in Times Square. It became a tremendous hit, running for six hundred performances. Chayefsky was at the opening and at numerous subsequent performances. On nights when he visited the Palace with Fosse, Chayefsky would stand at the back of the theatre and watch Verdon perform her show-stoppers. "*This* is the big time. *This* is Broadway," he would tell anyone who listened. And those two, Fosse and Verdon, embodied the true meaning of the words "musical-comedy genius."

Paint Your Wagon

In March 1967, Chayefsky was given the chance to work on another musical, this time as an adapter. *Paint Your Wagon* had originally been produced on Broadway in 1951. The book had been "a brute to write," lyricist/librettist Alan Jay Lerner said. It was also hard to follow, the critics complained. The reason for that was there was "too much in the pot." The story had a gold rush, a boomtown, sexually frustrated miners, incoming prostitutes, outgoing Mormons, an interracial love story, a town trial, and a prospector's drought, all of which were served up with eighteen songs and prolonged dance interludes by Agnes de Mille. Lerner said that during the run of the play he "never stopped tinkering" with the story. Sixteen years later, for the movie version, it was suggested that he bring in another writer, and Paddy Chayefsky was recommended.

Despite his fondness for musicals and his esteem for such a class act as Alan Jay Lerner (who had turned George Bernard Shaw's *Pygmalion* into *My Fair Lady*, a musical sensation on Broadway), Chayefsky expressed reservations about the assignment. He was from the Bronx and knew "nothing about writing a Western." Lerner proceeded to woo the writer. He told Chayefsky not to consider *Paint Your Wagon* as a run-of-the-mill tale of pioneer life in the Old West. This was a metaphoric fable of "wonderful courageous men who set out, as we all do in life, in search of the American dream, and somehow got lost along the way."

As the producer, Lerner also mentioned the budget for his movie. It was fifteen million dollars; so there would be no problem paying Chayefsky's fee ($150,000 plus a percentage of profits). The Paramount private jet would be available to take him to California for research and to Oregon, where the movie would be filmed. On the home lot in Los Angeles he would have his own office and secretary, and a private suite overlooking the pool at the Beverly Hills Hotel would also be put at his disposal. "He didn't have to sell me so hard," said Chayefsky, who needed the money and, more than that, the opportunity to be working again.

After reading numerous books on the gold rush era, Chayefsky went to work on his adaptation. In the Broadway version, Ben Rumson is a miner and widower with a daughter (whose relationship with a young Mexican was set up primarily so that Lerner's obligatory lush ballads could be performed). In his revisions, Chayefsky's first step was to get rid of the daughter and the Mexican. Instead he concentrated on the relationship between Ben Rumson and a junior miner, Pardner. The two become involved with a young woman, Elizabeth, whom Rumson buys from her Mormon husband for eight hundred dollars. In a liberated switch, Chayefsky then made Elizabeth the one who decides to have multiple spouses. She marries both Rumson and his partner. There wasn't any legal problem with that, because "California, being too young and innocent to have ever heard of polygamy, certainly had no laws against it," said Chayefsky.

With colorful peripheral characters and a sensational climax where the town built by gold is destroyed by greed, the final script was described by the director, Josh Logan, as "a preposterous story. Lusty. A mixture of Mark Twain, Bret Harte, and Paddy Chayefsky. It wasn't anything like the original stage show, except for its background."

The script fit him "like a glove," said character actor Lee Marvin, who, coming off his Oscar victory for *Cat Ballou*, agreed to play Ben Rumson for one million dollars. Clint Eastwood, star of Italian Westerns, after reading the Chayefsky adaptation, elected to play Pardner for considerably less. For the role of their shared wife, Alan Jay Lerner spoke to Jean Seberg. She read the script, agreed to test with Marvin, and was given the part. At that point, Chayefsky, who was looking forward to the summer production out west, was called to a meeting with Lerner in New York. Lerner tried to tell him that his script didn't have enough of "a musical structure," meaning that there weren't any story cues for where his precious songs could be introduced. Chayefsky's response to that was that the songs for *Paint Your Pupik* (Yiddish for "bellybutton"), as he referred to it, were essentially lousy, and anyway, Lee Marvin and Clint Eastwood couldn't "sing for shit."

Lerner, the producer, duly informed Chayefsky that he was fired. As merely the adapter, Chayefsky knew he had no power, but his contract with Paramount Pictures guaranteed that on or off the picture, he had to receive his entire fee plus a share of future profits. Commenting later on Chayefsky's dismissal, Josh Logan said that he was blessed for having been spared the trials of location shooting in the wilds of Oregon. Perpetual havoc, frequent brawls, some inter-star fornication, and the threat of a duel with pistols dominated the landscape *behind* the camera. In front of it, a cast of two hundred, including imported Chinese extras, per diem Indians, wandering hippies, plus numerous horses, mules, oxen, sheep, mongrel dogs, chickens, ducks, a bull, and a grizzly bear ran amok, oblivious to Logan's direction. As the budget escalated from fifteen to nineteen million, the new writer-cum-producer, Alan Jay Lerner, serviced and abetted by his personal physician, the amphetamine wizard Dr. Max "Feelgood" Jacobson, tried to take over the direction. But Logan's still devoted wife and ally, Nedda, and his lawyer, Deane Johnson, nipped that move in the bud. Hanging on until the end of location shooting, Logan said the final scene was filmed exactly as Chayefsky had written it. To effect the collapse of his "No Name City," all of the buildings had been erected on rockers and rigged to collapse on cue. When the cameras rolled and each structure came tumbling down, Logan said his heart rejoiced. "When the last building broke in two, we headed for Los Angeles."

When the film was edited and scored by André Previn, the report in Hollywood was that Paramount had a colossal hit on its hands. Paddy Chayefsky said he didn't believe a word of it. The movie was not only bad, he said, it was boring. The story had very little to do with his script. "I don't think there were six pages of mine left in the whole picture," he said. "A couple of my ideas were left but barely recognizable."

When Chayefsky told Alan Jay Lerner he wanted his name off the script, the producer said, "But Paddy, think of what you'll be missing out on at Oscar time." Chayefsky stuck to his standards, or to what was left of them. His name was removed as screenwriter, but he had to be listed as adapter; otherwise he would have forfeited his share of any eventual profits.

The reviews for *Paint Your Wagon* were noxious. "It was resoundingly booed at home—and resoundingly cheered abroad," said Lerner. "It grossed a startlingly large sum of money."

It didn't make a dime in profit, said Chayefsky, but it did provide him with enough upfront money, and the determination to resist working on adaptations ever again. As it turned out, the financial security also helped remove Chayefsky's creative block. This would result in the creation of a theatrical play that would bring his long, disastrous slide of the sixties to a tempestuous close.

A Return to the Theatre

The names of the hosts on the invitation were impressive: John Steinbeck, William Inge, Thornton Wilder, and Tennessee Williams. The occasion was a party celebrating the publication of Elia Kazan's book *The Arrangement*. The date was the evening of February 6, 1967, and the place was Brentano's bookstore on Fifth Avenue.

Cohost Tennessee Williams, bundled up behind dark glasses and a topcoat with an oversized fur collar, strolled in first, followed by Budd Schulberg; Kazan's second wife, Barbara Loden; and Andy Warhol "with his manic-depressive Chelsea girls." Passing up the champagne but making two trips to partake of the lobster Newburg set up in the rare-book section was Paddy Chayefsky. On the other side of the mezzanine, complacently looking down on the scene, was his old-time adversary, Arthur Miller, "sucking on a pipe in which there appeared to be no tobacco at all," said a reporter from *The Village Voice.*

Two years before, Chayefsky had indulged in yet another publicized skirmish with Miller. On that occasion they were part of a literary contingent invited to the White House to watch President Lyndon Johnson sign the Arts and Humanities Bill. Miller was opposed to the war in Vietnam and refused to go. His statement "When the guns boom, the arts died" made front-page news, attracting comments from other writers, including Chayefsky. "Does this mean he would have opposed the Civil War?" he asked. Zeroing in on the idea that war causes the death of creativity, he said that if this were true, "You'd have to overlook much of our literature, from *The Iliad* and Cervantes, all the way over to Hemingway and Norman Mailer."

By this time, the sporadic whacks at Miller, whose indifference remained steadfast ("I always liked him personally," he said of Chayefsky in 1991), could not have been provoked by professional envy. In the sixties, following the limited run of *After the Fall* and *Incident at Vichy,* Miller's stature as a playwright had declined with the times. In fact, surveying the collection of noted writers at the Kazan party, not one of these pillars of the traditional American theatre was currently represented on Broadway. Thornton Wilder, who had won the Pulitzer Prize for *Our Town,* had stopped writing plays and had returned to creating novels. Tennessee Williams had brought two different productions of *The Milk Train Doesn't Stop Here Anymore* to New York in the early sixties, and both had departed quickly. William Inge failed with *Where's Daddy?* in 1966 and said he had no intention of writing another play. And Paddy Chayefsky? In 1967 he had a play that Cecil Smith, critic of the *Los Angeles Times,* called one of "the best known unproduced works in the American theatre." The name of this was *The Latent Heterosexual.* It had been published in its entirety in *Esquire* magazine and in book form by Random House. Yet for inveterate theatregoers, it was a phantom piece, because it had never been seen on a public stage.

The concept went back to 1963. Immediately after the failure of *The Passion of Josef D.* to regain his "lost sense of stature," Chayefsky had hastily compiled a series of ideas for another play. One of these was on the "science" of tax evasion. The premise, he said, was "that all of modern life was governed by the morality of accounting. And what is that morality? To earn money and then keep it. Keep it from the government, that is, the Internal Revenue Service."

His interest in the subject, it should be pointed out, could be construed as personal. At the time Chayefsky and his accountant, Irving Gaft, were in dispute with the Internal Revenue Service over the sum of $86,770. That was the amount he claimed he had lost on the production of *The Goddess.* But the IRS ruled that Columbia Pictures had financed the film in its entirety and disallowed the loss. Naturally this set off a rapid exchange of heated phone calls, letters, and cables. It also stimulated Chayefsky's concern on *how* his tax money was being spent by the government. The idea that his hard-earned dollars were being used to subsidize bomb-testing and chemical-biological warfare was counter to his basic sense of pacifism. But protest "based on moral grounds was illusory, and useless, in a mass-democratic society," he conceded in a note to himself. "The point is, if you don't want to pay your taxes, let's not make a moral issue out of it, because that only gets you penalized and imprisoned, which is not to your advantage. They take your money anyway and put you in jail in the bargain. The trick is to avoid paying your taxes by realistic maneuver."

Having grappled with God in *Gideon* and harpooned the founders of communism in *The Passion of Josef D.,* in Shavian fashion—using his anger constructively—Chayefsky decided his next target would be the Internal Revenue Service. He would satirize its inane laws and expose its convoluted, arbitrary unilateral tax system.

"If a man was faced with a huge tax bite on personal income of one million dollars, how much could he save if he got married?" That was the question Chayefsky asked Irving Gaft on March 6, 1964. In subsequent conversations he spoke with his tax lawyers at the firm of Cuiffo and Spanbock. The vast amount of ways to limit and save on taxes—the shelters, the deferments, the loopholes, and abatements—"staggered the mind and the senses," he said. And the fervor and dedication the "tax scientists" brought to their work was truly religious in its intensity. "Corporate finance is the new capitalistic god, with its own 'Ten Commandments' furnished by the Internal Revenue Service," said Chayefsky with awe in his preliminary notes.

The Accountant's Tale became the working title of the project. In the first draft it focused on two clients who visit the offices of CPA Irving Spatz. One is a penurious man, suddenly rich, who must get married for tax purposes. The second is a divorcée with financial problems. Strictly as a business arrangement, Spatz decides his two clients must marry.

That was the plot, but who was the protagonist? Chayefsky asked. It couldn't be Spatz, the accountant, because he was "sort of god, a deus ex machina." His hero had to be the first client, the greedy man. But who was he and what did he do for a living? Obviously, he had to be eccentric if he was willing to marry a strange woman just to screw the government out of money. "What is the profession of a greedy, eccentric man?" Paddy pondered, before giving himself the answer. "A writer, of course, because a writer doesn't have to take care of anybody but himself."

His writer character is *not* a miser, Chayefsky elaborated further. "It's just that it's *his* money, and he doesn't want to give any of it, or at least only a tiny bit of it, to the government for which he has little respect and gets very little return from." The woman he marries also had to be induced by greed and self-interest. She could be frightened of living alone. "A divorcée who has gone through all her money, is broke, suicidal," he decided. "She has tried all the other illusions of life from hedonism to Swiss sanitarium sleep cures, etc. She agrees to the marriage out of desperation."

After the two characters were created and brought together, Chayefsky had them marry without emotion. "Selfishness and self-interest are the basic motivations of humans, and as long as we know it, we can get along very well in this world," was Chayefsky's philosophy. Employing one of the foundations of his own domestic arrangement, he deduced that neither one of his fictional newlyweds expected to be happy, because "they have discovered the pleasures of occasional misery."

For conflict and further dramatic intrigue a third main character was introduced. In Chayefsky's play the writer has become momentarily depleted. Bored with his work and "badly abused by the critics in his last few plays," he is vulnerable again. "In short he is ripe for an affair." In the accountant's office he meets a beautiful and spirited black woman. She infects the writer with morality, "a disease recognized by the symptoms of swollen platitudes and inflamed righteousness in his speech." She also influences his creativity, enabling him to master the difficulties of using jazz improvisation in his writing. Naturally she idolizes him, which gives the writer a sense of life.

After three drafts, Chayefsky abandoned the play. Over a year passed, during which he worked on *The Cincinnati Kid* and other adaptations. Then, in late 1965, he spoke with an actor who ultimately inspired and motivated him to revise and complete the work. This was Zero Mostel, star of *A Funny Thing Happened on the Way to the Forum* and *Fiddler on the Roof*, the current hit musical on Broadway. Mostel, according to Chayefsky, was, "along with Bob Fosse and Gwen Verdon, one of the most singular, brilliant artists to dwell on Broadway in half a century."

Chayefsky saw *Fiddler* a few times. After one show he went backstage and learned that he and Mostel had similar backgrounds. Both grew up in lower-middle-class Jewish families in New York, relished the Yiddish theatre, attended City College, and had the same English lit teacher, Professor Goodman. "He used to write on the board, 'You can't write like Thomas Wolfe.' And we used to write, 'In a pig's ass, we can't,' " said Mostel.

Chayefsky and Mostel discussed starting their own repertory group. Earlier that hadn't seemed feasible to Chayefsky. "Such a group implies we have a theatre and tradition of our own on which to draw, and we don't. We don't have any Shakespeare, any Racine. Our tradition is O'Neill," he said. But when Mostel suggested they present old and new works, specifically alternating James Joyce with Paddy Chayefsky, the latter listened intently. Mostel wanted to revive *Ulysses in Nighttown*, then follow with something fresh and original from Chayefsky. Paddy said he had just the project in mind for the actor. Verbally, he gave him the outline of a play in which a mad writer marries a stranger, just to screw the Internal Revenue Service out of their money. Having been blacklisted for many years, Mostel found the idea of opposing a governmental agency appealing. Referring to his political past, he might also have been giving his future partner a hint of what lay ahead in their professional relationship. "I was never a Communist," said Mostel proudly. "I was an *anarchist!*"

With Mostel committed, Chayefsky promptly went to work expanding and revising his tax story. The first major change he made was in his central character, John Morley, the writer. Adapting to Mostel's vast comedic and dramatic gifts, Morley was changed from an obstinate, articulate, but sexually conventional male to a flamboyant, outrageous, verbose homosexual. That would make the idea of his marrying a woman seem even more unusual and contentious. When this suggestion was made to Mostel, the actor reportedly "swooned" with the visions of what he would be able to do with such a role onstage.

Because he was writing specifically for Mostel, progress on the play went fast. Chayefsky's hero, after twenty years of composing mediocre poems, writes a novel about the gay community in Algiers. "With hot sperm spurting and smooth-skinned Arab boys on every page," and detailing one man's search for serenity, "a search presumably conducted with a proctoscope," the book becomes a best-seller and Morley suddenly is rich. To save on taxes, he visits a tax lawyer. One of the latter's suggestions is that Morley deduct the cost of his ample supply of narcotics as "development and research." Another is that he marry. Otherwise 80 percent of his recent windfall will go to the U.S. government.

Departing from his original story line, which featured two females, the wife and the black mistress, Chayefsky consolidated both into one distaff character, a "drop-dead, gorgeous blonde" named Christine whose looks and sexual mores could be compared to those of Marilyn Monroe. Except this new girl isn't an actress, she is a high-priced hooker, for the simple reason that the money is better. "I could get her a studio contract tomorrow," the tax lawyer says, "but do you know how much legitimate income she'd have to make as an actress to come off with an adjusted gross of fifty grand a year? She's better off whoring."

Morley agrees to marry Christine, but not before laying down the rules of his house. She has to stay out of the kitchen. That is his province. He also doesn't want her wandering around the house half-dressed. She will have her own room on the third floor with a view of the river, "if you crane your neck a bit." Said room is to be kept spotless, and there are to be no female undergarments left out to drip-dry in the bathroom. Furthermore, when his gay friends come to visit she is to stay in her room. "If, by hazard, you bump into my friends, just stride rudely off without a word," says Morley. "You will not show your transparent tolerance of us poor deviates. Above all, stay away from the boy who lives with me. He's mine. Resist that vanity common to all women that makes each think that she alone can straighten out a homosexual. If I catch you near Richard, I'll tear your eyes out. They're lovely by the way, where do you get that delicious gray eye shadow?"

In Act II there is an unexpected development. Despite the anomalous coupling, the gay poet and the high-priced whore fall "dementedly in love" with each other. It begins when she, with "a compulsive attraction to impotent men," seduces him. The seduction succeeds because Morley is not really gay, said Chayefsky, he has merely been frightened of women since puberty. The hooker, in exposing those fears, succeeds in raising his libido and his latent manhood.

"What happens when a howling faggot turns straight?" Chayefsky asked. He loses his outrageousness, his theatrical excesses. Permuted, John Morley in Act II swaggers onstage in stereotypical macho fashion: wearing boots and a lumber jacket and smoking a cigar. In the metamorphosis he also loses his literary sensitivity. Instead of writing he transfers his bountiful creative energy into monitoring his burgeoning financial empire. Introduced by his tax lawyers to the wondrous intricacy of domestic tax laws and foreign loopholes, Morley, in an apocalyptic swoon, says, "I have seen the face of God!"

In tailoring the lead role for Zero Mostel, Chayefsky was careful to consider the actor's physical limitations onstage. In 1960, Mostel's left leg had been crushed by the wheels of a bus. Four operations had left him with a permanent limp. When he was tired, the leg would swell and cause considerable pain, so for the second part of the play, Chayefsky concentrated on writing scenes in which Mostel's mobility would be minimal.

In Act III, John Morley emerges as a Kafkaesque abstract. Obsessed with his corporate identity, and with making more money, he becomes oblivious to all external stimuli. Devoid of his wife-whore (who seduces one of his lawyers) and bereft of his senses, he sits motionless before a ticker-tape machine that spews out his profit-and-loss statements each minute. The only visible sign of life comes when he is given news of his financial holdings. Otherwise he is catatonic, a corporate zombie. "If I had to describe Mr. Morley's condition, I would say he lives constantly exposed to the ultimate terror of life which is the existential state of all men. It must be insufferable," his lawyer says. Lacking even the will to commit suicide, he is given his final instruction by Spatz. "It would be of great benefit to your corporation if you were to die," the financial sage says. Morley agrees. Dressed in a kimono, he commits hara-kiri by plunging a pair of garden shears into his stomach. Our tragic hero has become the victim of "depersonalization in a bureaucratic society," said Chayefsky.

Upon reading the finished play Zero Motel reacted in character. Caressing Chayefsky's cheek, he wrapped his hands around the writer's head, then roughly pulling his face toward him, he gave him a big wet kiss on the mouth.

In June 1966, the Mostel-Chayefsky repertory venture was announced with director Burgess Meredith as part of the group. They would open the company in November with *Ulysses in Nighttown*, to be followed by *The Latent Heterosexual*. In August, however, it was learned that the stage rights to the Joyce adaptation would not be available for twelve months. Chayefsky suggested that they present his play first, and follow with *Waiting for Godot*. However, Mostel by this time had a film commitment, so *The Latent Heterosexual* was scheduled for the following spring. Then in March 1967, Mostel backed out of the project again, this time for another movie, *The Producers*. That conflict brought an end to the Chayefsky-Mostel-Meredith repertory company, but not to the publication of the play. In 1967, when *The Latent Heterosexual* appeared in *Esquire* and was published by Random House, offers for a Broadway production were made to Chayefsky. These he refused. "I'd be happy to give it to any professional repertory company in America. A Broadway production, even if it's a hit, is dead in a year and a half," he told the writer William Goldman. "If a play stays in a company's repertory five years that's worth something. What's important to me is that the play should live. I want the life, not the money."

Actor Douglas Campbell, who had appeared in *Gideon* and was instrumental in helping Tyrone Guthrie set up his repertory company in Minneapolis, was asked by Chayefsky to stage *The Latent Heterosexual* in that regional theatre. A report that they had agreed to this appeared in the New York papers, but for unknown reasons the Minneapolis production never materialized. "Paddy wanted me to do it, and I can't remember why I didn't, or couldn't, do it," Campbell stated later.

Zero Mostel was the reason, some surmised. When he heard that the play was going to be staged without him, he contacted Chayefsky. By December 1967, discussions were under way again. In January the first announcement appeared in *The New York Times*. *The Latent Heterosexual* would open in March, off-Broadway. In fact, the theatre was 3,000 miles away, in Dallas, Texas. When asked, "Why Dallas?" Chayefsky replied, "I want to be left alone to do my work as a writer. I have nothing against the commercial theatre, but I am not interested in hits." When the play was ready it would be staged in New York, not by a commercial theatre group but by the APA-Phoenix Repertory Company. Tickets would be sold by subscription, in advance, which would eliminate the danger of its being reviewed and "closed in a week" by the power-playing, presumptuous New York critics.

"This was such a deliberate slap in the face to the Broadway theatre community, and especially to the major reviewers," said one producer. "In essence, Paddy was saying, 'Hey, fuck you, guys! Who needs you? I'm doing the play *my* way.' He had this tremendous chip on his shoulder and the only way they could knock it off was by bringing the guy down. Which, as it transpired, was exactly what happened."

CHAPTER 25

Sabotage and Betrayal in the Provinces

By mid-February 1968, Chayefsky, Mostel, and director Burgess Meredith were in Texas meeting with Paul Baker, a drama professor and the managing director of the Dallas Theater Center. "We had a permanent acting company, part professionals and part amateurs," said Baker. Among the established playwrights whose works they had presented were Robert Anderson, Robert E. Lee, and Jerome Lawrence. "Naturally we were very excited about present-ing a new Chayefsky play, with Zero Mostel," said Baker. "This was a major coup for Dallas."

Having been absent for four years from the theatre, Chayefsky was happy to be part of the production process again. Sitting in on the auditions, he gave his approval of the thirteen actors chosen from the Dallas Theater's repertory group. These included Chris Richard, a twenty-year-old blond student who was asked to play the part of Christine Van Damn, the high-priced hooker; and Randy Moore, who was cast as Arthur Landau, an assistant lawyer. On the third day, unhappy with the performer chosen to play the Machiavellian tax expert, Irving Spatz, Chayefsky suggested that a professional actor, Jules Munshin, be brought in from New York as a replacement.

After ten days of preliminary readings, the play was put on its feet for another two weeks, on the stage of the Dallas Theater Center. The four-hundred-seat theatre, designed by Frank Lloyd Wright and situated on a hillside in a grove of trees, delighted Chayefsky. It had a rotating stage with multilevel turntables that could be used to effect the different transitions and moods of his play. The spare set, designed by Virgil Beavers, consisted of modern office furniture over which loomed a predatory clawlike group of figures, symbolizing impending avarice and corruption. The lighting, featuring the "new sixties pyschedelic strobes," was combined with a "twanging rock score" which would add a further touch of contemporary doom to the story.

The rehearsal period was "the happiest of collaborations," said Meredith. The character transformations for Mostel were collectively conceived. For the "fag poet" scene in Act I, Mostel came mincing on the stage wearing a black beret, made up with orange lipstick and rouged cheeks, and carrying a book and a daisy. "He was like a gay, crippled camel, and we all fell apart," said Randy Moore. Transformed into a virile male after the seduction, Mostel stomped on wearing rancher boots and a ten-gallon hat, with a cigar in his mouth, a booming voice, and a crushing hand grip. The final scene, where Morley, disembodied and paralyzed by his corporate identity, commits suicide, was carefully worked out with the help of Mostel's co-star, Moore. "Zero was bald as all get-out. So each night before the show he would ask me to pencil in hair on his head," said the Texas actor. "I would take an eyebrow pencil and cover his whole head with the pencil, and he would comb this long fringe from the back, over it." Mostel played the part looking like that, up until the moments preceding his self-immolation. "Just before the climax, he would step offstage, quickly pull the hair back, take a wet towel and completely clean the top of his head off, until it was shiny white," said Moore. "Then he would go back on stage wearing this Japanese kimono. The top of his head was completely white, the long fringe was streaming down. It was a startling transformation, a marvelous effect. He looked like some strange sort of samurai warrior as he plunged the garden shears into his stomach."

During the last week of rehearsal, prior to the official opening, the first signs of insubordination began to appear. As Mostel grew more confident in the role he began to experiment. In the midst of reciting one of Chayefsky's carefully created soliloquies, Zero decided that "the stage was getting too small for his emotions," Meredith told the writer Jared Brown. "He crossed the proscenium line and began to rampage the aisles. Then, still roaring Paddy's lines he disappeared through a far exit. We could still hear him perfectly as he prowled the basement below. The other actors, bewildered, shouted their lines to the floor. And then, like a Minotaur from the labyrinth below, exactly on cue, he erupted from the wings back onto the stage as the curtain fell."

Chayefsky was naturally alarmed by this transgression. Meredith, who had directed Mostel previously, assured him that the actor was "searching for his characterization" and would stick to the script, and the stage, in all future performances.

On March 19, two days before the opening, a much larger problem loomed. The playwright found out that he had been "betrayed" by the Dallas company. "Paddy had made Paul Baker promise that he would not invite any critics other than the two local Dallas ones to review the play," said Moore. "He said that the reason he was there was to do the play out of the limelight, and to work on it."

Paul Baker recalled that he was "in good standing" with the managing editor of *The New York Times.* "He called me and said that Clive Barnes, their drama critic, was coming to Dallas to review the play. When Paddy heard that, he said he would close the play. That would ruin us, I told him. We spent close to twenty-five to thirty thousand dollars on this production, which was a lot for our little theatre, and we were relying on the income from the subscription and ticket sales."

In a frenzy, Baker called back the *Times,* but Barnes had already left for Texas. "Paul actually got Barnes at the New York airport," said Moore. "He begged him not to come to Dallas, because Paddy was threatening to close the play down. Barnes said he would sign an affidavit saying that Paul had not invited him, that he was coming of his own volition."

Then Chayefsky learned it wasn't only *The New York Times* he had to fear. Most of the major reviewers he wanted to avoid were descending upon him in Texas. These included Wilfred Sheed from *Life,* plus the critics from *Time, Newsweek, The Saturday Review, The Village Voice, The Wall Street Journal,* and the *Los Angeles Times.* It was a deliberate attempt at sabotage, and the harried playwright didn't know whom to blame.

Baker assured Chayefsky again that neither he nor his press aides had invited these critics. The APA-Phoenix Repertory Theatre in New York had nothing to do with it either. "Paddy was naïve," said Moore. "Did he really think he could come to Dallas with a big star like Zero Mostel and Burgess Meredith, and put on a play that the rest of the country wouldn't hear about?"

Barnes said that even though Chayefsky insisted in a Dallas "theatre flyer" that his play was not "a tryout for Broadway," in fact this was a "world premiere." Therefore, as the official arbiter of taste for bona fide theatregoers at large he felt it was his duty to review the production. After the opening-night performance in Dallas, at a party in socialite Jane Murchison's house, while Zero Mostel worked the room singing snatches of songs and telling dirty jokes, Chayefsky remained in a corner, glowering at the guests and assembled critics. "If Dallas is the regional theatre, I want no part of it," he told Cecil Smith of the *Los Angeles Times.* "I'll write my plays and put 'em in a drawer."

ZERO MOSTEL TRIUMPHS IN CHAYEFSKY PLAY! was the headline of *The New York Times* review two days later. The direction had "great fluidity," the theatre was used with "great authority," and the play itself was "more interesting than totally successful," said Barnes. However, this was Chayefsky's most serious work, the critic believed, "if only because he seems at last to have lost the soft core of sentimentality that in the past reduced his finest thoughts to the level of fortune-cookie mottos."

There were two playwrights inside Paddy Chayefsky, said *Time.* One was a pixy, the other a preacher. "When the pixy handles the pen, it can turn out a funny, wryly perceptive comedy like *Marty,*" said the magazine. "When the moral preceptor is in command, the result is likely to be a chalk-duty lecture like *The Passion of Josef D.*" This latest work was an unsuccessful welding of the two Chayefskys, the newsweekly stated.

"In one sense the reviews were positive," said Randy Moore, "because most of them treated the play as a work-in-progress, and they encouraged Paddy to do more work on it. But he didn't and I think that may have been because of Zero. His reviews were all good." "If Zero Mostel is not America's greatest actor I would be extraordinarily interested to know who is," said Barnes. "It's not that Zero is funny—it's that he is ecstatic, intense, zealous . . . without Zero the play would be an idea wandering through limbo," said *Newsweek.* "The play is unimaginable without him," *The Village Voice* agreed.

The reviews went to Mostel's head, Moore recalled. "Everyone in Dallas lionized him, he was invited everywhere." An actor with a stupendous appetite for performing and being the center of attention, Mostel kept his momentum going by hosting parties backstage at the theatre or in his hotel suite. "I lived down the hall from him at the Stoneleigh Hotel," said Paul Baker. "He and Burgess Meredith were up all night, raising hell. Sometimes I could hardly sleep at all. This went on nonstop."

Paddy Chayefsky was not a part of the festivities. He deliberately stayed away from Mostel after the opening night. He was apparently still in a daze from the critics' assault. His work was in its embryonic stage when the bastards stuck their knives in. And praising Mostel while dismissing the play made no sense to him. How could any actor's performance be brilliant without the character and the corrosively witty dialogue created by the playwright?

After two days of brooding and sharing his grievances by long distance with his friends in New York, Chayefsky agreed it was best to ignore the critics. The point of being in Dallas was to rewrite and rework the play. Returning to the theatre, Chayefsky encountered further stress. His play was being battered each night by Zero Mostel's infamous deviations and embellishments.

Described by *Variety* as an "egomaniacal terror, who frequently alarmed his colleagues by improvising on stage," Mostel had been frequently reprimanded by his directors and producers for breaking the line of previous plays and the concentration of performers. His arsenal of distractions included leering, humming, crossing his eyes, breaking wind, and talking directly to the audience. In New York during one performance of *A Funny Thing Happened on the Way to the Forum,* he reportedly stepped to the rim of the stage and announced the results of a Sonny Liston–Floyd Patterson boxing match. The audience loved it. During a scene in *Fiddler on the Roof,* while in bed with his stage wife,

Golde, he ripped her nightgown off. The audience went crazy. On a subsequent night in *Fiddler,* when Mostel insisted on making faces during Golde's speech, Jerome Robbins, the director, turned the spotlight off and left the actor mugging in the dark.

In Dallas, Mostel never changed the words in Chayefsky's script. But he did distract the actors, particularly Jules Munshin. In one scene, Munshin was to deliver a page and a half of Chayefsky's complex dialogue about tax liens and foreign investments. Mostel was supposed to sit onstage and listen intently. "Zero was in a swivel, high-backed chair, with his back to the audience," said Moore. "All you could see were his hands. No one out front could see his face, so of course that gave him license to kill. He would mouth the words back to Jules Munshin. He would make faces. He would spit out paper spitballs. You name it. He did it. And here's Jules trying to give this exceedingly complicated speech. Eventually the only way he could do it was by keeping his eyes closed."

A distraught Chayefsky put the blame on Meredith, who not only failed to rein in Mostel but appeared to be in cahoots with him. "I know Paddy was very unhappy," said Paul Baker, "but I don't recall him losing his temper with Zero or Meredith, although he took it out on others." One day at the hotel, Chayefsky created a scene in the lobby with the management. "He told them that a watch or a ring of his had been stolen. That was a big disturbance," said Baker. "And meantime, at night, down the hall from him, the parties with Zero and his group were going on until the small hours of the morning. I'll tell you, when they finally packed up and left, I was damn glad because they were nothing but trouble."

From Dallas the company moved to Los Angeles. Producer James E. Doolittle and Chayefsky had made an arrangement where Doolittle would put up the money to produce the play for three weeks at the Huntington Hartford Theatre. Depending on the reaction there, they would take it to other cities, or move the play directly on to New York, and tour later. "Either way I would be the coproducer," said Doolittle. "It would cost me about a hundred-fifty thousand, but I figured we'd surely make that back in Los Angeles."

In Los Angeles, Chayefsky supervised the cast changes. He suggested that Alvin Epstein, who had played Trotsky in *The Passion of Josef D.,* be brought in from New York to play the lawyer, Arthur Landau. Randy Moore, who played Landau in Dallas, was reassigned to another part, and most of the other performers, including Paul Winfield, came from the West Coast ranks of talent.

With a renewed sense of adventure, Mostel and Chayefsky agreed to put the differences of Dallas behind them and work together to present the best production possible. Four and a half weeks were scheduled for rehearsals and rewrites. At a photo call during the first day's reading, Chayefsky and Mostel traded jokes and Yiddish insults of endearment. Socially, Chayefsky relaxed long enough to visit with Bob Fosse (in Hollywood preparing the movie of

Sweet Charity), and to sample what culture historians would later describe as "California's Summer of Love."

In May 1968, the streets of Los Angeles were filled with long-haired people and flower children wearing headbands and buttons proclaiming their new-found utopian connection. Randy Moore described himself as "this young, naïve actor from Dallas" whose head was turned around by what he saw and heard that summer. "Zero and Burgess sort of adopted me as their mascot," said Moore. "So we would go out together, driving down the Strip or along Santa Monica Boulevard. And you'd see all these kids. Everything was wide open, including the sexuality." Paddy Chayefsky was also exposed to his first "love-in." The writer who composed the rock music for *The Latent Heterosexual* invited him to a peace party in the California hills. Paddy said, "Why not?" and took off on the back of the guy's motorbike. According to Moore, "They arrived at this big log cabin in one of the canyons, and there's a sign over the entrance that said: 'Fuck for peace.' Paddy goes in, puts down the ten-dollar contribution they asked for, and this beautiful teenage girl comes up to him and says, 'Hi, you wanna fuck?' Paddy, who's this short little froglike guy, looks at this sexually active teeny-bopper, and says, 'Jesus Christ! This is crazy!' The whole thing just blew his mind."

Back at work, the love-in between Chayefsky and Zero Mostel ended sometime during the second week of rehearsals. Mostel allegedly began to complain that Chayefsky was negligent in supplying the necessary rewrites. The producer, James Doolittle, remembered things differently. "Paddy was a perfectionist, and he was fixing the play very intently, working at rehearsals every day in the beginning. But Zero kept playing everything very broad, and Paddy wanted him to hold to the story line."

Two of Chayefsky's writer colleagues, Robert E. Lee and Jerome Lawrence (*Inherit the Wind*), visited the theatre to offer him their moral support. "We would pace up and down the aisles of the theatre with him," said Lawrence. "I urged him, 'Paddy, work on it. It's a hell of a play.' " Lee also thought the play had great promise. "It needed some work. I had the feeling that Paddy didn't know exactly where he was going. He had a delightful idea and then it just sort of died in Zero's excesses. It got lost in its commingling with Zero's extravagant virtues and foibles. A playwright must be in control of his play and I think Zero took over."

In the scene where Mostel sits in the large winged chair with his back to the audience, he went wilder. "He was absolutely impossible," said Epstein. "He would start by crossing his eyes. He would go to unimaginable lengths—including feigning masturbation. He would do anything to distract Jules Munshin and me from trying to deliver those complex tax legalities that Paddy had written so carefully."

To add to the tension, a behind-the-scenes conflict was unfolding over the actress chosen to play the role of Christine, the hooker-wife. James Doolittle said that during the first week of rehearsals the part had been left open and it was his impression that it was to be cast from local Los Angeles talent. "A lot of actresses had called us because there was tremendous interest in the show. We sold out before we even opened, so every agent was on the phone asking if we would consider using one of their clients for the part." Chayefsky had his choice. He wanted Gwyda DonHowe, a tawny blond actress from the APA-Phoenix company in New York. "She was at the rehearsals in Los Angeles, but as far as I know had not yet been announced for the role," said Doolittle. "Then I learned that Zero wanted someone else, the girl [Chris Richard] who played the part in Texas with him. Obviously they were having a romance."

"She was a first-year graduate student," said Moore. "Very pretty, but really inexperienced for a leading role. But in the course of the performances in Dallas, Zero fell in love with her. So when we were ready to go to L.A., he decided he wanted her along."

Apparently Paddy Chayefsky knew nothing of these extraneous arrangements until the second week of rehearsals in Los Angeles, when Chris Richard, the understudy, proceeded to sit by Mostel's side at the main table. "She was apparently under the illusion that she was going to play the lead role," said Doolittle, "because that's what Zero had told her."

Randy Moore recalled being with Mostel when he ordered Meredith to get rid of Chayefsky's candidate. "He told Burgess, 'Do what you have to do to get that woman out and get Chris in.' And Burgess started giving Gwyda hell. I mean really going after this woman, making her life quite miserable. It was ugly and nasty."

Gwyda DonHowe, who had ambitions of her own, did not get intimidated. "They were trying to get her to quit," said Moore. "She refused to get upset because she knew what they were doing." She also had another strong ally in her corner. Norman Kean, who was the general manager of the APA Rep, was her husband. The latter connection was apparently not known to Mostel and Meredith. "I was having lunch with them at the Brown Derby," said Moore. "They were going on about the whole situation, and I mentioned something about Gwyda's husband, Norman Kean. Burgess stopped cold and said, '*What!?*' I said, 'You know, they're married.' Burgess was totally shocked, speechless. He said, 'Oh God, the things I've been saying to him about her.' And I'm thinking, 'Hey, why do I know this, and they don't?' And after that neither Burgess or Zero said another word to me about Gwyda."

It was up to Chayefsky to bring the situation to a head. "The Texas girl continued to sit in on things and this was getting on Paddy's nerves," said Doolittle. "Everyone at this point sort of knew what was going on but said nothing, until finally one day Paddy stood up in rehearsal and said, 'Zero! You can screw her on your time, but not on mine.' And he walked right out." With him went the production rights to the play. The following day Doolittle received a telegram in which Chayefsky withdrew permission for all further productions of *The Latent Heterosexual*. "We had a tour tentatively lined up," said Doolittle. "Every major city across America wanted this Paddy Chayefsky play starring Zero. Tickets were ready to be sold in New York. We also had a picture deal in discussion. Every major studio had called. But then the telegram came in from Paddy, canceling everything."

When Doolittle and Norman Kean tried to reach Chayefsky at the Beverly Hills Hotel, they found he had checked out. On opening night he did not show up.

Once again, the reviews were cool for the play but red hot for Mostel, and a battalion of movie stars and studio executives trooped backstage each night to compliment him. "Barbra Streisand came back one night," said Moore. "She was making *Hello, Dolly!* at the time, and it was fascinating to see her competing, locking eyes with Zero, as if to say, 'I'm better than you, buster.'" The deluge of attention for Mostel was part of a master plan, Moore believed. "He told me the main reason he went to Los Angeles with Paddy's play was to generate interest in him for movies. At that point he had only made two, and he hated them. 'Those directors keep cramming the camera up my nose, they need to use my body more,' he said. So this was his big chance. He rented a big house in Bel Air and used Paddy's play as a showcase, to become a movie star. He made no bones about it. 'Screw management!' That was his advice to me when I got my Equity card. 'Screw them before they can screw you,' he said. And I watched him do that for the rest of the time we were in Los Angeles."

A temporary cease-fire in the war between Chayefsky and Mostel was arranged by Norman Kean in the third week of the Los Angeles run. "Norman came to me and asked if I was still interested in coproducing a tour of the play," said Doolittle. "I said, 'Yes.' The potential was tremendous. The combination of Zero and Chayefsky, with a good actress in there—we could have easily sold that as a road show *without* the approval of the New York critics."

Tentative dates were made for San Francisco, Chicago, Detroit, and Boston, with a grand finish in New York for a limited run off-Broadway with the APA. Then the whole thing fell apart again, over the casting of the actress to play the hooker.

"Zero was insistent that his girlfriend be put back in as his co-star," said Moore. "He was absolutely infatuated with this twenty-three-old. I remember a few years later his son, Josh, asked me, 'What went on out there? My mother hit the ceiling about this girl.' Apparently this had never happened before. I think he wanted to marry the girl, and that affected the whole play. Even Burgess, who was close to Zero, said, 'Look, we haven't made any money so far on this. If we do the tour, we'll finally make something.' Also Jules Munshin, who got terrific reviews and needed the work, got down on his knees and begged Zero to change his mind. But he wouldn't budge. He wanted to stay in L.A. with this girl and make movies."

On May 23, shortly before the end of the L.A. run, it was announced that the tour and the play dates in New York had been canceled. "We could not agree on the casting of a leading role," Chayefsky said, offering no specifics.

"Paddy was really disgusted and deflated," said Moore. "He was obviously embittered by the entire experience. Here he had written this play for Zero. They were going to work on it quietly in Dallas and L.A., but that wasn't to be."

"It shows how fragile this business can be," said Doolittle. "You seldom get a team like Chayefsky and Mostel. It was a dream combination. And to have it totally fall part over a girl was most unfortunate. One would think that Paddy and Zero, who were two giant talents, would have been more dedicated to the theatre, because a great property like that could certainly have become part of the theatrical treasure. The dispersion left all of us feeling very sad."

"Sad and strange and wild," said Moore. "Just remember when all this happened." It was June 1968; one afternoon when the young actor was crossing Melrose Avenue, he heard a commotion. Coming down the street was a motorcade. "Sitting in the last open car was Bobby Kennedy," said Moore. "He reached out and shook my hand, and three days later, right after we closed the show, he was assassinated."

Moore went back to Texas, followed shortly thereafter by Chris Richard. Jules Munshin and Alvin Epstein went back to New York, along with Norman Kean, who years later would murder Gwyda DonHowe, then kill himself.

Zero Mostel stayed in Los Angeles, where he made one movie, *The Great Train Robbery*, as the second lead to Kim Novak.

In New York, Chayefsky had destroyed all his rehearsal notes for *The Latent Heterosexual*, when an offer came in from Joseph E. Levine of Embassy Pictures to buy the motion picture rights for $500,000. Paddy accepted the offer until he learned that Levine was buying the rights to star Zero Mostel, and refused to sign the contract. He would not allow his play to be performed by Mostel at any price. Mostel remained bitter toward Chayefsky for the rest of his life. "Zero hated Paddy's guts, really detested him," said the film editor Eric Albertson. "When his name came up in a meeting once, Zero became livid. He didn't want to be on the same planet as Paddy."

Some felt that Chayefsky was throwing out the baby with the bathwater in withdrawing the play from circulation. He would allow it to be staged in London ("They have a theatrical tradition . . . Shakespeare," he said), but this was the last production of the play, and the last complete play written by him. "I called Paddy in the spring of 1969," said William Gibson. "Arthur Penn and I were running the Berkshire Theatre Festival for that summer, and I said to Paddy, "Could you give us a play?' He said, 'What for? *The Latent Heterosexual* had a very nice production in London. And that's it.' He was absolutely down on ever writing for the theatre again."

And the Internal Revenue Service? Apparently Chayefsky's satiric attack on their complex tax system did not deter the federal agency from auditing his future returns. In 1978, the IRS served the writer with a bill for $26,000, for additional money they claimed he owed on his 1972 income. He insisted that he lost $51,780 that year, on Alamo 1972, a gas and oil enterprise that went bankrupt. "I've done nothing unethical! Nothing dirty! Nothing shifty! It's all complicated stuff," he said. And furthermore, he said, the government had no case, because according to *his* tax experts, the statute of limitations on the claim had expired.

A SPLENDID COMEBACK

CHAPTER 26

The Hospital

Although he stopped writing plays, Chayefsky remained an active member of the New York Dramatists Guild and attended its bimonthly meeting, "where the chandeliers would shake" from some of his strong debates with fellow playwrights. "There were never any gentle suggestions from Paddy," said Robert Anderson, a president of the guild. "He would be combative in a meeting and most of the time I would have to say, 'Calm down, Paddy, calm down.' "

Hippies, black power, Vietnam war protesters, radical chic—no cultural group or topic was immune from Chayefsky's scrutiny and loquacity. During the winter of 1969, in a Dramatists Guild seminar with Arthur Laurents, Israel Horovitz, and Leonard Melfi, Chayefsky's comments reflected the cynicism the decade had wrought in him. He no longer believed that war was immoral. "I'm ready to drop napalm on Cairo tomorrow," he said. Regarding the racial tensions in America, this was because black people wanted what white people had: "to be rich and despairing like the rest of us. They can have it!" The hippies were "the only distasteful group of all the action groups," and the young writers of the day were naïve and misguided. "Nineteen-year-old writers want more out of their writing than mere satisfaction. They want approbation, to change the world and many other things. Besides, at nineteen, he doesn't know his ass from his elbow."

"Paddy would take on anyone and everything," said Jerome Lawrence. "At guild meetings he would pace around the long table like a *bear*. At times his language was raw, even in front of the women like Lillian Hellman and Mary Rodgers, who were pretty gutsy ladies. Paddy really had passion—not only for playwrights but for life."

Chayefsky's manic intensity and rage had a purpose, Robert E. Lee believed. "I don't know of anyone who used anger more creatively than Paddy," said Lee. "On a personal level it created a wall which prevented contact with casual friends, but it was wonderful for the work, to sustain the creative energy."

"Absolutely!" Lawrence agreed. "Paddy's anger fueled his work. His characters really came to burning life under his beautiful writing. There was kind of a street poet about him. But his anger was directed. Some people can be angry at everything and it just sprawls. Paddy's anger, especially when the nineteen-seventies began, had a purpose."

In November 1969, previously dismayed, then contemptuous of the student riots at Columbia University, Chayefsky used the events for a story outline. When the students stage a sit-down in a university cafeteria, the dean arrives and says to them, "You want it—you got it." He throws the keys to the college at them, saying, "It's yours, you run it."

By January of 1970, with a new decade beginning, Chayefsky felt that the issue of campus riots, though widespread, was ephemeral. He discarded the theme but would use a variation of it in his next project, which he described as a "Gothic horror story," set in a metropolitan hospital that would also serve as a microcosm for all of the ills of contemporary society.

> When I say I'm impotent, I mean I've lost
> even my desire for work, which is a
> hell of a lot more primal a passion than sex.
> I've lost my reason for being, my purpose,
> the only thing I ever truly loved.
>
> Dr. Herbert Bock, *The Hospital*

Writer Herb Gardner and Chayefsky were walking along a New York street one evening when Paddy turned to him and asked if he knew of a good way to kill off nurses. "I think Susie had been in the hospital," said Gardner, "and Paddy was not happy with what went on there."

Susan Chayefsky, according to some people, was suffering from a neurological disorder and was in great pain. "The doctors did numerous tests, but could find nothing wrong," one friend recalled. When asked to submit to a research study, Susan Chayefsky refused. The staff tended to dismiss her ailments after that, which infuriated her husband all the more. So he decided to write a story that would expose the hospital staff's apathy and incompetence.

"Nothing got him going like anger," said Gardner. "Paddy was always best writing when he was pissed off about something."

"A fuck-up in a hospital"; that was the premise of the story he pitched to

David Picker, executive at United Artists in February of 1970. The timing for the material was ripe. Owing to the success of *Easy Rider* and *Butch Cassidy and the Sundance Kid,* original scripts were in demand. United Artists had also recently enjoyed a robust critical and financial return on their production *Midnight Cowboy.* Another acrid story set in New York, written by the man who had brought them their first Best Picture Oscar, made so much sense that Arthur Krim and David Picker offered Chayefsky a two-picture deal.

With the offer came a pair of basketball tickets. Chayefsky's guest was his lawyer, Maurice Spanbock. After the game the two had supper at a cafeteria. Throughout the meal Chayefsky discussed all the reasons why he shouldn't go back to the movies. It wasn't the theatre, and he was terrified of what other people might do to his work. By the end of the night he had talked himself into a decision. He would accept the offer from UA. He would return to the movies—but not as a screenwriter, as a playwright. That meant he would not only write his script for *The Hospital* in a full, spirited, theatrical style, he would insist on the same covenants the Dramatists Guild secured for its members: total involvement and authority. As "a picture maker," he would have full creative approval and be involved again in every detail of the production. "That's the only way you can make films as a writer," he said, "because film isn't essentially a writer's art, it's a director's art."

In March 1970, to ensure that his work was protected, Chayefsky joined forces with Howard Gottfried, a former lawyer who had worked in television supervising the production of "The Fugitive" and "The Outer Limits." As poker pals in the late sixties the two had gradually gotten to know each other. "Howard is a great showman, he knows story as well as anybody," Chayefsky remarked later. "He's a delight to work with. He's also an abrasive man. He has no interest in whether you like him or not, which is one of the reasons I like him so much." After working together on a tentative project for CBS TV, Chayefsky asked Gottfried if he wanted to be his partner. "He said he was thinking of returning to movies, and he wanted to work with somebody, not a studio, but a producer in New York," said Gottfried. Chayefsky would be the writer, Gottfried would handle the business aspects. As partners they would make the film together, but as the senior member, Chayefsky would have the decisive word. "He would have the final say because he was the creator, it was his vision. That was understood," said Gottfried, who would remain with Chayefsky for the next ten years. "There was nothing on paper between us. We never had a contract with each other for all that time. It was never needed."

Using the Hebrew form of his given name, Sidney, Chayefsky incorporated a new company, Simcha Productions, and hired a part-time secretary to handle the correspondence and answer the phone when he was out working on the research for his hospital story. This, he said, included everything "short of attending medical school." He read medical books and journals "by the truckload," and visited hospitals all over New York City and the metropolitan area. One emergency room in the Bronx, teeming with the sick and wounded, looked like "something out of a World War Two movie," he said.

Interviewing doctors, nurses, surgeons, anesthetists, interns, administrators, and ambulance drivers, Chayefsky learned that no one was reluctant to share the most intimate details of their work lives. Their accounts and the plethora of horror stories connected with working within the system of a big city medical bureaucracy were dutifully and gratefully accepted. "With Paddy, the record button was always on," said Herb Gardner. "He was always looking for information and was very quick to separate the truth from the bullshit. Paddy's perception of everything far exceeded everyone else's."

At night, in his office on Seventh Avenue, as he pored over the details of actual malpractice suits, a scenario began to emerge. The deaths in Chayefsky's hospital came first by mistakes and neglect, then by deliberate execution. It was easy for people to die by negligence or by design in an automated, machinelike society, where no one really knows anybody "and everyone is a number," he said. With the murders his story gradually turned from satire to black comedy. "Things grew with Paddy," said Gottfried. "That's why the stuff was so good. He was never locked in to anything. He wanted to develop it, and the characters, as it went along."

At the helm of his busy and error-prone hospital, Chayefsky created a hero, Dr. Herbert Bock. As a youth, this "boy genius" and "brilliant eccentric" was terrified of women, so he finds his purpose in life in medicine. Twenty-five years later, as the bitter, bruised, and betrayed chief of staff of a large city hospital, he feels his life is over. The fact that Bock would be Chayefsky's most popular character since Marty was again attributed to the personal traits he chose to reveal, most notably his despair and wrath. The anger that had been largely repressed in *Marty* would now be allowed to explode at full force in Dr. Bock. "Up until nineteen-seventy, my father was going through the same self-torture as Bock," said Dan Chayefsky. "During those last five years of the nineteen-sixties, he felt absolutely useless. He had done everything in the business and it meant nothing. All he had wanted was approval and he found out nobody cared anyway, which made him more despondent." At home at night, the boy would watch his father drinking in the dark. "He was never a heavy drinker, but he would sit in his study with a glass of scotch in his hand and a bottle of Johnnie Walker nearby. This was every night. I'd pass by the room and see him, sitting motionless, a silhouette in the dark." Everett Chambers, who had been the casting director for *Middle of the Night*, gave another impression. Prior to signing with UA to write *The Hospital*, Chayefsky had considered writing a TV pilot for Chambers, who was now a producer. Chayefsky's fee was $50,000, which Chambers agreed to. "Two days later Paddy called me in California and reneged on the deal. I asked why. 'I just decided I can't do it,' he said." Chambers immediately got on a plane for New York. When he arrived at Chayefsky's office the next morning he asked why the writer had pulled out. He had gotten a better deal for another project, Chayefsky admitted, then told Chambers to stay, that they'd have lunch. In the office, Chayefsky began a nonstop monologue, a harangue about money, life, and living in New York City. The crime and corruption were driving him crazy, he said. Looking up at a wall in the office, he pointed to his numerous plaques and citations. "Will you look at what I've done!" Chayefsky screamed. "The city should *pay* me to live here!"

Chambers loved his attitude. "But then he began to internalize a lot of anxiety, a lot of personal stuff. His life was miserable. He was going to commit suicide because the stress and strain were killing him. And two years later I go to the movies and I hear the exact same dialogue coming out of George C. Scott's mouth in *The Hospital*."

Suicide was very much on Chayefsky's mind during this period. What stopped him was not a sexual reawakening (as Dr. Bock would experience in *The Hospital*), but the realization that he was hurting his son by his destructive behavior. "He told me that he couldn't bear to have me watch him disintegrate, to see him not doing anything worthwhile for so many years," said Dan Chayefsky. "He felt he was really damaging me." The maudlin self-pity also got to him. "What am I doing here, feeling sorry for myself?" he said one day. "To hell with it. I'm getting off my ass." And not long after that he began to write *The Hospital*.

"When the moral fiber of a community erodes, it is the poets who have to stand up and establish some kind of a moral contact," Chayefsky said (paraphrasing T. S. Eliot). In *The Hospital*, through two disparate characters, Dr. Bock and Dr. Drummond, Chayefsky expatiated on the greed, the depravity, and the contagious incompetence that was crippling modern society. In Chayefsky's outline, the mad Dr. Drummond almost loses his life as a patient in the hospital. Revived and divinely guided, he seeks retribution, coshing the intern who made the misdiagnosis, then parking him comatose in the emergency room, knowing that as a patient he will be "promptly, simply forgotten to death." After viewing the carnage, which includes a "child sideswiped by a car, the old lady mugged in a subway, the derelict beaten by sailors, the paranoids, drunks, asthmatics, the rapes, the septic abortions . . . the whole wounded madhouse of our times," Drummond proceeds to knock off the other bungling medics in the hospital. Meanwhile, Dr. Bock, the conscientious, embattled chief-of-staff, is trying to hold on to his sanity and his sense of worthiness. In a drunken tirade he marvels at a medical establishment that can produce transplants and antibodies and manufacture genes while half the kids in the ghetto are left without shots for TB or polio. "We can practically clone people like carrots," Bock rages. "We have established the most enormous medical entity ever conceived, and people are sicker than ever. We cure *nothing*! We heal *nothing*! The whole goddamn wretched world is strangulating in front of our eyes."

The savage dialogue and the bitter, stark diatribes, which were more Swiftian than Shavian, certified how far Chayefsky had come from the simple, hopeful sentiments of *Marty* and *The Bachelor Party*. However, the extended speeches, later described by one enraptured critic as "a virtual violation and heresy of filmmaking," were met with some resistance. In September 1970, after Chayefsky had handed in his script of *The Hospital* to United Artists, he was told that the long sermons would have to be cut. "I don't recall being dissatisfied with the script," said Arthur Krim twenty years later. "I was delighted with it because I come from a family with a lot of people connected with hospitals."

An interoffice memo from Krim at the time did say the script was "too talky," with "an overemphasis on medical terminology," and expressed the hope "that Paddy would find it palatable to clean up all the dirty language by finding viable substitutes." David Picker believed that if UA indeed suggested the speeches be cut, they didn't mean it. "If you're going to do a movie with Paddy Chayefsky, you want Paddy, because he was a great, great writer."

"In any case," said Krim, concluding his original memo of 1970, he thought this was going to be an exciting picture, and the green light for production was given. The budget approved was $2.5 million, to be disbursed through Simcha Productions, of which $150,000 went to Chayefsky. Gottfried would receive $75,000, and 50 percent of the net profits would be split between them equally. As the independent producers they would hire the director and the cast, allowing UA "its usual rights of approval." The film would be made autonomously, with Chayefsky and Gottfried sharing absolute authority. "Nobody can fire me," said Chayefsky. "We do the firing."

The editing and final cut of the picture would be also be their province, with UA having its "customary rights." Chayefsky and Gottfried would have to be consulted on the marketing and advertising of the film, and there was a special provision stipulating that Paddy did not have to do any personal publicity unless he chose to.

Only one substantial change was made in Chayefsky's first official draft. At the end of the film, after Dr. Bock has his passion for life restored by the comely daughter of the mad Dr. Drummond, the couple decide "in typical sixties fashion" to run off to live a simpler life in the hills of New Mexico. But it wasn't like Chayefsky to run away from a problem. "So Bock stayed and fought," said Gottfried. "It shows the sense of responsibility over romance in the middle class," said Chayefsky.

With the script completed, the movie was scheduled to begin production in March 1971. Filming would be done entirely in New York, where "the climate of hatred was energizing," said Chayefsky. "It's significant for creative work," he explained. "In Hollywood you can go from your house to the studio, to [Wil] Wright's Ice Cream Parlor, to somebody's home for dinner, and back to Beverly Hills without ever coming in touch with reality. You walk one step onto a New York street, you're in a real place."

> My God, the incompetence here is absolutely
> radiant! I mean, two separate nurses walk into
> a room, stick needles into a man . . . tourniquet the poor
> son of a bitch's arm with adhesive tape, and it's the
> wrong poor son of a bitch. Where do you train
> your nurses, Mrs. Christie—Dachau?
>
> Dr. Herbert Bock, *The Hospital*

In his script, Chayefsky describes the leading male as "a bearlike man, with a beard." United Artists suggested two actors, Burt Lancaster and Walter Matthau. Chayefsky vetoed both. He wanted an actor from the "legitimate theatre." He wanted George C. Scott, who had the talent, the intelligence, the madness to play his Dr. Bock. "And George plays the greatest alcoholic," said Chayefsky.

With *Patton* in wide release at theatres, Scott was a very popular actor that year; he said no, then yes to Chayefsky's script. His salary demand of $300,000 was exorbitant, UA insisted. "They did not want us to make the deal with George. He was asking for too much money," Gottfried recalled. Rod Steiger was then considered, but his agent, Sue Mengers, "held us up for even more money," said Chayefsky. "So we went back to Scott and gave him what he was asking for."

With a start date of "on or about April 15, 1971," Scott was given approval of his co-stars and the director. The latter list included Arthur Hiller, who had directed *The Americanization of Emily*. "Arthur had just come off *Love Story* and he wanted to do *The Hospital*, desperately," said Gottfried. "But the size of his fee also caused a problem. It was too much for our budget. So Paddy and I flew out to meet with him. His agent, Phil Gersh, is a wonderful Hollywood old-timer, and he thought he'd be able to get us to pay Hiller's price. But we told him we couldn't."

David Picker of UA recommended another director, Michael Ritchie, who at thirty-three had one main credit, *Downhill Racer,* a feature that starred Robert Redford. "I felt Michael had the kind of edge that would be very good for *The Hospital,*" said Picker. Chayefsky met with Ritchie and found they shared a common interest. At one time they both had tried to adapt the book of William Bradford Huie's *Three Lives for Mississippi.* A preliminary discussion was held on *The Hospital* and Ritchie was hired as director for a salary of $100,000.

Scouting locations in New York City, Chayefsky, Gottfried, and Ritchie found the perfect medical complex for the film. The Metropolitan Hospital on the Upper East Side of Manhattan was owned by the city, and the permission to use it came directly from the top, Mayor John Lindsay. "His attitude was, if it's not going to disturb the patients, let's do it," said Chayefsky.

"The Lindsay administration were incredible," said Gottfried. "They gave us an entire floor, a new wing they weren't using. They loaned us beds, the furnishings, the medical equipment, and we paid them practically nothing." Trying to save more money, Chayefsky refused when told by the plumbers union that they would have to sign a separate contract with them. "They shut off the water for three days, until we signed," he said.

For their fictional surgery and recovery rooms, Michael Ritchie instructed Gene Rudolph, the set designer, to photograph and duplicate the Metropolitan's facilities, with space allowed for camera access. The resulting decorative ambience, however, displeased Chayefsky. "Paddy wanted his hospital to be old and seedy, with the greens, the tiles, etc.," said Gottfried. "Ritchie could not come up with what we wanted. So Paddy and I decided we had to do something about it."

The producers went to see David Picker. "Paddy came in and said that he just couldn't work with Michael, that he wanted to make a change," the executive recalled. "It was his and Howard's movie, so we went along with it."

It was up to Picker's assistant, Herb Jaffe, to let Michael Ritchie know that he was fired. "We met at a German restaurant near Times Square, the Blue Ribbon," said Jaffe. "It was not an easy situation. Michael was a young guy and though we agreed to pay him his full fee, I felt very bad about it. Then less than a month later, I read in *Variety* that Ritchie had already signed on for another movie, *The Candidate,* with his friend Robert Redford. On that deal he was also the coproducer, which meant Redford couldn't fire him. So I guess he learned something from Paddy Chayefsky."

With filming on *The Hospital* scheduled to start in five weeks, another director was promptly sought. "We decided to try Arthur Hiller again," said Gottfried. "We knew he still wanted it because after we signed Ritchie, Phil Gersh called us and was very emotional. Evidently Arthur had bawled him out because he had wanted our movie and the money was not the important thing to him." Keeping the latter in mind, Gottfried and Chayefsky called Gersh again and said, "Now here's the deal! We want Arthur, but now we only have so much money left." Offering less than the original sum, the producers assured the agent that the rest would be made up to his client in deferments and participation. They also gave him an hour to make up his mind. Two days later Arthur Hiller was in New York working with Chayefsky on the casting.

Earlier during the casting, agent Marion Dougherty brought in actor Barnard Hughes to meet with the producers. The actor was appearing on Broadway in *Abelard and Heloise*, "in which I castrated my daughter's lover. So I guess Paddy was impressed by my surgical skill," he impishly recalled.

The role he was asked to read for, that of a doctor who performs a hysterectomy on the wrong patient, was based on a true incident. "They wheeled in the wrong woman for the right operation and she died right there of heart failure," said Hughes. " 'Jesus H. Christ! Jesus H. Christ!' Those were my lines, as I looked down on this poor unfortunate soul lying dead on my operating table." Hughes was given the part, but when the directors were changed, Hiller asked him to take another role. "It was the part of Dr. Drummond, the old quack who goes around murdering the staff," said Hughes. "Naturally I was delighted because it was a much larger role."

"I like the best and biggest talent I can get at all times," said Chayefsky, approving the selection of other first-class New York stage actors for the remaining cast. These included Nancy Marchand, in her third Chayefsky work, as Mrs. Christie, the controlled but weary hospital administrator. Frances Sternhagen was cast as "the bitch from accounting," who will allow people to die in the emergency room if they don't give her their Blue Cross numbers. Donald Harron, who had been in *The Tenth Man*, was brought in to play a psychiatrist, and Richard Dysart was cast as the greedy doctor whose wealth comes from padded Medicaid bills. Others chosen for supporting roles were Katherine Helmond, Stockard Channing, Marilyn Sokol, Lenny Baker, Tresa Hughes, and Christopher Guest.

The last main part to be filled was the female lead, Barbara Drummond, the visiting daughter and ex-hippie who seduces George C. Scott in his office. Chayefsky's script describes her as from Boston, in her late twenties, with an attractive face and casual but distinct sensuality. United Artists favored Jane Fonda, as did Gottfried, but George C. Scott turned her down. The reason reported was that he considered Fonda to be "still too much of a hippie, and in need of a bath." Ali MacGraw and Candice Bergen were also considered, but by then Chayefsky had his own candidate. He wanted another professional from the theatre—Diana Rigg. A graduate of the British Royal Academy of Dramatic Arts and a leading stage actress, Rigg did have considerable colonial appeal due to the popularity of the imported TV series *The Avengers*, in which she played the efficient, smoldering Emma Peel.

From what can be determined, Chayefsky saw Rigg in *Abelard and Heloise* and was quite taken with her many attributes. Physically there were her regal height and carriage, and her seductive face and figure, which were fully displayed in the play's brief nude scene. On a dramatic level, there was the actress's extraordinary elocution, the verbal pyrotechnics that had audiences curled up in their seats, purring with pleasure at her every syllable. Along with her talent, form, and class, Rigg had another requisite for the Chayefsky work. Described by *Tatler* magazine as a performer who "could probably read Proust, understand it, and knee a villain in the crotch at the same time," Paddy knew that the British performer would be able to hold her own against her formidable co-star, George C. Scott.

After reading the script, Rigg said no to the part, that she was not suited to play a girl from Boston. That same evening, backstage at *Abelard and Heloise*, Barnard Hughes went to Rigg's dressing room for a "preperformance chat." She mentioned the film she had declined that day. Hughes recalled, "I said, 'My God!—you turned that down?' And Diana said, 'I shouldn't have?' And I said, 'My God!—starring opposite George C. Scott, in a Paddy Chayefsky film?' All of these things were absolutely impossible to say no to. And Diana, thinking about this, said, 'Well, maybe I should ring them up and ask to have the script sent back. That I'll read it again.' "

After Rigg reread the script she agreed she had been too hasty. She called her agent, who called the producers to tell them that she would indeed take the part. By then Hiller wanted someone else, but "Paddy dug his heels in and said, 'I definitely want her and nobody else,' " said Rigg. "Soon after, all of us went out for a very jolly lunch. And then the offer came through."

> I've always been mellow. I have been the most
> mellow son of a bitch you've ever seen.
>
> George C. Scott

Once, when asked how he would feel if he wrote the perfect script, had the perfect production with no hassles or delays, and it was released with no problems, made a pile of money, and won many major awards, Chayefsky replied: "I'd be bored shitless." On the set of *The Hospital*, thanks to actor George C. Scott, Chayefsky was seldom bored.

A few problems were anticipated with Scott. His reputation for "drunken rages, fistfights, and five broken noses" had preceded him. During the making of *Patton*, Scott, while battling the bottle, was said to be going head to head with Francis Ford Coppola over the script, which he considered "misleading and inadequate." In January 1971, three months before he was to begin the Chayefsky movie, arrant reports came in from Spain, where Scott was making *The Last Run*. These included tales of countless retakes, a few tantrums, and the dislodging of the director, John Huston, by the star. "George is a fine actor, but a total shit," Huston subsequently told *Rolling Stone*. In February, back in the United States, Scott was told that the Academy of Motion Picture Arts and Sciences had nominated him for a Best Actor award for *Patton*. This he refused to acknowledge, making him the first actor in movie history to decline the nomination, which meant of course that he did not intend to show up for their gala presentation ceremony. "Such a bloody spectacle—crying actors clutching a statue to their bosoms, and all that crap," was his blasphemous assessment of their prestigious affair. Gossip columnists and entertainment reporters naturally pounced on this unwonted conduct, fleshing out their stories with the accounts of Scott's current domestic situation. Having twice married the vibrant and magnificent Colleen Dewhurst, Scott was now rumored to be involved with his *Last Run* co-star, Trish Van Devere.

Shortly before the Oscars, both *Time* magazine and "60 Minutes" profiled the actor and the Oscar brouhaha, which pleased his forthcoming movie producers enormously. "You can't *buy* this kind of publicity," Paddy Chayefsky told United Artists, but the exposure soon had an effect on his production. On April 12, four days before the Oscars were to be handed out in Hollywood, George C. Scott failed to show up for his first day of work on *The Hospital* in New York. On days two and three he was on the set but he couldn't work because, according to the producers, he was drunk. "Along with the matter of the Oscars, George was going through his own private hell over his marriage to Colleen," said actor Donald Harron. "So he was literally living the character Paddy wrote in the film. He was drinking heavily and falling asleep in front of the television."

Scott's co-star, Diana Rigg, said gallantly that she wasn't aware of what was going on. "One day George was there. Then he wasn't. So Paddy and I played Scrabble and he cheated abominably."

At the Oscar event in Hollywood on April 15, when Goldie Hawn announced that Scott was the winner, the best actor was fast asleep in his bed in upstate New York. The following morning, with the press piled up at the front gates of the Metropolitan Hospital, Scott showed up clear-eyed and perfectly sober. He had learned about his Oscar victory when his son woke him up, he informed the reporters, then politely excusing himself he went to prepare for a three-page scene from Chayefsky's script, which he would complete in twenty minutes. In the sequence, as Dr. Bock, he tells the staff psychiatrist that he does not know why he is so depressed and suicidal. He is a man who is exhausted, drained, and riddled with guilt, the psychiatrist advises him, wherein the disgusted Bock regrets his confessional. "I feel humiliated and stupid," he says. "I've just got to pull myself together, and get back into my work."

The combination of the part and his own personal stress sent Scott on another alcoholic bender that weekend. On Monday morning, April 19, when the actor failed to show up for filming, a final warning notice went to his agent, Jane Deacy: If he didn't appear the next day, ready to perform, he would be replaced. "Up until that time neither Paddy nor I discussed firing George," said Gottfried. "It was a bad situation but we were hoping it would work itself out. And it did. He showed up the day after and he was prepared."

Barnard Hughes recalled the tension on the set when he filmed his first scene with Scott. "It was the part where I explained to him why I murdered all those people. The dialogue was very complicated, with a lot of medical terms, and I kept blowing the lines, one take after another. The more I blew my lines the tenser the set became. And finally I blew them again and I howled like a wolf. I didn't know George at the time, but right after I howled I reached over and bit him on the neck. And for some reason or the other he laughed and all that tension was released."

After that the filming went fast, and mostly without rehearsals. Gottfried recalled, "Paddy and I were totally devoted to rehearsals, but George was not. For theatre yes, but not movies. George's great talent is his sense of rage, and in certain scenes it worked well for him. He knew that in movies you've got to get it right when you film it, so he didn't want to overrehearse, to lose that performance. And for every scene, in every take, he was in possession of the moment and the character."

"He was spectacular," said the film's editor, Eric Albertson. "George was able to do pages and pages of Paddy's dialogue, which enabled Hiller to shoot enormous amounts of footage."

The only scene that Hiller rehearsed in advance was the one in which Bock rages at length to Barbara Drummond about the futility of his life and work, and his intention to end his life that night. On May 3 the monologue was rehearsed. The following day it was filmed in a room in the nurses' quarters across the street from the hospital. On hand with the two actors was a miminal crew. "The office was so small it could only fit the lighting man, the camera crew, the soundman, Arthur, Paddy, and myself," said the script supervisor, Barbara Robinson. The six pages of dialogue, timed at three minutes and thirty-two seconds, during which Scott devoured and chewed up, then spat out the pungent Chayefsky dialogue, was done with a maximum of three takes. "My flesh tingled when it was being done," said Robinson. "It really held you, it was so believable."

For her part Diana Rigg said she was grateful to have the writer there. "Paddy always talked to me at great length about the character I was playing. He was very specific about what he wanted. It was not a very easy film to make because the camera moved a lot, and there were tremendous chunks of dialogue, wonderful, rich dialogue."

Chayefsky tried to offer the same input and advice to George C. Scott. "I wanted him to play the doctor as a comic figure. I wanted him to be funny-true, not sad-true." "George has very strong ideas about the choices he makes in a work situation," said Gottfried. "That's part of what makes him such a great actor. But one day during a particular scene, Paddy was very upset about the way he was playing it. He kept yelling at me to talk to George. I said I would but he had to come with me. He was the writer. 'It's your vision,' I said. 'If he takes it from anyone, he'll take it from you.' "

Gottfried and Chayefsky entered Scott's dressing room somewhat apprehensively. "As it happened, George had a particularly hard day," said Gottfried. "He was sitting down in a chair, stooped over, untying his shoes. Paddy began his speech, about how he saw the character. When he was finished, George lifted his head, then got up, and pointing at Paddy, in an absolute fury as only George could do, he screamed, 'You do your fucking writing! And I'll do the acting!' And he pounded himself so hard at the 'I'll do the acting' part, I was sure that he had put his hand through his chest. So naturally, we scooted out of there real fast. And I don't believe Paddy ever approached him again."

> People often say to me, "You've done two
> pictures with Paddy, how did you get through it?"
> My answer always is, "When a genius speaks, I listen."
> He's really the only genius I ever worked with.
> He was way above the rest of us.
>
> Arthur Hiller

Although he had planned at the outset not to get into areas of filming that did not warrant his attention, Chayefsky's old obsession with control tripped him up occasionally on *The Hospital*. As the coproducer he couldn't help but cast his judicious eye on various details of the production. Barbara Robinson lived in upstate New York and came to work each day by car. "Someone on the crew had arranged a place for me in the hospital parking lot," she said. "Paddy saw this and got uptight. 'Whaddya mean getting a parking place?' he said. It was as if nobody could do anything unless he had the final say. *He* had to be the one making those decisions. It was Paddy playing God."

While diligently monitoring the lighting, the acting, and the sound, between scenes Chayefsky continued to prune his script. In preproduction the first draft of 170 pages was cut to 160. During filming, with the help of Arthur Hiller, the final shooting script came to 137 pages, with a total of 128 scenes shot. "We were working right to the end because there were areas we felt were a little broad in the last part of the picture. We pulled it in as much as we could," Hiller told *American Film* magazine.

Chayefsky admitted that there were script problems he couldn't lick technically. "I had a detective story, a love story, a drama, a satire . . . all kind of genres bouncing in the air at the same time." Years later he and Hiller were still talking about the changes they could have made. "There were things we felt we never quite got, which is why we kept playing with the script through production."

Looking at the final shooting script again in 1991, Barbara Robinson pointed out that there were only minor changes made during the filming. Names were altered, lines were rewritten, some dialogue was cut, and there were "ad-libs, a lot of ad-libs," said Robinson. Arthur Hiller recalled only one skirmish with Chayefsky over a suggested change. "One day a scene we were about to do didn't look like it was going to work. So I went over to Paddy and talked to him about it. He listened and said, 'You're right, the scene would be better that way, but you can't change it.' I said, 'Why not?' His answer was that it would affect everything that had been filmed before. I said I didn't believe that. We talked back and forth and he got very upset and finally stomped into his little office on the hospital floor. He shut the door and didn't come out for about four hours. And the next day, I was in the middle of preparing a shot and Paddy walked by. As he was passing he said, 'You were right.' And he kept on going." On June 15, *The Hospital* completed filming under schedule and under budget, and a rough cut was ready the day after the shoot. "That's rarely done on features, to have a rough cut so fast," said the editor, Eric Albertson. "But that was my first job. Arthur Hiller brought me in and I didn't want to let him down. I figured if Paddy and Howard discovered I wasn't any good, at least they would know I was quick."

Albertson's edit worked well, and the following week Chayefsky and Hiller worked on the opening narration. Originally Scott was to do this, but that idea was scrapped, along with the narration itself for a time. Chayefsky said he didn't want one. But when he realized that it enabled him to cut down on exposition, to compress three pages into a minute and forty seconds, he decided to use one. Hiller met with several actors to do the narration, but he couldn't get the quality he was looking for. "It had to sound real, with a touch of satire. Each actor's voice I auditioned sounded manufactured. Then it dawned on me: 'These are Paddy's words. He has the perfect voice to do this.'" Hiller asked Chayefsky to do the narration. "He almost fell apart with his insecurity. He was frightened. I told him this was just for the cut to show to the people at UA; we could change it later. So we went into a studio and Paddy tried it." The narration, which was to play over the introductory scene and credits, told of a horny young medical intern, Dr. Schaeffer, who, upon finding an empty hospital bed one night, decides to use it for some sexual activity with a technician from the pathology lab. "Dr. Schaeffer had been zapping this girl on wheelchairs, stretchers, pantry shelves, in the kitchen, the morgue, in the dark corners of corridors, standing up, sitting down. So you can imagine what an available bed meant to him," said Chayefsky in his droll Bronx delivery. With each take Hiller made him feel more relaxed and the narration was completed.

When the film, with the temporary Chayefsky overdub, was shown to United Artists, David Picker said the narration should be permanent. "They were supposed to go out and get a professional narrator, but I said, 'Paddy's voice is exactly right. Who could say it better?' So it stayed," said Picker.

Because Hiller was committed to begin work on another movie, *Man of La Mancha,* in Los Angeles, he, Chayefsky, Gottfried, and Eric Albertson packed up the reels of film and took them to California, where the sound mixing and final edit would be done. "Unfortunately, most of Arthur's time was spent with the other movie," said Albertson. "So that meant Howard and Paddy got involved in areas they shouldn't have. I don't mean the actual editing. Howard made some major contributions there. It was in the sound mixing." The sound mixer in L.A. was Buzz Knudson, who had worked on *The Sound of Music* and would later do *Jaws* and most of Steven Spielberg's films. "He was considered the best at the time," said Albertson, "but when he was equalizing the soundtrack of *The Hospital,* Paddy became very upset." Chayefsky said they were losing the gruff, guttural sound of George C. Scott's voice. "Paddy didn't know what the hell he was talking about," the editor continued. "He was used to hearing the soundtrack in the final cut. Buzz told him this, but Paddy got very upset. He told Buzz he didn't know what he was doing. 'Leave the guttural, don't equalize it!' he said. He was adamant, and when Paddy was adamant, that was it. He could be an ornery son of a bitch, and no one, not even Howard, could argue with him."

Chayefsky then took over the music scoring. "Arthur Hiller had chosen a very good composer by the name of Morris Surdin, a Canadian," said Albertson. "But he wasn't terribly adept at scoring movies. And Paddy, who had a terrible habit of getting up and directing, or editing, or whatever, when things weren't going right, said he wasn't happy with Morris's score. So he made him rescore the movie, in one week."

The scored and mixed film was then brought back to New York and shown to David Picker at UA. "This is ridiculous. Your dialogue tracks are muddy and your music score is lousy," Picker allegedly told the group. "So," said Albertson, "we went over to the Reeves sound studio. Dick Vorisek, who is the best technician on the East Coast, was there, and Paddy asked him for his opinion on who was at fault on the sound. Dick, very intelligently, said, 'I wasn't there. I can't tell you who was the one that dictated how the mix should be done. All I can say is I would have done it differently.' Which he did, from scratch."

Remixed and rescored, a final work print of the film was screened for the United Artists executives at a theatre on Long Island. The reaction was positive, but the following week some cuts were asked for. Faced with a possible X rating, Chayefsky and Gottfried were asked to consider changing the opening sequence. "Under the titles we had a shot that was really pornographic," said Paddy. "An intern was having sex with a nurse. Very graphic. When I learned that leaving that shot in would mean an X, I settled for a freeze-frame and a PG."

The first Manhattan preview was held at the Sutton, for members of the New York medical community. "Paddy was concerned about their reaction," said Gottfried, "but they loved it. There wasn't a moment in that movie that was invalid for them; dramatic license, yes, but the research was immaculate, meticulous. To this day that's why the greatest advocates of the movie are doctors and nurses."

"Everything that happened in the picture happened in a hospital somewhere at some time," said Chayefsky. "That's why after the screening the doctors and nurses came up to us and said, 'You got it right . . . at last, what really happens in a hospital.' "

On December 8 the first review appeared in *Variety*. It was negative. "A civilian mis-*Mash*," the trade paper said, predicting that the film might find its market "among slumming intellectuals, aspiring hard-hats, and insensitive juveniles." One of the first to call Chayefsky about the bad notice was George C. Scott. "My father was surprised to hear from him, because by the end of the picture he and Scott weren't talking," said Dan Chayefsky. Believing that the negative *Variety* review was the beginning of the end for *The Hospital,* Scott tried to comfort Chayefsky. "Hey, listen, we did our best, and it's still a damn good picture," said the actor.

The Hospital was officially released in New York on December 14, 1971, with Chayefsky's name second after Scott's in the main credits. The reviews from publications of secondary importance were mixed. "Preachy and stiff . . . about as much fun as an autopsy," said *Women's Wear Daily,* and the *Christian Science Monitor* found the series of plots "too absurd."

The notices from leading critics were another matter. "Clearly a writer's picture," Andrew Sarris wrote in *The Village Voice.* "Chayefsky was written off by the highbrows a long time ago, and now that we know he's not another Chekhov, it is almost a shock to be reminded what an intelligent craftsman he can be at his best." In a full essay in *The New York Times,* Walter Kerr lamented the loss to the theatre of Chayefsky's blunt, meaningful, and informed language. "The film had them [the words], the stage didn't."

That January *The Hospital* helped boost UA's much needed revenue. At the box office it was third in receipts to *Diamonds Are Forever* and *Fiddler on the Roof.* It succeeded where Chayefsky's last credited film, *The Americanization of Emily,* had failed, because "the public was ready for a sacred cow to be attacked," said one essayist. In January, when it went into national release, *The Hospital* still benefited from Chayefsky's vigilant supervision. To ensure that the paying public were seeing the film as he intended it, he went to neighborhood theatres in the Bronx and Queens, to check on the sound and to be certain that "the lens in the projection booth was clean."

With the absence of the stars to promote the film (Diana Rigg was in England, and George C. Scott remained remote), Chayefsky also volunteered to beat the drums at Oscar time. After giving interviews to *The New York Times* and the *New York Post,* he headed west, checked into the Beverly Hills Hotel, and began a "grueling round" of media interviews. Being interviewed at seven A.M. on the radio was "like talking into a computer," he said. "No personal contact, no real meaning for anybody—not for me, not for the interviewer, not for the audience." He knocked off seven other "congenial chats" during the next two days, including a coveted turn on Johnny Carson's "Tonight Show."

The campaigning paid off. When the Oscar nominations were released that February, *The Hospital* was cited for Best Actor and Best Screenplay. "We're going to deliver George C. Scott, if we have to drag him there ourselves," said Paddy. But on Oscar night only Chayefsky was on hand in Los Angeles. Standing in the lobby of the Chandler Pavilion with Alan King and Walter Matthau, he said he didn't think he would win, that he was there with his partner to show support for their picture. In the last half hour of the telecast, co-host Jack Lemmon introduced "the greatest living playwright in the Western world . . . Tennessee Williams." Changing his glasses to decipher the cue cards, Williams read off the names of the nominees for original scripts: Paddy Chayefsky for *The Hospital,* Elio Petri and Ugo Pirro for *Investigation of a Citizen Above Suspicion,* Andy and Dave Lewis for *Klute,* Herman Raucher for *Summer of '42,* and Penelope Gilliatt for *Sunday, Bloody Sunday.* Opening the envelope, Williams gave the faintest hint of a smile and said, "Paddy Chayefsky." Onstage, after embracing Williams, Chayefsky humbly praised "the high caliber of the other nominees." In the pressroom, holding the golden statue upside down, he told reporters, "Two years ago I was told that I was finished as a writer. I'm back, and I hope to write some more. Thank you."

Personal Alignments

There are no second acts in American lives, F. Scott Fitzgerald observed, but in 1972, with the critical and financial success of *The Hospital,* Paddy Chayefsky disproved the adage. His professional resurrection brought some distinct adjustments. He no longer cared about the fame aspect, or about what the critics said about him. "In the beginning he really wanted the attention," said Dan Chayefsky. "He may have complained but he really liked it. He was a man who wanted the spotlight. But after *The Latent Heterosexual* he turned in on himself and learned to be very lean about what he said to the press, or what they wrote about him. He began to make fewer and fewer mistakes about the things that made him feel bad about himself."

Working on *The Hospital* also enabled Chayefsky to seek medical help for a condition he had suffered from for most of his life, chronic depression. It had always been with him, he told his son. "He was absolutely gloomy a lot of the time," said Dan Chayefsky. "He wasn't just sad, he was miserable. Often I would look at him and he had this quality about him that had nothing to do with emotion or with esoteric problems like his work or career. The underlying depression was always there. It was almost like he woke up dispirited and he went to sleep that way."

Although his dark side was revealed in his work, he never openly discussed it with anyone, his son recalled—"except for the analysts he went to over the years, who never really helped him." Existential angst was a common burden for creative artists, Chayefsky had been told early on in analysis. When he switched to cognitive therapy in the late 1960s, his therapist suggested that his depression came from an incorrect way of thinking, which he tried to modify. He explored transcendental meditation, was officially initiated, and got his own mantra. He began to meditate whenever he could—at home, at the office, or in a cab. During one trance, when his head was slumped down, his son, thinking he was sleeping, tapped him on the shoulder. "Don't," Susan Chayefsky warned the boy, "he's meditating." The process of relaxing his mind and body brought calm and tranquillity, but Chayefsky didn't stay with it. "There was something about my father, perhaps the Paddy side of him, that always needed tension," said Dan Chayefsky. "He was not comfortable being peaceful. Hysteria is addictive and he felt it worked for him." When asked by a reporter why he didn't move to California and live like Neil Simon, with a nice house, pool, and servants, Chayefsky repeated that he was hooked on the dirt and tension of New York City.

During his research for *The Hospital*, Chayefsky learned that new methods were being used to alleviate depression. When Josh Logan, who suffered from manic-depression for thirty years, was successfully treated and went public with his illness, Chayefsky agreed to be diagnosed. His depression could be biological rather than psychological, he was told, and he was asked about hereditary influences. He revealed that he had an aunt (the model for the character of the dour Aunt Catherine in *Marty*) who suffered from depression; and there was his mother, Gussie, who had that "rage in her like fire."

In a series of tests for manic-depression, Chayefsky was told that although he was subject to manic episodes, they were not a prominent part of his condition. His other symptoms—the constant feelings of pessimism and impending doom, the obsession with details, the uncontrollable anger followed by guilt and abnormal eating, when he would gorge himself on food—were all due to a definite illness. "He was chemically depressed. There was a chemical imbalance in his brain. That's what the doctors told him," said Dan Chayefsky.

There was no permanent cure for his depression, but the symptoms could be alleviated by medication. For unipolar illnesses, such as chronic depression, tricyclic drugs were now available. But Chayefsky was apprehensive of taking *any* drugs. He feared that while sedating his brain they might also dilute his creativity, make him lose the hypersensitivity and "the edge" he needed for his work. "Some people love the idea of giving up control on drugs," said his son. "My father didn't want that. He needed full control of his mind at all times." When told that the drug Elavil would control only the condition, the way insulin does diabetes, and not impair his creativity, Chayefsky agreed to take the anti-depressant on a trial basis.

Within three weeks the medication began to work. Chayefsky's long-term depression was banished. The changes were striking. As the curtain on his gloomy self-absorption was lifted, Chayefsky became more aware and relaxed with people and with life around him. "I've become separated from my roots," he declared to Herb Gardner one day. To close the gap he considered buying a house in the Bronx. Upon visiting the old neighborhood, however, he found the changes were too drastic. So he went farther north, to upstate New York, and rented a house a few miles beyond the town of Newburgh. The locals were farmers and blue-collar workers. Chayefsky found he liked them so much he joined their regular bowling team. "He showed up in the office on Seventh Avenue one day with a black bowling bag," said Gardner, "and he said, 'I really miss the Bronx, where you used to be able to be part of a team and go someplace every week.' So for a long time he would meet once a week with his bowling team. When it got to be a Wednesday or a Thursday he would say to Bobby [Fosse] or me, 'Well, I'm off for my bowling night.' And you realized that for all the literary stuff and everything, there was still this Bronx kid inside of him who liked being part of a bowling team."

Malfunction in the Family

Chayefsky bought one hundred acres of land in Newburgh and met with an architect to design a spacious house—but it would never be built. The excuses were varied. It was too late to start a new life, he said, and living full-time in the country would be a hellish bore. The more pressing reason, and one not revealed, was that there were unmanageable problems within his family. Ironically, during the period when Chayefsky was diagnosed and released from his long-term depression, the damage it had inflicted on his family over the years had developed into serious discord. Susan Chayefsky was suffering from numerous ailments, intimated to be psychosomatic. A more serious casualty appeared to be the Chayefskys' son, Dan, who at the age of fifteen was said to be "a very troubled adolescent." The details were as usual kept from everyone, including Chayefsky's partner, Howard Gottfried. "It was never discussed," said Gottfried. "My impression was that it was never easy to be Paddy Chayefsky's son. Especially when you consider that the boy was ignored in the early years."

In June 1955, when Dan Chayefsky was born, the movie of *Marty* had just been released and won the Palme d'Or at Cannes. The Oscar came a year later, during which time his father also triumphed on Broadway. Next was *The Goddess,* with its myriad of responsibilities for Chayefsky. Dan's only recollection of that time was through a photograph, taken when he was three years old. "A stewardess is holding my hand, leading me to a plane, followed by my parents. They were fleeing from this country before the reviews for *The Goddess* came in. My father didn't want to see them because he thought they would be terrible." The first five years of his life were "absolutely insanity," said Dan

Chayefsky. "Through no one's fault. You cannot blame anyone in any way. My parents weren't psychologically ready for a child. My father once told me that the reason they had me was because it was the fashionable thing to do. In the fifties it looked good to have a pretty wife and to walk down the street with a baby carriage."

Dan Chayefsky was not the perfect baby. "I had a million things wrong with me. I had allergies, rashes, teeth that didn't come in right. I was brought constantly to the doctor. That made me highly emotional and hyperactive too. Which is why my father said, 'By the time you were five years of age, we had raised a very angry little boy.' "

While Susan Chayefsky, because of her own fear-induced childhood, was overcontrolling and overprotective of the boy, Paddy Chayefsky, with enormous needs to fill professionally, was either absent or impatient when his son sought his attention. "As a writer obsessed with his career, it was hard for him to understand the attention a small child needs," said Dan Chayefsky. "My father loved his work, more than anything in the world. I know he loved me very much, but his work gave him something that his family couldn't give him, a way of being in touch with himself that he could not get elsewhere." To say his wife and son were victims of Paddy Chayefsky's psyche would be an oversimplification. "There was much more to it than that," said Dan Chayefsky. "Early on it had more to do with both of us feeling left out, because of the focus he chose to be on, which he would not share with us. Also, in public, my mother and I felt overshadowed by all the attention he got. I was in awe of that attention."

As Dan grew older, his father found the role of a parent a little easier. They did the usual father-son things. Chayefsky took the boy to the temple regularly, and to baseball games at Yankee Stadium with the songwriter Frank Loesser and his son. On his birthday, Dan and his friends were treated to a Broadway show and to dinner in a restaurant. Chayefsky senior also tried to share his love of old movies, frequently taking his son to see revivals at the Thalia or Carnegie cinemas. "Preston Sturges comedies were a favorite of his," said the son. "On the way home he would always talk about what we had just seen. His pleasure and excitement were always contagious."

When he was eight or nine, Dan began to notice the contrasts in his father's personality. "He could be very loving and friendly, almost playful with people. He would greet the doorman of his office building with 'Hiya, Rudy! How's it going?' Like he was one of the guys." At other times the dark, brooding Chayefsky would emerge. "He could be suspicious of someone's good intentions. People on the street would congratulate him on things he didn't think he should be praised for, and he'd surprise me by snapping or barking at them."

At home, the unexpected fits of anger were also disconcerting to the youngster. Aware of how frightening his anger could be, Chayefsky tried to contain it. "Then all of a sudden it would explode, and it was scary," said Dan. "Especially coming from someone so gentle, such a caring father, who all of a sudden is in a rage." In the aftermath Chayefsky, concerned, would attempt to explain his behavior to Dan. "Even before I was old enough to know what a temper was, he would try to help me understand, so I would be able to deal with him when he was having trouble dealing with it himself. He was doing the best he could with his anger, but when you're that intense life can be really difficult."

He was not remiss from sometimes using the situation to create his own havoc, the younger Chayefsky pointed out. His parent's unorthodox conduct gave him the license to become rebellious and insubordinate. "Kids tend to take advantage of situations like that, and I did. It was like, 'Why should I grow up if my father acts bad, then feels guilty?' You hold it against him." When it was reported back to the parents that Dan was causing trouble in school, the family dynamics at home became even more chaotic. Eventually father, mother, and son were in regular counseling, each with his or her own therapist and agenda. "I think that in any family, everyone, including myself, takes the responsibility for what goes on," said Dan Chayefsky. "It was not like my father was this omnipotent god, that he was the one who caused all the problems. I caused a lot of my own. I also had a mother. We were like three chemicals you put in a test tube that explodes when mixed."

When he became an adolescent, the young man was urged by his father to appear more aggressive and outgoing. "He wanted me to be this fun type of guy, like Zorba the Greek, to develop a persona something like the one he developed for himself," said Dan. "He wanted me to be more like Paddy, not Sidney. But I was anything but a Paddy or a Zorba. I was withdrawn, often sullen. It would take me a long time before I could act happy like him."

During his teenage years the battle of wills on the home ground became more pronounced. Supremacy and control were always key issues with his parents, Dan Chayefsky recalled. "I grew up learning that to lose in a situation was the worst thing that could happen to you. In our house you were either a king or a beggar, omnipotent or nothing." The contests were terrifying and often disruptive. "Someone once asked my father if he ever wrote at home. And he said, 'Never!' It was like: 'Are you kidding? With all that turmoil, who could work?' "

In *The Hospital,* Chayefsky's fictional self, Dr. Bock, speaks of his son as a "pietistic little humbug" who preaches universal love but despises everyone. "He had a blanket contempt for the middle class, even its decencies," said Bock. "His generation didn't live with lies, he told me. Everybody lives with lies, I said. I grabbed him by the poncho, dragged him the full length of our seven-room despicably affluent middle-class apartment, and flung him out. I haven't seen him since."

When asked how close that passage came to their relationship, Dan Chayefsky said his father never called him a "pietistic little humbug. But I know my father and I know how he disguised things. There was a continuous rage between us, so I'm sure he had those feelings." After he saw the movie, Dan asked Chayefsky if that specific scene referred to him. The writer said no, that it was based on someone in his poker game. "I knew he probably wouldn't have told me the truth, anyway, because you never really know how writers feel," said Dan. "But there are moments when we react with fury at the people we love, and he did love me, so it wouldn't have surprised me if there was a lot of our relationship at that time in there."

When Chayefsky senior was diagnosed as a depressive and began to improve with medication, his son was skeptical of the change. "It's very hard when a parent changes like that. Here was a father who had spent my early years being self-focusing, very angry, and obsessive about his career. Then he changes and comes to grips that he has a son and he starts to really make an effort. That takes some adjusting on my part. I was not used to being dealt with by someone who was listening to me. I was used to being talked at and talked to, and with being blamed and ignored."

Chayefsky's old programs of past behavior did not change that easily either. The overbearing Paddy Chayefsky was still there. Aware of it, he consciously tried to hold back, to allow his teenage son to make his own decisions and mistakes. Whenever Susan Chayefsky would obsess about the boy's excursions beyond the house, Paddy would yell, "Let him be! Don't put this kid in a box." Freedom, however, was something that the teenager didn't know how to manage. "Sometimes I would deliberately stay out all night," said Dan. "I was hanging out with a truly irresponsible seventies crowd. We'd go to somebody's house, sit in a room with black lights, listen to Pink Floyd, and smoke reefers." Returning home the next morning, he noticed that while his father acted unconcerned ("I never did hard drugs, and I think he knew I had a strong streak of self-preservation in me"), his mother would become more agitated. "We were a typical codependent family," said Dan. "Today, I recognize that there was goodness in my parents' relationship, but back then, with all the tension and fighting, there was never much love expressed. There was far too much emphasis on pain in that house. And rather than pull away from it, as I would later learn to do, I became more sullen and inward, which led to more turbulence."

When the hostilities became too much even for Paddy Chayefsky to handle, he decided that a separation was in order. But instead of throwing his son out of the house, as Dr. Bock did in *The Hospital*, Chayefsky and his wife left and checked into a nearby hotel. "They went to live at the Navarro," said Gott-fried. "Neither Paddy or Susan wanted to abandon Danny. They felt more comfortable knowing he was in the house."

"They moved out in total desperation," said Dan. "I'm not proud of that time. It should have been the other way around, and I became twice as sensitive when people joked about it later. But my parents felt so guilty. We all did, especially my father. And as usual he took the burden of blame on himself, which was wrong, especially since there was enough there for all three of us."

The estrangement lasted three months, at which time, without any official reconciliation, the parents moved back home. "What happened was that my father said, 'Enough is enough. I feel terrible about this, but I've done my time,' " said Dan Chayefsky. "That's how he was. He would feel bad about something he caused, for a long time. Then he would drop it, forget about it, and move on."

> Paddy was an extremely complicated man.
> Usually he was very confident he could write any story
> he set out to write. But occasionally he would be
> troubled with just a touch of self-doubt. On one of those
> occasions I decided to cheer him up and bare my
> soul. I told him how much I admired his work. He modestly
> agreed. He also admired his work.
>
> Bob Fosse

Throughout the late 1960s and early 1970s, Chayefsky's closest confidant remained Bob Fosse, who was having private and professional crises of his own. In 1968, Fosse made his Hollywood directorial debut with *Sweet Charity*, starring Shirley MacLaine. The month before the movie was released, he had twelve offers to direct other films. The week *Sweet Charity* opened, to largely empty houses, the offers dried up. Nothing came in for sixteen months, until 1971, when Fosse was considered for the movie of *Cabaret*. He wouldn't get it, he told Chayefsky. The movie company wanted Billy Wilder or Stanley Kubrick. "If your name is on it, you'll get it," Chayefsky assured his friend. Fosse got the job. On location in Germany, he was on the phone frequently to New York. The producers were giving him a hard time and he thought of quitting. "If you quit, you don't get paid, and they'll give you a bad name," Chayefsky told him. "Stay and if they fire you, you'll be paid and they'll call it 'creative differences.' " Fosse stayed, and *Cabaret*, released in 1973, mopped up at the box office and won seven Oscars, including one for Best Director. He followed that up with an Emmy for *Liza with a Z*, and a Tony for the Broadway musical *Pippin*, which, although dazzling in movement and style, was primitive and slim in narrative form. The latter flaw had been glossed over by means of a suggestion from Chayefsky. "Cut the intermission," he told Fosse. "That way during the break the audience won't get the chance to discuss that there's no plot."

By this time Fosse's marriage to Gwen Verdon was strained, owing to his regular extramarital excursions. When the director-choreographer fell in love with a *Pippin* performer, Ann Reinking, it was officially acknowledged that he and Gwen Verdon had separated. There would be no divorce, however. Dubbed "the Empress" by Chayefsky, Verdon would remain close to Fosse's friends and associates, including a third member of their intimate circle, playwright Herb Gardner (author of the 1960 hit *A Thousand Clowns*).

"Herb is a painter and a sculptor as well as a writer. He is a real, honest-to-God, bohemian artist," said Chayefsky.

"You know, it's hard to remember when I *wasn't* friends with Paddy and Bobby," Gardner said in 1991. "They were key points on my life's map. You know, 'Take a left at Chayefsky, make a right at Fosse.' " When his career was stalled in the late sixties, Gardner used their offices to write in when one or the other was out of town. In 1970 he got his own office on the same floor. "Paddy was in Room 1104. I was down the hall, right opposite Bobby," he said.

In the mornings the three would often meet in the hallways and kvetch, Gardner recalled. "There was always some bad person out there who was trying to hurt them," said Ann Reinking. "Someone who was trying to change their work, so they were fighting the enemy *together*. They were very fighting people." Emotionally they complemented each other, Gwen Verdon said. "Both Herbie and Bob were so enamored of Paddy. And Paddy was so enamored of Bob and Herbie. It was just a love affair between three people."

Referring to Chayefsky's designated title "the Professor," Gardner recalled that he had a way of making writing very appealing. "For Paddy, writing just wasn't a career, a profession. It was footnotes of a powerful personality. Personality goes beyond writing. That's why he made it so inspiring for a lot of people. He made it look like 'Why would anyone want to do anything else in life but write?' "

Having two friends on the premises to listen to his stuff was invaluable to Chayefsky. And it worked for the others too, said Verdon. "The three of them listened and contributed to each other's work all the time. Bob and Herbie were always a little tentative about telling or suggesting anything to Paddy, because they were so in awe of his language. But Paddy always read film scripts that Bob was working on. And so did Herb. If the piece needed some humor, Herb, who was more of a philosopher, would talk about that. And Paddy would get in there about construction—the form of the piece.''

What was reflected in one another's work was not the contribution of any one individual, but the collective value of the "insane seminars that ran on and on over the years," said Gardner. "It's as if we were all students, and there was this school we were in. This little school, from which we would never graduate. We would go on talking, discussing, trying to understand, trying to get our diplomas, forever." As a student, everything fascinated Chayefsky. "Everything he didn't understand, that he wanted to learn about, was much more important than talking about what he really knew," said Gardner. "To understand 'What is that? What did he say? What does that mean? What can we find out here? What can we learn?' That was much more important to Paddy. And to Bobby, who was exactly like that."

Although they tried to help one another with their work, and to have serious talks, mostly they hung out and laughed, said Gardner. For lunch each day the trio went downstairs to the Carnegie Delicatessen, or to the Russian Tea Room on West Fifty-seventh Street. After that came the postprandial strolls. "We walked and walked, all over the city," said Gardner. "I would exhaust myself. I'd be five steps behind them. Paddy loved to walk and talk. It seemed to me we spent twenty years walking. We would walk and talk and on the way fall in love with at least six girls every afternoon. Usually it was Bobby who stopped and said, 'O.K., it's four o'clock. I don't know about you guys, but I gotta go back to work. I'll walk one more block and that's it.' To which Paddy always said, 'Fosse, you forgot. You have no work. You're finished in this business.' 'Oh,' Bobby would say, nodding in remembrance, 'that's right. I forgot.' And a half hour later it would be somebody else's turn to do the announcement and the reminder.''

They were lifetime pals, and they knew it, and reveled in the security by attacking each other's weaknesses, said Gardner. "I can still see Paddy hunched over with his evil cackle and Bobby with his head thrown back till he cried, one of us just having led a search-and-destroy mission on a weakness of the other." Of Chayefsky's frequent outbursts and manic monodramas, Herb Gardner said that he and Bob Fosse often kidded him about that. "Paddy could make an argument out of an egg-salad sandwich. And then he would say, 'Look at what I'm doing.' And make fun of himself. A lot of people used to make fun of Paddy, but nobody did it more than Paddy."

Gardner believed that nobody could write as well as Chayefsky did without being a good listener. "A man as vocal as Paddy was could listen to you by the hour without saying a word. People sometimes think of Paddy as this nonstop monologist—but the truth of his life is that he was a gifted listener.

You know from his writing that he was listening all the time, and not just listening for the purpose of being able to check characters for something he was writing, but listening to understand, listening to help, listening to give you an honest clear response."

In the period when Fosse was rehearsing the musical of *Chicago* by day and editing the movie of *Lenny* by night, he suffered severe chest pains and was taken to New York Hospital. The blood was being cut off from his heart and he needed open-heart surgery as soon as possible. Herb Gardner was tracked down at a performance of his play *Thieves,* and he immediately contacted Chayefsky. The night before the operation, Fosse asked his two best friends to witness his will. Gardner signed the document without reading it. Chayefsky wasn't so hasty. He took the time to examine the document in full. At the end of the thirty pages, he said to a weakened Fosse, "Hey, I'm not in here." Fosse explained it was immediate family only, that he was providing for Gwen Verdon and his daughter Nicole. "But I'm your oldest and best friend," Chayefsky complained, "and I'm not in your will?" Checking the last page again, Paddy paused, then shouted at his best friend, "Fuck you! *Live!*"

Herb Gardner described what followed. "Bobby started to laugh. He is rolling around the bed, pulling his tubes and wires with him, the heart-monitor screen looks like it's showing reruns of *Jeopardy!* Into this melee walks Bobby's surgeon, who appears to be twelve years old. The child surgeon proceeds to sketch the details of the bypass operation for Bobby, who leans forward, attempting straight-faced interest. The surgeon drops his pen, *clunk,* on the floor. There is a pause, and then the child surgeon says, 'Whoops.' Now, 'whoops' is not one of the things you want your heart surgeon to say the night before your operation. The surgeon bends down to retrieve his pen, Bobby turns to me and Paddy and whispers, 'Operation canceled.' The room explodes now, the laughter is wild and contagious. It's like we left that midnight room and are back at the Carnegie Deli."

CHAPTER 28

Chayefsky the Activist

The basic Jewish identity of survival has now
surfaced in me. It's an open paranoia right now.
That's all I really care about right now—to save the Jews.

Paddy Chayefsky, 1971

During World War II, when Chayefsky was in his early twenties and his "Paddy" persona had taken over the reins of his life, his attention to being Jewish and its religious obligations receded considerably. By the late 1950s, after success and its attendant miseries had arrived, he began to invest more time in his original creed. In December 1959, a month after *The Tenth Man* had opened on Broadway, he told friends that he was not celebrating Christmas that year. "On previous holidays our families used to exchange presents," said Audrey Peters. "But after *The Tenth Man,* Paddy, very graciously, told us he would no longer accept Christmas presents; Hanukkah, yes, but not Christmas presents. It wasn't phony, he was very sincere about it."

In the early sixties, when Dan was growing up, Chayefsky made sure that his son went to the synagogue regularly and attended Hebrew school three times a week, as his parents had done for him. "He never preached to me," said Dan Chayefsky, "but he believed in the Jewish tradition very strongly, as did the entire Chayefsky family." Dan remembered sitting with his cousins during the Passover seders, while his father and uncles joyously sang Yiddish songs all night long. When Dan turned thirteen, his father insisted that he be bar mitzvahed in a temple in Israel, where his mother had to sit on the open roof with the rest of the women. Arguments and differences of opinion on theological matters between father and son began soon after. Chayefsky believed in the Old Testament. His son leaned toward the New Testament. "Basically it was the stories in the Bible that my father was interested in, not so much the religious part," said Dan Chayefsky. "He also was very strong on tradition, whereas I felt that was just an excuse not to change." During the holidays, when Dan began to object to going to the formal services, Chayefsky protested strenuously. "He wasn't above trying to make me feel guilty, either. 'Two days a year, do something to make me happy,' he'd say. But again, he did allow me to make that choice, to not go to temple." The reverential aspect was not an abiding passion, Chayefsky told one reporter. "My children don't have to go to a synagogue and pray. They just have to know they're Jewish. That's what keeps them from going nuts when they're forty-five years old."

Politically, Chayefsky's fervor and activism expanded during the 1960s. "Someone once said that a Jew is a man with one bag packed in the hall closet at all times," he stated. He spoke to Arnold Forster, the general counsel for the Anti-Defamation League of B'nai B'rith, to discuss what he could do to help fight the fear and oppression. "Trouble had started a few years after Israel had been established as a state," said Forster. "Paddy wanted to know what he could do, not only for Israel but for Jews everywhere. So I invited him to come to some of our meetings and I put him in touch with other concerned people."

In 1971 Chayefsky went to Brussels as part of the American delegation to the International Conference on Soviet Jewry. Appearing before the gathering, Chayefsky spoke urgently for the freedom and release of the Jews suffering in the Soviet Union. He reminded the council of the Holocaust. "Six million went up with a snap," he said, "and there is little reason to assume anybody's going to protect the other twelve million still extant."

When the conference rejected the proviolence recommendations of Rabbi Meir Kahane (head of the newly formed Jewish Defense League) and insisted on adhering to a program of nonaggressive diplomacy, Chayefsky decided to appear on Belgium television. He called for a stronger policy on the defense of persecuted Jews in Western Europe. Speaking of the rise in anti-Semitism throughout the world, he warned that another half a million Jews were in danger of being exterminated in Russia. Paraphrasing Stalin, he said that just to tighten things up the Soviet Union was willing "to break a lot of eggs to make an omelet."

Frustrated with the pacifist stand of the conference in Belgium, Chayefsky was instrumental in starting a new activist group in New York, Writers and Artists for Peace in the Middle East. The founding members included Colleen Dewhurst, Frank Gervasi, Leon Uris, Gerold Frank, and Elie Wiesel. Wearing a Solidarity button, Chayefsky later appeared with Joanne Woodward, Joseph Wiseman, Beatrice Straight, and others as part of a public rally in Times Square protesting the Soviet detention of Valery Panov, the Kirov dancer. As he became more vociferous publicly on Jewish matters, especially those concerning Israel, it was said that this passion was just another outlet for his surplus anger. Chayefsky's concern, however, was neither misplaced nor arranged for extraneous attention. "Paddy felt it was always important to make a statement about a very serious situation," said Donald Harron. "He knew the persecution of the Jews was never going to stop. And he was right."

During the filming of *The Hospital*, Harron had asked Chayefsky what his next project would be. He said that he was considering writing about "a race of people who were about to disappear." Harron asked who they were. Chayefsky replied, "The Arabs." The topic was to be done "sympathetically," Harron believed.

The Middle East was "both the least understood area in the world today; and politically and dramatically, the most exciting," Chayefsky told *The New York Times* in July 1971. He said he was "up to his ears" in research for a story that was "a study of life within an Arab guerilla cell on the West Bank of the Jordan." That summer and fall, he went back and forth to Israel to work with Yisrael Stockman, an Israeli professor who was an expert on Palestinian Arabs. Arnold Forster was also there and recalled "barreling through Jerusalem, in cars and on foot," with Chayefsky. "He wanted to talk to everyone about the political situation. He wasn't just interested in the Israeli side, he had to talk to the Palestinians too."

The Habakkuk Conspiracy became the title of the work. It was "a political melodrama, much like *Z*, which I admired a lot," said Chayefsky. It would feature different genres, like *The Hospital*. "It was about a search for the Dead Sea Scrolls, but it finally became a murder mystery," said Howard Gottfried. "The time frame was the late nineteen-forties, in that period just before Israel was declared a state by the United Nations. So a lot of the intrigue that went on with the British, the Arabs, and the Jewish freedom fighters was in the story." "It had all of Paddy's attitudes about Israel and that world," said David Picker. "There was also a woman involved, a woman who was caught in the violence that was going on at the time." A love story between the woman and the younger brother of her husband, who had been killed early on, was the heart of the story. "It was a beautifully structured script," said Gottfried.

Gottfried and Chayefsky worked together for eighteen months on the project. "The script was completed and accepted by UA," Gottfried recalled. "They sent us back to Israel to scout locations." When the two returned to New York they learned that United Artists had canceled the film. "They turned it down because they had another movie in the works from Otto Preminger [*Rosebud*]," said Gottfried. "That also involved Israel and Palestine. I don't know what went on. It could have been Arthur Krim's relationship with Preminger. Paddy was furious, and rightly so. He had written a terrific script. To this day there are some old UA people who know that script and still talk reverently about it."

Chayefsky got paid in full for his script. He could have placed it with another studio but after the Yom Kippur War in October 1973, he said his story had "lost its significance." But he was resolved to continue to work on behalf of

Jewish causes. In December 1973, when the Arab oil embargo was crippling America's industries and complicating millions of people's lives, a full-page ad appeared in *The New York Times*. In big bold letters, one word appeared: OIL. Two lines below it read: IT CAN HEAT YOUR HOUSE. RUN YOUR CAR. AND BLACKMAIL YOUR COUNTRY. The ad, paid for by the A.D.L. (Anti-Defamation League), was written by Chayefsky. In it he warned readers not to let "a handful of kings, sheiks, and dictators" try to change Mideast policy. Profits were really at stake here, he said, because even pro-Arab countries like France and India had had their oil supplies cut. This was a seller's market, but the Arabs didn't want the world to think about that. "They want you to believe that they are strangling America more in sorrow than anger. They shed crocodile tears as they destroy our jobs and savings, force our factories to close, stop our transportation, and undermine our entire economy."

Four months later, another A.D.L. ad, composed by Chayefsky but uncredited, appeared in *The New York Times*. In this, the families of Israeli prisoners held captive in the Yom Kippur War asked the American public's help in finding out from Syria if their loved ones were dead or alive. "They are not just soldiers," Chayefsky wrote. "They are sons. They are not just men who fought for their country. They are husbands. And fathers." In plain prose, he invoked the agony and the helplessness of the parents, the wives, the children, who were left in the dark, waiting for the Syrian government to release the names of their loved ones. "Are they alive? Have they been murdered? Help us find out. Because there is no greater joy than finding the lost. And no crueler wait than for one who will never come."

Chayefsky still harbored some resentment toward United Artists for the way they had rejected his Israeli script. "They went ahead with Preminger's picture, and it flopped," said Gottfried. "Paddy remained a little bit bitter about the matter. He thought it wasn't fair of Arthur Krim to do what he did. So not long after, when the opportunity arose to fight back, he took it."

This was on another matter, concerning the ancillary rights to *The Hospital*. Gottfried and Chayefsky had met with the president of NBC, who wanted to buy *The Hospital* for a network showing. "Not only that, he wanted to give Paddy a lot of money to write a series based on *The Hospital*," said Gottfried. But UA co-owned those rights, and when the producer called them a few days later he learned that they planned to sell the movie as part of a TV package with some other films. "With a bunch of losers," said Gottfried. "That way we would not get nearly the amount of money if *The Hospital* was sold separately." When apprised of this, Chayefsky listened calmly, then said "O.K., Howard, what do we do?" Gottfried suggested they pay a visit to United Artists.

The meeting at UA turned out to be loud and nasty. "Things got very heated," Gottfried said years later. "Arthur Krim was called in to mediate, and David [Picker] told him that I had called him a liar. I said, 'Hey, if that's how you interpret it, fine.' " Arthur Krim then began to speak in corporate abstracts, about the honesty and good reputation of his staff and company. "He was saying things like 'Our people,' and he acted surprised that we would even think we were being exploited. Well, that infuriated Paddy even more. He knew that Krim was very smart, that he ran UA and ran it very well, so he began to get livid. He said, 'Ah, come on, Arthur, what are you trying to do here? You're screwing us out of a lot of money.' " Louder assertions of company honor were made by Krim, which drove Chayefsky crazier. "Arthur said he would talk 'to my people,' and he'd get back to us," said Gottfried. "And he did. But of course he stuck to the position that they were doing nothing wrong. And they sold our movie as part of their package."

Chayefsky and Gottfried deliberated about what they should do next. If they fought on the legal front, how would it look? In the industry they'd be called troublemakers. It would also be expensive. "Paddy didn't think too long about it," said Gottfried. "He also felt a precedent should be set here. Other writers and filmmakers were being exploited by these package deals, so he called Maury Spanbock and we went ahead and sued."

The suit went on for almost a year. In the end, Chayefsky and Gottfried won, but the money they got didn't cover the legal expenses. That meant that when Chayefsky's next script was completed, he would be ready to take on the entire company at UA. "And he did, much to their regret," said Gottfried.

CHAPTER 29

Network

In 1977, Paddy Chayefsky expostulated on the subject of his newest and most controversial script, *Network*. "Television? Forget it," he said. "It's all madness. People are instant now. I've sat through movies in theatres and thought, 'This picture needs more commercials.' Thanks to TV we have all developed a ten-minute concentration span."

Of course, he had begun to bite the hand that fed him, not to mention made him famous, many years before. In the beginning, the purpose of television was that of a small but conveniently accessible conduit, one that would bring art, information, and now and then, popular entertainment, to the deprived masses. But then the minor medium became a monster, sucking in millions of viewers, and instead of educating and enriching lives, television became "the most awesome, goddamned propaganda force in the whole world," said Chayefsky. While numbing, narcotizing, and influencing the "opinions of morons," the cathode-ray tube became the permanent nucleus of social control in the home, an unwelcome substitute for human interaction and communication. In giving the illusion of self-sufficiency and absolute unity with the outside world, television succeeded in obliterating that most precious quality of all—the viewer's selfhood.

In Chayefsky's own household, when his son was younger, television was often fingered as the culprit for irregular behavior. "I had allergies, and I was angry a lot of the time, and my father blamed it on my watching too much television," said Dan Chayefsky. Viewing was banned, except for special programs and times. "During vacations and on school holidays I was allowed to watch certain shows," he said. "I remember one Christmas, in *TV Guide* they listed a marathon festival of cartoons. I marked off all the ones I wanted to watch and I showed it to my father. He became very indignant. 'They're actually proud that they're showing this junk,' he said disgustedly. He thought it interfered with children's minds, that this nonstop television on a holiday could be better spent reading or talking."

In 1965 Chayefsky commented that when he was growing up, on Sunday nights and holidays people communicated with one another. "Today after dinner no one talks, except that fucking box in the corner of the living room." By the mid-1970s, Chayefsky felt that the cultural, political, and social control of television was in the hands of a small elite of corporate and network planners "who can make or break presidents, popes, and prime ministers."

In the wake of Watergate and with a new generation that idealized drugs and ambisexual rock performers, TV critics of a certain age were inclined to look back and pine for those halcyon days of unabashed innocence—the 1950s. Sighs of nostalgia and reams of copy began to appear about that era of innocence and simplicity—the Golden Age of Television. Heading most lists as the leading dramatist of that time was Paddy Chayefsky. Because of his still-sterling credits and his premature defection, the myth of his absence from TV had reached Garboesque proportions. This was unwarranted, because, his legend and his aesthetic objections aside, Chayefsky had never quite stopped writing for television. In fact, over the years, he created a number of scripts that for sundry reasons never got on the air.

In 1955, Chayefsky came up with his first spoof of the medium. It was called *The Man Who Beat Ed Sullivan*. The lead character is a minor TV host in Ohio who puts on a marathon variety show every Sunday night, featuring the local talent and eccentrics. The rustic variety show becomes a nationwide hit and beats out the CBS prime-time champion, Ed Sullivan. Chayefsky's script was enthusiastically discussed at NBC, but the length of his proposed show-within-a-show met with resistance. He wanted his spoof to be an actual three-hour talent marathon, thus bumping off not only Ed Sullivan, but also Steve Allen, Dinah Shore, Patti Page, and the rest of the TV variety hosts who appeared on Sunday nights.

Chayefsky's concept for a series on psychiatry came in 1958, but was rejected because he insisted on creative control. By 1965, the playwright was apparently willing to compromise a little. A TV series based on his most famous character, Marty, was planned. Actually, a sequel had been contemplated earlier by Delbert Mann and Ernest Borgnine. "We called up Paddy to ask what he thought about updating the story for a feature film," said Borgnine. "He said, 'I'll let you know in a few days.' " Chayefsky sat on this for some time, then told them, "No way. The movie has got to stand on its own." Time passed, and with it came a professional slump. Producer Harold Hecht was also caught in his own recession. So in 1965, he and Chayefsky decided to revive *Marty* as a thirty-minute sitcom for television. They pitched the idea to Screen Gems, who bought it. A script was written and a pilot was made, starring Tom Bosley, but no network wanted to buy the pilot or the series. "Son of a gun," said Ernest Borgnine years later. "I never even heard about that, which shows you what a secretive little guy Paddy was."

In 1969, Chayefsky apparently was ready for television again. He agreed to write a series for CBS: "social-satirical" dramas was the concept. The first episode was about "a bunch of guys, writers and actors, sitting around the Russian Tea Room, trying to come up with something significant for television," said Howard Gottfried. The fictional idea was to do an adaptation of *The Threepenny Opera* for TV, except it would be made in Harlem and cover such vital issues as racism, crime, and unemployment. The leading character, a writer modeled after Mel Brooks, would impersonate the late Bertolt Brecht and con the head of NBC television into making a deal. "Paddy had the conviction that most people don't really know who anyone is," said Gottfried, "and the need for quality programming on television was so desperate that the head of NBC really believes it's Bertolt Brecht on the phone."

As the plot unfolded, Chayefsky had his Mel Brooks character "turned loose in a major network." He impersonates John Schneider (a CBS vice president) and Senator John Pastore (head of the Senate Subcommittee on Television Communications). "You could see the script was a takeoff on television," said Chayefsky. "It was full of puns really razzing the system of programming," said Gottfried. But this was 1969, the year CBS yanked "The Smothers Brothers Comedy Hour" off the air because President Richard Nixon had pledged a government crackdown on network permissiveness. Certainly CBS was not about to add more ridicule to the bonfire by skewering their own. They explained to Chayefsky that his script was "irresolute . . . it posed a problem but didn't resolve anything." The rejection came with the payment of his fee of $75,000. "They tell you they're interested in drama," the writer said on his way to the bank, "but they're not. They'd just as soon run 'Bonanza' forever."

One further TV project followed, "Your Place or Mine?," a comedy series lampooning the 1970s singles scene, starring James Coco. When NBC rejected the pilot in May 1974, Chayefsky decided it was time to dissect the television industry itself. The area of news broadcasting irritated him the most. Controlled by mass ratings, the shows' substance and format had deteriorated drastically over the years. The most important events of each day were now being trivialized, condensed into brief capsules, accompanied by random images, to be scanned rather than understood. The tragedies of murder and crime and war were being sliced up and served on TV as thirty-second B-movie clips, followed by a solemn sincere gaze, a pause, then the cheery announcement: "We'll be right back with tonight's lottery winners."

The real tragedy of TV news, said Chayefsky, was that "it totally desensitizes [us to] viciousness, brutality, murder, death, so we no longer actively feel the pains of the victim or suffer for their lives or feel their grief. That is the basic problem of television. We've lost our sense of shock, our sense of humanity."

That July, the opening hook for his new script came when Chayefsky was watching a respected, supposedly learned TV anchor rattle off some scripted inanities on the evening news. "Jesus, how can these guys live with themselves? How can they deliver this garbage without becoming physically ill?" he asked himself. The following day, he had a tentative outline in his head. For validation he called a trusted friend at NBC, John Chancellor. Chayefsky asked Chancellor if it was possible for an anchorman to go nuts on TV. "Every day," replied Chancellor.

Within a week the first act of a rough draft was in place. One night, on the six o'clock news, an elderly anchorman, fed up with life and about to be dropped by the network, announces his intention to commit suicide on the air the following week. The network, in need of a ratings boost, decides to make a media event out of it. The attention is enormous, and the suicidal newsman, invigorated by the expanded audience, dispenses with the news and becomes a crusading, demoniacal pundit, preaching about modern-day doom to his captive viewers. As the popularity of his program soars, the anchorman disconnects further, eventually losing his mind.

Chayefsky named his mad anchorman Howard Beale. The "Howard" came from his partner, Howard Gottlieb, and "Beale" came from a current media story about an eccentric old lady, Edith Beale, an aunt of Jacqueline Kennedy Onassis, who lived in a run-down mansion on Long Island surrounded by cats and raccoons. Physically, Beale is a combination of John Chancellor and Walter Cronkite; but his rage and discontent, the lucid brain and the manic soul, are 95 percent Chayefsky. "Howard Beale came straight out of Paddy's own gut," said Howard Gottfried. "You couldn't write characters like that without being part of them. He never said that, but we knew it. The reason why these characters were so incredible was not only due to their validity, but because he dug into the deepest recesses of his own being and invested everything. There were things he wouldn't tell a psychiatrist, or anyone else, that he would insert in his characters."

As a counterpoint to Howard Beale, Chayefsky created a second prominent figure, Max Schumacher—a good guy, "the middle-aged hero," the president of the TV news division and a friend and ally to the tormented anchorman. He, too, was part Chayefsky and part Dave Tebet, a senior vice president at NBC. Decent and compassionate, Max Schumacher objects when the network opts to take advantage of Howard Beale's fragile mental state by exploiting him on the air. Schumacher is overruled and eventually loses his news show to the female villain of the piece, Diana Christensen.

A product of the TV generation who has learned about life "from Bugs Bunny," Christensen is the programmer of popular entertainment at Chayefsky's network. She sees that the American people have turned sullen. "They've been clobbered on all sides by Vietnam, Watergate, the inflation, the depression. They've turned off, shot up, fucked themselves limp, and nothing helps." The American people need someone "to articulate their rage for them," Diana says, and she finds just the man for the job, on the evening news. She takes over Howard Beale and his news program and proceeds to infuse both with a gaudy mixture of drama and entertainment that, she says, "will wipe that fucking Disney right off the air." This woman of "masculine temperament" was the strongest female character he had created since *The Goddess*, said Chayefsky. She was also self-inspired. "That part is me. She is a man," Chayefsky told a reporter from the *Soho Weekly News*. When asked why he made the character a woman, Paddy said it was because he needed a love interest. "It's a metaphorical love story," he explained. "She represents television, he [Max Schumacher] represents humanity; and it's the core of the picture."

By September of 1974, Chayefsky and Gottfried had won their suit with United Artists over the sale to television of *The Hospital*. The movie company, assuming that they and he were best friends again, asked Chayefsky if he would talk to them about his new movie script. "We were doing it on spec because of the litigation," said Gottfried. "We developed it but we would not show it to them, and they were dying to see it."

Chayefsky, being "a sentimental sort," agreed to let bygones be bygones and he met with the brass at UA. As a writer he pitched them his story about television, then stopped and put on his business cap. There were a few imperatives upfront, he told the movie executives. This project would not be like their prior deals, wherein UA had financed the script, he went off and wrote it, and six months later they decided to move or pass on it. What he was offering them, for $50,000 upfront, was an "option" for a first look at his first draft, which would be ready no later than January 1. They would then have seventeen days to make up their minds if they wanted to purchase the motion picture rights. If they passed he had the right to keep the $50,000 and take the property elsewhere.

On October 24, in an interoffice memo, Bob Bernstein, vice president of finance and legal matters at United Artists, confirmed to the company's executive staff that each one of Chayefsky's demands had been accepted. With the play-or-pay deal in his pocket, the writer proceeded full speed with the treatment. His research involved "watching hours of TV." On-the-job background was provided by Dave Tebet, who allowed Chayefsky to visit NBC at length and watch the executive machinery at work. Bumming around with management, he was invited to sit in on programming meetings during which he documented the "ambitions, the politics, the power struggles, the obsession with ratings and the insane pressures to be number one." As with his research for *The Hospital*, Chayefsky found that no one was shy or reluctant to reveal even the most derelict aspects of their work. "Most programmers told me that they didn't watch much television themselves," he said. "The programs they put on 'had to' be bad, had to be something they wouldn't watch. Imagine having to work like that all your life?"

Prowling the corridors at NBC, then CBS, Chayefsky's focus settled in on the news divisions. He took notes during their prebroadcast meetings, visited the control rooms and the makeup departments, and watched hopeful news anchors audition for jobs. The key word there was "audition," he said. "It's not how smart they are, but how they look, how they sound. They're models."

Within his fictional network, UBS (the United Broadcasting System), Chayefsky created his own popular entertainment programming. There were the obligatory game shows, including "Celebrity Mahjong." A "True Crime" reenactment series was followed by the legal defense flank: "The Young Shysters." Opposite ABC's Tuesday night's number one sitcom, "Laverne and Shirley," Paddy slotted his version, "Shirley, Pedro and Putz." The "Howard Beale Show," after it is appropriated by Diana Christensen, is populated with garish sideshow attractions, among them Sybil the Soothsayer, who "tells tomorrow's news today," a resident gossip columnist, "It's-the-Emmes-Truth Department," and a flashy but insipid weather reporter—all presented on a revolving set.

"Most of that came to pass," said Gottfried later. "Presenting the news as entertainment, the gossip columnists, the live cops and robbers shows—Paddy was prescient about all of it."

"He had a kind of Jewish Talmudic logic, which brought things to their eventual final conclusion," said director Sidney Lumet. "Paddy had that uncanny ability to see just where everything was leading."

In January 1975, the treatment for *Network* was completed and accepted by United Artists, which enabled Chayefsky to move forward, refining the plot and "punching up the jokes." Then he went to work on the "meat of the thing"—the passionate theatrical speeches delivered by Max Schumacher, Diana Christensen, and the mad prophet of the airwaves, Howard Beale. "I use insane people a lot because it allows you to be extravagant in your language, and insanity is a very contemporary theme," Chayefsky told writer Susan Horowitz.

One of Beale's feverish concerns was endemic to the writer's. It involved the buying up of U.S. companies and real estate by foreign concerns, including those from the rich Arab nations. In August 1974, another full-page ad appeared in *The New York Times*, placed by the Jewish Anti-Defamation League and written by Chayefsky. It urged the American people to protest U.N. Resolution 242, which called for the withdrawal of Israeli forces from Arab land occupied as a result of the 1967 war. If the retreat went into effect, the Arabs promised they would roll back their oil prices worldwide. That to Chayefsky was "patent propaganda." The resolution was in fact a matter of life and death for the Jews. "The Arabs have never made any bones about their ultimate intentions towards Israel, which is simply its obliteration," he said. And if Israel returned to its pre-1967 lines, "why not then return to the pre-1948 lines?" Chayefsky asked. And who could ensure that the Arabs wouldn't attack again? "France? Russia? England? Japan?—all these other powers who fell fawning to their knees at the first twist of a tap?"

Urging his TV viewers to fight back, Howard Beale tells them to call, write, send telegrams to the White House. "Now, listen to me, goddammit! The Arabs are simply buying us! They're buying all our land, our whole economy, the press, factories, financial institutions, the government! They're going to own us! A handful of agas, shahs, and emirs who despise this country and everything it stands for—democracy, freedom, and the right for me to get up on television and tell you about it."

So much of what Chayefsky had to say in his movies and plays came through different voices and different names, "but it was him, what he felt, what he cared about, what he was feeling at the time," said Herb Gardner. "Those speeches in *Network*, the issues he brought up, that's where he was at that moment. Those were little passionate weather reports on the prevailing winds of Paddy's life."

As he did with *The Hospital*, in the writing of his script for *Network*, Chayefsky employed a variety of styles. Combining realism and parody in the dialogue of the supporting characters, he imbued them with the nervous energy that dominated the TV business. "It's an industry built on hysteria," he explained. "You drop your rating share and a minute later hysteria sweeps through the network." And because manic, discontented people were involved, the rhythmic bombastic language in the key speeches was easy. The difficulty was in refining that language so one part of the movie audience would accept it as entertainment and another as poetry. "You have to make it sound as if they're talking realistically but with an articulate reality—characters who are capable of poetic reality."

The passage that contained the most popular and enduring catchphrase from the movie, the "mad as hell" statement, came from the writer's marrow. The depersonalization and paralysis of the human spirit was a concern that permeated his work and his personal life. "Everybody's out of work or scared of losing their job, the dollar buys a nickel's worth, banks are going bust, shopkeepers keep a gun under the counter, punks are running wild in the streets," says Howard Beale. He urges viewers to stop acting like frightened robots, to get past their feelings of apathy, shame, and manipulation, and go to their windows and scream out, "I'm a human being, goddammit. My life has value. . . . I'm mad as hell and I'm not going to take this anymore!" The speech was the easiest speech to write, Chayefsky said. "I wanted everyone, every man, woman, or child, to realize that they had a choice. I wanted them to know that they have the right to get angry, to get mad. They have the right to say to themselves, to each other, to the world at large, that they had worth, they had value. The speech wrote itself because that was Beale's battle cry for the people."

The writing of *Network* brought considerable hardship too. "Paddy was actually in pain when he was working on some of the speeches," said Gottfried. "I don't mean physical pain because of the difficulties or the hours, but the pain of having had to search within himself, of trying to discover, to invest the characters with a real truth. He spent hours and hours with Beale especially."

Red-eyed and drained by one of Beale's exhortations, Chayefsky decided to give the character his fatigue. At the end of one on-camera harangue, the TV anchor falls in a dead faint on the floor.

In late April the first draft of *Network* was completed and accepted by United Artists. In a memo dated May 16, 1975, Marcia Nasatir, who was in charge of script development on the West Coast, gave her opinion to her boss, Mike Medavoy, with copies to Arthur Krim, Robert Benjamin, and Bob Bernstein in New York. "Very funny . . . very pertinent; however major problem for me is no hero . . . no hope," said Nasatir. "*The Hospital* offered a committed man. Here it is all madness and bullshit philosophy. Accurate picture of TV and U.S.A. life but Chayefsky is too much of a do-gooding humanist to write a totally successful black comedy."

Nasatir went on to say that she thought it was a mistake for the Max Schumacher character to be dropped out of the story "except as boyfriend" (to Diana Christensen). Nasatir wanted him back at the network, and asked whether it was "logical to assume he wouldn't get another job?" Her summation: "Script is too wordy. Everything is punched home twice or even thrice. Let's discuss more."

On May 19, 1975, in good faith, believing that United Artists were very enthusiastic about his script, Chayefsky had his lawyer, Maurice Spanbock, send a letter to Arthur Krim at UA, giving their preliminary list of suggestions for a director. This was "subject of course to terms negotiated and a meeting of minds with Paddy and Howard about the production itself."

Among the names of directors submitted by Chayefsky and Gottfried were those of Hal Ashby, John Avildsen, George Roy Hill, Arthur Hiller, Stanley

Kubrick, Sidney Lumet, Joseph Mankiewicz, Elaine May, Bob Mulligan, Mike Nichols, Arthur Penn, Roman Polanski, Herbert Ross, and Martin Scorsese. "We put down the names of almost every first-line director around, just to get them moving," said Gottfried.

"Some of these names are ludicrous," Mike Medavoy said in his reply to Arthur Krim and Bob Bernstein. Among the directors he vetoed were Avildsen, Hiller, Lumet, Mankiewicz, Penn, Polanski, Ross, and Scorsese. Among those considered "O.K." were Hal Ashby, George Roy Hill, Elaine May, Mike Nichols, and Stanley Kubrick, who because of his success as writer-producer-director of *A Clockwork Orange* was being ardently wooed by UA.

Kubrick had never been their prime choice, Gottfried said. "His name was on the list because UA were driving us crazy to take a shot at him. It was a waste of time to send the script to him. When he sent it back with apparently a positive reply, they got very excited. But Kubrick was an auteur. Paddy never wanted that kind of director. If he had done *Network* it would have been a totally different movie."

Early in June, with no firm decision on a director, the producers were called to UA to formalize the deal for the film. As with *The Hospital*, Chayefsky acted as his own agent. "We had been told they were dying to do the movie," said Gottfried. "So we went in to talk to Krim. Now Paddy was one of the best agents in America. You're not going to con him with any kind of sweet talk. The bottom line is you had to be passionate about making his movie."

In this meeting Krim began to discourse on other subjects. He didn't mention the script at first; until, without offering any specific recommendations, he suggested that Chayefsky should consider making some changes. Chayefsky nodded politely, and as he and Gottfried were leaving, almost as an afterthought, Krim said that Bob Bernstein, the vice president for finance and legal affairs, wanted to talk to them. "We had done a lot of business with Bob before," said Gottfried. "He was exceptional, except he never knew when he had a good deal. He wanted to make it better. So we said O.K. Paddy figured he wanted to talk about the budget."

In Bernstein's office, the executive confirmed that everyone at UA was looking forward to making *Network*. Then came the capper: "Paddy, I would like to talk to you about the character of Howard Beale," said Bernstein. "Chayefsky in these preliminary meetings was always quiet," said Gottfried. "He was deceptive. He would always let me be the more aggressive one, the producer. But this time he said, 'What was that, Bob?' 'I want to talk to you about the character of Howard Beale,' Bernstein said. 'You want to talk to me about the character of Howard Beale?' said Paddy. 'Yes, I'm having some problems with him.' 'You're having some problems with him,' Paddy repeated, whereupon he gets up and leaves the office, leaves the floor, leaves the building. I turned to Bernstein and said, 'Bob, you schmuck, you know better than this.' It's not that Paddy objected to people talking about his script, he felt it shouldn't come from the guy in charge of business affairs."

Gottfried found Chayefsky back in his Seventh Avenue office on the phone with Maurice Spanbock, instructing him to take the script back from UA. "Maurice called Arthur Krim, who agreed to let it go," said Gottfried. "And within two hours of that, every studio in California was calling us. Apparently people within UA had spread the word, contacting friends of theirs at the other studios, letting them know that the script of *Network* was now in turnaround."

MGM producer Dan Melnick was in his office in Burbank when he was informed that UA executive Mike Medavoy was on the line. "Mike said to me, 'Do you know Paddy Chayefsky?' I said, 'Sure.' He said, 'You might want to give him a call, he has a very interesting project.' " Melnick got a copy of the script and called Howard Gottfried that evening. "He said, 'Howard, this is the single most important script I have ever read,' " said Gottfried, "which is the way Danny always talks, in hyperbole. But he was very impressed and he wanted to find out how he could get the movie. I spoke to Paddy and he said, 'Hey, why not? MGM is as good as the other studios.' "

However, the management above Melnick at MGM, like UA, were leery because the script came down too hard on television. "They didn't want to have anything to do with it," said Melnick. "They were very scared, which was understandable. At that time MGM was working on a very reduced budget. To get their money back on a movie they had to sell the ancillary rights to television. And their network division said, 'Forget this, it will never be shown on national TV.' "

In the meantime, Warner Bros. was talking to Chayefsky. "They were on the phone saying, 'We want it! We want it!' They hadn't even read the script but they were ready to talk a deal," said Chayefsky.

The following day, hearing of Warner Bros.'s interest, MGM called Gottfried and Chayefsky back with a firm offer. It would be a coproduction, they said. They had a partner on the deal, United Artists, which was distributing MGM's films at the time. "It was insane," said Gottfried. "UA was now begging to get back into the deal. Apparently overnight Arthur Krim felt he made a big mistake letting *Network* go. So he called MGM. He knew they needed product and between them they decided to produce the film. Paddy was cool and very amused by all this. So we said, 'O.K., let's talk a deal.' "

A few days later Chayefsky and Gottfried flew to California with Maurice Spanbock. On the plane, Chayefsky gave his lawyer the exact details of the deal he was insisting on. Along with creative approval right down the line, the financial compensation was a critical issue.

He was opposed to the industry standard wherein the director made far more money than the original creator of the project, the writer. "Paddy had a thing about directors being the kingpins of the movie business," said Gottfried. "He had a valid point, because Paddy's movies were essentially his vision. That's not true with other writers, but in Paddy's case it was. Most directors would agree with that. So Paddy felt he should do as well as they did in the financial arrangements."

In Los Angeles the negotiations with the MGM lawyers went on for days, with Spanbock arguing the creative points for his clients. At one point Chayefsky felt he wasn't being treated fairly. "It was late in the afternoon and the discussion had become antagonistic," said Gottfried. "So Paddy got up and left the room." The following morning he called his partner from New York. Without telling anyone, he had left Los Angeles and gone home. "There is no way I'm going to put up with their bullshit," he said. "I was upset with him, and so was Maurice," said Gottfried. "But you know what, it worked. Metro came across. We got the exact deal he wanted, which wasn't excessive because Paddy never overreached."

On July 2, 1975, the announcement was made that *Network,* Paddy Chayefsky's new film, would be produced by MGM and UA. Undisclosed was the writer's salary: a modest sum of $150,000 upfront, but with 23 percent of the eventual profits, to be shared equally with Gottfried.

Their first step was to appoint a director. Sidney Lumet, who had been nixed in the preliminaries by UA, always had "the insider's track," said Chayefsky. He knew Lumet from the early days of television and said of him, "He's sensational because he comes out of the theatre, but he knows everything about television and filmmaking." Lumet was also fast—"the only man I know who would double-park outside a whorehouse," said Paul Newman. ("Paul is wrong, actually," Lumet said with a smile in 1992. "I would never do that outside a whorehouse.")

Lumet and Chayefsky began by reading the *Network* script back and forth to each other. "Paddy wasn't a very good actor," said the director. "But what he was, was wonderfully clear about his intentions. He was always very intelligent about them."

Two months went into rewrites. "There were some structural problems, some language problems," said Lumet. "But basically the script was all there. The problems were minor, and Paddy was completely open. People always said that Paddy had this enormous ego; well, he did, but in the best sense. He was completely secure in his talent."

"Paddy was *meticulous* about his work," said Gottfried. "His concentration on his dialogue was extraordinary, so that one had to cut it with a certain amount of forbearance. He himself would go over and over the script. He would rethink and redo it if it needed it. He might object at first. 'Show me what to take out,' he would say. Then he would listen if he trusted you.''

"If your point made sense, there was no fighting," Lumet agreed. "He would say 'Gotcha!' And forty-eight hours later he would bring in a rewrite and it would almost never have to be done again. He would never have to go back to take another crack at it.''

The eventual shooting script was received with support from Dan Melnick at MGM, but the United Artists executives remained a bit apprehensive about the story's content and characters. Arthur Krim handled the matter circuitously, by requesting a meeting with Sidney Lumet. Krim was terrified of two things, he told the director. One was the specificity of the television jargon, mainly relating to audience shares and numbers. The second objection was to the length of the speeches. "Don't tell me how long the speeches are. Tell me how good they are, because if they're good, they're going to play," Lumet told Krim. "And don't worry about if the audience will understand 'homes per use' and 'share per thousand.' The people may not know exactly what that means, but they'll understand that it is true, that it's the way TV executives talk, and they'll not only go along with it, they'll feel they're in on something real.''

On November 19, 1975, another memo about the script was sent from Tom Parry in UA's script department to Mike Medavoy and Marcia Nasatir. This one said that the new draft of *Network* was "virtually unchanged from the previous draft." Only a total of thirteen pages had been cut, consisting of repetitions or peripheral material, but "not a single character has been dropped; nor any of the lengthy speeches cut by even a single line; or even an attempt [made] at beefing up Max's passive character." Also, the "technical rating references" had been left totally intact, which led Parry to believe that UA was "going to have major problems with the audience understanding and getting involved with the characters and the story unless someone gets Chayefsky to make substantial changes.''

"The thing of it is, they didn't want to get off the dime," said Gottfried. "They wanted changes, but Paddy wouldn't budge. And why should he? He was the genius, not they. These people were supposed to be experts, but they weren't. They put their criticisms in such didactic terms. Paddy was never that didactic. He was the genius and those nonentities were trying to tear his work apart.''

Chayefsky ultimately informed MGM/UA that if they had some constructive criticism to offer, he would listen and consider it willingly. If not, he was moving forward with the production and wanted to hear nothing further about changes. "The top brass knew well enough not to push it at that point," said Gottfried. "Because if they did, Paddy was ready to say, 'O.K. Don't do the movie.' And he'd take his script back.''

Casting and Production

In his script for *Network*, Chayefsky described Diana Christensen, the female lead, as "thirty-four, tall, willowy, with the best ass ever seen on a vice president of programming." Jane Fonda at thirty-eight fit that description and was the popular choice of MGM and UA, but Paddy Chayefsky would not hire her. "He thought that she was an exceptionally good actress," said Dan Chayefsky. "But he did not agree with her politically, because at the time she was involved with all kinds of anti-Israel movements." (A conspicuous spokesperson for the New Left, Fonda openly supported the Black Panthers, who were openly anti-Semitic and who were piercingly sent up in Chayefsky's *Network*.)

Jill Clayburgh, Marsha Mason, Candice Bergen, and Diane Keaton were also considered. "This was a script with two powerful male roles, and the woman's part was just as strong," said Gottfried, "so agents in New York and Hollywood were submitting their star clients."

By mid-September, Faye Dunaway was in the front line of contenders. "Sue Mengers wanted us to use Faye from the beginning, and Paddy and I were perfectly content with her," Gottfried said. Lumet felt Dunaway possessed two major prerequisites for getting the part: physical beauty—to play against the stereotype of the plain female executive—and she could act. The only question was, would she play the toughness, or would she insist on being loved? "After all, even in *Bonnie and Clyde*, although she and Warren Beatty were supposed to be cold-blooded gangsters, we were led to believe that at heart they were just two little lost children," said Lumet. "That wasn't going to happen in *Network*. There was no way I was going to vitiate Paddy's script."

To settle the matter upfront, before Dunaway was signed, Lumet arranged to meet with the actress, alone—without her usual retinue of handlers and without his producers. "Paddy did not come along," said Lumet. "On issues like those, with actors, I didn't think he was the best person to have around. Bless his heart, he knew that, too, so he kept his distance."

In her Central Park West apartment, Dunaway tried to broach the subject first. "I jumped ahead of her," said Lumet. "I said, 'Faye, this is presumptuous, but I think I know what you're going to ask me. 'Where is my character's vulnerability?' And right now I'm going to tell you, 'There isn't any.' And if the tears come in a performance, fine. You'll have that satisfaction that they came, but I'm telling you right now, I'll cut them out." This would be particularly relevant with the goodbye scene between Diana and her older lover, Max Schumacher. "If you think you can weep in that scene and show how lost she is, it won't play," Lumet warned her, "because she's not lost at all. She doesn't understand it, she doesn't understand a word he's saying. She feels terrible that he's leaving, but she feels terrible when other people leave."

Dunaway listened and bought Lumet's logic. "She didn't try to argue or to discuss it. There was never a moment of contention, then or later. She didn't try to sneak it in. She saw exactly what Paddy was going for." Her character, as Chayefsky wrote her, was "indifferent to suffering, insensitive to joy." Conditioned by television, she was "a humanoid."

The role of the second male lead, Max Schumacher, described as tall, in his midfifties, and craggily handsome, was cast soon after. The selection narrowed down to Glenn Ford (fifty-nine) and William Holden (fifty-seven). Of the two, Chayefsky preferred Holden, and the studio agreed. Having had a recent success and proven on-screen rapport with Dunaway in *The Towering Inferno,* Holden was the more commercial choice.

Third in billing, but the most important in terms of the script, would be the actor selected to play Howard Beale. Chayefsky's first choice was George C. Scott, who had played his frenzied mouthpiece in *The Hospital.* "As soon as we had a copy of the script, we went from our production office at 1615 Broadway, right across the street to the Circle in the Square Theatre, where George was directing and starring in *Death of a Salesman,*" said Gottfried. "We handed him the script and said, 'George, this is for you.' "

Scott turned them down. "I'm not sure why. He never gave us a reason," said Chayefsky. "I know why," said Lumet. "Apparently, years before, although we had never met, I did something to offend him. I don't know what it was, but George remembered, and he wouldn't work with me."

Marlon Brando, Paul Newman, and Henry Fonda were approached. "I don't think Brando or Newman even read the script," said Gottfried. "We talked about Fonda, because of the homespun American quality." A script went to Fonda, who refused the role. "A personal distaste for the material," was the reason given. The script was also sent to James Stewart and Cary Grant. "Stewart was turned off by the material," said Dan Chayefsky. "Cary Grant liked it a lot, but didn't think Howard Beale was an appropriate role for him."

Meanwhile, a young, aggressive agent, Barry Krost, after reading the script sent a copy to his client Peter Finch, who was living in semiretirement on a banana farm in Bamboo, Jamaica. "I was out in the fields, hacking away with a machete, when the script arrived," Finch said. Upon reading it, he rushed to the phone to call his agent. "But there had been a hurricane. All the lines were down. I had some anxious moments, because I was afraid the producers would give the role to someone else."

"Peter wanted the part desperately," Lumet recalled. "He was a wonderful actor. Paddy and I knew that, but he was British, Australian really, and we were very worried about the accent. *Network* was the quintessential American story, and the actors had to be Americans."

Advised of the accent problem, Finch decided to address the matter directly. "He did something no actor had ever done with me," said Dan Melnick. "I didn't know him at all, yet he put himself in the difficult position of pitching himself for the part. He called me from Jamaica, and said he loved Paddy's script so much, and that he had so much passion for the role of the anchorman that he was willing to fly in to New York at his own expense to meet with all of us."

Over lunch in New York with Melnick, Chayefsky, Sidney Lumet, and Howard Gottfried, the fifty-nine-year-old actor "auditioned." "He was as nervous as hell at that first meeting, he was like a kid reading for his first part," said Melnick. Being British was an obstacle, Finch acknowledged, but for Howard Beale the accent he intended to use would be neither a perfect regional American nor a non-American. It would be what he called Eastern Standard. "The way Peter described it to us, there was a very subtle distinction," said Gottfried. "It was the individual way he looked at it."

Finch told the luncheon group that when he got back to his hotel that evening he would tape the Walter Cronkite and the John Chancellor news broadcasts. When he returned to Jamaica, he would listen to the tapes, then record his interpretation of one of Howard Beale's speeches. "He promised to send us tapes of this in a week or ten days," said Lumet. "If we said 'no' there would be no problem. He did exactly that, and of course he was perfect."

Rounding out the featured cast, Robert Duvall read the script and sent word that he was willing to play Frank Hackett, the cold, efficient corporate hatchet man who decides that Howard Beale must be killed. Duvall also stipulated that although this was basically a secondary role, his name, owing to the success of *The Godfather* pictures, had to be placed *above* the title, in line with the other stars. Chayefsky, who admired Duvall's work, agreed, and he was signed as the fourth lead.

For the other lesser but potent roles, some theatrical heavyweights from Broadway were willing to audition. Colleen Dewhurst and Irene Worth read for the part of William Holden's loyal but discarded wife, Louise Schumacher. "Then Sidney Lumet asked us to meet with Beatrice Straight," said Gottfried. "After she read for us, Paddy and I were weeping." The role of Arthur Jensen, the chairman of the board who, in a closed power meeting, sends Howard Beale over the edge, had already been cast when Chayefsky discovered that the actor chosen wasn't right. He called a friend, Robert Altman, who had just finished directing *Nashville*. Altman recommended Ned Beatty, who read for the producers and the director and was hired.

On December 21, 1975, two weeks before rehearsals were scheduled to begin, Peter Finch arrived in New York to do some preliminary homework on his role with Chayefsky. The two went to visit John Chancellor at the NBC studios in Rockefeller Center. Before a broadcast began, Chancellor asked the British actor if he wanted to sit in his chair and read from the TelePrompTer. To Chayefsky's delight, Finch said "Thank you" in his "Aussie" accent, sat down, and in flawless "American" began to read the newscast. "His effortless transformation surprised me," said Chancellor. "He was not only a magnificent actor, but I thought he had the qualities of presentation which would have made him an ideal choice for our business."

On January 3, 1976, rehearsals began in a drafty ballroom at the Diplomat Hotel at Forty-third Street and Sixth Avenue. "I remember another place we used was a club called Le Jardin, a hot disco of the time," said Melnick. "People would disco at night and we would go there in the daytime. The first morning we went in, they left the sweepings on the side of the dance floor. Hundreds of crushed amyl nitrate capsules were piled up, which should give you some sense of the time and place. It smelled like an old gym."

When the rehearsals began, Chayefsky and Lumet told the actors they would welcome suggestions and ideas on the script and that they should feel free to improvise, "until we nailed it into place."

"*Network* was the only film I ever did that no one touched the script, because it was almost as if it were written in verse," said Faye Dunaway.

"It was exciting stuff, the script had incredible lines," said Melnick. "My favorite one, which I find myself using on occasion today, is when William Holden tells Faye—who is suggesting a romantic relationship—that 'You don't understand, I'm closer to the end than the beginning.' Paddy's insights and the use of language was extraordinary."

Voltaire, Chekhov, and Dostoyevski were writers who had the passion to take a moral stand, Peter Finch remarked at the time, and Chayefsky had some of that. "Paddy has something I call divine madness. There's a manic quality in his work that I adore." The dialogue in films is usually "monosyllabic—with no language with which you can manipulate thought," the actor continued. "In *Network*, though, I have long speeches that truly get to the heart of emotions—and of politics. It's very powerful."

William Holden agreed that the script was "simply the best" he had read in years. But like James Garner in *The Americanization of Emily*, Holden had some initial difficulty delivering his lines properly. "Paddy uses an entirely different pattern in approaching his subject matter," said Holden. "I'm not speaking of complicated words. I'm speaking of the structure of his writing."

Lumet said that Holden was "sort of overwhelmed by the honesty of the script. He was also not aware that his role was going to take so much out of him. I think he thought, compared to Peter and Faye, that his part was simpler, that of an older leading man. Then once we started rehearsals, and he saw the process that was going on, he was kind of stunned."

Unlike Finch and Dunaway, Holden had very little stage experience. His technique had been refined through acting in movies. At one point in rehearsals he went to Chayefsky and asked if he could change his lines. The writer gave his permission. A few days later Holden returned to Chayefsky and asked if he could go back to the original script. "What happens is that in rehearsal, you're still your individual self," said Chayefsky. "Then, as you get to know the character and make him your own, the lines begin to seem natural and right."

By the start of the second week, as the dialogue became easier, Holden had to be coaxed into infusing some attendant passion. "Bill never made eye contact," said Lumet. "He was always looking at either side of the actor he was talking to. When we went through the last scene with Faye, where he decides to leave her, I said, 'Bill, lock in on her. Get hold of her eyes and lock in on her.' He did, and the wealth of emotion that came pouring out of him was blinding. At which point I said 'O.K., don't do it again until we're shooting.' I knew that he was a very private man, and if we used that constant exposure, if he did it too often, it would eventually make him feel defensive or he'd retreat and start hiding it again."

By week two of rehearsals, Chayefsky felt that things were going too well. He had the perfect cast, the perfect director; they were scheduled to begin production the following week with everything already locked in to place. So where was the *tsouris* he needed to keep him on his toes. On day three, week two, it came.

In his previous movies and plays, Chayefsky had avoided scenes of overt affection. For *Network*, however, in pace with the liberated times, three scenes of explicit sex were written for the Diana Christensen character. The first had her in bed, watching Howard Beale on TV, while a young man was "fondling, fingering, noddling and nuzzling with the clear intention of mounting her," said Chayefsky. "Knock it off," says Diana, preferring instead to watch Beale's broadcast. The second scene came after her triumphant speech at the network convention in Los Angeles. Unable to descend after the high of the convention, Diana scouts for sex in a gay bar. Catching the eye of a male stud with his shirt unbuttoned to the waist she says, "You go both ways?" He nods. "How much?" she asks. "Fifty bucks." "Let's go," she says. Cut to her hotel-room bed. She is staring at the ceiling, with tears streaming down her face, as the stud services her.

By the time the shooting script was completed the first of these scenes had been refined and the second was cut. A third sequence was extended. It began as a weekend rendezvous between Diana and Max Schumacher (William Holden). Driving to East Hampton, Diana talks TV business nonstop. She's about to "steal" a package of James Bond movies (from United Artists) for the network. In a series of shots in East Hampton, on the beach, through dinner at a local restaurant, entering a motel room, and then undressing, she keeps talking of her ambitious programming plans, until, fully naked, in bed, she sits on top of Max, when, grinding away and crying out about ratings, she climaxes.

During the second week in January, Melnick was in California when he received a call from Chayefsky and Howard Gottfried. "We have to replace Dunaway," they told him. "Why? What do you mean?" he said. "She refuses to do the nudity scene," they answered.

"That scene was pivotal to her character," said Gottfried. "It was never written as a sexual scene. It just so happened that was the only way she was turned on, by talking about business, about TV ratings. Paddy felt the only way to show that was physically."

"Faye was nervous," said Lumet. "She had never done this before. To show an orgasm is tough. And whatever tough time she was having, what about Bill Holden, who was going to be nude and lying under her?"

Network was no *Deep Throat,* Holden commented. Their sex scene was not meant to be pornographic. "It was a valid scene, a confirmation of the weirdness of Diana's character."

"Absolutely," said Lumet, "that scene said it all. She has the orgasm over the TV ratings, not because she's sitting on his cock."

During their initial talks with Dunaway, the producers had been very meticulous about explaining to her that there was nudity. "She said that wasn't a problem, as long as it was done in good taste, and all the rest of that," said Melnick. "Then when the scene came up in rehearsals she changed her mind."

"She really put us on the spot," said Gottfried. "Production was supposed to start the next week. So Paddy and I told Melnick that we wanted to fire her and find a replacement right away."

Melnick told Chayefsky and Gottfried that he didn't want to replace Dunaway, "as long as there was a chance that we didn't have to." He flew into New York and met with the actress. "We spoke at great length. I reminded her that she had agreed to do that scene. I told her, 'You signed on for it—we made our plans on this.' She had some terrific fights with Sidney and Paddy and Howard," said Melnick.

"There weren't any fights," said Lumet. "Just arguments, with me saying, 'It has to be, Faye, it has to be.' And her saying, 'I can't, Sidney, I can't.' "

"Faye loved Paddy," said Gottfried, "but she wouldn't budge on this. So I called her agent, Sue Mengers, and said: 'Sue, believe me, Faye is out of the picture. She is getting fired. We are not kidding.' Sue gave her hell. So did her lawyer."

With the additional threat of being liable for the costs if the production shut down while a replacement was sought, Dunaway began to relent. "We played brinkmanship," said Melnick.

"Faye was a game-player. She wanted to see how far she could go," said Gottfried. "I told her, 'You won't see anything graphic in that scene. You can look at the dailies. You can look at the final cut.' " Finally, "very graciously," Dunaway relented. "You know, I'm probably wrong. I'm probably scared. I'm sure it will be O.K.," she told Melnick. "The irony came later," he said, "when she got the Oscar for playing that part."

On January 19, 1976, filming on *Network* began in Toronto at the CFTO-TV studios. Chayefsky had previously discussed using TV studios in New York and Los Angeles, but they were all tied up. Then a letter arrived from the Toronto company offering their studios. "We went up there," said Lumet. "It was a gigantic television plant, with superb studio space and modern equipment, which they put at our disposal. We didn't know how good their technicians would be, but they turned out to be sensational."

For the opening scene, when Howard Beale announces his suicide plans on TV, the broadcast was shot live on one floor, while three floors above, Lumet had another unit shooting the reaction of the technicians and actors in the control room. The economy and momentum of the dual filming was appreciated by Chayefsky, but not the clarity of the performances.

"Paddy had very definite ideas on how certain scenes should be played, and in a few specific instances they differed with Sidney's," said Gottfried. "This was the first instance. The way Paddy wrote that opening scene: Peter Finch is on TV, he announces he's going to blow his brains out the following night but the people in the control room aren't listening to him. Paddy's vision of that was clear as crystal. The people in the control room aren't paying attention or even watching Finch. The A.D. [assistant director] is sitting there talking to the technical director; the producer is standing against the wall, feeling up his secretary. Everybody is doing his own thing."

Lumet's concept was to play that scene with frantic energy. "He wanted the actors to react immediately, to get hysterical when Finch says he's going to kill himself," said Gottfried. "Which was completely contrary to how Paddy saw it. It was a volatile issue for a while, but Sidney went with Paddy's way. He honored his vision."

And Chayefsky respected Lumet. "Sidney has a peerless sense of authenticity, and we had a grotesque story," the writer said. "I knew that Sidney would make it look real."

For the broadcasts of the "Howard Beale Show," as refurbished by the Dunaway character, Lumet brought in art director Phil Rosenberg to design the elaborate revolving set. To enhance and further exaggerate the dramatic impact of Beale's fervid TV sermons, a circular panel of stained glass was set at the rear of the set. The celestial shafts of light that beamed down on him during his manic ravings were created by cinematographer Owen Roizman. "In preproduction we had many discussions on the lighting and the visuals for the movie," said Lumet. Over the course of the picture it was their intention to "corrupt the camera," he said. "That's what *Network* is about, corruption. So we began the movie in absolutely naturalistic style with Bill Holden and Peter Finch. By the end of the movie, where Faye and the rest of the executives are sitting in Bob Duvall's office, it looks like a Ford commercial. That was done gradually. And only Bill Holden's character was kept in the naturalistic light."

One of the reasons the Howard Beale broadcasts worked so well on the screen, Chayefsky felt, was because the audiences could see how the TV show was being done. "We had these two huge TV cameras circling like modernistic dinosaurs, lifting and dipping and zooming in on Peter Finch as he delivered his broadcasts, while in the bleachers there were about three hundred extras listening to his every word."

There was another authentic touch provided from the old days of TV. "It was hilarious," said Lumet. "Off to the side of the stage you could see these two fat stagehands pushing the turntable for the revolving set. It was this crude mechanical way of doing things, which we had in TV in the early days, and probably still do."

In Toronto, when asked how he managed to master the energy and volume of his galvanic speeches, Peter Finch confided his secret to his co-star William Holden. Each evening at his hotel, after sending his wife and small children out of the suite, the actor locked himself in the bathroom and practiced his dialogue. "Then the maids come in to turn the beds down and they hear this man ranting and going berserk in the bathroom. They think I'm absolutely insane."

Searching for the core of his character, Finch admitted, there were moments when he was afraid. "Every role you pick looks marvelous, but then the fear sets in. This role I found particularly difficult. Paddy and I sat in this bar until four A.M. He told me that if my character were a raving lunatic and nothing more, then he would be a bore. There had to be a suggestion that he was eminently sane underneath the madness, and that he did, in fact, have a kind of revelation. That's a very thin edge to play."

Faye Dunaway said that she also sought the writer's help. "My character was in fact a murderess. But what intrigued me was why, and how she did that, and what she was giving up of her own personal soul. Paddy and I talked about that. The challenge was to infuse it with a moment here and a moment there that gave you the sense that she was a human being." And because of the "no vulnerability" edict set up by Lumet at the outset, Dunaway had to insert these moments on the sly. "I had to sneak it in," said Faye, "to do it very, very obliquely."

"Very, very, *very* obliquely," Lumet agreed. "And one expects that from an actress of Faye's caliber. She is an artist who puts her entire heart and soul into the characters she plays, so she never stops giving."

Filming was right on schedule when the company moved to New York City. Interior scenes were filmed at a number of locations: a bar near the Warwick Hotel, the New York Public Library at Forty-second Street and Fifth Avenue, Elaine's restaurant, and the Althorp co-op apartment building on the Upper West Side. For the balance of the newsroom scenes, a set was built in a vacant store on Fifty-sixth Street, with the bulk of the office and executive boardroom sequences filmed inside the MGM Building on Sixth Avenue. Across the street from MGM was the Office Pub, where the actors and the producers invariably spent their lunch hours. "They were worth more to me than my salary," said Gottfried. "There was Bill Holden, Peter Finch, sometimes Bobby Duvall, and Paddy and I. Sidney never came, because he took naps during his lunch hours. And Faye liked to stay in her trailer, going over her next scenes."

The lunches at the Office Pub consisted of the group swapping jokes and telling stories of their varied backgrounds. "The beauty of it all was that you had Paddy and myself, who were both brought up in the Bronx," said Gottfried. "You had Bill Holden, this major old-time Hollywood movie star. He would talk about Duke and Spence—John Wayne and Spencer Tracy— who were his buddies and our idols. He was not putting on airs, just reminiscing, sharing these wonderful stories of the old days. And then there was Peter

Finch, who was born in Australia and worked with all the major theatre people in England, including Laurence Olivier, and had affairs with these incredible women, including Vivien Leigh and Shirley Bassey. Paddy, who had a million stories of his own, just reveled in all this."

Chayefsky and Lumet had their second disagreement during the filming of the exteriors for the "mad as hell" sequence. When Howard Beale tells his viewers to open their windows and take to the streets in protest, the director had planned a variety of reaction shots. He wanted to have people standing on street corners, and cabdrivers sticking their heads out of cars, screaming, "I'm mad as hell, and I'm not going to take it anymore."

"I wanted to do a hundred things," Lumet said. "I had twelve or fourteen locations already picked out. I wanted to shoot it in two nights, not one. By getting as many reactions as possible, I could build the scene higher." "But Paddy wouldn't have anything to do with that," said Gottfried. "He stopped the show. He wanted the scene shot as he wrote it, with less drama."

The tight restriction on the budget also had a lot to do with that, Lumet surmised. "Paddy as a producer was always a good man with a buck. He didn't want to spend the money on it. He wanted the scene shot in one night and not two. I lost. He won. It was simple as that."

The critical sex scene between Faye Dunaway and William Holden was scheduled for last. "We did that deliberately, because we wanted to get everything out of the way first," said Gottfried. The day before the shoot, he was called to Dunaway's dressing room. "I went to her trailer and Faye is in there with her lawyer. He hands me a sheet of paper to sign. On it it says there will be 'no nipples' shown in the scene. And that she had to see the dailies and the final cut too. I signed it. And as I'm leaving her trailer, Faye says to her lawyer, 'Well, I guess we lost that one.' Which showed what a little devil she could be."

The setup scenes were filmed on the beach and outside a motel in East Hampton. The motel room was duplicated in a small studio on Manhattan's West Side. The set was closed. Only essential personnel were on hand, which by Dunaway's request did not include the writer or the producer. "Believe me, neither Paddy nor I wanted to see Faye's tits," said Gottfried.

There would be *no* breast shots of Dunaway sitting on top of William Holden, the actress was assured during her makeup session that morning. "I explained exactly how I was going to shoot the scene," said Lumet. "We would open with a high shot of the two in bed, then the camera would dolly in behind her. I assured her that the bedsheet would be high enough that we would see no crack of the ass. As we moved in closer, her arm would be at such an angle it would cover her breast. And during filming we stuck to that agreement. I would not violate it, because among other things, Faye had to play the scene. It wouldn't have been good, much less funny, if there was so much tension she couldn't act."

Holden received scant attention. "Talk about an actor being used," said Lumet. "He had to lie there under Faye, and was not allowed to say a word, or act anything. I don't think I even made a reaction shot of him."

Filming on *Network* came in under schedule and under budget. To celebrate, Chayefsky and Gottfried hosted a wrap party at Sardi's. William Holden arrived with Stefanie Powers; Peter Finch was with his wife, Eletha; and Sidney Lumet brought his wife, Gail. Paddy Chayefsky came stag. This was the best work experience he had had since the stage production of *The Tenth Man*, he told Finch and Holden. The sentiment was repeated to Sidney Lumet. "Paddy said that this was only the second time in his career that the original vision of his work was realized. The first was with Tyrone Guthrie on *The Tenth Man*, and now, with me on *Network*. I took this as an enormous compliment." The director also hoped the relationship would endure during the editing to follow.

Eric Albertson, who had worked on *The Hospital*, recalled seeing Chayefsky at this stage. "I was working on 'Kojak' as the supervising editor, and one day I let Sidney and Alan Heim, his editor, use my cutting room. Paddy came in with them and I remember smiling to myself as he began to dictate certain things he wanted from them. But Sidney was a master. He not only knew actors, he knew story. And he knew how to handle Paddy."

By then, there was a high level of trust between them, Lumet said. "I did the editing with Alan. He showed the first rough cut to Paddy, who made some notes. I went back, made some more cuts. And then, towards the end, before we went into mix, I felt we were a little bit long, that we could pop out lines here and there. And since I knew how precious the dialogue was to him, I said, 'Paddy, come up to the cutting room. Come sit at the Moviola and let's see what we can trim.' So he was there for that, for the tiny trims which can get you off two to three minutes."

The MGM/UA brass were nervous when they saw the first cut of *Network*. Prior to this they asked Chayefsky to eliminate the copious swear words the TV executives used. He downplayed this request until after the first viewing of the rough cut, when a company aide delivered a memo to him on which was noted how many times the words "Jesus," "goddamn," "Chrissake," "holy shit," "son of a bitch," "ass," "fuck," "schmuck," and "bastard" were used. Those words were all relevant to the characters, Paddy insisted. Network executives always cursed like troopers. Later he would regret not yielding. "I overdid it. I wanted to cut some of them out, and I didn't, and I'm sorry I didn't," he told John Brady.

The studio also persisted in trying to persuade Chayefsky to give them a "softer" ending. They felt that the audience for *Network* would be much larger if the movie ended at the point where Max Schumacher split with Diana Christensen and returned to his wife. To take the film further and show Peter Finch being assassinated before a live audience was not only immoral, it would repel a large segment of mainstream ticket buyers. "There was always a lot of stuff about the ending," said Lumet. " 'How can we allow this? It's crazy. It's wild. And so on and so forth.' I was nervous too at first. I wondered if the audiences would buy it. The way that Paddy wrote it, the assassination occurs, then we cut to the control room, where it is seen on the monitor. There's a freeze-frame and we go to a commercial. After I shot it, I sat down with someone who works extensively on TV commercials. We decided to wrap up the ending like a commercial, with very fast cuts to different monitors. It was a tough stylistic problem, but like Paddy, my answer to those problems was not to back off but to go further into them. When it was all put together and I saw it, I knew we were in hog heaven, that it would be a powerhouse."

The first screening before an audience was in San Francisco and, according to Lumet, it was "glorious. It worked right off the bat. They were screaming." A second screening was held in Los Angeles, in a packed theatre in Westwood. On hand were selected members of the out-of-town press. The mood was one of alertness and connection. They paid special attention to the scene where Max Schumacher tells Diana that if he doesn't leave her he'll be destroyed: "Like Howard Beale was destroyed. Like everything you and the whole institution of television touch gets destroyed! War, murder, death are all the same to you as bottles of beer. . . . You are madness incarnate, Diana, virulent madness, and whatever you touch dies with you."

"That's telling 'em, Paddy, old boy," said the *Washington Post* critic Tom Shales, as the theatre erupted into wild applause.

Chayefsky knew that the real test would come from "the hard-assed critics in New York." On October 26, 1976, the first public showing took place in the Paramount Theatre, in the Gulf & Western Building on Manhattan's West Side at Columbus Circle. "Audiences stomped their feet and erupted into uninhibited cheers and whistles," said the columnist Earl Wilson. The following week the balance of the national press, along with radio, TV, and college newspaper reporters, were brought to New York to see the film and to talk with the stars and filmmakers.

At ten A.M., after a screening the night before, a press conference was held at Shepheard's, an East Side nightclub. Gathered on stage were Sidney Lumet, William Holden, Peter Finch, Paddy Chayefsky, and Howard Gottfried. Arriving an hour late, making an entrance "worthy of Garbo," was Faye Dunaway. After kissing everybody on the dais, the star sat down and the conference began. William Holden, when asked why a nice guy like his character would fall in love with such an immoral woman as Diana Christensen, paraphrased the old saying: "When a man gets an erection, his brains slide into his backside." Amid gasps and chuckles, Holden added dryly, "I hope, just for the marvelous experience of living, that has happened to you." Faye Dunaway, when asked whether her portrayal of the ambitious but malevolent Diana would upset feminists, sighed, "Ah . . . the feminist number." If after fighting for years to get out of stereotypical, traditional roles, feminists now objected to actresses playing "women who are *not* wonderful, I think that is hypocritical," the actress replied.

Writer-producer Chayefsky, wearing a navy pea-jacket and smoking a pipe, "all of which make him resemble a cross between a satyr and a sea captain," said one reporter, told the gathering that his film was "an affectionate satire." He had many friends in the TV industry: anchors and executives he considered "incorruptible." This movie was not directed at them, he said, but at "those decision-makers who are part of a larger corporation." He also wanted to stress that the inference in the ending of *Network*, "that a corporation will even kill as a normal, everyday executive decision," was a sardonic point. That was the license of a satirist, to take what is true and proceed with it to its logical finish. Furthermore, if he had made a film about General Motors or U.S. Steel or the Teamsters Union, he didn't think anyone would been compelled to say, "Hey, Paddy, come on! You don't really think that they would really consider murder just to ensure four million dollars' worth of profits!"

"Early rumors have it that the networks don't know whether to kill Chayefsky or thank him for all those suggestions on how to jazz up their network news shows," said reporter Allan Wolper of the *Soho Weekly News* after a second screening and press conference. Nothing "traumatic" had happened to him in television, Chayefsky told this group. He had not written the film out of rancor. His rage was not against television, his rage was against "the dehumanization of people."

"At that point, Paddy stopped kidding himself. And the audience," said Wolper. Where are the good TV documentaries? Chayefsky asked. Where are the splendid TV correspondents like Edward R. Murrow, who knew what a news story was and how to follow it up? "There is no such thing as objective journalism on television," Chayefsky told Wolper later at lunch. "It is impossible to maintain objectivity on television news. They always get blandness, not objectivity. You put a camera in front of a cop and suddenly the crook becomes 'a perpetrator.' A newspaper reporter can just go over and ask, 'Hey, what the fuck happened?' "

When the matter of advance screening was first discussed at MGM/UA, studio executives suggested that it would be best if the critics from the major TV news shows not be invited until a few days before the official opening.

"The fear was that if we let anyone in TV see the movie early on they would run back and tell their bosses that we were saying some very nasty things about their business," said Chayefsky. He told MGM he had nothing to hide or to fear from people in TV. "Let 'em see the film upfront, with everyone else," he said, hosting a special showing for Walter Cronkite and others in New York. On the West Coast another screening was held for old friends and foes in the medium. "This is not a satire, it's a documentary," said Norman Lear. Gore Vidal agreed: "I've heard every line from that film in real life."

Obviously the intention to rattle the cages within the corporate branch of the TV industry worked. "In Los Angeles, network executives watching a screening of the movie were on the edge of their seats, almost clawing at the armrests in indignation," said *Time*. As news of the movie circulated through the rest of the broadcasting world, the press offices of MGM on both coasts were besieged with requests from other TV personnel to see the film. At the same time, editors of every major magazine and newspaper instructed their reporters to get in there and cover the fray.

On November 14, a full month before the film was to open nationally, some New York critics, eager to beat the rest of the competition, jumped the date with their reviews. "A blazing, blistering indictment of television by the brilliant probing mind of Paddy Chayefsky," said the *Daily News* critic, Rex Reed. On the same page, the paper's TV editor Kay Gardella wrote that the film was much more than a bilious attack. "It is a remarkably incisive movie, brilliantly conceived, which sustains an artistic perception of network television that is both outrageously funny and, with a good stretch of the imagination, quite believable."

In the weeks that followed, the rave reviews from the New York press piled up, with a few negative slams on the side: "Pedestrian plot and shopworn prose," said John Simon. "Patriarchal Jacqueline Susann," said Pauline Kael. "There were some snotty notices," said Gottfried, "but they didn't matter. Nothing could stop this movie because by the time *Network* was released it was a national event."

For their part, some film critics employed by the major TV networks chose to downplay the release of the Chayefsky movie. Gene Shalit of NBC said he was "unfamiliar with the subject matter, which I guess makes me even with Paddy." "That man is a professional clown," said Chayefsky, describing most TV critics as "frustrated actors who try to be cute in ninety seconds." *Women's Wear Daily* ably led off its coverage with quotes from the major real-life TV anchors. Walter Cronkite said it was "a fantasy burlesque . . . an amusing divertissement but nothing more. I'm not sure whether Paddy Chayefsky, who is a personal friend of mine, had his tongue in his cheek or not." Edwin Newman of NBC thought it was not a true representation of TV, and found the movie itself incompetent. "I've rarely seen a drunk scene worse than the one that opened the film," said Newman. Harry Reasoner of ABC, who had refused to allow Lumet and Chayefsky to use footage of him in their opening and closing monitor scenes, said that the last movie he saw was *The Best Years of Our Lives*, thirty years before, so he was skipping *Network*. Barbara Walters of ABC News, whose recent $1 million contract was half paid by the network's entertainment division, said she was troubled because the movie might lead the public to believe that television news was on par with "show business."

In *The Washington Post*, Tom Shales also gathered some choice bites for his coverage. He quoted Paul Friedman, the producer of the "Today" show, as saying that *Network* was "heavy-handed and outrageous." Friedman thought "it would be a shame if it were a big hit, because it gives a distorted picture of people who work in television." The medium was not as powerful as Chayefsky thought it was, the producer said, and he feared that "the incredible inferiority and hate complex on the part of the people in the print media" would capitalize on this. Barbara Walters repeated her concern to Shales, saying that the exaggerated story of *Network* was "the result of Paddy Chayefsky's bitterness toward what happened to him in television."

"I've never had any bitter experiences in television," said Chayefsky, surprised that Walters didn't like his movie, because he was "just saying terrific things about her." ("She has no malice," he said. "She pushes just hard enough to get the answers.")

Walters told Shales she feared that the Chayefsky movie would harm the image of TV broadcasting, and that there would never be "that kind of show-biz approach to the news" that *Network* portrayed. "We've been accused of that, but it could never happen, because we will never let it happen," she said. "If anything, the entertainment side of television is more respectful of the news side now than at any other time in the past."

Laughing uproariously, John Chancellor said he had not seen the movie, but had read the script. "It's about an anchorman who goes crazy, isn't it?" he asked. "And isn't there a marvelous scene where the woman programming executive sort of rapes the head of the news division?"

In early December, as an advance holiday present, MGM's press department distributed fifty thousand bumper stickers reading I'M MAD AS HELL to the public. Audiences responded by jamming movie theatres across the country to see *Network*. At the end of the month, when the reviewers compiled their annual Top Ten lists, the movie was voted number one by many. At the New York Film Critics party at Sardi's, Chayefsky showed up and was photographed lodged between his old friend, a "squealing" Elizabeth Taylor, and Robert Redford (the object of her squeals).

The competition for Oscar nominations would be tough; Chayefsky knew that. Along with the other strong films in the race—including *Rocky, All the President's Men,* and *Taxi Driver*—his two male co-stars in *Network* would be competing against each other. "Bill Holden loved and respected Peter Finch," said Howard Gottfried, "but this was Bill's last shot, and he would have loved that final Oscar." When Finch was asked by MGM to step down to the supporting category, he refused. Howard Beale was not a secondary role, he said, and furthermore he wanted that leading nomination. "We're all so dreadfully egocentric in this business," the actor candidly told reporter David Barry of *Women's Wear Daily.* "The nomination lets people know you're there—for a moment at least."

After doing an estimated two hundred interviews with domestic and foreign press over a three-month period, on the morning of January 14, 1977, Finch walked the one and a half miles from his new home in Benedict Canyon to the Beverly Hills Hotel, where he was to meet Sidney Lumet. The two were to appear on a TV news show. While waiting for Lumet in the lobby, Finch suddenly moaned and fell to the floor, suffering a heart attack. "I was walking down the staircase towards him," Lumet recalled. "Peter was sitting on the banquette, and I saw him go right over. I ran over and started to give him mouth-to-mouth resuscitation. I didn't know what [the problem] was, but it was clear he was in deep trouble."

Within two minutes, the L.A. medics were there. "But he was gone as they put him into the ambulance," said Lumet. He packed up and headed back to his family in New York. William Holden, Paddy Chayefsky, Howard Gottfried, and David Tebet of NBC had dinner that night at the Palm Restaurant in Los Angeles. The mood was solemn, until Chayefsky reminded the group that Finch would rather they mourn "in merriment rather than sadness." "And before you knew it," said Tebet, "our talk turned into a vicious tirade against the film business and how it could kill a man like Finchie. But Paddy Chayefsky said, 'You can't blame the business. It's what we do to ourselves. We're all impulsive and neurotic about it.' " Intent on lifting the congregated spirits, Chayefsky added, "But you know something, in spite of all that, it's better than threading pipe."

Three weeks later, both Peter Finch's and William Holden's names appeared on the nomination list for Best Actor. *Network* in total received ten nominations, including Best Director, Best Picture, and Best Original Screenplay.

"To me the Academy Awards are like trying to catch lightning in a bottle," said Lumet, who along with Chayefsky and Gottfried attended the proliferation of Oscar parties that preceded the big night in Hollywood. "I didn't know what was going to happen," the director continued. "I figured we'd catch some, because we were up for so many. I was pretty sure about the script and Faye. Then out there, going to the parties, and all of that, it got to be quite heady. You start to believe everything. And Paddy, talk about being prescient, when I said to him, 'Hey, I think we're going to win because everybody keeps coming up to me, saying, "I voted for you," ' he said, 'Sidney, I'm nervous about that *Rocky.*"

The ceremonies were held at the Dorothy Chandler Pavilion on March 29. Peter Finch's widow, Eletha, wearing a mink stole and corsage, mingled in the lobby with Chayefsky. Faye Dunaway arrived with her rock-star husband, Peter Wolf. On stage the alternating TV hosts were Richard Pryor, Jane Fonda, and Warren Beatty. During the first hour *Network* failed to win anything. Then, at the top of the second hour, Sylvester Stallone announced the Best Supporting Actress category. Competing against Jodie Foster for *Taxi Driver* and Piper Laurie for *Carrie,* Beatrice Straight won for *Network.* In her speech she thanked Chayefsky, "who writes what we all feel but cannot express." *Network* then lost for Film Editing to *Rocky,* and for Cinematography to *Bound for Glory.* Before announcing the writing awards, Norman Mailer launched into a story about Voltaire patronizing a gay whorehouse of long ago. "Once a philosopher, twice a pervert," Mailer commented, then read off the nominees for Best Original Screenplay, including Lina Wertmüller for *Seven Beauties,* Walter Bernstein for *The Front,* Paddy Chayefsky for *Network,* and Sylvester Stallone for *Rocky.* The winner: "Paddy Chayefsky . . . for *Network.*"

Chayefsky spoke briefly, accepting his statue, "in the name of all us perverts," then moved backstage. A short time later, he was back to accept the Best Actor award for Peter Finch. "For some obscure reason, I'm up here accepting an award for Peter Finch, or Finchie, as everybody who knew him called him," he said. "There's only one person who should accept this award—Mrs. Peter Finch. Are you in the house, Eletha? C'mon up and get your award."

After delivering an eloquent speech, Eletha Finch was ushered off by Chayefsky, who was ambushed in the wings by the awards show's director, William Friedkin. Prior to the broadcast, Chayefsky had been told not to bring Finch's widow onstage, because Friedkin didn't want any depressing "boo-hooing." It was a spontaneous gesture; he never planned to do it, Paddy said innocently. Later that evening he would reveal that he had not only planned to call Eletha Finch onto the stage, he had written her acceptance speech. "Friedkin said he didn't want any sentimentality and I didn't want to get in a fight," Chayefsky explained. "So I said I'd do it his way—but I figured if Peter won, I'd call on Eletha to accept. I thought this is what movies are all about—'This is Mrs. Norman Maine.' "

CHAPTER 31

Behind Closed Doors

In his Oscar acceptance speech for *Network*, Chayefsky had remarked that as a rule he never spoke in public about his private feelings, "but I think it's time that I acknowledge two people who I could never really thank properly or enough. My wife, Susie, and my son, Danny." Afterward, however, at the Governor's Ball, those well-wishers who sought an introduction to his family were disappointed. Chayefsky's wife and son were not in California with him. On this, his big night, his escort was his lawyer, Maurice Spanbock.

Chayefsky had invited his son to the awards ceremony, but he was in college, and furthermore he said he wasn't equipped to handle the onslaught of attention his father received at such events. Susan Chayefsky was also a very private person, her husband explained. She was uncomfortable in the spotlight. "That's understandable," said Arthur Penn. "There's something about not liking the limelight, but what about coming out in the daylight?"

Others noted that Susan Chayefsky hadn't been seen in public with her husband for years. "Paddy went everywhere by himself," said David Shaw. "I have no idea what the trouble was. He was very private about it. He always said he loved Susie very much and that was all that was ever mentioned."

Why should she choose to be a part of his professional life? That was another consensus. Chayefsky had made it clear to his wife years before that his work came first, before her, before everything. "The hostility between those two was enough to light up the city. It goes back a long time," said Penn. "There's nothing like a woman scorned."

The precedence of the work over her was only part of the problem, for Susan Chayefsky's behavior at this stage exceeded what could be considered that of a shy, retiring woman. She was said to be suffering from a psychological disorder called agoraphobia, a chronic fear of public places. When left untreated, it could lead to physical symptoms and even paralysis.

According to the medical experts, two thirds or more of agoraphobics are women who have been emotionally or physically abused at an early age. Those components certainly existed in Susan Chayefsky's childhood. She came from a family system where her feelings were ignored and her attempts to establish her worth were crudely discouraged. Shamed when she attempted to display her skills, she learned to become self-effacing, and to rely on altruism to bolster her lack of self-esteem. When her own needs and emotions required attention it was easy to dismiss or deny them, because they had never been acknowledged before. After her marriage, when a genuine force offered help or encouragement, it was too late, because by then the process of retreat and acute paranoia had begun.

Susan Chayefsky's first known inclination toward withdrawal came during the early years of her marriage. In 1951, when Paddy was invited to visit Elia and Molly Kazan in California to work on his play, Susan refused to accompany him. She became sick when she traveled, she said, urging Paddy to go on his own. He handled the situation calmly that time, explaining with humor that even Sigmund Freud had a morbid fear of travel and hated trains. As Chayefsky became successful and socially desirable his wife's preparatory rituals began to dominate and undermine the actual social events. Invited to a dinner or even an informal gathering, Susan Chayefsky would spend hours, sometimes days, getting ready. It was no longer an issue of being perfectly turned out, of having gloves that weren't creased like Jacqueline Kennedy's. Mrs. Chayefsky's entire appearance had to be checked and rechecked before she left the apartment. And Paddy, who considered a pressed suit and a close shave—*sans* specks of toilet paper applied to dry up the nicks—to be good grooming, was said to be "climbing the walls" at his wife's obsessiveness. One night, pulling up outside a theatre for the opening night of a friend's play, Susan Chayefsky suddenly became ill and couldn't get out of the car. At a subsequent awards banquet, fearful that the other guests were staring and ridiculing her appearance, she panicked and had to be taken home. In time, Chayefsky stopped insisting that his wife accompany him. At the public dinners and parties, his excuse to inquiring friends was that his wife was "feeling under the weather." After a while, people stopped asking.

In the mid-1960s, concurrent with the decline of Chayefsky's career, his wife's reclusiveness abated somewhat. She traveled with him to Europe, then joined him when their son was bar mitzvahed in Israel. She also went to the Newburgh house on summer weekends, where she appeared to get on well with his blue-collar friends. For a while Susan Chayefsky also allowed his urban poker pals to converge on their apartment. Those gatherings were short-lived, however. Accustomed to ordering in "Chinese or deli," and dining from cardboard containers, the players became uncomfortable when, striving for social perfection, Susan Chayefsky insisted on having the meals for the poker games catered, replete with fine linen and silver.

Howard Gottfried recalled that in the early years of the 1970s he and his wife dined out on occasion with Paddy and Susan Chayefsky. "My wife was pregnant at the time and Susie shared her experiences with her," said Gottfried. "She liked the idea of being the senior one, of giving advice to a younger woman." At the Carnegie Deli one evening, Chayefsky came in and told Herbie Schlein, the maître d', that he wanted him to meet someone. "We went out to the street and there was a limo parked at the curb. He opened the back door and said, 'This is Susie, my wife.' " Years later, after Chayefsky's death, when Schlein was ill, he said he was surprised when Susan Chayefsky called him, offering medical advice and financial assistance. "We became very close," said Schlein in 1991, ten years after Chayefsky's death. "Today Mrs. Chayefsky is one of the dearest, sweetest, most supportive people in my life." That support, however, was never rendered in person. Their relationship for the entire duration was conducted solely by telephone.

"It is strange, isn't it?" Gwen Verdon commented. "Through all the years that I've known Susie, I've seen her five times at the most. The rest of the time we've spoken on the phone, which is always great, because Susie is witty and sounds just like Jean Arthur."

During the mid-1970s, when Ann Reinking was with Bob Fosse, she was one of the few who was allowed access to Susan Chayefsky. She and Fosse visited the Chayefskys when they were staying at the Navarro Hotel. "I was surprised by how pretty Susie was," said Reinking. "She had the kind of skin that doesn't need powder or makeup. She changed her hair color when I knew her. One time she was blond and the next time she was brunette." Reinking also met their son. "He was a very gentle young man. Paddy cared for both of them very much. He was a good husband to Susie. I liked her. She was real easy to talk to. She would call on the phone a lot. My impression was that she had her own life, which from all appearances remained largely separate from Paddy's."

"I don't think anyone really could know what their relationship was," said Verdon. "Paddy adored Susie. But whether or not he was upset about the fact that she would never go anyplace with him, I honestly don't know, and I wouldn't presume to guess."

In November 1977, when the publicity campaign for *Network* was launched, "60 Minutes" wanted to profile Chayefsky, but he turned it down because it would have meant allowing the TV news team into his home. All other media requests to talk to or about his wife and son were also firmly declined. Even in casual conversation with friends, when the topic of his family was raised Chayefsky became uncharacteristically mute. If his wife's well-being was mentioned he gave one of two responses: "The same," or "Don't ask."

Susan Chayefsky's health had in fact declined considerably by this time. She had entered the secondary stage of her phobic condition, which was cyclical. Appearing calm and lucid for months, she could never predict when the panic would strike. One day in public she was suddenly overcome and went berserk in a telephone booth. The terror of future outings instinctively made her body shut down. She also suffered from severe muscle spasms which made her legs feel paralyzed. Dr. Milton Reder, who treated many celebrities, including Yul Brynner, was in his office one day when he received an emergency call from Paddy Chayefsky. His wife was lying on the floor of their living room, screaming in pain from her twisted, tortured legs, and she needed the doctor's immediate attention.

Perhaps because of Reder's publicized and controversial treatment, which consisted of daubing or injecting a cocaine-derived solution into the nostrils or into the affected area of the patient, it was rumored for a time that Susan Chayefsky's reclusiveness was due to her dependence on narcotics. This was inaccurate. Dr. Reder treated Mrs. Chayefsky for only a short time, and according to Dan Chayefsky his mother was opposed to drugs, to even "the taking of an aspirin." When asked why she or his father didn't seek professional help from any one of the specialists now available to treat the condition, Dan Chayefsky replied: "I don't think my mother saw herself as agoraphobic. She considered herself as private, reclusive. Also, in the earlier time, when she was making efforts, it was the days of psychoanalysis, not therapy. Both of my parents spent hundreds of years in analysis. It produced a lot of insights and a lot of tears in the office, but not much change."

Perhaps his father could have helped more, Dan Chayefsky added. "He could have given her more of a push out of the nest. By allowing her to become more and more isolated, he catered to her fears." Other sources said that Paddy Chayefsky made numerous attempts to get his wife to seek counseling, which she resisted with denial. Of the two, his father was more willing to change, Dan felt. "My father would say, 'What's the scariest thing I can do? What would be the most challenging, take the most courage?' " Susan Chayefsky was the opposite. In choosing to indulge her fears, the only way she could cope was to feel wounded and withdraw, while blaming others, especially her caretakers.

"I will never leave her," Chayefsky said of his cloistered wife, but whether or not his attachment was because of responsibility, loyalty, or his own generous portion of pathology was uncertain. In 1993, when asked about his parents' relationship, Dan Chayefsky said that there was genuine love between his parents but that it remained largely hidden under the dynamics of their relationship, which he never understood. "It's still an enigma to me," he said. "And I would think to anyone. They would wonder what degree was love, what degree was habit, what degree was anger—the addiction—and what degree was mutual dependence, and a simple fear of change."

The real tragedy, and the professional loss, was that Chayefsky the writer never used any of this material in his work, some of his associates stated. "Paddy was a writer who aspired to greatness, to be recognized as a serious playwright on a par with O'Neill and Arthur Miller," said producer Milton Perlman. "So why didn't he use his background more? O'Neill and Miller bared the deepest recesses of their personal lives in their work. Paddy revealed himself only in his frustration and anger at institutions and other people. The private aspect of his life was never exposed, which is a shame because the purpose of any artist is to grow."

But Chayefsky did use parts of his grim, unstable private life in his writing. Arthur Landau, the brittle, self-communing lawyer in *The Tenth Man,* was based on him; and Evelyn, the possessed girl, who described herself as "not a dangerous schizophrenic; I just hallucinate," could be compared to Susan Chayefsky, whose outbursts of alienation alternated with long periods of clarity and coherence. A further analogy could be found in *The Goddess* and *The Passion of Josef D.* In the latter, the character of Nadya, Stalin's wife, which Chayefsky admitted he fictionalized considerably, was a woman who sees only despair in the changing realities of life. Subject to strange seizures, one day she is found whimpering on her hands and knees in public. Chayefsky's Nadya apparently also enjoys her torment. Extremely moral people shatter easily, she tells Lenin during a critical passage in the play. She is aware that her husband is a boor and an assassin, but they are suited to each other, she says, because love is an act of terror and he "couldn't endure life alone any better than I."

Attendant to his attraction to the bizarre, what apparently enabled Chayefsky to cope and continue in this strange relationship was his ability to physically remove himself at times. When the situation became too tense he would leave and spend the night at Bob Fosse's apartment. During one prolonged, tumultuous spell, after their neighbors complained about the screaming to the building's management, Chayefsky moved out indefinitely. "He lived on his own for a while at the Navarro," said Howard Gottfried. There was also the luxury of the frequent business trips he took to Los Angeles and London. On those occasions he led an entirely different existence, a seemingly happy and carefree existence that his family knew very little of.

The collection of people who were part of Chayefsky's social circle was as varied as his two distinct personas. For Sidney, the serious intellectual, there were the evenings spent at the home of Robert Jastrow, a science writer. Following their astute analysis of current events, Chayefsky and Jastrow would retire to the music room, where they would perform classical duets. "I don't know what they played," said Herb Gardner, who was at one meeting, "but it sounded good to me." The author-historian Arthur Schlesinger, Jr., was also an academic confrere. "Paddy was a deeply if erratically cultivated man, endlessly curious, widely read in literature, history, science," said Schlesinger. "He would often come to our home. My wife and I introduced him to the Kennedys, to Jean and Steve Smith. Because Mrs. Chayefsky never went out, Paddy was a marvelous extra man, and would often be invited to dinners. His exuberant imagination and that elegant, irrepressible wit always made him a valuable addition to any group."

At the other end of the social stratum was Eddie White, a Damon Runyon–type character who wrote songs, produced records and concerts, and was friends with many sports figures, including Rocky Graziano and Jake La Motta. White used to meet Chayefsky at the Business Men's Club, a private health club located in the YMCA on West Sixty-third Street in Manhattan. Celebrity members included Jerry Stiller, Dan Rather, and Frank Gifford, but White had the locker next to Chayefsky's. "For a long time I didn't talk to him because I heard he was a difficult man to know," said White. One day, having no one else to bother, Chayefsky began to grill White about his background. His father was Max Rotheburg, also known as "Broadway Jack," a colorful minor gangster. "When he walked out on my mother she couldn't afford to keep us, so my younger sister and I were sent to live at the Hebrew Orphan Asylum in Harlem. When Paddy heard that he wanted to know every last detail."

The two became friends. White was naturally flattered, "because Paddy was so bright and I hadn't finished high school." Their common ground was their love of sports. "One day when we were talking about football, I told him he didn't know the difference between a middle linebacker and a squeeze play," said White. "And Paddy agreed. He didn't know. And he asked me what the difference was. I didn't know either. When it came to sports, we were really the gang that couldn't shoot straight."

Personal things were never divulged. White knew nothing about Chayefsky's family life, his long-term depression, or that he was taking medication. "He would talk about Dustin Hoffman seeing a shrink for so many years, but never about himself," said White. The usual topics on the agenda, after sports, were local crime and political skulduggery. White said he would sometimes have to yell for the chance to express an opinion. "Then Paddy would scream at me, 'Go ahead, shoot; let's hear it, Voltaire,' and I would forget what it was I wanted to say." Another favorite ploy of Chayefsky's, if they were with Bob Fosse or other friends, would be to instruct White to tell "the joke that you always fuck up." "He would make me so nervous," said White. "I'd screw up the line. The guy could be cruel. But later, if he felt he hurt my feelings, he'd call me up. He'd never apologize. He'd say something like 'Hey, Eddie, guess where I'm taking you tomorrow night. To a party at Elaine's.' "

There were also some impressive females among Chayefsky's friends. One of them was Lucille Ball. Every time he went to California, one of the first people he called was the famous redhead. In England, a regular partisan was Diana Rigg. A measure of Chayefsky's continuing regard for Rigg was that he used her first name for the female lead in *Network* and told her about it. Shortly after that, when Rigg was profiled for a cover story in *Time*, Chayefsky spoke about his "unending devotion" to her. "Diana's a very unusual lady. No hang-ups," he said. In return, Rigg said of him, "Paddy was always one of the kindest, nicest people I've ever met. And the funniest. And cleverest. When he came to London we would always have dinner." Of the speculation raised by one of the British tabloids that their friendship went beyond dinner, the actress delighted in her reply. "Well, we did have a very uncarnal, loving relationship. And it was always a highlight when he came into town and I saw him."

In New York, there were "a lot of women who were crazy about Paddy," said White, "and some of 'em wanted to get to know him better. But he never made a move on any of them."

Chayefsky had an innate respect for women, Ann Reinking believed. "He never talked down to you. When I first met him I was just a kid in the chorus. But he really liked what I did. He was very easy to talk to. You always got the sense that he appreciated you for who you were. After I got my first principal part on Broadway he started calling me 'Reinking.' Like a Hepburn, as if I had done something important."

"I can only tell you about parties, when Paddy would go with Bob [Fosse] and me," said Gwen Verdon. "These actresses would always flock around us, because they wanted *him*. They were always auditioning for him. And Paddy knew it."

"He *loved* the attention," said Howard Gottfried. "When he would go to California, for the Oscars or whatever, Paddy would disappear into his hotel room with his little black book. Then later, we'd be downstairs in the coffee shop or the Polo Lounge and the calls would begin to come in." Over the loudspeaker system Chayefsky's name would be paged every five minutes. He was his own best press agent, Gottfried said. "He would let a select core of people know he was in town. Part of it was that he didn't want to be alone. And the other part was, he loved being with stars. And they loved being with him. It wasn't just lip service. He was so bright, very funny, and very stimulating to be with. He had a very unique original personality. He could talk about anything, to anyone."

Making the rounds of pre–Academy Award parties for *Network*, Chayefsky drew a stellar group into his circle. "Warren Beatty, David Geffen, Barbra Streisand, they all gravitated towards Paddy," said Gottfried. "These people always wanted to get their clutches on him to write for them, to curry that kind of favor. And why not? You're only as good as your material. Streisand knew that. We went to her house in Beverly Hills at least twice. She wanted him to write *anything* for her."

Marlo Thomas was a name that could get features made in Hollywood at that time. She wanted to make a film with her father, along the lines of what Jane Fonda would later do with Henry Fonda in *On Golden Pond*. "Marlo was going with Herb Gardner, so she got to know Paddy pretty well," said Gottfried. Angling to get Chayefsky to write a script for her, during one of his California visits Thomas set up a Sunday breakfast meeting in her Hollywood home. "She must have bought out Nate and Al's Delicatessen. There was so much food, we could have had a wedding reception," said Gottfried. A half hour after they started to eat, her father walked in. The group continued breakfast, talking, until Thomas senior excused himself, left the table, and didn't return. Wandering out to the kitchen later, Chayefsky found the famous comedian with his hands in the sink, washing and rinsing the dirty dishes. "Apparently Marlo's maid had the day off, and Danny was running around, acting like he was the help," said Gottfried.

Chayefsky never wrote for Thomas or Streisand or for any of the Hollywood power group who tried to seduce him. "Paddy enjoyed being pursued," said Gottfried. "He loved being a part of the glamour and all that. He'd dismiss it if the subject was raised, but he loved it. The funny thing was, Paddy was almost seduceable, because he was so impressed. The thrill of being close to people like Cary Grant or Elizabeth Taylor never went away, because with all his talent and celebrity and wit and brilliance, deep down inside that little guy from the Bronx was still there."

CHAPTER 32

Tutelage and Chastisement

In June 1977, CBS paid five million dollars for three showings of *Network*, the movie that Chayefsky had been told "would never be shown on television." *Network* was sold with the satirical plot intact and some of the swear words sanitized. "When we were looping the sound we covered ourselves," said Sidney Lumet. "We used the word 'fugging' for 'fucking,' 'bullsop' for 'bullshit.' " When asked to comment on the sale, Chayefsky replied, "Like I said, they'll do anything for a good rating, even eat their young."

As the only writer to win three Academy Awards, he found he was frequently lionized by new young writers wanting to know his "formula" for success. When he had the time, he answered each call and letter soliciting advice. "My father had such a caring for people starting out, for writers who were not sure about themselves at the beginning," said Dan Chayefsky. "He knew how difficult it was. Sometimes he would take me to the clubs to see the new comics. At the end of their act they would wind up talking to my dad about their work. And he was always generous with his advice and suggestions." Budd Schulberg, after the Watts riots in 1966, had opened a workshop in Los Angeles for young writers. In the early 1970s he established an extension in New York City. "It was basically for minorities, for potential writers in inner-city areas." When contacted, Chayefsky enthusiastically lent his name, his money, and his participation to the workshop. "If a young writer has talent let them know it; encourage them," Chayefsky stated. "But also let them know that if they want an enduring career, they will have to be willing to go out of fashion a lot. Don't expect to be accepted all the time."

As a member of the Screen Writers Guild, Chayefsky often spoke at seminars. The secret of any good film, of any lasting film, was not the stars, the director, or the special effects, but the *story*, he said. As a playwright he also tried to get the same contractual rights and benefits for screenwriters that the Dramatists Guild secured for its members. "Possess and protect your work," was his repeated counsel, urging all writers to do their own revisions and to be on guard against egotistical producers and directors who tried to appropriate their work and ideas. "He wanted screenwriters to have more dignity and more money," said Elihu Winer, one of the pioneers of the Screen Writers Guild. "As a writer he never had any illusion that he was better or more famous than anyone else. He knew he was smart and talented and he made himself heard. He could be very steadfast, and when stung, he would scream. Essentially he was a lovable guy and a 'charming bastard,' and one did not cancel out the other."

In a course conducted by Winer for aspiring playwrights, Chayefsky was a guest speaker. During the discussion, a writer called Owa, a self-styled black radical, made some "unsentimental remarks" about Zionists. Chayefsky, taking this as an attack on Israel, became very agitated. "In very belligerent tones, he asked exactly what I meant," Owa recalled. "I said something to the effect that I believed that Israel did not belong to the Jews. It didn't belong to the Palestinians either, as it once was a part of Africa, but I didn't say that. Paddy was extremely sensitive when I mentioned the Jews. He jumped up on the table. Some of the other writers in the room, who came from the Eugene O'Neill school where I was studying, decided they would speak for me. 'No, he didn't mean it, he didn't mean it,' they said. When they were finished, I said, 'Well, if he wants to accept *their* answer, fine with me.' "

After the meeting, Chayefsky gave Owa his office number, and asked him to contact him. He did, and a professional relationship began. "Paddy taught me a lot about writing, about the craft of writing," said Owa. "He would evaluate my work and he gave me a lot of encouragement."

On the subject of Jews and Zionists Chayefsky remained vehement. "The code word for Jew in left literature, as it was in Nazi literature, is 'Zionist hoodlum/hooligan/imperialist/murderer/gangster,' " he told Owa. Jews didn't have a chance in Arab countries, he insisted. "Hitler didn't introduce the Yellow Star of David to be worn on the arm of Jews; that was an invention of Haroun El Raschid, the great caliph of Baghdad," he said. "The plain truth is Jews have been butchered, shot, gassed, stomped on by elephants, chopped up, and shit on by every two-bit looney looking for a power base, and, between you and me, I'm tired of it. If every Jew in this world was wiped out tomorrow—not entirely an impossibility—the world would still be the same treacherous whorehouse and abattoir it is right now. Oil prices would still go up every time OPEC felt like it, the various Communist and Trotskyite and New Left groups would find some other bullshit to rationalize their own impotence."

On Thursday, October 31, 1974, an ad placed by the Anti-Defamation

League of B'nai B'rith appeared in Section 1 of *The New York Times.* The copy asked why the Palestine Liberation Organization, with less than ten thousand members, was going to be allowed to represent all of the Palestinian Arabs, who numbered "over a million and a half," at the United Nations. Listing the recent atrocities credited to the P.L.O.—the murders of Christian pilgrims and of Israeli men, women, and children; and the hijacking and destruction of planes owned by Pan Am, TWA and KLM—the ad, written by Chayefsky, said that what the P.L.O. really represented was a promise "of violence, terror, and murder."

On September 21, 1977, another full-page manifesto appeared in the *Times.* This was in memory of the eleven Israeli athletes who had been killed at the Munich Olympics five years before. Placed and paid for by the Writers and Artists for Peace in the Middle East, the signatories included Saul Bellow, Colleen Dewhurst, Melvyn Douglas, Bernard Malamud, Eugene McCarthy, Arthur Miller, Leon Uris, Herman Wouk, and Elie Wiesel. Chayefsky's name was also listed and he composed the message: MURDER SCREAMED 11 TIMES AT MUNICH ON SEPTEMBER 5TH, 1972. THE KILLERS WERE THE PLO. AND WE SHALL NOT FORGET!

That November, a controversial two-hour documentary supporting the Palestinians was screened for potential distributors in New York City. The film was narrated and coproduced by Vanessa Redgrave, a self-styled Trotskyite. The news of the documentary brought an immediate cry of denunciation from Rabbi Meir Kahane of the Jewish Defense League and from the American Jewish Committee. They informed Twentieth Century–Fox, the producers of Redgrave's latest movie, *Julia,* that they intended to picket theatres showing the film unless Fox issued a statement denouncing her political activities and vowing never to hire her again. Fox ignored the demand and the J.D.L. reacted "by letting white mice loose in theatres showing the picture," said *Variety.* Neither the Anti-Defamation League nor Paddy Chayefsky took part in any public censure at this time. Abiding by the First Amendment, Chayefsky exercised restraint and refused to comment for the record on Redgrave or the documentary.

Redgrave was hardly unknown to Chayefsky. He had admired her work as far back as 1966, when she appeared in her American breakthrough film, *Morgan.* In 1967, when she was making *Camelot* in Hollywood, Chayefsky took his son to the set to meet her and director Josh Logan. In the mid-seventies, Jane Fonda, who named her daughter after Redgrave, approached Chayefsky about writing a movie for both of them. "She wanted him for a script about two female pirates," said Dan Chayefsky. "His reaction was 'Why on earth would they want me for a story like that?' It was something he would not do, although he admired Jane Fonda's talent and he would have liked to work with her."

In 1976, when *Network* was being cast, both Fonda and Redgrave were bypassed by Chayefsky because of their anti-Israel leanings. "Vanessa was my first choice for *Network*," said Sidney Lumet, who had worked with her the year before on *Murder on the Orient Express.* "I wanted her, and needless to say, Paddy wasn't going to have one minute of that. When I said, 'But, Paddy, you're blacklisting,' he said, 'She can work wherever she wants, except not with me.' "

At one juncture Redgrave attempted to change Chayefsky's mind. She visited him in his office and "tried to convert him regarding the Palestinians and the Trotskyites," said Dan Chayefsky. "But he wasn't having any of that." Even as she spoke, Chayefsky was helping Redgrave into her coat. He escorted her out of his office, into the hallway, and that was the end of the proselytizing.

The actress went on to make *Julia* with Fonda, and in February 1978 both were nominated for Academy Awards. Of the two, Redgrave was the more unpopular candidate. Because of her P.L.O. documentary, not only did she have the Jewish extremists against her, there were many prominent Jews in Hollywood who also opposed her. When the ballots were being cast, the Jewish Defense League strenuously urged the Academy members to vote against her. At the Oscar ceremony on March 29, five hundred extra police were on hand for protection. Across the street from the theatre several hundred members of the J.D.L. were waving anti-Redgrave signs, while nearby a smaller group of P.L.O. sympathizers demonstrated in her support. As Redgrave arrived at the rear of the theatre in an ambulance with two burly bodyguards, another ambulance on duty out front picked up two men in Nazi uniforms who were jumped on by Jewish supporters. Watching the melee as he embarked from his car was Chayefsky. A winner the previous year, he was there to present the writing awards.

Inside the theatre, the awards ceremony proceeded. Presenter John Travolta announced the first winner, for Best Supporting Actress: Vanessa Redgrave. As she graciously thanked her co-star, Jane Fonda, and her director, Fred Zinnemann, the members of the Academy sighed in relief: she was not going to indulge in politics. "And I *salute* you, my dear colleagues," Redgrave continued. "I think you should be very proud that in the last few weeks you've stood firm and you refused to be intimidated by the threats of a small bunch of Zionist hoodlums—"

"Everyone stopped listening after that," said Jane Fonda, sitting in the audience.

"I was so startled I did something I never did before or since," said Dan Melnick. "I booed."

The film editor Eric Albertson said he was watching the telecast at home with his father, who was "an old left-winger and a ranking member of the Communist party." "That's the problem with these famous people," Albertson senior said of Redgrave's remarks. "All they care about is the enjoyment of the battle, they forget there is a goal to win."

As the gasps and boos "and a smattering of applause" echoed through the auditorium, Chayefsky sat in his seat next to Howard Gottfried, steaming. "He was so upset, he was speechless," said Gottfried.

At intermission, when the break for the commercials came, Dan Melnick ran down the aisle to Chayefsky's seat. "It was such a stunning and terrible thing she did. I said to Paddy, 'You have to do something.' "

"Paddy waited," said Gottfried. "He was sure that as the show proceeded somebody would say something. When no one did, it became obvious that he would have to do it."

"I met him in the men's room during the second hour," said Johnny Friedkin. "He was wandering back and forth furiously. He said, 'I've got to say something. I can't let that bitch get away with it.' I told him, 'Paddy, for once in your life, keep your mouth shut.' "

"I didn't ask Vanessa Redgrave to get up and make that stupid, vicious statement," Chayefsky remarked later. "I sat there praying somebody would say something. But they didn't and I wasn't going to stand around and let somebody make cracks about Jews without doing anything about it."

Melnick and actor Alan King also spoke to Chayefsky in the men's room. "He was debating it. I was pushing him to do something, and so was Alan," said Melnick. "He still wasn't sure whether it was the right thing to do."

Back in his seat, Chayefsky made some notes on the back of an envelope. "In his usual way, he sat there, thinking about it," said Gottfried. "He wanted it to be right. It's so easy to be wrong on how you do it. His eyes were closed half the time. I know he was working it out in his head. How could he convey this without making a grandstand, without being antagonistic, without getting involved in name-calling as she did."

Following the award for Best Director, the next presenter, Chayefsky, walked out on stage. "Before I get on to the writing awards," he began, "there's a little matter I'd like to tidy up . . . at least if I expect to live with myself tomorrow morning."

"Uh-oh, trouble," said Redgrave's sister, Lynn, watching the show at home.

"I would like to say, personal opinion, of course," he continued, "that I'm sick and tired of people exploiting the Academy Awards [loud applause and bravos] for the propagation of their own personal propaganda [more applause]. I would like to suggest to Miss Redgrave that her winning an Academy Award is not a pivotal moment in history, does not require a proclamation, and a simple 'Thank you' would have sufficed."

"It was a simple, eloquent speech, and the whole auditorium stood up," said Gottfried. "Paddy got so thrown off by the reception to what he said that he was about to open the envelope without announcing the nominees."

Backstage, to the delight of the press, the controversy continued. After telling reporters that hers was not a political statement, Redgrave asked to meet with Chayefsky. "She tried to speak to me and I cut her dead," he said.

At the Governor's Ball, Redgrave sat with her bodyguards, largely ignored, while across the room, people had gathered to pay their respects to Chayefsky. "United Artists had taken two tables. They had won all the major awards for *Annie Hall.* Yet the crowd at our table was greater. People were lined up to shake his hand," said Gottfried.

The next morning the press gave their views on the fractious evening. "Paddy Chayefsky is a hypocrite," said Denis Hamill in the *Los Angeles Herald-Examiner.* "Anyone who castigates another person for exercising the right to free speech is making a political statement."

Quotes from celebrities were naturally stirred into the cauldron. "I guess it's fine. But I'm not a well-read person," said Jack Nicholson. "What are these Zionists anyway? Are they Reds? There've been threats? I've been skiing." Hollywood was "split right down the middle," said syndicated columnist Liz Smith. The movie community did have a surprising number of people taking Redgrave's side, the gossip reporter stated. "You may be amazed to learn that these include Henry Winkler, Joan Hackett, and Debbie Reynolds." Saying that the movies had already distorted history to the point "where many Americans believe it was the Indians who were the bad guys who tried to steal America from the white man," Smith asked, "What does Chayefsky want Redgrave to do—conform to a character he wrote in *The Americanization of Emily?*"

"My new hero is Paddy Chayefsky," said a voice from the far right, William F. Buckley. Redgrave's speech showed her bad manners, Buckley commented in an editorial. She was "as unapproachable as Goebbels."

"I haven't taken back or regretted *anything,*" the British actress said as the smoke cleared and she left L.A. "I thought it out beforehand. What I regret is the reaction to the speech."

When he got back to New York, Chayefsky was anxious to hear if he had done the proper thing. Eric Albertson said that as much as he disagreed with Chayefsky politically, he thought, "Paddy was dead-on, absolutely correct that night. Redgrave was just plain fucking stupid. Eventually her friend Jane Fonda learned, if you want to win over people there's a way of doing it."

Chayefsky's concern for Israel and other Jewish matters would continue to rule his behavior. "He became terribly paranoid, with this great fury," said Albertson. "He was almost professionally Jewish." Producer Sonny Fox recalled having lunch with Chayefsky one day. "All through the meal he was very agitated about what was happening to the Jews all over the world. He got me so scared that when we left the Carnegie Deli and went out on the street, I fully expected to see brown-shirted men on horseback rounding up all the Jews on Seventh Avenue."

A Plethora of Proposals

In Hollywood, the criterion for your next movie is always how much money your last one took in. After *Network,* Chayefsky had no difficulty staying employed. Among the deluge of offers there was one from Lew Wasserman, the chairman of the board of Universal/MCA. He wanted Paddy to write the script for a multimillion-dollar twelve-hour TV miniseries entitled *The Holocaust.* "Wasserman was a giant in Hollywood, and a very strong supporter of Israel," said Howard Gottfried. "He was very concerned about enlightening the world about the persecution of the Jews and of course Paddy was the perfect writer for that. They were willing to give him the studio if he'd do the script."

What could *he* bring to this project?, Chayefsky asked. Would this be just a straightforward dramatization of actual events? And why the Jews? Pogroms had been going on since before the Spanish Inquisition. What were the roots of anti-Semitism? And why had the animosity toward, the fear and persecution of Jewish people persisted down through the years?

"If Paddy was going to do the series, he had to provide some fresh insights, something deeper, not just a chronological narrative of what happened in Nazi Germany, but *why* it happened," said Gottfried. "His greatest motivation, and this is reflected in all his work, is that there had to be a relationship to some *meaning* in life, to the individual, to the human being. He was constantly searching for some explanation of what we were all doing here. It wasn't just what happened in the pogroms or that kind of persecution, it was *why* it started, and *why* they were picking on the Jews."

The subject would have been "simply too painful," Chayefsky told writer John Brady, and if he proceeded he would have to "make a soap opera of the whole thing." American television demanded that. They needed regular high-emotion moments for their "damn ten-minute intervals"—the commercials. Those marketing interruptions would trivialize the story. However, if NBC agreed not to insert breaks every ten or fifteen minutes and presented the script exactly as he wrote it, he would do the series. "But they couldn't agree to that," said Chayefsky. "They had to make the series their way so they could sell it to mass advertisers."

The July 4, 1976, raid on Entebbe, when Israeli soldiers rescued the 103 hostages hijacked aboard an Air France airliner by Arab terrorists, was another dramatization that seemed suited to the talents and interests of Chayefsky. "When that happened the phone didn't stop ringing. Every studio—Universal, Warner's—wanted him to do the script," said Gottfried. "They were offering buckets of money. Paddy said, 'Let me think about it.' We spent a month or three weeks discussing what happened at Entebbe. 'It's a good story,' Paddy said, 'but what can I bring to it? They don't need me. Any writer can do this.' And he passed."

Other offers to write adaptations of books, plays, actual events, came in, all of which Chayefsky turned down. There were fortunes involved, which were tempting to his partner, Gottfried. "I used to kid him, 'Paddy, you can afford to say no. I can't,' " he said.

"Writing was never a business for Paddy," Herb Gardner said. "In that way of always caring, he retained an inspired-amateur standing. It was never 'How many can I write?' He operated on passion and had to feel for what he was writing about. He would not take on a project unless there was something there, unless there was meat on the bones."

Enter Warren Beatty and his Russian project. As Beatty told it, back in the mid-1960s, he had visited the Soviet Union with his then girlfriend, Natalie Wood, whose parents had come from Russia. In Moscow, they met a woman who told Beatty she had been the lover of John Reed, "the most famous American hero in Russian history." Beatty read up on Reed, the upper-class, idealistic journalist from Portland, Oregon, who covered the Russian Revolution in 1917 and became an ardent Bolshevik supporter.

In 1972, Beatty went to Moscow again. During this visit he was urged by the Soviet authorities to join them in making a movie based on John Reed and his book, *Ten Days That Shook the World.* Beatty knew the book and was still taken with Reed, but not with the Soviet Union. If he worked on a movie of Reed's life, it would have to be done his way, as the actor-producer-director, with an American crew and cast. Back in the U.S., Beatty had spoken to numerous writers about doing a script, when the name of Paddy Chayefsky was raised.

His credits and plaudits notwithstanding, Chayefsky was also of Russian stock, and had written *The Passion of Josef D.*, which made him an expert on the revolution. In 1976, Warren Beatty began to lay siege at Chayefsky's door, but Chayefsky told him he wasn't interested. The "bullshit" of the Communist movement was old hat to him. Furthermore, the idea of writing for an actor who intended to direct himself was a dangerous situation. "Actors have no business directing a show they are in," said Chayefsky. Where Beatty was concerned, there was another encumbrance. Along with his multitudinous creative and producing skills, Beatty considered himself something of a writer on his movies. "Beatty does not write as much as he supervises, in the manner of an architect," said the author-scenarist John Gregory Dunne. "Teams of writers in effect work under the pseudonym Warren Beatty." And Paddy Chayefsky, as the entire world knew, worked very much alone.

But Beatty persisted. "Warren had energy, a keen intelligence, and more chutzpah than any Jew I've ever known," said Elia Kazan, who had directed Beatty in his first film, *Splendor in the Grass.* Like Marilyn Monroe, Warren also had a formidable talent for seducing writers, regardless of sex, creed, or age. Lillian Hellman was well into her seventies when, after one meeting with Beatty, she was said "to be ga-ga—like a sixteen-year-old girl." Robert Anderson, in the days when he was a hot playwright, recalled that Beatty would always approach him and ask when he was going to write something for him, "which is always the way to come on to a writer," he said.

The lunches between Beatty and Chayefsky began at the Carnegie Deli in New York, followed by dinners and invitations to parties in California. In between there were the interminable, inveigling phone calls the actor was famous for. "Warren was all confused about the lead character, John Reed, who was basically a very naïve man," said Howard Gottfried, "and nobody knew more about that whole thing than Paddy because he had done so much work on *Josef D.*"

Eventually Chayefsky agreed to do some research. He read books and articles on the early life of John Reed, and two specific adductions emerged. When the reporter-turned-radical worked with the International Workers of the World, he resisted America's entrance into World War I. Aligned with his pacifist beliefs, Reed and his lover (later wife), Louise Bryant, were also very much involved with the young playwright Eugene O'Neill, a figure who had at one time intrigued Chayefsky.

"In all, Paddy spent about three months on the research for *Reds,*" said Gottfried. "But he didn't take any money upfront. He wasn't sure if he still wanted to write the script."

The decision to do the Beatty movie came after Chayefsky had spoken to some old Bolsheviks who lived in New York City. They had helped him with his Russian play and knew firsthand of John Reed, who had helped found the Communist Labor party in America. Chayefsky was told that shortly before Reed's death at the age of thirty-two in Russia, he had become disillusioned with communism and had tried to resign from the party. In 1964, a similar political retraction had been presented by Chayefsky in *The Passion of Josef D.,* and was ignominiously refuted by the critic from *The New York Times.* With an old score to settle and a new passion kindled, Chayefsky called Beatty: he would do his Russian movie. Beatty in turn began the negotiations with Chayefsky's lawyer, but the contracts were never signed. "I don't know what happened," said Howard Gottfried. "But for whatever reason, Warren didn't make the deal. Warren was not very nice to Paddy. He double-crossed him in my opinion. Paddy had many meetings with Warren. I am absolutely certain Warren utilized a lot of the ideas he got. I don't mean that to be libelous, but he did use Paddy."

"If Paddy had done *Reds* with Warren, they would have killed each other," said producer Max Youngstein. "Warren's idea of collaboration is that you do whatever he asks you to do." Beatty and Chayefsky could not view the world through the same telescope, Youngstein believed. As an actor, Beatty had talent, but his ego demanded that he do everything, which vitiated his potential. "Not that Paddy didn't have ego," said Youngstein. "He did, and he played the games also. You could depend on that with Paddy. But once the deal was made that was it. He stuck to it."

> I want to be alone. I have a great deal of unfinished business with myself. I need to confront myself, because the self I have at the moment is a very shoddy, makeshift thing, contrived, illusory, unreal, lacking truth and substance, constantly pretending, constantly lying, shifting, taking different forms. I want to find my true self, an immutable self.
>
> Eddie Jessup, *Altered States*

By the spring of 1977, Chayefsky had his next project locked into place. It was a dissection of "another hot area nobody's tapped into—the scientific community." The physical scope of the film, *Altered States,* would be "epic, immense, never attempted before," he said. On a fundamental level it was "about a man in search of his true self. It's about what constitutes humanity. We will explore what it means to be a human being. When you strip away all the nonsense and get right down to the nucleus, what is that nucleus? I think it will be a startling film."

Despite the serious aspects of the story, the genesis for *Altered States* began under comic circumstances. Herb Gardner volunteered this account: "Somewhere around 1974, Bob Fosse, Paddy, and I were asked to do a remake of *King Kong*. It was a mad notion of either [agent] Sam Cohn or [producer] Dino De Laurentiis, or maybe it was just a way to keep us off the streets." Although the three had graded one another's work for years, some "animal instinct" had prevented them from collaborating on one joint enterprise. "If we did we would kill each other," said Gardner. "We were three little demons. But this project we decided to take seriously. Afterward we admitted that each one thought the other needed the money. Also the idea of collaborating lent a certain dignity to our hanging out."

Their first meeting on *King Kong* was held at the Russian Tea Room. Fosse immediately assumed the role of director and assigned Chayefsky and Gardner their jobs. "Paddy," he said, "*you* will handle the dignified thematic part of the script; that is, the Boredom. Herb, you will do your usual semicomic lyrical bullshit, the Whimsy. And *I'll* shine it up so somebody'll come to see it, I'll do the flash.' "

After naming their corporation Boredom, Whimsy, and Flash, they held a second staff meeting, with Chayefsky and Gardner already into the introductory concept of the film. "*Our* story would begin after Kong had already become a big movie star celebrity," said Gardner, "wearing an enormous velour jumpsuit, a silver pendant, and shades, unable to face the fact that he was now just another fifty-foot Hollywood has-been. In the opening shot, at the Beverly Hills Hotel pool, there is one giant close-up of a cabana. We hear a voice over the public-address system: 'Mr. Kong . . . Mr. Kong . . . telephone call for Mr. Kong.' At which point, the mighty Kong himself bursts out of his giant cabana, a tree-sized joint in one hand and most of the Polo Lounge Bar under his arm, trudging through the pool like it's a foot-bath, displacing two dozen starlets on his way to the phone booth; then picking up the entire phone booth and roaring into it, 'O.K., O.K., Sam, I'll *do* the series.' "

The *Kong* project did not proceed any further than that. The celebrated trio knew that their close friendship required their staying apart professionally. "The way to keep this group intact was not to work together," said Gardner. "What we were good at was patching up the debris from our separate enterprises."

However, the simian aspect of the story continued to intrigue Chayefsky. He read Sigmund Freud's anthropological essays, *Totem and Taboo*, which had been influenced by Darwin's *The Descent of Man*. Did man spring from apes? The answer for Chayefsky was no. For him the human spirit came from a divine source, a tenet retained from the religious training of his youth. Man, however, did have licentious urges. Beneath his seemingly benign exterior, there lay a beast who subsisted on rage and lust, an animal who, if unduly provoked and unleashed, could feast on destruction and genocide. Where did that beast come from?

The entire history of man's evolution was contained within the human brain, Chayefsky was certain of that. Memory was energy, it was still in there, it never disappeared. Surely there was a way to tap that primeval recall? Modern man, through science and physics, had already conquered outer space, and landed on the moon. So why couldn't he explore *inner* space and move back in time to an earlier consciousness, and find his original life force, his true self? Hypnosis had been used for years to induce memories of childhood. On a professional and recreational level, drugs were also being used to induce mystical levels of consciousness. Surely, under the proper administration and supervision, they could enable a man to regress, to revert to "some proto-human state."

"Then I hit on the old theme of *Dr. Jekyll and Mr. Hyde*," said Chayefsky, "and I knew I had something—an updated version of the classic, with a philosophical twist."

Different sides—light and dark—exist in everyone, but to what extent Chayefsky examined his own many facets for this new work could not be ascertained. In any event, in the construction of the story, as he did with his previous leading characters, autobiographical elements were added. Dr. Edward Jessup, a Cornell psychophysiologist, was raised in Yonkers, New York. In his childhood he was "a whiz kid, a genius." But instead of displaying his prodigious gifts on the piano, or in precocious discourse, as Sidney Chayefsky had done, Eddie Jessup had religious visions and spoke in miraculous voices. People came from all over to hear him and he planned to become a minister. At the age of sixteen, however, the boy lost his faith when his father suffered a prolonged and painful death from cancer. Sitting by his bedside, as Chayefsky had done with his mother, the young man tried to comfort the dying man. The lips of his yellow waxen face moved but no sound came out. "Did you say something, Pop?" the young man asked. He put his ear closer to the dying man's lips. Two words were hissed. "Terrible, terrible," said his father. So the end was tragic even for the good people, the boy said, and that night he dispensed with the idea of God altogether.

Possessed of a monomaniacal mind, and a "merciless gift of finding the defective links" in another person's reasoning, Jessup as an adult becomes frustrated with the fragmentation of his being. He wants to tap in to his earlier consciousness. The key to psychic solidarity can only be found in his primal roots, he believes. "I think that true self, that original self, that first self, is a real, mensurate, quantifiable thing, tangible and incarnate. And I'm going to find the fucker," he says. He is not alone in his quest. He is encouraged by a female companion. Her name is Emily. She is an anthropologist, lovely, intelligent, and spirited, but a handmaiden to his abiding articulation and wishes. When she first meets Jessup at a party in New York, he does all the talking, about his exploratory work with schizophrenics, and about isolation, and sense deprivation. Emily is taken with his zealous self-absorption and that night she goes to bed with him. Expecting "the fumblings of an inhibited scholar," she is spiritually and physically surprised when she finds herself "harpooned by a raging monk." In postcoital repose, when she asks Jessup what he was thinking about during sex, he says, "God, Jesus, crucifixions." "Well, as long as it isn't another woman," she sighs.

It isn't the sex, which is inconsistent and at times abrupt and violent, akin to "the quality of the lancing of a boil," that makes Emily fall in love with Jessup. It is his genius. Like Newton, Darwin, Einstein, he is a visionary, intent on exploring every mystery in life. When his mind suddenly vaults into untracked areas of speculation "and he would give himself with abandon to outrageous and poetic hypotheses," she feels chills go up and down her spine "and a swift stirring of sensuality within her." When he proposes to her, Jessup lets Emily know that she'll never be able to compete with his work. She accepts this and marries him. They have children and are happy for a while, but consumed with his research and resentful of intrusions, Jessup acknowledges that he is simply too selfish to be a husband and a father. "I'm not a complete son of a bitch. I'm not cruel," he says. "I did try to put on a good show of being a good husband and a good father. But that's what it was, a show. There wasn't an ounce of truth in it. It's all shit. It's all artifice."

The confinement of marriage forces Dr. Jessup to examine his relentless rage, a formless seething emotion he finds very hard to contain; at times he suspects himself of imminent madness. At first he thinks it is caused by his wife, his child, the demands of domestic minutiae. But when he removes himself from that environment, the fury stays with him. To determine its cause, to "get down to the embedded rock of life," Jessup decides to regress, to use himself as a guinea pig in his laboratory experiments. "If I can't find God, I at least want to find myself," he says.

For his research on genetic regression, Chayefsky spoke to doctors and professors at the departments of anthropology and human genetics at Columbia University and the American Museum of Natural History. "Fumbling with the original ideas," he then went to Boston, where he met with Dr. Mary Stefanyszyn of the Harvard Medical School, who introduced him to the community of scientists, anthropologists, and endocrinologists, and to the members of the school's psychophysiology department. Other talks were held with the medical and research staff at Duke University, at the Maimonides Medical Center in Brooklyn, and at the City University of New York. "Paddy was an inspired scholar," said Herb Gardner. "So many subjects fascinated him. Everything he didn't understand he wanted to listen and learn about. That was much more important than what he already knew or what he could posture and lecture about."

After absorbing the works of Aldous Huxley and Dr. John Lilly, both pioneers in mind exploration, Chayefsky went to Stockton State College in California, where he was introduced to his first isolation tank. He described the experience as "a warm return to your mother's womb." He also participated in progressive forms of yoga and meditation. As a writer, he already had highly developed verbal thinking, the language. Meditation gave him a more refined ability to "image." "He never spoke about it, but I truly believe when he meditated he went into an altered stage, another planet, so to speak," said Dan Chayefsky. "But he never heard voices like Howard Beale, or anything like that. My father was too painfully attached to reality for that."

Integrating the accumulated material with the help of various medical research assistants, Chayefsky then proceeded to outline the scientific aspects of his story. Monitored by a medical associate Jessup begins his first auto-experiment. He immerses himself in an isolation tank filled halfway with water which is spiked with a 10 percent solution of magnesium sulfate and heated to 93 degrees Fahrenheit. The darkness and silence at first bring shock and fear. He feels alive. Piercing images soon follow. He sees the face of Christ on a handkerchief, then his own body, lying nude on a surrealistic landscape of white beach. He sees part of his brain, then everything turns red, "the color of rage." Moving into his brain, Jessup's self-awareness takes the shape of a "swollen, obviously aroused vagina, into which his whole body was plunging with trembling anticipation." The vagina changes into the form of a beautiful young woman writhing on the beach. Her face is that of Jesus Christ, the one on the handkerchief, and despite the crown of thorns on Christ's brow, his face is distorted in sensual pleasure. In a flash of red brilliance, Jessup explodes into orgasm. As it recedes he finds he is back in the isolation tank, "floating effortlessly, serene, peaceful, and hooked."

Chayefsky's Jessup, addicted to the danger and discovery of self, decides to combine hallucinogenics with his tank therapy.

During his next out-of-body voyage, strange animallike noises are heard on the monitoring lab recorder. When the tank is opened, Jessup's face is covered in blood and he is aphasic, he cannot speak. That night, in bed with a female student, he awakens to find his body being physically transformed. He watches as bulges and ripples shoot up and down under the skin of his arms, and his stomach swells to grotesque proportions. Frightened but obsessed with going further, against the advice and without the supervision of his medical backup, Jessup opts to take the ultimate trip, alone. In the lab one night he increases the hallucinogenic dosage and the time spent in the tank. When the lid of the tank finally opens, a prehuman creature emerges. Dr. Jessup, said Chayefsky, has regressed totally, into "a fucking gorilla."

The finished treatment came to eighty-seven pages. When Chayefsky showed it to Dan Melnick, now at Columbia pictures, the executive said, "Put hard covers on that, and they will call it a novel." But becoming a novelist did not appeal to Chayefsky. "I consider writing novels déclassé," he said. It was much classier to write plays and scripts. "After all, drama has been around since the Orphic rites; the novel has been around only since Cervantes or thereabouts."

"Paddy hated the whole idea of doing *Altered States* as a book," said Arthur Penn. "He repudiated it. He wanted to do it only as a script. But either Melnick or Sam Cohn prevailed upon him to do it first as a novel."

"Paddy wasn't crazy about the idea," said Melnick, "but I told him the book would be a wonderful weapon in selling the picture."

Melnick and Cohn were right. After the extended treatment had been sold as a novel to Harper & Row, Melnick brought the outline to the attention of David Begelman, the senior executive vice president and studio head at Columbia Pictures.

Begelman was "a crapshooter," Gottfried believed. "He already had *Close Encounters of the Third Kind* in production. *Star Wars* was a monster hit. And here was a project with a forthcoming script by Paddy Chayefsky that required special effects. Big money was in the air. Begelman knew that, he was no fool." Nor was Chayefsky. When he and Gottfried arrived at the Columbia studios in California to meet with Begelman he knew exactly what he wanted for his work-in-progress. "O.K., guys, here's the deal," he said. Begelman and his assistant, vice president Stanley Jaffe, listened, then excused themselves and left the room. When they came back ten minutes later they gave their answer to Chayefsky: "Yes."

The details of the deal were kept secret, but it was unprecedented in screenwriting history. "He got close to one million dollars," said Gottfried, "and along with that Paddy insisted on a time-completion guarantee. Columbia had a certain amount of time to make the movie and if they didn't adhere to it, they'd have to give the script back to him. But he would be allowed to keep the million dollars."

Dan Melnick, the executive producer for Columbia, knew from past mediations on *Network* that there could be no nickel-and-diming with Chayefsky on the financial *or* the creative aspects. Hence, the contract for *Altered States* was approved and signed in a very short time.

Over the summer of 1977, Chayefsky went to work on the first step of the two-part project—the novel. Jessup's voyage-exploration in the book would span ten years. While his hero went in search of the Great Truth, his journey would enable the writer to honk at a few road marks and social traditions along the way. One sharp Bronx cheer would be given to the liberals and dopeheads of the 1960s who tried to invade everyone's consciousness through loud rock music, grass, and LSD. An even more articulate thump would be given to the current decade's rapt absorption with the self. Introspection obviously was a pursuit reserved for artists and scientific types, and should not be indulged in by amateurs or the masses. "We're all weekending at est or meditating for forty minutes a day or squatting on floors in a communal *om* or locking arms in quasi-Sufi dances or stripping off the deceptions of civilized life or jumping into a swimming pool filled with other naked searchers for self," says the critically jaundiced Dr. Jessup.

Combining technical scientific language with dramatic dialogue in a cohesive dramatic narrative form was, again, an exhausting and depressing process for Chayefsky. At times he felt the subject matter was beyond him. The relentless probing and validation of what he and Jessup were looking for often carried him through a labyrinth of dark paths and deep recesses, where further fear and doubt dwelled. Each profundity revealed led to another intangible, so dense and inpenetrable they frequently caused Chayefsky's brain to shut down or to spin out beyond his control.

"The work on *Altered States* took a long time and really sapped him," said Gottfried. "Paddy immersed himself in that whole world, the scientific community. That's the only way he would write. He went through a lot of pain, investing the characters with parts of his own being. Also he was struggling very hard for an ending to Jessup's story. He had seven or eight different endings at one time."

"The original ending was that Jessup died, because he went too far with his experiments," said Dan Chayefsky. "It was written that way, and then he said, 'No, I don't believe that. I don't feel that.' He believed that it was a matter of turning back from what is in front of you. 'Isn't that what life is all about?' "

Before the last chapter was completed, Chayefsky collapsed. "The stress of the entire thing gave him a heart attack," said Gottfried.

"At least this proves that I'm mortal," Chayefsky told his son when he visited him in the hospital. Along with the medical tests the heart specialists gave Chayefsky a behavioral-stress quiz. "It was one of those 'Type A' personality tests," said Dan Chayefsky. Are you aggressive? Compulsive? Impatient? Do you get irritated waiting for elevators? Cross on a yellow light? Do you enjoy working under pressure, and living in New York City? He scored "yes" on all of them, the patient said proudly.

When he was released, Chayefsky was put on a strict diet and told to exercise. The diet prohibited caffeine, tobacco, and salt. The latter restriction meant giving up his favorite pastrami sandwiches at the Carnegie Deli. The weekly poker games were avoided because of the temptation of junk food, but the "Monday Night Football" show with Fosse, who had his own heart problems, continued. "Their idea of something healthy was to eat Jarlsberg cheese and to drink 'light' beer," said Ann Reinking. If Fosse tried to smoke, Chayefsky stopped him. "Once during the rehearsals for *Chicago,* we were invited to attend a run-through," said Herb Gardner. "When we walked into the theatre, Fosse was standing near the stage with a cigarette in his mouth. Paddy, in front of the entire cast and the stage manager, went up to him and said, 'Give me that fucking cigarette.' And he pulled it right out of his mouth."

The one thing that Chayefsky could not give up was "the work." In the hospital when he asked that a portable typewriter he brought to his bed, the request was denied. So he got his daily fix by writing each morning in a school notebook that he had smuggled into the room.

The ending of *Altered States* still concerned Chayefsky. Originally the relationship between Dr. Jessup and his wife, Emily, had been much more antagonistic. Emily, jealous of his quest and self-involvement, calls Jessup "a Faust freak," a man who would sell his soul for the great truth. "Nothing in the human condition has any reality for you because it's uncertain, imperfect, transient," she says. "You have to have some great immutable truth. You're still looking for God's truth, any truth, even a godless truth, as long as it's ultimate, absolute, permanent, everlasting." But there isn't any such truth, Emily insists. Everyone is born screaming in doubt and they die suffocating in doubt, "and human life consists of continually convincing ourselves we're alive."

Jessup decides to divorce Emily, so he can concentrate more fully on his work. Emily resists this move. "She insists she's in love with me, whatever that is," he tells a colleague. "What she really means is she prefers this arbitrary structure we've created to being alone. She prefers the senseless pain we inflict on each other to the pain we would otherwise inflict on ourselves."

When asked how closely this situation resembled Chayefsky's own domestic situation, his partner Gottfried said he wasn't sure, but in the early drafts of *Altered States,* the conflicts between Jessup and Emily went much deeper. "It was based on so many areas. There was one great battle over some of his findings, with this incredible research he was doing on the unknown. They have these incredible battles and at one point she steals his papers and burns them. It became a wild scene between them."

Chayefsky conceived of Jessup going much further in his experiments, and of his ultimately being destroyed in the process. Following his heart attack, Chayefsky changed that ending. After his heart attack, Chayefsky eliminated the scene of violent discord between Jessup and Emily. He then added a climactic pronouncement. "I found the fucker," says Jessup to Emily after his last major regression. "I found the final truth all of us have been treasure-hunting for. . . . I can tell you what it is! It is nothing, simple hideous nothing! The final truth of all things is that there is no final truth! Truth is the illusion! Life is the only substance we have!"

At that point Jessup wants to destroy his files. It is Emily who tells him to save them. She praises his mind and his passion, and urges him to keep his research for future use. As he tells her that this is too late, that the drugs he has taken have a latency factor, his body begins to change shape and form again. He starts to regress into a protohuman again. Emily screams at him to defy it. "You made it real! You can make it unreal. If you love me, Eddie, defy it!"

That was the ending of his story, Herb Gardner told Chayefsky. Jessup is saved through the love of Emily.

After dedicating the novel—"For my wife, Susan. For my son, Dan"— Chayefsky dispatched the completed work to Harper & Row. He took three days off, then started in again on the screenplay. "All the holes came out," he said. "I tried to follow the book, but it didn't work." He completed the first draft in March 1978, at which time the movie, which had been scheduled to begin filming that summer, was postponed. The delay had nothing to do with Chayefsky's health or his script. It was attributed to "internal problems" at Columbia Pictures. David Begelman, the production chief who had paid one million dollars to Chayefsky for his script, was about to be indicted for forging and cashing company checks.

It was fortuitous that Begelman's temporary replacement at the studio was Dan Melnick, who assured Chayefsky and Gottfried that despite the scandal and changes at Columbia, *Altered States* would not be affected. It was scheduled for production that fall, with a budget of $9 million. That generous financial allocation was due to the "tremendous faith" the studio had in Chayefsky's script, and because *Close Encounters of the Third Kind* had raked in $75 million in the U.S. alone over the past five months.

That June *Altered States* was published to mixed reviews. It was not a bestseller, hindered perhaps because Chayefsky did not promote it. He had been offered the cover of the Sunday *New York Times Magazine* to pen an article on why and how he had written the novel. That exposure would have helped the book enormously, but the writer refused the assignment. "He told me that he didn't think he was a novelist, that the book was essentially only a blueprint for the screenplay," said Dan Chayefsky. "Also, he was tired. The book knocked him out considerably."

That summer Chayefsky's energies were expended further, on the preproduction of the movie version. Sidney Lumet was on board to direct, until a snag occurred over his contract. "I thought *Altered States* was a hell of a script, and it would be a wonderful movie," said Lumet. "But Paddy was very tough about money. I had a deal on *Network* and I wanted the same one for *Altered States*. I couldn't understand it. We had worked so well before and here we were stalled, not over the basic money, but on the percentage, which was stupid because you never see percentages anyway. I don't know what got into him, but Paddy would not give me the same deal. He kept saying, 'We'll work it out, we'll work it out.' I kept saying, 'When, Paddy, when?' "

When Lumet was offered another movie, he called Chayefsky and told him he had to know about *Altered States* by the end of that week. "Paddy said that he was going out to the West Coast, and that he would call me by Thursday. 'Don't worry about it. We'll work it out,' he said. Thursday came and he never called. On Friday I took the other picture. I felt so bad about it. It broke my heart. I loved it. First of all I thought *Altered States* would make a wonderful movie. Secondly, if I had done it, perhaps none of the heartbreaking things that happened on that movie would have happened."

Lumet's agent, Sam Cohn, suggested another director client, Arthur Penn.

He had worked with Chayefsky during the Golden Age of Television and his subsequent sterling movie credits included *The Miracle Worker* and *Bonnie and Clyde*. Chayefsky enthusiastically accepted Penn and the two went over the script. Although Chayefsky was "gifted and original," Penn felt "that dramaturgy was not his strongest suit." In their initial meetings, the pair had some disagreements over the leading male character. "I felt Eddie Jessup, the doctor, was too cold, too deadly, and that the story wasn't going to be intimate enough," said Penn. "I kept saying that it's got to be more of a love story for this kind of operatic event. It had to be embedded with some kind of deep emotional statement. Jessup was this kind of destructive scientist, very much self-centered. Paddy didn't agree with me. He made some revisions, but they were minor."

The two were in complete accord over the casting. "Columbia wanted names for the leads and he wanted actors, good actors," said Penn. "Whenever you're dealing with a Hollywood studio they all want 'movie stars.' We stuck to our guns, that we wanted good actors, *unknown* actors."

In the book of *Altered States*, Chayefsky described the hero as twenty-four, flaxen-haired, with a pale complexion, gold-rimmed glasses, and "a look of Calvinist authority." Newcomer William Hurt fit that description. Hurt had no movie experience, but had done two dramas for public television, *The Best of Families* and *Verna the USO Girl*, copies of which went to Chayefsky for viewing. The producers then went downtown to the Circle Repertory Theatre to see Hurt in Lanford Wilson's *Fifth of July*. The script of *Altered States* was delivered soon after. The actor said he cried for forty-five minutes after he read it. "I couldn't stand for another twenty," said Hurt. "I was trying to express something in my own life, something I wanted so badly. I never had a friend as great as Emily who could get me across a river that wide."

When Hurt was chosen, Dan Melnick's reaction was " 'Oh my God, these guys have gone and hired one of those New York guys. Some creep is going to show up in the lead of this big movie.' Then Melnick met Bill and his heart jumped when he saw him." said Gottfried. "Here was a guy who was on the cusp of movie stardom."

Actress Blair Brown was vacationing in France with her boyfriend, actor Richard Jordan, when the script of *Altered States* arrived. The cover letter and the title page were missing. "We didn't know whether it was for Richard or me or what," said Brown, "so I just read it because I was so thankful to read anything in English." She was intrigued by the story, and when she got back to New York, she auditioned repeatedly for Penn and Chayefsky. "I was there so much, I felt like I was doing a one-woman show of Emily." She *willed* the landing of the role, she said. "I really wanted it. They told me at the end, after they tested somebody else, 'We're giving it to you not because we think you are particularly right for it, but because it was your time. You seem to be the one to play it.' "

Lacking stars in the cast, Columbia Pictures felt that an important selling factor for the picture would be the production team they brought in to create the altered-states sequences. The men they hired were true stars in their field. Joe Alves was the art director on *Close Encounters of the Third Kind* and John Dykstra was responsible for the special effects in *Star Wars*. In New York, Arthur Penn hired Dick Smith, the makeup artist whose credits included *The Godfather, The Exorcist,* and *Taxi Driver*. His elongated employment on *Altered States* was "wild, bizarre, from beginning to end," said Smith. During the initial conferences, Chayefsky told the makeup and production designers that he was willing to adapt his script to their suggestions. "Paddy was wonderful," said Smith. "He told us upfront, 'You guys can change anything you see fit.' " In the months that followed, complications arose. During the summer of 1978, the New York contingent met with the West Coast team every third or fourth weekend in Los Angeles. Chayefsky's script called for three "cosmic makeovers." The first comes when Jessup emerges from his isolation tank transformed into a five-foot apelike creature. That was no problem, said Dick Smith, and not "too exciting because . . . hell, everybody's done apes."

The second and third cosmic changes were harder to translate. Number two required William Hurt to be in the isolation tank when it explodes. He emerges from the vaporous solution in a succession of monstrous shapes and forms, as his wife watches, horrified. In the final mutation, Blair Brown as Emily, while trying to save her husband, is consumed by the primal energy. Her body begins to swell and burn and crack. "She no longer had eyes or a mouth to scream with. She knew where she was going, to the lifeless, arctic, final isolation," said Chayefsky. Whether or not these last two sequences would be done through optical means or through elaborate makeup was a continual puzzlement to the principals. "We never could decide on a single approach," said Smith. "We would have regular meetings which would cancel each other out."

Eventually it was decided that rubber body suits would be the most effective way to convey the cosmic transformations for sequences two and three. In New York, a full body cast of Bill Hurt had to be made from which to construct the head-to-toe foam latex suits. For one sequence, as outlined in Chayefsky's script, the actor's right arm was supposed to be attached to the top of his head with his hand grabbing his left cheek. "To make a suit that would fit him in that position," said Smith, "we had to recast his head and shoulders *in that position*."

To decrease the actor's discomfort, and accelerate the casting process, Smith assembled a group to help him. In Smith's garage in upstate New York, Hurt stripped to his Jockey shorts and Smith had two assistants stand in front of him and two in the back, each one holding a large bucket of quick-set plaster. After inserting a large plastic tube in Hurt's mouth so he could breathe, the team went to work. "We all plunged large pieces of burlap into the plaster and literally threw them at his head and body," said Smith. "It was a horrendous experience for him."

Then it was Blair Brown's turn to be assaulted and cast. "It was just so bizarre," she said. "It was beyond sex." Two different latex suits were created for the actress, with separate sections for the hands, feet, body, and head. One suit was supposed to make her look scorched to a cinder. "We called that one 'Burnt Brown,' " said Dick Smith. The other looked as if her skin had burned off. "That was called 'Bare Blair.' "

Bladders of various sizes and shapes were fashioned from urethane rubber. These could be attached to the latex suits or skin of the actors, so that on cue, Bill Hurt's forearm and brow could expand, and Blair Brown's stomach could explode. "We threw out a lot of ideas," said Smith. "Her transformation was going to be truly grotesque."

Meanwhile, on the West Coast, John Dykstra, Joe Alves, and their teams were constructing the sets for the tank-room scenes. When finished these did not meet with the approval of Chayefsky and Gottfried. "We had been very specific in saying that we did not want a super-duper scientific set, where you have all the modern technological looks," said Gottfried. In the script, the tank room was in the basement of the Harvard Medical School, which was supposed to look like a regular basement. "But Arthur Penn, working with Alves, had put together a set that looked like the Planetarium, in the most high-tech fashion," said Gottfried. "This was totally inconsistent with Paddy's concept. At that point we sat down and agreed that Arthur was not really the director for the movie. Paddy and I were very disappointed. We felt that Arthur Penn should have been more on top of things. Frankly, he should never have undertaken this movie. Sam Cohn had talked him into it, and I think that maybe it was the wrong movie for him."

"Arthur is a brilliant director, wonderful," said Sidney Lumet. "But what Paddy needed was a combination of intellect—because his ideas were so complex—and nutsy, wild passion. And Arthur when he works is very, very quiet, rather detached, separated. Every method of directing is legitimate, there is no right or wrong way. But on a personality level, I just knew that Arthur wouldn't work out. Paddy needed equal abrasiveness coming back at him."

According to Penn, the main disparity was over the isolation tank. Chayefsky did not like the color and said it was too big. "I tried to explain to him that when we used only a section of the set it wouldn't look too large.

'No, no, it's too big,' he said. That was the substance of our basic quarrel—the size of the isolation tank."

Any and all problems that might surface could never be resolved when Penn found out that Chayefsky, in his contract with Columbia, had complete authority over the director and the entire film. "I was amazed to learn that Dan Melnick and Columbia, in order to seduce Paddy into signing with them, had given him this incredible power. He had the power to veto everything, and I didn't find that out until we were getting ready to shoot."

He and Chayefsky were clearly on a collision course. "It was fine with me that Paddy had approval over the script and any changes," said Penn. "But for him to veto what I was doing, or to intervene in areas where he wasn't knowledgeable or even competent, was wrong. Set and camera angles my ass, Paddy didn't know or want to know how it was done. Paddy was a results guy. He understood there was a process involved, but he did not want to really engage in it."

To help ease the impasse, the writer and the director were called in to meet with Frank Price, the new head of studio production at Columbia. "We met to discuss where the power should reside," said Penn. "On the set, decisions have to be made fast, especially on a movie like this, and you have to feel sure they will happen and not get shot down by an outside force. We spoke about this with Frank Price a few times. Paddy and I were still amicable. He and I went back a long time, but in this instance, the problem was not going to be resolved because he was not going to relinquish his control. And I was not going to make the film under those circumstances."

The director also knew that if he quit, he wouldn't be paid. "That seemed nuts to me. I had worked months on the picture, and not to receive some remuneration was crazy. So under Sam Cohn's advice, I went back to the house I had rented in Los Angeles, and I waited for the telegram to come removing me from the film."

The names on the list of directors sought by Chayefsky to replace Penn were impressive. They included Orson Welles, Fred Zinnemann, Martin Scorsese, Francis Ford Coppola, Bernardo Bertolucci, Arthur Hiller, Sydney Pollack, and Nicolas Roeg. Unfortunately each one could not, or would not, direct the movie. "Perhaps they were wary because we had gotten rid of Arthur, who was a very respected director," said Gottfried.

Chayefsky called Steven Spielberg and they met for lunch. "We wanted him very much for *Altered States*," said Gottfried. "He loved Paddy. He admired the hell out of Paddy's work, but this wasn't a movie for him. Spielberg's stuff at that time was a lot more simplistic. Paddy's writing had more depth."

There were directors who called *them,* the producer said, but they weren't interested. "We needed someone who could handle the visual and the drama."

The name of Ken Russell was submitted by his agency. "Paddy didn't know his work," said Gottfried. "I did and I thought he would be worth considering. Ken has tremendous visual talent. Of course, in hindsight, if I knew he was going to be such a putz, such a miserable son of a bitch, I would never have recommended him."

A former seaman, RAF cadet, ballet dancer, actor, and photographer, Ken Russell got his start at the BBC television network in London.

He had directed controversial drama-documentaries on the lives of Debussy and Isadora Duncan, followed by the movie version of D. H. Lawrence's *Women in Love*. The latter brought Russell an Oscar nomination as best director. It also enabled him to produce and direct a subsequent cycle of films that provoked *Time* magazine to anoint him "the cinema's dilly Dali," running "amok through the lives of the great composers like a hyperactive adolescent." Vulgar, camp, hysterical, and "a hymn to sadomasochism" were some of the other judgments passed on the director's work, which included *The Devils, Mahler, Tommy,* and *Lisztomania.* Evidently indifferent to these opinions, the director placed a framed sign across the portal of his future productions. "Russell's the name, bad taste is the game," was the proud proclamation, which led some to believe that this was not the man suited to Paddy Chayefsky's finer sensibilities. "The combination of Russell and Paddy was just wacko," said Arthur Penn.

"I don't know," said Lumet. "When I heard about Russell I thought that it was a marvelous idea. Because, no doubt there would be the abrasiveness, and there is an intellect with Ken. He's a very brilliant man, and visually he's a suberb director, which Paddy's pieces needed. They required a real visual attack, which Paddy wasn't too interested in, so the director had better be. I felt it would work with Ken but I knew it would be volatile."

To acquaint Chayefsky with the director's work, Columbia arranged a series of private screenings. Understandably, the movie company omitted Russell's *Mahler,* in which the Jewish composer, after converting to Catholicism, was forced to eat a plate of ham and drink pitchers of milk, while his companion, Cosima Wagner, dressed in a Nazi storm trooper's outfit, whipped the composer and herself "through an anti-Semitic lyric chanted to the tune of 'Ride of the Valkyries," said critic Carrie Rickey. Columbia's pride and profit was in *Tommy* ("the greatest opera since *Wozzeck,*" said its director humbly), and when it was shown to Chayefsky he said he was "amused" by two scenes in particular. Deaf and dumb and blind from childhood, Tommy is taken for a cure to various holy shrines, including one for St. Marilyn (Monroe). The second sequence has the boy's mother (Ann-Margret) becoming a veritable victim of consumer commercials, when the TV screen in her living room explodes and she is drowned in a deluge of baked beans and melted chocolate.

By happenstance, Russell was in America when Chayefsky expressed interest in talking to him. Courtesy of Columbia he was brought to New York, put up at the Sherry-Netherland Hotel in a penthouse suite overlooking Central Park, then treated to lunch at the Carnegie Deli by Howard Gottfried. The producer knew from *Tommy* that Russell could handle the surrealism in *Altered States,* but what about the straight scenes?

Russell referred Gottfried to *Savage Messiah,* which he said was as "low on fantasy and high on acting as anything I'd ever done." Personally financed from a double mortgage on his house, the film was about the sculptor Gaudier-Brzeska, who, poverty-stricken, steals a tombstone, creates a nude from it, and when the dealer who commissioned the piece refuses to pay for it, wheels it through the streets and tosses it through the merchant's gallery window. "It was about revolution and fuck-the–art dealers of Bond Street and Madison Avenue and fuck Pinewood and Hollywood, who never made a proper film on an artist yet," said Russell, arranging a screening for Chayefsky.

The following day, after seeing *Savage Messiah,* Chayefsky was taken to meet with Russell and the two embraced. After congratulating him on his brave art film, Chayefsky handed the director a dog-eared copy of his *Altered States* script. Russell was happy and relieved. This film was his last chance to pull himself back to acceptability and to establish himself with the big Hollywood studios, he said, but later he had some doubts. Back in his hotel that evening he called his wife in England. He had never before made a film "just for the money," or been dictated to, he told her. She tried to assure him that he would "turn it into a Ken Russell film yet." But he couldn't work with Chayefsky, the director countered. "He's a complete egomaniac."

"Then you should get along just fine," said the discerning Mrs. Russell.

CHAPTER 35

The Titans Collide

The day after he was hired to direct *Altered States,* Russell learned that the courtship phase of his induction was over. He was now on the production payroll, so he was moved out of the penthouse to a cheaper room at the back of the hotel, with no view of the park. The hasty script meetings, held in Chayefsky's musty office on Seventh Avenue, were equally cheap and cheerless, he complained,

Much to his amazement, Russell then learned that his function on the film would be limited to directing only. Apparently his producers did not know that aligned with his genius for staging, the director had keen literary capabilities, having co-written or revised considerably the scripts of *Women in Love, The Music Lovers,* and *The Devils,* among others. But Chayefsky, while welcoming Russell's suggestions and ideas for the hallucinatory sequences, made it clear he did not need any help whatsoever on his dialogue or the narrative, which Russell felt had too soppy an ending. "Paddy could never readily accept any idea that was not his own," the director said, detailing in his memoirs that when they visited the primate house at the Bronx Zoo, his guide, Chayefsky, "who had rather long arms and a pronounced stoop," gave an impression of an agitated chimpanzee when a critical remark on his script was made.

In California, Russell was confident that he would be able to ditch Chayefsky and proceed with the film as he saw fit. But in February 1979, when preproduction on the film began in Los Angeles, the director said he could not shake the writer. "The monkey on my back was always there and wouldn't let go."

A disparity in lifestyles was soon established. While the parsimonious scribe-producer lunched on turkey sandwiches and decaffeinated coffee, his director had sirloin steak and rare French wines served to him in his own private office on the Columbia lot. And rather than bunking down at the Beverly Hills Hotel, where Chayefsky and Gottfried had checked in, Russell insisted that he be given a private house in Beverly Hills. The one he chose belonged to Shelley Winters and came equipped with a kidney-shaped pool. When coproducer Chayefsky complained about the cost, Russell told him it was none of his business, it came out of the Columbia budget.

To curtail the expenses on the production itself, Russell promised the studio he would use the set already erected by Arthur Penn. He kept his word. He used the timber. Russell had the sets demolished, and the wood converted to a carpenter's shop erected on one of the soundstages. He also brought in a fellow Britisher, Richard McDonald, as production designer to replace Joe Alves—"who had resigned, I heard tell," said Russell, "when Paddy walked onto the set with a chain saw and hacked off the bits of his sets that he didn't approve of."

When the new sets were constructed, Chayefsky expressed his displeasure with the color and lighting of the new isolation tank. "In the scene our hero is supposed to be in complete sensory deprivation," he said. "Russell had him in an upright bronze boiler, dog-paddling around, and the whole thing is lit up like a Halloween scare."

"What's it to you if you don't like it or not? You're only the writer," Russell replied.

"Remarks like that would normally drive Paddy crazy," said Gottfried. "But there was no way he was going to get into a confrontation publicly with Russell, who was also very devious, a game player. He gradually began to align certain people, the creative staff—whom he called 'my team'—on his side, against us, particularly against Paddy."

Meanwhile, the actors, William Hurt and Blair Brown, who had been kept on salary, were nervous about their jobs when Russell was brought in. "I was sure I would be replaced," said Brown. William Hurt told New York journalist Stephen Silverman that when he was summoned to a meeting, he noticed that the director had Betty Boop on his socks and he knew he was safe.

Choosing the supporting actors and extras in L.A., the director was irked when Chayefsky, as was his custom, sat in on the auditions. Every time he spoke up, Russell became more annoyed. "Paddy was meticulous about the casting for his scripts," said Gottfried. "For example, at the Harvard Medical School, the security guards on campus, most of them were described as black. And Ken brought in a bunch of Mexicans for the parts. Paddy said, 'Not in my movie.' Ken snarled back, 'What do you mean not in *your* movie?' Paddy told him that there were no Mexicans in Boston. It was a totally valid point, but to Russell it wouldn't have made a bit of difference."

At his home in Los Angeles, to acquaint himself with Chayefsky's scientific subject matter, Russell had his first "out-of-body" experiment. On a free weekend he ingested a hallucinogenic mushroom. The trip was endless and exhausting, the visions malevolent and savage. The bad vibes flowed over to Monday morning when, coming down with a heart-sickening thud, he was told that Columbia Pictures, "finally tired of Paddy's shenanigans," was dropping *Altered States.*

The new head of the studio, Frank Price, had become apprehensive about the project, Gottfried stated. "In the beginning, when Price was reporting to Danny Melnick, he professed his great love for *Altered States.* Then, when Ken Russell was brought in, Price started to get a little testy. He had to write off some money to pay Arthur Penn; there was also the cost of the sets which we scrapped. Maybe in all it came to $1.5 million." The original budget of $9 million now stood at $12.5 million, and before shooting was completed, it could go higher, the studio feared.

"Everyone insists that money was not at issue, but what else does Hollywood get nervous about?" asked the reporter Helen Dudar.

Altered States had been Dan Melnick and David Begelman's baby, as was *All That Jazz,* the Bob Fosse bio-musical. The budget on the latter had also ballooned, from $6.5 million to $9 million. The Fosse project seemed a safer bet, so Columbia kept that film, bringing in Twentieth Century–Fox as a co-financer. *Altered States* was then put up for bids from other studios, along with Steven Spielberg's next science-fiction project, a "kiddie movie" called *E.T.*

As it transpired, *Altered States* found a buyer almost immediately. In the Hollywood tradition of studio leap-frogging, executive Dan Melnick had left Columbia for Warner's, where he secured an independent deal. The two studios shared production space in Burbank and Melnick suggested that Warner's pick up the new Chayefsky project. "We met with Danny and Ted Ashley and others at Warner's," said Gottfried. "Paddy was there, along with Ken Russell. Everyone was very impressed with the script, and with Ken. He was on his best behavior, because he desperately wanted to hold on to his job."

Russell outlined his concept for the film and the special effects to the Warner executives, followed by the producers, who gave their estimated cost. "The budget wasn't that exorbitant," said Gottfried. "We made it for fourteen million, I believe." ("It came in at $14,910,481," Melnick said.)

After the deal with Warner's was signed, Ken Russell dropped the congeniality act and proceeded to establish that he was the principal authority on the picture. According to Gottfried, when he was first hired, Russell was very respectful of Chayefsky's script. "He was all sweetness and light. He would pay respect and be very decent about it." On March 1, 1979, the first day of rehearsal, that esteem turned to scorn. Sitting around a table in a deserted storeroom at Warner's, every time "the writer" started talking, the director became tense and irritable. "Russell began to treat Paddy as a nonentity," said Gottfried. "He would try to demean him by being mean and sarcastic."

In his account of that initial reading, Russell said that the dialogue was loaded "with scientific mumbo-jumbo which the actors spat at each other across a long table watched over by Paddy and myself at either end. Paddy wanted everyone word-perfect." When the actors had completed the first reading of the script, Chayefsky said, "Perfect for me. Over to you, Kenny." "You can't improve on perfection, Paddy," said Russell, then snidely suggested that they rehearse the scene "where Jessup fucks Emily on the kitchen floor? I'd appreciate your input on the grunts." The shocked silence was followed by Chayefsky growling like "the big, bad wolf," then calmly saying that in matters of grunting ape-men and moaning lovers, the director had carte blanche, because Chayefsky was concerned only with the actual dialogue.

In the days that followed, Russell "started to beat the shit out of the script," said Gottfried. "He would make real lousy remarks. Just anything to get Paddy upset. He was really looking to dislodge Paddy from any position of authority, that was obvious. He more than baited Paddy. He wanted to debase him, to irritate him."

Critic Andrew Sarris of *The Village Voice* noted that the conflict was hardly new: this was part of the same power struggles and unresolved dialectics that had affected movies since 1905. "The word still mars the image, the story still compromises the spectacle, the director and the writer are still at each other's throats, and the star is never fully satisfied with anything," said Sarris.

The unconditional power that Chayefsky had in the theatre could not work in films, Arthur Penn believed. "In movies there are too many areas of expertise that are not available to the writer. I don't care how smart Paddy was, he didn't know about lenses. He didn't know about sets or sound. In movies you have to rely on the expertise of others, because film is a collaborative medium."

Collaboration in film was fine with him, Chayefsky said, as long as it was geared toward the realization of the script *he* wrote, with the original intrinsic vision and values intact, or better still, enhanced.

On *Altered States,* once production started, he agreed that it was the director who was in charge. "Paddy knew and accepted that," said Gottfried. "It was perfectly fine with him. What he wanted was to be there and to have a rapport with Ken Russell. That's all he was looking for." But Russell was anti-authority. As soon as anyone who had more power stepped into his domain, which was his movie set, "forget it, he was going to destroy them."

But Paddy was a scrapper. In previous work-crusades he obviously thrived on the battle and the conflicts.

"Yes, but this was a different kind of battle," said Gottfried, "this didn't stimulate him. You're perfectly right, Paddy *could* be stimulated by a good fight. Paddy was never passive. But this wasn't conflict, this didn't invigorate him. Ken never came out in the open about it, he never confronted Paddy directly. This was a duplicitous, mean man. To the cast and studio executives he could be charming, brilliant, even lovable. He was like that old saying about a child: 'When he's good, he's very, very good, but when he's bad, he's horrid.' Well, he was horrid to Paddy. During rehearsals, Ken would cast aspersions about 'the precious script,' which was an area that Paddy was particularly vulnerable about."

"That's what this whole fight is about, isn't it, the dignity of the work," said the daughter to her struggling father in *The Big Deal* twenty-five years before.

On Friday, March 23, principal filming began. The first scene to be shot was between William Hurt and actor Charles Haid, in the basement of the Harvard Medical School. At this point Chayefsky and Russell were no longer talking. "Paddy by now was very depressed," said Gottfried. "There was no way that he was going to accept what Ken was doing. We were standing a short distance away from the set. Ken was with the actors. They did a few takes. And Paddy started to get very nervous. 'What is he doing?' he kept saying, in a whisper that you could hear on Burbank Boulevard."

Chayefsky's concept was from the theatre, Russell said, dismissing the writer's qualms. "He sees things in terms of scenes, on a stage, almost flat. I'm a great believer in the choreography of the camera, like it's one of the actors."

That afternoon, when filming resumed, the second assistant director went over to Gottfried and told him that Russell wanted to see him. "I walked over to where he was and he turned and snarled at me. 'I can't possibly direct this movie with all your incessant talk going on,' he said. He was real loud, just to embarrass Paddy. Ken was overwrought. He wasn't looking to ameliorate the situation. He was using it to assert his authority. Everything was tense. The actors knew what was going on but couldn't say anything."

The conflict was that of a composer interfering with a conductor's interpretation of his music, Russell stated. During a performance you "can't have two conductors."

That weekend, Chayefsky had dinner at writer David Shaw's house in Los Angeles. Also present was director Delbert Mann, who recalled Chayefsky's frantic tales of working with Russell. "We were laughing hysterically," said Mann. "Paddy's ranting and raving and carrying on put us on the floor. Although I don't believe he thought he was being funny."

On Sunday morning in his hotel, Chayefsky typed a letter to Owa, his playwright protégé back east. Apologizing for the rush and the typos he said: "I'm out here in California trying to make a movie, which has been a horror from the beginning. Right now, it's a low point, if you can pick out the low points from each other. There has been no highpoints at all that I can remember. We started shooting the fucker last Friday, and the director not only has turned out to be a monster, but a monster with not enough talent to make it worthwhile. Man, I'm tired of battling, I truly am."

On Monday morning, March 26, shooting resumed at an Italian restaurant on Santa Monica Boulevard. The scene was a dinner celebration for Dr. Jessup, who is about to depart for Mexico to conduct some experiments with hallucinogenic mushrooms.

In the bar area, with a headset on, Chayefsky monitored the first of the key speeches he had written for Jessup and the other characters. "Everybody's looking for his true self. We're all trying to fulfill ourselves, get ahold of ourselves, get in touch with ourselves, face the reality of ourselves, explore ourselves, expand ourselves," Jessup says. "Ever since we dispensed with God, we've got nothing but ourselves to explain this meaningless horror of life."

After numerous takes, the dialogue, as heard by Chayefsky, was becoming more and more incomprehensible. The fault obviously lay in the direction. This was supposed to be a festive occasion, hence Russell had instructed the actors to partake freely of the food and drink that the restaurant had provided. By take 5 of the scene, as instructed, William Hurt was circling the table with a bottle of wine hoisted to his lips, delivering Chayefsky's important speech. To add to the chaotic jumble, the director was matching the actors drink for drink, take for take, and had become quite inebriated.

"When Ken drank, he became quite vicious," said Gottfried.

In his account of the events, Russell claimed that during a break, Blair Brown told him that Chayefsky had been "hanging around the lavatories," cross-examining the actors on his directions and "giving them contrary advice."

"Horseshit," said Gottfried. "I'm sure he spoke to Bill Hurt, but Bill Hurt spoke to everyone. He was a guy who was open to everyone."

Russell proceeded to give a verbal lashing to Chayefsky, who abruptly left the set.

That afternoon, according to Brown, "a lot of lawyers, grown men in suits," arrived on the set. "We finished shooting and Ken was screaming and yelling all afternoon. And Bill Hurt and I were crying in the bathroom. We thought, Well, this is all going to be over, isn't it? We've now waited for six months, nine months to do the film. It's the big break, a thrilling prospect, and we all think it's done for."

That night, "all hot and bothered," Ken Russell went home and jumped into Shelley Winters's pool. While cooling off, and still drinking, he overheard his wife and his agent "plotting" in the living room. He shouldn't rock the boat, they felt. He "counterattacked" by screaming back at them that no film could have two directors. Grabbing a nearby phone, he called Chayefsky at the Beverly Hills Hotel and asked him what the hell right did he have in counteracting his directorial instructions. Chayefsky in turn asked why the director insisted on making the actors play a perfectly normal scene drunk, and shooting everything at a distance. "Why can't you shoot scenes like other directors in a long shot, medium shot, and close-up, for chrissakes?" Chayefsky asked. "So that you can re-edit them after I've gone?" Russell shouted. "And don't think I fucking won't," Chayefsky screamed back. Firing one last fusillade over the phone, the mad dog of the British cinema told the obstreperous three-time Oscar-winning writer from the Bronx to "take your turkey sandwiches and your script and your Sanka and stuff it up your ass and get on the next fucking plane back to New York and let me get on with the fucking film."

Crowing triumphantly, Russell said he had won that round. The following morning when Chayefsky did not appear on the set, it was rumored that the director had had him barred from the studio. "Ken Russell never had that kind of power," said Gottfried. "The decision on what to do lay only with Paddy."

"From what I heard, Paddy tried to fire Ken, but they wouldn't back him on that," said Sidney Lumet.

"What really happened was this," said Gottfried. "Paddy came to me and said, 'I want you to fire Ken Russell.' He was miserable. I said to him, 'Paddy, there is only one way we can get away with this. You and I will go to the front office tomorrow morning and we'll tell them we're letting Ken Russell go, and that you're taking over the direction.' " But Chayefsky knew he was not a director. He had found that out on *The Passion of Josef D.* Individual scenes with actors he could handle, but the aggregate staging was beyond him.

On Tuesday, March 27, Chayefsky made his decision. "He called me very early that morning," said David Shaw. "He said that if he didn't leave it was going to cost him money, points. So he packed his bags and went back to New York."

But this was *not* an exit in defeat, he told Warner Bros. The rushes of each day's filming would have to be sent by Air Express to him in New York. And nothing in the script could be altered without his prior approval.

"We could not change a single word," said Blair Brown. "We could not add a hello, a thank-you, an excuse me, nor could we delete anything."

"That's the kind of power Paddy had—that I found absolutely unbelievable," said Arthur Penn. "Certainly if I had stayed on the picture—knowing Paddy—we wouldn't have that kind of restriction on the language. He did that defensively. He invoked his contractual rights and boom!—down came the steel door."

Stubbornness did play a part in the inflexibility imposed on the script,

Gottfried admitted. "Paddy was a very proud guy. You don't become someone like him and not have a certain ego. Also, this *was* a very serious piece of work to him."

All that spring and throughout the summer, as filming on *Altered States* continued in Los Angeles, each day's rushes were sent to Chayefsky in New York. With Bob Fosse immersed in his own production angst editing *All That Jazz,* and Herb Gardner working on a stillborn musical with Jule Styne, Paddy used some of his other pals as a sounding board for his frustration. "When the rushes would come in he would call me," said Eddie White. "I'd go over to his office and he'd say, 'We're going to order lunch in and watch the film, but don't talk, don't give me an opinion.' Then we'd watch the rushes and all Paddy would say was, 'Look! Look! What do you think of that shit?' He would start to cry hysterically—'Eddie, what are they doing to me?' Then he would call Los Angeles."

"Every day at one o'clock New York time, ten o'clock California time, the studio secretary would come on the set and say, 'Your phone call is here, Mr. Gottfried.' And for the next two hours that's all I did, listen to Paddy"

"YOU SON OF A BITCH! YOU MOTHERFUCKERS! THIS IS NOT THE WAY I WROTE IT! THEY'RE USING DIFFERENT DIALOGUE AND BODY LANGUAGE," he would shout at Gottfried and Melnick and whomever else he could get through to at Warner Bros.

"He would drive himself crazy," said White. "I'd tell him, 'Calm down. You got a bad heart, Paddy. Calm down. Don't call these guys no more.' But he went on and on tearing himself up. He ate his insides out. Eventually I'd get him to lie down on the couch in his office and I'd cover him. He'd close his eyes but he'd keep on mumbling to himself, 'They're destroying my script. They're wrecking my beautiful story.' "

He described the destruction to his son as "an abortion . . . a major separation from something you've invested in and cherished." The pain was magnified by the return of his depression, which could no longer be treated with medication. "Two years before when he suffered his heart attack the doctors told him he could no longer take anti-depressants," said Dan Chayefsky. "Much later they discovered other drugs, which helped people like William Styron, Rod Steiger, and Dick Cavett. But at the time they had nothing. So he had to learn to live with it, to allow the depression to coexist with the pain and frustration of seeing the work that he spent three years on be destroyed."

Howard Gottfried said that "not one word of Paddy's script was changed. I wouldn't let Ken Russell or Bill Hurt or any of the actors do that."

Russell stated that at the outset Chayefsky had agreed that there was too much dialogue in the script. At that time they pared some of it down together. During shooting, the director proceeded to shoot the script "as it was—typos and all. But I shot it in such a way that the excess dialogue could be junked later." Chayefsky contended that to circumvent the strict covenant on adhering to the script, Russell instructed the actors to eat while talking, or deliver their speeches at a fast, incomprehensible speed. "It was clear that Russell had contempt for the screenplay, by rushing the actors through the dialogue," said Dan Chayefsky.

"Paddy thought they were doing that on purpose, just to upset him," said Eddie White.

But it was Chayefsky who suggested the fast pace and overlapping dialogue, the director insisted. "During rehearsals he told me he had spent time researching the way scientists talk and what I was doing was right. It was simply a matter of creating a reality. People who know their business speak quickly." And quick speech patterns convey enthusiasm, is what Russell claimed Chayefsky told him.

Blair Brown believed that "a lot of the breakneck speed had to do with the fact that we could never have rewrites to accommodate sets and camera moves and things like that. That's why there are long stretches in which nobody says anything."

"It didn't sound like the actors that I knew," said Arthur Penn. "When I saw the film, I remember Bill Hurt just rattling through certain sections."

In fair defense of Russell's direction, there were previous indications that Chayefsky had intended to burlesque certain aspects of his story, including the overly erudite articulation of the scientific community. "*Altered States* did have dialogue that was hard to digest, but that wasn't handled best by having the actors steamroll through it," said Dan Chayefsky. "Also, Ken Russell intended to cater to an audience who didn't want to listen to words, which is why he made the movie such a visual assault."

Chayefsky's partner believed there were many brilliant things in *Altered States*. "The production design was exceptional, and there were many scenes that Ken Russell did that were superb. But Paddy could not see any of that." If the director had been more amenable to at least talking with the writer about his objections, and about his suggestions for changes, the matter could still have been resolved, Gottfried believed. "I don't think Ken ever realized how much he alienated Paddy by his abuse. Paddy was really hurt by him, so he put up his armor, his shield. He could never differentiate or rationalize the abuse he got from Ken the man, who was despicable, and Ken the director."

In time, as his anger and depression increased, Chayefsky began to turn against his partner. "Paddy felt that Gottfried wasn't staying on top of Ken Russell," said White. "On weekends he used to come to my apartment and he'd call Gottfried and scream at him. Then he'd hang up, go to my kitchen, and stuff himself with food that wasn't any good for him. Once I caught him eating a whole salami from my refrigerator. When I yelled at him, he turned around with the meat in his hands and glared at me. I swear to God, he looked like a madman. I pleaded with him, 'Paddy, stop this. It's not worth it. Fuck Ken Russell. Fuck the movie.' But he wouldn't and couldn't let go of it. He couldn't stop torturing himself."

In a desperate attempt to turn things around, Chayefsky told White one day that he had found the solution. He was going to fire Gottfried and make Eddie White his new partner and the producer on *Altered States.* "He told me we were going to fly to California. We would check in to one those bungalows at the Beverly Hills Hotel and work from there," said White. "We weren't going to go to the set, maybe look in once in a while to see the rushes. I guess the idea was for him to get his hands on the finished movie and fix it."

But after making a few calls to the executives at Warner Bros., Chayefsky was told that it was best for all concerned if he stayed in New York. "The people at the studio didn't want him anywhere near the production. They felt he was making too much trouble," said White.

At this stage of the multimillion-dollar production, apparently the entire company were up to their necks, literally and figuratively, with the problems connected with the film's altered-states sequences. "It was a madhouse," said the makeup designer, Dick Smith. "They'd have endless variations of the tank-room scene, with various figures coming out of the tank. One day it would be Bill Hurt in a suit, the next day an inflatable figure. It was grueling."

In one sequence, after the tank exploded, Blair Brown was to wade through the flood in the room, looking for what remained of her husband. For this, it was suggested that instead of using water, they should use a heavier substance. "They bought this tankful of gook which was basically K-Y jelly," said Smith. "When I heard about it I was horrified. How would anyone be able to stand up in it? Fortunately when they were unloading the stuff outside the Burbank studio, they spilled a little of it. People were falling down all day in front of the entrance. Soon we were back to using good old water."

Then there was the matter of getting the actors in and out of their rubber suits. It took three hours each morning to fit the various layers on Blair Brown. "At one point, I had small lightbulbs attached to my eyelids and false eyes glued over them," said Brown. "I had a harness attached to my back and I was yanked down the length of the hall. The only parts exposed of me were my nostrils. I could breathe and that was it. I couldn't see. I would be yanked into this door over and over again. After a while, your body takes a defensive attitude and goes into a dead zone."

For the scene where Jessup is transformed into an apelike man, it was originally agreed by Chayefsky and Arthur Penn that they would use a Nigerian, a five-foot-tall soccer player made up for the part. When Ken Russell took over, he decided to replace the Nigerian with a Mexican ballet dancer who would be more agile. "That meant we wouldn't have an authentic primitive-man profile," said Smith. Large dentures and various appliances were created, and at Russell's request, the ape-man was given blue eyes like Bill Hurt's.

To affect a further animal resemblance, hair had to be pasted in an anatomically correct manner on each section of the Mexican ballet dancer's body. The process took four hours each morning, and because the creature was very active during filming, patches of hair fell off during each shot and had to be replaced.

Prowling on all fours around the city zoo and surrounding streets, the ape performed on par, and soon after, the rushes were dispatched to Paddy Chayefsky in New York. This was done as a courtesy. There was no dialogue involved, hence he had no veto. He had a reaction however. Watching his hero-turned-ape go through his scenes Chayefsky began to make some animal noises of his own. His script called for the "simian creature to be glimpsed fleetingly," he said. Russell, however, decided to make an entire terpsichorean production out of it. Using the diminutive dancer as a double for William Hurt, the director had the sequence lit and choreographed like a grotesque modern ballet. "Up to that moment, the scene is completely realistic," said Chayefsky. "The janitor hears something in the lab and creeps in to check. Then the ballet dancer suddenly jumps out of the tank doing a grand *jeté*. You're into *Planet of the Apes!*"

After seeing this Chayefsky called his lawyer. A meeting was arranged with the legal heads of Warner's in the offices of Spanbock & Carro on Sixth Avenue. Chayefsky arrived and was relatively calm until the conversation turned to the latest scenes directed by Ken Russell. In describing how the ape was loping around the basement, the writer started loping around his lawyer's office. Then suddenly, in front of the entire group, Chayefsky let out a bestial roar and jumped up on the windowsill.

When the shock and uneasy laughter subsided, Chayefsky came down off the ledge and delivered a mandate to the Warner Bros. lawyers. They could proceed as they wished with *Altered States,* but without his participation. He was officially removing himself from the production.

The War Within

Who, or what, is this Imp of the Perverse,
but a portion of the ego separated out from the
rest, which seeks the destruction of that
from which it is separated.

Edgar Allan Poe, "The Imp of the Perverse"

In his memoirs, Ken Russell said he was perplexed as to why, at the eleventh hour, Chayefsky withdrew from the production of *Altered States*. "Rumours were rife," said Russell. "Paddy was ill. Paddy was humiliated. Paddy was mad. Paddy was paralyzed with anger. Paddy had suffered a nervous breakdown. Paddy liked the film so much he was ill with envy. Paddy hated the film so much he couldn't bear to think about it. Paddy was schizophrenic."

Paddy was exhausted, his son explained. "He told me he didn't have the energy left to fight anymore," said Dan Chayefsky. "And in a way, I think that afforded him some relief, from his own demons."

The schizophrenic aspects of Chayefsky's condition were manifest during the summer months when the rushes of *Altered States* were being flown to New York for his inspection. Beyond the hurt and the hatred he felt for Ken Russell, what impaired Chayefsky's judgment and caused his ongoing disintegration was the struggle he was waging within himself. During the entire disruptive process, two distinct voices kept playing on a split soundtrack in his mind. One belonged to Paddy, the producer, the administrator, the omnipotent boss of the production. The other voice was calmer, more rational. It belonged to Sidney, the creator, the writer, the artist, who, although concerned with preserving the work, wanted balance and harmony to reign. Outwardly, while Paddy, in simian fury, was bellowing about unconditional adherence to his words and vision, inwardly Sidney was desperately striving for fair play and basic trust. "On *Altered States* it was a constant inner battle between my father and his ego," said Dan Chayefsky. "His inner self was trying to cope with and accept the changes, but the ego kept insisting, 'No, no, do it my way.' "

It was the crux of the matter that overruled logic or reason. The most enduring thing in a man's life was his work. That static force, left for future generations, was "man's sole way to achieve immortality," James Joyce said in *Portrait of the Artist as a Young Man*. Chayefsky's writing had been his primary sustenance, his raison d'être, the source of his invincibility for so many years. And now, as it was being sullied and torn asunder by hostile outsiders, his rage and frustration were compounded because he could not fathom how this had happened. He had the best deal, the best contract on this movie. He had carefully and painstakingly set himself up as all-powerful, as creatively invincible, yet everything was now falling apart, and he felt helpless to prevent it. "My father had spent all of his life controlling," said Dan Chayefsky. "He was always a man very taken with images—of the protected writer, the husband, the father. He was a man in love with images and one by one they were beginning to slip away from him."

Although he may not have recognized it as such, this final round in Chayefsky's long journey into himself was closely allied to the one fought in *William Wilson*, the classic story of duality by Poe. In *William Wilson*, the protagonist, an imperious, materialistic young man, is followed everywhere by a masked figure who tries to obstruct and impede his ambitions. The shadowed figure whom he calls his companion, his namesake, his rival, can only speak in a whisper, but at every turn he mocks his double's vanity, his vices and soulless charades. Expelled from Oxford, Wilson flees to the Continent but is pursued by his tormentor. At a masked ball in Naples, he finally confronts him, challenges him to a duel, then stabs him in the heart with his sword. Under his rival's mask he finds his own image, the bloodied specter of himself. He has destroyed his soul. "You have conquered and I yield," his dying conscience tells him. "In me didst thou exist, and in my death, see by this image, which is thine, how utterly thou hast murdered thyself."

On the night before his meeting with the lawyers at Warner Bros., Chayefsky spent the hours alone, desperately trying to decide on a final course of action for *Altered States*. His physical and mental resistance to surrender was enormous. "Don't give up! Don't give in! Don't let the miserable bastards win!" That was Paddy's constant war cry. "Walk away. Let it go. It's only a movie," said the softer, more sober, and always more serious-minded Sidney Chayefsky. The crossfire of dialogue and the explosion of counterschemes that kept playing on that endless loop in his mind began to shatter his entire being. His disorientation was such that the solution he chose to end the chaos was the same as William Wilson's. To stop the pain and save his "damned dignity," Paddy Chayefsky was now prepared to sacrifice his soul, his creative conscience—Sidney.

On September 21, 1979, the lawyers at Warner Bros. were informed that the name of Paddy Chayefsky had to be removed from the script of *Altered States*. When instructed that someone had to be listed as the screenwriter on the movie, Paddy gave them a pseudonym. This move would cost him. He would lose all his percentage points from the film, he was told, but he remained adamant. Sidney Aaron was the name he wanted listed on the credits. At the same time, he instructed Irving Gaft, his accountant, that he wanted the company named for his original self, Simcha Productions, dissolved.

His immediate response to the truncations of Sidney was one of tremendous relief. Paddy slept soundly for the first time in years. Rested and inspired, he then went back to work. With a renewed wildness he seized upon story ideas for a new independent enterprise. However, none of these ideas stuck. The reasons were simple. The outlines were derivative. Everything he came up with was a variation on characters and situations that had been done before. He was stealing from himself. His originality had dried up, he feared, until one morning he examined the ephemeral process more closely. The concepts, brilliantly conceived each day, were being discarded overnight by that enduring, judgmental presence within, Sidney Chayefsky. Presumed banished, Sidney was still very much there, holding center court and passing comment on the entire creative flux.

Over lunch, Chayefsky told Bob Fosse of the predicament. "The little fucker will not die," said Paddy. Fosse laconically, but wisely, replied that perhaps Chayefsky was trying to nail the wrong culprit. "You can stomp on the talent but *never* kill it," said the director, whose recently completed film, *All That Jazz,* was an attempted purgative unmasking of his own slick and self-destructive alter ego, Bob Riff (known in the film as Joe Gideon).

Although he never spoke openly about it, Chayefsky was conscious of the extremes in his personality. "He was always a very insightful man," said Dan Chayefsky. "Even about his own folly. When he was trapped in his own neuroses he was ultra-aware of it." During the early 1970s, in his ongoing effort to get to the root of his psychic discord, Chayefsky tried hypnosis. It didn't work because his resistance was too strong. In California he had once considered trying the hallucinogenic LSD, which actor Cary Grant had used successfully under medical supervision. "It worked for Grant," said Dan Chayefsky. "It enabled him to actually see what went wrong when he was Archie Leach [Grant's former childhood self]. But my father wouldn't take the drug. He was scared of the aftereffects."

Through his ongoing analysis and therapy, it wasn't hard for Chayefsky to see how Paddy, his alter ego, evolved as the guardian of the more fearful and vulnerable Sidney. For a time, especially during the struggling years, the two were a compatible pair. Sidney had the intellect, the sensitivity, the talent,

Paddy had the drive, the energy, the courage to get things done and to make sure the world appreciated their worth. Paddy also had optimism in abundance. He was the card, a show-off, the happy-go-lucky, tough little guy who was always there with a quip or a word of cheer for the masses.

That was a myth, a façade, an illusion, Sidney came to realize. Paddy had his down times too. In fact, the base of their childhood depression began with him. During the early 1930s when Harry Chayefsky lost the big house in Mount Vernon and all their money, it was Paddy, not Sidney, who fell apart. Paddy was spoiled. He loved the luxuries, the privileges, and lived for the lavish attention and applause. When it was all taken away he became stricken with doom. For years it was Paddy and not Sidney who hung on to the melancholy, to the sense of loss and dreams of retrieval for what they had once had. Of course he never showed that. Concealment and secrecy were always second nature to Paddy. A pro at putting on a front, he had a knack of drawing people around him while keeping them at a distance. By closing off and deliberately holding back his love, he really believed it would protect them from further pain. But instead, it alienated them, especially Sidney, from the ones who truly mattered, including his only offspring. "I wish I had known Sidney more," said Dan Chayefsky, "because do you know how hard it was to live with Paddy? Very hard. I don't think I could ever feel Paddy's love as a father. He was so busy with images. His image. My image. People like that are so chaotic, that it's almost impossible to know who they are or what they feel. They can say, 'I love you.' But you can't feel it. That's a terrible thing for anyone to feel from a parent. It makes you yearn for emotions."

Control was Paddy's prime addiction. Protection of the work was fine. Original vision and good work should not be tampered with. Sidney held firm with that belief and the insistence that it be put in writing, legally. Paddy, however, tended to overreact when anyone approached or encroached on what he considered his turf, his territory. He would lash out, behave abominably, accuse even the most earnest of meddlers of sabotage. His hysterics were such that one might think he had written the damn stuff himself.

Born of conflict, Paddy really believed he had to carry it everywhere. When it wasn't there he created it. The prolonged insanity and absurdity of living in New York City was a strict canon of Paddy's. He relied on the chaos to "energize the work," he said. That was another fallacy, Sidney believed. The inflated idea that pain and discomfort are associated with higher creativity and productivity was an exaggeration. Sidney could write *anywhere,* and what was wrong with a little peace and quiet as they got older? But no, Paddy needed the urban grind, the daily fix of noise and hostility. It made him "feel alive," he said, ignoring the fact that each accumulative blow left Sidney feeling more deadened and diminished. And whenever he would try to raise his voice to complain, to ask, "Why are we here? Why are we doing this to ourselves?" Paddy would patronizingly reply, "For the work, dummy. For the work." That was the true bullshit, Sidney learned a long time ago. The work was Paddy's escape, his bogus strength, his only force, and if it had held up he could have continued the deception of bulldozing his way up that infinite illusory mountain of fame and success.

In the fall of 1979, with spartan discipline and sheer will, Chayefsky started the difficult process of separation from his personal dybbuk, his monster ego. Sidney took command from the minute they woke in the morning. Humility, constraint, and forbearance were in order. In public, the self-aggrandizement, the wry observations, the clever quips and comebacks, were banished. Not an idle thought of individuation or a speck of grandiosity was tolerated.

The exorcism went into a second week, with Paddy resolutely staying on and Sidney coming close to extinction through despair and exhaustion. "It was a very hard time for him," said Dan Chayefsky. "People spend their entire lives without confronting their dark side. But he knew he had to do it. He had taken enormous risks for the work, but never really for himself." The terror was in not knowing what came after the surrender. What if there was nothing there to fill the void? "The devil you know is better than the devil you don't," his mother had always said. Was that the hellish predicament? Was he supposed to be locked into this conflict and torment all of his life?

The confusion and strife continued until one day, in a match of wills, Sidney was led into examining his own ignoble side. Unusual, because he never believed he had one. In recalling their first serious breach, when success came in the early fifties, Sidney was reminded of how unsettled he became when he began to suspect that people only liked him because they thought he was funny, because he entertained them. Was it possible that the lofty, cerebral Sidney was *jealous* of Paddy? The thought seemed preposterous, but pursuing it, Sidney discovered he *was* resentful of the attention that Paddy received over the years. In a further examination, he found other defects masquerading as virtues. The appropriate redress came from elsewhere. Transpersonal Psychology, a popular therapy of the time, stated that ego chastisement was wrong. Only by recognizing the positive and negative aspects of a person's divergent selves, and raising or demoting each accordingly, could a possible fusing and more serene existence begin.

"After enlightenment, the laundry," the Zenrin coda said. In the sorting, Chayefsky made a list of some of his virtues and all of his faults, endeavoring to find out which belonged to whom. Paddy laid claim to the drive and humor, which remained. To be discarded were his speed and impatience. Even now, he wanted their synthesis and recovery to be accomplished *immediately*. Perfection and control was a crossover compulsion. The bent for brilliance began with Sidney. "Do better . . . be smarter . . . try harder" was part of the strict work ethic he was raised with. The ensuing control was Paddy's province. To him perfection signified uniqueness, being better than others. But excellence was a hopeless taskmaster. It brought success and admiration but narrowed their life to a lean and isolated scale. To do one's best was more reasonable and human. Other possible alignments were listed, but the steps made to effect them continued to be slow and painful. "At his age it was very difficult to change," said Dan Chayefsky. "But he kept trying and it was strange to watch. It was as if I was now the parent and he was the son. He was finally getting a grasp of life and I was really proud of what he was trying to do."

The final and most difficult thing for Chayefsky to let go of was his renowned anger. It was in his wrath that Paddy felt electric, alive, important. The sensation was eventually instilled in Sidney, to use as expression in the work, as a cry for help, a legitimate means to effect change and order for the people. Anger became their literary insignia. Being mad as hell was the Chayefsky crest, their banner, a standard unfurled in the name of justice and social causes. In the process Sidney also became hooked. Anger stimulated his mind, made sense of the incomprehensible and, more important, for a time, made him feel at one with Paddy. But as with any addiction, when the dosage and frequency were increased, the benefits declined and perversity ensued. Sidney's anger became childish, petulant; Paddy's turned to virulent rage. With time the passion became a poison and the fury was used indiscriminately, as a weapon for punishment and oftentimes spite. Gluttonous, when the fury began to feed on itself it made Paddy corpulent, and Sidney a skeleton, begging to be heard before they were both destroyed.

In recovery, Sidney, the stronger now, insisted that their anger be dispensed with entirely, which alarmed Paddy considerably. In a city like New York, where short tempers and instant spleen were as easily displayed as holy medals at the Vatican, Paddy felt naked, defenseless without his armor. But Sidney helped, counting to ten or distracting Paddy with calm mental sketches when the daily urban aggravations arose. The larger issues were also subdued, until the day a dispatch arrived from Warner Bros. *Altered States* had completed principal photography two weeks before, with ten months of special effects production to follow. Having removed himself from the project, Chayefsky wanted no further involvement. But the studio insisted on sending him the first optical sequences. When the tape arrived he swore he would not look at it. But he did. A familiar swell of nausea and terror gripped him for approximately twelve seconds, whereupon Chayefsky stood up, stopped the machine, took out the tape, carried it outside to the incinerator closet in the hallway, and dropped the tape down the garbage chute. Then he left for lunch.

With that, the fear and anger he had known for close to fifty years began to dissipate. It was a slow, impermanent abatement, but Chayefsky began to feel better, more at peace within himself. His imperfections, his weaknesses, the madness would always be there, but through strength and grace he hoped to reduce them. "At the end he merged better," said Dan Chayefsky. "Those two different extremes fused into a more integrated person—he wasn't so fragmented. He began to really know who he was. He wasn't turned on or off, not hyper as he was before. He became a real pleasure to be around and a lot less self-focused. He no longer felt he had to regulate everything around him. He still had his depression, but he knew he would have to live with it, without medication. He accepted that. He also stopped putting himself down, he stopped criticizing himself for it."

His brothers, Bill and Winn Chayefsky, also noticed the changes. "His evolution was remarkable," said Winn. "Up until then Paddy's awareness was a development thing with him, a work-in-progress. He was just beginning to touch his soul and his genius."

Outsiders commented on the new spontaneity, on how for a time Chayefsky began to relax and to smile more, and be kinder. "He became more open and trusting," said Herb Schlein. "There was less of that hard-ass, no-nonsense, get-off-my-back attitude he used to have." said Eddie White. "He began to say nice, almost affectionate things to me. He would ask me about my son, Peter, and he'd talk about his son, Danny."

"A lot of Paddy began to merge with Sidney," said Dan Chayefsky. "He could be Paddy in public, go out there and have fun, but at the same time let Sidney emerge. He became very straightforward and direct and heartfelt at the end. And that to me was Sidney. It was a beautiful thing to experience because I no longer had to deal with multiple people."

That October, Chayefsky, becoming more socially active again, went to a special screening of Martin Scorsese's *Raging Bull*. It was held at the Sutton Theatre, where *Marty* had played twenty-four years before. "This brought out the kid in him," said White. "We sat in the balcony and he sent me to the candy stand to buy red licorice, which we both loved. We were like two kids, teasing each other, seeing who could eat the red licorice faster. Then he began to reminisce about the candy they used to sell in the theatre lobbies in the old days. We had a candy shootout. Paddy would say 'buttons on paper,' and I would say 'rock candy.' He'd come up with 'jawbreakers,' and I would answer 'chocolate twists.' "

When winter came, Chayefsky attended the closed-circuit championship fight parties that Roone Arledge of ABC-Television hosted at the Plaza Hotel. Other A-list invitees included Frank Sinatra and Henry Kissinger. At one gathering Woody Allen showed up with his new companion, Mia Farrow.

They stayed in a corner all night, kissing and holding hands, until Chayefsky spotted them. "Look at them," he said. "They're so skinny and scared they look like two starving kids released from Dachau."

"Every now and then he'd make a mistake and he'd say something out of line at a party, which made him feel terrible later," said Dan Chayefsky. "But he knew that he had to go through that, that he would have to learn to monitor and control his behavior. And he began to do that, which made him twice as special."

A Final Drama and Divulgence

The calls for movie assignments never stopped. MGM/UA wanted him to adapt *Gorky Park;* director Robert Altman asked for "a collaboration"; and Barbra Streisand was persistent in sending him her numerous scripts and ideas for her forthcoming vanity production of *Yentl.* Chayefsky was always happy to read what Streisand sent him and give her his feedback, but no matter how much she pleaded, he would not work with her. "Both of them demanded too many creative controls," said Dan Chayefsky.

By January 1980, the writer had decided to start all over again, to return to his first true calling, that of a playwright. He began an outline for a new play, set in America during the red scare of the late 1940s and early 1950s. "There was something about the memory of that time, the kaleidoscopic changes and the idealism, that appealed very much to him," said Herb Gardner. When questioned, Chayefsky said the play was about Alger Hiss, the former Harvard lawyer and government official who had been accused of spying for the Russians in the late 1940s. But the Hiss affair, it was later determined, was only a dramatic backdrop for the piece. The protagonist at front and center was again Chayefsky, and the theme was to be an assessment of his part in a critical period of history that hitherto he had carefully remained silent about.

In 1947, when the Cold War between the United States and the Soviet Union had become solidly entrenched, the House Un-American Activities Committee in Washington commenced a series of hearings on suspected subversives in the motion picture industry. Its first victims were a group of writers and directors called the Hollywood Ten. Cited for contempt for refusing to reveal their own or others' past or present involvement with the Communist party, the ten were subsequently sentenced to prison. A prominent group from the film industry, including John Huston, William Wyler, William Holden, Henry Fonda, and Katharine Hepburn, came to their defense. Rallies were held, money was raised, and petitions were circulated. "Has it anything to do with communism? Of course not," Lillian Hellman told the members of the Screen Writers Guild. Politics, bias, and fear motivated Washington and Hollywood, where pictures about the American Negro were prohibited by "men who only in the last year allowed the word 'Jew' to be spoken in a picture," said Hellman, urging her writer-colleagues to stand up and "fight!"

Paddy Chayefsky obviously heard that call. He was in Hollywood at the time, writing for Universal Pictures. But in retrospect, his response to the plight of the Hollywood Ten was clouded to some. Michael Gordon remembered seeing him at meetings in Hollywood and Santa Monica. Chayefsky was very vocal about the political witch-hunt but no one was sure if he ever signed his name to a brief or petition. Betsy Blair's recollection was that Chayefsky was a Social Democrat. "Paddy was anti-Marxist, anti-Stalinist, and certainly anti-Communist," she said. "Most of our arguments and discussions at that time revolved around those issues."

In the period that immediately followed it seemed as if the hysteria over communism had subsided. In 1949, however, a violent confrontation occurred in upstate New York. At the end of the summer a group of Manhattan artists, writers, and others gathered for a week of recreation and conferences in a camp on the Hudson River near the town of Peekskill. To close that year's assembly a special fund-raising concert featuring Paul Robeson was planned, to benefit the Harlem chapter of the Civil Rights Congress. When the town's residents and American Legionnaires heard about this, they became incensed. What inflamed them particularly was that the visiting concertgoers would be not only "Reds," but also "niggers and kikes." On the evening of the show 150 people, many of them women and children, were seriously injured, attacked as they left the concert site and surrounding area. The following day, the American Civil Liberties Union issued a report critical of the state and local police, who were present and did nothing to prevent or stop the assault. A deluge of objections were also sent to President Truman in Washington. One telegram, dated September 15, protested the "flagrant whitewash of state and county law officials' open connivance in the Peekskill outrage." The signers of the telegram demanded that Truman order the Department of Justice to fully investigate the vicious attack and that "police officials and the proven attackers be brought to trial." The Justice Department did not comply and the Peekskill matter was allowed to slide by. However, a copy of the September 15 telegram was sent to the F.B.I., which made up an official dossier for each signed name. In due time four of these signatories would be subpoenaed to appear before

HUAC. Two other names on the telegram were those of Mr. and Mrs. Paddy Chayefsky, who had been present at Peekskill and who would now be assigned their individual F.B.I. files.

By 1952, with the war in Korea escalating, Senator Joseph R. McCarthy was waging his Red Menace Campaign in Congress and the House of Representatives had reactivated its committee hearings on suspected Communists in the movie industry. One of the first subpoenaed was Larry Parks, star of *The Jolson Story*. When asked to name names—of people he knew or suspected to be Communists—Parks respectfully refused. "This is not the American way," he said. "To force a man to do this is not American justice." Through coercion, Parks was forced to reconsider. "What the Committee wanted, in the old witch-hunt tradition, was public denunciation, public purgation, a purification of the convert by means of his public humiliation as he betrayed his old friends and comrades," said David Caute, author of *The Great Fear*. The names Parks gave were those already known to the committee, but his capitulation seriously affected his esteem and his Hollywood career. Parks was ostracized by many in the theatrical community when he looked for work in New York. Paddy Chayefsky was an exception; he took Parks up to the Bronx for a home-cooked meal from Gussie Chayefsky. At about the same time actor Howard Da Silva was blacklisted, and Chayefsky was one of the hosts of a rent party for him in Greenwich Village.

In quick succession, other Chayefsky friends and associates were brought before the HUAC investigators. These included Elia Kazan, Budd Schulberg, Harold Hecht, and Abe Burrows, all of whom cooperated by naming names. Michael Gordon was subpoenaed, refused to recant or inform, and was subsequently unemployed for eight years. That summer, with a national presidential election looming, red-baiting soon became the rival platform of both parties. The incumbent Democrats declared that they were on top of the Communist threat. The attorney general announced that six detention camps were being built to incarcerate alleged spies and saboteurs. To help fill up the camps, a number of independent crusaders volunteered their services, for patriotism and for profit. Naming names and hounding suspects from their jobs became the full-time duty of such publications as *Counterattack, Red Channels, Aware,* and *Spotlight*. The most powerful and feared vigilante group of all was the American Legion, which had its own anti-subversive investigative team in Washington and its own anti-Communist news sheet, *The Firing Line*. The latter was aimed specifically at the radio and especially the burgeoning television industry in New York City. On December 7, 1952, a month after the United States exploded its first H-bomb (to be followed shortly by the Soviet Union with its version), *The Firing Line* castigated the Columbia Broadcasting System for allowing its Theatre Guild of the Air program to employ suspected subversives. Among the names listed was that of Paddy Chayefsky. "How can so many objectionables slip through the screen?" the Legion asked, giving no specifics yet urging its members to write to U.S. Steel, the show's sponsor, and ask why it couldn't find American actors and writers "without front records" to put on the airwaves.

In retrospect this hitherto unpublicized imputation of Chayefsky raised a few questions. What was his reaction and how did he clear himself? The latter process put in effect by the major Hollywood studios called for complete atonement. Any employee fingered by the Legion was required to write a letter to or appear in person before James P. O'Neil, the head of their anti-subversive office in Washington. A full confession of past political sins, with a fervent denouncement of the evils of communism, was to be tendered, and if this was accepted, absolution would be granted. But this was not to be construed as "a political clearance," said O'Neil. What the Legion was trying to do was establish a climate of employment for "the innocent, the stupid, and the repentant guilty," he said. And the bigger the name the more public and humiliating the penance. Edward G. Robinson, after writing two letters, had to go to Washington and grovel before O'Neil. Further contrition was asked for, whereupon Robinson duly signed his name to an article, "How the Reds Made a Sucker out of Me," which appeared in the Legion magazine.

In December 1952, the same month that Chayefsky's name appeared in *The Firing Line,* John Huston and José Ferrer were also indicted. Under the threat of having their latest motion picture, *Moulin Rouge,* picketed at theatres across the country, the two were advised to make hasty amends with the Legion. On January 15, 1953, a bulletin sent to Legion posts told its members to lay off the director and the actor, because "they are displaying the type of cooperation we have requested in the past." Their names were not cited again by the Legion, nor was Chayefsky's. It was unlikely that his name was simply dropped. Once listed it was near impossible to be expunged without some form of repentance or influence. Betsy Blair was in the Legion's bad graces in 1954. To get cleared for the movie of *Marty* she was told she had to write a letter. She asked Chayefsky to help her compose it. He couldn't. MGM chief Dore Schary intervened with the Legion in Washington. She made the film and won many glowing reviews and tributes, but no further Hollywood work came because her name remained on the Legion's list. Two years later, when she questioned her agent, Lew Wasserman, she was told that she had to write the letter. "I couldn't then, and I can't now," Blair replied, and she moved to Europe. "There were certain rights involved," the actress said in 1993. "That letter was alien to everything I believed in."

Another alternative for Chayefsky was to fight the Legion through a lawyer. Among those who specialized in this was William H. Fitelson. He was with the

A.C.L.U. and was also the managing director of the Theatre Guild of the Air. He knew Chayefsky at this time, and may have urged the guild to ignore the Legion listing and to continue to employ him. Except by then Chayefsky had moved on, to the Philco-Goodyear series at NBC, where clearances were strictly enforced. Another such lawyer was Arnold Forster. He represented blacklisted actor Albert Dekker and was helping to "rehabilitate" John Garfield when the actor died from the stress of the HUAC investigations. Forster knew Chayefsky. Later they would work closely together on behalf of Israel and the Anti-Defamation League. In 1992, when asked if he had helped clear Chayefsky's name with the Legion, Forster's reaction was one of surprise. He had never known that Chayefsky was listed.

The matter of the Legion's charge against Chayefsky might have remained unnoticed and unessential if not for an incident that occurred during the making of *The Hospital* in 1971. Eric Albertson was the film's editor. His relationship with Chayefsky was good, he said, up until the point where they "got into a few arguments that were political." Albertson's father, William, once imprisoned, had been on the executive committee of the Communist party in New York and Detroit, and through him his son had heard of Chayefsky's earlier involvement. "Paddy was leftist," said Eric Albertson, "but as far as I know he was not a member of the party." During the editing of *The Hospital,* Albertson asked Chayefsky "why he cooperated, why he re-canted," which caught Chayefsky off-guard. Then Chayefsky responded. "He blamed it on Elia Kazan," said Albertson. "Kazan talked him into it. That's what he said."

In an ad placed in *The New York Times* two days after his HUAC testimony in 1952, Kazan had urged others to follow his example. "Secrecy serves the Communists," he said. "The employment of a lot of good liberals is threat-ened because they have allowed themselves to become associated with or silenced by the Communists. Liberals must speak out."

"*Shit* no!" said Kazan in 1993, when asked whether he told Chayefsky to cooperate with the Legion. "It was none of my business."

"Gadge talked him into it. That's what Paddy said when I confronted him," said Albertson in a follow-up conversation. "I remember because that was the first time I had heard Kazan's nickname."

"Everyone made up their own mind about the blacklist," Kazan insisted. Regarding Chayefsky: "I didn't give him advice and he didn't ask for it."

Albertson's distinct impression was that Chayefsky *did* recant. "If I'm wrong about it, why did he react?"

"Paddy was clean! No one touched him during the blacklist," his sister-in-law Terry Chayefsky later insisted. But again, neither she nor his brother Bill nor Paddy's close friend Herb Gardner were even aware of the Legion listing.

What Dan Chayefsky recalled from that period was a pervasive sense of fear in their household. "Every time a letter arrived from the government addressed to Sidney Chayefsky my parents were terrified," said Dan Chayefsky. "They were sure it was a subpoena."

Speculation could be made that it was the ongoing terror that motivated Paddy Chayefsky to seek the psychiatric help that began at this time. And the guilt, if he did recant, the inner dissent for a man who had made a career out of fighting and noncompromise, might account for the desolation and fury that began to pursue him. The possibility that he did bow before the Legion might also explain Chayefsky's continued antipathy toward Arthur Miller, who when faced with the threat of being put in prison did the brave and "honorable thing," steadfastly refusing to cooperate with any witch-hunt committee. And what was the effect of all this on Susan Chayefsky? She had her own fears and anxieties to contend with, and certainly it could not have helped her mental equilibrium to see so many of the people she knew and grew up with in the Allerton co-ops being hounded and stripped of their civil freedom and their right to work.

Chayefsky's fear of being subpoenaed continued until the late 1950s, his son recalled. "One day he said, 'To hell with it. I'm not going to let this rule my life.' " In November 1958 he began work on a TV play about a man with a "social aberration." Entitled *The Communist,* it dealt with the emotional pattern and deterioration of a man who belonged to the party. The network, CBS, passed on that script. In 1962, Chayefsky decided to write about the diseased roots of the movement itself, in *The Passion of Josef D.* That consumed two years of his life but it did not alleviate his hate and anger. For the next sixteen years he would castigate "the Commies" and scoff at the Trotskyites, without true catharsis or revealment—until 1979, when after successfully confronting his own duality and duplicity, he may have found it was time for a more thorough and honest appraisal.

Old habits die hard; hence, when the word was spread that Chayefsky was working on a new play, those who inquired as to the subject matter were carefully deflected. It was about Alger Hiss. That was the continued refrain. Chayefsky, however, the master of research, never did contact Hiss, who was still alive and lived in downtown Manhattan. Herb Gardner said later that the new play had "more to do with self-examination, and betrayal and loyalty. It involved the emotions and idealism of an individual, somebody not unlike Paddy in some ways."

There were two leading characters in the play. The victim is a man who is visited one day by government agents. Assuring him that he is not a suspect, they want to know about various people from his political past. When their pressure increases he consults an attorney. The lawyer agrees with the victim that he did the right thing by telling the agents to "go fuck themselves." Together, they sift through the past and endeavor to unravel the enigmatic line between actual guilt and innocence.

Among the lawyers Chayefsky consulted in connection with his play were William Fitelson and his own attorney, Maurice Spanbock. He also spoke at length with Elia Kazan. "We were now in the same office building," said Kazan. "I was on seven and he was on eleven. He used to come down to see me and talk about the play. We discussed everything: Alger Hiss, the Communists, the blacklisting, all of that."

Chayefsky started the work with a certain intention, he told his son. "He wanted to prove or disprove something," said Dan Chayefsky. "And the more he explored it the more he disagreed with his primary intention. It developed into a completely different thing."

The play was "something right on his game," said Herb Gardner. "He was all caught up in it. You could hear him typing away through that door— chortling to himself and yelling and carrying on. He was back in business."

In September 1980, Chayefsky's absorption was curtailed. The movie *Altered States,* integrated with the special effects and soundtrack score, was now ready for release. After a successful preview in Los Angeles, Warner Bros. embarked on an ambitious marketing campaign and they prevailed upon Paddy Chayefsky to let bygones be bygones and allow them to put his name back on the credits. Gottfried tried to talk to him, as did Dan Melnick, Ted Ashley, and others. Producer Marty Ransohoff lunched with Chayefsky at the Russian Tea Room. "The guys asked me to intercede," he said. "It was not a lot of fun, believe me. He was still very angry, and he wouldn't budge."

In December 1980, when the film was released, Richard Corliss of *Time* said he was pleasantly pleased. "Laugh with it, scream at it, think about it. You may leave the theater in an altered state," he said. No other writer could move from behavioral parody to dead-serious paranoia the way Chayefsky had in *Network,* Corliss stated, but in *Altered States* he went "further, higher, conceptualizing great notions like a tragic tenor in an orgiastic Rand opera." And nobody could overwrite as Chayefsky could, with his endlessly reflective, articulate characters, the critic observed: "Spitting out litanies of adjectives, geysers of abstract nouns, chemical chains of relative clauses . . . and yet Chayefsky's voluptuous verbosity is a welcome antidote to all those recent dialogues of the carnalities—movies in which brutal characters speak only words of one syllable and four letters."

During this time Chayefsky gave a rare extensive interview to John Brady for his book *The Craft of the Screenwriter.* While acknowledging that during the making of *The Goddess* he had been a very "presumptuous fellow . . .

screaming at everybody, yelling at everybody, going into tantrums over and over again, and carrying on very badly," Chayefsky steered away from mentioning the trouble on *Altered States*. His only desire, he told Brady, was that the film would make enough money to allow him to finish his play.

Two acts were finished, with some slight "plot problems" in the third act, Maurice Spanbock said, "but it had marvelous speeches, some brilliant stuff in it."

"It was truly good," Herb Gardner agreed. "We were talking about it, at that point every week. He had only a month or so to go on it, then he became ill."

Early that winter, Chayefsky developed a bad cough that led to pleurisy. "He would never discuss what was wrong with him," said Eddie White. "He was seeing different doctors and he went into the hospital for some tests. In the past when he did that he would let it be known through his friends in the press that he was on a cruise or a vacation; which didn't fool anyone because everyone knew that Paddy never took vacations."

When he came out of the hospital he had lost a lot of weight, and his hair and beard had turned gray. Many attributed this to the continued stress of *Altered States*. Following the trouble with Ken Russell a lawsuit had been filed by a medical research assistant.

"The research guy wanted to be credited as 'co-author,' " said Dan Chayefsky. "And that devastated my father. He still had that great pride about his work. He could have settled the case for very little money, but he refused. He spent close to a quarter of a million dollars fighting the guy. It also cost him maybe two to three extra years of his life."

J. P. Miller believed that Chayefsky's basic self-destructiveness led to his physical decline. "There are fights and turmoil connected with every picture," said Miller. "That's the way the movie business works. Paddy got sick because he never took care of himself."

At the gym, Eddie White tried to get Chayefsky to exercise by running. "He would tell me, 'Force me to do it.' Instead I'd encourage him to run one lap with me. 'Let's try it,' I'd urge him. And he'd say, 'All right! But *don't* leave me alone after it's all over.' "

When White wasn't there, Chayefsky goofed off. "Mostly he hung around and schmoozed with us in the locker room," said the lyricist Joe Stein. "We schmoozed about everything. As a matter of fact Paddy kept us from exercising. I don't remember ever seeing him on the track, and certainly not in the pool. I think he spent most of his time sitting on the locker bench, talking. Talking was his idea of exercise."

"He was constantly breaking his diet," said Arthur Penn. "And he began smoking again. He and Fosse had this ferocious humor about smoking; it was like 'Are you dead yet?' "

With the illness Chayefsky's black pessimism and anger returned, but he no longer had the energy to fight. At Elaine's restaurant one night, Chayefsky was seated with Dyan Cannon, Darren McGavin, and Eddie White. A dispute arose when the news reporter Denis Hamill dropped by. He had covered Chayefsky's altercation with Vanessa Redgrave on the Oscars a few years before. Eager for an update, Hamill mentioned that the actress had recently appeared on television as the Holocaust survivor Fania Fenelon, in *Playing for Time* by Arthur Miller. "That prick purposely hired her to play a Jew," Chayefsky said to Hamill, "just because she's for the P.L.O."

"I kept saying to Hamill, 'Leave him alone, he's a sick man. Let him eat his dinner in peace,'" said White. "But Denis kept prodding him. 'You've got to separate the actress from the politics,' he said. The more he spoke the more upset Paddy became. His face went red, then white. The blood drained out of him. I don't think Denis realized how ill Paddy was. He was too weak to argue. He tried, but he didn't have the energy. He whispered to me, 'Take me home.' So I got him out of there and brought him home in a cab. When we got to his apartment, I wanted to take him upstairs, but he said, 'No,' and he staggered into the lobby of his building."

> It is all right for the bulk of men to fear death,
> for in death they fear me. But, in truth,
> there isn't anything to it at all. Nothing happens,
> nothing changes; the essence of things goes on.
>
> God, *Gideon*

In January of 1981, Bob Fosse hosted a birthday luncheon for Chayefsky at the River Café overlooking the East River. The guests were Herb Gardner and his wife, Barbara Sproul; agents Sam Cohn and Arlene Donovan; Bill and Winn Chayefsky and their wives, Saranne and Terry; and Bob Fosse and his current girlfriend, actress Julie Hagerty. "It was a very festive occasion," said Terry Chayefsky, "with Paddy and Fosse trading their usual jokes and backhanded compliments." After the meal, Fosse had two birthday cakes wheeled out for dessert. One was inscribed to Paddy Chayefsky, the other to Sidney Aaron.

The following month, when the pleurisy returned, Chayefsky returned to the hospital for more tests. The diagnosis was cancer but he refused to be operated on. "No way. I won't let them near me," he told Eddie White. "He meant the surgeons," said White. "He had that terrible fear, 'They're going to get ahold of me and cut me up because of that movie I wrote about them.' He was convinced if they got him on the operating table he would not get up alive."

Opting for chemotherapy treatments instead, when his hair fell out, Paddy began to wear a cap. "He no longer wanted to go into the Carnegie Deli, so we would have lunch down the street," said Maurice Spanbock. Sometime later, Howard Gottfried recalled seeing Chayefsky sitting with Herb Gardner at a window table in the Mayflower restaurant on Central Park West. "As I passed by, Paddy waved," said Gottfried, "and I remember thinking, 'His hair, it's turned completely white.' "

That wasn't his hair, it was a wig, Gwen Verdon explained. "After the chemo treatments, Bob went to see Romain Greene, who designed wigs for all the Broadway shows. They went up to see Paddy in the hospital, with all these different wigs. It was like he was playing a part. Is he going to look like Rasputin? Or does he want to look punk? It was a very funny situation and of course, Paddy loved the absurdity of it all."

"He'd show up at the Dramatists Guild meetings wearing the wig," said Robert Anderson. "It was very sad, very touching—obviously everyone was very fond of Paddy. But he was always—'Let's not talk about it'—very gruff—or he'd make a joke about it."

In his private life, Chayefsky continued to try to repair the damage that had been inflicted on his son. "He knew mistakes had been made and he tried to make up for them," said Dan Chayefsky. "Towards the end he was very open and loving. It helped me greatly later on to realize how honest he had become."

Ann Reinking told of a luncheon that she attended with Chayefsky. "It was at La Côte Basque, with a group of people brought together by Bill Fitelson." Also at the lunch were executives from Columbia Pictures and the investment banker Herbert Allen, Jr., who had recently married Reinking. "My life had some sort of a direction at that point and Paddy was very happy for me," she said. "When he came in, he hugged me and said, 'You look really great and I'm so pleased.' He was fatherly, just so good. But he also looked very pale, very unhealthy. But no one discussed it. And that was the last time I saw him."

"He left a message that I was to meet him on the street outside his office building," said Eddie White. "He looked more gaunt than ever. He kidded and joked, but when we said goodbye I instinctively knew that I would not see him again."

"He called me," said David Shaw. "He told me he had been sick, then recovered, but was now going back into the hospital, that they found something else wrong with him. And he said, 'Pray for me.' "

At Columbia Presbyterian Hospital, Garson Kanin was visiting his brother, Michael, when he saw Chayefsky coming down the hall in his bathrobe. "He was attached to an IV tube, with a nurse or orderly holding up the bottle. We stopped and talked and he was quite cheerful. I said, 'What's going on?' And he said, 'Ah, it's a lot of bullshit. You know, the doctors have to make money, and I'll be out of here in a week.' "

The black humor was there to the end, Herb Gardner recalled. "During the last weeks, when Bobby and I visited, Paddy was at the point of doing death-joke scenes. We'd be talking to him and he'd go, 'It's getting dark, fellows.' As we were leaving he would do his worst idea of a corny death scene, with this terrible dialogue from forties films. 'It's getting dark, fellows! It's getting very dark.' We would hear him from the corridor. It was such hilarious stuff. We couldn't help but laugh."

Within a short time his condition began to deteriorate rapidly. "It was very confusing," said Dan Chayefsky. "I never knew what exactly was wrong with him. When I asked him he said it was 'floating cancer cells.' For all I know he may have had a large tumor that he didn't want me or my mother to know about."

Susan Chayefsky, under sedation and with the help of a friend, made it to the hospital, where she left notes on the door of her husband's room, in which she told Bob Fosse and Herb Gardner to cut their visits short and not tire the patient. Winn and Bill Chayefsky also visited with their wives and were given "the Paddy performance." The medical tests were wrong, he told them. He was going to fight the cancer and get well. "It was scary, actually, because he was losing so much weight from the chemotherapy," said Dan Chayefsky. "When I would go to hug him, I felt he was disappearing on me."

> I am truth. It is God that is fiction.

> Eddie Jessup, *Altered States*

Emotionally, Chayefsky wanted to believe in God, but intellectually there was always resistance. "My whole nature utterly *revolts* at the idea that there is any Being in the universe superior to *myself*," Edgar Allan Poe had written in his 1847 cosmic essay "Eureka." Chayefsky dramatized his position in 1961 with *Gideon*, which pitted man's obduracy and vanity against God. "My father *was* Gideon. He truly felt that his talent and intelligence set him apart from others," said Dan Chayefsky. "People who are lonely and desperate also tend to make phony claims for themselves. In his pain, rather than destroy himself or go crazy, he said, 'I'll be my own God.' " That self-will and approbation stayed with him until after his defeat on *Altered States*. As he moved toward becoming more complete within himself, Chayefsky began to look at God as more loving and benevolent than the vengeful, shaming, fire-and-brimstone figure portrayed in the Old Testament. His son was more inclined toward the New Testament, and Chayefsky found himself reviewing those possibilities. "To my mind, the happiest people are those who trust they have a Higher Power, no matter what happens to them. Only then can they let go of their control over everything," said Dan Chayefsky. "Some truly wicked things had to happen to my father on *Altered States*, with the movie and the lawsuit. Then on top of that to lose control of what was happening to his body must have devastated him. But he knew it was for a purpose, to make him grow."

The hardest thing to part with was his sense of being special and self-sufficient. "It is all but a gift from God. There is no honor that reflects to me in it at all, merely that I am beloved of God," he wrote in *Gideon*. The fact that God was and is "the final truth of all things" was something Paddy Chayefsky still had difficulty yielding to. "I must aspire, God," was his repeated entreaty, until he could no longer speak.

In the hospital that July, Chayefsky woke up from one of his nightmares extremely agitated. He was suffocating, choking to death, but awake. When he tried to scream, no sounds came from his mouth. His lungs were filled with fluid, and the doctors had to perform an emergency tracheotomy to save his life. In intensive care it seemed he might not survive, but he rallied, and although he could no longer talk, he could communicate by writing on a pad. The notes he wrote to Fosse and Gardner, his brothers, his son, were cryptic and still combative. Paddy went on fighting, even when he slipped into a coma. Hooked up to tubes, he tried to pull them from his body. When the medics taped his arms to boards he tried to rid himself of the wooden slats. "He wasn't conscious but he kept yanking the tubes out," said Dan Chayefsky. "We'd say to him, 'You can't do this. These tubes are feeding you.' But he didn't want to be restrained. Even in his sleep he was like a caged tiger."

After one exhausting, contentious night, Chayefsky woke up completely calm and peaceful. "It was the strangest thing," his son recalled. "I don't know if he had been battling God or himself. But he had some kind of an after-death experience. It was as if during the night he had gone to the other side and saw something he needed to know. When he woke up he stopped fighting against a lot of the negative things that he had been holding on to. He was so alive and optimistic. He knew exactly what was wrong with him and how he should correct it. And then, ironically, shortly thereafter he let go of life itself."

On August 1, 1981, Paddy Chayefsky died. He was fifty-eight.

His last words were to his wife, written on a pad of paper. "I tried. I really tried," he said. He was referring to the work.

CHAPTER 38

Epitaph for a Playwright

"When Paddy died, we called each other up. It was as if the boy who carried the flag had fallen," said Tad Mosel, his colleague from the Golden Age of Television.

"I was in Canada when I got the call. It was so unexpected, because I didn't realize he was so was ill," said director Arthur Hiller.

"I was on a plane and I read it over someone's shoulder," said William Hurt, "and I yelled out, 'No! It can't be true.' I owed him much more than I realized."

"He was first of all a playwright, with a love of words. In Hollywood he was that rarity, the writer as auteur. . . . His movies, with the exception of his last, belonged to him, not to his director," said *The New York Times*.

Ever the efficient organizer, Chayefsky had left instructions for his interment. "I was born a Jew, took pride in being a Jew, and I want to die a Jew," he said, but he did not want an Orthodox service. The funeral should be simple and conservative, with both men and women attending, and he wouldn't mind a eulogy. "I think they're nice at funerals," he said. "But I do not want to be eulogized by a rabbi who never met me in my life (since I don't know that many rabbis anyway). A few kind words about me from people who mean it would be appreciated."

Bob Fosse stepped in to stage the ceremony, with Herb Gardner, David Picker, writer Noel Behn, and Maurice Spanbock handling the arrangements and invitations. The response was so enormous that two rooms had to be booked at the Riverside funeral home on West Seventy-sixth Street. It was "a full house, standing room only," said Fosse, "just the way Paddy would have wanted it." The *Times* put the number at 500 mourners. Placed at the front with the family were some of Chayefsky's favorite people—the writers: Garson Kanin, Ruth Gordon, Tad Mosel, David Shaw, J. P. Miller, Peter Stone, James Goldman, E. L. Doctorow, Arthur Laurents, David Mamet, Kurt Vonnegut, Melvin Van Peebles, Alice Childress, Sidney Kingsley, Ira Levin, Shana Alexander. Even his old faithful adversary, Arthur Miller, showed up. ("Paddy admired Miller and Miller admired him," said Herb Gardner. "Finally the things they cared about in life were so much the same that it made no difference what happened before.") Among the others who came to pay their respects were Elia Kazan, Howard Gottfried, Sidney Lumet, Arthur Penn, Arthur Hiller, Mike Nichols, Betty Comden, Adolph Green, Sheldon Harnick, Joseph Stein, Martin Balsam, Celeste Holm, Jerry Stiller, Marian Seldes, Alan Manson, Jack Weston, Charles Grodin, Robert Merrill, and Jan Peerce. "I was in the second room," said the playwright Owa. "There was an old man next to me, crying, because he felt he should have been in the main room with the celebrities."

Laughter, drama, and the appropriate intrigue were supplied. "Everyone was kind of straining their necks when 'the widow,' Susan Chayefsky, was helped down the aisle," said Eddie White. "This was the first time many of us had seen her."

"Paddy is dead, and when he finds out he's going to be mad as hell," said Herb Gardner in his opening eulogy, describing how the departed writer "always looked like he was ready to go fifteen rounds with Western civilization."

"In hollow times he was a man of passion, and his work and life had the lucidity of his passion," said Arthur Schlesinger, Jr. "His theme became the corrupt and lunatic energies secreted by our great modern organizations. He had a rage against pomposity, a rage against stupidity, a rage against injustice, a rage for humanity."

"The only thing I know best about Paddy is that he is my brother and there was never one small second when he was not," said Winn Chayefsky. "I know that he is a very complex person, but the brother relationship between the three of us is a clear and simple thing, and nothing between us has ever been complicated. With three different personalities, we lived three different lives. But we only have one feeling toward each other. And it is the same—a true and good feeling. I never said any of this to Paddy or Bill, but I am certain they knew it."

For the finale, Bob Fosse said he hoped he was not going to offend anyone, but he and Paddy had this pact. Whichever one preceded the other out of this life would do "this silly thing," a brandish at death, a soft-shoe routine. Whereupon he began to dance beside the coffin.

"It was a shuffle," said Tad Mosel. "I wished he had gone all out and done a big number, because Paddy would have wanted it that way."

At the finish of the dance, Fosse, wracked with sobs, leaned over and touched the coffin. "I can't imagine my life without you," he whispered.

The final interment was at a cemetery in Valhalla, New York. Chayefsky had given instructions that Kaddish be sung and that the ceremony be "as brief and painless a burial service as possible, and then back to the comfort of some-body's home where I honestly wish everybody a good time."

That night "a blast," a farewell party, was held at Herb Gardner's house. Guests were told to tell "Paddy stories," with no tears. Arthur Hiller recalled a subsequent gathering, at a special screening of *The Americanization of Emily.* "I got up to speak, and as I started, I became very emotional," said Hiller. "I started talking about Paddy and couldn't finish. I was angry with God for taking him away. We hadn't had enough from him. Normally I am very calm, but that night I was almost screaming at God. It was as if Paddy was talking through me, saying, 'Why, God? Why now, when I had so much yet to give?' "

"Five more projects, that's what he told me he had in him," said Dan Chayefsky.

"If he had lived, he would have been after everyone, with such hilarity. Paddy had the ability to see the ridiculous, to see the madness," said Sidney Lumet.

"Whatever it would be it would have to be about mankind, about humanity, and it would be caring and compassionate," said his son. "It would also probably be pretty biting, with a lot of humor in it."

On March 5, 1984, three years after his death, at a black-tie dinner in Los Angeles, Chayefsky was inducted into the First Annual Television Hall of Fame, along with Edward R. Murrow, William Paley, Norman Lear, and Lucille Ball. Accepting the posthumous award for Chayefsky was Bob Fosse. In his speech, he told the audience of a time when Chayefsky was in despair and questioned his worth as a writer. "I reminded him of his incredible range—from the uncommon common-man language of *Marty* to the poetry of *Gideon,* [from] the black comedy of *The Latent Heterosexual* to the fierce eloquent anger of *The Hospital* and *Network.* I even threw in a few extravagant phrases critics used about him—'acerbic,' 'witty,' 'powerful.' But the doubt remained, and then Paddy spoke. 'Fosse, I would like to be remembered,' he said. 'I think the most modest of us aspire to that. But this is a very fickle business. I'll be lucky if they remember I'm the guy who wrote the lines 'What are you doing tonight, Marty?' and 'I'm mad as hell and I'm not going to take it anymore.' "

As those lines were spoken, loud applause broke out in the banquet room. Fosse paused, then gave his closing. "Paddy, you're wrong," he said. "You are remembered. Some of us will never forget you."

ACKNOWLEDGMENTS

This book's existence is largely due to the generosity and time given by those who worked with or knew Paddy Chayefsky. They include his colleagues from the "Golden Age of Television": J. P. Miller, Tad Mosel, David Shaw, Gore Vidal, Horton Foote, Sumner Locke Elliott, Ethel Winant, George Baxt, Milton Meyers, and Delbert Mann, who also directed three of Chayefsky's earliest motion pictures, including *Marty*.

From the Dramatists Guild, I am grateful to playwrights Garson Kanin, Robert Anderson, William Gibson, Robert E. Lee, Jerome Lawrence, Arthur Miller, John Guare, and especially Herb Gardner, Chayefsky's peer and durable friend, who provided a perspective and color that otherwise might have been missed.

Among the actors, directors, producers, production designers and managers, script supervisors, editors, studio executives, publicists, and others who worked on Chayefsky's plays and movies, I owe my thanks to Betsy Blair, Ernest Borgnine, Douglas Campbell, Everett Chambers, James Coburn, Alvin Epstein, Lee Grant, Donald Harron, Steven Hill, Betty Lou Holland, Barnard Hughes, Werner Klemperer, Martin Landau, Alan Manson, Nancy Marchand, Randy Moore, Lee Philips, Audrey Peters, Diana Rigg, Gene Saks, Arthur Hiller, Sidney Lumet, Arthur Penn, Milton Perlman, David Hays, Marty Ransohoff, John Calley, Paul Baker, James Doolittle, James Hill, George Justin, Charles Maguire, Dick Smith, Marie Kenny, Maggie Janes, Barbara Robinson, Eric Albertson, Herb Jaffe, Arthur Krim, Daniel Melnick, David Picker, Max Youngstein, Johnny Friedkin, Bernie Kamber, and Walter Seltzer. I am also beholden to Chayefsky's longtime lawyer Maurice Spanbock, and to Howard Gottfried, Chayefsky's partner and coproducer who made himself available for lengthy interviews and follow-up discussions over a long period of time.

Gwen Verdon and Ann Reinking graciously gave their recollections and help in re-creating the deep friendship between Chayefsky and Bob Fosse. Other friends who added their private and professional remembrances were Michael Gordon, Elia Kazan, Budd Schulberg, Mel Goldberg, Arthur Schlesinger, Jr., Dan Barton, Mike Kelly, Eddie White, Herbie Schlein, Owa, and Abe Pasternak and Larry Mayer (who knew Chayefsky during his school and war years). Stanley Donen, Ginger Rogers, Sonny Fox, Chris Chase, Tino Balio, Arnold Forster, Martin Gottfried, Elihu Winer, Marian Seldes, Joseph Stein, Barney Rosensweig, Gordon Sander, and Esther Pollock also assisted with information or suggested other leads.

Regarding Chayefsky's personal life, a large debt of gratitude is owed the writer's son, Dan, who over a period of ten months, under sometimes difficult circumstances, spoke honestly and incisively about his father's life and about their close but complex relationship. Without him this book as it stands would not have been possible. Terry Chayefsky, Paddy Chayefsky's friend and sister-in-law, was instrumental in getting the family to cooperate and I am more than appreciative. Bill Chayefsky, Paddy's eldest, surviving brother, was also forthcoming and extremely helpful.

For assistance in the research I would like to single out Eileen Tuohy, who gave freely of her time in Los Angeles, searching and making copies of Chayefsky press items and interviews, and looking through photographs and stills at the Academy of Motion Picture Arts and Sciences. Harold Miller, the reference archivist at the State Historical Society of Wisconsin, where Chayefsky's papers and the United Artists files are stored, was of enormous assistance. I thank him and his staff, and Ben Brewster, the assistant director of the film and photo division, for providing the needed material. In New York, the staff of the Billy Rose Theater Collection at Lincoln Center were as always courteous and efficient in sharing their files and in making suggestions where other documents could be found. From the film and photo still department of the Museum of Modern Art in New York, I am grateful to Ron Magliozzi, Mary Corliss, and Terry Geeksin. Raymond Daum of the Humanities Research Center at the University of Texas in Austin gave other valuable assistance, as did Peter Eliot in London, providing reviews and news items covering Chayefsky's frequent visits and stage productions.

For her continued support as a friend and adviser, I owe more than I can express here to Kathy Judge, M.S.W., of Killington, Vermont. Along with providing insights and clarification on important details, she supplied an endless flow of encouragement, humor, and patience. In her free time she also managed to track down a rare copy of William Bradford Huie's novel *The Americanization of Emily*.

Another staunch ally was Peg Judge of Southampton, New York, who listened with enthusiasm to every Chayefsky story, then went over the first completed draft of the book with her astute tutorial expertise. Stephen M. Silverman of Manhattan, a friend and colleague, also painstakingly went over the same draft, and his sharp judgment was equaled only by his wit and precision.

Special thanks to my agent, Kris Dahl, at ICM, who believed in and supported this book from the beginning; and to Dorothea Herry, her ever-efficient literary assistant, who helped field the calls and handle the emergencies when they arose. At Random House, David Rosenthal was the executive editor, and I am thankful for his taking a chance on this less-than-commercial prospect. His assistant, Tad Floridis, compiled the photo insert and very ably marshaled the completed manuscript, with Ruth Fecych, Benjamin Dreyer, and Katherine Scott adeptly handling the final cuts and the copyediting, for which I am grateful.

Lastly, I wish to acknowledge a special and powerful patron, Saint Jude, who always comes through without fail.

BIBLIOGRAPHY

BOOKS

Ansky, S. *The Dybbuk and Other Writings*. Edited by David G. Roskies. New York: Pantheon Books, 1992.

Baker, Carroll. *Baby Doll*. New York: Arbor House, 1983.

Balio, Tino. *The United Artists Story*. Madison: University of Wisconsin Press, 1987.

Barnouw, Eric. *Tube of Plenty*. New York: Oxford University Press, 1975.

Brady, John. *The Craft of the Screenwriter*. New York: Simon & Schuster, 1981.

Brown, Jared. *Zero Mostel*. New York: Atheneum, 1989.

Brown, Peter Harry. *Kim Novak: Reluctant Goddess*. New York: St. Martin's Press, 1986.

Caute, David. *The Great Fear*. New York: Simon & Schuster, 1978.

Chayefsky, Paddy. *Television Plays*. New York: Simon & Schuster, 1955.

———. *Middle of the Night*. New York: Samuel French, 1956.

———. *The Tenth Man*. New York: Samuel French, 1960.

———. *Gideon*. New York: Random House, 1961.

———. *The Passion of Josef D*. New York: Random House, 1964.

———. *The Latent Heterosexual*. New York: Random House, 1968.

———. *Network*. A novelization by Sam Hedrin. New York: Pocket Books, 1976.

———. *Altered States*. New York: Harper & Row, 1978.

Clum, John. *Paddy Chayefsky*. Boston: Twayne Publishers, 1976.

Corliss, Richard. *The Hollywood Screenwriters*. New York: Avon Books, 1977.

Cottrell, John. *Julie Andrews*. London: Arthur Baker, 1968.

Faulkner, Trader. *Peter Finch*. New York: Taplinger Publishing Company, 1979.

Fine, Marshall. *Bloody Sam*. New York: Donald I. Fine, 1991.

Goldman, William. *The Season*. New York: Harcourt, Brace & World, 1969.

Gornick, Vivian. *The Romance of American Communism*. New York: Basic Books, 1977.

Gottfried, Martin. *All His Jazz: The Life and Death of Bob Fosse*. New York: Bantam Books, 1990.

Henry, William A., III. *Jackie Gleason: The Great One*. New York: Doubleday, 1992.

Hoffman, Daniel. *Poe Poe Poe Poe Poe Poe Poe*. New York: Paragon House, 1990.

Huie, William Bradford. *The Americanization of Emily*. New York: E. P. Dutton, 1959.

Hunter, Allan. *Faye Dunaway*. New York: St. Martin's Press, 1986.

Kahane, Rabbi Meir. *The Story of the Jewish Defense League*. Radnor, Pa.: Chilton Company, 1973.

Kanfer, Stefan. *The Journal of the Plague Years*. New York: Atheneum, 1973.

Kazan, Elia. *A Life*. New York: Alfred A. Knopf, 1988.

Klemo, Larry. *Kim Novak: On Camera*. New York: A. S. Barnes, 1980.

Kobal, John. *People Will Talk*. New York: Alfred A. Knopf, 1986.

Logan, Joshua. *Movie Stars, Real People, and Me*. New York: Dell, 1978.

McClintock, David. *Indecent Exposure*. New York: William Morrow, 1982.

McGilligan Pat. *Backstory 2*. Berkeley: University of California Press, 1991.

Miller, Arthur. *Timebends: A Life*. New York: Grove Press, 1987.

Navatsky, Victor S. *Naming Names*. New York: Viking Press, 1980.

Plimpton, George, ed. *Writers at Work: The Paris Review Interviews*. First Series. New York: Viking Press, 1958.

Richards, David. *Played Out: The Jean Seberg Story*. New York: Random House, 1981.

Russell, Ken. *Altered States*. New York: Bantam Books, 1991.

Selznick, David O. *Memo from David O. Selznick*. Ed. Rudy Behmer. New York: Viking Press, 1972.

Silverman, Kenneth. *Edgar A. Poe*. New York: HarperCollins, 1991.

Simon, John. *Reverse Angle*. New York: Crown Publishers, 1982.

Strait, Raymond. *James Garner*. New York: St. Martin's Press, 1985.

Wiley, Mason, and Damien Bona. *Inside Oscar*. New York: Ballantine Books, 1987.

ARTICLES

American Film Magazine. "Dialogue on Film: Arthur Hiller." October 1979.

Barry, David. "Arts and Pleasures." *Women's Wear Daily*, October 11, 1976.

Barthel, Joan. "TV Will Do Anything for a Rating." *The New York Times,* November 14, 1976.

Blumenfeld, Ralph. "New York's a Film Festival." *New York Post,* June 6, 1971.

Brender, Alan. "Blair Brown Talks About Altered States." *Starlog,* May 1981.

Buckley, Tom. "Ken Russell on Altered States Controversy." *The New York Times,* January 16, 1981.

Buckley, William. "Vanessa and the Use of Oscar." *New York Post,* April 6, 1978.

Broeske, Pat H. "Carolyn Jones." *Drama-Logue,* n.d.

Cagin, Seth. "Ken Russell's Altered Ego." *Soho Weekly News,* January 14, 1981.

Carroll, Kathleen. "Hollywood Zaps the Boob Tube." *Sunday News,* March 14, 1976.

Chayefsky, Paddy. "In Praise of Reappraised Picture-Makers." *The New York Times,* January 8, 1956.

————. "Art Films—Dedicated Insanity." *The Saturday Review,* December 21, 1957.

————. "The Goddess." *Esquire,* March 1958.

————. "From the Notebooks of Josef D." *New York Herald Tribune,* February 2, 1964.

Corliss, Richard. "Invasion of the Mind Snatcher." *Time,* December 29, 1980.

Crist, Judith. "What Price Laughter?" *New York Herald Tribune,* November 8, 1964.

Crowther, Bosley. "In Praise of Cowardice." *The New York Times,* November 8, 1964.

Denby, David. "Blissed Out." *New York,* December 22, 1980.

Dryansky, G. Y. "Chayefsky: Save the Jews." *Women's Wear Daily,* February 26, 1971.

Dudar, Helen. "Paddy Chayefsky: A Portrait." *New York Post,* January 4–7, 1960.

————. "A Mind-Blowing Battle." New York *Daily News,* December 1980.

Ebert, Roger. "Altered States: Pure Energy." New York *Daily News,* January 23, 1980.

Gardella, Kay. "Notes of a Concerned Critic." New York *Daily News,* November 18, 1976.

Glover, William. "Chayefsky: Sick of Broadway." New York *Daily News,* June 3, 1962.

Gross, Ben. "Unimportant Folks Are Interesting." New York *Sunday News,* May 26, 1957.

Gussow, Mel. "Chayefsky: Writer with Love of Words." *The New York Times,* August 3, 1981.

Horowitz, Susan. "Paddy Chayefsky Speaks Out." *The Saturday Review,* November 13, 1976.

Klemesrud, Judy. "The Hospital." *The New York Times,* December 31, 1971.

Knight, Arthur. "Paddy Chayefsky Becomes Part of the Big Picture." *Los Angeles Times,* March 26, 1972.

Lahr, John. "Betsy Blair." *New Theater Review,* Fall 1989.

Manning, Robert. "A New Era for Playwrights." *Life,* July 25, 1955.

Mills, Donia. "A Movie About TV." *Washington Star,* November 3, 1976.

Mills, Nancy. "Altered States Alters Director's Life." *Boston Herald American,* February 27, 1981.

Mitgang, Herbert. "Chayefsky: A Man of Passion." *The New York Times,* August 5, 1981.

Moss, Robert F. "The Agonies of a Screenwriter." *The Saturday Review,* May 1981.

Naha, Ed. "A Cosmic Love Story." *Future Life,* March 1981.

———. "I Create the Body Cosmic." *Fangoria,* April 1981.

Norton, Elliot. "Chayefsky Learned by Copying a Play." *Boston Daily Record,* March 7, 1957.

Phillips, McCandlish. "Focusing on Chayefsky." *The New York Times,* January 3, 1972.

Rickey, Carrie. "How Would You Like to Tussle with Russell?" *The Village Voice,* January 21, 1981.

Russo, Vito. "Network." *Soho Weekly News,* December 13, 1976.

Sayre, Nora, and Robert B. Silvers. "An Interview with Paddy Chayefsky." *Horizon,* September 1960.

Schiff, Stephen. "Spaced Odyssey." *The Boston Phoenix,* January 27, 1981.

Shales, Tom. "Network: Hating TV Can Be Fun." *The Washington Post,* October 24, 1976.

Shanley, J. P. "Big Decision on a Bronx Gridiron." *The New York Times,* December 12, 1954.

Sharp, Christopher. "Home Watch." *Women's Wear Daily,* August 26, 1981.

———. "Dunaway and Holden." *Women's Wear Daily,* November 12, 1976.

Sheed, Wilfred. "Paddy's Gold Jag in Dallas." *Life,* April 19, 1968.

Smith, Cecil. "Chayefsky: Disciple of Making It Right." *Los Angeles Times,* November 7, 1954.

———. "The Golden Years of TV." *Los Angeles Times,* August 23, 1981.

Taylor, Clarke. "Paddy May Have a Hit on His Hands." *Los Angeles Times,* September 21, 1976.

Unger, Craig. "Blair Brown." *Interview,* November 1989.

Winsten, Archer. "Rages and Outrages." *New York Post,* January 17, 1972.

Wolper, Allan. "TV Goes to the Movies." *Soho Weekly News,* November 11, 1976.

Zolotow, Sam. "Chayefsky Plans to Be a Director." *The New York Times,* June 26, 1963.

Upon request, under the Freedom of Information Act, the U.S. Department of Justice submitted copies of F.B.I. records on Paddy Chayefsky. Included was a copy of the American's Legion's *Firing Line* report, dated December 1, 1952, in which Chayefsky was accused of being associated with a number of Communist front organizations. The Justice Department, having presumably considered these charges, stated further, in a letter dated July 13, 1993, that upon searching its central records system no information was found "to indicate that Mr. Chayefsky has been the subject of an investigation by the F.B.I."

The American Legion, when contacted in August 1993 with a request to examine its files on *The Firing Line* and whatever documentation it had on Chayefsky, stated that these records were no longer available. "That material had all kinds of legal liability," said Philip Budahn, the Legion's official spokesperson in Washington, D.C. "When it no longer beame appropriate for us to be involved in those kind of issues, the files went into the furnace." In assessment of the Legion's former anti-subversion investigations, and the damage it undoubtedly caused those who were arbitrarily named, Mr. Budahn stated: "I would like you to understand we are aware that there were things done by our organization—the blacklist, and some of the radical stuff—that isn't accepted today. We think it's important to do our part, to acknowledge exactly what happened."

INDEX

SHAUN CONSIDINE was born in Brooklyn and raised in County Clare, Ireland. He is the author of two previous books, and as a journalist and photographer his work has appeared in *The New York Times,* the *Los Angeles Times,* the *Chicago Tribune,* and approximately forty other leading publications. He lives in Manhattan and is currently working on an original screenplay.

ABOUT THE TYPE

This book was set in Galliard, a typeface designed by Matthew Carter for the Mergenthaler Linotype Company in 1978. Galliard is based on the sixteenth-century typefaces of Robert Granjon, which give it classic lines yet interject a contemporary look.